J. K. Lasser's
Business Management Handbook

J. K. Lasser's Business Management Handbook

Bernard Greisman, *Editor*

Director, J. K. Lasser Tax Institute

THIRD EDITION, Revised and Expanded

McGRAW-HILL BOOK COMPANY

New York   San Francisco   Toronto   London   Sydney

658.082
LAS

J. K. LASSER'S BUSINESS MANAGEMENT HANDBOOK

07-036555-5

3 4 5 6 7 8 9 K P K P 7 9 8 7 6 5

PREFACE TO THE THIRD EDITION

This Handbook stems from J. K. Lasser's lifelong interest in serving the businessman. He developed this book with the objective of providing the businessman with a source of advice in areas that require a particular expertise, and the Institute has continued to follow his objectives. This new and expanded edition contains thirteen entirely new chapters and nine revised chapters, all of which were written to bring businessmen advice that will educate, stimulate, and lead to profitable decisions.

Leaving it to the experts can often be a sophisticated way of "passing the buck." The executive needs to comprehend every facet of his organization. No responsible businessman will want to develop his business planning and make his decisions without such knowledge.

Business Management Handbook brings the know-how of specialists to the executive. It presents the advice of experts for ready and constant reference. Each author is an authority in his field and has developed his material in clear and concise terms. A perusal of the Table of Contents will immediately give the scope of the book.

J. K. LASSER TAX INSTITUTE
Bernard Greisman, Director

CONTRIBUTORS

William J. Casey, a member of the law firm of Hall, Casey, Dickler and Howley, holds several important directorships. Writer of some 30 books on legal, tax, and financial subjects, he is chairman of the board of editors of the Institute for Business Planning and has lectured for the American Bar Association and other professional organizations. He has served as chief of OSS Intelligence Service, European theatre; Associate General Counsel, Marshall Plan; and adviser to Senate Finance Committee.

J. C. Dine, Electric Bond and Share Company, is a former Massachusetts newspaperman who has had extensive industrial, broadcasting, and corporate public-relations experience.

Elmer I. Ellentuck, whose law offices are in New York City, was formerly senior editor of *Practicing Attorney's Letter* (Prentice-Hall, Inc.). He currently participates in the editing of business, law, and management periodicals, and is a coauthor of *Employee Discipline* (Man and Manager, Inc.).

Roy A. Foulke is a distinguished financial analyst. He was a vice-president and director of Dun & Bradstreet, Inc., until his retirement in 1961. He is the author of *Commercial Paper Market, Behind the Scenes of Business, The Sinews of American Commerce,* and *Practical Financial Statement Analysis,* and coauthor of *Practical Bank Credit.*

James Greene, formerly a vice-president of Business International Corporation, is a senior specialist in the International Operations Department of the National Industrial Conference Board, a major fact-finding laboratory for American industry. He has made studies of business operations and investments in the international area, and has written and spoken widely on the subject.

G. Dryver Henderson is director of marketing for the Industrial Valley Bank, Philadelphia. His previous business experience includes marketing and organization consultation, and sales for a national brand package-goods manufacturer. He holds a Master of Business Administration degree.

Lee H. Hill, partner and board chairman in a firm of New York City management consultants, also heads a management-counsel firm in Florida. Drawing on wide experience as an electrical engineer and in business management, he has written and coauthored a number of books. His principles of continuously improving profit are set forth in *Upward in the Black* (Prentice-Hall, Inc.).

James B. Kobak is managing partner of the international accounting firm of J. K. Lasser & Company, with headquarters in New York City. Among his duties is the supervision of the management consulting operation of the firm.

Joshua Levine is an attorney-at-law and a partner in the firm of Davis, Gilbert, Levine & Schwartz in New York City.

Curtis B. Lilly served as assistant insurance manager in both the mercantile and manufacturing fields before joining a firm of insurance analysts. After becoming a senior analyst and secretary of the corporation, he left to organize his own firm, which provides corporate insurance management and advisory services for major manufacturing firms, retail operations, public utilities, and other large and complex entities.

Lawrence L. Lipperman, a staff member of the International Business Machines Systems Research Institute, has worked as an electronics design engineer, participating in the design of computer equipment. He has helped to design and install computer systems in various business enterprises. At present, he is engaged in computer applications and education. He also serves frequently as a management-science consultant.

John H. McMichael, an assistant professor of accounting at the Wharton School, University of Pennsylvania, is coauthor of an accounting book, cost-accounting study guide, and cost-accounting practice sets. A CPA, he has been a consultant to government agencies, a telephone company, and manufacturing enterprises.

Edward McSweeney is founder of Edward McSweeney Associates, management and marketing consultants, and a director of a number of well-known corporations. He is a member of the American Arbitration Association and the author of numerous articles on management and marketing.

D'Alton B. Myers has an extensive record as an adviser on business problems, based on 46 years of experience in business, Federal government, and education. He is now living in Texas, engaged in management consulting as member of the Amarillo chapter of SCORE (Service Corps of Retired Executives).

John J. W. Neuner, a CPA, a practicing accountant and management engineer, is also professor of accounting at the School of Business and Civic Administration, College of the City of New York. He is the author of more than 25 books on accounting, office management, insurance, and other business subjects.

Maurice E. Peloubet, a CPA, has acted as a consultant to government departments and is the author of *Audit Working Papers.* He is now a retired partner of Price Waterhouse & Co., with which his own firm, Pogson Peloubet & Co., combined in 1963.

Carl A. Polsky, a CPA and tax lawyer, is an assistant professor of accounting at the Wharton School, University of Pennsylvania. A partner in the law firm of Bluestine, Diamond, Polsky, and Bauer, he is the author of a number of articles published in accounting and tax journals.

J. Richard Schneider is in product management with the Maxwell House Division of the General Foods Corporation. He has experience in all aspects of marketing, including advertising, promotion, sales, and new products. He holds a Master of Business Administration degree in Marketing.

Howard Schwartzberg, a member of the bar of the State of New York, is assistant general counsel of M. Lowenstein & Sons, Inc.

David Scribner, president of David Scribner & Associates, Inc., is a consultant to real-estate investors and a real-estate investment analyst for corporate and individual investors, underwriters, and industrialists.

Charles H. Sevin has had much experience in management consulting. He is now employed by EBS Management Consultants, New York; responsible for quantitative methods of analysis in marketing. He has written *Marketing Productivity Analysis* (McGraw-Hill Book Company, 1965), *Distribution Cost Analysis,* and *How Manufacturers Reduce Their Distribution Cost.*

Jerrold G. Van Cise, a partner in the law firm Cahill, Gordon, Sonnett, Reindel & Ohl, has served as chairman of section on antitrust law of the American Bar Association, and of the New York State Bar Association. A member (1953–1955) of the Attorney General's National Committee to Study the Antitrust Laws, he has written *The Federal Antitrust Laws, Understanding the Antitrust Laws,* and is coauthor of *How to Comply with the Antitrust Laws.*

George S. Vanderwende served the Federal government for over 27 years as a procedures and management analyst on both domestic and foreign assignments. In various agencies, he was instrumental in the development of forms control, standardization of forms, and the organization of forms and records control units.

William E. Weber, a CPA, has been associated with Manhattan College since 1949 and holds the rank of associate professor in accounting. He has offices in Irvington, New York.

CONTENTS

Section 1

HOW TO FINANCE A BUSINESS

BY

WILLIAM J. CASEY

HOW TO FINANCE A BUSINESS [1]

1. The capital structure

The financial requirements of a business will depend upon its scale of operations and its method of marketing. Conversely, the scale of operation of the business and its methods of marketing will be limited and controlled by the amount of financing available to it. Thus the very efficiency and competitive vitality of the business will frequently turn on its financing.

The sound way to develop a business is to get it going on a modest operating scale—enough to achieve the operating economy which it needs to be competitive. Then, after it has proved its right to live, it can be expanded. This kind of a two-step approach will not only minimize risks but enormously simplify financing. Getting the money necessary to launch a new enterprise and getting the money needed to expand a proven enterprise are two very different problems. We shall look at them separately.

Questions which must be answered. In developing any financing plans and seeking financing, these basic questions must be answered to the satisfaction of both borrower and lender—both the person who puts up money and the person who accepts responsibility for using it:

How will the money be applied—to what purpose and on what time schedule?

How will the money turn over, and from what sources will repayment come and on what time table?

Will the use of the money be profitable?

What kind of a return (interest rate or dividend yield or capital depreciation) will it show to the investor?

The first two questions can best be answered by projecting a cash budget. It should be scrutinized carefully to see that all possible contingencies have been considered and allowed for. From the cash budget it can be determined how full repayment will come from amortization of fixed assets, from liquidation of inventory or other assets, and from anticipated profits after tax. Profitability will be shown by a projected-earnings statement—a projection of a profit-and-loss budget as distinguished from a cash budget. The projected

[1] Substantial portions of this section are based on the author's *How to Raise Money to Make Money*, published by the Institute for Business Planning, 2 West 13 Street, New York, N.Y. 10011, first printing 1966, and adapted or reproduced here with the permission of the copyright owner.

profit-and-loss budget together with pro forma balance sheets based on budget projections will show dividend prospects and potential capital appreciation.

How much financing?   An initial budget is needed to show (1) the probable amount and timing of cash requirements; (2) the kind of balance sheet the company will have on which to attempt to secure borrowed funds as needed; (3) a forecast of the margin required for profitable operations and the probable time needed before the inflow of cash will exceed the outlay, and thus the time needed to repay borrowed funds; and (4) a demonstration that operations will yield profit sufficient to justify the investment.

First, the factual basis for budget projection must be obtained.   How long will it take to reach profitable operations—to develop, get in production, and market effectively a standardized product?   How long to secure machinery, materials, labor, funds, and sales orders and to organize their flow?   What are production and selling costs?   What volume is probable—what prices and discounts?   A hardheaded investor or lender will dig at all these points and apply a skeptical eye to them.   Successful financing requires a conservative estimate of factual factors with strong supporting details, precedent, and comparisons.   It is difficult to put forward an exact answer to these questions and to coordinate sales expectations, production runs, the time it will take to lift sales to a point which minimizes production costs, and the rate at which manufacturing, administration, and sales overhead will be absorbed.   The difficulties are so great that a high, a low, and a medium budget level may be, and frequently are, developed.   The first profitable month and the date of cumulative breakeven can be calculated by drawing up estimated profit-and-loss schedules by month to show how cumulative profits offset cumulative losses.

The cash-requirement schedule is prepared from much the same data.   It will show the cash required for capital equipment and improvements, organization expense, acquisition of patents, and such items which do not appear in profit-and-loss schedules.   The most important financing function of the cash-requirements schedule is to show the lag or lead on every major item of incoming expense.   How soon will customers pay their bills?   How soon must machinery be bought, and how soon paid for?   How large must inventories run?   When must an inventory be acquired, and how soon paid for?   How often must payrolls be met?   When are insurance or tax payments due?   What selling expenses must be incurred before the current sales income materializes?   What initial advertising is contemplated, and when must it be paid for?

Careful reflection of these factors in a cash budget may substantially minimize financing requirements or avoid unanticipated shortage of funds.   This process must be done so as to determine financial requirements and to justify a lender or investor in making funds available.   The comparison of projected profit and loss in the cash schedule may show the necessity to adapt the operation or its scale so that it will conform with the availability of financing.   It may suggest a preservation of cash by forgoing quantity purchase discounts and cash discounts, forgoing the economies of long production runs, holding back on promotion, etc. It will also show how final success creates need for additional financing to achieve profitable expansion. This may have considerable bearing on the character of initial financing, in calling for the holding back of certain stock and collateral for use in raising additional funds later on.

Rule of thumb for estimating financial needs. Carefully worked out budget projections are highly desirable for even the smaller business. Yet rough approximations can be quickly developed from the ratios, profit margins, and turnover frequency which prevail in a particular line of business.

Probably sales volume may be determined from a study of the market. Operating ratios will tell how much net this should yield and how much rent should be carried.

Turnover experience and prevailing markups will tell how much inventory will be needed to do that volume. If the volume potential seems to be $40,000 and in the particular line inventory should turn over four times, money required for inventory will be $10,000 less the trade discount or prevailing margin. If the margin is 35 percent, $6,500 should acquire beginning inventory. Add to this the rent and operating expenses for a 90-day period, plus the cost of fixtures and equipment.

Another way of going at it is to determine how much profit will be needed to make the business worthwhile. Determine how much volume that will require. After investigation establishes that the necessary volume can be attained, determine how much inventory and how much equipment will be needed to attain it. If $10,000 profit is needed and the ratio of net to gross is 10 percent, $100,000 must be grossed and 200,000 units of a 50-cent item must be produced and sold. From there, space, equipment, inventory, and working-cash requirements can be developed roughly. To pin down the flow of cash and other requirements takes one back to budgeting.

What kind of money? In addition to determining the amount of money which is needed, it is equally important to determine what the money will flow into and how it will revolve. Money which will go into buildings and equipment will be fixed capital and therefore will have to come from stock and long-term loans. This money will revolve slowly, and as money invested in fixed assets is turned back into cash via depreciation charges, it can be used to amortize debt or for additional working capital, but always with the proviso that some day it will be needed to replace fixed assets which have worn out or become obsolete. Money which is required to carry the organization until it is converting money into goods and back again into money fast enough to meet incoming bills should also be part of the permanent capital of a business. Similarly, a reserve of cash to meet emergencies should be part of the permanent capital.

Over and above these requirements is the ordinary daily working capital which the business will need. This is made up of the funds which are put into inventory and payroll, converted by sales into accounts receivable, and then converted back into cash as customers pay their bills.

The importance of adequate working capital is too well known to be labored. It is important to determine how much of the working-capital requirements should be available as permanent capital and how much can be obtained by short-term financing. Where there is a long production or selling cycle and inventory is readily salable, or where there are peak requirements at certain seasons of the year, current financing can be relied upon for much of the working-capital requirements. Where there is quick turnover, working-capital requirements will be lower and a larger portion should come from the permanent capital of the company. There should be careful study, with bankers and other financial advisers, to see that business policies are shaped to bring working-capital requirements in line with available resources and that there is enough permanent financing to sustain the amount of current financing which is anticipated. The amount of capital needed to execute the necessary turnover of the company's operations will depend on how customers pay, on terms set in selling, on terms obtained in buying, on the volume of business and the rate of its expansion, on the time consumed in manufacture, and on the rate at which inventory is turned over. The amount of permanent capital which will provide for safety over and above that needed to acquire fixed assets will depend on how hazardous or how stable the business is and on the practice of bankers in making current financing available to the particular line of business. The planned relationship between permanent financing and current financing, taken together with the way in which money will flow, should be such that the business can be expected to meet the tests which will be applied to determine its credit worthiness when it seeks current financing.

Exactly how these tests will be applied to a particular line of business must be determined by canvassing the outlook with a seasoned banker, but the financial plan must be such that, on the basis of the projection of a cash budget, an income budget, and pro forma balance sheets, it seems likely that they will be met.

The rule of thumb is that the ratio of current assets to current liabilities should not be allowed to fall below 2:1. Where this ratio prevails, liquidation of current assets at 50 percent of book value will clean off current liabilities. The ratio of current assets to liabilities at 2:1 means that the company, via stock, surplus, or long-term debt, has provided as much of the capital over and above fixed assets as short-term creditors. Thus if a 2:1 ratio is satisfactory in a specific line of business, it follows that to get a specified amount of short-term financing, a business will have to count on having a definite amount of permanent financing over and above that needed to acquire fixed assets.

Then the projection must show that the cash account will bulk sufficiently large compared with total current assets and current liabilities. This again will vary with the type of business, but should not run less than 5 to 10 percent of current assets.   If current debt is to be held at 50 percent of current assets, cash should run 10 to 20 percent as much as current debt.   There are companies which keep less than 10 percent cash, and there are companies which keep enough cash to meet current liabilities.

Promoter's interest and control.   Frequently, persons setting up a new business bring to it an idea, experience, or skill; and they have the problem of carving out an interest for themselves adequate to reflect this contribution and their continuing efforts, while at the same time raising money from outside investors so that the business can be developed.   To work out a financial plan in this kind of a situation, we have these requirements:

The promoters must secure their control over the key elements needed for the successful development of the enterprise.   This is necessary to nail down and justify their position and stake in the business and to attract the additional financing necessary

The promoters must convert these key elements into their own interest in the continuing business

The promoters must give sufficient security, stake in the enterprise, and income potential to get necessary financing from investors

This must be done on a basis which will not result in the stake received by the promoter being taxed to him too heavily, if at all.   This is a critical point.   Issuing stock options and warrants to the promoter may result in his being taxed on the spread between the option price and the value of the stock at the time of exercise.   Issuing stock to him at the time the business is set up may result in that stock being valued at the price at which it is sold to the investors putting up the money and the value of the stock being chargeable to the promoter as fully taxable compensation.   A further consequence of this would be that if the stock treated as compensation amounted to more than 20 percent of the total stock, the formation of the corporation would no longer be tax-free, so that any stockholders who contributed property for stock would become subject to capital-gain tax on the difference between the cost of their property and the value of the stock received.   There are several courses that can be followed to avoid or minimize this risk—

Set up a leverage capital structure so that the promoters can buy their proportionate part of the equity stock without being required to put up their share of the bond or preferred-stock money

If the promoters can put in a patent, or drawings, or models, this may justify their proportionate share of the stock.   There does not seem to have been much effort to look behind the value the venturers have put on such intangible property.   But the Treasury can try to break down stock received for such intangible property into the value of the property and compensation for services

Have the promoters form the corporation in the first instance and bring the money in at a later stage.   If this is merely a formal separation of a single deal into two steps, the promoters can be charged with the receipt of compensation on the net effect of the total deal. However, if the promoters make some progress on their own and increase the value and the prospects of the enterprise, they should incur no risk of being charged with the receipt of compensation when they subsequently issue additional stock for cash or property at a higher price than they paid

Have the business carried on as a joint venture for a period of time, then incorporate the joint venture and bring in most of the financing at that point. This may also permit the financial backers to charge off their share of the loss on the joint venture in the early stages of developing the enterprise

In attracting outside financing to a new venture, it is desirable for those who put up the money to get debentures or preferred stock. This gives them the fullest security available for their investment and the opportunity for them to get their money back off the top and, if debentures are used, on a tax-free basis. This also makes it possible to give the promoter a larger share of the common share for his contribution of ideas, control elements, services, and managerial skill.

To get control over the key elements on which the enterprise will depend, these possibilities should be explored:

The basic idea. Protection of an idea is extremely difficult. However, it can be done by contract. Sometimes there is an agreement through which the idea is disclosed against a deposit of cash in trust to be turned over to the contributor of the idea if it is exploited within a specified time. Merely reducing the idea to writing and delivering the idea to a new corporation for stock can be sufficient to justify the issuance of a stock interest

Options or contracts. Provide for the acquisition of property, such as a unique location, equipment, patent rights, or other assets which will be needed for the proposed business. These options or contracts can be traded in to a new company for stock on a tax-free basis

Patents and copyrights. Application for a patent or copyright provides tangible control over an asset which may be licensed or turned into a new company for stock

Leases. Occupancy of real estate needed to develop a new business, or even an option to lease an important site, can be traded to a new corporation for stock

Franchises and concessions or distribution agreements. These, from governmental units or private companies, can be traded to a new company for stock

Contracts for the services. Contracts with individuals who have special talents or skills on which the operation of a business will depend can constitute a control element which can be traded to a new corporation for stock

Capital structure. After determining how much money is needed, how it will flow, and the proper balance between long-term and short-term funds, the next step is to determine how money will be raised, the securities which will be offered, and the sources of funds. Many considerations come into play here, and the correct decision will require a judicious balancing of all of them. The final decision is frequently governed by the kind of money which is available and the terms on which it may be had. Nevertheless, it is highly desirable to make a serious effort to formulate the most correct and desirable financial structure. To the extent that the business does not justify the kind of financing thus formulated or that the kind of money needed is not available, the owners of the business will at least know what they want and go only as far from that point as forced by trading necessities. The questions to be asked are—

What financial structure will be most profitable?
What structure will yield the best margin of safety and best provide for future emergencies and possible expansion?
What securities structure will yield the desired control features?
What structure will be most advantageous taxwise?

In most cases the capital structure which shows the greatest profit potential will be least satisfactory as to provision for future requirements. The reverse is also true. This is the kind of balancing which is needed to achieve a desirable financial plan. This balancing should be done even though the ultimate capital structure reflects as much money as can be obtained on a risk basis and as much as can be obtained on a loan basis. Understanding and balancing of these factors are important in selling the investment.

Fundamental economic principles should determine the financial plan. If a plan is formulated which reflects fundamental principles accurately, it will facilitate the obtaining of money from both equity and loan sources. The old rules were that bonds could be issued only when future earnings of a corporation promised to be liberal and reasonably certain; that the preferred stock would be issued when the earnings were irregular but, over a period of years, promised a fair margin over the preferred stock dividends requirements; that only common stock would be issued when the earnings were uncertain and unpredictable. These principles are no longer automatic, principally because scarcity of equity capital and tax advantages in borrowing have brought about a shift from stock financing to loan financing.

Profitability and capital appreciation. The smallest possible proportion of equity investment (common stock or partnership interest) and the highest possible proportion of debt payable in a fixed amount will produce the highest potential return on capital investment and the largest potential for capital appreciation. This is called trading on the equity. A business borows money in the hope that it will be able to make that money pay more than the interest rate payable on borrowed capital. Obviously, failure to earn the rate of return higher than interest payable on borrowed money will eat away basic capital and possibly result in creditors taking away the assets of the business.

To illustrate, consider a business with $100,000 in capital stock which can make 10 percent on capital. If it borrows another $100,000 and maintains a 10 percent earnings rate on the capital it uses, there will be a 14 percent return to common stockholders after paying 6 percent on the borrowed money. If the earnings rate can be kicked up to 15 percent, common stockholders will receive a 24 percent return. However, if the rate of earning on the capital employed should decline to 5 percent, common stockholders will receive only 4 percent on their capital. If the corporation should earn only 2 percent on capital employed, 6 percent will still be payable on the borrowed money and the common stockholders would have their capital dissipated by 2 percent a year.

Thus we see that the higher the proportion of borrowed capital, the greater the rate of return to equity owners as long as they can make the business show more than the interest rate. As earnings fall below the fixed interest rate, the higher the proportion of borrowed money, the more rapidly the equity owners lose their capital. Increased earning power, inflation, or any other factor which enhances the dollar value of assets will benefit common stockholders exclusively. Owners of fixed-value notes or bonds or preferred stock do not benefit. Thus the owners of the business will profit more from appreciation in value, and lose more substantially and more rapidly, where there is a low proportion of common stock and a high proportion of fixed value obligations.

Safety factors. Maximum safety requires all common stock and no fixed obligations to pay annual interest and redeem loans. Yet debt may be desirable to produce sufficient capital and to maximize income and capital-gain possibilities. A business must therefore determine how far it can go into debt. To a considerable extent this will be determined by the caution and prudence of lenders. As a generality, a lender is apt to insist that the borrower have as much money at risk as he has. For practical purposes, this may restrict borrowing to somewhere between 40 and 60 percent of total capital. Frequently the owners themselves will want to advance money to a business on a temporary basis, and this will make it possible for the proportion of debt to be increased.

The limits of prudence on the proportion of capital to debt will vary with each situation, depending on the stability and prospects of the business and on the experience and financial position of its operators. The following factors will suggest setting a conservative limit to the debt assumed:

Instability of prices and volume
An unusually high burden of fixed costs
A high rate of turnover
A low ratio of profit to sales

By way of illustration, a merchant's business will be well advised to borrow less than an apartment-house venture or a printing plant with a large fixed investment in machinery.

Provision for future requirements.   Where a substantial expansion is likely to be necessary or desirable, sound financing calls for a high ratio of stocks to debt to provide borrowing power for future needs.   However, should the owners be sure of the prospects and earning power of the business and feel that after some experience and an opportunity to demonstrate profitability they will be able to issue stocks at a higher price, it may be better to hold back as much stock as possible, and to use as high a proportion of borrowed money as is available. Similarly, if a business is successful, capital requirements will almost always increase sharply, and careful consideration must be given to holding back enough stock so that additional stock will be available for expansion financing without too great a dilution of the owner's control and interest.

Control elements.   To work out a financial plan that will bring in enough outside money and at the same time maximize control requires careful planning. It is usually accomplished by giving the common stock sole voting power and making the issues small.   There is always great danger that control will be lost and the owner's interest diluted when they do not anticipate the scale of financial requirements that successful operation will bring.   When those requirements do arise, the owners may have to let go too large a portion of their holdings to satisfy them.   A preferred issue is usually used to secure the investors' money when some of the group contribute intangibles in the form of services or special skills or patent rights and are entitled to a large share of the profits over and above a normal return on tangible cash investment.   But here again the owner of the underlying equity stock must look ahead to see that the financial requirements of successful business can be obtained without causing him to lose control and dilute his interest by having to issue so much new stock that his proportionate interest dwindles rapidly.   The use of preferred stock permits retention of a more substantial proportion of the common.   Later on, when a business has reached a certain size, the issue of additional voting stock may actually strengthen control of the management by making it more difficult for another group to purchase control.

2. How taxes affect financing

Tax savings play a vital, but too frequently overlooked, role in financing a business.   It is a multiple role.   Tax savings can—

Represent cash which can be used directly to meet the money needs of the business

Reduce the net cost of money

Attract money from outsiders in two ways, by (a) giving them favorable tax treatment on any gains they will realize and (b) minimizing their risk by cushioning any loss they may sustain

Tax rules to guide your financing.   In the tax planning of financing, we seek these results—

Favorable tax on the investor's gain—capital gain on leverage stock
Favorable tax cost to the user of money—fully deductible interest or rent rather than nondeductible dividends
Cushion against loss by getting the maximum charge-off against income through a limited partnership, or loans, or guarantees, or by investing in a small-business corporation and taking an ordinary loss on sale of the stock or its worthlessness if the business goes bad
Tax-free recovery of capital through repayment of debt

How to minimize the cost of money.   Interest on debt is deductible.   A dividend paid on stock is not.   This means that it costs almost twice as much for a corporation in the 48-percent tax bracket to use money obtained by issuing a 6-percent preferred stock as it does to use money obtained by issuing a 6-percent debenture.

How to get new money back tax-free.   If new money is put in for common stock, the investor will probably have to pay tax on dividend income when he gets his money back from the company—unless he is prepared to give up his entire interest in the company.   The same result may follow with a preferred stock.   But by putting money up as a loan, we can get it back tax-free.   But if it is not a real debt or if the capital structure is top-heavy with debt, both the deduction of interest and the tax-free character of any repayment made out of the company's earned surplus may be lost.   In other words, the debt may be considered equity capital.   What to do to avoid this result is discussed later on in this section.

How to get a capital-gain position for new money.   We get a capital-gain position on stock we buy.   But we cannot get the advantages of deductible interest for the borrower and tax-free repayments to the investor on stock.   To get these, we must give him debts.   We can try for the best of both worlds by giving him one of the three following alternatives:

1. Convertible debentures
2. A package of low-value stock and debt
3. Warrants with the debt

Of these three alternatives, the warrants are least to be recommended, because the government has indicated that the spread between warrant price and stock value at the time of exercise may be ordinary income as additional interest.   A package of low-value stock and debt gives the investor both capital-gain opportunities and a chance to pull out a good portion of his investment without tax.   The debt when repaid will be tax-free.   And any increase in the value of the business as a result of its successful operation will be reflected in the increased value of the stock.

Convertible debentures allow the investor to decide later (after he sees how the company is getting along) whether to continue his debt position or cash in on the growth of the company by converting his debt to stock and putting himself in a position to realize capital gains. The conversion from bonds to stock is a tax-free transaction. But by converting, unless dealing with a publicly traded stock, he then puts himself in a position where he can realize his capital gain only by giving up his entire position in the company. A less-than-all redemption of his stock will likely result in a dividend. But it is possible, through a disproportionate redemption, to cash in on part of his gain by having enough stock redeemed so that after the redemption the percentage of all the stock in the corporation that he owns is less than 80 percent of the percentage of the outstanding stock he owned before the redemption. What is more, he cannot end up with the 50 percent or more of the outstanding stock after the redemption. In addition, in applying these rules, stock owned by his family, fellow stockholders in other corporations, partners, or partnerships all count in figuring the various percentages. Where we are dealing with a publicly traded stock, of course, we do not have these problems, since the stock can be sold off piecemeal on the market at capital gains.

How to use tax money for financing. Individuals in the top tax brackets can use heavily taxed income dollars, sometimes worth as little as 30 cents to them, to finance a business. This can be done in one of two ways:

1. Invest in a joint venture or limited partnership in which losses can be deducted by the partners on individual tax returns
2. Invest in a corporation having 10 or fewer stockholders and elect to have it taxed as a partnership under Subchapter S of the Internal Revenue Code

When this kind of an investment gets out of the loss state, it can be converted into a real corporation, so that the corporate rate ceiling comes into play and the stock interest can be cashed in at capital-gain rates.

Where the deal involves an existing corporation in which the Subchapter S election is not possible, it may still be possible to put up new money on a tax-deductible basis by forming a new entity to develop a new product or a new market and then, after the job has been done, merge the new entity into the existing corporation for stock.

How to cushion the risk of loss. An investor can always be attracted more readily if any loss he should suffer stands to be substantially offset by a reduction in his tax bill. A loss on the usual stock purchase or on a loan will almost always be available only on the limited capital-loss basis. When that happens, the loss is usable only to offset capital gains, plus an additional $1,000 available each year until exhausted as on offset against ordinary income.

The availability of capital losses only, should the investment go sour, takes a good deal of the incentive away from a number of investments. Investor incentive is dampened by the amount of time it may take to recover a loss out of after-tax income where the loss has to be handled on a capital-loss basis.

So our efforts are generally aimed at arranging for the loss to offset ordinary income in full. To do that, we have these possibilities:

Have the investment made via a partnership

Have it made through a corporation electing to be taxed as a partnership (Subchapter S)

Have the investment take the form of "small-business stock" under Sec. 1244 of the Internal Revenue Code. Loss on this stock is fully deductible up to $25,000 a year ($50,000 for husband and wife on a joint return). Note that Sec. 1244 stock can be used when setting up a Subchapter S corporation, too. While it may not be needed while the corporation qualifies under Subchapter S (since the stockholders deduct the corporate losses as if they were their own), it may be handy to have the Sec. 1244 stock outstanding in the event the Subchapter S status is later lost and then the corporation's fortunes take a downturn.

Have the investment take the form of the purchase of depreciable assets to be leased to the business.

Debt financing costs less than stock financing. When a company borrows money, all the money earned by the new money carries through to cover interest costs. At a 48 percent corporate-tax rate, a profitable corporation risks 52 percent of the interest due on its debt. The balance is absorbed by the tax saving on the deduction of the interest.

Annual Results from $10,000 of Borrowed Capital for a Corporation in the 48 Percent Bracket, Without Reflecting the Added Income That Such Capital May Produce by Being Invested in the Business

	Interest rate, percent				
	3	4	5	6	7
Yearly gross interest cost	$300	$400	$500	$600	$700
Reduction in normal and surtax—48 percent	144	192	240	288	336
Actual interest cost	156	208	260	312	364

When money is raised today by issuing stock, the company must earn enough to pay the corporate tax and have enough left to pay the dividend rate if it is to service the financing. Thus, at a 48 percent tax rate, a corporation must earn slightly less than 10 percent before taxes to carry a 5-percent preferred stock. It can carry a 5-percent debenture if it earns 5 percent of the money. A company must earn almost twice as much on new money to finance by a 5-percent preferred stock as by a 5-percent debenture. Also, 48-percent of the cost of the debt financing is underwritten by tax savings even if the new money is not profitably employed. The common stockholders risk 52 percent of the cost.

But if money raised by a 5-percent preferred-stock issue is not employed at a profit, 100 percent of the cost falls on the common stockholders.

But stock financing at high prices brings in tax-free money and tax-free appreciation. At a certain stage in a growing business, we are apt to find that the sale of additional stock to the public will seemingly do the wrong things taxwise but achieve the right tax results for the owners. The sale of additional shares will require the owners to share some of the rights to corporate income and require the corporate institution to pay nondeductible dividends for the use of this new money. However, it will bring new cash into the business tax-free. If the business has prospects, it will improve the equity position of the owners even though they share some of their rights to the future income and the total assets of the business. It will create a public market and facilitate the gradual conversion on the part of the owners of some of their remaining rights in the business income to capital gain.

This combination of tax and financial management can best be illustrated by an example:

The original book value of a company before financing was $55,000. The company successfully floated an issue of 100,000 shares of common stock at $3 a share. The original stockholders kept 200,000 shares, thereby retaining 66⅔ percent control. Underwriting costs were $6,000, so that the proceeds to the corporation were $240,000. The total book value of the company was now $55,000 plus $240,000, or $295,000. Since the original stockholders retained two-thirds control, their book value had increased after the financing from $55,000 to $196,667.

How did the financing affect the market value of the company? The market value before financing presumably was equal at best to the book value of $55,000, and probably even less because there actually was no market for the stock—it would have been difficult to sell at all. After the financing, the original stockholders had 200,000 shares of common stock which had sold at $3 a share, or $600,000. In other words, their market value had jumped from no more than $55,000 to $600,000.

If the business prospers, as it did in this case, the market value of these shares will increase further. More important, as long as the additional capital dollars, which, in turn, make additional debt capital available, and the marketability of the stock cause the stock to be capitalized at a multiple of earnings 50 percent in excess of that which would be applied in valuing the stock if it had not been made public and marketable, the original holders will always be ahead in capital value in addition to being in an easier estate-tax position and more readily able to realize on portions of their capital as they go along. It is not at all uncommon for a business, which could not be sold for more than six times earnings if it were privately owned, to be valued at ten times earnings when its stock is properly traded and when investors, who would not be able to buy the entire business, can buy some of the stock. Also, this permits the

holders to sell off a little at a time and still retain control. If the original
owners sell one-third of the business to the public, as in this case, they will
have as much value as before as long as they have increased the price-earnings
ratio of the stock from six times earnings to nine times earnings; if they increase it to ten times earnings, they will have more total value in the two-thirds
of the business they retain than they would have had in the entire business if
they had not made the stock marketable.

Here is another example of how these factors work:

A company plans to have a capitalization of 150,000 shares. The owners
will hold 90,000, or 60 percent, of the shares for their equity, which has a book
value of $200,000 (possibly understated). They will sell 60,000, or 40 per-
cent, of the shares to the public at $5 per share, which will bring in $300,000
of new capital.

Suppose it takes $50,000 to pay for underwriting costs and commissions, con-
sultant and legal fees, printing costs of the prospectus, etc.   The company nets

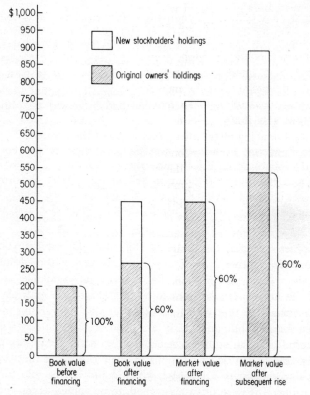

Fig. 1. Example of results of successful stock
financing (in thousands of dollars)

$250,000 in exchange for 40 percent of the stock, thus increasing the total book value by that amount, to a new figure of $450,000. The book value of the original owners' 60 percent holdings is now $270,000, or $70,000 more than the 100 percent they had before the financing.

Everybody has gained. The financing has established a market for the stock. The original owners now have something they never had before—market value (or what others are actually willing to pay for their stock) of $450,000 for their 60 percent. And supposing the stock rises, say to $6 per share, as should in fact happen if there is effective use of the new working capital and the rate of earnings increases. Then the original owners' holdings will be worth $540,000 at market value—and the new stockholders, the investors, also will have what they are looking for.

The chart on the previous page illustrates how these factors work.

How income bonds afford some of the advantages of stock financing along with those of bond financing. Income bonds, on which interest is payable only if earned, make the cost of financing tax deductible without imposing the fixed commitment usually required with debt obligations.

Despite the fact that interest is a contingent rather than a fixed charge, interest payments are deductible from income for tax purposes. As long as the corporate tax rate continues high, therefore, the right of a corporation to deduct income-bond interest payments in determining its taxable earnings is an important advantage. Under modern tax laws, it means that large corporations paying bond interest can reduce their tax burden by 48 percent of what they would pay if this amount had been disbursed as dividends on preferred stock.

In the organized exchanges, income bonds are likely to trade "flat." This means that the purchase price of the bond includes all accumulated interest. The price will tend to drop by the amount of the payment, as in the case of common stock after payment of the expected dividends. Fixed-interest bonds, on the other hand, trade on the basis of "and interest," which means that the seller is entitled to the interest that accumulated during the period he held the bonds. This can have tax advantages for the investor in giving him capital gain rather than fully taxed interest.

How to protect your capitalization. The government can raise the question whether debt financing is real debt or disguised stock. This can occur, if (1) the debt obligation is not definite enough, or (2) the debt is top-heavy in relation to the equity.

If the government is successful, it can deny deduction of interest and tax repayments as dividends.

You can insure against the first risk by following these rules—

The debt securities should have a definite fixed maturity

A reasonable interest rate should be definitely payable regardless of earnings

The holders of the debt should have the unrestricted right to sue or enforce payment on default

The holders of the debt should not have voting rights, as such

The debt should be treated as debt in the corporation's financial statement

There should be a substantial investment in stock

There should be a bona fide debtor-creditor relationship

Debenture-preferred stock should not be held out as capital

The big emphasis in court decisions which determine whether what you call debt is really debt or disguised stock is on the intention of the parties.

The following steps will help insulate you against a contention that the capitalization of your corporation is too thin:

The amount of capital invested should compare favorably with other businesses in the same industry. If possible, there should be enough of an investment to acquire all the assets essential to carrying on the business. It may be wise to explore the possibility of operating on a limited scale to show that the invested capital is at least adequate for that purpose. Consider entering into leasing deals

Try to create a reasonable amount of debt (one that can be paid off through normal operations). Debt which earns interest should be kept within the limits of projected earnings

Make sure the debt instruments are clear and unambiguous. They should show an unconditional obligation at some certain future time at a reasonable rate of interest. Avoid subordination or predicating debt payments on earnings

Give some form of collateral whenever possible

Keep records to show the debtor-creditor relationship. Listing the transactions in the minutes and all financial accounts is helpful

On transferring assets to the corporation in exchange for both stock and debt, allocate the consideration clearly on the books. Separate transactions are preferred where possible. The assets should be valued at their true appraisal value

Do not make loans in proportion to shareholdings. If it becomes necessary to default on the notes, selling the debt for capital gain or loss in a bona fide transaction may avoid an unfavorable inference. This is another way of substituting an outside loan for the inside debt

Borrowing in spurts instead of in a lump sum usually indicates that they are loans made to fulfill an urgent need. Lump-sum borrowing connotes investment

Where possible, different types of debt instruments should be made. This acts as a preventive against all debt being thrown out in one shot and provides the background necessary for partial relief

Have the financial records (including correspondence, minutes, and other documents) indicate good business reasons for debts. Nontax considerations for debt have been frequently cited as all-important by the courts

Weigh the debt against the risk of repayment. If it appears too risky, the
chances are such loans will be considered to be capital

When payments of interest and principal are not discharged on time, creditors should take some sort of realistic approach to enforcing the obligation.
Written demand for payment should be made

Do not disregard the debt-equity ratio even though current decisions soft-
pedal it. Ratios in the 1:1 to 3:1 range cannot harm the stockholders,
but a higher ratio (over 4:1) is an ever-present hazard

3. Equity financing—ways and means

The investment banker. The investment banker undertakes to funnel the
savings of the public into productive use. An experienced investment banker
will be of great value in developing the most desirable financial structure. In
formulating the correct ratio between common stock, preferred stock, and bonds,
between long-term and short-term debt, he will be able to contribute seasoned
experience in appraising the immediate and future financial need of business
ventures and also an up-to-date knowledge of what types of securities and what
rate of return will attract public funds.

Ordinarily the investment banker does not invest any of his own funds. He
is a middleman or an agent in procuring the funds of the public. He may
underwrite an issue, that is, guarantee that it will be sold and that he himself
will buy any portion to which the public does not subscribe. On companies
which do not have an investment record, it is more likely that he will limit his
commitment to undertaking to sell the company's securities to investors, without committing himself to purchase any shares which the public does not take
up within a specified time period. In almost every city in the United States
there are security dealers who may undertake to sell a new issue of common
stock to the local investing public. It is the business of these security dealers
to know and appraise companies and their securities and to be in touch with
local investors. Most local security dealers do not underwrite or purchase
securities for resale to the public. They limit themselves to an agency basis
under which they undertake the sale of securities on a best-efforts basis.

Cost of flotation. The cost of selling securities to the public, whether common stock, preferred stock, or bonds, goes up sharply as the issue becomes
smaller. The two main reasons for this are that a larger issue absorbs fixed
costs such as printing, legal fees, etc., over a larger number of securities and
dollars. Also the smaller issues are likely to come from companies whose investment merits are unproved and therefore require more costly and intensive
selling efforts.

What does it cost to go public? For a full registration, the cost will probably add up something like this—

Legal fees. These will be from $15,000 to $30,000, most of which will go to the lawyer for the company, who usually does most of the work. The underwriter's counsel will usually confine himself to reviewing the documents of the counsel for the company. If, however, the latter is inexperienced and the lawyer for the underwriter has to do a large portion of the work, he gets a larger portion of the fee. Counsel for the underwriter usually does the blue-sky work because that depends on the states in which the underwriter expects to sell. If it is necessary to do blue-sky work in a number of states, the legal costs will increase somewhat

Accounting fees. These will vary with the size of the company and the amount of work which has to be done to bring the company into shape for a public offering. A rule of thumb on this would be somewhere between $5,000 and $10,000

Printing costs. This will depend on the size of the registration statement, the number of proofs necessary, the extent of the revisions made in the proofs, and the number of copies which the underwriter will want to give to prospective purchasers. These printing costs can be expected to run between $6,000 and $12,000

Stock certificates. The cost of a simple lithograph certificate is not great. If a great deal of art work and engraving is dreamed up for the certificate, it becomes expensive

Securities and Exchange Commission registrations fee. This is 0.01 percent of the maximum aggregate public offering price of the security, with a minimum fee of $25

Federal issue and transfer taxes. Only the Federal tax is necessary unless part of the offering is made on behalf of selling stockholders, who will have to pay transfer taxes, or the closing occurs in a state which taxes the original issue or transfer of securities

Blue-sky filing fees and expenses. Depending upon the number of states in which the underwriting group wants to offer the stock, these costs can run from $1,500 to $3,000

Registrar and transfer agents' fees. This depends on the number of certificates issued and registered and can be expected to run upward from a minimum of about $1,000

Insurance. Lloyd's of London will insure underwriters and selling stockholders against liability under the Federal Securities Acts arising from erroneous statements or omissions in the registration statement. Up to $1 million, this insurance costs about 1 percent of the underwriting; and after that it ranges down to less than ½ percent

Securities and Exchange Commission. The Federal Securities Act of 1933 seeks to protect investors by requiring companies which offer securities for public sales to disclose financial and other information about the company's business, its principals, and the securities to be issued. It also prohibits misrepresentation and other fraudulent acts and practices in the sale of securities. Disclosure of information is provided by the filing of registration statements with the SEC and by requiring delivery of an informative prospectus (selling circular) based on the registration statement.   Issuance of common stock and other securities may be exempt from SEC requirements if it fits into one of these categories:

Private offerings to a limited number of persons

Offers to the residents of a single state by companies organized and doing business in that state

Offerings not in excess of $300,000 made in compliance with specified conditions laid down by SEC

The fraud provision of the law applies to all sales of securities in interstate commerce or by use of the mails, whether or not they are exempt from registration.

In general, the registration forms call for disclosure of information such as (1) description of the registrant's business and its development, (2) description of the significant provisions of the security to be offered for sale and its relationship to the registrant's other capital securities, (3) information as to the management, how much it is paid by the registrant, and what dealings it has with him, and (4) certified financial statements, including a balance sheet, profit-and-loss statements, and detailed supporting schedules.

Private sources.   Small business needing capital of under $100,000 rarely obtains it by selling shares to the general public, nor is it economical for a small business to seek capital that way.   Such enterprises depend to some extent on bank borrowing and trade credits.   For the equity money they look to their own personal savings, to friends and relatives, to a limited number of local businessmen who may be ready to go into a new venture, and sometimes to companies which they supply or services to which they constitute an outlet. Companies sometimes get equity money from employees, from their customers, and from dealers and suppliers.

There are many individuals who, because of tastes, interests, their tax position, like to take a position in promising situations.   There are some of these individuals in almost every sizable community.   There are some who range nationwide for promising situations in which they can take a position at an early stage.   Some investment-banking firms will find or put up equity money to bring a promising company with growth opportunities to the point where it is ripe for public investment.   Private investors can be found through investment-banking firms, through your local banker or his larger correspondents in the larger cities, and by the simple method of advertising what you have to sell in business-opportunity sections of newspapers, trade magazines, and financial media.

The private investor will be looking for a shot at capital gain with as little risk as possible.   He also wants to conserve his capital for another venture if one should come along.   This means that he will probably want to lend money to the venture on a subordinated-debenture basis so that he can get paid back out of earnings without having those earnings treated as taxable dividends. He will probably want detachable warrants as the medium for realizing his capital gain. Sometimes, if there seems to be a lot of risk in the deal, he will want IRC Sec. 1244, or "small-business," stock so that he can charge off any loss against ordinary income.

This Sec. 1244 stock permits high-income investors to invest in small business ventures on much the same tax basis that they can drill for oil. If it is no good, they can sell their stock, and if the loss is $25,000 ($50,000 for husband and wife), it can be charged against that year's income. If it is good, they can hold or cash in at capital-gain rates.

Another way to attract a private investor is to show him that his money can be charged off against his personal income as it is spent—that he does not have to wait until the venture is bankrupt to get his charge-off. This can be done in two ways: (1) by starting the venture as a limited partnership or joint venture (this permits losses of the venture as reported on the partnership tax return to be deducted proportionately by the partners), or (2) by creating a corporation having no more than 10 stockholders and electing to have it taxed as a partnership.

When either form of venture stops losing and starts making money, it can be converted to the usual corporate taxpayer, paying 30 percent on the first $25,000 of net and 52 percent on additional net. The stock becomes the medium of capital gain.

The important thing is to show the private investor—

That he is risking only his after-tax dollar worth 10 cents or more, depending on his tax bracket

That each $1 of investment can be worth $5, $10, depending on the potential of the venture and how optimistic he wants to be. To do this properly takes some carefully worked out projections

That each $10 of future value can be cashed in for $7.50

That he is thus risking only his after-tax dollar, say 30 cents, to shoot for say a 10:1 return, which can be cashed in at $7.50. Thus he is really risking 30 cents to shoot for a 25:1 return, although the risks and potential of the venture, without the tax factors, indicate only a 10:1 return

Common stock. The individuals who buy the common stock of a corporation bear the ultimate risk. It is they who will enjoy the major fruits of its success or take the first loss of its failure. An individual bears this risk of buying common stock in the hope and expectation that his investment will be secured by the assets into which his money will be converted and that the enterprise will create enough value to pay him a return on his money. As a common stockholder he gets no guaranty of return or rate of return, and he will not receive anything until interest has been paid to creditors and dividends to preferred stockholders, if any. For assuming the brunt of the risk, an individual putting his savings into common stock usually wants some expectancy that earnings available for common stock will be enough so that, after the enterprise has proved its capacity to earn, less venturesome individuals will be willing to pay more for his stock and take a smaller but now more assured rate of return.   That is how capital values are enhanced as earnings mature and the risk is shaken out of an enterprise.   That is why an investor in the common stock of a new enterprise wants to see that the business may be capable of earning more than a normal investment return.   That is why, in offering common stock to prospective investors, it is necessary to project a possible and a probable rate of return.   A cautious investor will want to see that prior charges will be serviced and that he will get an investment return on his money if the business, for example, operates at from 50 to 75 percent of its capacity. The working figure will vary with the risk element in the enterprise and the stability of the particular line of business.   Such prudent discounting of maximum results should be presented to give the investor some degree of safety. Then the compensation for remaining risk will have to come from the prospect of substantial profit and capital appreciation, if the business should exceed the discounted level and achieve maximum volume and profit ability. In judging the rate of return which will be attractive to investors, one should compare the probable investment yields with those shown by profitable companies.   At a time when going companies with years of successful experience are selling at a price where the established dividend rate yields 8 percent, it will be necessary to show the prospect of a substantially higher return in order to interest a prudent investor in taking the risk of an unproved enterprise. When securities are selling below their book value and at a price where dividend rates show a high rate of return on money used to buy securities available and salable on public exchanges, it becomes very difficult to raise money for a new company or to expand an existing company without seriously diluting the equity of present stockholders.

Preferred stock.   Investors may be more willing to put capital into an enterprise if they are given a prior right to dividends and a first claim on assets if the business should be terminated and liquidated.   This is accomplished by issuance of preferred stock.   In financing a small company, preferred stock may be particularly appropriate where the individuals who are to be active have put up only a small proportion of the available money.   Investors who are not to be active may be given a participation in the ultimate success of the business by buying common shares at a relatively low price and may also be given priority as to the major portion of their investment by the issuance of stock preferred as to dividends and distribution.

There are many varieties of preferred stock.   It may be cumulative or noncumulative.   If, when a company fails to pay the prescribed rate of dividend on preferred stock, the arrears are accumulated and the accumulation must be paid before dividends can be declared on the common stock, preferred stock is said to be cumulative. If dividends on preferred stock are payable only as earned, and failure to pay the dividend in any one year does not create any obligation to make up the deficiency in subsequent years, a preferred stock is said to be noncumulative. Preferred stock may be callable or noncallable. If, at a specified time, it may be retired upon payment of a specified redemption price, a preferred stock is said to be callable. If it carries no such provisions, it is noncallable. A preferred stock may be participating or nonparticipating. It is participating if it is provided that after the common has received a specified rate or amount of dividends, additional dividends are to be shared with the preferred on some specified basis. The participation itself may be limited so that after the preferred receives a specified dividend over and above the required rate it no longer shares in profits beyond that point. If the preferred stock is to receive only the specified rate of dividend and that is the limit no matter how high the dividend on the common, then it is a nonparticipating preferred stock. The issuance of a preferred stock may provide that a sinking fund is to be established to redeem the preferred stock. The requirements and existence of a sinking fund usually improve the attractiveness and the value of a preferred stock.

Conversion privileges. If the ordinary limited returns upon preferred stock or upon bonds is insufficient to attract investment money, a further attraction may take the form of conversion features. This privilege permits the holder to convert his stocks or bonds into a stipulated number of common shares whenever he believes that it is to his advantage to do so within specified time limits. Thus, in addition to a prior claim on earnings and assets, the holder of a preferred stock or bond can be given a participation in the appreciation of value which will come to the common stock if the business is successful. Whenever the value of common stock exceeds the rate at which preferred stock can be converted into common, sufficiently to compensate the holder for the priority he gives up, the conversion option will normally be exercised. If a preferred stock has a face value of $100 and is convertible into four shares of common, the preferred stockholders get an extra run for their money because, when the value of the common stock moves beyond $25 and looks as though it will stay there, a profitable conversion can be made. The existence of a conversion privilege is frequently considered a sign of financial weakness. It is an indication that the company could not obtain funds entirely on its own credit standing. On the other hand, when conversions are made, a company strengthens its financial structure because it is relieved of fixed charges and enhances its equity base. Its capacity to issue new securities to meet emergencies and to expand is improved. The trick in using conversion privileges to advantage is to place the price at which the privilege may be exercised low enough to make it attractive, and yet not so low that it will unduly dilute the per-share value of the common stock and so injure the position of the original holders of common stock. The conversion price must be placed somewhat above the market price of the common stock at the time the new security is being sold. If it is placed too high above the prevailing market price, its value in attracting investors to the new security is diminished. If it is placed too close to the market price, the present common stockholders will share the profits from the risk they have been bearing at too early a date. If a preferred stockholder has the option of acquiring common stock at $50 per share, and the stock appreciates to $80 before any conversions are made, the conversions will dilute the value of the equity and bring the per-share value of the common stock down below $80. Earning power per share will be similarly diluted because a given level of earnings applicable to common will have to be shared with that many additional holders of common stock. The interests of the common stockholders may be protected to some extent by so arranging the conversion privilege that the conversion price will be raised by gradual steps over a period of years.

Convertible, participating preference stock. A new type of preference stock offering maximum flexibility to the investor and which, therefore, should be effective in attracting new money, is illustrated by Litton Industries' issue of "convertible preference stock, participating series." Here is a rundown of the main features of the stock—

> The holder is entitled to cash dividends if cash dividends are declared on the common stock. The rate of dividend is equal to the amount declared on the common multiplied by the number of shares of common stock into which the preference stock is convertible
>
> Conversion ratio of the preference starts out on the basis of one share of common for each share of preference and increases each year for 24 years until it finally reaches the point where the holder is entitled to 2.0145 shares of common for each share of preference
>
> As an alternative to converting, the holder may sell up to 3 percent of his preference shares each year without reducing the number of shares into which the remaining preference stock is convertible
>
> It is expected that the proceeds of future redemptions (which will be for a higher amount each year) will be taxable at capital-gains rates

Sale of additional stock to stockholders. Going concerns sometimes finance their expansions by offering, at least initially, new common stock to existing stockholders. Most corporations have charters which give existing stockholders preemptive rights on the issue of additional common stock. This is done in order to give stockholders an opportunity to preserve their control and their share of surplus and goodwill. The new stock is offered for less than current market or book value. The technique of offering existing stockholders privilege subscriptions to new stock usually involves the issuance of rights or warrants. Such rights are readily transferable and have a market value that depends upon the spread between the market price of the stock and the subscription price at which the rights may be exercised. An offer of a security by the issuance of rights to existing stockholders may be underwritten by investment bankers.

The offering of subscription rights will fail if the market price falls below the subscription price during the subscription period.   This risk may be calculated and hedged in these terms—

   The issue must be small enough to be absorbed.   Existing stockholders are
      much more likely to absorb another 10 percent addition to outstanding
      stock than a doubling of outstanding stock.   For this reason, it may be
      desirable to spread an expansion program over a period of years and offer
      rights in a succession of small amounts rather than in a single large offering
   The greater the spread between market price and the price at which new
      stock may be acquired, the greater the chance that the market price will
      stay above subscription price and that the offering will be a success
   The investment quality of the stock, its market performance of the past, and
      the general business outlook must be gauged.   Finally, the distribution of
      stock holdings, the kind of stockholders (wealthy, medium, or small; safety-
      minded or speculation-minded) and the size of their holdings must be care-
      fully evaluated

Employees as stockholders.   Many large companies make stock available to their employees as a regular practice.   Sometimes this is done through employer-financed stock-purchase plans, bank-financed stock-purchase plans, or savings and profit-sharing plans in which the funds are invested in company stock.

Although stock-purchase plans are generally adopted to provide incentive for employees, they are also an excellent method of financing the needs of a growing business.   The capacity of employees to generate equity is substantial.   If, for example, 50 employees each make purchases of stock amounting to $300 per year, the company will be raising $15,000 per year.   In 5 years, this amounts to $75,000; in 10 years this figure is doubled.

How employees become owners.   Employee ownership is being accomplished in different companies and in different industries by a wide variety of methods. These methods range from the formal and direct employee-purchase plan, through the indirect method of having employee-benefit trusts buy company stock, to informal arrangements between owners and their executives and other employees.

Methods being used today are—

   Formal stock-purchase plans.   The employer offers newly issued treasury
      stock to employees and has the employees pay for it through payroll de-
      ductions or other methods.   American Telephone & Telegraph has prob-
      ably the largest program of this character
   Stock-options plans.   Employees get the privilege of buying stock, but are
      not committed to buy, and probably do not buy until a rise in the market
      has made it very attractive.   Eastern Air Lines has made such a plan
      available to all rank-and-file employees, and a large portion of that com-
      pany is now owned by employees

Stock bought through a bank. Some companies make stock available to employees, arrange with a bank to finance the purchase, and then the employees are on their own

Informal stock-purchase plans. In some companies, the employees get together informally and commit themselves as a group to buy blocks of stock in large enough denominations to save brokerage commissions. A group of the employees of the Chemical Bank New York Trust buys stock of the bank on this basis

Purchase through employee organizations. Executives of the General Electric Company have had an investment trust buying company stock for a long time. Employees of the Phillips Petroleum Company are helped to buy company shares by a fraternal and charitable organization established by employees of the company. The group buys in round lots, thus saving brokerage commissions, and helps individual employees finance their purchases

Employee internal exchange for employee purchases and sales. In some companies whose stock is not traded, the price is established by conducting an employee exchange for the sale and purchase of shares of the company stock

Purchase of shares by profit-sharing trust. More and more profit-sharing trusts are following a regular program of buying company stock. The Sears, Roebuck profit-sharing trust has been doing this for a good many years and now owns more than 25 percent of that company

Outright purchase of a business by an employee trust. Sometimes a pension or profit-sharing trust will buy all the stock of the company which created it. This happened with Cleveland Pneumatic Tool and with a chain of meat markets in Chicago. The employee trust of the Arthur D. Little research firm bought a large block of that company's stock previously owned by a charitable trust created by the founder

Stock bonuses. Many companies bring their executives and employees into ownership by the practice of paying year-end bonuses in company stock

Awards made in stock. It is becoming an increasingly common practice for companies to award stock as prizes under suggestion systems, sales contracts, etc. Another example in this category is the program at General Electric where employees are given shares of stock as an incentive to save through the purchase of government bonds

Insurance-funded stock-purchase plans. In many closely held companies, a program has been set up under which executives insure the lives of the working owners and contract to use the insurance proceeds to purchase the stock of the company on the owners' death

Sales to executives. The pressure to meet impending estate-tax liability and the effect of income taxes in minimizing the ability of individuals to save enough money to buy an important interest in the business have combined to cause many owners to work out a program to sell the business to a group of executives. This is sometimes done by the owner during his lifetime. It is sometimes the only way in which an executor can dispose of the business interest of a deceased owner.

How the stock is paid for. The employees may pay for their stock (1) in cash, (2) through deductions from the payroll, or (3) by means of loans from the employer with the stock held as collateral.

The first two methods are simple in operation: The stock is turned over to the employee when he finishes paying for it. The third method is more complicated. The transaction takes place as a sale on credit. The employee buys the stock immediately at the current price, but the company keeps it as security for payment of the loan.

There is a tax danger in the third method; the Treasury may claim that the loan is actually compensation with the stock-purchase factor not genuine. To forestall this possibility, the purchase plan should make it clear that an employee acquires ownership of the stock when he enters the plan and has no right to rescind the purchase. These elements should be present:

Sale price equals fair market value of the stock at the time of purchase
Full ownership of the stock, including the right to dividends, passes to the
    employee
A fair rate of interest is charged on the loan
The employee is legally liable for the full purchase price (it is all right to
    permit him to assign his dividends to be applied to the purchase price)
The loan installments should be over a reasonable period of time, with
    appropriate installment terms. The employee need not remain with the
    company throughout the entire installment period

Intercompany financing. It is not uncommon for large companies to give financial aid to smaller companies to whom they sell or from whom they buy. The advances of the larger companies in such cases are not viewed as investments that return a yield but as a common-sense method of promoting an outlet for goods or of preserving a source of supply. In a seller's market the flow of funds is from large companies to small company suppliers. In a buyer's market the flow is from large companies to smaller company customers.

Investors with an interest hope for more than a satisfactory return on their investment. As a rule such an investor looks forward to a long period of mutually profitable trade transactions between himself and the debtor. More often than not, the profit to be derived from these transactions dwarfs the return promised on the investment and renders safety a matter of secondary importance. Back in 1903 a certain large mail-order house advanced $30,000 to one of its suppliers. The eyes of the officials who decided upon this advance were focused not on the interest charged on this loan but on the profits that would accrue to the larger company from the sale of the debtor's product during the course of the next 50 years. An economic by-product of this particular loan was the conversion of a small struggling producer into the world's largest manufacturer in the line. Today the company boasts nine factories and four display rooms. A portion of its product is still marketed through the mail-order

house, but it also sells to a large number of independently owned retail outlets, many of whom owe their existence to the aid given them by the manufacturer.

There are three types of intercompany aid:

1. The most common form of intercompany financial aid grows from the
   practice of selling merchandise on credit.   When the seller himself cannot
   afford to finance the sale, he often takes the buyer's note for discount.   In
   this way his credit standing causes bank credit to be made available to
   buyers who normally would not be able to demand bank accommodation.
   Examples of seller financing through intercompany loans are easy to cite.
   It is common practice in the automobile field.   Most of the large trucking companies that exist today started when a driver made a down payment on a truck, agreeing to pay off the balance on an installment basis.
   Small road contractors frequently purchase equipment in this manner.
   The chief disadvantage of ordinary trade credit is that, like bank loans,
   it is short-term credit and must be renewed from time to time.   If business activity declines, the supplier of the credit may become alarmed and
   curtail his aid, and this would deprive a small business venture of credit at
   a time of its greatest need.   The only restraining influence on such cur-
   tailments is the desire of the larger company for a combined outlet for its
   goods.

2. Of much greater value to a small company is a grant of credit by one
   of its suppliers for purposes other than to finance a sale by the latter and
   on terms such as do not make it necessary to renew the contract periodically.   Examples of such advances are purchases by large companies of
   the common stock, preferred stock, or long-term bonds of a smaller company.   The interest of the larger company in such cases is almost always
   to conserve or to strengthen an outlet for its own products.   Thus in
   1939 we find a certain large oil company purchasing $400,000 of the 3
   percent notes of a national trucking company.   During liquidation proceedings for a prominent furniture company, it was revealed that a large
   radio manufacturer (who was a customer of the furniture company) and
   a certain truck company (who sold transportation services to the furniture
   company) had jointly advanced the company $950,000 of funds.   The
   pages of Moody's Investment Manuals contain numerous examples of
   companies that have purchased the stocks and bonds of the smaller
   companies to whom they sell.

3. It is even more common practice for large corporate buyers to extend
   financial aid to smaller corporate sellers, the motivating interest of the
   larger company being to conserve and to strengthen an important source
   of supply.   The effect is often to develop the weaker company into a
   strong producer.   An officer of a large mercantile corporation writes:

   Our company has for many years given financial assistance to smaller companies, many
of which are our most valued sources.   Capital is made available in three ways:
   1. Direct lending of money to small manufacturers during their peak production season.

2. Investment of money in factories through the purchase of stock.
3. Arrangements through field warehousing financing companies.

That such aid proves beneficial and is appreciated is obvious from the
following comment of the treasurer of one of the recipient companies:

In the early years of our company, some 25 or 30 years ago when our business was very
small, one of our large corporate customers did at times render financial assistance to us
by advancing sums of money upon request when we were in special need of it. In that way
they were a very direct assistance to a small struggling company. Although we might have
secured funds elsewhere, nevertheless they did give us assistance when the need was great
and thereby, no doubt, were instrumental in developing a strong source for the products
which we manufacture for them.
I believe that large companies often do just that in assisting their smaller sources of
supply, especially in difficult economic times.

Customers as stockholders. Utilities and railroads have sold stock extensively
to customers. Distributors have purchased stock in companies making products which they handle. The United Drug Company was financed by druggists
who handled "Rexall" products manufactured by the company. Customer
stock ownership is sometimes an effective and an economical way to raise
capital. It is frequently conceived as a method of tying the customers to the
company and ensuring continued business with them. This method may backfire, particularly when the fall in the value of stock creates dissatisfaction in a
customer who may be satisfied with the product and the service he is receiving.

Contract advances. Some companies have been able to do some of their
initial financing and expansion financing by getting customers to make deposits
or to advance money on contracts. Large companies will give this kind of aid
to companies which they seek to develop or maintain as supply sources.

Franchising. Over the last 5 years, many businesses have turned to franchising or licensing distributors, local outlets, and local service organizations as
a means of accelerating their expansion. Today it is estimated that there are
over 400 companies offering franchises on a national basis and 100,000 small
businesses operating under a franchise.

Franchising is a method of adding capital. The president of one franchiser
has stated: "By franchising, we can grow with the other fellow's capital."
But it is more than that. With the capital comes another distributor. He is
a distributor who has put his money into the business and who stands to lose
it if he does not perform and to realize significant rewards if he does; thus,
franchising strengthens the organization and adds marketing power, in addition
to bringing in money for rights, training, advertising material, inventory,
equipment, etc.

Franchising is a licensing arrangement. A company which owns a branded
product, method, or service can arrange with a group of dealers to handle its
retail distribution. The franchiser retains control over the merchandising
methods. He gets his revenue through either a fee or sale of equipment or
material, plus, in many cases, a percentage of the gross. What does the

franchisee get for his money and his effort? He gets access to a tested and accepted product or service, together with all the merchandising, research, management, and promotion know-how of the franchiser.

The usual franchise specifies a capital requirement. The franchisee will have to put up a specified amount of money. Some of this money may go for a royalty, or admission fee, or training. Most of it will buy the inventory or the equipment necessary to carry on the business locally. Sometimes it is necessary to buy land and a building to carry on the franchise operation. For example, it is estimated that anyone who establishes a Howard Johnson franchise motor lodge will have to invest about $1,000 a room for land, building, supplies, and equipment. One paint-store chain requires $7,000; a water-conditioner franchise for one company requires an investment running between $75 and $100 per customer. A Manpower, Inc., franchise, providing part-time workers to local industry, calls for a training-course fee running between $1,000 to $2,000 and a first-year investment which may run to $15,000.

This money is put up to launch and operate the franchisee's business. But much of it goes back to the company offering the franchise, in a one-shot purchase of equipment, payment for training or rights, or in a continued flow of orders for inventory, or continued royalty payments. This additional flow of money makes it possible for many companies to expand more rapidly and with less financing via the franchise system than would be possible in any other way.

It is possible to bring the distribution power built up by franchising back into the parent company. For example, Holiday Inns has built or licensed scores of motels throughout the country. All but 15 percent of them are franchised. Now, Holiday Inns is willing to buy up franchised motels through exchange of stock, on the basis of one share of common and three shares of Class A common for each unit. The deal is planned so that each share will bring the company pretax earnings of $5 per share. The arrrangement enables the franchisee to convert his equity into stock with a market value. In one instance, where an individual operated a St. Louis inn, the franchisee had made an initial investment of $400,000, on what was originally a 100-unit motel—later expanded to 304 rooms. Subsequently, he swapped this property for $1 million worth of Holiday Inns' stock. Holiday Inns expanded much more rapidly by franchising than it could have by building the motels directly. Now, by issuing additional stock to some of its franchisees, it is able to incorporate these franchise units back into its permanent capital structure.

4. Debt financing—ways and means

Bond issues. Bonds give the investor a fixed claim on assets and a fixed income rate. They give the owners of a corporation financing without diluting their control or ownership. Prevailing low interest rates and deduction of interest in computing corporate tax make bond financing cheap. Bonds carry a fixed charge which may be burdensome in adversity. They also have a fixed maturity value, which gives the equity owners the full value of any increment in value enjoyed by corporate property.

Bonds which are secured by mortgage on the corporation's real property, such as mortgage bonds, or by other tangible property such as equipment trust certificates, or by securities or intangible assets, pledged in trust as collateral trust bonds, can usually be arranged for longer maturities and at lower interest rates.

Debenture bonds are secured only by the general credit of the company. It may be provided that if a mortgage is issued in any subsequent financing, outstanding debentures will share in the lien equally and ratably with the new financing. In closely held companies, in order to bolster general credit, it is sometimes provided that debentures issued to stockholders will be subordinated to the claims of general creditors. Debenture bonds may be given extra attraction by making them convertible into stock, or by issuing a warrant to each bondholder which gives the bondholder the right to purchase common stock at specified prices. This gives the bondholder a share in the prosperity of the first-risk stockholders, if the company is successful.

Bonds have been issued which give bondholders a right to participate in stock earnings over and above a certain level. This is a doubtful practice. Where it is desired to give bondholders an equity stake, it is probably better to sell them a package with some low-cost stock with each debenture. This permits each bondholder to separate his two investments and sell each off separately and gives the corporation a more rational capital structure.

There are such things as income bonds which require payment of interest only on an "as and if earned" basis. This practice is doubtful because it runs into a question whether the securities are really bonds or preferred stock, and whether the payments are deductible or nondeductible interest for tax purposes. It also opens up endless dispute whether the accounting, which shows either income or the lack thereof, is valid.

Requiring the establishment and maintenance of a sinking fund to retire a bond issue enhances its value. Financing flexibility is imparted by the provision that bonds may be called before maturity.

Tax counsel must be consulted to assure that bonds are not likely to lose their tax advantages by being treated as preferred stock—

Because the ratio of debt to stock is inordinately high
Because bonds are subordinated to bank loans and creditors
Because interest is contingent on earnings
Because stockholders hold notes in the same proportion as they hold stock

Any combination of these factors makes it possible for the Treasury to contend that the bonds are in fact the equivalent of stock.

Mortgage loans. Of the different ways open to the businessman for raising cash for his enterprises, the mortgage is one of the most widely used, since it furnishes a quick and easy way of raising money.

If you are thinking of making a mortgage loan, you should know the different types of mortgage loans that are available to you and the institutions which are in the business of making those loans. You should also be familiar with the tax advantages of mortgaging, as well as with its other advantages.

You should know, for example, that you can get property worth more for less cash and still get your depreciation on the full value of the property—not just your equity. In this manner, you can cut your taxable return from the property without cutting into the cash income. A rise in value belongs to you even though your equity in the property may be far less than the mortgage debt on it. But, of course, by the same token, any decline in the property is your loss, not the mortgagee's.

Appreciation of the effect of mortgages on real estate also involves knowing how and when to sell your property because of the mortgage situation and when and how refinancing is to be attempted.

How to apply for a mortgage loan. If you are seeking to finance your venture by way of a mortgage from a large institutional lender, you will find that the proper preparation of your mortgage application will go a long way toward making your efforts successful. Most important to keep in mind is that every detail of the proposed development should be put in writing.

What type of mortgage suits your purpose? Mortgages are either short-term (usually 1 year) or long-term (over 5 years). In terms of priority, mortgages are either senior or primary (first mortgages), or junior or secondary (second, third, or fourth mortgages). Different lenders specialize in different types and each type has its own use.

How short-term mortgages are used for interim or construction financing. The most important use of the short-term (first) mortgage is to provide financing for construction of new buildings or improvement of existing structures. Some lenders are restricted by law from making these loans and others do not do so from choice. The furthest these lenders will go is to issue a commitment for a "permanent" mortgage when the building is completed (known as a "takeout" commitment). There are two reasons why construction loans involve extra risk. First, possible delays in construction or unanticipated costs can result in failure of the project. Second, changes in the real-estate or economic picture can make it impossible to obtain a profitable rent roll.

Short-term construction loans are made, however, by commercial banks, some savings institutions, and private mortgage companies and investors who are attracted by the higher return. The loans usually run for 1 year, although shorter periods can be arranged.

Long-term mortgage money. The long-term mortgage loan provides the businessman with a means of obtaining a loan up to 75 percent or more of the value of his property for a term of anywhere from 15 to 30 years. The major sources of long-term mortgage money are insurance companies, pension funds, saving and loan associations, mutual savings banks, and commercial banks.

Virtually all long-term mortgages are primary liens on the property. The occasional long-term second mortgage is usually a purchase-money mortgage which has been extended by the seller in order to make the sale. Long-term loans are mainly distinguished by the extent to which they are amortized prior to maturity. Generally, this type of loan is made with the expectation of full or partial amortization.

Term loans. A business loan which runs for a term of more than 1 year with provisions for amortization or retirement over the life of the loan is a term loan. Such a loan, even if secured, will depend upon the bank's appraisal of the long-range prospect of the company, its earning power, and the quality of its management. The term is sometimes a maximum of 10 years, but more often 3 or 5.

Term loans are usually restricted to large companies whose organization precludes the possibility that repayment of the loan will hinge on the abilities of a few key individuals. Lines that are stable, such as merchandising and foodstuffs, are preferred; and it is difficult for those in an industry with sharp ups and downs, like construction, to obtain term-loan financing.

The current position of the company is very important. In some cases the bank will require that current assets exceed current liabilities in at least the traditional 2:1 ratio. If the company shows considerable fluctuation in earnings over a period of several years, the required ratio may be much higher. The banker may require that the ratio of equity capital to debt shall be more than 1:1.

A term loan may be for short periods and for small sums. A small term loan is usually secured by real estate or equipment, with repayment in equal installments within 5 years.

Many term loans are backed by collateral security, but the bank must still rely primarily upon the ability of the company to repay the indebtedness out of earnings over the life of the loan. This means that the ability of the businessman to operate his business on a profitable basis is more important to the bank than the liquidation value of the security. Fixed assets disposed of at forced sale seldom realize more than a small portion of their book value. The additional security merely strengthens the possibility that the banker will be able to recover his loan with interest during its life.

Equal installment payments are not the only form of repayment. Repayment may follow along seasonal lines—calling for a large payment when income is high. The loan may be repaid on almost any agreed basis. For example, monthly, quarterly, or annual payments may be stipulated, depending upon the nature of the borrower's business and the use to which the funds are to be placed. Early payments are usually relatively small, with large final payments, again depending on the surrounding circumstances. Also, the agreement usually provides that in case of default on any installment, the balance of the loan becomes due at the lender's option.

Interest charges for term loans run higher than rates for short-term loans, and the smaller term loans are even more expensive. The term loan is tailored to meet a specific situation, and so no standard interest rates can be quoted. Overall, the larger the loan and the better the company collateral, the lower the interest rate.

Under a term loan, the bank will usually insist that the company follow certain definite operating policies. Therefore, these loans are usually covered by a comprehensive agreement calculated to protect the bank against drastic changes in the value of the security or in the business income available for repayment of principal and payment of interest. The agreement binds the borrower to maintain working capital at an agreed level and to secure bank approval before making capital expenditures over a certain amount, limits the amount to be paid in salaries and bonuses, keeps assets free of encumbrances, and applies a certain portion of net profits to loan repayments, over and above the amount stipulated in the borrower's note.

Trade credit. Credit granted by the seller to the buyer of materials or merchandise is called "trade credit." It is highly important, particularly for the small business which has difficulty in raising capital from other sources. Granting of trade credit by suppliers of parts and raw materials to manufacturers, by manufacturers to wholesalers, and by wholesalers to retailers is a well-established practice and is at least as significant a source of financing as bank credit. A trade creditor looks at his extensions of credit quite differently than does a bank. Trade credit is considered a requirement and aid to selling. It is usually covered by a profit margin more substantial than usual interest rates. Bad-debt losses are not regarded as net loss until the net-profit margin on the business has been wiped out. A seller may even feel that if he rejects a class of business because of the credit risk, he will lose the contribution that business makes in covering fixed expenses as well as the possible profit margin. Likewise, in extending trade credit the seller is looking forward to establishing a continuing source of repeat sales. Forward-looking companies seek to build up trade customers and their credit rating by extending credit and helping them to merchandise and operate effectively.

Trade credit is normally extended on the basis of the credit reports of Dun & Bradstreet and other mercantile agencies and credit bureaus. This may be supplemented by checks with banks and other supply sources and credit references supplied by the buyer. The availability of trade credit will vary with the following factors:

The seller's own position will govern his willingness and ability to use liberal credit in his method of selling his goods

When inventories are heavy or moving slowly, and when the price outlook is dubious, trade credit will become more generously available

With the introduction of all products to a new market and of new products to a general market, easy credit terms are frequently used to stimulate sales

Longer credit terms may be expected on merchandise which moves slowly and has a long turnover period. The need to help distributors carry such inventory usually creates a trade practice of fairly long terms. Thus a retail jeweler would expect longer terms than a butcher

Similarly, the more standard the article, the more likely credit terms are to be generous. On novelty items which are difficult to sell, credit terms are held very tight

Customers located a long distance away from a source of supply may be able to get longer credit terms on the theory that they have to stock for a longer period of time

In a general depression, competition tends to extend credit terms and, even though credit terms are used to stimulate sales, to make sellers weed out weak customers and restrict credit to their more stable customers

The cost of trade credit may be calculated in terms of this discount offered for cash. When sellers offer a 30- or 60-day credit term, cash discount is ordinarily allowed for payment made within some specified period of 5 or 10 days. This time is calculated to cover the shipping period and to give the buyer a chance to check the merchandise before making his remittance. Where a 2 percent discount is allowed for payment within 10 days and the buyer is required to pay the entire bill at the end of the 30-day credit period, he is paying 2 percent for 20 days of credit if he fails to discount his bill—an annual rate of interest of 36 percent. When there is a 2 percent cash discount for payment in 10 days on a bill payable within 60 days, a buyer not taking the discount is paying 2 percent for 50 days of credit. When the situation is analyzed in this way, most companies will find that bank credit is ordinarily cheaper than trade credit, beyond the cash-discount period.

Selecting a bank. The choice of a bank is important in the development of proper credit facilities, and a good banking connection once made is a valuable asset. As a general rule, it is not necessary to shop around for a banking connection—a local bank can usually meet the company's banking needs in a thoroughly satisfactory manner. Some companies deliberately patronize more than one bank with the idea that if one bank turns down a request for a loan, the other will grant it. But this may backfire. One bank may want quick repayment for fear that the other will get repayment first. Where the local bank has restrictions which make it unable to meet the company's requirements, it is wise to go to another bank. But ordinarily it pays off to give one bank all your business, in the expectation that the bank will take care of a good customer in time of financial stress. Banks prefer the exclusive arrangement. In times of financial need the bank whose officials have a good working knowledge of a company's operations and financial background can take care of its credit needs more quickly and effectively. Start to develop this close relationship at the time the first bank account is opened.

The company should study the resources, experience, and policies of local banks and make a choice as soon as possible.

The first factor to be considered is the *size* of the bank. The company wants a bank that has financial resources to satisfy its maximum anticipated needs. And the relative sizes of bank and company are important. A small company may get more consideration from a small bank than from a large bank handling the accounts of huge corporations.

Second, consider the bank's *lending policy*. Banks differ in this; and it is important to ascertain just how much the bank likes to lend, for how long a period, at what interest rate, and with what security. Some banks have special experience and feel sure of their judgment in particular lines of business. Discussions might be held with the bank officials to determine the bank's experience in and understanding of your kind of business. The bank you finally select should be the one that seems to understand and be willing to cooperate with your company's plans.

Third, weigh the bank's *safety* factor. A bank is a company as well as a possible lender. Study the bank's financial statements and any other information you can get. Analysis of the bank's financial reports can minimize the danger in suffering loss and embarrassment from bank failure. Deposits in banks participating in the Federal Deposit Insurance Corporation are insured up to $15,000, but many companies will anticipate deposits in excess of that figure.

In determining the safety of the bank's financial position, a company may rely upon ratio analysis. The three basic ratios to consider are—

1. The ratio of net worth to total deposits or to total risk assets (all assets less cash and short-term government securities)
2. The quick-assets ratio (cash and short-term government securities as a percentage of deposits or assets)
3. The ratio of liquid funds to business loans

These are not the only ratios to consider. Any figure on the bank statement that appears to be out of line should be analyzed. The company may be interested in the bank's earnings ratios expressed as a percentage of total capital assets. Usually, if a bank's assets are predominantly quick assets, it is a better credit risk than one wherein risk assets predominate. But predominantly quick assets also mean that the bank's management is ultraconservative—or too satisfied with small earnings to find a more profitable way to invest funds.

Look, too, at these factors:

Bank personnel. Check the services the bank offers and how experienced in financial arrangements its personnel appear to be

The experience of the bank in your line of business and its credit problems

The bank's location and overall facilities (such as parking, night depository services, payroll services, and banking-by-mail privileges)

The bank's corresponding relationships. Good relations with larger banks provide useful contacts and become particularly important when your credit needs exceed the bank's loan limits

Ability to borrow from a conservative and well-known bank and to use it as a financial reference can enhance your company's prestige and credit standing.

Your approach to a banker. When you ask a banker for a loan, you are a potential customer. Do not put yourself in a position of asking for a favor. Know what you are entitled to, how much credit your position justifies, what price you should pay for the money, what security you should give. Know how much you need, exactly what you need it for, and when you wil be able to repay it. Be in a position to spell this out so that it will make sense to the banker in his terms. His terms are, "When do I get the money back, and how much certainty can I get that any loan I make will be good?"

Have all the necessary facts and figures about your own business, about competitive conditions and opportunities, and the problems in the industry. Lay all the cards on the table. Tell the banker all your problems and possible pitfalls. You want to establish a permanent relationship, and you do not want the banker to experience any unpleasant surprises. The banker will draw you into a discussion about your business. He will want to see whether you have the ability to step aside and evaluate the condition of your business and the problems it faces, whether you are aware of future contingencies, whether you have business ability. At the same time, he will be informing himself about conditions and circumstances in your business so as to be better able to judge your loan application. Carry on this discussion with complete frankness, and be sure you have full knowledge of the current business situation inside and outside your business.

Frequently the discussion will indicate that the bank will not find it possible to lend you all the money you need, but that if you can get additional equity capital into the business, you will qualify for credit.

Small businesses can usually get bank credit only for seasonal purposes—manufacturers who have to buy inventory for fabrication and sale later on; distributors, jobbers, and retailers who must accumulate inventories preparatory to cold or warm weather, school, or holiday demand. Banks will sometimes lend money pending the realization of profits or the collection of receivables. Then, less regularly, loans for longer periods of time may be obtained against equipment and real estate.

The banker will want to know the use to which the borrowed funds will be put. Back up your loan proposal by showing that reasonable achievement of the purpose of the loan will provide an adequate margin of safety for the repayment of the loan without impairment of your capital. Do not ask for a bank loan for a purely speculative purpose. Suggest a repayment plan that you can reasonably meet. Show the banker a cash projection which you can back up and meet and which will retire the loan you want.

How the banker looks at you. The banker is going to need additional information which he will get partially from discussion with the prospective borrower, partially from checking his credit files, and partially from checking with other creditors. The customer's or prospect's credit file and the accumulated information about a particular business and its owner are of tremendous importance in every loan decision. It is a marked trail which leads the experienced lending officer back through the history of the organization and its officers, and enables him to uncover and evaluate information that might not otherwise be made available to him.

The banker will want to know these things about the prospective borrower:

His character, ability, and capacity. Is the principal reliable? Does he make good on his commitments? Does he have the ability and the energy to carry out his plans? Does he have proven management ability? Does the organization have depth of management?

What kind of capital resources does he have? Is the equity of the business enough to carry the job? Are his own assets fully committed to the enterprise? Does the borrower have ability to supply further funds? Could he raise equity money outside? Is there a proper relationship between the capital commitments of the business and the amount of the loan requested, together with other debt which the business may be carrying?

What kind of business organization is it? How good are its executives? Do they know where they are going? What has been the sales trend? Does it indicate acceptability of products? How competitive is the business? Is there product diversification? Is too much money going into new products? What is its reputation in the trade? How effective is its sales organization? Are its plant and equipment old and uncompetitive? Are its financial records and controls adequate? Has the profit trend been healthy? Are its margins good enough to support the present level of overhead? Are disbursements for dividends, salaries, and bonuses in balance with sales, profits, net worth, and working capital?

Will the loan be a sound one? Is it for a proper purpose? Does the cashflow projection show that it can be repaid on the due date? Is working capital after scaling down past-due receivables and stale inventory sufficient to cover a reasonable loss and still provide reasonable protection for the loan and other creditors? Does the applicant have enough of his capital in the business as evidenced by net worth in relation to advances from trade creditors, other creditors, and the new bank loan? Are any of the following conditions present to an extent which would throw doubt on the financial soundness of the business—
Heavy inventories in relation to sales?
Excessive dividends and salary withdrawals?
Heavy loans to officers of subsidiary organizations?

Large past-due receivables?

Top-heavy debt?

Too much investment in fixed assets?

An overextended position, indicated by excessive inventory receivables and debt, scrambling to apply income and funds to pay the most insistent creditors?

A revenue structure which indicates that any sharp drop in sales would throw the business into serious financial trouble?

Types of bank accommodations.   A company should familiarize itself with the various kinds of loan accommodations a bank is willing to extend.   It is advantageous for the company to know the different types of loans a bank will grant—the interest rates, terms, and security requirements of each.

Line of credit.   A line of credit is merely a declaration by a bank that, until further notice, it is prepared to lend up to a stated maximum amount on certain terms and conditions to the prospective borrower.   Since the line of credit is only a declaration of intent, it can be canceled at any time.   The availability of a line of credit is very valuable because, instead of fixed credits which call for continuing interest, only amounts of money actually used, plus a small commitment fee on any portion of the original commitment not actually consumed, are charged, which adds up to inexpensive financing.

The application for a line of credit is not an application for a loan, but simply an arrangement under which the bank agrees to make loans if funds are nedeed.   But even so, a bank conducts an intensive investigation before granting a line of credit.

It is not a requirement that the borrower must utilize the total amount of the line of credit; but if the borrower wants to formalize the line of credit into a written agreement (a standby contract), a fee is charged on the unused portion of the line of credit, usually a fraction of 1 percent.

Once the line of credit has been agreed upon by the bank and the borrower, it becomes the governing rule for the borrowing relationship.   As the borrower needs funds, it borrows against the line of credit.   Advances are evidenced by short-term notes, which are periodically reviewed and repaid, reduced, or extended.   If the loans must be cleared up annually, the borrower may have to borrow from another source or forego discounts and withhold payments to trade creditors.   When the borrower must clean up the loan annually, the company should accumulate any idle funds during the year by refraining from paying dividends and bonuses until the loan is repaid.

The establishment of a line of credit is a protection for the borrower, since ordinarily a bank will not reduce or cancel a line of credit without substantial cause.   The bank will keep a careful eye on the borrower's financial statements and the industrial and economic factors influencing the borrower in particular operations, so that the line of credit can be revised to meet new conditions.

A line of credit is not difficult to establish for a company which is seasonal and has the kind of inventory turnover which creates a peak financial need. In such cases, the line of credit is a highly desirable and flexible arrangement and should be the answer to most financial problems.

Short-term loans. Short-term bank loans are obtained either by individual borrowing or by obtaining a *line of credit* (above), against which advances may be obtained. Short-term borrowing is available to companies that have sufficient credit to minimize the bank's risk. The loan is granted on the basis of a study and analysis of the financial position of the company. The security for these loans is an installment note or a series of promissory notes which evidence the cash advance. These notes have maturity dates calling for repayment within a specified time period, usually within a year, at which time they are reviewed, repaid, reduced, or extended. Short-term loans are particularly effective for seasonal financing and building up inventories or to keep things running smoothly during spurts of seasonal activity. Before granting a short-term loan, the bank may require that between 10 and 20 percent of the loan actually made be kept on deposit, or that the loan be cleaned up at least once a year to assure the bank that the business is remaining liquid, to prevent the use of bank credit as permanent funds.

Interim financing. This is simply a high-interest short-term loan to tide you over until you can get permanent long-term financing. It is suited to the company that has a good competitive position and has met an opportunity to make a profitable business provided it can come up fast with a sizable sum of new money. It may also be suited where interest rates on a long-term financing are high and the company expects that they will decline by the time the short-term loan matures. If you are in this position and are already using a full credit line at your bank, you can get the necessary funds in one of two ways:

1. Get a standby commitment from a bank or other lender in this way. You get an interim financer to stand by—that is, he agrees that if you default, he will take over the loan. The bank, now protected, will lend you the money
2. Get a direct loan by putting up the collateral and paying the agreed-upon interest

Character loans. These are short-term, unsecured loans, generally restricted to companies or individuals with excellent credit reputations. If the businessman has high credit standing, he may be able to trade on this to obtain short-term funds.

Installment loans. Larger banks generally grant this type of loan. Installment loans are made for almost any productive purpose and may be granted for any period that the bank allows. Payments are usually made on a monthly basis; and as the obligation is reduced, it often may be refinanced at more ad-

vantageous rates.   The installment loan can be tailored to the seasonal requirements of the company, with heavy repayments in peak months, smaller payments
in the off season.

Equipment loans.   An increasingly popular method of raising funds is to
borrow money against machinery and equipment.   There are two main ways
of handling equipment loans.   The first is to pledge equipment to which the
company has an unencumbered title as security for the loan.   The second
method is via an installment-financing plan.

Time-purchase loans.   Many special types of time-purchase loans are available to finance both retailer and consumer purchase of automobiles, household
equipment, boats, mobile homes, industrial and farm equipment, etc., and are
made for varying periods of time, depending on the product.   This category
also includes accounts-receivable financing, indirect collections, and factoring.

Inventory loans.   These loans are available if the merchandise or inventory
can qualify as collateral.   The requirements are stiff and the loans are limited
to certain classes of inventory.

Accounts-receivable loans.   Small banks are not usually equipped to offer
this type of loan, and the majority of their business customers are too small to
take advantage of it.   Under this loan, the bank takes over the company's
accounts and notes receivable as collateral for the loan.

Warehouse-receipt loans.   Under this plan, goods are stored in warehouses
and the warehouse receipts are used as security for a loan to pay off the supplier.
As fast as the company is able to sell the merchandise, it pays off the bank loan.
This loan permits the company to get along without a large investment in
working capital.

Collateral loans.   A company may be able to obtain bank loans on the basis
of such collateral as chattel mortgages, stocks and bonds, real-estate mortgages,
and life insurance (up to the cash surrender value of the policy).   Even with
collateral, the bank will still give great weight to the company's ability to repay.
The bank may turn down the application for a loan, no matter how good the
collateral, if there is not a clear showing of ability to repay.

The bank does not expect to liquidate the collateral unless forced to and then
will probably not realize the book value of the collateral on a forced sale.
However, the collateral affords the bank some security, and a collateral loan
is easier to obtain than a line of credit or unsecured loan for a new or somewhat
risky business.

Equipment financing.   Equipment financing has two connotations.   It is a
financing vehicle when presently owned equipment is offered as security for a
loan.   It is an expansion vehicle when new equipment is purchased and its cost
is financed through use of equipment-financing methods—installment-plan purchases and the like.

Equipment loans may be based on existing installations or on new purchases,
but the equipment used must be of general purpose and removable.   A security

interest in the equipment until the loan is repaid will be reserved. Equipment loans usually have an intermediate term maturity (1 to 6 years) based on a period considerably less than the minimum anticipated productive life of the equipment.

Equipment-loan financing can be used to purchase new equipment. Or borrowed money can be put to other uses, with equipment presently owned pledged as security for the loan. There are two ways of handling these loans. One method is the installment-financing plan for the new equipment. A note and a security agreement are signed and a monthly repayment schedule is set up to amortize the total loan balance in equal payments. Another method utilizes a pledge of new or valuable used equipment to which the borrower has an unencumbered title as security for the loan. A formal security agreement and note are also drawn. The latter method is the customary bank advance and is widely used on medium-sized and large equipment loans. The situation of the borrower will dictate whether the equipment loan will be used to finance a new acquisition of equipment or whether existing, already purchased equipment will be offered as security for a loan.

Application of the Uniform Commercial Code. Prior to the adoption of the Uniform Commercial Code, which has now been adopted in most of the states, equipment financing would generally involve either a conditional sale or a chattel mortgage. Both forms are known as "chattel paper" under the code. If a code form is used, it is known as a "security agreement." Under the present rules the conditional sale becomes a "purchase money security interest" in "goods." The code does not eliminate the old forms of agreement. Under the code, it is immaterial whether title is in the buyer or seller. If the parties, for tax or other reasons, want title to remain in the seller, they may use the conditional-sales form.

Thus, in seeking financing for your equipment you may still encounter the terms "conditional sale" or "chattel mortgage," but the provisions of the code will prevail in interpreting the agreement.

Equipment as security for a loan. Money can be borrowed by using existing unencumbered equipment as security for a loan. When a company needs funds that cannot be obtained on an open loan at the bank, or a company cannot repay quickly enough to meet bank requirements or has exhausted its ability to finance on receivables or inventory, equipment financing may offer the best method of raising funds.

A company needing quick cash can resort to an equipment loan secured by a security agreement on its equipment and removable fixtures. The form set out immediately preceding the discussion of equipment as security is typical of a security agreement using equipment as collateral. These loans are usually short-term, with high interest rates and possibly a "bonus" charge. The cost of loans secured by existing equipment is usually higher than the cost of financing newly purchased equipment under a security agreement. This is because the value of secondhand equipment varies on the open market and because of the possibility of obsolescence or shrinkage in value of the security. This kind of money when obtained from a financing company may cost as much as 15 to 20 percent a year on the actual money lent. And the borrower may be required to pay a bonus charge to cover handling costs or additional risks.

There is another, less expensive, source of these funds. A company should explore the possibility of getting the equipment loan from a bank. Bank rates run about 8 to 10 percent per year. Many banks do not like to make equipment loans, because the ordinary bank interest rates are too low to justify the cost of appraising the equipment before making the loan and the expense of disposing of the equipment in case of default. When the bank does grant a security-agreement equipment loan, it is usually in conjunction with a loan secured by real property, using the security agreement only as additional security.

Most of the loans made by security agreement are small loans, ranging from $1,000 to $10,000, on equipment in small business establishments. Sometimes the larger finance companies make substantial loans, from approximately $25,000 to $250,000 or more, where the company borrows against receivables and/or inventory and the lender is willing to accept a security agreement on equipment as supplementary security.

Since a security-agreement arrangement is expensive, a company should reflect upon the situation before entering upon the plan. A company must be sure it will be able to meet the payments required. The company can roughly calculate the loan cost as 10 percent of the face amount of the loan. A cash-flow analysis should be projected for the loan period in order to get a clear picture.

Inventory loans. Inventories are not so liquid as accounts receivable, and a bank or finance company will generally want to secure its advances by accounts receivable and go to inventories only after the business has exhausted its ability to borrow on receivables. Receivables convert into cash automatically, they present fewer legal problems, they do not go out of style or become technologically obsolete or suffer drastic price declines. But inventory financing is important, particularly to businesses that must build up a stock to meet a seasonal demand.

Inventories can be thawed out, if these conditions are met:

The inventory is readily salable, that is, no great sales effort would be required to turn it into cash to satisfy the loan if that should become necessary

The inventories consist of basic commodities which will not deteriorate or become obsolete within the period of the loan

The legal technicalities necessary to protect the lender's position in the event of bankruptcy can be met

Do you have the right kind of inventory? You will be able to borrow, if at all, only on your stock of raw or finished merchandise. Work in process has no value for borrowing purposes.   No lender wants the responsibility for finishing and selling work in process.

Inventory loans are normally confined to raw materials which have a ready market such as oil, wheat, coal, lumber, etc.; or basic materials which are always in demand and have standard specifications, such as pipe, wire, sheet metal, etc.; or standard type units used in assembly, such as small electric motors, tires, pumps, etc.

Finished articles which can be converted into cash without too much effort also may be used as collateral.   The marketability of the inventory will determine not only whether you can borrow at all, but whether you can borrow 40 percent of the value or 80 percent of the value.

Here is what a lender will want to know about your inventory before he decides whether and how much he can lend on it:

Is the price fairly stable or does it fluctuate sharply?
How broad a market is there for the commodity?
Are there any governmental restrictions on its sale?
Under what conditions may the commodity be stored and for how long?
Is the item closely graded by the trade?
How does the condition of the commodity affect its value?
Is the commodity usually sold in certain standard sizes and does the commodity under consideration comply with those standards?
Is there any danger of obsolescence in the near future due to technological changes?
What would the cost of liquidation, such as sales commissions, packing, and transportation charges, be?
Can the commodity be hedged by the purchase of futures?

Four methods used for borrowing on inventory.   There are four methods which a lender will frequently use to get greater protection on an inventory loan, and the borrower should familiarize himself with them.   They are—

1. *Floating lien.*   The Uniform Commercial Code which is now in force in virtually all states has made possible the creation of a valid lien on a shifting stock of inventory remaining in the debtor's possession.   Before the adoption of the code the validity of such liens was in question, except to the extent that they were recognized under various factors acts

2. *Factor's lien.*   Before the Uniform Commercial Code was adopted, many states had so-called factors acts which gave factors a general lien on all goods and merchandise from the time consigned to or pledged with them, and upon any accounts receivable or other proceeds resulting from the sale or other disposition of the goods, for all the loans or advances to or for the account of the person creating the lien.   The goods need not be in existence at the time the lien is created.   They may come into existence or be acquired subsequently by the person creating the lien

    A number of states which had these factors acts repealed them when they adopted the code. They have not been repealed in every state, but this is something which primarily concerns the lender rather than the borrower. Any institutional lender will know how local law stands on this

3. *Warehouse receipts.* Warehouse receipts can be used when the inventory can be segregated and kept in a public warehouse or a field warehouse located on the premises of the business which owns the inventory

4. *Trust receipt.* This is a document executed by the borrower, by the terms of which he agrees to hold goods as trustee for the lender solely for the business of shipping them to the buyer and collecting money for his account

Public and field warehouse financing. A business can get money on its inventory by delivering it either to a public or field warehouse and causing the warehouse to issue a receipt for the goods to the lender. This can be done with goods which must be purchased for manufacture or with finished goods, but this can only be done with goods which can feasibly be segregated and, through the warehouse, placed under the control of the lender for the duration of the loan.

Warehouse receipts may be issued against goods placed in either—

1. *A public warehouse.* This is a building operated by a corporation in the business of storing goods for the general public. Use of a public warehouse can be cumbersome and expensive, because it necessitates transferring the goods to and from the borrower's premises

2. *A field warehouse.* A field warehouse is a branch public warehouse maintained at the borrower's premises by a warehouse company, such as Lawrence Warehouse Company, American Express Company, New York Terminal Warehouse Company, Douglas-Guardian Warehouse Corporation. Since it is established at the borrower's own plant, the transportation problem and some of the storage cost are eliminated

The field warehouse is created by the warehouse company leasing, at a nominal rent, a portion of the buyer's premises where the pledged inventory is to be stored. This space is segregated from the rest of the buyer's premises by a partition, wire fence, or other appropriate means. Separate locks are installed to prevent any person from entering the storage space without the consent of the warehouse company. Signs are usually posted all about the leased premises, indicating that the space is under the control of the warehouse company and not the borrower. The purpose of this is to assure that the borrower's creditors will not be misled into thinking that they can lay claim to this inventory or that they are secured by the fact that this inventory is on the borrower's premises.

The warehouse company hires a custodian, usually putting on its payroll a stockman who has been looking after the inventory for the borrower.

Commercial finance companies have worked up a method of handling the whole chain of transactions from the acquisition of raw material to finished inventory for accounts receivable. Withdrawals from the warehouse are replaced by a steady stream of new raw materials and finished goods going into the warehouse. The sales invoice goes into the hands of the commercial finance company to replace finished goods shipped out of the warehouse. The new effect is to add a substantial increment of working funds to the business. As the finance company furnishes funds to buy raw materials, it is repaid out of advances of the finished product and then gets repaid for these advances out of cash paid upon the collection of the accounts receivable created when the finished product is sold.

Trust receipts. A trust receipt is a financing instrument in the form of an agreement between a bank (the lender), called the "entruster," and a person, firm, or corporation (the borrower), called the "trustee." It shows that certain goods or property, or evidence of title to these goods or property, having been acquired for financing purposes by the lender, are released by it under specified conditions to the borrower. While the goods are in the borrower's possession, the lender retains ownership until the goods or property, or the evidence of title to goods or property, are properly accounted for by the trustee to the entruster. This accounting is through payment or otherwise, as set out in the instrument.

The trust receipt is used for interim financing of staple commodities when it is necessary to release pledged goods from a warehouse in order to sell or process them. Another wide use is in financing, under a "floor-planning" arrangement.

Floor planning. This term refers to the use of the trust receipt to finance the purchase by dealers or distributors of motor vehicles, household appliances, and other products that may be readily identifiable as to specific units and that have other than a nominal unit value. Under such a financing arrangement, the products are actually paid for by a bank or other lending agency, which obtains title through the payment of the purchase price by a draft with bill of lading attached or through a bill of sale, or otherwise. Then, in effect, the products are released by the lender to the borrower for inventory and sales purposes against the borrower's note and trust receipt. The trust receipt provides, in effect, that the borrower will hold the products in trust for the lender for the purpose of sale at not less than a specified minimum sales price per unit and will, pending sale, return the products to the lender upon demand. Or, upon sale, the borrower will keep the proceeds of sale segregated and deliver such proceeds to the lender immediately.

Floor-plan terms. Frequently, the lender will advance for the original purchase up to 90 percent, but never more, of the invoice cost of the products to be financed. It will usually require the monthly curtailment of any advances outstanding at the end of 3 months, with complete liquidation required within 6 months after the date of purchase. Interest on daily loans outstanding is usually billed to the borrower at regular monthly intervals.

Floor-plan procedures. During the period when advances are outstanding, the lender will have a valid security interest (except against an innocent purchaser for value) in the products held by the borrower under trust receipt provided they are clearly identifiable and the lender has observed all requirements of law surrounding trust-receipt financing. These requirements may vary to some extent with the laws of each state; but usually they include the necessity of placing on public record a "Statement of Trust Receipt Financing," which, in effect, is merely a notice that the borrower is engaged in trust-receipt financing with a specified lender. At frequent but irregular intervals, the lender will make a detailed physical check of the products held by the borrower under trust receipt to establish their continued availability and to inspect their condition.

Observing floor-plan terms and procedures. The business using this method of inventory financing must take exceptional care to see that when floor-planned products are sold, the proceeds of sale are delivered promptly to the lender to apply on outstanding advances. As the name implies, a trust receipt arrangement requires the trust of the lender in the integrity of the borrower, and the latter must avoid any appearance of irregularities that might lead to the destruction of that confidence.

Accounts-receivable financing. Accounts receivable are accepted by some banks and most commercial credit companies as collateral for a line of credit. Individual banking practices vary, however, and the borrower should become familiar with local banking requirements.

The financing of accounts receivable involves the assignment by the borrower to the lender of the borrower's accounts receivable. These accounts receivable are security for advances which the lender makes to the borrower simultaneously with each assignment. As the proceeds of the assigned accounts are collected, they are turned over to the lender and applied to reduction of the indebtedness, the excess being returned by the lender to the borrower. The borrower remains responsible for the payment of the debt, even though the primary source of payment is the proceeds of the assigned accounts receivable. If the proceeds of the assigned accounts receivable are insufficient to repay the amount advanced, the borrower is liable for the deficiency. This is one important difference between accounts-receivable financing and factoring. The factor purchases the accounts receivable from the borrower and assumes the risk of loss from any bad accounts.

Accounts receivable may be financed on a notification or a nonnotification basis. Under a notification plan, the receivables are pledged and payment is made directly to the lender, but the borrower remains responsible for the payment. The lender notifies the borrower's customers that their accounts have been assigned and directs them to make payments directly to him. Under the more satisfactory and more commonly used nonnotification plan, the borrower collects as agent for the lender. This method is preferable because the relationship between the borrower and his customers is not disturbed, and the financing arrangement remains confidential.

Functions of accounts-receivable financing. The primary function of accounts-receivable financing is to release funds tied up in these accounts, thereby giving a company working capital. Financing of receivables may put a borrowing company in a stronger position for sales expansion and may improve its credit standing by providing funds to discount its own payables.

Accounts-receivable financing should be employed in conjunction with a cash forecast and financial plan. The financing will be used according to the plan's estimate of how much cash will be required before the expended cash comes back from customers. Whenever there is a shortage of working capital, but accounts receivable that are not yet due are available, the borrower is in a position to raise cash to meet his current needs. Of course, this financing is not the final answer to the problem of inadequate working capital, but it is a means of temporary relief, especially in seasonal industries where receivables are concentrated in a short period of the year and so are not acceptable collateral for long-term financing. The basic question to ask yourself is: Will the financing of receivables sufficiently speed up the turnover of the company's cash so as to assure the timely payment of obligations as they mature? If this question can be answered in the affirmative, then accounts-receivable financing may be the best way to raise needed cash.

Mechanics of accounts-receivable financing. Before accounts receivable are accepted as collateral, the lending agency will evaluate the risks and investigate the facts involved. Through analysis and investigation of the borrower's financial history and related factors, the lending agency can decide whether it wants to assume the risk, and how the risk can be minimized. At the outset it should be emphasized that certain types of businesses do not lend themselves to receivable financing. Most service enterprises fall into this category. This is because a serviceman may damage the customers' goods and offset any receivable that may be due. The same risk appears in businesses that furnish special orders. And generally factors do not look with favor on unstable industries, such as the dress industry.

Other considerations involve the accounts themselves. The lender will look to see whether the accounts are acceptable for financing. Usually, any account that represents a bona fide obligation owed to the borrower from a creditworthy customer without the probability of setoff or the like is available for financing. Under certain conditions, partial billings against unfinished contracts may be financed. The lender will have to be assured that these invoices are payable on regular terms and will not be unduly delayed. Under most circumstances, long-term dating will not disqualify the receivables unless there is undue hazard in their collection.

After the lender has satisfactorily completed his investigation, a basic contract which defines the rights and obligations of the lender and the borrower will be executed. The contract is generally needed because accounts-receivable financing contemplates a series of transactions rather than a single, isolated loan. Many lenders require yearly contracts. While the agreements vary with the situations, a typical agreement might provide that the borrower assign all accounts receivable, or a selected group of them, to the lender as security. In return, the lender agrees to advance funds up to 80 percent of the face value of the accounts receivable pledged, usually specifying a dollar maximum which can be borrowed. Periodically, schedules of customers' invoices are submitted to the lender to replenish borrowing power. Under this type or arrangement, the borrower, when cash is needed, simply lists the invoices which he wants to finance on the lender's standardized form, and the lender advances the cash upon presentation of the form. The borrower should avoid arrangements where it is necessary to get clearance on each individual invoice. Blanket deals are much easier to administer, since invoice schedules are simply submitted periodically on accounts that have blanket approval, and the lender worries about individual account limits.

Under the wording of most finance company contracts, the borrower does not borrow; the contract reads as a sale of the accounts receivable with recourse (as distinguished from factoring in which there is no recourse). The recourse provision of the contract will legally be interpreted as a loan arrangement in almost all cases. Banks will adhere to the older method of taking a note secured by the receivables, rather than disguise the arrangement as receivables financing.

Under the agreement in a nonnotification plan, the borrower will act as collection agent for the lender. The borrower collects the balance of the account and turns over the remittance directly to the lender. If there is any dispute, the borrower must settle it at his own expense. If the customer is slow in paying, the borrower must use his own credit facilities to collect the account. When the payment is made and the check turned over to the lender, the borrower must find out exactly how the lender credits the account for collections. Most institutions make up schedules of collections periodically and credit the borrower's account from the schedule. This results in payment of additional interest for the period between the time when customers' checks are cleared and the time when the collections are reflected in the account. Interest cost can be increased as much as one-third by this delay.

There may be a further clause in the agreement whereby the finance company reserves the right to determine what percentage of the value of the collateral will be given to the client upon presentation of the accounts. The percentage agreed upon can be varied by the finance company, if it so wishes, during the term of the contract. The percentage given will depend upon the quality of the accounts and any other factor which might affect the value of the accounts during the term of the contract.

Another important clause which may be included in the agreement concerns the remittance of the balance due to the lender. The lender will require that the borrower turn over the customer's remittance in its original form. The lender will endeavor to endorse the original payment in such a manner that the customer will not know the account has been assigned. The lender will deduct the charges and the reserve percentage from the customers' remittances, and the borrower will be entitled to the balance. If he has already drawn on this figure, the finance company will keep it as payment on the advance; otherwise the borrower is entitled to the surplus.

The agreement may provide that payment will be made by the lender to the borrower provided the borrower guarantees that all accounts assigned are bona fide and all information contained in the invoices is correct; that the accounts assigned are not subject to any claims from the customer which are not a direct result of the accounts sale; that the accounts assigned have no encumbrances on them; and that no other party has a claim against them. This clause protects the lender in case it is not protected sufficiently by the accounts; it still has legal recourse against the borrower. In addition, the agreement usually states that the finance company has full recourse against the borrower for all accounts which have been assigned or sold by the borrower under this arrangement.

Accounts-receivable financing is a revolving-fund plan that is self-liquidating. It is a continuing arrangement under which the borrower sends his periodic billing to the lender, who pays out daily to the borrower about as much as he receives on old billings. The advances are self-liquidating since as the account remits its balance due, a previous advance is paid off. It is as if the borrower had taken out a series of loans, each one being satisfied by one of his customer's remittances on an open account.

This method of financing does not involve complicated bookkeeping records. The borrower continues to maintain its regular bookkeeping system with but a few simple changes. The borrower will prepare a schedule of sales, which is a list of open accounts receivable ledger accounts. The lender will keep a debtor's ledger, which is nothing more than a copy of the borrower's accounts receivable ledger. These accounts should always equal each other. Periodic schedules will be submitted to the lender to determine whether there are any discrepancies. Individual finance companies may require certain notations on the accounts receivable ledger indicating that the accounts have been pledged. Furthermore, the lender will conduct periodic audits at the office of the borrower.

Sometimes the lending agency will set limitations on the amount of credit it will extend. The maximums are based on a study of the borrower's financial statements and financial prospects. If the lender is a finance company, it will probably offer the highest line of credit consistent with the borrower's needs. There is really not too much risk on the finance company, since it does not purchase the receivables outright. The risk is still on the borrower, so most of the finance companies will offer funds to the fullest capacity of the borrower's ability to do business. In this financing arrangement, the borrower suffers other risks also. His credit rating may suffer, since he has tied up his most liquid asset. If the funds obtained from this arrangement can be put to beneficial use, it will more than compensate for the pledge of the receivables and the credit rating should not suffer too greatly.

Factoring. Factoring is primarily a credit business in which the factor checks credits and makes collections for his client. He also purchases his client's accounts receivable without recourse, thereby guaranteeing the client against credit losses. This is the basic service of a factor; and for this service he receives a fee, ranging between 3/4 to 1½ percent of the purchased receivables. Normally the account debtor is notified that the account was purchased by the factor and that payment thereof is to be made directly to the factor.

In this operation, the factor checks the credits, makes the collections, and assumes the loss in the event the accounts are not paid. Up to this point, however, the factor has passed no funds to his client. He has purchased the accounts and has agreed to pay for them on their net due date.

Under the standard factoring contract, the factor buys the client's receivables outright, without recourse, as soon as the client creates them by shipping merchandise to customers whose credit the factor has investigated and approved. Cash is made available to the client immediately on shipment, and thus, in effect, he sells for cash and can turn his receivables into cash as fast as he creates them. The arrangement is flexible, however, to the extent that the client may withdraw prior to the due date. Thus he has a 100 percent demand privilege on the funds available to him, but pays interest only on funds actually used.

However, the factor will make cash advances to the client on the receivables prior to their maturity. For example, let us suppose that the factor purchases accounts receivable amounting to $40,000 from his client, without recourse, due in 60 days. In this case, the factor owes the client $40,000 which must be paid in 60 days. The factor, however, will advance, say, $35,000 to the client immediately, to make operating cash available. The other $5,000 will be paid when due. The factor will charge interest on the funds advanced to the client, and this amounts under today's rates to about 7 percent. If these advances are not enough to meet the needs of the client—and this occurs frequently in seasonal business—the factor will also make short-term, supplementary loans secured by inventory, fixed assets, or other acceptable collateral.

Bank and factor in combination. Frequently, a commercial bank cannot provide all the loan funds a growing company needs. Its balance sheet is not liquid enough, or it cannot clear off the bank debt every 6 or 12 months. A factor can provide funds to clear off bank loans periodically or make additional bank credit possible by guaranteeing accounts or replacing accounts receivable with cash.

Here is an example: A bank had furnished unsecured credit to a client for about 25 years. For the 3 years immediately preceding the loan application, expanding sales had prevented the client from annually cleaning up its loan. During this period, the manufacturer's sales had increased by more than 50 percent, but the bank was able to furnish only about two-thirds of the $600,000 needed as additional working capital. In addition, while the bank wanted to continue the relationship, it had to have an annual cleanup of the loan.

The bank discussed with a factor a mutually beneficial solution to the problem. In examining the manufacturer's business condition, the factor noted that about half its net worth was in fixed assets and that about 65 percent of its working capital was in inventory. Coincidental was the relatively lengthy collection period, averaging 40 days. Ratio of current assets to current liabilities was 2.9:1, a sound situation, but the firm's working assets were in accounts receivable and inventories.

The factor agreed to work with the client and began by substituting cash for the company's receivables. The manufacturer turned over to the factor all its $800,000 in receivables. The factor, in turn, advanced payment on them up to 80 percent of their face value. This first $640,000 advance became a continuing, flexible fund, expanding when sales were up and contracting when sales dropped.

The bank entered into a participation agreement with the factor in its receivables-financing contract. The bank participated in loans for 40 percent and the factor kept a 60 percent interest but maintained the collateral, and the factor's staff provided the entire day-to-day close management and supervision and the required field auditing.

The factor, of course, kept the bank informed of developments by sending it complete reports of assignments, collections, and so forth, as they were completed by the auditors. Perhaps even more important from the bank's view was that the factor made arrangements whereby the bank could be completely paid out every year and could remain out of the picture for 15 to 30 days, thereby eliminating objections from bank examiners.

The arrangement was ideal for the bank. It was investing its funds on a secured basis and at an attractive rate. It was assured of a yearly cleanup and, simultaneously, had a partner who provided responsible supervision of the account. It maintained its good relations with the client. The borrower benefited additionally by the fact that the cost of the bank's funds in the participation were at the bank's rate—6 percent, plus a small servicing percentage to the factor on the bank's share of the loan—thus materially reducing the overall normal cost of the financing arrangement.

For the firm which a commercial banker might consider to be overtrading in relation both to working capital and net worth, factoring can provide an efficient vehicle for cleaning up a long-standing bank loan. At the same time, it can create a foundation for comfortable financing of even larger sales.

Reasons for factoring. Many of the companies that turn to factoring do so because they are interested in the risk-sharing advantages of the factoring arrangement even more than the financial accommodation. Through factoring, the borrower shifts credit risks to the factor. Larger sales to one customer are made possible when the company does not carry all the risk. Credit and collection expenses are reduced or eliminated, with the result that a fixed factoring cost is substituted for varying credit losses. With less risk of loss, the company has a better financial position. And the company gets working capital to increase its volume of operations or its current ratio position. Valuable, too, are information and advice many factors provide concerning financial and merchandising problems.

An example of the benefits that can accrue where factoring is employed will be seen in this chapter of the HF Company:

HF Company sells its $100,000 receivables for $95,000 cash (factor holds back $5,000 for reserve for returns and allowances).

	Before factoring	After factoring	Results after use of funds
Cash	$ 15,000	$110,000	$ 40,000
Receivables	100,000	5,000	5,000
Other current assets	15,000	15,000	15,000
Total current assets	$130,000	$130,000	$ 60,000
Fixed assets	70,000	70,000	70,000
Total assets	$200,000	$200,000	$130,000
Accounts payable	$ 60,000	$ 60,000	$ 30,000
Notes payable	10,000	10,000	
Other current liabilities	30,000	30,000	
Total current liabilities	100,000	100,000	30,000
Long-term liabilities	30,000	30,000	30,000
Net worth	70,000	70,000	70,000
Total liabilities and net worth	$200,000	$200,000	$130,000
Working capital	$ 30,000	$ 30,000	$ 30,000
Ratio of current assets to current liabilities	1.3:1	1.3:1	2:1

As can be seen, not only does HF get the immediate use of funds to pay off its currently due liabilities and build up cash, but the company's whole financial position is basically improved. The company is now in a liquid position and has a better chance of obtaining credit through banking channels should the need arise. The company has $40,000 in cash instead of $15,000; it has borrowed no money and signed no notes and has increased its ratio of current assets to liabilities to the theoretical ideal of 2:1.

Pros and cons of factoring. Certain disadvantages of factoring should be considered. There is a loss of the close relationship the borrower might have maintained with its customers. The company no longer dictates the methods of payment or credit arrangement. In some businesses, this may affect the sales volume; but usually practices introduced by the factor improve collections and minimize the risk of bad-debt losses.

The net cost of factoring may run to around 6 to 9 percent of sales after considering the savings on credit, collection, and bad-debt losses. Part of this is payment for services rendered—only a portion is payment for borrowed money. If the cost cannot be readily absorbed by the anticipated profit margin, factoring should be avoided.

Credit insurance. Commercial credit insurance gives a company indemnification against abnormal credit losses arising from failure of business debtors to pay. Most of the credit insurance in this country is written by the American Credit Indemnity Company of New York, with headquarters in Baltimore, Md. It is a subsidiary of Commercial Credit Company and is known as ACI. The London Guaranty and Accident Company, Ltd., an English company, also writes credit insurance in this country. Commercial credit insurance is used by several thousand manufacturers, wholesalers, and service organizations dealing with business firms. The policyholders represent more than 150 lines of industry. Credit insurance is used by firms having capital of as little as $20,000 and by those having resources of millions of dollars. Most of the insured firms have annual sales of less than $10 million. Firms having sales as low as $100,000 use credit insurance.

Credit insurance is not available to retailers and other businesses on accounts owned by consumers. Nor is it available to manufacturers, wholesalers, and other firms on accounts owed by businesses in lines where the loss experience has been so erratic that there is no sound actuarial basis for the calculation of insurance premiums. It is not available to firms selling their output on a title-retention basis. It is also withheld from firms having an unsatisfactory record, involving the tendency to abuse credit, to gamble, or to make speculative shipments to questionable risks. Credit insurance is not of sufficient value to justify it for a firm selling its output to the government, those factoring their receivables, those selling for cash or COD, those selling on conditional bills of sale, those leasing instead of selling their products. Any other business may qualify for credit insurance and find it very useful.

What does it cost? Over a period of years, the total premium writings of the American Credit Indemnity Company have consistently represented about 0.1 percent of total covered sales. In a credit-insurance policy, the insured company assumes an agreed-upon primary loss. It is indemnified for loss only in excess of that amount. The combination of credit-insurance premium and primary loss assumed will represent less than ¼ percent of total sales. These are averages. Premium rates are tailor-made for each insured. For each business, its premium will depend on the risk classes of accounts covered and the amounts of coverages stipulated, the total sales volume covered, the policy amount, the terms of sale, and the special endorsements, if any, attached to the policy. The premiums paid by most policyholders range between $\frac{1}{20}$ and $\frac{1}{5}$ percent of covered sales.

What will credit insurance do for a firm? Credit insurance protects a company from dissipation of its working capital through credit losses. It is particularly valuable for firms whose sales are concentrated in a few accounts, or in one line of business, or in a particular region, or for firms that do custom manufacturing in significant amounts so that recovery of the product when an account goes bad would not be very helpful. Those who have a lot of small accounts, those who have been selling for cash or COD and who want to shift to a credit operation, and those who find that it is necessary to accept greater credit risks in order to maintain or increase sales volume will benefit through credit insurance.

Of course it protects a firm's working capital against excessive credit losses. In addition, it provides a collection service. When a claim is past due, it is placed with the insuring company for collection. There is no charge on a collection which is made within 10 days from the insurer's first demand on the debtor. When collection of an account requires more time, effort, and expense, a fee is charged for collection. This fee is based on an experienced mass-collection operation and is likely to be lower than the cost which the insured would incur if he had to place each account in the hands of some other third party for collection.

Credit insurance will help a company maintain its sales volume by making it possible to avoid undue tightening of credit policy, to give customers larger credit lines, and to penetrate the market more deeply. These steps to loosen credit in order to maintain and increase sales volume cannot be carried to the point of loose credit policy and lax collection procedures.

Credit insurance is granted on a year-to-year basis and it will be withdrawn if credit policy extends beyond the bounds of reasonable prudence.

Finally, credit insurance can substantially improve borrowing power and credit standing. It can encourage trade creditors to extend longer lines of credit to a firm, and it can encourage banks to lend more freely and generously. When a banker or the credit man of a supplier looks at your balance sheet in order to determine how much credit you are entitled to, the chances are that he will arbitrarily slice a substantial chunk off the accounts receivable figure on your balance sheet. If you can tell him that your accounts are insured, he is likely to take the figure as it stands. This can substantially improve your borrowing power and credit standing. This factor alone can justify the cost of the credit insurance and make it an important element in your overall financing plan.

Installment-sales financing. The marketing of consumer durables—automobiles, refrigerators, washing machines, television sets, etc.—and industrial machinery and equipment, ranging from a dentist's drill to factory and road-building equipment, depends on being able to sell these products for a down payment plus regular installment payments. To make installment selling feasible for most businesses, it is necessary for them to be able to convert the paper they receive into cash. Sales finance companies make this possible.

For installment selling to be feasible, a product should have these characteristics:

A useful life longer than the life of the prime payment obligation

The merchandise must be relatively uniform and have a value that can be readily known or estimated in advance, so that its worth as collateral can be determined, and model changes and improvements in the product cannot be so drastic as to render obsolete articles which have been sold on time and are serving as collateral. As a concomitant of this, the merchandise must have a predictable ready resale value

The product must be mobile, so that it can be repossessed if necessary

The price must be high enough to make 12, or 24, or even 36 monthly installments sufficiently large in amount to warrant the handling and bookkeeping expense involved

To make installment payments attractive to sales-finance companies, these attributes are necessary:

There must be a big enough down payment to commit the buyer fully and to cushion the usually large drop in value which occurs when the product is put to use and converted from new to secondhand

The period of repayment must be short enough so that the obligation is reduced faster than the value of the merchandise is reduced by depreciation

The purchaser must have a good credit standing, so that collection trouble is unlikely

Most installment sales are made on conditional-sales contracts, which provide that the seller can take back the goods, resell them, and still hold the buyer for any deficiency. Most states require the recording of the conditional-sales contract in order to validate it against creditors of bona fide purchases from the buyer. The seller usually sells the installment contract to a sales-finance company and thus gets the same funds he would have received if he had sold the goods for cash. The big question here is the liability the seller assumes if the customer does not pay. In a full-recourse arrangement, the seller agrees to buy back any defaulted contract. Without recourse, the finance company takes the whole credit risk. In some arrangements, the seller has no continued liability on the customers' obligations, but does agree to buy back the equipment if the finance company has to repossess it. The purchase price of the equipment will not be its value at the time of repossession but will depend on the amount of debt outstanding at that time. The seller and the finance company will have to negotiate such vital terms as interest rates, the

amount of the purchase price to be held back by the finance company as an
additional credit and safety factor, the seller's participation in the interest
earnings or reserve, etc.

Tapping government sources. There are many different governmental programs designed to aid companies, particularly small business, find capital.
From the Federal government there are the following potential sources:

Commercial, industrial, and financial loans
    Small Business Administration
    Treasury Department
    Federal Reserve System
    Federal Home Loan Banks
    Maritime Administration
    Area Redevelopment Administration of the Department of Commerce
Agricultural loans
    Farm Credit Administration
    Rural Electrification Administration
    Farmers Home Administration
    Commodity Credit Corporation
Housing and community development loans
    Office of Transportation
    Department of Housing and Urban Development
        Mortgage Credit Administration
        Renewal and Housing Administration
        Metropolitan Development Administration
Veterans loans
    Veterans Administration
Natural resources loans
    Department of the Interior
        Bureau of Reclamation
        Bureau of Commercial Fisheries
        Bureau of Indian Affairs
International loans
    Export-Import Bank, Washington, D.C.
    Agency for International Development

Under the Department of Housing and Urban Development are several
programs of particular interest to the private business. Included are a program for direct government loans for the provision of housing facilities for
elderly and handicapped persons, and nine programs of Federal mortgage insurance under the National Housing Act: multifamily-housing mortgage insurance, cooperative housing insurance, urban-renewal housing insurance and
insured improvement loans, moderate-income projects mortgage insurance,
housing for the elderly insurance, mortgage insurance for the financing of the
construction of nursing homes, condominium housing insurance, and land-
development mortgage insurance. Under mortgage insurance the government

guarantees the lender against risk in a manner similar to the regular home FHA loan.

By far the most important programs from the point of view of small business are the programs of the Small Business Administration. These are the loans and guarantee programs, and the program to establish small-business investment companies. Small-business investment companies (SBIC) are privately formed entities, the purpose of which is to serve as a source of equity capital and long-term credit extension to small business concerns. The Small Business Administration may lend an SBIC a sum equal to 50 percent of its paid-in capital and paid-in surplus, in order to provide working capital.

Small-business loans are made to finance construction, conversion, or expansion, to finance the purchase of equipment, facilities, machinery, supplies, or materials, and to supply working capital. Such loans are administered by the Small Business Administration (SBA) through its regional offices. The SBA can make loans up to $350,000, for periods up to 10 years, at a rate of 5½ percent interest. An applicant for a loan must satisfy two general criteria: (1) It must demonstrate that satisfactory assistance is not available elsewhere, and (2) it must qualify as a "small-business concern."

To satisfy the first criterion, the applicant must present proof of refusal of the required assistance from two banks in cities with a population of 200,000 or greater. It must also appear that the required funds are not available on reasonable terms by either the public offering or private placement of securities, through the disposal of assets not needed in the conduct of the applicant's business, through the use of the personal resources or credit of the owners or partners of the applicant, or through any other type of government financing.

In determining the size of a concern, the SBA takes account of all the applicant's affiliates. Generally, there are three criteria in the definition of a small-business concern: (1) It must be independently owned and operated; (2) it must not be dominant in its field of operation (that is, it must exert no controlling or major influence on a national level in a kind of activity in which a number of business concerns are engaged); and (3) it must meet the specific size requirements contained in the regulations. These requirements vary by type of industry, and the standards are based both on dollar value of annual sales and number of employees.

There are four basic types of loans available:

1. *Guaranteed loans* Under this program, a financial institution makes the actual loan, but the SBA obligates itself to purchase up to 90 percent of the loan if the borrower is in default for longer than 90 days
2. *Immediate participation loans* These loans, which are not available if a guaranteed loan is available, are made either by the SBA or a financial institution; whichever does not make the actual loan agrees to purchase a participation in it immediately upon disbursement. The SBA's share may not exceed 90 percent

3. *Direct loans* These are made directly by the SBA to the borrower, and
are not available if either a guaranteed or a participation loan can be made
4. *Limited loans* These loans are available only as guaranteed or participation loans. They are for borrowers who cannot pledge sufficient collateral to qualify for a regular loan, and are available only if the borrower
has a good earnings record, a good credit record, and competent management

Participation of the SBA in loan programs is naturally dependent on congressional appropriation of funds. There have been periods when the SBA has
been unable to implement one or more phases of its loan programs because of
lack of funds. You must, therefore, check with your local SBA office to find
out the present status of the program.

The role of small-business investment companies in financing arrangements.
The Small Business Investment Act became law on August 21, 1958. Today
there are some 700 licensed small-business investment companies in the United
States. The phenomenal growth of these companies is due, in good part, to
the tax advantages they offer to investors so as to minimize the risk of their investments.

The purpose of these companies is to supply capital to so-called small businesses (they may actually be quite large, as we shall see), which, for the most
part, are having difficulties raising the money elsewhere. Businessmen who
are unable to raise long-term capital from their usual sources find that a small-
business investment company (SBIC) is willing to take a greater risk than a
commercial bank or an insurance company. Relatively new firms or firms
which do not have a past record of profitable operation find that an SBIC will
not turn them down. In addition, SBICs are willing to make an investment in
an amount bearing a higher ratio to net worth than banks and insurance companies.

By the same token, businesses seeking capital from SBICs have to be prepared, for the most part, to pay more for their money than they would have
to pay in conventional money channels if these were available to them. The
"more" that is required is not necessarily more interest—although SBICs do
get as much as 15 percent for their money in some situations. The average
interest rate on SBIC loans and investments runs about 8 percent. More
likely, the "more" will be in possible dilution of capital, since SBICs may either
purchase stock outright, buy convertible debentures, or take debentures with
warrants attached. If the borrower's business succeeds, the SBIC will likely
convert its debentures or exercise its warrants. Thus, the SBIC then attains
an ownership interest instead of requiring a repayment of its loan. And the
borrower has had to give up some equity, or possibly control, in order to get the
the money it needed. However, this possibility of capital dilution is not
necessarily a deterrent to the borrower. Usually, exercise of conversion rights
or warrants will give the SBIC a substantial ownership position, but not enough

to deprive old management of control. And ownership by an SBIC of a substantial portion of the company's stock may well enhance the company's credit position. What is more, once debentures are converted, interest will cease and the outstanding loan no longer has to be repaid.

SBIC funds must go to small business. Not every business concern needing money is eligible to receive it from an SBIC. Only small-business concerns as defined by the Small Business Administration (SBA) can qualify. To be eligible, the borrower's total assets should not exceed $5,000,000 and its net worth should not be over $2,500,000. Average net income for the two preceding years should not be more than $250,000 after Federal income taxes. In addition, the borrower cannot be dominant in its field of operation.

What is more, the borrower will likely have to be a corporation. While that is not a requirement in the law, most SBIC deals involve taking a potential equity position via convertible debentures or warrants. And that is possible only when dealing with a corporation. Outright loans are available to some extent, but most SBICs are looking for a big return via capital growth in the situations that pay off, to compensate for the many deals they will enter into which are likely to turn sour.

Equity investment and long-term loans. The law as originally passed in 1958 provided that SBICs would supply equity capital to small business concerns only through the purchase of debentures of the borrowing companies, convertible into the common stock of the borrowers. While convertible debentures worked well, there was a demand in many quarters for greater flexibility in the types of equities that might be acquired by SBICs. In 1960, Congress answered the demand with an amendment of the law. And SBA, under the amendment, permits SBICs to acquire common stock, preferred stock, notes, debentures (convertible or otherwise), stock-purchase warrants, or any combination of such securities. However, an SBIC may not, except in unusual circumstances, acquire more than 49 percent of the stock of a small business concern. The price paid for common stock, whether purchased initially or on exercise of options or conversion rights, may not exceed sound book value on the date of closing.

The law itself says little about the terms on funds advanced by SBICs to small concerns, except to provide that the maturity on the loans shall not exceed 20 years (with extensions of an additional 10 years permitted to "aid in the orderly liquidation" of loans) and that the interest rates shall be subject to SBA approval. SBA's regulations provide that both equity investments and long-term loans shall be for a minimum of 5 years, but regular amortization is permitted on either. Loans may be repaid at par at any time without penalty.

As for the interest rates, SBA charges 5 percent on all funds which it advances to SBICs. It was thought at the outset of the program that SBICs would be held to relatively low interest rates and that the net return on investments, disregarding conversions, would not be profitable, particularly after paying SBA 5 percent for its money.   But such has not been the case.   Where local law sets a legal limit on interest rates, SBA requires adherence to that limit.   The fact is that the majority of all SBIC commitments to date have been to corporations. Many states set no limit on the interest rates that may be charged to corporations.   Those that do usually put them at a much higher level than the limit permitted to be charged on loans to individuals.   In Florida, for example, the legal rate is 6 percent, but the law permits corporations to be charged up to 15 percent.

The result has been that SBA has adopted a policy of permitting SBICs to earn up to 15 percent return on their funds in those jurisdictions where the law is silent on interest rates or where the law permits interest in excess of that amount.   In practice, SBICs usually charge about 7½ to 9 percent plus a so-called "sweetener" in the form of a stock option.

Tax breaks.   The law setting up SBICs extends the following special tax benefits to them:

Under an amendment to Sec. 243, where the SBIC acquires stock of a small concern, dividends received by the SBIC on that stock are entirely tax-free. Other corporations are taxable on 15 percent of dividends received

Under the new Sec. 1242, persons investing in the stock of an SBIC are allowed an ordinary loss deduction, rather than a capital loss, on losses arising from the worthlessness or sale of the stock.   The law sets no limit on the losses to be claimed under this provision, and it should not be confused with Sec. 1244, which limits ordinary losses on so-called small business stock to $25,000 ($50,000 on a joint return). Treasury regulations make it clear that Sec. 1242 makes ordinary losses available not only to original investors in an SBIC, but also to subsequent purchasers of SBIC stock

Under the new Sec. 1243, where the SBIC incurs a loss on stock which it acquires from a small concern, it is treated as an ordinary loss rather than a capital loss

Section 542 (c) (8) of the code grants SBICs an exemption from the personal-holding-company surtax.   It was recognized that SBICs would receive little else but personal-holding-company income, and the threat of the 75 to 85 percent surtax would cause many high-bracket taxpayers to pass up the program

Regulations under Sec. 533 provide that earnings and profits of an SBIC reinvested in accordance with the provisions of the Small Business Investment Act will not be regarded as surplus accumulations subject to the 27½ to 38½ percent penalty

Sale-leaseback financing.   Here, a company sells its property outright to an insurance company or other institutional investor and gets back a long-term lease to assure its continued occupancy.   The lessee assumes all the risks, taxes, insurance, maintenance, and other costs of ownership.   The lessor, who puts up the money and takes title to the building, gets a lease commitment that assures him that he will get his money back over a predetermined period of time at an adequate interest or other charge for the use of his money. In addition, he gets a kicker in the form of the residuary value of the property, or continued rentals at a reduced rate paid by the lessee, after the lessor has gotten his money back.

Often, the sale-leaseback accomplishes the equivalent of mortgage financing; but the seller of the property, since he is in the position of a lessee, is entitled to tax deductions for the rental payments that he makes to his purchaser. As in the case of a mortgage, the seller-lessee keeps the use of the property (although he will lose it when his lease expires) ; and he pays a constant net rental, which can be conceived of as representing both interest and mortgage amortization. But in the case of a mortgage, the owner gets only a tax deduction for the interest that he pays, not for mortgage amortization.

In the sale-leaseback, since the rentals paid to the purchaser, in effect, are equivalent to interest and amortization on a mortgage, mortgage payments are now put on a tax-deductible basis. This may more than compensate for the loss of the depreciation deduction by the seller.

The investor-purchaser owns the building and is entitled to depreciate it. He is fully taxable on the rent he receives and part of this rent represents amortization of his investment. But his depreciation of the property may provide enough of a tax deduction to make up for this. Nowadays, sale-leasebacks are often entered into with institutional, tax-exempt investors. But deals are still worked out even where the investor is not tax-exempt, particularly where short-term leases and high building–land-valuation ratios exist. In this way the investor shelters from taxation, by way of the depreciation deduction, most of the portion of his rent which represents amortization and recovers this "amortization" in a short period of time.

Small as well as big businesses can get sale-leaseback financing. A number of life-insurance companies, pension trusts, foundations, and other institutions are now interested in buying properties worth anywhere from $100,000 up. Purchase-lease financing can be used for new construction as well as where buildings already exist. In new construction, the user usually builds to his specifications, and the purchaser agrees to buy the building and lease it back on completion, provided that it meets the prearranged specifications.

Here are general considerations common to all sale-leaseback deals:

Major weight is given to the company's credit standing, earnings record, management ability, and fundamental industry position. From the standpoint of the buyer, it is a bond deal. He is getting his money back with interest, plus a "kicker." He is interested primarily not in the real estate, but in the credit rating of the lessee

Nevertheless, location and quality of the real estate are important factors. The poorer the location, the better must be the credit rating of the tenant. General-purpose commercial buildings are favored over industrial property, and thus rental costs on factory buildings tend to run higher

The lessee assumes all costs of operating the property, paying taxes, and other charges, including capital expenditures, to keep the property in good condition

Rent covers the required rate of return, plus amortization of the purchase price over the fixed term of the lease

Leases usually run for an initial term of 20 to 35 years, with renewals for additional periods at reduced rentals, to be determined by negotiation

Sometimes a rejectable offer is provided. This permits the lessee, after a period of time, to make an offer for the property at the then unamortized balance of the investment, plus a percentage of that amount as a penalty. If the offer is accepted, the property is conveyed. If the offer is rejected, the tenant has the option to continue in possession or vacate. This provision gives the tenant some "out" on his commitment

How a sale-leaseback can improve financial condition. Sale-leaseback financing tends to effect a big improvement in a company's balance sheet. The rental obligation, which is subject to cancellation in bankruptcy, does not show as an obligation on the balance sheet. However, good accounting practice footnotes the liability, to show its existence.

Here is how a sale-leaseback transaction can make a huge improvement in a company's current financial position and in its earning power:

Assume a sale-leaseback transaction in which a company sells its buildings and land for $550,000, realizing a long-term capital gain of $50,000. The lease is for 30 years at 5½% ($30,250) a year. A renewal provision for another 25 years at 2 percent ($11,000) is also included. Here is how such a deal can work a tremendous improvement in the company's current financial position. Note how the proceeds are used to pay off a $350,000 loan and build up cash at the same time.

	Before net lease	*After net lease*
Cash	$ 75,000	$ 275,000
Other current assets	700,000	700,000
Total current assets	$ 775,000	$ 975,000
Equipment (net)	100,000	100,000
Land and buildings (net)	500,000	—0—
Total assets	$1,375,000	$1,075,000
Notes payable	$ 350,000	$ —0—
Other current liabilities	150,000	162,500
Total current liabilities	$ 500,000	$ 162,500
Capital stock	$ 400,000	$ 400,000
Surplus	475,000	512,500
Total liabilities	$1,375,000	$1,075,000
Net working capital	$ 275,000	$ 812,500
Working capital ratio	1.6 : 1	6.0 : 1

Now follow through on an earnings basis, assuming that the additional $537,000 working capital will earn 15 percent ($12,500 of proceeds goes for capital-gain tax) :

Net operating profit	$ 250,000	$ 330,625
Depreciation on building	15,000	—0—
Rental charge	—0—	30,250
Profit before taxes	235,000	300,375
Federal income taxes	106,300	137,680
Net income after taxes	$ 128,700	$ 162,695
Additional cash available for reinvestment of dividends		$ 33,995

When is it better to own than to lease? It is all a matter of arithmetic. On one hand, the corporation will be saving the net after-tax rent cost. On the other hand, it will have after-tax operating expenses and loss of income on the money invested in the plant. However, it will have an additional release of cash equal to the tax saving caused by the depreciation deduction. If the net costs of owning the building are less than the after-tax rent costs, the corporation will be cash ahead by switching to ownership. If the residual value of the property is added to the total of the cash saved during the life of the building, you have the total value of the plant as an investment.

Example. Assume a corporation pays rent of $100,000 per year. It can buy a plant with a 25-year life for $600,000. Land is worth $100,000; the building, $500,000. Realty taxes and other expenses come to $30,000. If the corporation invested the $600,000 cash at 6 percent, it would have made $36,000 a year —$17,280 after taxes, assuming a 48 percent corporate-tax rate.

As a lessee, the corporation's after-tax cost of its rent was		$52,000
As owner, its after-tax expenses are	$15,600	
Its after-tax loss on investment of the cost of the plant is	$17,280	32,880
Thus, its after-tax cash outlay as an owner is reduced by		19,120
But, in addition, the depreciation deduction of $20,000 (4 percent of $500,000) reduces the income tax and releases additional cash of		10,000
That makes the total cash benefit, per year, to the corporation as a result of owning instead of leasing, a total of		$29,120

On a 25-year basis, the savings will total $728,000. At the end of 25 years, however, the building (theoretically) is worthless—it has been completely depreciated. But it should be possible to determine what the building will be worth in 25 years—whether it will have some resale value or whether land values will hold up enough to make demolition and reconstruction feasible.

In our example, we have used straight-line depreciation. Declining balance is more favorable in the early years. There depreciation will be reduced yearly and so will cash benefit, although the 25-year total will be about the same. (But if you use accelerated depreciation, then in the event of an early sale, the so-called "recapture" provisions of Sec. 1250 of the Internal Revenue Code would apply.)

The corporation might consider paying only partly in cash and giving a mortgage for the rest. Whether this is advisable (where the corporation has all the cash) depends on whether the company can earn more with the money it does not put into the building than it will pay for mortgage money.

Sale-leaseback of machinery to increase working capital. Your company has machinery and equipment having a depreciated book value of $288,000. A leasing company purchases these assets for $288,000 and leases them back over a 5-year period at a semiannual rental of $34,560. Here is the effect on the balance sheet:

Balance Sheet Assets

	Before	After
Cash	$ 49,500	$112,500
Notes receivable	3,600	3,600
Accounts receivable	109,800	109,800
Inventory	369,000	369,000
Total current	$531,900	$594,900
Land and building	$ 45,000	$ 45,000
Machinery and equipment	288,000	—0—
Investments	9,000	9,000
Other receivables	10,800	10,800
Total assets	$884,700	$659,700

Liabilities

	Before	After
Notes payable	$225,000	—0—
Accounts payable	6,300	$ 6,300
Accruals, taxes, etc.	34,200	34,200
Total current	$265,500	$ 40,000
Capital stock	162,000	162,000
Surplus	457,200	457,200
	$884,700	$659,700

Balance Sheet Comparisons

Dollars	Before	After
Net quick assets	($102,600)	$185,400
Net working capital	$266,440	$554,400
Tangible net worth	$619,200	$619,200

Ratios	Before	After
Current assets to current liabilities	2×	14.7×
Fixed assets to tangible net worth	54%	7.3%
Inventory to net working capital	138%	66%
Current debt to inventory	72%	11%
Total debt to tangible net worth	43%	6.5%

Results of sale-leaseback—

Retirement of notes payable
Increase in cash position
Increase in net quick assets and
    net working capital position
More favorable ratios
Bank line freed for future borrowing

Equipment leasing versus purchasing.   Leasing equipment is an increasingly important method of raising money.   Instead of laying out cash or borrowing to purchase equipment which will appear on its balance sheet, a company can acquire the use of productive and service equipment by merely obligating itself to pay regular rentals over a specified period of time, usually 3 to 5 years, and use the cash or borrowing power for additional working capital or other purposes.   However, in leasing equipment, the company has fewer fixed assets than if it had purchased the equipment, and the obligation to pay rent is just as definite as the obligation to pay interest and amortize the debt.   Also, while leasing may make for a better balance sheet for the reason that the lease will not appear on the liability side of the sheet, sophisticated lenders will take leasing obligations into consideration; and accounting practice calls for footnoting those obligations.

Rentals paid for equipment are deductible on income-tax returns.   Money laid out for equipment is not deductible; but, over the life of the equipment, its cost can be charged off by depreciation allowances.   Companies which use the 200%-declining-balance depreciation or sum-of-the-digits depreciation will find that this depreciation, in most instances, gives them as much tax benefit as the deduction of equipment rentals. Indeed, in short-life equipment, 3 to 5 years, they will be able to make larger deductions in the earlier years if they purchase equipment than if they lease it.

Does equipment leasing pay?   A lot of controversy has been raised over this question.   It is a little more expensive than bank borrowing, but on the whole it is a means of credit which goes beyond bank borrowing. It usually adds to the total credit that a company can command.   It is less expensive than raising money by selling securities to the public.   A prominent underwriter, writing in the *Harvard Business Review,* admitted that equipment leasing imparted a healthier glow to a company's balance sheet, but then raised this question: "What is taking place to justify this marked improvement?   The company has exchanged one obligation for another carrying a higher interest rate, and in the process has given away title to its plant and with it any residual value that it may have at the expiration of the lease."   Proponents of leasing point out that it protects users from equipment obsolescence and that there may be maintenance advantages in leasing.   They contend that these practical factors outweigh any loss of residual values.   Moreover, options to renew at reduced rentals frequently give the lessee the equivalent of the residual value in the equipment at fairly nominal cost.

If we compare five methods of acquiring equipment valued at $100,000 with a usable life of 10 years and no scrap value, we will find that the total outlay required for financing the equipment would line up this way:

5-year lease with renewals	$140,000
10-year conditional sale with 25 percent down payment	131,875
5-year 100 percent bank loan	112,000
5-year 75 percent bank loan	109,000
Cash purchase	100,000

Thus, we find that leasing the equipment costs an additional $40,000 over 10 years, on the basis of the rental rates charged top-credit companies by the Booth Leasing Corporation, one of the well-known leasing companies operating on a national scale. Though it costs $40,000 over a cash purchase, it costs only $8,125 more than the best credit terms which are usually available to a purchaser of equipment. If a company had to pay a 6 percent interest rate, a 5-year bank loan would cost $118,000 instead of $112,000.   But leasing the equipment would still cost $22,000 more over the 10-year period.

The question is: How much can the company earn on the cash which is freed by leasing?   If the company can earn 25 percent a year on this cash, the lease of equipment as a financing device would result in more than a $50,000 additional net profit over the 10-year period.   Leasing permits the user of the equipment to pay for fixed assets out of the earnings which those assets produce. It may also provide a cash-flow advantage by virtue of the fact that the rental payments are deductible from income as an expense.   Finally, because bankers tend to view rental obligations as future operating costs and in a different light from debt obligations, leasing equipment will usually make more capital available to the business.   The test of whether leasing is a good proposition for the individual company is whether it can put to work at a profit the extra cash which is made available.   In making this evaluation, consider that leasing does not save taxes, but may postpone them.   Thus, the tax significance is primarily that it may also add to the amount of cash available for other purposes.

Advantages of leasing.   The main advantages of leasing are—

It normally conserves capital, giving the lessee 90 to 100 percent financing as against a possible one-third or one-fourth down payment required on many purchases

On types of equipment which are subject to a high rate of obsolescence or uncertainty as to obsolescence, leasing can operate as a form of insurance against obsolescence.   At the end of the term, lessee will be able to modernize his equipment and processes

On types of equipment not permanently needed, such as construction scaffolding, bulldozers, and cranes (where the lessee is not in the construction business), leasing offers a means of satisfying a temporary need at a definite cost in place of the uncertainty of buying and having to resell such equipment in an uncertain market

On types of equipment where service and maintenance are important considerations, a lease of equipment to be serviced by the lessor will relieve the lessee of having to maintain his own service department or relying on independent contractors to provide maintenance and service

Leasing may make for a better balance sheet. The lease will not appear on the liability side of the balance sheet. Hence, proponents say leasing makes for lower debt ratios, increased borrowing capacity, freedom from debt and budgetary limitations and restrictions, and, as a side effect, increases the value of stock of the lessee corporation. However, sophisticated lenders will take account of leasing obligations and accounting practice calls for footnoting such obligations. Also, debt and budgetary limitations or restrictions may be drafted so as to take in lease obligations. Further, if property were purchased on an installment contract, while the debt would be reflected on the liability side, the value of the equipment would appear on the asset side

Leasing will not involve the control and supervision of operations that often attend traditional debt financing, will not threaten voting control as equity financing may, and will not involve the costs of underwriting a stock or bond issue

Leasing often permits postponing taxes via higher deductions than are obtainable with interest and depreciation deductions in case of installment purchases of equipment. Lease payments may be adjusted to match the declining-balance or sum-of-the-digits approach to depreciation

Leasing can offer virtually the same advantage as purchase with respect to investment-credit provision of Federal income-tax law. A lessor of new equipment can elect to pass the credit through to the lessee

Disadvantages of leasing. The main disadvantage of leasing is that it normally costs more than buying on time. But there are several factors that may, in a particular situation, narrow the cost differential to nil or even swing the balance in favor of leasing. Here are the factors:

Leasing companies may by reason of mass purchasing power be able to buy at better prices than the lessee

If the lease calls for service and maintenance by the lessor, he may be able to effect savings thereon by reason of the scale of his operations and greater efficiency which he may pass on to the lessee

Leasing companies are generally able to do better in disposing of property at the end of the term or when it has reached the point of diminishing returns; and this factor may also help to offset the cost to the lessee

Arc leasing. A small, growing company may find a new setup in equipment leasing, so-called "arc" leasing, helpful in getting through tight-money days. Under an arc leasing plan for fixtures and equipment, payments are lowest during the early years of the lease, when a business is growing and needs ready cash the most. As sales go up, the lease payments increase; but they get smaller again in the later years of the lease. A company to qualify under the plan must meet the requirements set up, as, for example, that it show a profit for 3 years, that it lease only new equipment, and that it lease a $5,000 minimum.

The lease-or-buy decision. Here is an illustration of how a contractor analyzed his lease-or-buy decision. He has current assets of $175,000 and current liabilities of $100,000 at a consequent ratio of 1.75:1. He needs $35,000 of equipment. The tables below show sample leasing transactions and the cost of each to the contractor.

CASE I *Customer desires to lease equipment costing $35,000, including sales tax and freight, for 4 years (base period) and for an indefinite number of annual renewals or with option to purchase:*

Initial equipment cost (including sales tax and freight)	$35,000.00
Lease term	4 years
Rate factor (rent per $1,000 of initial equipment cost per month) ..	$ 25.40
Deposit, last 4 months rent, payable in advance	3,556.00
Monthly rental, balance 44 months	889.00
Annual renewal rent: After base period (4 years), annual rent is payable in advance for each year. Annual rent per renewal year is 3½ percent of initial equipment cost	1,225.00
Purchase option (if requested by lessee): After base period (4 years), 12½ percent of initial equipment cost	4,375.00
After 4 annual renewals after base period (8 years total), 6¼ percent of initial equipment cost	2,187.50
Total cost of equipment	42,672.00

CASE II *Same as in Case I except that the leasing company will always have complete ownership of the equipment and there will be no option-to-purchase clause:*

Invoice cost (including sales tax and freight)	$35,000.00
Lease term	4 years
Fourth year's rent in advance: 10 percent	$ 3,500.00
36 monthly rental payments	1,060.50
Annual rent, fifth and succeeding years	350.00
Total cost of equipment	41,678.00

This is how the three alternatives of buying for cash, borrowing, or leasing would affect his financial status.

(1) *Cash Outlay for Equipment*

Current assets	$175,000
Current liabilities	100,000
Ratio	1.75:1

Purchase $35,000 worth of equipment, paying cash:

Current assets	$140,000
Current liabilities	100,000
Ratio	1.4:1

A current asset-liability ratio of less than 1.5:1 is not in good standing to borrow money from the bank to conduct operations.

(2) *Funds Borrowed from the Bank*

Current assets	$175,000
Current liabilities	100,000
Ratio	1.75:1

After borrowing $35,000 from the bank for equipment:

Current assets	$175,000
Current liabilities	135,000
Ratio	1.29:1

Still unable to borrow money to conduct operations.

(3) *Lease Arrangement*

	Before	After
Current assets	$175,000	$175,000
Current liabilities	100,000	110,668
Ratio	1.75:1	1.58:1

After lease arrangement, the first year's payment is included in current liabilities as in good accounting procedure.

As you can see, the contractor is in good standing to borrow money from the bank to conduct his operations efficiently.

5. Financing by lease

The leasing of land, buildings, and equipment has become an important method by which a business acquires the use of assets needed for its operations. Leasing offers an effective way to minimize capital requirements. In effect, a business which obtains land, buildings, or machinery, on long-term lease is borrowing money from the owner rather than from a bank.

Long-term lease of locations. Securing control of land suitable for business operations by long-term lease is the equivalent of borrowing the value of the land. Although not showing up in the balance sheet, such a commitment represents a fixed charge and has very much the same effect on profitability of the capital structure that long-term debt has. The annual rental should be arrived at by taking between 3½ and 6 percent of the fair value of the land. Sometimes the rent goes up as high as 10 percent of appraised value, but there is room for a lot of negotiating in setting rates, values, and final rents. Bear in mind that the owner of property relieves himself of paying real-estate taxes, which are normally assumed by the lessee. He also converts property into an income producer without going through the process of sale and payment of capital-gains tax. If the property has doubled in value over the owner's cost, he will net more from a 5 percent rent than from a sale with investment of the proceeds at 5½ percent. A lessee may be able to minimize his fixed commitment and get some trading value by offering the lessor some inflation protection by negotiating to pay a low basic rental plus a percentage of sales or profits over a specified level.

When land is leased, the problem of getting mortgage funds to improve it becomes much more difficult. This may be overcome by having the owner improve and lease both land and building or by getting the owner to join with the tenant to get a building financed and built. A lessee can trade quite heavily on the fact that he commits himself to improve, or to contribute to improve, leased land, and that these improvements inure tax-free to the lessor.

6. Financing expansion and refinancing

Financing expansion. Careful study will have provided satisfaction that the reasons for expansion are valid and that the dangers of overexpansion have been appraised and guarded against. Up to a point, the financing of expansion will resemble the normal financing of a healthy and growing business. The usual methods of issuing additional stock and borrowing money from a public or credit institution may be followed. Again, up to a point, expansion may be financed by accumulated profits not distributed as dividends and by growing depreciation reserves. Wise management will look toward long-term growth and, in financing early expansion, will retain their best security for last. They will raise money with stock and debentures as far as possible. To pave the way for later expansion, they will refund bond issues into stock. The desirability of keeping open the way to further expansion and further financing, and of minimizing fixed charges, will have to be weighed against the low cost of borrowed money today, the advantages of trading on the equity and of a thin capital structure, and the requirements of maintaining maximum control. This decision may boil down to a question of weighing the profitability of maximum expansion, conservatively financed, against the profitability of expanding more slowly so as to maintain tax and control advantages without placing too great a risk on equity ownership. The risk of overexpansion is compounded when financed by short-term credit. Income and short-term borrowing may be drained off to build up big assets or expanded inventory, leaving the business vulnerable to the first cold wind of bad times. The nature of the financing used to carry out expansion will also be conditioned by the state of the stock market. If stock prices are high, it becomes possible to sell additional stock without unduly diluting the equity of existing stockholders. If stock prices are low, new stock can usually be sold only at a price which gives away too much of the business. Under these circumstances, such expansion financing as is desirable may best be carried out with borrowed money.

Acquisition of other businesses. The most advantageous type of expansion is frequently effected by issuing additional stock to acquire another business which will expand or diversify existing operations. The fact that other companies can be obtained by tax-free expansion frequently permits the owners of an acquired business to avoid capital-gains tax on their sale and to improve their liquidity with little if any loss in investment yield.

For example, if stock having a cost basis of $400,000 is sold for $1,000,000, the owners wind up with $850,000 after paying $150,000 capital-gains tax. But, if the deal is a tax-free exchange, the owners wind up with $1,000,000 in securities. Return of 5 percent on the securities would yield roughly as much as a 6 percent return on the proceeds of a sale.

The acquiring company builds up its equity in several ways. First, the volume of earnings of the acquired company may be expanded by using the more powerful resources of the acquiring company. Also the established earnings and the method of financing can build up equity by retiring obligations, thereby building up earning power of the remaining stock.

In addition, major benefits may flow when the acquiring corporation has so proved an established earning power that its stock is valued at a higher multiple of annual earnings. The stock of the acquired company would normally be valued at a lower multiple of earnings, and the incorporation of the acquired firm's earning power into the acquiring company's structure will automatically bring about an important increment in value.

Take a corporation whose stock is currently the subject of high investment popularity. Suppose it has 1,000,000 shares of common stock outstanding, backed by $10,000,000 of assets, or $10 per share. Because of its popularity, promise, and earning power, the stock is currently selling for $20 per share. If this corporation acquires a company at a value of one and one-half times its net asset value, acquiring $600,000 net asset value by the issuance of 45,000 new shares, it achieves a 6 percent increase of asset value for a 4.5 percent increase in shares, and each share thereby gets a 1.43 percent enhancement in asset value.

Again, an acquisition deal may be made mutually attractive by the superior credit standing of the acquiring company, which permits it to acquire funds on a low yield basis and to purchase properties of businesses less fortunately situated as to credit standing. The higher valuation set upon the earnings of a large corporation by the securities market means that the acquiring corporation can offer shares that are extremely attractive to the owners of the acquired business, and acquire earnings greater than its own shares are able to report. These earnings are then translated into the higher value for all its shares, including those newly issued.

Refinancing and recapitalization. The capital structure of a company may be changed by refinancing or recapitalization for the purpose of (1) achieving a more balanced financial structure; (2) paving the way for additional financing; (3) improving the appreciation potential of junior stockholders, the safety of senior stockholders, and the liquidity of both; (4) eliminating arrearages and preferred stock dividends; and (5) saving interest and other financing costs. Such capital changes fall into these categories:

Funding essentially involves the extension of maturities. Short-term debt is converted into long-term debt. Such a move is called for when a balance sheet shows a current liability practically equal in amount to current assets. It's possible only when underlying assets and earnings are adequate to support permanent debt and higher fixed charges.

Refunding involves calling bonds for redemption and paying off with the proceeds of new bonds issued. Such a move is called for to reduce financing charges when either interest rates have dropped or credit position has improved so that money can be acquired at lower cost.

Refinancing debt with stock involves calling bonds or preferred stock with funds realized from the sale of additional common stock. Such a move may be desirable when common stock values are high or when it is important to improve safety or to pave the way for future expansion by removing fixed charges and maturities.

Recapitalization involves revising capital structure by getting holders to exchange existing securities for new securities, on a voluntary basis. Substitution of junior securities for senior securities will improve safety, reduce fixed charges, and pave the way for future financing. Substituting senior securities for junior securities will provide a bigger gamble for those who retain junior securities, and greater safety and liquidity for those who make the swap.

7. Checklist for planning the financing of a business

Study the business to determine the operating ratios, profit margins, discounts, and rate of turnover which prevail

Determine the scale of operations for which the business will strive. What volume will make it a going concern, and what are the probable and desired stages of growth?

Determine how much will be needed for plant, machinery, fixtures, and such fixed assets

Project a cash budget to determine the probable amount and timing of cash requirements and a profit-and-loss budget to determine the extent to which prospects justify the risk of capital

Start fitting the capital requirements, as determined in the first four steps, to the availability of capital to the owners. This may mean revising the scale and projected growth of operations

Determine how much capital can be raised by investment in equity (common and preferred stock) and how much it is desired to spread ownership

Set aside enough of this amount to cover promotion and early development costs and to provide a fund for contingencies and a cushion over and above short-term working-capital requirements

Determine how much long-term loan financing (mortgage, equipment, term) will be justified by the remaining equity and the collateral value of assets needed

Determine how inventory, payables, and receivables will turn over and explore ways and means of carrying these assets—advances from customers and trade credit, bank loans, inventory loans, loans on receivables

Determine desirability of leasing or licensing rather than owning assets such
as plant, trucks, machinery, patents

Look around for trouble.   What would be called for if expansion ran ahead
of available capital?   What would happen if necessary volume were slow
in developing?   Draw off pro forma balance sheets from budget projections and test them to see how credit-worthy the business promises to be at
selected intervals

Test the capital structure indicated by the availability and desirability of
different forms of capital against tax factors

Section 2

STARTING A BUSINESS

BY

D'ALTON B. MYERS

STARTING A BUSINESS

You have turned to this chapter because you want to check your thinking before you start to set up a business of your own.

You have been asking yourself, "Can I make a success in business for myself?" Perhaps two or three of you are talking over the prospects. Or it may be that several of you are planning to launch a medium-size corporation—a manufacturing or wholesaling concern. Regardless of the size, type, and scope of the contemplated business, now—before it is started—is the time to stop, read, and check.

We could do a much better job of helping you get the answers to all the questions that are flooding your brain if we could talk them over together. That is out for the present; so condensed into this short chapter are the highlights of hundreds of talks with men and women who have asked the same questions. Regardless of whether they were production engineers with large manufacturers, buyers or merchandising managers for large department stores, salesmen, office managers, Army and Navy officers, government workers, secretaries, or GIs; whether they were experienced business managers or novices; whether they had $500 or $50,000 to invest, the conferences invariably started with, "I am thinking about going into business for myself. Do you think I should?" Or "A group of us is considering starting a new corporation. I'll be one of the owners and managers. What do you think of the idea?"

The answer to the first question involves you and what, where, how, and when. Answering the second question increases in difficulty in more than direct ratio to the number of men who will participate in the management of the proposed company. It is a safe assumption that the success of the venture and your participation in it rest to a great degree on how well your group probes into the abilities and temperaments of the members and is able to integrate them into a working team.

The same general problems face all businesses regardless of their type and size. However, the fact that these problems may be dealt with differently in the various types and sizes of business tends to increase or to lessen their importance in any specific case. In the small one-man business all problems must be handled by the owner-manager. As businesses increase in size, more and more problems must be dealt with by division heads and other subordinates. Only major problems reach the top management.

Similarly the questions that should be thought about before starting a business will vary in importance with the size and type of the venture; nevertheless they remain basically the same. The larger the business, the more detailed the advance consideration must be. This is not so much because of the increased size of the financial risk, but rather because the larger the organization, the less flexible it tends to be in adjusting quickly to new and unforeseen developments —of which any new business will have plenty.

But to get back to the first question, "I am thinking of going into business for myself. Do you think I should?" In this section we will subdivide the question that involves you, what, where, how, and when, into six. Two questions I will ask of you; four you will ask of me.

Before getting into a discussion on the specific questions some orientation into the world of small-business economics might be helpful to you.

The question is frequently asked, "What do you mean by 'small business'?" During the past 25 years there have been many attempts to quantify the term. Retailers having net annual sales of less than $50,000 were considered small by the U.S. Department of Commerce, as were manufacturers employing fewer than 100 people. Various government agencies and economists employed different quantitative terms, none of which were really descriptive. More and more, those working and studying in the field of small business realized that quantitative terms confused the issue. They realized that what was really meant by "small business" was those enterprises that were independently owned and operated, and were not dominant in their fields of operation. Criteria such as dollar volume of business or number of employees were useful only in refining the definition.

The United States in one respect is a land of small business. According to the Internal Revenue Service, there were approximately 10,500,000 businesses, including agricultural units, in the United States in 1962. Even excluding the agricultural units—which an increasing number of economists are considering as businesses—there are at least 7,000,000 businesses in the United States, about 5,000,000 of which are sole proprietorships, 900,000 partnerships, 1,100,000 corporations. By any definition, small businesses comprise approximately 95 percent of our total business population. If farms are included, the figure is closer to 98 percent. Perhaps this explains why small business is so often referred to as the seedbed of the American economy.

There can be no doubt that small business is a seedbed, for approximately 450,000 new enterprises are started each year, started by men and women who like yourself think they see a way to a better life and perhaps financial independence. But the analogy with an actual bed is not really sound, for by knowing what kind of seed has been planted we can forecast the shape and size of the plant. But no one has ever formulated a method of predicting the ultimate size of a newly started business. Nor has anyone ever formulated an accurate system of predicting success. There are too many variables. About all that can be done is to say that businesses that are now successes had such and such policies and operating methods, and if you understand why they had them, your chances for success are greater if you adopt them in your business.

If you look at the statistics on the number of businesses, their receipts, and net profits, or if you just look closely at the business sections of our cities and towns and along the highways, you will see that, numerically speaking, the vast majority of businesses are small, started small, and have never grown. Actually over 90 percent of the businesses in the United States have less than $50,000 in net annual receipts—not profits—and the average is less than $20,000.

Statistics, according to some authorities, tend to conceal more than they reveal. Personally, I think this is somewhat true about the statistics on small business. It is impossible to get data on how our businesses are growing except for our large corporations or by case studies of the exceptional business that started small and has grown into a large enterprise. The history of American business is full of such cases; and many of them, such as Sears, Roebuck and Co., are well known as having started on the proverbial shoe-string.

There is another economic fact that you should consider. It is estimated that there are over 400,000 business closures each year. Some are bankruptcies, but in the majority of cases the owners just quit and folded up their businesses. Here, too, the figures are not complete, but the statistics on bankruptcy cases show that between 55 and 60 percent of the failures occurred within 5 years or less of the opening of the business, and 75 percent in 10 years or less.

In my opinion, what I have been saying about the "business seedbed," the numbers of businesses in the United States, the annual number of closures, and the failure rate is pertinent only if they make you see the need of being growth-minded. In this day and age, when more and more economic power is being concentrated in the hands of giant corporations, there is definite social and economic need for aggressive smaller companies to grow and be able to step on the heels of the giants. What we want from our smaller businesses is for them to grow and to keep injecting competition into our economy. Actually, as far as the individual small business is concerned, only a very few would mourn its passing—the family, a few friends, perhaps a bank, and a handful of creditors. But the existence of dynamic, progressive small businesses with growth-minded owner-managers is essential to our entire economy. That is the role in which you should see yourself.

Since World War II much has been done for small businesses. The Federal government has been active. During World War II the Smaller War Plants Corporation was effective in helping smaller manufacturers contribute to the war effort. The U.S. Department of Commerce through its Office of Small Business worked to help in the improvement of management, work subsequently taken over by the Small Business Administration. The Department of Justice and the Federal Trade Commission work to curtail unfair competition.   The policies of our commercial banks have undergone quite a change in the postwar years, making loans more avaliable to small businesses either independently or in cooperation with the SBA.   Small-business investment companies have been started which provide private funds for small businesses that show growth possibilities.   Our university schools of business administration have played an active part in endeavoring to improve the managements of our smaller businesses.   And last but not least, there has been an increasing awareness on the part of our large corporations of the social and economic value of smaller companies, a greater willingness to help them and to refrain from using their greater financial strength unfairly.

Actually, the whole thing boils down to *you*—your attitudes, your ideas, the way you think about business.   Business has come into its own "space age," and the policies and practices of a less turbulent time, economically speaking, are no longer effective.   In simpler times, one used to see in retail stores signs such as "The Shop That John Keeps; the Shop That Keeps John."   There are thousands of shops keeping Johns, but the data based on income-tax returns show that the vast majority are keeping John on a relatively low level of income.   In addition, if John is being kept at a very substantial level of income, you can rest assured that competition will spring up.   One only has to look into our department stores to see many lines of goods being handled which were once sold exclusively by independently owned specialty shops.

There are small businesses—relatively a small percentage of the entire business population—that do make a good living for the owner-managers.   But if you are thinking in terms of real success, you must think in terms of growth. If you do, and if you can formulate policies and practices that can make for growth, you can find plenty of help.   The importance of growth is perhaps best indicated by the standards set by many of the small-business investment companies that are constantly looking for well-managed small companies in which to invest funds.   They want a company to have a growth rate of at least 15 to 20 percent annually and to be able to go public—that is, to sell its stock to the public—within 5 years.

At this point, I would say that if you are not familiar with or have not read the histories of businesses that started small and have become sizable—perhaps not the giants—during the past two decades, you should give this top priority. You will find many stories in magazines on business, such as *Forbes,* available in practically all public libraries.

But back to the six questions again.

1. Do you really want to start a business?

You will have to answer this question objectively and completely before we can get down to a sound discussion of your particular business.   Most likely if we were talking this over, you would be able to convince me of your earnestness in a few moments and we could move right on to the main topic—your business.   These are the points that I would raise with you:

Have you analyzed carefully the security provided by business ownership and compared it with that possible if you remained an employee?

Have you compared earnings and salaries of business owners with the wages and salaries of workers?

Have you carefully considered the negative aspects of business ownership? The dangers of losses?   The "mortality" or failure rate of business?

What is driving you toward business ownership?   Need to earn more?   Desire to be independent?   Wanting to be the "boss-man"?   Dissatisfaction with present job or work?

Here are some facts and opinions on these points:

Business ownership and security.   Security is not guaranteed by business ownership—neither immediate job security nor that for old age and retirement.   In fact, the "mortality" or discontinuance rate of businesses is so high that authorities state that out of every 1,000 new businesses started during a year, 250 disappear before the end of the year.   By the end of 5 years, only 350 remain; and no more than 190 of the original 1,000 start their eleventh year.   These figures apply pretty much to all types of businesses.

Business ownership is synonymous with risk taking—at least it should be. Risk taking involves both the possibility of profit and that of loss; if the unprofitable operations exceed the profitable, closing up the enterprise is just a matter of time.

By placing this emphasis on the mortality rate of business there is no intention to deny that in this country today there are tens of thousands of smaller businesses that produce good incomes for their owners—or rather, it might be said, that enable their owners to earn good incomes through capably managing them.

Business ownership does offer a particular form of security: security against arbitrary and sudden dismissal.   Perhaps this is one of the reasons you have for wanting to start a business.   If so, good; but the way may be long and hard before you can get your enterprise to the point where the security begins to mean something tangible.

The question of security should be at the bottom of the list.   But because so many people talk about it first, I have considered it early in this section.

Too much emphasis on the security possibilities of business ownership can easily get you on the wrong track in starting a business.   In the final analysis the only real security for the individual rests in his making himself more and more qualified for the job to be done.   If he is an owner, it means running a business that so pleases the customers or clients that they will support it or buy its products.   And, of course, that is what so many men mean when they talk about the security of business ownership.   They feel that they can produce, and they do not want to be blocked by some boss who has unsound business policies or uses out-of-date business methods.

The fear of insecurity has kept many people from launching businesses for themselves. Perhaps you have been asking yourself whether you should not stay on your present job—whether you are not foolish to venture into the unknown. If your friends and relatives know that you are considering starting a business, the chances are ten to one that they are saying, "Don't be foolish. Stay where you are."

If the fear of insecurity is holding you back, or the desire for security urging you on, then I think you had better ask yourself the question, "Do I really want to start a business?" If the desire for security outweighs all the other reasons for starting or not starting, then, in my opinion, you are not mentally or emotionally prepared for business ownership.

Jobs with big corporations provide very little in the way of real job security. Even men in the top positions are subject to sudden and arbitrary dismissals by boards of directors or controlling interests. Face-saving letters of resignation are accepted, but the results are the same. All you have to do to check on this phase of insecurity is to watch the shifts in management of well-known corporations.

The insecurity of key executives in our large corporations was impressed on me several years ago when I listened to a series of sales talks designed to recruit salesmen for an insurance company. They had been put on seven double phonograph records; 14 sides in all. Two records were devoted chiefly to case histories of former business executives who had found real economic security only after they had set up their own insurance offices. In each case, the man had held an important position with a big corporation, had drawn a good salary, and had thought he had security. Then there had been a sudden change in management or policy, and the man had been let out. If the facts given were accurate—and they must have been, for names of companies and individuals were stated—they would certainly dispel the idea that top jobs in large corporations provide security.

Business ownership and income. Many people who claim that they want to go into business for themselves point to large earnings of businessmen and to the fact that they can pay themselves large salaries, that is, draw out a lot of the earnings for their own living expenses and personal investments. You most likely have heard stories of men who started a few years ago in their own businesses and today drive around in Cadillacs, own swanky homes, and always seem to have plenty of the folding "green stuff"—certainly far more than they would ever have had "working for someone else." Many of these stories are true, although perhaps a little exaggerated, but they do not tell the whole story.

The facts are that, on the whole, the range of incomes of the owners of unincorporated businesses or of closely held corporations is about the same as the range of the earned incomes of wage earners and salaried employees. In other words, lots of business owners do not draw out of their businesses any more money for their own use than the average full-time worker draws in wages.

On the other hand, there are business owners whose share in the profits, withdrawn in cash, will run into hundreds of thousands of dollars each year. But it is also true that the top employees in some of the larger corporations draw similar amounts.

Maybe you have convinced yourself that, because someone is paying you a salary or wage, he is making a profit on you which you could keep if you were your own boss. Perhaps you are right, but you had better check your thinking once more. No general rule holds true in all cases. In some, the individual is valuable only as a member of a team, and the so-called profit of the owner is on the work of the team as a whole, not on the individual members. The minute you leave such a team, your value drops, even to yourself—that is, until you are able to form another team that is just as efficient. Perhaps the business principle that it is not good business to begrudge the other man a reasonable profit—even on your efforts—should be applied more often.

Your business proposition may be just the opposite; that is, highly individualistic. Perhaps it is similar to the case of the young European who evaded the Iron Curtain, got into this country, and wanted to get started in the importing business. All he had was his knowledge of materials and a list of contacts with whom he had previously done business. My advice to him was to start his own business immediately. For personal reasons, he felt that he had to get on a payroll, so he spent several weary weeks calling on importers, trying to sell them on hiring him for what and whom he knew. He could get no bona fide offers from reputable companies, so he finally launched his own company. In a short time, he was on the road to success. My reasoning was that it was he as an individual who was valuable. Being a member of a team would not add one iota to his worth to any company. Apparently this was obvious to all the businessmen he interviewed, for each figured that, since whatever they paid him during the early months was being staked on one person, not on building a team of workers, the possible returns had to be very high. Furthermore each implied—some even asked—the question: "If you are worth the salary and expenses you ask us to advance, why don't you go it on your own?"

If it is the envy of someone else's making a "profit" on you that is causing you to want to start your own business, why not talk it over with your boss and tell him of some of your ambitions? This assumes that you are currently working for a smaller company, which is all the more reason for considering such a move. If you start the same type of business as you are now working for, you will have to build it into more than a one-man enterprise. That is, if you want it to grow, you will need an organization. Perhaps your present boss has some ideas along the same line. Therefore, unless you have some very valid reasons for not doing so, I would talk things over with him. But do not be surprised if at first he takes a negative view of the whole idea. It is my observation that most small businessmen are immediately suspicious and resentful of employees who approach them with the idea of getting in on the ownership of the business. It is a perfectly normal reaction, so recognize it as such. Word your proposition so that you do not have to consider his first reaction—if he is opposed—as a turndown, but rather as the basis for further study of the idea.

Recently during a talk on business management I urged the small businessmen present to start building organizations in their firms by taking their employees into their confidence and giving them as much responsibility as possible. In the question period following, one man challenged the idea. According to him, I was all wrong. "If you let an employee learn about your business, he will quit as soon as possible and start up for himself." I asked him why *he* had gone into business for himself. He replied, "The guy I was working for wouldn't give me a chance to become part owner. He wouldn't even let me learn the important parts of the business." I felt that he was helping me make my point very clear, so I asked him if he would have left his old boss if he had been given such an opportunity as I now urged him to give his employees. My point was made!

Let us ask the basic question in another form: Why do you want to start a business? This, of course, includes buying out a business as well as acquiring part interest in a going concern.

The specific answers that men give to this question are manifold. It is my observation that if you can get your real reason out in the open where you can analyze it thoroughly, you will be taking a long step toward getting launched in a successful business, or avoiding a false start.

Profits are supposed to be the prime reason why men go into business. If you mean by *profits* the difference between the sum of money a business takes in during a year or any other period of time and what it pays out during that period (including what the owners get, what is set aside to replace the equipment when it wears out, and what it has promised to pay later on), then, in my opinion, it is safe to say that the majority of businesses are not operated at a profit. Actually, most of the so-called "profitable" businesses produce for their owners no more than reasonable salaries plus a nominal interest on their investments.

Self-expression through business ownership. As previously implied, I do not think that many men or women become business owners because of the possibilities of big earnings or because they see real security in it. It is my opinion that they become business owners because they see, or think they see, an opportunity to create something—an opportunity for self-expression. Is not that the basic drive that is behind your thinking about starting a business? The "grand openings" of markets, retail stores, theaters, factories, and in fact all types of businesses are not just advertising stunts; basically, they are a desire to present the new business, just created, in all possible glory. I have seldom met a man who could any more conceal his pride in a new business than he could his pride in his first-born son.   And the men who seem the proudest to become business owners invariably are former executives of big corporations.   They are like an acquaintance who telephoned wanting to see me for a few minutes.   For years he had held important positions in one of the largest rubber companies, and he just wanted to stop in to tell me that he was now in business for himself.   I had never seen him so happy or so proud, despite the fact that *his* company would not do as much business in a year as the big corporation he had just left would do in half a day.

The desire for a better income from business ownership is a perfectly legitimate justification for wanting to go into business.   Perhaps it is your desire; perhaps, the wife's.   The latter is just as good; many a man who claims to be self-made is actually wife-made.   But if the desire for profits takes precedence over that of making your business render a real service, it is my opinion that your chances for success are definitely lessened.

American businessmen are often kidded about their ideas on *service*.   Businessmen in many other countries scoff at the idea and think the Americans are either naïve or hypocritical.   But we seem to have learned that service pays dividends.   "Rendering a service" is just another way of saying "solving a problem."   And that is just what most businesses do for us day in and day out. The fact that we create many of our problems does not alter the situation, nor does the fact that we are frequently talked into having problems by high-powered advertisements.

It has been said that if you can find 30 people who have a common problem, or who can be convinced that they have, you have the basis for starting a business.   You can think of hundreds of businesses that will illustrate this point. I always think of diaper laundries.   We had been having babies for a considerable number of years and the home washing of their diapers had always been a burden, but in spite of this it was not until 1932 that the first commercial diaper laundry was started.   It had taken businessmen a long time to see this problem and do anything about it.

The problems that businesses are set up to solve may range from the simple to the very complex.   They may be problems that are causing serious losses and great worries, or they may be problems whose solutions just simplify life, make it more enjoyable, and give people more time to do all those things they really like to do.

Let us take a simple situation that may illustrate not only the problem-solving role of business but also the relationship of profits to service.   A chap with less than $1,000 of capital came to a California town where he wanted to live and where he wanted to start a business.   The businessmen in the town had lots of problems, but one that seemed universal was the distribution of handbills.   The high school boys they hired were usually too careless about where they stuck the handbills; sometimes they even put them down the storm drains to speed the distribution. In a few days the newcomer convinced enough merchants that he could solve this problem for them, and he was in business for himself. It was profitable right from the start. The merchants appraised the service in terms of the increased effectiveness of their handbills plus their savings in money, time, and worry. They wanted him to make a profit and to stay in business as long as he solved their problem.

Businesses that solve one problem frequently create whole series of problems the people will want solved. The automobile industry is a well-known example of this. Even after 70 years of the motor car, companies and individuals are still solving the problems of motorists.

Perhaps you are starting your business because you want to be the "boss-man," or because you would rather be the big frog in a small puddle. That is very understandable and, if kept within bounds, perfectly all right. The danger in this approach to business ownership is that it overlooks the fact that many workers do not care to work in so-called "one-man" businesses where their interests are likely to be at the mercy of one individual's whims. Rightly or wrongly, labor today wants to broaden the area of its interest in the management of businesses. More and more, professional managers of businesses are recognizing the value of labor-management teamwork even on such matters as sales and advertising programs, production costs, the introduction of new labor-saving machinery—questions that a few years ago were strictly management's job to solve.

If the drive to be boss is at the top of your list of reasons for starting a business, ask yourself whether you would want to work in that kind of business. If it is not good enough for you, it most likely will not be good enough to attract capable workers. It may be hard to build business teams, but when you can get a good one going, it certainly pays off. Being boss does not need to mean that you have to "lead the band and play all the instruments in it." On the contrary, in some well-managed and profitable small businesses the boss is the least conspicuous. Before you start your business, you may want to answer very thoroughly the question: Can I build a real business team?

A word about franchises or dealerships. Perhaps you are considering setting up or buying a business based on a franchise or dealership. Frequently this is a very good idea, for it can combine the advantages of individual ownership with those of being part of a large organization. The parent company frequently provides excellent training in both the technical operations and the management. Also, many such companies put on nationwide advertising campaigns from which local dealers benefit. There are, however, negative aspects of franchises and dealerships that must not be overlooked. Much of a franchisee's or dealer's success in many instances is dependent on the success of the parent company. If it fails to play a dominant role in its industry, you, as one of its dealers, may find all your money and efforts have been wasted. In the early days of the automobile industry when over 200 companies were started, thousands of dealers lost out because the parent company failed or went out of business.

If you take on a franchise, you should do so only after you have carefully analyzed the financial strength of the company and investigated its management policies. You should also continue to study its financial condition and policies as you would if you were the owner of a block of its stock. And speaking of stock, if you take on a franchise or become a dealer you should, like other key workers, be granted an option to buy at specified prices stock in the parent company, whose growth will be dependent to a large extent on men like you. Taking on a franchise or dealership is no sure road to success. Contracts or agreements pertaining to them need to be scrutinized most carefully from both an economic and legal point of view.

Larger ventures. The larger the business-to-be under consideration and the more owner-managers involved, the more important it is that you discuss the basic problems of ownership and the questions of security and income to achieve a meeting of the minds regarding them. Not only the basic policies for the business must be agreed upon but also the objectives of the owners of the enterprise. Let me illustrate:

Recently I watched a sound business break up and disappear—not because of lack of orders or of capable operating management. The breakup was due solely and entirely to a conflict among the owner-managers over top policies and the main objectives of the concern. Some of them felt that security and income—that is, their personal security and income—were furthered by keeping the business relatively small. Others felt that growth provided the most security and that income—that is, their current incomes—should be restricted in order to help the business grow.

The damage done by this cleavage was irreparable. The records revealed that this basic policy had never been explored prior to starting the business. Each man had entered into the deal with his own preconceived ideas as to the objectives of the enterprise.

The variation in the Federal personal-income-tax rates is another reason for achieving agreement on the business policy affecting security and income. This is particularly true in those cases where some of the owner-managers of the enterprise have sources of personal income other than the business in question, while others are dependent solely on it for their total incomes. The problem is complex and no single general advice can prevail. Help of experts should be obtained when the problem is under discussion—that is, before you start.

All that we have been doing so far in this section is to get you to check whether or not you realy want to go into business. If you are satisfied that you really do, we can move on to the next question from me to you. But before we do, you may want to make certain that you have the facts which will justify the following statements by you:

I want to go into business [1] because—

    I believe there is greater security for business owners than there is for job-holders

    I believe my average profits over a given period of years will greatly exceed my average wage or salary income for the same period

    I believe I can develop a business that will prove to be a genuine service to my customers and will solve one or more problems for them

    I believe that I can build an organization in which others will enjoy working. In short, I believe that I have qualities of leadership and am justified in my desire to head an organization

    I believe I understand the importance of growth in today's business economy and that I have the knowledge and ability to make my business show a steady growth

2. Are you prepared to start a business?

Whether or not you are prepared—that is, adequately prepared—to start a business depends, of course, to a large extent on the kind of business you are thinking of starting.

There are fields of business you cannot enter unless you pass professional and/or technical knowledge tests and are granted permits or licenses by governmental or other agencies. Pharmacies, beauty parlors, and plumbers are typical examples of businesses in this category. But actually such businesses are very few and in most of them it is an individual, not a business, that needs the license. Such men can be hired as skilled workers in many cases.

I am assuming that the business you are considering is either one whose legal requirements you can meet or one for which there are none.

Similarly, we will skip the question of whether or not you are financially prepared—that is, whether you have adequate resources. During the past few years this aspect of business ownership has received a lot of attention. In part, this situation was due to the fear that many men and women would try to start businesses without full appreciation of the financial problems and would go broke. Writers who got their information from credit managers, bankers, and government officials tended to stress the amount of money that it takes to get established in a small business. It is my opinion that not enough stress has been placed on the need of being prepared for financial management of business. The amount of money you have is not nearly so important as how you use what you have. Understanding how to use money—your own and that which you can borrow—is a key point on which you should be prepared. Are you?

Before we discuss this question, let me cite a case that is all too typical. As a

---

[1] If your business is to be a partnership or corporation, substitute "we," "our," and "us," for "I," "my," and "me" in the above statements and similar ones that appear in subsequent parts of this section.

member of SCORE—Service Corps of Retired Executives—I was asked to give management counsel to a man who had borrowed $40,000 from the Small Business Administration and a participating bank. He was in default on his payments.

A survey of the situation revealed the following: His bank account was practically zero. He was drawing from the business barely enough for groceries. His books and records were months behind, for he had no funds for a bookkeeper or secretary. On the positive side and from a technical or production point of view, he seemed well qualified and had designed what seemed to be an efficient small plant. But what he had overlooked was the need of balance in the uses of his own funds and those he had borrowed. He had put practically every dollar of his capital—his own and borrowed—into land, a building, and equipment. These, plus his inventory, much of which was slow-moving, tied up 95 percent of the capital. On top of this, he had lost several thousand dollars on bad credit accounts.

I could find no evidence that he had really planned his operations in keeping with his financial resources. He was typical of so many men who get into business for themselves via the production route and are ignorant of financial management, if not actually hostile to the controls that sound financial management imposes on any business, large or small.

His case made me think of one authority's summation of the contrasting views of small and big business:

Today's operations—the concern of the small
Planning—the concern of the big
Hogging the show (a one-man operation)—the concern of the small
Developing managerial talent—the concern of the big

Financial management. Preparation in financial management is all-important—unless, of course, you conceive of your business as one that will remain relatively small, a sort of shop. If you have visions of its growing into a large concern, you had better be prepared in financial management or make haste to become so prepared. Borrowing money—that is, using one's credit—is not all there is to financial management, but it is an important part of it. This is especially true today, for the business owner never knows when he must either expand rapidly or lose out to his competitors. The superabundance of investable funds and the thousands of men and women who are looking for business opportunities are constant threats to existing businesses. It is estimated that at least 45 billion dollars out of the 450 billions of individual savings is available for investment. That is, while the owners of these funds have them invested, it is on a temporary basis, and they are always looking for more remunerative places to put them.

There is an aspect of financial management that must be faced up to: the danger of the original owner or owners of a growing business losing control

of it and being forced out.   This is frequently referred to as the "squeeze out."
There have been thousands of cases in the history of American business.   Some
men say stay small and no one will want to take over.   But they overlook the
fact that lack of growth on the part of an established business is exactly the
reason a more aggressive, growth-minded individual or group starts a competitive enterprise.   You only have to observe what is happening in the motel industry to have this confirmed.   In this day and age, smallness—whether actual
or relative—is seldom a protection in American business.   You will find that
even businesses that stress that they give more personalized service because they
are relatively smaller than competitors, or that they try harder, are growth-
minded.   And you can rest assured that if they ever get into first place they
will quickly change their advertising appeal.   You can get legal advice on how
to protect yourself against a squeeze out, but in the final analysis, the best
protection is to so manage the business that your services will always be wanted.

Human relations.   Perhaps the most important question under preparation
is: Are you prepared in human relations?   This is a term that is usually applied to relations between management and labor or between boss and workers.
But in a broader sense adequate preparation in human relations means that
you know how to work with people, deal with people—in short, get along with
your fellow human beings as equals.   No one is ever fully prepared on this
score.   Most of us bat only about .200 at the most when we come right down
to it, but if we recognize the importance of good human relations, there is much
that each one of us can do.

You can get lots of help in becoming prepared as far as human relations are
concerned.   There are many excellent and well-written books on the market.
You will find them very readable, and they can help you acquire a scientific
basis for most effective dealing with your customers, the people you buy from,
the people who work with you, and your fellow businessmen.

When you check into what is adequate preparation in human relations, you
will see that it is chiefly *you* that is involved.   It is the way you act, what you
say, and even how you think that determines what the other fellow does or
says.   You cannot make people buy from you, but you can so conduct your
business that they will want to buy from you.   You cannot get loyalty from
your workers and associates by command, but you can earn it by your understanding of them, their ideas, their hopes and aspirations, and their problems.

Let me illustrate by a couple of short stories from real life.   Both happened
in a Midwestern manufacturing company whose top management has a keen
appreciation of good human relations.

The first involves Joe, a janitor, and the building of a second-floor addition
to the main office building.   It was not much more than a routine construction
job to provide more space for the engineers, draftsmen, and general office force.
As such, it did not seem that it would be of much concern to the rank and file
of the workers.   But the general manager knew that Joe, like most of the em-

ployees, lived with his family near the plant. On Sundays now and then he had seen Joe with his two small sons walking past the plant while Joe, the big shot in their eyes, pointed out things of importance. The general manager could foresee the questions they would ask just as soon as construction started, and he could sense Joe's embarrassment and hurt if he were unable to tell his sons what *his* company was doing in this latest development. So on the bulletin boards were posted the details of the expansion, complete with blueprints, architect's sketches, costs, and explanations of the need for the expansion and just what it would mean for each department. Joe and the other working fathers were never embarrassed for lack of information about *their* firm.

The second story involves supervisors and the difficulties of really getting to the root cause of a problem. According to this company, supervisors or foremen find it hard to understand and to apply good human relations. And the more recent their promotion to the supervisory positions, the more trouble they seem to have. One such supervisor complained that one of his men, Brown, continually ignored instructions and did work below the standard acceptable in this plant. Reprimands were of no avail, and finally it reached the point where Brown's dismissal was being considered. His production record made such action possible under the terms of the union contract. When the case reached the general manager, he urged that shop friends of Brown find out what had happened to him during the last 6 months. Word came back promptly that Brown had lost his hearing and was afraid that he would be discharged if his deafness was discovered. The general manager allayed his fears and pointed out that several of the executives wore hearing aids. Brown immediately acquired one, and the problem was solved. But the real payoff for the company resulted from the better understanding by the supervisors of what really constitutes good human relations.

Perhaps we can restate the question for this part of the section: Do you consider that you are temperamentally and emotionally prepared for business ownership? I am not trying to scare you away from business ownership, but I do think that you must answer that question frankly and honestly to your own satisfaction. And your answers must be made with present-day business conditions in mind. Competition is keen, business as a career has attracted many of the country's most able men, labor (for the most part) is well organized, and customers are well informed.

If your business venture is to be a partnership or corporation—that is, a medium-size or larger small company—then the question is: Is each member of the group of owner-managers adequately prepared in human relations?

The relationships among the owner-managers of businesses of these sizes must usually be very close, and it is vital that each man in your group be able to bring emotional maturity and judgment to the problems of the business.

You can help develop sound human relations if you are party to developing an organization in which the responsibilities, duties, and authority of each member are clearly defined and in which each feels that there is confidence in his ability and integrity.

If the need for these is not clearly understood by each member of the group or if there are conditions existing in their private lives that would prevent or retard the development and continuance of sound human relations in your group, then no further action should be taken until this problem is satisfactorily dealt with.

Good human relations among owner-managers of a concern do not require that discussions and arguments be avoided or that they agree on all matters. On the contrary, desirable human relations develop best under conditions that bring up problems for frank and open discussion and, in the event that unanimity cannot be reached on important policy questions, provide for arbitration of the disputed points. Excellent work in the arbitration of business matters is being performed by the American Arbitration Association, 140 West 51st Street, New York, N.Y., whose services are available to all businessmen.

Experience. I have left *experience* as the last factor to be discussed under preparation because, frankly, I think that is where it belongs—at the bottom of the list. As with training (and it is really only a phase of training), experience is absolutely necessary in some businesses. There are some things that can be learned only by doing; for example, the shortcuts, the so-called tricks of the trade, and the establishing of the many personal contacts so necessary in all types of businesses.

The Second World War dispelled a lot of the myths about the need of experience. We discovered that jobs which workers had formerly claimed required many years of experience to learn could be mastered in a few weeks. Men moved into important jobs in industry, government, and the armed forces in which they had absolutely no experience and did remarkably fine work. But we will most likely go back to putting a high—perhaps too high—premium on the repetition aspect of experience rather than on the ability of human beings to learn very rapidly when properly motivated.

Another reason why I put experience far down on the list is that it tends to put the stamp of approval on what has been done in the past or on how people are doing things now, and to avoid the question of how things can be done better.

All this boils down to the observation that experience is a great teacher, provided that what experience is teaching is the best that can be taught. As far as this applies to your preparation for business ownership, it means that you have to check your experience against the best in the business. For example, if you are considering the restaurant business, your experience should be measured against that obtainable if you worked for the most efficient and profitable restaurant in the class you are considering starting.

Your experience as a user of a product or service is frequently more important than your experience as a producer. Many of the most successful hotels, motor courts, restaurants, service stations, and even manufacturing and retailing businesses have been started by men and women whose only claim to experience was that they knew "a good one when they saw it." Many had never actually operated a business of any type, but they had been keen observers of what the buying public likes and will support. To people with enough brains to observe accurately, the problem of learning efficient operating management of most businesses is relatively simple. They are usually better qualified than the ex-GI who claimed he wanted to start a cocktail lounge. He stated he was experienced, so I asked him where he had worked. And he replied, "I have never worked in one, but I hang around them every night." Since at that time a lot of fellows were dreaming of getting rich by serving drinks, I had made a point of talking with a number of bartenders and cocktail-lounge owners myself. So in a few minutes I was able to get the ex-GI to realize that his experience as a consumer was not teaching him very much about the business.

You will be better qualified to answer my question as far as experience is concerned if part of your experience has been in the role of an observant user of the product or service you are going to deal in. You can get a form of this experience from reading magazines published for the many types of businesses. There is practically no business for which a trade magazine is not published. If you do not know the titles for your business and cannot find out from your local public library or chamber of commerce then write to the Director of Trade Associations, United States Chamber of Commerce, 1615 H St., N.W. Washington, D.C., or to the Small Business Administration, Washington 25, D.C.

There is just one other phase of preparation that I want to ask you about, and this assumes that you are married. Is your family prepared for you to start a business? This applies particularly to your wife, for without her understanding of all that is involved, your chances are considerably lessened. The importance of this part of preparation for business ownership will, of course, vary with the kind and size of the business, its location, and the personalities involved; but for many men considering business ownership, it should be the first question under preparation, not the last.

Before we move on to questions about your business, the following list may help you to evaluate your preparation for business ownership:

I believe that I am prepared to start my own business because—
    I possess the necessary skills and can obtain the required permits and licenses. I have made arrangements to employ men having those I do not possess or cannot obtain
    I understand the importance of financial management and the need for being ready to increase the size and scope of my business
    The experiences I have had with my kind of business have made me familiar not only with all phases of it but also with the reactions and opinions of its customers and clients. I know how the better businesses of its kind are managed

I get along with people. I know how to work with customers, employees, suppliers, and fellow businessmen for the most mutually satisfactory results

My family—and particularly my wife—approve of my going into this business

3. What about my business?

You most likely have a specific business in mind; also a specific community where you would like to start your business. Most people do, when they ask whether or not they should go into business for themselves. Obviously, in this section or even this entire work, we cannot talk in terms of specific enterprises. What we attempt to give you are facts, ideas, principles, and techniques that are applicable—more or less—to all businesses. Another thing that we should like to do is to stimulate your imagination and broaden your vision as to the possibilities in business. So in answer to your question, "What about my business?" I am going to talk about business opportunities.

Have you ever been curious about how men get started in the businesses they are in? That is, why they selected a particular type of business? I believe that if you asked businessmen why they chose the businesses they did, you would be intrigued with the discovery that many, if not most, just landed in them by chance. Sometimes luck is with them and their careers get written up as "success" stories in later years. But that only proves the hazards of relying unnecessarily on chance to determine your fate.

Specialization in business. No one has ever made satisfactory descriptive lists of all the different kinds of businesses in the United States. Even if one had been made (and one is highly desirable), it would have to be added to almost daily because new businesses or new forms of old businesses are being set up constantly. A great deal of specialization is taking place in the business world. In many cases the specialized businesses are actually new types of enterprises, although they may be classified under a common term. The diaper laundries are a perfect example. Although technically listed as laundries, the service they were set up to render is so unique that they should be considered as a separate kind of business. In retailing, the specialty store is very common, particularly in women's wear; but even in men's wear we find stores devoted exclusively to the sale of such items as neckties. Frequently these stores will specialize in merchandise at one price only. Specialization in manufacturing and processing is even more pronounced. Companies not only specialize in products, but in many lines they specialize according to prices, types of materials used, styles, sizes, and other factors. For example, in the women's dress industry, a successful company does not just make dresses—it makes dresses to sell at certain prices or for certain sizes of women.

Specialization is one of the earmarks of an advanced business economic system.   You seldom find specialized businesses in so-called "pioneer" or primitive communities; there the general store is most common.   Usually it is not until a considerable volume of trade has developed that people set up stores, shops, or factories to sell or produce just certain things.

The ability of specializing firms to reduce costs and selling prices was most effectively shown to me when in France in connection with the drive to improve productivity of French industry.   In the U.S. Bureau of Labor Statistics we had made studies of a number of American industries, including the men's shirt industry.   We had found that the total time to cut, sew, press, bag, and box a man's shirt in some factories was less than 11 minutes per shirt.   French men's shirt manufacturers doubted our figures and with some justification, because they could not dream of a shirt manufacturer making only men's white shirts of practically one style with only a few variations in the collars.   French manufacturers whose plants I visited made not only men's shirts, but men's pajamas and underwear, children's clothes, and women's dresses—in fact, about anything that could be put together by a sewing machine.   Under these conditions, productivity—the output per worker hour—could not be high.

Of course, there is another side to this story.   The French manufacturers had a smaller national market to serve, also French labor laws demanded a very steady employment of factory workers; and so our concept of very highly specialized factories was practically unknown and French manufacturers had reason to doubt that our policies and procedures would be successful in their country.

One of the fascinating stories of growth-mindedness and specialization in American business is that of the Clark Oil and Refining Corporation of Milwaukee.   Starting in 1932 with only one service station, Emory T. Clark, its president, has built a chain of over a thousand stations and is adding at the rate of 60 to 90 a year—this in an industry purportedly dominated by giants.

Clark is a cut-rater as well as a specialist.   His stations sell only premium gasoline—meaning gasoline of antiknock rating suitable for extra-high-compression engines—and at only 2 cents above the price of regular.   He sells only gasoline and oil—no tires, batteries, grease jobs, or repairs.   Practically all the stations are operated by franchised dealers, with 1-year contracts, which facilitates better supervision.   The towns and locations are selected by Clark; the stations are built according to strict specifications, attractive design, colors orange and white, no garage or grease rack, and plenty of shrubbery, trees, and flowers.   The station attendants are noted for their spick-and-span white uniforms and the dispatch with which they fill the tanks.   There is no waiting.   It took vision and courage to launch on a program so contrary to the established business methods, but apparently it really paid off.

The demand for specialized businesses is far greater than most people realize.   In fact, it is in the performing of special services or in the providing of special goods that are to be found, according to some authorities, the greatest opportunities for business ownership.

One way to stimulate your imagination as to all the different kinds of specialized businesses is to get a directory of businesses—for example, the classified section of a telephone directory—and study all the various types of activities and enterprises that are listed.

Of course, specialization can be carried too far or may be attempted in a town or area where the people are not ready to support it. To find out those specialized businesses that the people in any community will support calls for some real checking, some real market research. But if you can find that the people of a community are saying that they would certainly like to have a particular type of specialty store—for example, a bookstore—you have something to work on. Of course, you have to make certain that their demand will be large enough and steady enough to support your venture. This is just another way of saying that if you can discover a problem which a number of people have in common and can set up a business to solve it, you have at least laid a good foundation for future success.

Strange as it may seem, I have found that many people want to start businesses and sell things which they personaly like but which their customers do not like. I do not mean that your likes and tastes are not important; they are. But I do mean that they had better be secondary to those of your customers. I saw a perfect example of this when a former secretary decided that she and her husband would start a restaurant specializing in well-balanced meals, with vegetables and salads. Nothing I could say would stop them. They located near a group of municipal buildings. Because of their location and the general surroundings, their main patronage came from clerks and office workers. This was as they had anticipated, but what they had not anticipated was that their customers did not want to have their dietary habits changed. For two months they struggled to get the clerks and secretaries to take their well-planned and balanced meals, but to no avail. The last time I saw them, they were dishing out the fats, starches, and sweets. The vegetables and green salads had all gone by the board. And they were looking for a buyer for the business.

If you say that only a greenhorn would do such a thing, let me remind you that Mr. Childs, founder and developer of the Childs chain of restaurants, tried to force his dietary ideas on his customers. The results were disastrous. Even Henry Ford had to lose many millions before he was convinced that the public no longer wanted his idea of motor-car transportation—the Model T.

The business population. Right now, you are concerned chiefly with one business, the business you are considering starting. That is as it should be. But I have been trying to get you to compare or check your business with other possibilities that are open to you. Maybe you already have the perfect business in mind. If so, fine. But the chances are that you can afford to take one more look before you leap.

As pointed out in discussing the economics of small business, there are around 7,000,000 businesses in the United States. It would be impossible to classify these with any degree of accuracy by specific things they make or sell or the services they render. We do know, however, that the service businesses and retailing account for approximately half the total number, and that over the past couple of decades the services have been increasing very rapidly in number. Many authorities estimate that it is in the field of services that the greatest opportunities exist for starting a business, also that there are many types of service businesses that have real growth possibilities.

We also know that the business population has grown considerably since World War II. In 1950 there were approximately 4,000,000 firms as compared with the 7,000,000 today. And we know that the size of the business population ebbs and flows with economic conditions. For example, during World War II about 560,000 firms disappeared. Then after that war there was an increase of approximately 1,100,000 firms, many of which were reopenings of businesses closed by men entering the services or taking employment in war industries.

One thing you can be assured of is that any abnormal or unusual condition in our economy will cause a rapid increase in specific types of businesses. For example, the housing shortage after World War II resulted in doubling the firms in the contract construction industry within a very few years. While many of these disappeared when the housing shortage was met and others remained relatively small, a few grew into really large enterprises making their founders extremely wealthy men.

Another question for you to ask yourself is, "How did I get interested in the type of business I am considering starting or buying?" If you have been influenced to a large extent by a salesman wanting to sell you machinery or equipment or an initial inventory, you may be well advised to "Stop, Look, and Listen!" Without trying to make you so skeptical that you will never venture becoming a business owner, I do know from hundreds of conversations that all too many men and women have started businesses—or for that matter taken jobs in businesses—where their chances for personal success and happiness were definitely limited.

Sources of information. There are many sources of information and suggestions as to different businesses that you may want to check in comparing your proposed business with other possibilities. I have mentioned telephone and business directories, also the Small Business Administration. The best procedure with the latter is to visit one of their 60 field offices. If you cannot locate their office locally, write to their Washington, D.C., office. The SBA has also set up many chapters of SCORE (Service Corps of Retired Executives) throughout the country. You will do well to tap the pools of experience of these men who have been successful in many types of businesses—both large and small. Do not overlook the chambers of commerce, power and light companies, banks, local newspapers, and other organizations interested in the development of their communities. Many of the states have excellent industrial-development commissions that can be very helpful. In some communities, labor unions are becoming increasingly aware of the need of encouraging new companies. Do not think that the emphasis is on helping just the large companies. More and more community leaders are realizing that 50 companies hiring about 50 employees each can make for more stability than one company that hires 2,500.

You may wish to discuss your ideas with one or more small-business investment companies. These are private financial enterprises which are organized to provide both equity capital and long-term loans to small businesses. There are several hundred in the 50 states. They are usually listed under Investments in the yellow section of the phone book. The Small Business Administration can supply you with the names and addresses of those in your area or state.

The policies, interests, and attitudes of SBICs vary greatly, for they are profit-motivated enterprises and their greatest profits come from providing equity capital to small companies whose managements are both capable and growth-minded. Small businesses that remain small or business owners who are small-minded have little appeal to the majority of them. Those I have talked to are quite hard-boiled and skeptical about investing in small businesses, for they know from experience that less than 1 percent of all the small business owners are capable of so organizing and managing a business that its chances for real growth and success are reasonably high.

The time and energy which you will expend in starting your business will most likely be many times more than you anticipate. Once launched in the enterprise you will be unable or reluctant to change, for you are making a long-time contract with yourself—maybe a lifetime contract—when you start a business.

Your decision in the selection of your business is so important that one more "I believe" is offered for your guidance:

I believe I have selected the kind of business that is best for me because—
    I have carefully surveyed the business world as to types of business opportunities
    I have chosen a business in which I can happily and sincerely cater to my customers' tastes and requirements
    I have chosen a business in which I can be of real service to my customers in the solution of their problems

4. Where should I start my business?

The answer to this question, as to the previous one, depends in most cases on the type of business you have in mind and on you—your personal likes and dislikes.

The vast majority of people who start businesses are as much interested in where they will live and work as they are in the type of business. Top managers of larger corporations, when they are selecting sites for the relocation of their plants or the setting up of branch plants, must, of course, consider such factors as the availability of raw materials, power, and fuels, transportation facilities and freight rates, and access to markets. In recent years, noneconomic factors have been playing a very important part in the decisions on site selection by top management. As the percentage of highly trained and educated employees has increased in industry—as it has been doing since World War II— there has been a realization that with our ever-increasing standards of living and leisure time many workers will take positions or jobs only in communities where the educational, cultural, and leisure-time facilities are superior. Practically gone are the old types of company or mill towns with their dismal housing and wide gulfs between the top management and factory "hands."

From your point of view—that of a man or woman launching a new business for yourself—you will find great agreement today between managers of large corporations, employees (both union and nonunion), and independent businessmen and professional men about what constitutes a good community in which to live.

Checking communities. There are many sources which you can tap to help you choose the community for your business. Perhaps just looking it over is the best start. The conditions of its public buildings, schools, parks, and streets is a good indicator of the existence or lack of the spirit of progress. One acquaintance who has been successful in picking smaller communities says all he looks at are cemeteries, for he considers them the best gauge of the overall philosophy of the community. Of course, there is much printed material that you can draw from. The census of business contains a vast amount of information. Bureaus of business research at state universities frequently have much information on the trends of individual communities as do chambers of commerce, power and light companies, railroads, and industrial commissions. From these sources you can get facts about populations, tax rates, bonded indebtedness, number of workers, incomes from manufacturing, wholesaling, retailing, agriculture, etc., educational backgrounds of citizens, purchasing power, and a score of other things, from which you can begin to evaluate and compare communities.

An excellent source for information on economic and business trends is the Center of Economic Projections of the National Planning Association, 1606 New Hampshire Avenue, N.W., Washington, D.C. Their projections by areas and states cover population growth, labor force, and per capita income. They compare each area and state with the projections for the nation as a whole. This is the type of data extremely valuable in the selection of a location for any new business or expansion, especially for those whose management is growth-minded.

Statistical facts are seldom enough to give the whole picture. There are some things that you can learn only from a personal check of local conditions.

Communities of the same approximate size vary tremendously as to their possibilities as locations for businesses. Sometimes it is very obvious why a town is exceptionally good or bad as a business center; in other cases it is not easy to put your finger on the real cause.

It has been my observation that the first thing to check into is the community government; that is, discover who actually runs the town or city. If you find a broad and democratic participation in the government by all groups—including labor, businessmen, professional men, women's groups, and public employees —you will most likely find the community a good location for your business. If the leaders in business and labor have sincere mutual respect for each other, if industry is diversified (not concentrated in one or two large companies), and if the surrounding agriculture is supported by good soils, you have found a good place.

Any community that depends on one industry or resource is in a vulnerable situation, and so is the businessman who locates in it. Industries are continually migrating, and individual companies usually have to follow the trend in order to keep in line competitively, regardless of their feelings in the matter. There are literally hundreds of "ghost towns" in the country, the results of the sudden and wholesale migration of one industry, the depletion of a basic resource, or the development of a new source of supply or substitute. It always seems that in these cases it is the homeowners, the merchants, and other smaller businessmen who suffer proportionally the most.

This does not mean that you should never select this type of community for your business. It does mean that when you do, you should understand fully the hazards involved and should plan your operations accordingly.

Most of the material written about locations for businesses is directed toward manufacturing companies, mainly the larger ones. Regardless of how well it is prepared, it is my opinion that if the smaller businessman follows it uncritically, he may overlook a number of excellent communities as possible locations for his business. Perhaps this will illustrate:

A Brooklyn manufacturer of leather goods wanted to move his business to California and made a trip to pick a location. Santa Barbara appealed to him as a place for his home, but when he talked of locating a manufacturing business there, everyone was shocked. The standard remark was, "Santa Barbara? Why, that's a millionaire's town. You'll never find workers for your plant there." But he was fairly sure that the clerks he had seen in Woolworth's and the other chain stores were not debutantes working for the fun of it. So he started asking these same clerks if they would like to work in a leather-goods factory when he started one. In less than an hour he had assured himself of an adequate labor supply.

The larger the business and the greater its normal marketing area, the more important is the role its location plays in making it a success; and so, if your venture is on the larger side, you will undoubtedly want to give more consideration to the economic aspects of communities than to your personal preferences.

The following are the main factors in selecting plant location as incorporated in the checklist used by the National Planning Association in its study:

   I. Raw materials
      1. Immediate or potential availability
      2. Assembling costs
      3. Raw material reserves
      4. Quality of raw materials available
      5. Disposal of raw-material by-products

  II. Power and fuels
      1. Immediate or potential availability of electric power, coal, gas, oil, coke, wood, and waste fuels
      2. Power and fuel costs at the plant
      3. Disposal of fuel by-products

 III. Water
      1. Immediate or potential availability of adequate supply of proper quality water
      2. Water costs

  IV. Transportation
      1. Availability of water, rail, truck, and air transportation with relation to plant site
      2. Costs of transporting raw materials
      3. Shipping costs to markets
      4. Possibilities for arranging special commodity rates
      5. Local transportation facilities for material and personnel
      6. Adequacy of highway facilities for company's own transportation

   V. Labor
      1. Immediate or potential supply of labor
         a. Total labor force within commuting distance
         b. Availability of required skills
         c. Male-female supply
      2. Facilities for training personnel
      3. Wage rates and labor costs
      4. Extent and character of unionization
         a. Local history of labor relations
         b. Labor attitudes to technological changes
         c. Community attitudes
      5. Extent of labor-market domination by other industries

  VI. Financial
      1. Availability of local capital
      2. Adequacy of local banking facilities

 VII. Management and technical
      1. Availability of management and supervisory personnel

    2. Availability of technical personnel
    3. Availability of testing and research facilities
       a. Business institutions
       b. Educational institutions

VIII. Marketing
    1. Economic relation to market or main marketing center
       a. International
       b. National
       c. Regional
       d. Local
    2. Future trend of markets in relation to location
    3. Availability of marketing services and specialists
    4. Relation to competitors
    5. Geographical location and pricing pattern

IX. Relationship to established concerns
    1. Relationship to other plants of same company
       a. Ability to integrate plant into company production pattern
       b. Possibility of interchanging personnel and materials by company
    2. Relationship to plants of other companies
       a. Availability of other companies as source of materials or as outlet for production
       b. Economies of specialized service owing to existence of manufacturers locally within same industry
       c. Domination of community by some established concerns
    3. Corporate interrelationships

X. State governmental influences
    1. Tax structure
    2. Minimum wage and hour laws
    3. Workmen's compensation
    4. Laws of incorporation
    5. Incentives to new industries
    6. Attitude of legislators and government

XI. Community influences
    1. Housing
    2. Local government attitudes and local business attitudes
    3. Physical attractiveness
    4. Fire protection and insurance rates
    5. Social structure
    6. Recreation facilities
    7. Community spirit and progress
    8. Special inducements

XII. Building
    1. Costs of new construction
    2. Use of old plants

XIII. Site
     1. Costs of building
     2. Space for expansion

Business population shifting. The center of our business population, just like the center of the population, has been moving toward the West and Southwest rather consistently during the past 50 years. This trend, which was intensified during the Second World War, has continued unabated during the postwar boom.

The selection of the location (the community) for your business is closely associated with the selection of the site or actual spot where your business will be housed. Care in both selections is an important factor in the success of your enterprise. Methods for choosing the most desirable sites will be discsused in Section 6. For some kinds of businesses, site selection has been reduced almost to a science, but when it comes to the selection of the community for a new and smaller business it is invariably the personal desires of the owner that prevail, and strictly economic factors are given secondary consideration. For this reason, it is all the more important that you stop, check, and consider once again the community you have selected. Does the following coincide with your observations of your community? If so, it should be a good location for your business.

I believe I have selected the right community for my business because—
    There is a wide diversity of industry for the size of the community; *or,* industry is concentrated in a few companies, but I have checked carefully and found that these companies are well managed, have stable employment records, and are well financed
    There is a good wholesome democratic spirit among all segments of the population and a sharing of the responsibility for solving the community's civic problems
    Labor has a fair cooperative attitude toward the industries, and this is reciprocated by management with the development of fair, workable labor-management programs
    The natural resources of the surrounding territory are being developd and used soundly, particularly fuels, water, and soil resources. The farmers are progressive; crops are diversified
    The materials, supplies, and labor I will need are available
    The community is in line to benefit from recent shifts in industry and commerce

5. What are my chances for success?

If the answer to this question is to be based strictly on the statistics of business successes and failures, it must be admitted that your chances for success in any new business are not very good. As already stated, 25 percent of new businesses disappear before the end of the first year, and only a handful survive for 10 years.

But one of the chief reasons for the high mortality rate among businesses is that the vast majority of them are started by men and women who do not check thoroughly into the things we have been talking about so far in this discussion. In my opinion, the very fact that you are trying to evaluate your personal capacities and ambitions and to compare the opportunities afforded by various kinds of businesses and locations puts you in a class apart from that of most people who start businesses. So, assuming that you have the skills or techniques that are absolutely necessary for the day-to-day operations of your business, I would say that you have already increased your chances for success severalfold. But in the final analysis your chances for the successful development of your business will depend on you and your managerial ability, particularly your capacity to inaugurate sound business policies and to carry them out.

In this part we discuss six conditions relating to management and the making of policy decisions. We ask that you use these six as a check list against which to measure your present ideas regarding your role as manager of your business.

Time for decisions. The making of sound policy decisions is without doubt the most difficult task in business. As a general premise, it may be said that your ability to make such decisions increases in direct proportion to the constructive time and energy you can devote to them.

One of the main deterrents to the growth of the average small business is that the owner fails to realize how much of his time will have to be devoted to considering, evaluating, and selecting policies. Invariably he becomes so involved in performing the daily operating tasks of the business that he has no time to contemplate and to study some of the long-range possibilities of his business.

Planning for the most effective use of your time in the business is a job that only *you* can do. When you are your own boss, no one can force you to plan and no one can compel you to reserve time and energy for this type of work. If you now realize how important it is for you to have time to devote to the formulation of policies and to what are frequently called the "problems of top management," you will have placed another strong foundation stone under your business.

Organization essential. The second managerial prerequisite to success is a good organization, for without this you cannot be free to function effectively in your key position of top management. Your ability to build an effective organization will depend on your capacity to delegate responsibilities, to encourage initiative, to permit self-expression, and to create an atmosphere where in the eyes of all concerned the enterprise becomes "our business."

The questions you need to ask yourself at this point are: Do I have the know-how for building an organization? Can I develop good human relations in my business?

Multiplying yourself. Third on the list of managerial skills essential for success I list the ability to multiply oneself. By this term I mean possessing both the willingness and the capacity for making known to all members of the organization the policies and decisions that have been made.

Here is a very simple illustration of what I mean by multiplying yourself. The sales price you set on a piece of merchandise or a service to be rendered requires a decision. You, or someone to whom you delegate the responsibility, has to say such-and-such will sell for so much. Now if every piece of that same merchandise is marked with the price, if every clerk or salesman who has to sell the merchandise is told, preferably in writing, the price and special points about the price, then you and your decision have been multiplied effectively.

If all the decisions that you and your associates make relative to hours of work, the vacation and holiday schedules, overtime, etc., are reduced to writing and made available to all, you have multiplied yourself and simplified your personnel problems. Likewise, if your decisions regarding the granting of credit, the delivery of goods, the cashing of checks, and the acceptance of returned merchandise have been reduced to writing, and the procedures for dealing with them clearly stated, you have multiplied yourself.

Failure to grasp the importance of multiplying oneself and to learn the techniques is another reason many businessmen fail to expand their businesses. The block to progress and growth is the boss himself. How many times have you gone into a store, liked something you saw, tried to find the price on it, asked a clerk who did not know, and then finally found the "boss" who had to look it up in a little notebook that he kept tucked away in a littered drawer of his desk?

Yours has to be the decision as to whether you are going to be a *multiplier* and help your business grow or be the *indispensable man* who makes all the decisions and makes them over and over again. The tools of multiplying are simple and readily available: manuals, price tags, instructions, directives, staff meetings, illustrations, and, as your business grows, slide films and movies. The determination to use them must be yours.

Financial management. You have already been asked, in connection with your preparation for starting your business, to check yourself on your ability in financial management. We are again bringing up the question, but this time with particular reference to the role of financial management in the successful expansion of your business. We are emphasizing this point because the importance of the know-how to successful financial management is not understood or appreciated by the majority of men starting in business.

There are many definitions and interpretations of the term "financial management," but in this section I refer to ability in financial management as the ability to obtain control of the other man's money and resources and to use them effectively. It means much more than keeping an accurate set of books, or paying your bills promptly, desirable as these may be.

Perhaps you do not like the expression "use the other man's money." Perhaps it implies sharp practices or even dishonesty. Or perhaps you are like so many smaller businessmen who say that they never want to go into debt. If so, all right; but your chances of heading up a growing dynamic business are considerably reduced and your chances for survival lessened.

This is why:

Businesses get money for growth from two sources: earnings and investors. Taxes, particularly the Federal income tax, reduce considerably the amount of earnings that can be retained for expansion purposes. The ploughing back of profits, one of the methods by which many businesses grew from small companies to large corporations, does not provide an adequate method for meeting the growth requirements of smaller companies, which frequently find that they must expand or lose out competitively. It is even doubtful that granting special tax exemptions on the earnings of smaller companies would solve the problems of financial management associated with growth.

This means that, more than ever, expanding businesses must depend on investors as the source of funds for growth. It is particularly true in those instances where mass advertising and the public's acceptance of the product or service create almost overnight a sudden and heavy demand. This creates a sort of business vacuum into which will flow money and resources.

If your business is of this type, you will not be able to stop the flow of money and resources from investors. The question will be whether you have the ability in financial management to induce people to place their money and resources at your command rather than to start competing companies which may soon dominate the market you have developed.

This problem is intensified by the fact that savings of individuals and corporations are at an all-time high (estimated as $450,000,000,000 to $550,000,-000,000 by various authorities). Interest rates are relatively low, and the owners of a considerable portion of these savings are continually looking for better or more remunerative places for them.

On the other hand, the superabundance of funds means that the skillful manager has innumerable sources of money to tap. It should never be forgotten that using the other man's money is synonymous with providing him with an opportunity for investment or speculation; also that to the extent that your use of his money is based on sound judgment, effective business policies, and honesty, an investment in your enterprise will be desirable from his point of view. If you have the ability to understand and appreciate that borrowing (or creating a need for more capital) and investing are two sides of the same coin, it is one of the signs that you know the importance of financial management.

Management tools. The fifth factor that will enhance your chances of success is your understanding, appreciation, and use of the tools of management. These tools for planning the operations of a business and for controlling those operations have increased both in numbers and accuracy during the past few years.   By tools of management we mean not so much the mechanical devices and equipment that have been developed and improved but the accounting systems, budgetary methods, stock and inventory controls, production controls and cost accounting, and statistical methods that are now available to businesses of all sizes.   Today, the business owner has no valid excuse for not knowing at all times the exact condition of his business.   In many progressive, well-managed businesses the men and women responsible for the top-level decisions know · at the start of each workday morning just how things stood at the close of the previous business day.   Are you satisfied that you are qualified in this area?

Customers and competition.   The customer is the real imponderable in business.   You might almost call him the great unknown.   Psychologists have studied the reaction habits of consumers.   They know quite accurately the colors, and the words, and other factors that encourage people to buy.   They have taught advertisers a great deal concerning the instinctive and conditioned reactions of human beings.   All this has tended to make selling and advertising more "scientific," but the fact still remains that people are individuals, and no two human minds work exactly the same at all times.   This, plus the increasing keenness in competition, is the reason why top management in the larger corporations is more and more actively concerned with customers.   It is likewise the reason why it is so important that you build the type of organization and use the techniques of planning and controlling which will leave you free to work on the customer problem.

When you talk about customer relations, selling, and advertising, the question always comes up: What about competition?

You will have plenty of competition.   And if you do not, you had better find out in a hurry just why it is absent.   The question is not one of competition, but of the type of competition that you will encounter.

When discussing locations and sites (or spots) for businesses, potential business owners often say that they are picking particular places because there is little competition.   What they all seem to want is a nice little monopoly, although they are not thinking in those exact terms.   To get them thinking straight about competition, I frequently ask them where they go fishing.   When they tell me, I ask if other people fish there also.   If it is a popular spot, I ask them why they do not go to some other spot where there are no other fishermen —and usually no fish.   So it is with competition.

It is not the number of competitors, but the number of actual and potential customers in relation to the number and size of your actual and potential competitors that you should study.   If your business is based upon rendering a real service, if it is well planned, and if its policies are consistent with the desires of reasonable customers, you should never find yourself in an unfavorable competitive position, provided you are not the victim of unfair or concealed competition or monopolistic practices by other businessmen.

Unfair methods of competition vary considerably in their frequency and intensity among the different types of businesses.   Some industries are practically free from them; others are continually plagued.   On the whole, the American business system is conducted on relatively high standards of conduct.   You, undoubtedly, have sought to avoid, in your choosing, those businesses where unfair methods seem to be prevalent.   But if you do encounter what you consider to be unfair methods, you can get advice and assistance from many different agencies.   Locally, there are usually better business bureaus, fair trade committees in chambers of commerce, and neighborhood business groups that are working on this problem.   A number of states have boards or commissions that will assist you.   The following Federal agencies and offices are interested in various aspects of the problem of unfair methods of competition, particularly as they affect the small businessman: the Federal Trade Commission, the Department of Commerce, Senate Subcommittee on Small Business, and the House of Representatives Select Committee on Small Business.

Competition that is concealed is harder for you to deal with.   In connection with financial management I have already mentioned the competitive threat from the large amounts of savings in the hands of potential businessmen.   Actually, when competition is concealed, it means that the businessmen engaged in the practice are trying to eliminate competition as far as they are concerned. If they are powerful enough to create a monopoly or even to concentrate control in a few large companies so that your access to raw materials, goods, services, or markets is restricted and your competitors favored, then you are definitely up against an impossible competitive position and need to turn to the government for assistance.

Another type of competition that is extremely hard to meet exists when a group of businessmen operate one business on a break-even or loss basis solely to provide them with the opportunity to carry on a second and *very profitable* enterprise.   There is nothing illegal about this method of operating; but if you are in competition with their break-even business, you may find it very tough going.   Let me illustrate:

The consumer-credit or small-loan business has been very profitable.   The big problem and cost in this type of business is getting the loan accounts "on the books."   People will borrow money for many reasons: to pay hospital bills, take trips, etc.   But some businessmen believe that the best way to get people to borrow is to sell them something in return for a small down payment and a promise to pay at terms that are very favorable to the businessman.   They are willing to split even on the sale of merchandise, and make their profit on the financing charges.   If you have to make *your* profits solely from the sale of the same type of merchandise, your chances for successfully competing with them and staying in business are considerably lessened.

The larger the business you are planning to start, the more important it becomes that the six conditions discussed in this section be understood by the owner-managers and provided for.

In launching a full-blown business of medium or large size—that is, one employing 250 or more workers—all the problems of a new business are intensified. However, such businesses are usually undertaken only by experienced men who thoroughly understand the importance of the six conditions.   Many of the most successful launchings of such enterprises have been directed by large, experienced, and successful companies either as subsidiaries or as semi-independent companies.   This is particularly true in industries where the investment in the plant, machinery, and equipment is heavy and where a relatively large volume of production is needed in order to compete effectively from the start.

The production of men's work clothes as compared with that of women's sport clothes in the garment industry provides a good example.   Men's overalls and work shirts are so closely priced that a plant must be able to produce several hundred dozen garments per day and operate at near-full production every day if it is to make a profit. Women's sportswear, on the other hand, in which style and design are the important factors, can be produced with a profit in relatively small factories.   As a result, most new factories for work clothes started during the past 25 years have been branch plants of large established operators, who were able to provide production and marketing know-how right from the start.   On the other hand, in the women's sportswear industry hundreds of small independent companies have been started.   Quite a few, despite the inexperience of their founders and their limited original resources, have developed into profitable enterprises.

The financial problems of a new business tend to be intensified when you start a business in an industry such as men's work clothes.   Operating expenses can consume working capital very rapidly during the initial period, and if it is ever reduced to the point where the company is unable to avail itself of every possible financial gain such as the discounting of accounts payable, the chances of successful operations and survival are virtually ended.

To summarize: Your chances of success to a large extent depend upon *your* managerial ability.   If your chances of success are to be well above the average, you must be able to subscribe honestly and fully to the following:

I believe I will succeed because I understand how to—
  Provide time for me and my associates to make sound policy decisions
  Organize my responsibilities and those I delegate so that I can function
    effectively as the top manager of my business
  Multiply myself by the use of proved techniques so that my associates
    can carry out my decisions efficiently
  Use my own and investors' funds to expand my business operations as
    the growth and success of my enterprise necessitate
  Use such tools of management as accounting systems, budgetary methods,
    stock and inventory controls, production controls, cost accounting and
    statistical methods; and to make top-level decisions based on the facts
    provided by these tools

Develop sound customer relations in the competitive situations existing in American business today

6. Should I start my business now?

Most questioners have the booms and busts of the business cycle in mind when they ask this question. They have decided on the type of business and the location, and they feel that the situation within the industry or trade is favorable. But, they say, what about business conditions in general? Are we likely to have another depression? Are we likely to have inflation?

When you reach this question, you are right down to the point of paying out your money and assuming many financial obligations. You have passed through the thinking and planning phase and are entering that of action.

The fluctuations of the business cycle have, in the past at least, been the hazards or risks of business ownership most difficult to deal with. In fact, it is doubtful that there is any adequate method by which the individual can protect his business against them. The ordinary methods of risk shifting by insurance or hedging are not applicable, nor can one truthfully say that efficient management contains the answer. American business provides too many case histories of well-managed businesses that were forced to close their doors by causes beyond their control. There was nothing their managements could have done that would have saved them.

Generalizations as to the desirability of *any time* being the time to start a business or not to start a business are dangerous. So much depends on you and the kind of business. Even the normally sound advice of "Don't start a business at the top of a boom!" does not hold true in all cases. Sometimes it is only during booms that you can get the customers and financial support needed to justify your starting the business.

Basically, it is the rapidly changing value of money during the various phases of the cycle that causes the trouble. Many business transactions and contracts require businessmen to make "dollar commitments"—that is, to agree to make payments in fixed amounts of dollars regardless of the value of the dollar in terms of other commodities and labor. When prices drop drastically in a depression, these dollar commitments can take such an unduly high percentage of business income that heavy losses and failures are inevitable. This was the situation in the early 1930s.

As a result of these experiences, businessmen try to avoid fixed commitments and seek to make contracts in which the number of dollars to be paid during any period can be adjusted to meet the changed conditions. Real-estate leases that call for monthly or yearly rentals figured as given percentages of net sales are examples of this type of contract. In the same category are salary and wage contracts, long-term purchase agreements that contain clauses to keep these fixed expenses in reasonable ratio to income during any future periods of national depression. Frankly, because yours will be a new business, it is doubtful that you will be able to obtain this type of "depression-relief" clause in most of the longer term contracts you have to enter into in starting your business. But the more you can, the more you shift the risks of the fluctuations of the business cycle.

Their experiences during the past depressions have convinced many people—including a large number of businessmen—that it is impossible for the majority of individuals to cope with the forces of uncontrolled economic fluctuations. This belief has led to the demand that the Federal government act to prevent violent ups and downs and to produce a relatively stable but expanding economy, one in which both the fear of depressions and that of inflation are reduced to the minimum.

Whether violent fluctuations in the business cycle can be eliminated by governmental policies and actions remains to be seen. Much appears to have been learned during the past 30 years of the fiscal policies and monetary controls which seem to ensure against violent downswings. But the effectiveness of governmental controls against booms—particularly inflationary booms—is not so clear.

The answer to your question is further complicated by the fact that any attempts at the control of the business cycle become involved in national politics. To some people, government actions affecting business inevitably produces statism, the welfare state, or socialism; all of which, according to them, would mean the end of the present American business system. To others, government actions including those taken to prevent or lessen the fluctuations of the business cycle are steps that must be taken if we are to preserve the system. Regardless of the correctness of either point of view, it cannot be doubted that the American people believe in action by the Federal government when their economic well-being and interests are at stake and that no political party will remain long in office if it permits uncontrolled fluctuations in the business cycle and the value of money.

I am not sure that from your point of view as a potential business owner seeking the answer to the question, "Is now the time?" this discussion of the business cycle is specific enough. The question has to remain unanswered, for no honest answer is possible. However, this discussion of your question will have served its purpose if it has caused you once more to stop, read, and check:

Am I certain that I really want to be a business owner?
Am I prepared for business ownership?
Have I selected the business with the greatest possibility?
Have I selected the right community?
Do I have the essentials for success?
Is *now* the time?

7. A checklist

When you are thinking about starting a business or joining with a group to set up a partnership or corporation, you need to consider hundreds of things; you are about to make an important decision. Careful thought in advance will prevent many mistakes and will go far in assuring the success of your venture.

The following checklist will suggest some of the questions which you will want to ponder seriously and investigate carefully. As you read them, you will note that they probe into personal attitudes, basic policies, and business philosophies rather than the details of getting a factory ready for production or a store ready to open its doors to customers. These details are dealt with in various sections. You should consider this list only a starter—a stimulator of your thinking. It will help you most if you will not only go through it question by question, but also add questions that have occurred to you while reading and discussing this section.

A check or notation in this column will show you have considered each point

Personal attitudes toward business

Do you feel that you have a clear-cut picture in your mind regarding the possibilities and hazards of business ownership?

Have you checked the records of success and failure in business?

Do you have a definite personal objective in starting a business? Is it psychologically sound? That is, do you see in business an opportunity for service, or are you just using it as a means of escaping from an existing unpleasant situation or job?

Do you consider that business ownership assures you security?

How do your present earnings compare with the incomes of men in the type and size of business you plan to start?

Can you stand the emotional and financial strain of an irregular income? (Relatively few new businesses are able to pay their owners steady incomes.)

Does your wife understand that your income may be very irregular? Does your family?

Have you sought to participate in the ownership of the business where you are now employed?

*A check or notation
in this column will
show you have con-
sidered each point*

Personal attitudes toward business

Have you analyzed carefully your reasons for wanting to start a business?   Do you think they are
reasons that increase your chances for success?

What problems of other people will your business
solve?

Do you think your personal attitude toward business
is such that people will want to be in your employ?

Have you and your associates-to-be discussed the
problems of business ownership?   Do your attitudes and objectives seem to be compatible?
(There are few human relationships, except
those of husband and wife, in which mutually
determined objectives are more important than
those existing among owners of smaller business
organizations.)

Personal qualifications

Do you possess the professional or technical skills
needed in your business?   If not, can you hire
them?

Do you believe that you can meet all the problems
of financing the business?

Have you tried to foresee the problems—particularly the financial problems—you may experience if your business starts to grow rapidly?

Do you consider that you have had sufficient experience and training in human relations?

Do you believe that you have the capacity to build
an efficient organization?

Have you ever supervised people?   Have you ever
conducted training programs?   Have you ever
hired people?

Do you rate your experiences as being those that
would best qualify you to start and operate your
type of business?   Do you really know the best
managerial policies and methods?

Are you thoroughly satisfied with the qualifications
and personal attributes of your partners-to-be?

Have you discussed and agreed upon with your

A check or notation
in this column will
show you have con-
sidered each point

Personal qualifications

partners the major objectives and policies of the
business?

Do you understand the techniques of getting your
policies and decisions over to your employees and
associates? That is, do you know how to *multiply* yourself?

Do you consider yourself adequately skilled in the
use of the tools of management? Do you understand accounting, budgeting, purchase and
production controls, and statistical methods?

Have you checked carefully into the type of competition you will encounter? Do you feel that
you have the ability to compete effectively?

Do you appreciate the need for your having time
for the study of your business problems and the
making of policy decisions?

The business and location

Have you compared the possibilities of your proposed business with others you are qualified to
start?

Have you carefully analyzed the needs of the community for your business?

What problems of consumers or other businessmen
will your company solve?

Is the demand for your type or kind of business on
the increase?

Have you checked carefully to determine that you
will like to serve the types of customers who will
normally patronize your kind of business?

Have you and your partners-to-be discussed the
project with businessmen and others qualified to
advise you?

If your employees will be union members, have you
discussed your ideas with local union officials?

Have you considered the growth possibilities or limitations of your business-to-be?

Are you satisfied you have picked the best location
for your business?

Have you considered all the major economic factors

*A check or notation
in this column will
show you have con-
sidered each point*

The business and location

of the community, or are you selecting strictly for
personal reasons?

Have you checked carefully the local ordinances
and regulations?

_____

Are you satisfied that you have selected a progressive community?   Is it efficiently managed?   Is
it new-business-minded?   Does it encourage the
newcomer?

_____

Does your community have a sound economic base?
Are its industries diversified?   Are its natural resources long lasting?   Is farming diversified or
is it confined to one or two crops?

_____

Have you checked carefully general trends in locating your type of business?   Is the industry shifting geographically?

_____

Are you satisfied that now is the time to start your
business?

_____

Are you satisfied that the costs of starting now are
not so high that you would be at a disadvantage
with your competitors?

_____

Have you taken any precautionary measures against
a drastic decline in business activities and prices?

_____

Have you investigated thoroughly all the various
types of competition that exist for your type of
business?

_____

Do you appreciate the importance of planning for
growth?   In other words, are you growth-
minded?

_____

Section 3

ORGANIZATION FOR
MORE EFFICIENT MANAGEMENT

BY

Edward McSweeney

ORGANIZATION FOR
MORE EFFICIENT MANAGEMENT

Organization is the art which multiplies a one-man business enterprise into a large-scale, coordinated undertaking. Without organization—the controlled and directed teamwork of other people—there are distinct and rigid limitations on what one man can do.

For many centuries—perhaps ever since the dawn of history—men have practiced the art of organization to realize their greatest accomplishments. Had they not done so, monuments would never have been built, governments would never have been founded, and institutions would never have endured. Business as we know it today would be unthinkable without the organized structuring and direction of human effort.

As a businessman and consultant, my interest in organization has extended over a lifetime, a working span of some 45 years. The time involved has been comparatively short. Yet more has happened to change the *structure* of management than in all the centuries before. One of the chief contributing factors has been the introduction of electronic data processing.

Today's computer can accomplish tasks which no individual, or even group of individuals, could possibly have achieved in the past. It can, for example, automatically post accounts, control production, update and replenish factory inventories. Most important of all, it can collect and store vital business information to speed up, coordinate, and improve the quality of executive decisions. In some cases it can obviate the necessity of decision making entirely.

Without question, the computer will have a far greater impact on management techniques during the twentieth century than any technological development since the Industrial Revolution.

Yet, much as the methods of management have changed and are changing, the *principles* of organization remain substantially the same. This is not merely my own view, but that of hundreds of businessmen with whom I am in contact.

As this is written, some of these executives underscore the rising importance of marketing, research and development, automation, and international trade on the current business scene. Chiefly, they emphasize electronic data processing as the force that will change the face of management irrevocably. But the *principles* of organization are concerned with getting things done through people, no matter what the contemporary situation.

This section, then, is concerned with principles: planning, deputizing, supervising, controlling, and other activities that bring men into cohesive units and multiply the effectiveness of their work. So long as human society endures, these basics of organization are likely to remain.

It always takes *people* to grow. The difference between an independent grocery store grossing $800 to $900 a week and a supermarket grossing $20,000 to $25,000 is largely a matter of organization. The merchant who personally unpacks shipments, stacks goods on shelves, wraps packages, and acts as cashier has that much less time per day for waiting on customers. But one manager, plus an organization, can handle thousands of transactions daily.

The proprietor of a printing shop expands by putting on a salesman. The garage man sees a step ahead and adds a wholesale department to sell parts and equipment to other garages. The village upholsterer starts selling furniture in addition to repairing it, and winds up on a main highway with several floors of merchandise, including floor coverings, radios, and appliances. And now he has people selling goods for him, people delivering his wares in trucks, *people* installing television sets and air conditioners. Lacking organization, he could not function effectively.

Lester Jones and Wallace Smith both start out in comparable lines of business. Jones is a near genius in his field, and he quickly outstrips Smith, who is a plodder. But Jones "does everything important" himself and reaches a point where, for lack of hours in the day, he can go no further. Smith, on the other hand, gradually acquires, trains, and organizes personnel. Eventually, he passes Jones and keeps on forging ahead. Paradoxically, the bigger his business grows, the more time he has for creative forward planning. In short, he has an organization, and has multiplied his effectiveness many times over.

Hiring people is only part of the organizing process. They must be welded into a unified whole, freed of overlapping and conflicting functions, held together by a common bond or morale. They must be carefully trained for the roles they are to assume and periodically retrained as their responsibilities grow.

History abounds with instances where organizing genius triumphed over numbers—the Macedonian phalanx against the Persian hordes; the Roman legions against numerically predominant Goths and Gauls; the few hundred Spaniards under Hernando Cortez who conquered Mexico. Time and again, a handful of trained, disciplined, coordinated men have overturned an empire.

Procurement for war has always stimulated the organizing process among civilians. It was George Washington's compelling need for muskets, for example, which spurred Eli Whitney into mass-producing flintlocks on an assembly line—the world's first employment of interchangeable parts as a basis for production.

The next great advance was stimulated by the Second World War. The war developed many improvements in technology, but one of its greatest contributions was in the development of business organization. Time was vital, and war production could not wait on decisions from above. Consequently, top management rapidly extended the delegation not only of tasks, but also of authority and of responsibility for carrying them out. At the same time, the war draft required an analysis of what each man was doing and a classification of his job. And the wartime wage regulations required a statement of his authority and responsibilities.

The outcome was a highly developed system of job analysis and delegated authority, which had the advantage of freeing top management to deal with the shifting wartime emergencies of materials, labor force, transportation, taxation, and finance.

Though 15,000,000 people were lifted out of the labor force of the country for the armed forces, our war industrial production was multiplied two and a half times in 3 years.

In recent times, the race for space exploration has involved the largest and costliest scientific organization in the world's history.

To the businessman, the reasons for organization should be self-evident. Organization not only multiplies his capacity to produce and distribute. It gives him access to others' capital, thus providing financial sinews for growth and operation. It frees him from slavish devotion to detail and enables him to work at his highest skill—managing his business. And it means that after his death or retirement the business will continue, with all that it holds for his associates, employees, and dependents.

The process of organization may be classified as a science because it depends so much on precise definition of function, authority, and responsibility. The process of management which directs an organization may be considered an art, because it depends on human reactions, which cannot be relied upon to be always sternly logical.

1. The principles of organization

The only constant that applies to business is a situation of constant change. Industry has traditionally operated in a state of flux, but the process has now been enormously accelerated. Scientific advancement and the rapid growth of markets have each contributed to the speed of transition. From these have evolved certain functional management changes, of which three are of predominant importance:

1. *Electronic data processing.* The function of computerizing and disseminating basic information to guide decision making in all phases of a company's operation. In general, computer applications serve four basic purposes: to reduce operating costs, to lower working-capital requirements, to improve the ability of a company to serve its customers, and to enhance the possibilities of long-range improvements
2. *Marketing.* The function of advancing the company's competitive prospects in relation to products and sales. The marketing operation has

become a "total" concept. It is concerned with market research, improvement of sales management, advertising and sales promotion, selection and training of salesmen, product planning, product and brand management, reduction of distribution costs, and pricing

3. *Research and development.* The function that is concerned not only with the development of new products, but with the production of more useful materials, devices, systems, and methods. Research and development is also directed toward (1) the increase of scientific knowledge in general, and (2) the application of scientific knowledge to specific industrial uses

These and other changing managerial functions will be enlarged upon as they occur in succeeding pages. For the moment, it is important to reemphasize that the concern of this chapter is with fundamentals, not with their changing manifestations. Just as the accomplished portrait painter must be acquainted with the elements of composition, so the businessman must master the underlying principles of business organization before he can become a professional manager.

Organization, in the traditional sense, then, is the management tool which enables the owner or top executive of a business to coordinate the "four Ms"—men, money, machines, and materials—retaining control over their use and performance, so that all factors in the business move ahead according to plan. It is the key to eliminating waste and lost motion—and also the means of expanding opportunities for employees and executives. The business which does not meet these tests is not yet fully organized.

Defined in still another way, organization is the wedding of authority and responsibility, because in its essentials it consists of assigning specific functions to designated people or departments, with authority for them to be carried out, plus accountability to management for the results obtained.

Each of the following steps in setting up an organization involves a major principle.

Determine objectives. "What are we aiming at?" is the beginning of wisdom in organizational planning. The aim is not merely to make money, which is the first essential. Is it to capture a *measurably* larger share of the industry's business within a certain area? Is it to introduce a new or improved product? Is it to purchase and merge another company? To launch a subsidiary? Or to extend the company's operations abroad?

From questions such as these, other questions arise. If the company is dissatisfied with its present business, what business or businesses does it wish to enter? Is it realistic to try to make the transition? How much time will be needed to achieve results?

Only when specific goals or targets of this nature have been defined is it possible to weigh their feasibility, to see whether they are in harmony with the organization's other goals, and to estimate what may be required in terms of financing, facilities, and personnel in order to accomplish each objective.

Corporate goals, it should be added, are both long-term and short-term. A short-term goal may be to increase product sales within a 6-month period. A long-term goal, such as entering a new enterprise, may require planning as far as 5 or 10 years ahead. Increasingly the emphasis is on the far-distant future—on regarding "the present situation as already obsolete."

Formulate policies. Administering a business, like administering a state, depends for continuity and consistency upon the *policies* prescribed. The constitution, laws, and court decisions, plus the regulations of administrative agencies, provide the great body of policies and precedents in the field of government. In business, policies are made or confirmed by the board of directors and carried out by the management. Through practice and precedent, the latter also builds a policy structure no less important than that of the directors.

Here are a few typical questions, the answers to which become a part of management policy; they must be answered before subsequent steps can be taken in setting up and administering the organization. The best procedures for developing the correct answers to most of these questions are discussed in other sections—

How should additional capital be obtained, if needed? Through the sale of shares? By borrowing? By converting other assets into cash?

Should the distribution of the company's products be direct, or through jobbers, selling agents, etc.? Should dealerships be exclusively franchised?

Should the company make or buy parts or other components? Should it own or rent the facilities for manufacturing, warehousing, the office, etc.?

Are operating executives overburdened with paperwork? Conversely, are they deprived of strategic decision-making data? How can company communications be simplified and at the same time be made more meaningful?

Where should specific executive jobs be placed on the organization chart? In all cases where the question is applicable, should the particular executive's function be "line" or "staff" (operational or advisory)?

Should certain functions of the business be carried on by departments, divisions, or subsidiaries?

How much information should be supplied to stockholders, and what should be contained in the annual report?

What research projects should the company engage in? How much should be spent each year for this purpose? Should it be done by company specialists, by outside laboratories, or jointly with a college or the Federal government?

It is the nature of business policies to be *cumulative*. If arrived at after mature reflection based on all considerations, one policy supplements another.

The existence of this corpus juris (body of law) greatly expedites future decisions.   It also enormously diminishes the hazard of conflicting verdicts and incompatible, ill-assorted ventures.

Classify or functionalize operations.   Traditionally, there are four major, or basic, groups of functions in a manufacturing organization: financing, production, marketing, and accounting.   With the exception of certain advisory functions—personnel, law, economics, public relations—practically everything a company does can be allocated to one of these four functions.

More recently, some companies have added research and development and electronic data processing to the basic four already mentioned.   This development has been due, in part, to the growing importance of the computer.

The computer has added a major side effect—the emergence of the concept of total company planning instead of management by bits and pieces.   Functions are becoming much more critically related instead of operating separately.

For example, the planning of manpower for future needs necessarily involves all functions of a company, requiring the cooperation of individual managers to act with dynamic totality.

But this growing subordination of the parts to the whole does not invalidate functional operations.   Indeed, the very fact that functions are interrelated emphasizes their need in the first place.

It still remains true, then, that such activities as taxes, payroll, insurance, etc., normally fall under accounting; purchasing, safety, plant layout, and maintenance come under production; market analysis, advertising, sales management, dealer relations, etc., are classified as part of marketing; the raising of funds and the conservation of assets clearly belong under financing.   In most companies today, electronic data processing comes under the direction of the controller.

Departmentalize.   Once the separate functions become clear and their relations with others clearly understood, it is possible to set up departments to handle particular functions.   In addition to a major function, each may have one or more related minor functions.   Where the volume and nature of an erstwhile minor function justify, it can be given departmental status.   For example, in many larger companies, internal auditing has become a separate function, no longer tied in with accounting.   The internal auditor—who performs for the management what the certified public accountant does for the stockholders and directors—usually reports directly to the president.

When organizing departments, due consideration should be given to administrative ease and control.   Anything which needlessly increases the volume of reports, or which adds unnecessarily to the number of executives having direct access to the top official, impairs rather than improves business efficiency.

Centralize control.   The man at the top of the organization should *hold the reins* or else have them held by executives under his direct supervision and control.   According to Col. Lyndall Urwick, well-known management consultant, "No superior can supervise directly the work of more than five or, at most, six subordinates."   However, Colonel Urwich qualifies this statement by adding that if individuals under the chief's supervision have extremely specialized areas of activity which do not bear on one another in a highly interlocked way, the span may be considerably greater.

The control function, which will be enlarged upon in subsequent portions of this section, is largely a matter of records and information flow (plus interpretation) based on standard of performance.   Devising such standards, and providing for their proper use, is of major importance to top management.

Recruit and train personnel.   The procurement, selection, and training of personnel—both executive and rank-and-file—are vital factors in building and maintaining an organization.   Obtaining the right people is only part of the job.   The training responsibility is far greater, because it is training which makes an employee invaluable, once he has been properly selected.   This last has particular pertinence in our age of automation, when jobs are rapidly diminishing in some areas and just as rapidly increasing in others.

Training is not just a personnel-department responsibility; it should continue, at all times, through all levels of the organization.   Ideally, every job should be regarded as an apprenticeship for something better.   The department head who is not training his subordinates to undertake higher responsibilities is failing in his duty to them and to the firm.

In short, long-range policies and provisions for the selection and training of future executives and other personnel should be part of the organizing process.

Ensure coordination.   Cooperation and teamwork, both within and between departments, are essential to the success of any organization.   These cannot be left to hit-or-miss efforts, but are the fruit of continuous and constant application of management policy.   Communications and meetings are two dependable instruments, but even the best of these will fail without positive backing from top management, which, through its powers of delegation and control, can coordinate activities.

Coordination is increased when the organization chart provides for executives with *coordinating powers.*   The marketing of two products which are sold to the same type of customer might, for example, be more expeditiously handled by a single manager than by two managers with coequal responsibilities.

In larger companies, the use of committees comprised of key executives is another method of promoting coordination.   If all the company managers concerned with a particular decision are required to meet for the purpose, they will have participated in the decision-making process and will probably carry out the decision more quickly and efficiently.

Another alternative is to designate a project director to study the feasibility of a specific venture—for example, the development of a new substance to withstand intense solar heat—and to obtain the consensus of all executives who might report directly to the president, or to the vice-president in charge of research and development.

Top management must be free to manage. A chief executive whose day is uncluttered with details—especially details not of his own choosing—can be truthfully said to head a good organization. He must be free to devote his full time to management functions—to administer, to troubleshoot, to create new ideas, to plan for the future—unencumbered by operating details. Whatever *can* be delegated *should* be delegated, always assuming clear-cut responsibility and tight control.

2. The two prime objectives of good organization

The two most basic, fundamental objectives of good organization are (1) to permit delegation of authority, and (2) to exert control. In other words, they provide answers to the questions, "Who is to do this work?" and "Is it being accomplished correctly, at the right cost, and on time?"

To permit delegation of authority. When a problem arises, management's first task is to evaluate it, i.e., project it against the organization chart and see whether it is routine and therefore referable to a given department or executive. If not, the problem must then be broken into fragments, and each piece assigned where it logically belongs, with provision for assembling the solutions. Or, perhaps, the organization chart may have to be redrawn to accommodate the new situation.

For example, fault is found with a price. Was it properly computed? Did *accounting* accurately evaluate and assign the elements of cost? Is it a *cost-reduction* problem, which might involve *production* economies, or even research and an improved design? Is the cost too high because of uneconomical marketing? If so, marketing may have to come up with the answer. Or the marketing function may find, as one executive put it, that "our organization chart is the most obsolete thing around this place."

A problem of a different sort might be that of establishing a pension fund for employees. To *accounting* fall the details of the plan—whether, for example, a trusteed or an actuarial plan appears best—and also the computing of probable cost to the company and to the employees. *Personnel* or *industrial relations* must weigh the plan's impact upon the workers, including collective-bargaining connotations. To *public relations* may fall the task of selling wide acceptance of the plan.

Delegation, of course, takes place at all levels. The foreman or supervisor who gives orders also endows the worker so instructed with some of his own delegated powers. He is *authorized* to proceed along a given course of action. Every step in the chain of command, from the board of directors down to the individual worker, involves a greater or lesser right to delegate responsibility and the authority to carry it out.

Much of top management's direct delegation is concerned less with the day-to-day functioning of the business than with the collection and interpretation of *facts* to use as the basis of planning. It is here that the computer exerts its magic.

Consider, for example, the fact-finding which must precede decision making in regard to a new plant. Where should it be located? Are transportation facilities adequate? Is new construction more advantageous than buying and modernizing an old building? Is it better to borrow new money for the purpose, or to use cash (to the possible detriment of dividends), or perhaps to let an insurance company build and own it, with the manufacturer taking a long-term lease? Will the local labor force be adequate without importing others? What group of seasoned, well-trained employees, supervisors, and executives should be transferred from an existing plant to provide an expert nucleus? How much additional business must the company handle each year in order to absorb the various outlays and justify the expansion?

When the head of an effective organization needs facts like these, he usually delegates his executive assistant, a project director or perhaps a committee, to investigate all angles and submit a report with recommendations. Sometimes an outside consulting organization is retained to make a study, working in close liaison with an assigned executive of the company. Either way, the delegation carries with it authority to obtain facts and figures from all departments and especially from the centralized computer service, where pertinent data are stored in quantity and instantly available for retrieval.

One would think, from reading material printed on the subject, that delegation normally originates with the top executive. This oversimplifies the process. More typically, it is an act of *confirmation,* carrying with it authority, which sharpens in detail as it proceeds outward from the top administrator.

Here is an illustration. A report from the controller or chief accountant reveals that sales in a certain market are decreasing in relation to those of competitors. The marketing manager, when acquainted with this condition, decides after investigation that more intensive direct mail will help recapture the market. The advertising manager is brought into the picture and instructed (the first true delegation) to map a test campaign. From this point on the delegation spreads—to the advertising-agency account executive, from him to the copy chief and art director, and eventually to the printer who produces the literature.

This simple illustration shows that delegation is not a magic process, with the president sitting somewhere on Olympus, dreaming up ideas and pushing buttons to translate them into action. Rather, it is a process of stimulating others to think and communicate their ideas to management, which acts upon them. In short, delegation is a two-way street.

To exert control. Control is the obverse side of delegation. The larger the organization and the more far-flung its activities and personnel, the greater is the need for formalized control, which is another name for being kept informed about all aspects of the business. The pilot of an airplane has automatic instruments which tell him at a glance his altitude, speed, stability, fuel consumption, direction, wind resistance, and other vital factors. The controls which the head of a business organization exercises play a similar role. They tell him where he is and how he is proceeding, so that he can see where he is heading.

The president who says to an operating executive, "Do such and such, and we'll go over it on Wednesday," is exercising control in its simplest form. By fixing a date for the completion of the work and providing for his inspection of the results at a particular time, he has made what businessmen would call a "tight delegation." It is "tight" because it includes the measures for control. A follow-up file of dated reminders is another rudimentary example of control.

Organizationally, the control function is related to that of accounting, information, and records, which explains why, in the larger companies, the controller is the chief accounting executive as well as the director of electronic data processing. In small and medium-sized firms, the top executive may act as his own controller, guided by the reports and records prepared and submitted by the accounting department.

It may be interesting to note in passing that in most companies today—even very large companies—the computer is more closely related to the controlling function than to any other activity. More typically than not, the computer is utilized in applications such as payroll, sales analysis, inventory control, billing, shipping, and the like. In some companies, computers also play a part in long-range planning, but this role at present is limited.

Control, which might also be termed "evaluation," because one of its major purposes is *measuring results,* gives management a reasonably automatic check on all aspects of the operation. Without adequate controls to keep him informed, the head of a business cannot effectively hold the reins on his organization. More on this subject later.

3. The three major functions of organization

A business organization has three major functions: planning, operation, and control. Without the first, it grows haphazardly, if at all. Without the second, the real base of any business, organization is meaningless. Without the third, it is headed for the shoals of loose administration.

The planning function. Planning is the translation of objectives into concrete procedures and assignable responsibilities, determining what shall be done and who is to do it. It represents the generalship of business, including both strategy and tactics. It has long-range and short-term connotations, and it is successful to the degree that it is kept balanced and elastic.

The legendary autocrat who growled, "I'll do the thinking around here!"

is the polar opposite of the more enlightened businessman whose organization provides the plan, probably with alternatives from which he can select the course best suited to his purpose.

Forecasting and budgeting are two specific instances of high-level business planning. The first step in forecasting is *appraisal* or *review*. What was our performance in the period just ending? How did it compare with that of comparable firms in the industry? What can we reasonably expect to do in the period to be covered by the forecast? What depressing or stimulating factors exist or can be anticipated in the general economy? What do we have to go on, in the sense of materials on hand or arranged for, work in process, products or projects in development, inventories, plant and equipment, cash resources?

As a rule, the sales forecast is the foundation of the overall prediction. Because sales are usually equivalent to gross receipts, most other factors in the business forecast are related to the anticipated volume of sales. But the marketing manager's opinion alone does not suffice. He is expected to look on the bright side of things, to minimize obstacles, and to reflect in his forecast an optimistic and enthusiastic point of view. Organization provides the needed checks and balances—from the "figure men" or accounting-minded executives, from research and development experts, and from those concerned with production and procurement difficulties, who visualize the bottlenecks, internal and external, which may restrain the flow of goods into the market.

Great strides have been made in the art of business forecasting during recent years. Business cycles are better understood. Economic facts are more readily available through the statistical services of trade associations and the Department of Commerce. Furthermore, business organizations themselves possess a greater store of past-performance data, particularly since the emergence of the computer.

The techniques of budgeting have also advanced conspicuously. Few companies of any size, for example, make one rigid budget any longer. The growing practice is to make not one forecast but two or more, with a budget keyed to each. Then, if the lower volume of sales eventuates, there are budget categories to fit, without the need for complete rebudgeting. The so-called "flexible budget" has many advocates. Under this method, outlays are automatically reduced in proportion to periodic drops in sales.

This section is not concerned with the merits of any particular type of budget, but rather with the forecasting-budgeting process as an example of good organizational planning. Instead of being masterminded at the top and imposed on those below, it flows from the department heads themselves, and is accepted by them as a democratic device to facilitate their operation—and cooperation.

Forecasting and budgeting, of course, are only two aspects—albeit vital ones —of planning. Research, marketing, electronic data processing, production, purchasing, personnel, training, compensation of executives and employees—all require planning. But the applicable techniques are all the same. Regardless of the particular problem involved, the organizational approach is the best for any business to follow.

The operational function. The operational function of organization is to eliminate the need for intervention in the operating process by those who constitute top management. The goal is to make the business *run itself* so far as possible, and limit management's intervention to improving methods, i.e., further organizing operative details, whenever this seems advisable. Only to the extent that this goal is attainable can management be really free to manage.

This objective is achieved by routinizing operations via the establishment of systems, and by safeguarding their performance with controls. Standards are set up for every task, and records provided for, so that results will be measurable and subject to check. All operations are conducted within a functionalized framework of executive and supervisory personnel to whom appropriate delegations of authority have been made.

The requisitioning of materials constitutes a simple illustration. Only in the smallest shops does a workman have to go to the boss for what he needs. All others have a system of forms, authorizations, and sometimes automatic checks, which ensure a ready flow, combining records and control. The separation of toolmaking from production machining is another case in point. This simple, practically universal idea is management's assurance that (1) enough taps, dies, drills, files, etc., of the right type and variety will be on hand at all times; (2) all tools will be kept in top condition; (3) production-machine operators will not waste their time sharpening or adapting tools, with the concurrent risk of spoilage. In short, the supplying and maintenance of tools has been *organized*.

The extent to which operations have been organized is apparent in many ways, from every perspective. To the rank-and-file employee, it shows up in such terms as convenience on the job (plant layout); lack of delays due to hitches in the flow of work from machine to machine or department to department; protection against accident, injury, and other health hazards; a clean and attractive workplace, with adequate washup and toilet facilities; a formalized grievance procedure; helpful and understanding supervision; a compensation method which he understands and accepts; and a feeling that he is being regarded and appreciated as an individual, rather than as a machine or just a number on the payroll.

To the customer, a business is well organized if his needs are anticipated and planned for; if the deliveries are made on time; if the company's salesman calls at regular intervals; if invoices are accurate and submitted in time for discounting; if the goods themselves are up to standard; and if, when occasional things go wrong, remedial steps are promptly taken.

Suppliers have kind words for their customer's organization if orders are clearly stated, shipments promptly accepted, bills paid on time or discounted, requirements estimated far enough ahead to keep rush requests at a minimum, etc.

Stockholders, bankers, investment counselors, and others whose concern is financial also have criteria for judging a company's management and ability to organize. Regularity of earnings, health of growth, cash position, debt management, treatment of reserves, depreciation policy, executive continuity (ability to attract and retain the services of competent people), freedom from proxy fights and other disputes over control, the absence of litigation or controversies with government—these are among the signs that the financial community goes by in evaluating a business organization.

The best systems for obtaining these desired results are not haphazardly conceived. As a rule, each is the result of considerable study and actual test, plus regular revision and overhauling to keep in step with changing requirements. And when things go wrong, organization-minded managers ask, not "What's wrong with the man?" but "What's wrong with the system?"

The chief auditor of a large company recently remarked that a cash defalcation on the part of an employee is as much an indictment of the firm as of the embezzler. It raises the point, "What is wrong with our controls if they tempt —and permit—one to steal?" The same philosophy applies to waste of materials, accidents, absenteeism, and other drains on efficiency.

Almost all contemporary concepts of operating organization stem back to F. W. Taylor's discovery of "scientific management," which combined at every point the following conditions:

Standardization of the operation, including machines, tools, and methods
Selection and training of the right individual to perform the job
A cooperative spirit on the part of the worker

None of these three conditions is *static*. Standards for even the more elementary jobs require constant revision, because of improvements in machinery, changes in materials, changes in other jobs related to the first, etc.

Automation is a case in point. Originally developed to simplify or accelerate line production, automation has been successively applied to many other uses: quality control, for example; detection of variation in chemical purity; the measurement of size, weight, and form; the regulation of product coloration. The computer itself is nothing more than the application of automation to record and information handling.

As C. E. Knight and C. H. Falkner of Monsanto Chemical describe the impact of automation on company organization:

Paradoxically, the trend toward disappearance of direct human contribution to product creation is accompanied by an increased need for recognition of workers as people and more tolerance for the constructive nonconformist.

As has been remarked many times over, the human element is one which requires constant attention. The quality of supervision, plus the general level of human relations prevailing, are basic factors in keeping systems operating with maximum efficiency.

The control function. Positive, centralized executive control as a function of management is a relatively new concept. Prior to the 1930s, few companies numbered a *controller* in their list of key executives. The control function, in other words, was divided among several people, from the president down. The trend today is to concentrate the various aspects of control in one executive or department.

For a number of years, until recently, decentralization was characteristic of large American businesses. Such businesses almost invariably operated manufacturing plants at distant geographical locations. Product divisions were commonly dispersed. As a result, certain executives were given prime responsibility for the success of an individual unit.

With the expansion of electronic data processing, and with modern emphasis on total marketing and research, centralization has returned to favor. Centralization reduces the risk of duplicating or overlapping information or effort. It facilitates the adoption and enforcement of uniform policies and decisions.

Centralization also permits greater standardization and specialization, with attendant economies in operation and equipment.

An idea of what control involves can be gained from the following summary of the duties and responsibilities of a controller:

Determination and promulgation of accounting policies and office procedures

Office management and office services, including provision for central filing and information processing; standardization of office machinery, equipment, and forms; and supervision of certain services, including systems and procedures

Maintenance of the accounting records of the company in adequate form to disclose all needed information

Determination of income, costs, and profits of the company from its various activities, including all necessary preliminaries, such as taking and valuing physical inventories, classification of receipts and expenditures, allocation of costs and income as between accounting periods, etc.

Preparation and interpretation of financial and statistical reports of the company, including government reports and forecasts of probable results in coming periods

The making of recommendations for suggested executive actions indicated as necessary by the reports or forecasts, i.e., in conjunction with other officers and department heads, to initiate and enforce measures and procedures whereby the business may be conducted with the maximum safety, efficiency, and economy

Administration of control practices and procedures with respect to assets, receipts, and expenditures, including budgetary controls

Preparation of tax returns and the supervision of all matters relating to Federal income taxes, Social Security taxes, state income and franchise taxes, etc.

Administration of internal-audit procedures, including the continuous audit of all accounts and records of the corporation, wherever located; the verification of the company's securities and other property; the verification of the adequacy of insurance carried, etc.

The organization of the controller's department is as important in setting up the overall pattern as is the organizing for production, marketing, and research and development. As in these other instances, functional lines are followed. The organization chart for a small or medium-sized company would probably show two executives reporting directly to the controller: the office manager and the plant accountant. The former would have authority and supervision over receipts and disbursements, general accounting, and budgets, while the latter would be in charge of payrolls, plant accounting, production and shipping, and costs. The functions of auditing, taxes, and so forth would be performed by the controller himself, or by an assistant controller.

In a larger, more involved establishment, the controller might be aided by three or more assistants—say one in charge of manufacturing accounting, to whom the plant accounts report; a second in charge of sales accounting, to whom the office managers of the various branches report; and a third in charge of general accounting, assisted by an accounting director for general accounts and an accounting director for taxes. To these might be added a treasurer, a purchasing director, a credit manager, an insurance manager, and, not least of all, a manager in charge of information processing. In still larger setups, there are divisional controllers who report, as a rule, to the general manager of the division.

Although the title of controller is rarely found in small companies, the idea of centralizing records, accounts, and controls under one executive is rapidly spreading. Even where no such office exists, the fact remains that the controller's functions still have to be performed, and it is better organization to concentrate them in one department than to leave them scattered across the board.

4. How to develop a pattern of organization

Formulate and communicate top management goals. A company is often described as "the lengthened shadow of one man." It follows that one of the prime duties of the chief executive is to make clear what corporate objectives are and to communicate them again and again. Unless the organization feels a sense of participation, however, there can be no enthusiastic response. This means that communications must also travel in an *upward* direction to advise, alert, and inform.   Unless there is an atmosphere of give-and-take, friction and misunderstanding almost inevitably result.

Define responsibility by preparing job description.   As previously stated, having people working for one is not the same as having an *organization,* with all that the word implies.   The first step in converting a relatively unorganized group of employees into a real organization is obvious: to find out what they are doing at present, so that their duties and responsibilities can be defined and realigned.   This calls for a *job description* of each function.   When these descriptions have been written down and examined, it is possible to reassign duties on a more efficient, more logical, and more equitable basis.

Delegate authority sufficient to handle responsibility.   Hand in hand with the redefining of the job should go the delegation of authority sufficient to discharge the duties.   It is unfair and impractical to assign responsibilities without delegating the powers which go with them.   It is inefficient and confusing to have authority and responsibility divorced, but this does happen in industry —most frequently at the supervisory level.   The foreman who has no right to hire, fire, or discipline, who is bypassed in the grievance procedure and overshadowed by the union shop steward, does not have authority in keeping with his responsibility.

When defining jobs and delegating authority, it is important to avoid or eliminate overlapping.   A delegation is effective only if it is clear-cut and if its scope and definition are known to others in the organization.   Limiting authority is as important as imparting it.   In short, the executive should know how far he can proceed without trespassing on another's territory.

Some businessmen who are good in every other sense make two cardinal errors in this regard: (1) They prefer to let authorities be implied, rather than stated; and (2) they do not respect the boundaries which they themselves have laid down, but feel free to "cut across channels" whenever they so desire.   Such actions are subversive of an organization, and are the frequent cause of resignation, frustration, and resentment on the part of executives so treated.   By the organization, the cost is paid in terms of waste, lack of cooperation, and impaired control.

Compensate fairly.   *Compensation* is of supreme importance in reorganizing a business or setting up a new one.   The salary paid to a specific executive must be in line with those paid for comparable jobs in the company, in the area, and elsewhere in the industry, and it must fairly reflect the nature and scope of his responsibilities.   A salary is significant not only in terms of the purchasing power and living standards which it represents to the person receiving it, but also as a measure of his importance and prestige.

An executive's salary should be sufficiently larger than that of his best-paid subordinate to substantially reflect the difference in their ranks.   It is a mistake, for example, except under abnormal conditions, for a company to pay supervisors less than the workers under them receive.   Such a condition was prevalent during wartime, when production employees' pay was swelled by high piece rates, shift differentials, and overtime. As a result, the foreman's status was badly undermined.

No one, employee or executive, should have his responsibilities increased without receiving a comparable increase in pay. The stabilization rules of the Second World War took this into account, and one dependable way for an employer to win approval of a wage or salary increase was to demonstrate an increase in responsibilities. Incidentally, this rule stimulated the healthy practice of job analysis, job description, and job evaluation as a basis for fixing compensation. It also caused widespread adoption of job classification—the setting of a range for every job, from the minimum or starting wage to the maximum for that position. Many companies which lacked such classifications went to work and installed them, and a few months' trial sufficed to prove the value of the innovation as a permanent device.

Length-of-service increases, within the range set for the particular job, were also recognized in the wartime regulation, and were generally adopted and retained by employers.

Of course, once a maximum has been set for a particular position, the question arises of what to do with the employee who has achieved the maximum. One cannot go on increasing the maximum; this would not only upset and confuse the compensation schedule, but would also lessen the employee's incentive to take on additional or higher responsibilities. The way to meet this difficulty is through a policy of promoting individuals to higher jobs and training them to move ahead.

In the more important positions, the value of salary increases as incentives has been greatly impaired by income taxes. The same is true of a bonus, which is treated as taxable income by the Treasury, and the tax treatment of stock options to employees has also deprived them of their former importance as incentive rewards.

Some companies have partially overcome this condition by granting special privileges to executives in lieu of substantially higher pay, once the tax "bite" becomes confiscatory. These range all the way from more luxurious offices and more assistants to deferred compensation, longer vacations, and larger personal expense accounts. Everything possible is done to increase the individual's feeling of significance, such as encouraging him to take a larger part in trade-association activities, allowing him to speak for publication, giving him greater opportunities for travel, and admitting him to the inner councils.

Retirement pay is an important part of the compensation problem, especially in regard to higher executives. Again, tax restrictions interfere with a company's right to determine retirement payments, and few pension plans give an adequate retirement allowance to the higher-paid executives and officials. This has been met in some quarters by *not retiring outright* the victims of this discrimination, but giving them responsibilities of an advisory or consultative nature, which do not take up all of their time but keep them on call when the need for their help arises. Such duties, of course, must be tangible, because otherwise the Federal tax authorities would disallow the expense of such salaries as not representing services rendered.

The so-called "fringe benefits"—vacation pay, hospitalization, health insurance, education allowances, employees' pensions, etc.—are becoming more and more a regular part of the compensation plan. Economists estimate that from 5 to 20 percent of the payroll is for such benefits, and that the burden will increase, rather than diminish. Obviously, a company is not prepared for future contingencies unless it has made tentative provision for this "hidden payroll." Social-minded government combines with aggressive labor-union leadership to impose these costs upon industry.

Evaluate progress at stated intervals. Another "must" to keep in mind is to evaluate progress at stated intervals. This includes not only the progress of individual employees, as measured by merit rating, but also that of departments and of the company as a whole. No company stands still; it either grows or shrinks. Therefore, it is important for the organization to include provision for periodic reviews and soundings to show which way the firm is heading.

One way to keep growing is to keep the individual employees and executives adding to their stature. If their progress is regularly checked and recorded, a basis is provided for recognition of their growth. This keeps the organization on its toes, and passes the benefits down the line.

Select carefully and train thoroughly. Whenever and wherever new personnel is required, the emphasis should be on careful selection and thorough training. If jobs have been properly analyzed and standards of the right sort devised, the personnel department will be guided in its choice of applicants. Final selection, of course, should rest with the department head to whom the new employee must report.

Training should be dynamic and long-term, rather than haphazard and confined to learning the immediate job. It has been wisely said that "authority to supervise includes responsibility to teach." Unfortunately, there are some high executives in industry who never had supervisory experience and who are equally unprepared to train and teach. The facts regarding such conditions should be known to management, which then—and then only—can take steps to supply the deficiency. A program combining attendance at outside institutions, plus appropriate on-the-job training, will go far to remedy such a situation.

There is another corollary, which holds that no employee is fully trained for a given position until he is able to supervise others in doing the work. It follows that employees who show any promise at all should be early instructed in the art of supervision.

Training also involves indoctrination in the company's policies and procedures, acquaintance with the rules and regulations surrounding various jobs and departments, plus knowledge of its products and of its position in the industry and the community. The preparation of an employee manual, so that a copy can be given each new recruit, is a constructive step in this direction. Needless to say, it should be graphically attractive and up-to-date, and not just one more piece of dry-as-dust "literature" to be put away and forgotten.

Following is a restatement of some of the previous points as formulated by the American Management Association:

TEN COMMANDMENTS OF GOOD ORGANIZATION [1]

There are two kinds of efficiency: One kind is only *apparent* and is produced in organizations through the exercise of mere discipline. This is but a simulation of the second, or true, efficiency which springs, as Woodrow Wilson said, from "the spontaneous cooperation of a free people." If you are a manager, no matter how great or small your responsibility, it is your job, in the final analysis, to create and develop this voluntary cooperation among the people whom you supervise. For, no matter how powerful a combination of money, machines and materials a company may have, this is a dead and sterile thing without a team of *willing, thinking,* and *articulate* people to guide it.

1. Definite and clean-cut responsibilities should be assigned to each executive
2. Responsibility should always be coupled with corresponding authority
3. No change should be made in the scope or responsibilities of a position without a definite understanding to that effect on the part of all persons concerned
4. No executive or employee, occupying a single position in the organization, should be subject to definite orders from more than one source
5. Orders should never be given to subordinates over the head of a responsible executive. Rather than do this, management should supplant the officer in question
6. Criticisms of subordinates should, whenever possible, be made privately, and in no case should a subordinate be criticized in the presence of executives or employees of equal or lower rank
7. No dispute or difference between executives or employees as to authority or responsibilities should be considered too trivial for prompt and careful adjudication
8. Promotions, wage changes, and disciplinary action should always be approved by the executive immediately superior to the one directly responsible
9. No executive or employee should ever be required, or expected, to be at the same time an assistant to, and critic of, another
10. Any executive whose work is subject to regular inspection should, whenever practicable, be given the assistance and facilities necessary to enable him to maintain an independent check of the quality of his work

5. The levels of organization

Any organization can be broken down into levels of delegated authority and responsibility. These levels of organization are important only in checking actions to make certain that they are being handled at the right level. The majority of decisions will fall under these levels of organization:

Policy decision
Planning and recommending techniques
Supervision
Detail work

[1] Reprinted by permission of the American Management Association.

The actual working of these levels of operations is covered so thoroughly in the other parts of this section that they are being listed at this point simply for checking.

6. The growth pattern of delegation of authority

Most business organizations are the result of an expanding pattern for delegating authority. The process starts with the original one-man business. The proprietor begins organizing when he engages an assistant to whom he delegates a portion of the work. As business increases, he adds additional assistants, and they, in turn, acquire personnel to help them. In time, the assistants become heads of departments and report to the owner.

As the business becomes more complex, outside services are retained: a public account, who for a time provides all the accounting services required; legal counsel; an advertising agency; public-relations and management counsel, etc. Often outside services fill an awkward gap, because the business is still too small to justify full-time specialists on a salaried basis.

Gradually, the business acquires a full-time staff. Accounting detail has grown and the need for audits and reports has sharpened. So the rudiments of an accounting department appear. The volume of advertising has also grown to a point where someone must keep in constant touch with the agency, so an advertising manager is engaged to operate under the direction of the marketing manager. Technicians of various kinds, depending on the nature of the business, are added to the payroll, which by now also includes an office manager (who probably doubles as chief accountant), a purchasing agent, and a sales manager.

By this time, the need for capital in keeping with the enlarged scope of the business has made it necessary to sell securities to the public—which in turn has resulted in the election of an active board of directors. The owner has now become the president, and with the directors' help he rounds out the organization, so that he can function as an administrator, effectively carrying out the policies of the board.

As one of the major steps in completing the structure, the company obtains a controller, whose function—besides managing the accounting, tax, and related departments—is to keep the president informed where the business is, so that he can see where it is heading.

7. The importance of controls

In order to function properly, the head of an organization must retain control over key activities, including—

Acquisition and sharing of information. The function of top management is to insure *direction* of an enterprise instead of "flying by the seat of one's pants." This requires the constant acquisition of basic data to appraise one's position and to change it, if necessary, in the light of current conditions. No higher duty accrues to the president than to *remain informed* and to make sure that his subordinates keep up to date

Budgeting and control of funds and expenditures. The company budget is the basic instrument of such financial control, supplemented by daily balances of condition, summaries of receipts and disbursements, etc. Before any check is signed, the payment is checked against the proper budget category, as are authorizations to commit the company to buy in excess of certain amounts

Materials en route and in process. A control is kept on all such items, so that warehousing costs, material prices, demurrage on freight, and other losses are kept to a minimum, and so that production stoppages are not caused by delays in arrival of materials at the plants

Plant and equipment. These are under constant and positive check on their adequacy, depreciation, maintenance, comparative production costs, etc. The newest and latest devices for materials handling, inspection, speeding up and improving quality of output, and so forth, are studied and tested

Resources and suppliers. The quality of materials received is established by test, and the dependability of one source as against another is kept a matter of record. Such matters as labor stability and financial and credit status are studied from time to time, and any development which may affect the supplier's delivery capacity or credit is quickly investigated. Otherwise employment in the organization's own plants may be unstabilized, with a consequent impact upon employee morale and customer satisfaction—not to mention profits

Personnel. Personnel here includes employees, consultants, and agents. The entire field of employee relations, including collective bargaining, morale building, promotion, and training, should be subject to periodic surveys and examination. Manpower needs should be *planned ahead* in the same manner as new products and markets are planned for. Never so intangible as they first appear, employee relations are measurable and definite. Just as the military commander's first thought is for his men, so does the happiness and prosperity of his employees loom large in the top manager's thinking

Outlets and markets. Control in this sense over outlets and markets greatly exceeds mere credit management, which is only one of the factors to be considered. A good organization is "choosy" about those to whom it sells. Price-cutters, chiselers, and others of that ilk may have the best of credit, but the firm may suffer from doing business with them. Care is also taken not to overreach into distant markets, where the cost of doing business may exceed the total volume from the area.

It may be interesting to note in passing that the United States' stake in European investment is relatively small, amounting to less than 5 percent of total investment. But interest and optimism are growing fast. It is estimated that in the next few years, companies will increase overseas investments by 20 percent, spending a record $7.4 billion. Already a few corporations derive 50 percent of their total earnings from foreign sales.

As noted earlier, many executives predict that international trade will have a vital bearing on the future of management. For this reason, some companies equate international trade on a par with electronic data processing and research and development—giving it an equal place with financing, production, marketing, and accounting as one of the basic functions of the manufacturing organization.

Control of markets, then, must be positive as well as negative. The wide-awake organization constantly surveys new markets, as well as restudying those already established. It never lacks the facts on which to base its decisions regarding territories, consumer demand, etc., and is ready on short notice to move in and capitalize on any favorable situation.

8. Basic helps

There are a number of basic devices which top management can use in building and administering an organization. Here are some which have proved their utility:

Separation of functions. As previously stated, functions must be clear-cut and sharply delineated if delegation is to be clear. Otherwise, those who perform the functions will be fuzzy in regard to them and to their own measure of authority and responsibility. This does not rule out the desirability of functional coordination—the meeting of committees or department heads to plan for the overall company welfare

Organization chart. This is a means of defining functions, job titles, and their relation to other functions and other jobs. It is the nature of organizations to keep developing and changing, and so the charts which portray them must also be kept fluid. One prominent corporation, for example, makes a practice of changing its organization chart every 6 months

Clear delegation of work and authority. This has been dwelt upon before, but is an absolute essential, and hence worth mentioning again and again

Budgets and accounts. These are management's keys to control, the basic instruments in keeping a business concern a going (and growing) concern

Accurate costing and forecasting. Without these, budgeting cannot be accomplished, which would rob top management of its most essential controls

Reports to management. These include control reports and summaries, trend and analytical reports, financial reports, etc., as well as special studies made at the request of management or the board. The facilities for gleaning information, making comparative studies, etc., are of vital importance in conducting an organization and keeping it moving ahead. This is why electronic data processing has become widely accepted, and continues to grow as a tool for facilitating management decisions

9. Errors to avoid in building an organization

In building a business organization, certain mistakes are possible—even probable, under certain conditions. The most commonly made include—

Excess personnel and resulting high cost of management. It is human nature, under pressure of time and necessity, to *add people* to the organization, rather than to restudy the setup and see how *change,* rather than expansion, will enable it to absorb a higher load. It should be remembered that while some functions wax, others wane, and this in itself provides a certain elasticity

Confusion over line and staff functions. The line executives and departments are those in the direct chain of command from the top executive; they execute orders with the authority and responsibility implied. Staff executives and departments, on the other hand, are those with a purely advisory function, except in regard to their own department personnel. Accounting, auditing, public relations, etc., are staff, rather than line, activities

Loss of initiative at the top, especially in the formulation of policy. When moves and decisions are *forced* "by conditions beyond control," management to that degree has lost its ability to manage

Too great a burden of reports, interoffice communications, and so forth. This is deadening to the people who must read and act upon them. One of the current complaints against the computer is that so large a volume of data is being produced that action is delayed by a constant flow of paper. The effort should always be to diminish, rather than to increase, the volume of communications, and to require summaries, rather than detailed reports, whenever abridgment and condensation are possible

Undue emphasis on some one particular activity—accounting, production, research, and so forth. Organizations thrive on *balance* and are bound to suffer in effectiveness if the direction at the top is one-sided. After all, one of the primary purposes of having an organization is to permit it to move ahead on all fronts

10. How to check your organization efficiency

The top-management search for organization efficiency is a continuous examination of how your organization is doing what it is supposed to do. The following headings are suggested as major checking points for such an examination. Obviously, they are not all the points that must be checked, but if you look for improvement in these areas, you will undoubtedly identify the special points at which the efficiency of your own particular business organization can be raised.

Organization. Have you an organization manual, defining functions, authority, and responsibility of your personnel? Is the organization charted for easy grasp by all involved? Have standard practices been reduced to writing? Are the manual, the chart, the standard practices maintained on a current basis? Are they circulated?

Personnel. Have you a policy and a program for selecting, placing, and advancement training of all personnel? Are salary and wage rates, from common labor to top management, established by job evaluation? Is an individual history and job record for each employee kept up to date? Are salaries and wages increased only under pressure? Or by seniority? Or on performance?

Product. Do you ensure market acceptability of your product by close cooperation with your marketing division? Is your engineering aimed at a competitive cost? Are your marketing and research-and-development teams looking for product improvements and for new products?

Production. Is your production completely planned and scheduled to control the economical purchase of raw materials, to progress the work through modern machinery, processes, and layouts, to utilize labor under efficient supervision and incentives to cooperation, to gear the inventory of finished goods to the sales requirements and manufacturing capacity? How much attention is given to increasing the automation of equipment and the quality of product?

Distribution. Do you determine your customers' needs by market research and current sales records? How closely do you follow the efforts and results by salesmen, territories, customers, and products? How alertly is your sales force directed? How well is it compensated? How does your delivery system meet customers' requirements competitively?

Planning. How much of the volume and nature of your business is based on guesswork and impulse, and how much on data and the judgment of divisional heads? How much attention do you pay to your progressive position in the industry, and the position of the industry in the economy, and the state of the economy as a whole? Are your plans definitely stated and understood by those who are to carry them out? Do you participate in trade and business associations? How are your public relations?

Financing. Do you forecast and schedule your money requirements for the business volume you have decided to undertake? Do you budget your intake and output and reserves to keep your capital continuously at work?

Control. Do you recognize that control figures are the checkup on current efficiency—the road to prompt corrective action under a forward-moving plan? Does your accounting supply you with daily, or weekly, or monthly reports on the performance of all departments, showing you what was planned and how the plan is working out? How is departure from the plan signaled and how is the necessary correction determined? Do you get enough control reports and not too many? Are they on time? Do you need better accounting equipment and personnel? Does your accounting secure the necessary data on costs and variations without encumbering operations with forms?

Section 4

HOW TO FACE THE RISKS IN BUSINESS

BY

Roy A. Foulke

HOW TO FACE THE RISKS IN BUSINESS

Anyone in business for himself, or planning to start a new enterprise, recognizes that he runs the risk of becoming a failure statistic. Recognition of the possibility of failure is one way to ensure against it. In this handbook can be found ways and means intelligent management uses to avoid risks in business and to operate as a profitable concern. In this section, we shall discuss some of the reasons why many commercial and industrial ventures end in bankruptcy, foreclosures, or attachments.

Business failures have been attributed to many divergent factors: lack of working capital; the increased intensity of competition; changes in the technique of production and distribution; changes in styles, fads, and habits; the introduction of substitute products; overtrading and undertrading; the personal extravagance of officers or partners; and, last but not least, the greatest overlord of all of the masters, "general business conditions." Failures have been attributed to every reason under the sun and also to some reasons under the moon, the stars, and the planets.

Essentially, failure may be said to result from managerial inexperience or inefficiency, mental or physical inertia, or ill-considered judgment. In a competitive economy, other factors help or retard progress, but they are of secondary importance. The finest plant, the most meritorious product, the greatest potential market are liabilities under poor management. Examine these situations:

1. Lack of working capital

If a business begins to manufacture folding card tables on a net working capital of $40,000 when a minimum of $60,000 is essential, the very organization of the concern with insufficient working capital is the result of incompetence and lack of financial knowledge and experience. Say the business was started with a net working capital of $60,000 and in 3 years losses reduced excess current assets to $40,000. Again, inefficient or incapable management must be blamed for the loss.

2. Extreme competition

If the effects of competition were actually beyond the control of business management, a philosophy of fatalism would be needed. Thought, energy, and conscious effort would be largely superfluous.

Suppose that there are 59 motion-picture–theater supply houses in the United States and that each dealer handles a wide variety of supplies for the typical motion-picture theater—projection machines, seats, curtains, carpets, sets, projector repair parts, lamps, accessories, and carbon. Say competition becomes keener, prices are cut—first on carbon, then on projector repair parts, lamps, and accessories. Profits are turned into losses as the gross margin on carbon is cut from 30 percent to 10 percent, and the gross margins on other items are materially reduced. One concern after another liquidates its affairs, pulls down the shades, and closes up shop. Finally, 39 remain. But why were only 20 forced out of business? What saved the other businesses?

Obviously, the 20 which felt the results of keener competition were the marginal concerns. The managements of the liquidated concerns lacked the aggressiveness to hold business and failed to acquire new business on more profitable lines, such as television, radios, tape recorders, sound, and air-conditioning equipment, the type of film equipment that could have been sold to clubs, schools, and churches. The surviving concerns responded to the stress of intense competition with new lines, aggressiveness, and the will to go after and acquire profitable sales. As always, managements with the greatest ingenuity, keenness, and foresight survive, and those which lack the competitive instinct, the will to work, and the ability to create a hard, tight-functioning organization are the first to fail.

3. Changes

Change may take place in production technique or in popular demand for a product. Even the responsibility for failure said to be the result of new technological development, or of the whim of a public following style or a fad, may rest nowhere except with an executive staff. An aggressive, alert management generally realizes that changes are taking place behind the scenes many months—and, at times, years—before they come to light. Consequently, improvements and changes are made in products or in the methods of manufacture well in advance of actual needs.

Less wide-awake executive staffs watch their sales shrink to the vanishing point and then, when it is too late, place the onus on the "changing times." Every manufacturing and wholesaling business, and most of the larger retailers which have been in existence 25 years or more, have had to meet and overcome changes in the demands and needs of customers, in manufacturing processes, and in methods of distribution. A constant change is in process, a change which is quietly taking place in the method of operation of all concerns whose managements have a firm grasp on reality.

The ability to develop with the times and the wisdom to know what to change and when to put such change into effect are essential to today's business leaders, whether they guide vast corporations or small plants in outlying communities. It is the alert management that acts, and does so at the right time. The businessman who stays with yesterday's methods too long invites failure.

The responsibility of management. Every policy and decision of an executive staff can be seen in the healthy or unhealthy proportions of assets and liabilities on the balance sheet, income statement, and in the surplus account of a business. Managerial inefficiency, mental or physical inertia, or ill-considered judgment may be seen in heavy liabilities, excessive inventory, top-heavy fixed assets, excessive receivables, inadequate sales, heavy operating expenses, poor location, or competitive weakness. Each of these conditions, in turn, may be brought to light by secondary factors such as poor business conditions, changes in the accepted technique of production and distribution, changes in budgetary and accounting controls, and fluctuations in wholesale commodity prices. Consider these points:

4. Top-heavy fixed assets

This condition, indicating a lack of working capital, burdens the operating account with more than its normal share of yearly depreciation. Such a condition in a manufacturing business results from the desire of the management to expand the capacity and the facilities of the concern, often during a period of "good business." When the business cycle turns, the concern is distressed by idle plant capacity. Such a situation is doubly dangerous when new construction and additions to plant capacity are financed with borrowed funds.

The same situation occurs with retail establishments when large sums are spent to improve the frontage or the furnishings of a store, when an addition is made to an old store, and when new units are taken over either by the purchase of the properties in fee or under leaseholds. This condition may also be brought about by continual heavy losses, withdrawals, or dividends for several years by the management of a business which at an earlier date had maintained a satisfactory relationship between its fixed assets and its tangible net worth.

5. Excessive inventories

This manifestation of managerial incompetence may be brought about by the manufacture or distribution of too many products or lines for the size of the business; by speculation in merchandise, that is, by buying heavily in anticipation of a rise in prices that too often fails to materialize; by poor judgment of future markets, that is, by overbuying; by the production or handling of a product that is off-style or not in public demand; by unknowingly having prices that are high competitively; and by not keeping the inventory neat and up-to-date.

An executive who speculates in merchandise, purchases in excess of reasonable needs, and whose business subsequently becomes bankrupt as the result of the ensuing drop in wholesale prices, certainly lacks both knowledge and foresight. The drop in wholesale prices was not the cause of the failure, but merely the means through which the inexperience of the management became evident. The fundamental error was in the decision to pile up an inventory far in excess of reasonable needs.

6. Understanding figures is essential to avoid difficulties

For the successful operation of commercial and industrial businesses, the fundamental, clear, definite understanding of three sets of figures is essential. This does not mean that a business executive, a commercial or investment banker, an investor, a speculator, a business counselor, a mercantile credit man, or a financial analyst must know how to prepare these three financial statements; trained accountants are available in every city in the United States for that purpose. But the unchallenged ability to interpret these three sets of figures intelligently and accurately is essential to an understanding of the operations of business enterprises in a highly competitive profit economy. These three financial statements are the *balance sheet,* the *income statement,* and the *reconciliation of surplus.* When gross profits and net profits are decreasing, or when black figures have turned into red figures, the active management of the typical business enterprise generally follows two policies simultaneously: Sales are pushed just as hard as the aggressiveness, the energy, and the ingenuity of the organization will permit; and the amount and the percentage of each expense item in the detailed income statement are compared with the amount and the percentage of the corresponding item for the previous fiscal period to ascertain where expenses may be reduced. The emphasis is primarily on increased sales and on decreased expenses. It is a natural and logical emphasis.

Over a period of years, the author has found that the typical business executive knows his income statement thoroughly. He can always find some place where expenses may be cut, perhaps the advertising budget, perhaps salesmen's expenses, salaries, wages, telephone, or even postage. Probably not more than one business executive out of ten gives a particle of thought or analysis to the balance sheet of his business. If he recognized the implications in the relationships between items in the balance sheet as clearly as he sees the implications of the relative size in individual items in the detailed income statement, he would realize the effect that operating policies which anticipate profits and losses have upon the future financial condition. With this understanding, he would be more careful in making decisions which once made cannot be changed, and so often result in anxiety, sleepless nights, and the necessity for the subsequent study of the income and expense figures.

Here are examples. If receivables are heavy and include a large number of past-due or questionable accounts, a charge-off for bad debts that is greater than usual will make inroads upon subsequent operating profits; if the inventory is top-heavy and prices should fall, nothing can stop a write-down, generally to that well-known accounting convention of "cost or market, whichever is lower," which will reduce or possibly wipe out operating profits; if fixed assets are excessive, the annual depreciation charges will represent an overbalanced charge to expense; if a large funded debt exists, the interest on that debt will eat into net profits. These conditions become evident from an analysis of the balance sheet. Skilled management realizes the intimate effects of these unbalanced conditions upon the future income statement, and so determines and follows financial policies that prevent such unsound conditions from arising in the first place. To do so, however, the individual must know what represents sound and unsound relationships in a balance sheet.

Therefore, the fundamental importance of understanding the delicate shades in meaning of balance sheet proportions must be emphasized. If a balance sheet is out of line in any important respect, intelligent operation and consistent sound financial policy are essential to bring affairs into a healthy condition over the years. No balance sheet will recover a healthy condition by itself; the management staff must guide the business consciously. Too many businesses are constantly adrift, blown by the variable winds of the season, and the conditions of their balance sheets are the unfortunate results of extraneous influences instead of conscious managerial direction. One should keep in mind that every management policy, or the absence of managerial policy, is reflected somewhere in the figures—in the balance sheet, in the income statement, or in the reconciliation of surplus. The extension of credit to customers in excess of their reasonable needs will be shown in excessive receivables and a heavy collection period; the purchase of merchandise in excess of reasonable requirements, because an executive officer is "sure" that prices are going up, will be shown in a larger inventory and a slower turnover; and expansion in plant facilities, home offices, or retail stores will be reflected in a large proportionate investment in fixed assets. The payment for an insurance policy will appear in the expense account, the return of merchandise will be evident in the income statement, and the payment of dividends will show in the surplus account.

In conclusion

There is no sure way to avoid risks in business, but there are tried methods for handling them, danger signs to look out for, and steps to take when faced with specific situations such as the following:

Fire, floods, earthquakes, hurricanes, tornadoes. Some areas of the country are more vulnerable than others to natural disaster. Keep such possibilities in mind when you set up your plant. Insure to cover these catastrophes

Migrations of population or industries with or without government instigation. These do not happen suddenly. They can be anticipated if you study the political and economic scene

Government fiat. Watch social trends; anticipate laws (police laws, health laws, zoning regulations) that may put you out of business

Cutthroat competition by monopolies. Tie up with other independents (in union there is strength); call on government for aid; sponsor legislation remedying situation

New legislation, such as tariff-law changes, wage and hour and labor laws, industry regulations. Anticipate these possible changes by keeping informed on trends. Join with others to see that such laws are fair and not discriminatory

Competition from new sources that have better products. Recognize the change, and make the more accepted product. Try to be the first to develop such products. Consider merging with powerful competitors

Foreign competition. Seek legislative protection; meet the competition with better products or lower cost

Shifts in consumer demand because of population decline, change in taste, changed standards in living, wider knowledge. Watch trends. Anticipate these social changes; improve your products or make new uses

Fluctuations in business. Anticipate them. Know when to expand and when to contract. Timing is important

Poor management (failure to plan or budget, lack of definite policy). Know what to do and how to do it. You must plan for the long term and budget for the short term. Guide your factors of sales and production and hold the reins of your business. You must fulfill and consummate your plans. Get vital information currently from your accounting and statistical departments to prevent lack of efficiency, spoilage, waste, theft, and embezzlement, and to detect high costs

Corrupt management. Get responsible management whose personal interests do not conflict with business aims, including profits for owners. Watch especially when there is absentee ownership. Use internal checks and controls. Have internal and independent audits; also professional surveys

High costs. Remedy this by such steps as: new equipment if this means lower costs after deducting interest, maintenance, and depreciation cost; check on relative costs of laborsaving equipment and equipment-saving labor; check on idle plant capacity—perhaps you can dispose of such plants and eliminate high depreciation charges; check on plant location to see whether it should not be changed; often you can write down the plant valuation to meet the true situation, and your current costs are not too high after all; slough off "deadwood" personnel; check on your techniques and modes of operation—are they obsolete?

Section 5

HOW TO BUY AND SELL A BUSINESS

BY

JAMES B. KOBAK

HOW TO BUY AND SELL A BUSINESS

1. Reasons for buying or selling a business

The reasons for buying or selling a business are many and varied. They can, from the buyer's point of view, range from an individual looking for a means of livelihood for himself (and involve a comparatively small investment, such as the acquisition of a retail outlet from a national chain under a franchise) to the acquisition of a substantial, multimillion dollar company by another of equal or greater size for diversification purposes.

As for the seller, he may want to retire, seek diversification, get financing, or have any number of other reasons for selling.

In many cases, while we speak of a buyer and seller, we are really concerned with a combination of two or more going businesses. And while one of the two will usually be the *survivor* in the combination (hence, the buyer), the objectives of both buyer and seller may be somewhat similar (for example, where diversification is sought).

Let us therefore first examine some of the reasons why companies are bought and sold, since the objectives of the buyer and seller must be clearly understood before a particular proposed purchase or sale can be intelligently appraised.

Diversification. Getting into other businesses may help a business grow and produce greater total profits than it can produce within the framework of its present operations. Additional profits may then help the company finance still more expansion, since its increased total assets plus profits may justify expanded credit lines from financial institutions. Diversification can also help overcome the problems of cyclical businesses—businesses which have peaks of manufacturing and selling seasons and then have periods of the year where there is very little activity. Heavy financing may be needed in certain periods of the year while the cash flow from the products produced and sold does not come in until a later period. A company like this may want to acquire a company whose operations are on an even keel throughout the year and which can produce the cash needed for the peak periods of production in the cyclical business.

Economies of operation. Combining two businesses that have similar operations (but perhaps in different markets) permits the combination of similar departments in both companies into one department. This eliminates a number of employees and equipment with resulting economies. For example, after a merger, the purchasing, engineering, or some other department of one of the companies may no longer be needed, with one department handling all the details for the combined company.

Acquisition of an existing function or product rather than developing a new one. A company may find it cheaper, more efficient, and a lot quicker to acquire from another company what the other company has already developed or has available than to develop its own. Thus one company may acquire another in order to—

> Pick up a product line the other company has rather than invest in developing that new product line itself
>
> Acquire a source of raw material
>
> Acquire an existing sales organization that can also handle its products or products it intends to develop rather than develop a (or expand its existing) sales organization
>
> Acquire the use of machinery and other equipment that the acquired company has rather than invest in the acquisition (including possible construction) of new machinery and equipment—and often have to wait a considerable period of time before the required machinery is finished and installed
>
> Acquire the use of research facilities and research personnel rather than undertake to set up its own research department
>
> Acquire the services of other key or specialized personnel that it might otherwise find difficult or impossible to acquire

Making use of excess capacity. A company may have excess plant capacity, or underutilized sales force or other employees. By acquiring an additional business, it can use this previously unused capacity and employee availability without any appreciable additional cost.

Retirement or estate planning. Where a company is closely held, selling may be part of a retirement or estate-planning maneuver. Sale of stock (or a substantial portion) can give the selling stockholder a substantial capital gain on which he may retire. (Or, while parting with most of the stock in the company, he may still retain some ownership, or stay on as an employee, adviser, or consultant.)

From an estate-planning view, the sale of a closely held family business to a publicly held, possibly highly diversified business—where a tax-free exchange of stock is the vehicle used for bringing about the sale—gives the sellers more easily marketable stock, stock that is easier to value. Part of this stock may later be sold off for capital gain; it may be used to make family gifts to transfer income to lower-bracket taxpayers (e.g., children and grandchildren). And the exchange of stock gives the former owners of a business which was perhaps in one line a holding in a business that is diversified and has more growth potential.

Diversified investment may also be an objective within the estate-planning objective.   Sale of a family business may produce proceeds that can then be invested in a number of diverse areas.   Sometimes the corporation will be kept intact as a holding (investment) company after it sells off the operating assets. In a number of cases, after the operating units were sold off, the companies invested in portfolios managed by the managers of a mutual fund or a closed-end regulated investment company with a further view of merging the company into the mutual fund or closed-end company after several years.   As a result, the owners of the stock in the family business, several years after the sale of the assets, ended up owning shares in a regulated investment company and thus got their diversification of investment that way.

These are just *some* of the reasons that a business is bought or sold.   Other reasons include attempted use of the net operating loss carry-over of one company by the other, squabbles among stockholders, attempts to avoid penalty taxes for unreasonable accumulations of earnings in closely held corporations, the desire to get rid of a losing proposition, and as many other reasons as there are business situations.

2. Information you need

The buyer, before it can determine whether it wants to acquire a business and how much it is willing to pay for it, obviously needs a good deal of information about the seller's business.   Where the deal is really a combination of two businesses—even though one is being acquired by the other—each side needs a lot of information about the other.   (The seller is often, in a sense, a buyer— as when the seller's stockholders are going to end up with stock in the buying company and the seller's business is going to be continued as a going entity within the framework of the buyer and the seller's executives and other personnel are going to continue in the capacities they occupied before.)

Before the deal is closed between the parties in principle—subject to considerable investigation, verification, occurrence of future events—the buyer will have at least examined the seller's industry, seller's status therein, and what information about the seller can be obtained from published and public records —which may range from newspaper and magazine articles (in the financial and trade press) to annual reports, proxy statements, and statements filed by the company with the SEC and stock exchanges (in the case of listed companies).

Once a tentative agreement is reached between the buyer and seller, it will almost always be subject to many conditions—verification that facts as represented by the seller are so, which usually involves a detailed investigation by the buyer and his specialists, the production of certain proofs or the giving of certain warranties by the seller, as well as the possible need of clearance from governmental or other public bodies (such as the Justice Department where antitrust problems may exist; the Internal Revenue Service about tax consequences of the transaction; the SEC about required registration statements; stock exchanges about listing requirements; and special regulatory bodies, where appropriate, such as the Federal Communications Commission, the Interstate Commerce Commission).

The investigation by the buyer may be conducted by the buyer's own executives who are experts in specialized areas (e.g., engineers, sales, marketing, or purchasing executives) as well as outside specialists—usually, at least, the buyer's attorney and accountant.

Depending on the nature of the business being acquired, the investigation will likely concern itself with some or all of the following areas: financial, legal, tax, production, marketing, management, and personnel.

Financial information. In examining the financial information about the seller, the buyer will, of course, want to be sure that the financial statements of the seller—the balance sheet and income statement—fairly present the seller's financial position. To this end, the buyer may want an audit of the seller by the buyer's accountant. Where the seller is regularly audited by a firm of certified public accountants, the buyer's accountant (and buyer) may be willing to rely on the other accounting firm's work sheets (if made available) to some extent.

It is very important in analyzing the accounting data of the seller to note the differences between the accounting methods used by the seller and the buyer. These differences can produce significantly different results, and the buyer must be aware of them when evaluating the benefits it expects to derive from combining its business with the seller's business. For example, differences may produce an entirely different amount of earnings per share than the buyer is anticipating.

Some of the items to be watched in this connection are—

Valuation of inventories. Does the seller use the LIFO (i.e., last-in–first-Out) method of valuation while buyer uses FIFO (first-in–first-Out)? Substantial differences in inventory values mean substantial differences in net profit (In a rising market, use of LIFO will produce a lower profit than use of FIFO.)

Depreciation methods. An accelerated depreciation method—e.g., 200%-declining-balance; sum-of-the-years-digits—bunches the depreciation deductions into the early years of the life of an asset and tends to reduce profits in those years

Research and development costs. Are these costs being charged off currently or are they being deferred and written off over a 5-year period, for example? An immediate charge-off, of course, will reduce current profits more than a spreading of these costs over a period of years

Funding of pension plans. Are both past service and current service costs being funded? Funding of past service costs will cut current profits

Executive compensation. Deferred compensation in one company may have to be compared with current bonus payments in the other. Current payments give current reductions and reduce current profits. Deferred arrangements—for example, stock options—will result in no current deductions

An examination and analysis of all the balance sheet and income statement items will be made.

Thus each of the asset accounts will be examined—

Cash flows will be projected
Receivables will be valued and turnover determined
Inventories—as to quantity, condition, sufficiency—will be examined
Working capital will be determined
Investments will be examined
Loans to officers will be investigated
Properties—depreciation policies, insurance coverage—will be analyzed
Other assets, such as goodwill, prepaid expenses, will be analyzed

On the liability side, all the liabilities will be examined and their status determined. Here, bank loans, accounts payable (is the seller taking advantage of sales discounts?), taxes payable, and any contingent liabilities will be examined.

On the income statement, sales income will be analyzed—probably including an examination of the trend over 10 or so years. An analysis of the manufacturing costs will involve looking into each major category and determining trends of each type of cost as related to the total costs. Similar analyses will be made with selling and general and administrative expenses.

Other analyses may include the profits from each type of operation (in a multioperation business) and from each branch or division in a multibranch or division business.

The profit trend over the past 10 or so years will be examined. Comparisons will also be made with other businesses in the field and with the buyer's own business (to determine, for example, the expected increase in profit per share after the acquisition of the seller's business). An examination of the seller's dividend policy and record will also be made.

Legal information. The extent of the lawyer's investigation may differ somewhat depending on the type of acquisition that is being made. If the buyer is acquiring assets only, for example, the possibility that the seller may have contingent liabilities that may not be disclosed would not matter to the buyer. But if the buyer were acquiring the stock of the selling corporation, any contingent liabilities that the seller had would be of vital concern to the buyer.

Here are some of the more important areas the legal investigation should cover:

Corporate status under state law. Rights of its stockholders; provisions in state law, what board of directors may do in negotiating sale, and what stockholder approval may be required

Corporate status and powers based on its own bylaws. Prior actions by the board of directors and approval of stockholders, status of its stock (fully paid for), outstanding stock options and employee agreements

Laws and regulations, state and Federal. Bulk sales laws, possible registration requirements (state and SEC), possible stock exchange requirements (where listed company is involved) of stockholder approval where there is no legal requirement for such action

Contracts by seller have to be examined. Status of licensing agreements, distributorships, collective-bargaining agreements, contracts with suppliers or customers, questions of enforceability, assignability, antitrust violation, renegotiation clauses have to be considered in connection with the contracts

Liabilities of the seller must be examined. Restrictions on seller's activities required by lenders, for example. Determination that there are no undisclosed contingent liabilities. Action to be taken to protect buyer against possible undisclosed liabilities (including keeping payment to seller in escrow for period of time)

Seller's properties. Examined and analyzed with a view to determining seller's title, encumbrances or liens on the property, leases on the property to others, chattel mortgages on personal property, intangibles such as patents—and strength of patent position, time left for patent to run (similar analysis for trademarks, trade names, copyrights)

Antitrust considerations. Will acquisition of seller create antitrust problems? (consultation with Justice Department may be necessary) ; does the seller itself have potential antitrust problems or has it had any?

Is a broker involved? Who will pay his commission?

Tax information. For the most part, the tax considerations will be concerned with the acquisition itself, i.e., will it be a tax-free or taxable acquisition? If tax-free, what route will be followed, who is to apply for a ruling from the Internal Revenue Service (if a ruling will be applied for), or is counsel's opinion to be relied on? If taxable, how will the purchase price be allocated over the assets to be acquired?

In addition, the tax status of the seller will be examined to determine what years have been examined by IRS and what years are still open and unexamined. Are any tax problems on appeal within the Internal Revenue Service? Or in the courts? Are there any claims for refund outstanding? Does the seller have a net operating loss carryover and is it available?

Production information. Production information will deal with just what methods of production the seller uses, materials handling, assembly methods, quality control and inspection, storage and warehousing, efficiency, safety, and similar items.

Marketing information. Here, the buyer will want to analyze the product line, acceptance of the product, markets and pricing policies, types of distribution used, advertising policies and budgets, sales organization and sales methods, sales planning, and forecasting.

Management and personnel information. The buyer will be interested in the managerial structure (the organization chart), officers and directors and their duties, number of departments and employees in each, key employees, employment contracts, management leadership abilities, lines of succession, whether key employees will leave if seller is taken over by buyer, whether there will be an overlap of personnel after the takeover with economies dictating the release of some of the seller's personnel, union contracts, job classifications, working rules and regulations, compensation arrangements (bonuses, fringe benefits, vacation policies).

3. Types of purchases and sales

The purchase and sale of a business involves either the transfer of assets of the business or transfer of ownership to the business entity. Thus, the buyer can either buy individual assets or the stock of the corporation owning the assets.

The purchase can be for cash, for stock of the buyer, for obligations of the buyer, or a combination of two or more of these. Where the buyer uses its own stock to make the purchase, we are able to have (if the tests are met) a tax-free transaction. That means that the seller will not have immediate taxable income at the time of the sale on the gain he realizes. (Because where the gain is not recognized for tax purposes, the seller's basis for his stock is not "stepped up" to the value which he received on the sale, the tax impact on the gain has merely been postponed until the ultimate disposition of the stock received by the seller in the transaction.)

Purchase of stock versus purchase of assets. Tax considerations loom large, of course, among the considerations involved in the purchase or sale of a business.

Stockholders of the selling company usually prefer to sell stock. If the sale is a taxable one, the gain will likely be a long-term capital gain, taxable at favorable tax rates (the tax will not be more than 25 percent of the gain). If the corporation has to sell its assets, special precautions must be taken to avoid a double tax: once, at the corporate level, when the corporation sells its assets; again, when the proceeds are distributed to the stockholders in liquidation of the selling corporation.

The buyer, on the other hand, normally prefers to buy assets. For one thing, the buyer will get as its basis for the assets it acquires what it pays for them. Thus, it can then compute its depreciation deductions on this basis. If, however, the buyer acquires a company by buying its stock, it will pay fair market value for the stock (which will reflect the fair market value of the assets held by the corporation being acquired). The assets may have greatly appreciated in value in the hands of the corporation being acquired. So the corporation's basis for those assets may be considerably less than their fair market value. Nevertheless, since only the corporate stock has been sold, the corporation has remained intact and that lower basis will continue to be its basis after the stock ownership has changed hands. This, of course, is a very undesirable result for the purchaser. It is possible, however, for the corporation to buy stock, liquidate the purchased corporation within 2 years, and step up the basis of the assets received in the liquidation from this newly acquired subsidiary to the amount paid for the stock. (This purchase and liquidation route, however, may not be used if the transaction is to be tax-free to the seller.)

A major nontax consideration, from the buyer's viewpoint, that militates in favor of a purchase of assets rather than a purchase of stock, involves possible undisclosed liabilities. Where assets are purchased, the buyer does not have to be concerned about any possible liabilities of the seller that are not apparent at the time of the purchase, but which come to the fore afterwards. If, however, the buyer acquires stock, the corporate entity of the purchased corporation remains intact, and liabilities that had their origin in actions or events taking place before the purchase may first arise afterwards. To assure against undisclosed or contingent liabilities, the buyer will usually require some sort of warranties from the seller, possibly even retaining part of the purchase price in escrow for a period of time to provide the funds to repay the buyer should these liabilities arise.

4. Purchase or pooling of interests

Where the purchase is made with the buyer's stock and the price paid for the seller's business exceeds the book value of the seller's assets, the excess—if the transaction is treated for accounting purposes as a "purchase"—is then shown on the buyer's books and financial statements as goodwill.

On the other hand, if the transaction can be treated as a "pooling of interests" rather than a purchase, the respective book values of the buyer's and seller's assets are added together and the excess that would show up as goodwill if the transaction were a purchase is charged to surplus.

The advantages to the purchaser of a pooling-of-interests treatment over the purchase treatment lie in the reporting of earnings after the acquisition.

If goodwill was entered on the books—if the purchase approach has to be used—the goodwill will normally be amortized over a period of years (10 years is quite common). That means that in each of the 10 years, the purchaser will show a deduction on its income statement for one-tenth of the goodwill, thus reducing its current earnings and earnings per share reported to its stockholders. At the same time, the purchaser will not be entitled to a tax deduction for the goodwill amortization deduction each year.

Assume the buyer pays $2,000,000 in stock for the seller. The seller's business produces $200,000 a year in profits after taxes. But the goodwill factor in the purchase is $1,500,000. Consequently, each year for 10 years, the buyer will write off $150,000 of goodwill, thereby reducing the reported earnings from the purchased business to $50,000.

At the end of 10 years, instead of showing that it has recouped its entire purchase price from the earnings of the business it purchased, the buyer will show only that it has recouped 25 percent of the purchasing price.

Where a pooling-of-interest approach is used, no goodwill is shown, and the full $200,000 of annual profits will be shown.

When pooling-of-interest approach is available. The criteria for the allowance of the use of the pooling-of-interest approach as recognized by the Securities and Exchange Commission for listed companies and the American Institute of Certified Public Accountants as a guide to the accounting profession are as follows:

> The seller's owners, to a substantial degree, have to continue as owners of the combined business. Hence, the pooling of interest approach is available only where the buyer pays all or most of the purchase price in its common stock
>
> The seller's business has to be continued after the acquisition by the buyer. If the buyer disposes of a large part of the purchase or discontinues it, the pooling-of-interest approach is not available
>
> Generally, the management of the seller has to continue to have a voice in the management of the business after the combination of the two
>
> The AICPA research bulletin on pooling of interests assumes that if the seller gets no more than 10 percent of the buyer's voting interest, the transaction will be a purchase rather than a pooling of interests. However, the SEC has approved pooling of interests where the seller has acquired substantially less than 10 percent of the voting interest in the buyer

5. Allocation of purchase price

Where there is a sale of assets in a taxable transaction, it becomes important for the parties to allocate the purchase price among the assets transferred. In an arm's-length transaction, where each side negotiates from an interest opposite to the other (which will often be the case as far as tax considerations go), the values that they put on the various assets in allocating the purchase price will usually stand up for tax purposes. Where one side is indifferent to the allocation—or not aware of the tax consequences (and not advised by a qualified tax practitioner)—the values set for the advantage of the other side may subsequently be overturned by the Internal Revenue Service or the courts when the tax consequences of the transaction come under the scrutiny of the tax people or the courts.

Normally, buyer and seller will have diametrically opposite desires in allocating the purchase price to the various assets.

The sale of goodwill and land will give the seller capital gain and it will want to assign as high as possible value to these assets. On the other hand, neither of these assets are depreciable by the buyer; consequently, it would like to assign relatively low values to these assets.

On the purchase of depreciable assets, the buyer is willing to allocate a fairly high value because the cost is recoverable via depreciation deductions—and accelerated depreciation (i.e., 150%-declining-balance) may be available. The seller is able to get capital gain on the sale of depreciable property used in its business. It would thus seem, at first blush, that the seller, too, would be willing to allocate a fairly high value to depreciable assets. However, to the extent that the seller's gain on the sale of these assets reflects a recovery of previously deducted depreciation, there may be "depreciation recapture." And depreciation recapture, to the extent it does not exceed the gain, is taxable as ordinary income.

With personal property (e.g., machinery, equipment, other non-real-estate items), the amount of depreciation that is subject to recapture is any depreciation claimed after 1961. With buildings, depreciation recapture is limited to the excess of accelerated depreciation over what straight-line depreciation would have been. (Here, we are concerned only with depreciation taken after 1963.) And not all of the excess of accelerated depreciation over straight-line is subject to recapture—for each month in excess of 20 months that the property was held by the seller, the amount of depreciation subject to recapture is reduced by 1 percent. Thus, if the property were held more than 10 years there would be no depreciation recapture (10 years equals 120 months, and the 100 months in excess of 20 months of holding period would eliminate 100 percent of the depreciation subject to recapture). Also, of course, if the seller had claimed only straight-line depreciation, there would be no excess depreciation subject to recapture.

Another problem involved in allocating the purchase price to depreciable property is the investment credit. The buyer, to the extent it is buying personal property, will be entitled to an investment credit of up to 7 percent of the cost of the property (subject to certain limitations as to expected holding period, its current taxable income). The seller, on the other hand, may have received the benefit of the investment credit on certain items it is now selling. If those items have not been held for the period of time upon which the investment-credit computation was based, the seller may now have to repay part of the investment credit to the government.

The tax benefits and detriments that may arise for either side on the sale of depreciable assets will usually be taken into account in arriving at an allocation of values to these assets.

When we come to inventory items—items the buyer will sell in the ordinary course of the business—the buyer will want to allocate as high as possible values. The higher the value, the less taxable profit the buyer will realize when it sells these items in the ordinary course of the business. The seller, of course, wants to allocate as low as possible values to inventories because the gain it realizes on the sale of these items will result in ordinary taxable income to it.

Another area that may present allocation difficulties involves the seller's agreement not to compete. There are two problems here: (1) the nature of the agreement, and (2) the allocation of purchase price.

Payments to the seller for its agreement not to compete are fully deductible by the buyer and are taxable as ordinary income to the seller. On the other hand, if the payments are part of the package of the purchase of goodwill and the noncompete agreement is really a means of protecting the goodwill, the buyer's payments are deemed part of the purchase price of the goodwill with no deduction for the buyer and capital gain for the seller. Thus, if the payment is clearly for noncompetition, the buyer will want a high value allocation to the payment and the seller will want a low value set for it. On the other hand, if the payment is truly for the purchase of the goodwill, the buyer will want a very low value allocated to it while the seller will want a high value set.

When the noncompete question comes before the courts, they are likely to recognize a separate noncompete agreement if—

It is separable from the other assets

It is bargained for between the parties realistically and in good faith. The fact that the covenant not to compete is listed separately in the contract between the buyer and seller with a price allocated to it goes a long way to help establish that there was a separate covenant bargained for

There is a basis in fact for the noncompete agreement—that is, reasonable men in similar circumstances would bargain for such an agreement; there was a real business need for it. In other words, without the agreement, there was a real possibility that the seller could and would go into competition with the buyer after the sale

The price set for the covenant was reasonable and not merely arbitrary (It is also helpful to show that the other side was aware of the tax consequences to it from the allocation of part of the purchase price to the covenant)

From the foregoing, it is easy to see that in an arm's-length transaction, the buyer and seller will have opposite aims for the most part (due to the tax consequences to each) in allocating the purchase price to the various assets being sold. Knowing what all the tax consequences are enables them to bargain hard and arrive at an allocation that will probably be fair and stand up for tax purposes.

6. Taxable transactions—the buyer's considerations

A taxable transaction, whether it takes the form of the purchase of assets or stock, will usually be for cash or cash and obligations of the buyer. Because of the tax consequences to both buyer and seller, the transaction may be cast in specialized forms. Let us first examine some of the buyer's problems and methods used to solve them.

Using the purchased company's own funds to help pay for the purchase. The corporation being acquired may have a surplus of cash. The buyer would like to use that cash to help pay for the stock. (If the seller's stockholders attempted to withdraw that cash from the corporation prior to the sale and thereby reduce the value of the company and the funds needed by the purchaser to buy it, the seller's stockholders would likely end up with a taxable dividend.)

A solution to this problem is to have the buyer buy only a portion of the seller's stockholders' stock from them. Then the remaining stock the seller's stockholders own will be redeemed from them by the corporation, using its cash-surplus funds. Since the sellers will be parting with their entire interest in the corporation at the time of the redemption, the redemption will not be treated as a dividend. And after the redemption, the stock the buyer bought will be the only outstanding stock of the corporation; so the buyer will have acquired ownership of the selling corporation. In two published rulings, IRS has given approval to this approach.

Using the purchased corporation's future earnings to help pay for its purchase. By making an installment purchase, requiring payment of the sales price over a period of years, the buyer can use the purchased company's own future earnings to help pay for its purchase. It is important that the obligation to pay the purchase price be in the same company that has the earnings. Otherwise to get the earnings from the company having the earnings to the company or individuals owing the money may involve a taxable dividend.

Where the purchaser is a corporation, it can liquidate the purchased company (where it has purchased stock) and acquire all of the purchased company's assets in that way. Then, the future earnings will arise in the purchasing corporation and it will have them to meet its obligations on the purchase price. (Where assets are purchased in the first place, of course, the purchaser will have the new business within its corporate entity to begin with.) If the purchase was negotiated by individuals, e.g., where the stockholders of a company propose to buy the stock of the stockholders of the selling corporation, it is important for them first to organize a corporation and have the corporation (not the individuals) buy the stock. Then the purchasing corporation can liquidate the purchased corporation as indicated above.

Stepping up the basis of the assets of the purchased corporation. As previously indicated, a big problem when the buyer must buy stock is that the value of the assets in the corporation being acquired may have appreciated considerably in its hands.   But the basis of those assets remains unchanged within the corporation being bought, even though the purchase price paid by the buyer reflects the appreciation in value of the assets in the purchased corporation.

It is possible, however, for the purchaser to step up the basis of the assets in the purchased corporation by liquidating that corporation.   The tax law provides for this step-up.   To get it, the buying corporation has to buy at least 80 percent of the stock of the acquired corporation within a 12-month period. Then, if the corporation whose stock was bought is liquidated within 2 years of the last purchase of the stock that gave the purchaser the required 80 percent (pursuant to a plan of liquidation adopted within that 2-year period), the assets received in liquidation of the purchased corporation take as their bases a proportionate part of the basis of the stock that was bought.   The price that the buyer paid for the stock is allocated among the assets received in liquidation of the purchased corporation in proportion to their relative market values.

7. Taxable transactions—the seller's considerations

As previously indicated, where the seller sells assets, it will realize capital gain on some items and ordinary income on others.   Land, goodwill, and depreciable assets (to the extent the gain exceeds any depreciation recapture) will result in capital gain.   Sale of inventory and payment for agreements not to compete will give ordinary income.   Allocation of the sales price (as previously indicated) thus becomes extremely important.

When the assets are sold by a corporation with the intention of going out of business, a problem of double taxation may arise insofar as the stockholders of the selling corporation are concerned.   The corporation will have one tax on the gain it realizes on the sale of the assets.   Then, when the corporation is liquidated, the stockholders will receive the after-tax proceeds of the sale and will be taxed again to the extent that the proceeds they receive exceed their bases for the stock in the liquidated corporation.   That is one reason the stockholders prefer to sell their stock; then there is a "clean" capital-gain deal. The stockholders realize capital gains for the difference between the sales price and the bases for the stock they are selling.

Where a sale of stock is not possible, a double tax can be avoided on the sale of assets by the corporation if the selling corporation goes through a so-called 12-month liquidation.

How the 12-month liquidation works.   The selling corporation adopts a plan of liquidation.   It must then distribute all its assets in liquidation within 12 months after adoption of the plan of liquidation (except to the extent it holds back assets to meet liabilities of the corporation).   During that 12-month period, to the extent the corporation sells its assets (including bulk sale of its inventories) it is not taxed on any gain.   The stockholders are taxed in the usual way when the corporation is liquidated—that is, they have taxable gain to the extent that the value of what they receive in the distribution in liquidation exceeds their bases for the stock in the liquidating corporation.

Since the corporation pays no tax on the gains it realizes during the 12-month liquidation period, there is only one tax paid on the sale of the assets—the tax paid by the stockholders as a result of the liquidation.

Note that the rule that makes the gains nontaxable to the corporation during the 12-month period also makes losses nondeductible by the corporation. Thus, if some of the assets are to be sold at a gain and some at a loss, the corporation might first sell the assets at a loss before it adopts its plan of liquidation. These losses would then be deductible to offset the corporation's operating income. Thereafter the corporation can adopt its plan of liquidation and sell the other assets at a gain and avoid the tax on the gain.

The difficulty with the 12-month liquidation approach is that it will not work where an installment sale is made. Why this is so is explained below.

How installment sales work. As previously indicated, buyers will often want to pay for the business out of future earnings. Consequently, it is not at all uncommon that a taxable sale will be for other than all cash. The buyer will pay part cash and part in the form of obligations. (This can be the case whether the buyer is buying assets or stock.)

Since the seller is not receiving all cash in the year of sale, it usually does not want to pay the tax on the entire gain immediately—it, or its stockholders, would like to spread out the tax over the period that the payments from the buyer will be received. This is permissible under the tax law if the seller elects to report the sale as an installment sale. To do so, the seller may not receive in the year of sale more than 30 percent of the sales price.

For example, if the sales price is $1,000,000 and the gain is $250,000, 25 percent of each payment received will be treated as income in the year received, provided, of course, no more than $300,000 (30 percent of the $1,000,000) is received in the year of sale.

Where the buyer is taking assets subject to (or is assuming) obligations (for example, a mortgage on one of the properties being transferred), the gain is compared to the so-called contract price (sales price minus obligations taken over by the buyer) to determine what portion of each payment is taxable. In our example above, if of the $1,000,000 sales price, $250,000 is being paid by the buyer by taking over certain properties subject to the $250,000 obligation, the gain would still be the same, $250,000. However, one-third of each payment ($250,000/$750,000) would be taxable. Since the seller would be receiving only $750,000 from the buyer when all the payments are made, the seller would still be taxable only on $250,000. In this case, too, the 30 percent requirement still applies to the sales price, and so installment sale reporting would be available as long as no more than $300,000 was received in the year of sale.

Because interest is taxable as ordinary income while the gain on the sale is likely capital gain, a practice was often resorted to of not calling for interest on the unpaid installments. The sales price was adjusted to, in effect, provide for the interest. The tax law was amended, however, to take care of this situation. If less than 4 percent simple interest is called for in the contracts, a 5 percent interest rate will be imputed. Each installment payment is discounted back to the date of sale at a 5 percent rate to find the value of that installment at the date of sale. The difference between that discounted value and the full amount of the installment is then treated as interest and taxed as such.

In addition to creating ordinary interest income, the discounting back of the installments reduces the sales price. That can create disastrous results for the seller. If the sales price is reduced sufficiently, the payments received by the seller in the year of sale may exceed 30 percent of this recomputed sales price and the entire gain may thus become taxable in the year of sale since installment reporting will not be available. Consequently, the safest course to pursue is to call for interest on the unpaid installments in the sales contract— at a rate of at least 4 percent simple interest.

Why installment sales are not available in a 12-month liquidation. As indicated above, when there is a 12-month liquidation, the corporation pays no tax on the sales of the assets. However, the stockholders do have a tax to pay on the liquidation. And the gain on liquidation is computed by comparing the fair market value of the properties distributed to the stockholders with the bases of their stock in the corporation being liquidated. Among the assets distributed to the stockholders will be the buyer's installment obligations. And the value of these obligations will be included in the package of assets being distributed to the stockholders. The stockholders will have to pay a tax immediately on the gain determined by including the value of the installment obligations in the proceeds received. Only to the extent that the fair market value of the buyer's obligations are worth less than face value, will the stockholders escape an immediate tax. Then, when the full face value of the installments is paid to the stockholders, when the obligations are paid off, the difference between the face value of those obligations and the value placed on them at the time of the liquidation will be taxable at that time. But that difference will be treated as ordinary income even though the transaction giving rise to the obligations resulted in a capital gain at the time of the sale.

There are two highly specialized situations where you can sell corporate assets and still get the benefits of installment sales, however. One deals with a so-called 1-month liquidation. The other requires that the selling corporation be a Subchapter S corporation.

How to use a 1-month liquidation. In a 1-month liquidation, the gain to the stockholders on liquidation is computed in the usual manner. That gain is then compared to the corporation's earnings and profits. To the extent of the earnings and profits, the gain is taxable as ordinary income (capital gain, if the stockholder itself is a corporation). Then, if the corporation had any cash and stock or securities acquired after 1953, the total of the cash and stocks and securities is first reduced by the amount of the corporation's earnings and profits and the excess is taxable to the stockholders as capital gain. Any gain remaining after applying the earnings and profits and the cash and stocks and securities is not taxable to the stockholders.

For example, assume the gain to the stockholders (computed in the regular way) would be $1,000,000. At the time of liquidation, the corporation had $100,000 of accumulated earnings and profits and cash plus stock and securities acquired after 1953 totalling $150,000. In this case, $150,000 of the $1,000,000 gain would be taxable to the stockholders—$100,000 as ordinary income and $50,000 as capital gain. (If the stockholders were corporations, the entire $150,000 gain would be capital gain.)

As can easily be seen, the 1-month liquidation is valuable only where the corporation has a negligible amount of earnings and profits, cash, and stocks and securities acquired after 1953, but does have considerable assets that have appreciated in value.

Where the corporation has no earnings and profits or cash or stock and securities problem, it can go through a 1-month liquidation and liquidate its assets to the stockholders, who would receive those assets without paying a tax on the gain. The stockholders' bases for the assets received, however, would not be their market value; the bases would be the stockholders' bases for the stock they had owned in the liquidated corporation. But the stockholders could then sell those assets in an installment sale and report the sale under the installment method.

If this approach to the sale of assets is used, it is important that the sale be negotiated on behalf of the stockholders and that in no way it can be said that the sale was really negotiated on behalf of the corporation. Otherwise, IRS will step in and say that the sale was really made by the corporation, that the corporation realized the gain and then made the distribution to the stockholders. That was the position the government had taken in many sales made after liquidation before the 12-month liquidation rule was put on the books. And the 12-month liquidation rule was enacted into law to avoid the problems of showing whether the sale was really made on behalf of the corporation or the stockholders. Since, in this case (where the installment sale method of reporting the gain is desired) the 12-month liquidation route is not available, it becomes extremely important that the negotiations to sell be clearly made by the stockholders on their behalf and not on the corporation's behalf.

If the 1-month liquidation is to be used, certain technical rules must be met. The corporation must first adopt a plan of liquidation. Then the stockholders must file elections with the district director to have the 1-month liquidation rules apply. These elections must be filed within 30 days after adoption of the plan of liquidation. Elections have to be filed by 80 percent of the voting power of the noncorporate stockholders, and 80 percent of the voting power of corporate stockholders must also elect. After the elections have been timely filed, the corporation must make a distribution in liquidation within 1 calendar month of all of its assets (other than assets needed to meet liabilities). The month of liquidation need not be in the same year in which the plan of liquidation was adopted, however.

Use of Subchapter S corporation. To begin with, since a Subchapter S corporation can have no more than 10 stockholders or one class of stock, its availability is limited.

Where a corporation is a Subchapter S corporation, however, it does not pay any tax on its income or gains—these income and gains are passed through to the stockholders in proportion to their stockholdings. So, were a Subchapter S corporation to make an installment sale of all of its assets, it could elect the installment method of accounting and pass through the gains to the stockholders each year as it collected the installments. (In other words, the Subchapter S corporation would be kept alive after the sale for as long as it collected the installments.) Consequently the corporate assets could be sold, the installment method used, and only one capital-gains tax paid—by the stockholders.

The availability of this approach was severely curtailed by legislation passed in 1966 affecting taxable years beginning after April 14, 1966. Under this new rule, unless the corporation was a Subchapter S corporation for the 3 years preceding the year in which it realizes a capital gain (or unless it has been a Subchapter S corporation during its entire corporate life if it has not been in existence during all of the preceding 3 years), the capital gains can be taxed on the corporate level and only the after-tax gain is passed through to the stockholders (to be taxed again to them as capital gain). This new rule has effectively blocked the switchover to Subchapter S in anticipation of the sale of the corporation's assets. Where, however, an installment sale is made, but the gain recognized each year does not exceed $25,000, this Subchapter S approach to the sale of the corporate assets in an installment sale can still be used. The reason: The new rule does not tax the first $25,000 of capital gain to the Subchapter S corporation.

Note this, however, if you use the Subchapter S approach: A Subchapter S corporation loses its status as a Subchapter S corporation if more than 20 percent of its gross receipts consists of interest, dividends, royalties, and capital gains from the sale of securities. Where an installment sale is made, the selling corporation will have interest income (either called for in the contract or imputed). It is thus necessary to watch the figures closely if the corporation is to retain its Subchapter S status.

8. Nontaxable transactions

The sale and purchase of a business can take the form of a nontaxable transaction. To qualify, the transaction has to be part of a plan of reorganization. This requires the formal adoption of the plan by the parties to the reorganization.

The transaction, in a nontaxable sale and purchase, will take one of the following three forms:

1. A statutory merger or consolidation
2. An exchange of the stock of the selling corporation solely for voting stock of the purchasing corporation
3. A transfer of substantially all of the assets of the selling corporation for voting stock of the purchasing corporation. Here, if solely voting stock is given for at least 80 percent of the assets, other types of property may be given for the other 20 percent

Statutory merger or consolidation. In this type of acquisition, the selling corporation is merged into the buying corporation and they become one. (Technically, in a consolidation, the buying and selling corporation both become part of a new third corporation. However, the line between mergers and consolidations is not that clear, because the statutory language in the various states differs.) The important thing to remember, however, is that the merger or consolidation must be made pursuant to the laws of the state or states of incorporation of the various corporations involved in the transaction.

The merger in fact resembles the acquisition of the sellers' assets by the buyer (with the seller going out of existence). The seller's stockholders then turn in their stock in the seller corporation and receive stock or securities in the buying corporation.

To the extent that the seller's stockholders receive nothing other than stock and securities of the buying corporation, the transaction can be entirely tax-free. (It makes no difference whether all the stock received is voting stock or not; it may be partially preferred stock, for example.) To the extent the seller's stockholders receive other than stock and securities, they have "boot." Also if the face amount of the securities (e.g., bonds) received by the seller's stockholders exceed the face amount of securities given up by the seller's stockholders, that excess is also boot. (Thus, if the seller's stockholders give up no securities—only stock—and receive some securities, the face amount of the securities received constitutes boot.)

Boot can be taxable. To the extent the boot does not exceed the gain to the stockholder, the boot is taxed. Where the boot has the effect of a distribution of a dividend, it will be taxed as a dividend; otherwise, the stockholder will have capital gain.

For example, in a statutory merger of Corporation B into Corporation A, a stockholder in Corporation B turns in one share of Corporation B stock for one share of Corporation A common, one share of Corporation A preferred, a Corporation A debenture, and $5 in cash. Assume the following values:

One share of A common	$100
One share of A preferred	50
One Corporation A debenture	20
Cash	5
Total	$175

Assume the stockholder's basis for his one share of B stock he turns in is $100. His gain is $75. But only $25 of the gain (the debenture plus the cash) is taxable since the boot of $25 is less than the gain.

The basis of the assets acquired by the purchasing corporation in the merger —or in any tax-free reorganization—is the same basis as the transferor had for the assets increased by any gain taxable to the transferor.

As for the stockholders, their basis for the stock or securities received is the basis of their old stock or securities reduced by the amount of boot received and increased by the gain realized. Where the entire boot is taxable, the net result is that the basis for the new stock and securities is the basis of the old. (The basis of any boot received is its fair market value.) In our example above, the stockholder would have a $20 basis for the debenture (the fair market value of that boot); cash, of course, is worth the cash. His basis for the A common and A preferred would be the $100 basis he had for his old B stock, allocated according to relative market value. So, the A common would get a basis of $66.67 and the A preferred would get a basis of $33.33.

Stock-for-stock transactions. In this type of acquisition, the purchaser pays *solely* voting stock of its corporation for the stock of the selling company. After the exchange of stock, the buyer has to be in control of the seller. That means the buyer has to end up with at least 80 percent of the voting power in the selling corporation plus 80 percent of the total shares of all other classes of stock. Since the requirement is that the buyer have control immediately after the acquisition, it need not acquire control in the transaction. For example, Corporation A may already own 25 percent of the stock of Corporation B. A subsequent transaction in which it acquired at least another 55 percent of the B stock could qualify as a tax-free, stock-for-stock transaction. And the acquisition of the 55 percent over a reasonable period of time (for example where a company advertises for tenders of stock of the corporation of which it is seeking to acquire control) will be treated as one transaction.

The stock-for-stock approach is useful mostly when the selling company's stock is in the hands of a few stockholders. Where there is a publicly held, widely distributed stock issue involved, the only way the buyer can acquire the necessary 80 percent control is to ask for tenders of the stock. This is usually done only when management of the company sought to be acquired is not amenable to the acquisition.

Another difficulty the stock-for-stock approach presents is basis. As indicated above, the acquiring company's basis for what it gets in a tax-free reorganization is the transferor's basis. Where a stock-for-stock approach is used, the acquiring corporation's basis for the stock it gets (and, eventually, for the assets of the acquired corporation if it is liquidated after it is acquired) is the total of the bases of each of the stockholders of the acquired corporation whose stock the acquiring corporation acquired. This presents several problems: first, the need of getting each transferring stockholder's basis for the stock he has turned in (this can be a tremendous problem where more than a few stockholders are involved). Another problem is that the acquiring corporation will not know what its basis for the acquired corporation will be (regardless of how much it pays for it) unless it knows in advance what basis each of the stockholders of the corporation to be acquired has for his stock (again, an impossible task when you are dealing with more than a comparatively small number of stockholders).

Where the stock-for-stock approach of acquiring a company is used, there cannot be any boot. The law specifically states that the transfer of the selling company's stock to the buying company must be *solely* for the buying company's voting stock. And that "solely" requirement has been strictly construed by the Supreme Court. (It is, however, possible to use cash to round off fractional shares in an otherwise stock-for-stock exchange.)

It is also possible to give contingent rights to additional stock in a stock-for-stock exchange without violating the "solely" rule. The Treasury has ruled that a valid stock-for-stock exchange had occurred where the agreement called for the issuance of additional voting stock to the transferors of the other company's stock if the earnings of the acquired corporation reached a certain level. What influenced the Treasury to rule favorably was that only additional voting stock could be issued, the right to the additional stock was not assignable, and the transferors were not entitled to receive any dividends on the possible additional stock issued to them.

Stock-for-assets acquisition. In this type of acquisition, the acquiring corporation acquires substantially all the assets of the selling corporation. In exchange, the acquiring company gives solely its voting stock. However, the requirement for solely voting stock is not so strict here as in a stock-for-stock exchange. Here, if solely voting stock is given for at least 80 percent of the value of the assets acquired, other property (cash, securities, etc.) may be given for the remainder of the assets. But the other property is treated as boot and rules for the taxation of boot (as explained in the previous section on statutory mergers) would apply here, too.

In a typical stock-for-assets exchange, Corporation A would acquire all the assets of Corporation B in exchange for voting stock of A (plus, possibly other property—within the 20 percent allowable limit). Corporation B would then distribute the A stock (plus any other property) to its (B's) stockholders in exchange for their B stock. If all the B stockholders received was A stock, the B stockholders would have a completely nontaxable transaction. If boot were also distributed, the B stockholders could have some taxable income (as explained in the section on statutory mergers).

Corporation A may acquire the assets of Corporation B or it may have its subsidiary acquire the assets even though A issues its own stock for the assets. If, however, part of the stock issued were A's stock and part voting stock of the subsidiary, there would not be a tax-free reorganization.

It is not unusual for the acquiring corporation in a stock-for-assets transaction to assume liabilities of the corporation whose assets it is acquiring. If the acquiring corporation is given solely voting stock, the assumption of liabilities presents no problems. The assumption of liabilities is ignored in determining whether the rules for a stock-for-assets acquisition has been met. If, however, boot is also given, the assumption of the liabilities is added to the other boot to see whether the boot exceeds the 20 percent limit on boot explained above.

9. Acquiring loss corporations

Often a major motivating factor in the acquisition of a business is that the business has a net operating loss carry-over for tax purposes. If that loss is usable by the acquiring company, it means that the acquiring company can earn profits up to the amount of the loss carry-over without having to pay any taxes on that profit, since the carry-over loss deduction will offset those profits. Consequently, the availability of a loss carry-over may make a company an attractive acquisition. However, there are many barriers to the acquisition of a loss carry-over and the possibilities of having it available after the acquisition must be carefully explored.

Nontaxable transactions. Where there is a tax-free reorganization (other than a stock-for-stock acquisition), the carry-over loss of the acquired corporation is available to the combined entity (that is the acquiring corporation in a statutory merger or where substantially all of the assets of the loss corporation were acquired for solely voting stock for at least 80 percent of the assets). But even there there are some restrictive rules.

The stockholders of the loss corporation must end up with at least a 20 percent stock interest in the acquiring corporation if the acquiring corporation is to get the full use of the acquired loss carry-over. For each percentage point below 20 percent that the loss corporation stockholders lack, the acquiring corporation loses 5 percent of the loss carry-over. For example, if Corporation A acquires all the assets of Corporation B in exchange solely for A voting stock and, as a result, the former B stockholders end up with 15 percent of the total

A stock outstanding, Corporation *A* is entitled to use only 75 percent of *B*'s carry-over loss.

In addition to the restriction on the use of the carry-over loss in terms of the stock interest with which the loss company stockholders end up, other restrictions (e.g., tax-avoidance motives) can prevent the use of the acquired loss carry-over. (These restrictions are discussed later.)

Taxable transactions. If Corporation *A* buys all the assets of Corporation *B* in a taxable transaction, there is no way it can claim any carry-over losses to which *B* was entitled. *A* is a corporate entity separate and apart from *B*; and the loss arose in Corporation *B* (which could even still be in existence after selling all of its assets to *A*).

If Corporation *A* buys all the stock of Corporation *B*, *B* continues in existence as a separate corporate entity and can continue to use its carry-over loss— if certain rules are met. These rules apply where there has been a change in ownership of 50 percentage points or more. (Where Corporation *A* buys all of *B*'s stock, there has been more than a 50 percentage point change of ownership). In that case, the acquired corporation must continue to carry on substantially the same trade or business as before the stock ownership change for a stated measuring period or else the entire carry-over loss is lost forever. The measuring period is the remaining taxable year in which the stock ownership change occurred plus the next full taxable year.

While the corporation must continue to carry on substantially the same trade or business during the measuring period, new businesses may be added to it; thus, the acquiring corporation can add other businesses to the acquired business so as to produce profits (which can be absorbed by the carry-over loss). But it must continue the old business as well. The continuation must not be a mere minor portion of the old business but *substantially* the same business. In this connection, the Treasury and the courts have been at odds on the consequences of carrying on the same type of business but at a different location and with different customers. The Treasury argues this is not substantially the same business while the courts say it is.

Here, too, if you meet the tests above for deducting the loss carry-over, tax-avoidance purpose may still rise to plague you and cause the loss not to be allowed.

Liquidation of company acquired in taxable transaction. As indicated earlier, a corporation may buy the stock of another and then liquidate the purchased corporation in order to step up the basis of the acquired corporation's assets to the price paid for the stock. Suppose the acquired corporation has a loss carry-over.

This same rule that permits the acquiring corporation to pick up the carry-over loss of an acquired corporation in a tax-free reorganization (detailed above) also applies to the liquidation of an at least 80-percent-owned subsidiary. However, the corporation which bought the stock of another corporation within 2 years of the liquidation does not have this rule available to it. As long as the liquidation will result in a step-up in the basis of the assets (as a liquidation within 2 years of the purchase of the stock will do), the carry-over loss does not pass to the parent corporation under the tax-free reorganization rule.

Thus, if Corporation *A* buys all the stock of Corporation *B* and *B* has a carry-over loss, what *A* can do is keep *B* in operation for 2 years. (During those 2 years, *A* might put some profitable operations into *B*—but make sure to keep *B*'s preacquisition business substantially unchanged—and attempt to use some of the loss that way.) After 2 years have elapsed, *A* can liquidate *B* into itself and get the advantage of any remaining carry-over loss. Keep in mind, however, that each year's carry-over loss lasts for only 5 years, and so the 2-year waiting period to use it may reduce or defeat its value. Also remember that if the 2-year waiting period is used, the liquidation will not result in a step-up in basis of the assets of the acquired company.

Tax-avoidance purposes. Even if the rules above are met for allowing the use of the acquired loss, the Treasury may attempt to disallow it (and the courts have sustained the Treasury in a number of cases) where the acquiring company has no good business purpose for the acquisition (other than the availability of the carry-over loss). The principal purpose of the acquisition has to be other than to get the available loss carry-over. Even where a loss corporation continues in substantially the same business after its acquisition, but the acquiring corporation adds new lines of business, the Treasury says the tax-avoidance rules can still knock out the loss.

Thus, it becomes essential to show a good business purpose for the acquisition. Two instances where good business purpose was sustained in recent cases were—

1. Acquisition of the seller's company as part of a "package deal" to acquire needed land by a real-estate developer
2. A national rubber company looking to expand its tire manufacturing operations in the South acquired a poorly run, loss-ridden company and by good management made it profitable. The company was also able to show that the availability of the loss carry-over did not affect the price it paid for the company's stock

Section 6

HOW TO FIND THE BEST LOCATION FOR YOUR BUSINESS

BY

DAVID SCRIBNER

HOW TO FIND THE BEST LOCATION
FOR YOUR BUSINESS

1. Pattern of the metropolitan district

Location. Location is everything or nothing. It is the aspect of a site. In a positive sense it is labor, management, raw products, and finished goods; in a negative sense it is just a spot on the map.

There is probably more sentimental rationalization concerning the location for a business than there is reasoning. The factors which make a location ideal for one business may or may not apply to another.

Locations must be sought to serve the individual needs of business, which for the sake of clarity we may divide into three components: retail, which comprises the vast majority of business enterprises; wholesale, which is a specialty; and industrial, including research, development, and engineering.

In the retail trade, there has grown up a sort of patois used to describe location. One hears of "100 percent locations" where large chain stores are located, or prosperous department stores attract crowds, and other stores bask in the reflected prosperity of the big advertising budgets of the center of attraction. For a good retail location, your business may be of the type that depends upon a large volume of small purchases and requires a 100 percent location, or one bordering on it. Other stores attract people to them by the special goods or services they have to offer.

In the typical regional shopping center, where there may be two department stores with areas in excess of 200,000 square feet of retail space, it is interesting to note those local stores which do well in the vicinity of the larger, well-known department stores. These are invariably specialty stores which offer a more personalized service, or an unusual quality of merchandise, or which cater to a certain snob appeal of women buyers.

An example may be seen in the case of a women's-wear specialty store in Brooklyn. The store is on a side street—a decidedly secondary location when compared with that of the large department stores one block away on a busy thoroughfare. A pedestrian traffic count shows about 10 persons on the side street for every 100 persons on the main street. Now, if the main street is a 100 percent location (and there are a dozen good stores to prove it), then this would appear to be only a 10 percent location. But further examination shows that 90 percent of those who turn into the side street go to the specialty store which caters essentially to the outsize and the taller woman, and to the buyers of maternity clothing. The store has demonstrated in many cities that it does very well in a secondary location.

Corners. The advantages of a corner location are stressed by many retailers. This location is compared with a site in the middle of the block and the advantage of the corner is called "corner influence." This added value reflects in the land, and although the building may be designed to take advantage of it, the increment is to the land. Added value for a corner location may be 10 percent or 50 percent. There are many formulas and curves to chart the added value of corners with inside lots, depending upon the corner. The added value for corner location is dependent upon the additional patronage which may be obtained by exploiting two streams of traffic rather than one, and it applies to the 20 or 25 feet on the corner. The 20 or 25 feet adjoining the corner is called the "key" and the key influence is usually only 20 percent of the corner influence. The weighing of the factors involved in this measurement is solely that of the trained real-estate appraiser who knows how to interpret earnings, capitalization, and comparable sales. In general, it is well for the man inexperienced in real estate to calculate the corner lot value as follows:

Determine the value of a typical inside lot of the same size on each of the two streets

Apply the unit values to the lot in question

Example. A 40-foot (frontage) by 100-foot (depth) lot on Main Street is worth $40,000, and on the side street it is worth $10,000.

40 by 100 ft. on Main Street	$40,000
100 ft. on side street at $250 per ft. would equal $25,000, but corner influence extends only 20 ft., or one-half area of the lot	12,500
Key influence for the balance of the lot at 20 percent of corner influence	2,500
Total	$55,000

There are corners in all big cities which crowds pass like cattle in a chute, and which offer little or no advantage, except for advertising, over inside locations, but again for the retailer who depends upon a volume of trade, the corner location is important and often worth the added cost. Corner influence should be considered only in good retail locations. In secondary locations it has a declining influence in ratio to the general lack of retail desirability of the location.

Other factors. There are many arguments as to the east side of the street versus the west, and the north side versus the south. The influence of these factors varies with the type of establishment and from one part of the country to another. In general, there is no rule for this, and each city must be examined by itself.

There are cases where a heavy flow of traffic discourages customers from crossing the street and makes for a concentrated retail section on one side of the street while the opposite side may become a secondary location.   More often, however, locations in proximity to the large advertisers such as department stores are desirable for volume stores of the 5-and-10-cent type, and specialty stores.   In this case, being directly across the street from the large advertiser is often more desirable than being around the corner or farther down the block on the same side.   Directly opposite R. H. Macy's great store on 34th Street in New York is a better location for a specialty shop than on the same side in either of the adjoining blocks. Location on a block is often important if the blocks are very long.   Another factor of importance is a curve in the street, where the problem of visibility is of concern.

There are many examples where a prestige location is captured by good architecture which takes advantage of the intersection of two main thoroughfares, or an interchange of high-speed highways, and where there is uninterrupted view of the location.   In downtown core area locations, the predominance of the building brought about by open space may be very important, such as a women's quality store in White Plains, which occupies the high point on a curve of a street, thus standing out above its neighbors.

Technical Bulletin 56 by the Urban Land Institute handles in some detail "Store Location and Customer Behavior" and is recommended reading on this subject.   This monograph reads in part as follows:

If a locational decision creates a situation which gradually alters the retailer's identity, it also alters his ability to attract and sell to customers at all of his locations, with resulting effects upon his profits. If he can attract a large number of desirable customers to a developer's shopping center, then his bargaining power with relation to real estate costs will increase, with resultant decrease in his costs. Thus, he must consider the long-run effect of today's decisions on the future development of his *retailing identity,* because of its influence on his future ability to secure locations under favorable terms and also upon his long range profit picture.

It is a good rule to look at the rents being paid by other retailers as a guide. If, for example, a shoe store has a 20-year lease at a high rental, and other stores of national chain type have high rentals, the chances are that they enjoy a high retail volume and the business risk for a similar type business is reduced. At the same time, the venture of starting a service-type business or one which does not depend upon volume is risky, as this type of business seldom would pay the premium for 100 percent location.

· Another guide is sidewalk-pedestrian counts.   These have a great bearing on volume retail trade, but have little influence upon the quality or so-called "carriage trade" type of enterprise.   An analysis of traffic counts and pedestrian counts showing the predominance of men or women has a more important bearing than mere numbers.

Even the best of retail streets are affected by such "dead spots" as churches, libraries, monuments, and parks.   The influence of St. Patrick's Cathedral is not so noticeable on New York's Fifth Avenue as is the influence of St. Thomas

Church, a few blocks to the north, where the volume of trade on the opposite side of the avenue is higher than that enjoyed by the shops on either side of the church. In the first instance, Rockefeller Center more than offsets the influence of the cathedral, while in the second instance, there is no such compensating factor.

Experience has shown that there are certain physical features about retail space that are desirable and other features that are undesirable. Basements are important, as they provide the ideal space for excess inventory, packaging, and shipping, and often may be used to supplement the regular display space during busy seasons. Good basement display space for which adequate escalators or elevators and stairs are provided is generally considered superior to second-floor space for retail purposes.

Mezzanine space is desirable for office work and sales space, but for the latter it should be at least 9 feet above the main floor and have the same clearance height, in order to provide adequate ventilation and lighting. This added height tends to create awkward space in shallow stores, but it is desirable in stores of sufficient depth to offer attractive display space. It is difficult to display small objects in a store 19 feet high, but the same space may be ideal for furniture, antiques, rugs, cars, or other large objects.

Another important aspect of stores is that they should be neat, not gaudy. Clear signs—single color or clear white neon lighting—against the facade are far superior to hanging signs or multicolor flashing signs.

Transition areas. When a section of a city is known as a "transition area," it should be regarded by the prospective tenant or purchaser with a very jaundiced eye. The term usually refers to a section which has been jumped over in the development of the city pattern, or an area of the city which has been left behind in the city growth. It is characterized by marginal industry and retail and wholesale trade which does not depend upon either sidewalk or vehicle traffic for customers. The used-car, used-furniture, office-fixture, hotel-supply, and similar forms of enterprise that inhabit such a section are necessary for each city, but are not characteristic of good downtown established locations. These are frequently very profitable business firms, and if the merchandising is aggressive, customers may be attracted in spite of the location, but generally the firms must go out after the customers.

The direction of transition is important. Many downtown core areas now tenanted with first-class retail establishments are actually dying because of the competition caused by outlying sections which can attract the vehicle-borne trade, while the central section, which cannot provide adequate parking, cannot serve its customers. In this case, the downtown area is in transition from a profitable retail section, and the outlying area is in transition toward becoming a good retail section.

Secondary locations. There are a great many business enterprises which need not be located in a high-volume business section and for which the cost of occupancy in such locations would be prohibitive. Home outfitters who have large inventories, food stores, including supermarkets, chain stores of the Sears, Roebuck type, and many of the service businesses are found in secondary locations. Food stores, particularly supermarkets, are the cornerstone of such locations. About 28 percent of all retail dollars go into food and related merchandise.

It has been the experience of a chain store in a city in which it is established that when it opens one of its large supermarkets, it is able to close three or four of its older retail outlets. While the other stores were central and depended upon pedestrian customers, the newer stores are in secondary locations and depend upon vehicle-born customers. The impact upon small independent retailers is drastic. The effect of the trend to supermarkets, larger per-customer purchases, and more rapid turnover of inventory is the more intensive use of secondary locations.

Parking area requires large plottage, which is just as important as the actual retail space. The Urban Land Institute examined a great many shopping centers in peripheral locations and found that the ratio of 2 to 3 square feet of parking space per square foot of retail space prevailed. The newest shopping centers of this type are now being designed with 4 or more square feet of parking space per square foot of retail space. Factors which have a bearing upon the ratio are many, and it is dangerous to rely upon a rule of thumb. For years there was a standard rule that 200 square feet of space per car was sufficient, but this no longer may be taken for granted. The newer car doors are larger, requiring greater aisle space; and longer overhang in the front and rear requires greater turning radius. The figure is probably closer to 250 square feet per car than 200. While supermarkets put customers through their turnstiles rapidly, restaurants, barbers, hairdressers, dentists, and dress shops are very much slower, with a consequent greater number of car hours per square foot of parking space.

This retail trend has been called "decentralization." It is not limited to shopping centers where an overall plan exists for the use of common facilities by many tenants, but is also found among independently owned retail outlets.

Combination retail and manufacturing—or retail, wholesale, and manufacturing—businesses are often found in secondary locations. Likewise, banking facilities are usually adequate. When they are not, something is wrong.

It is here that the prospective owner or tenant should carefully regard the real-estate situation. He should look at the vacant plots and determine whether a building can be created to his specifications at less cost to him than the cost of renting an existing structure. Another factor is the proximity of steadily employed wage earners as a backlog for any business enterprise which may be undertaken. When this factor is favorable, it may be found that the location is a good one for his own labor as well as the customers; when this factor is unfavorable, the contrary is likely to be the case.

Quantitative factors.   It has been taken for granted for many years that 10 shops in a cluster could be supported by 500 families, and above the 10 basic shops of a neighborhood group, one shop for each 100 families.   Such rules are not reliable, but should be considered as a very rough approximation. Likewise, the method of allowing for 65 to 75 linear feet of store front per 100 persons should be taken for merely a working estimate.   The reason for the lack of accuracy of these methods is that they apply to an urban area and not to any specific subsection thereof.

Studies of the Urban Land Institute (*Community Builders Handbook*) show that—

When the number of expected customers is multiplied by the averages of annual expenditures for consumer items, the sales potential of the trade area comes into focus. Another factor, the variation in expenditures by the type and amount for the different income groups, must then be applied. Other methods for measuring the buying power of the trade area are possible. Income can be estimated by taking the normal ratio of income to home value. There is a fairly close relationship between value of homes owned and family income. . . . Where there is a state income tax, it is possible to secure the total number of families by income groups in a city or county. Thus state income tax returns can indicate the number of high income families in the trade area.

David Bohannon has used a detailed form of this method in evaluating a shopping-center location which he has developed and which illustrates the kind of survey warranted in the larger center.

The economic aspects of the survey were prepared by McConnell's Economic Surveys, and cover the following items:

Determination of the economic trading area tributary to the shopping center
Present population, families, and purchasing power for—
    The entire county
    The trading area
    Ratio of trading area to county
Population, families, and purchasing power for the trading area estimated
    for the current year
Annual purchasing power after deducting other expenditures of—
    Federal taxes
    Automobile-transportation costs
    Mortgages and rentals
    Local taxes
    Insurance, savings, etc.
    Retail sales in other centers within the economic area
    (Deducting these six items from the gross purchasing power leaves the
      commodity dollars spent elsewhere)
Analysis of competitive retail-shopping areas
Analysis of the proposed shopping center regarding type of stores and the
    priority of their establishment in the center

An item of interest is the stress which has been laid on provision for parking.

The center as now designed provides for all the automobiles in the tributary area to park on the average of three times a week, assuming a 5-hour shopping day.   This is considered a nearly ideal provision.

2. Price that a business can afford

The cost of occupancy is the primary limiting factor, and the determination of just what a business should pay for its rent or ownership is always a matter of debate.   It depends in great part on the character of the business—whether it is retail, wholesale, industrial, or of the service and professional type.

Retail—commercial.   In the case of retail establishments, the following table of experience shows what the average rental of space has been found to be (i.e., this may be taken as what these businesses can afford to pay for rent) in terms of percentage of gross sales:

Leases, Percentage Rates 1966 Percentage Lease Table *

* This table is based upon one prepared by the National Institute of Real Estate Brokers, associated with the National Association of Real Estate Boards, and is modified by other data and the author's experience.

Type of business	Range, %	Type of business	Range, %
Art shops	5–9	Jewelry (exclusive)	4–10
Auto accessories	3–5	Leather goods	5–9
Auto agencies	2–4	Liquor stores	3½–6
Bakeries	4–7	Meat markets (individual)	3–5
Barbershops	8–12	Meat markets (chain)	3–5
Beauty shops	7–15	Men's clothing	4–7
Books and stationery	4–6	Men's furnishings	4–10
Bowling lanes	6–10	Men's hats	7–10
Candy	6–10	Men's shoes	4–8
Children's clothing	5–8	Men's shoes (volume)	4–6
Cigars and sundries	5–8	Men's tailors	6–8
Cocktail lounges	4–6	Millinery	7–12
Credit clothing	5–8	Motion-picture theaters	8–12
Department stores	1½–4	Office-supply stores	3–6
Drugstores (chain)	1½–4	Optical stores	5–10
Drugstores (individual)	4–6	Paint, wallpaper supplies	3–8
Dry cleaning and laundry	5–10	Parking lots	30–60
Electrical appliances	3–7	Photography shops	5–10
Florists	6–10	Pianos and musical instruments	4–7
Fruit and vegetable markets	6–8	Radio and television	4–6
Furniture	3–7	Record shops	5–7
Furs	5–8	Restaurants	3–10
Garages (storage)	30–50	Shoe repair	6–10
Gas stations, center per gallon	1–2	Specialty stores	6–10
Gift shops	5–10	Sporting goods	4–7
Grocery stores (individual)	1½–5	Taverns	4–6
Grocery stores (chain)	1–2	Women's dress shops	4–8
Hardware	3–6	Women's furnishings	3½–10
Hobby shops	5–6	Women's shoes	5–10
Hosiery and knit goods	6–8	Women's shoes (volume)	4–6
Jewelry (cheap costume)	7–10	5–10¢ or 25¢–$2 stores	3–6

Wholesale.   Most wholesale establishments handling food have found that to be competitive they must take merchandise in lots, break them up into components, store them, assemble them into orders, and load them on out-going vehicles for a total cost of under 5 percent to the retailer.   In many instances, this has been reduced to 3.5 percent.   Of this total, that portion which is the cost of occupancy is usually less than one-quarter and often closer to one-tenth.

The greatest advance in planning for the most efficient use of space has taken place in the wholesale and warehousing fields.   Not long ago, when labor was getting 50 or 60 cents an hour, any old building would do; but today, with labor getting at least four times that figure in most cities, and still capable of manually moving only 6 tons per day, good use of real estate means efficient space, mechanical lifts, and other aids.   Here location becomes increasingly important, and analysis of ton-miles of haul to serve customers is indicated, as well as a thorough study of transportation.

Any new building should be designed so as to have as great a distance between columns as possible, in order to be able to install equipment to handle heavy and awkward loads, and to stack them as high as possbile.   Modern warehousing calls for fewer and fewer people to handle more and more goods mechanically.   It is becoming the usual thing, rather than the exceptional, to see computerized devices which pick up quantities of goods, place them in containers, label the containers, and then place the containers in a vehicle so that they will arrive sealed at a destination.   All this can be done by the more sophisticated equipment now available.   Any new warehouse must be readily fitted to handle long-distance rail shipments, as well as shorter-distance truck transportation.   Trucks may be used for piggyback containers on long-distance rail shipment and for delivery purposes for a shorter distance at either end.   It is only a question of time before it is generally accepted that heavily loaded pallets can move on a cushion of air with very little human effort, and that overhead cranes can supplement the forklift type of operation with many more tons and packages per hour, and at a substantially lower payroll factor.

The wholesale business is the distribution business, and its use of real estate is limited to the means of distribution (or transportation).   For this purpose *all* means of transportation are important.   Good sites with rail and highway locations zoned for industrial use are hard to find in many cities, and rail, highway, and water transportation is even more difficult to obtain.

In New York City, so much of the good waterfront property has been diverted to highway use, housing, or public use that its great mercantile position is endangered.

Establishing truck bypass routes so that truck, truck-trailer, trailer, and semitrailer vehicles are excluded from central business districts has been the rule in many cities.

Location of a wholesale establishment must be such as to serve the majority of its customers in an economical manner with the greatest efficiency.   A large grocery cooperative in the New York metropolitan region called in a firm of real-estate consultants to find the best location for a new warehouse. The site finally selected is very close to the theoretical center of population of the city as a whole. It is on an excellent rail line and is connected with the main arterial truck routes serving the entire metropolitan area. This cooperative is owned by the 400 or more independent grocers, who, in order to compete with the chain stores, must be very efficient. Thus one progressive wholesaler met the location problem and solved it.

The downtown loading and unloading problems are often expensive to solve. Unless the wholesaler can deliver the goods to the retailer on a competitive cost basis, he is in trouble. Phasing the delivery of goods to retail outlets through the off-hours has seldom worked except deliveries to department stores, which usually have off-street loading facilities anyway. Most cities, particularly the older ones, have a one-way street pattern. In spite of all of the laws to the contrary, double parking persists and the trucker spends more of his time muscling loads between vehicles, over curbs, and into stores than he does behind the wheel of his vehicle. If there is a solution for this problem, the traffic experts seem not to have found it. In newer areas, including urban renewal projects, off-street facilities for unloading have been the rule rather than the exception since 1960. For these areas, this factor alone often has made them competitive with the shopping centers.

Unless and until the wholesaler is able to locate where he can receive the goods, sort, store, assemble, ship, and deliver, he is not performing the function for which he is paid and he will fail. Location, for the wholesaler, is a factor of the highest importance. This involves an understanding of a city as a whole, and the wholesale trade, perhaps more than any other is dependent upon the entire metropolitan area.

There are many ways to collect the necessary data in order to pass judgment upon competitive locations for wholesale and distribution purposes. One of the best techniques, however, is to take a large-scale map of the metropolitan region and superimpose upon it the proposed highway planning. It is almost impossible to put dates upon proposed highway plans, but some kind of priority can usually be found out from local planning officials. In any event, with such a map and overlay, it is possible to anticipate central interchange locations.

Around most metropolitan regions there are now federally subsidized peripheral highways. Many of these have not been completed; some are only a dream on the planners' board. But where these peripheral highways intercept main arteries to the core of the city are opportunities for distribution which should be exploited. Not only are they between the main part of the city and its suburbs, but they can take advantage of the time-honored arterial routes into the core of the city from the area that the city serves, as well as speed the distribution of goods over other arteries, both into and out of the metropolitan region.

If the direction of growth is to be properly anticipated, census tracts of those areas where the largest growth of residential population has taken place must be examined, and the nature of the terrain surrounding these clusters must be analyzed, so that with the information already obtained from the highway maps, it may be possible to prognosticate scientifically greater than ordinary population growth, and in this manner to anticipate future growth patterns.

Information from the Bureau of Public Roads indicates that in the 10 years 1955 to 1965 the family automobile increased substantially. In 1955, 73.5 percent of American household units owned an automobile, and 10.1 percent had more than one. By 1965, 79.6 percent of the families owned a car, and 20.6 percent had more than one.

Industrial. Industrial space does not fluctuate to the extent that is characteristic of other real estate. An example of this is shown by the statistics of occupancy of loft buildings in New York City, which in the 20-year period 1929 to 1949 (which included the Great Depression and World War II) averaged about 90 percent occupancy with a low of one year at 80 percent. This may be compared with office-building occupancy, which during the same period averaged about 85 percent and showed 5 years of occupancy below 80 percent. Since 1949, industrial space generally in the major metropolitan regions was 92 to 95 percent occupied. In the 1959 to 1961 recession, only the very large plants built years ago for consumer durable goods manufacture became available. This was a technological change, and by the end of 1961 they had been absorbed for other purposes. Since then, through the first quarter of 1967, when high interest rates became felt, industrial construction continued with occupancy nearly 100 percent in good general-purpose structures.

Manufacturers seeking industrial space will always find outmoded space available in any city, for the excellent reason that unless the space is efficient for general use, the chances are that it will not be good enough for a new business except at very low cost of occupancy.

There is no rule of thumb for the cost of occupancy of industrial space. A concern with excellent credit, good standing, and proven experience may be able to occupy quarters on a basis of as low as 6½ percent of the book value, plus real-estate taxes, maintenance, and repairs. This is the leaseback technique, and in industrial real estate this method is available only to the strongest concerns.

When a city or group of adjacent cities are dependent upon a concentration of one specific type of manufacturing endeavor, it is similar to having one large manufacturer which dominates the area. Both cases are an element of danger, for a single-industry community may be dominated, for good or evil, by a few labor leaders or a handful of the most prominent businessmen, or both. Then, too, the demand for the products manufactured is the controlling item in the economic life of the area. This demand may be altered by a technological improvement or a new product which is made elsewhere.

Long-range trends in industry have a great deal to do with this, and the vast quantities of vacant industrial space in such cities as New Bedford and Fall River, Mass., after the cotton industry moved South, were testimony to the inability of a city to absorb its vacant space when it was placed upon the market in large quantities. Such cities often offer the greatest opportunity to a young industry, as the whole community will go out of its way to make conditions favorable. Such conditions are known to the various state industrial boards and industrial departments of railroads and public utilities.

In the past, manufacturing was characteristic of the section of our cities surrounding the central business district. This section, in turn, was surrounded by the industrial workers' dwellings. In our older cities these industrial sections, subdivided between the downtown core area and the slums, still exist. It is here that the multiple-story lofts are found. Many of the heavier industries have moved out of these buildings, leaving them for the lighter manufacturing processes. The result of this is that there has developed a transition in which the lighter and more numerous small industries have displaced the heavier industries and the latter have moved on to a peripheral location.

Most heavy-industry complexes gather around them other allied industrial companies with which they do business, on a more or less regular basis, and geographical propinquity is desirable. Such is the case, for example, in the areas surrounding oil refineries, where other components of the petrochemical industry which use the by-products of the refining process can find a profitable location. So it is also with steelmaking complexes. Forest-product plants are often located near paper-products manufacturers. As these centers become more important as the originators of payrolls, satellite communities may spring up in the vicinity, thus creating an economic unit which itself is a satellite of the largest metropolitan region.

These industrial complexes form the basis for a network of highways joining them and tying them to the interstate highway network. In all heavy industrial complexes, rail and sometimes water transportation are important. Rail still accounts for the bulk of the long-haul tonnage, while highways account for the short haul.

Industrial plants cannot spend a great deal for land, and they need a greater area than is generally realized. Rail lines are usually important, but also the trailer-truck must be accommodated. The cars of employees, executives, salesmen, and visitors all must be accommodated in today's factory grounds, as well as the loading platforms and a place for trailers awaiting unloading, loading, or pickup. Add to this a one-story or, at most, two-story plant, and the land-use ratio (ratio of total land area to manufacturing space) becomes more like that of a shopping center than like one of the old factories.

This concept of low density has led to the development in many parts of the country of so-called "industrial parks." They used to be known by the more accurate term, controlled industrial districts. In any event, the landscaping and other amenities have changed the name to industrial parks. It is here that many small buildings housing branches or distribution facilities of larger national companies can usually be found, as well as manufacturing plants. One of the elements attracting industry to such industrial parks is that of security. By having a controlled entrance and exit to the park, pilferage can be minimized. Furthermore, internal traffic can be controlled so as to permit 24-hour operations where it is desirable without disturbing the neighbors, and to facilitate delivery to customers with optimum efficiency.

There are numerous advantages accruing to the community in which the industrial park is located. In the first place, no additional city services are required. The park creates no school problems, rather it helps to solve a good many others: inasmuch as there is no population, police and fire protection are reduced. Frequently, the interior roads are privately owned and maintained, and a solid tax base is created.

In the spring report of the Federal Reserve Report (1967), there is an interesting statistic. In the period 1950 to 1965 inclusive, the manufacturing output of the United States doubled. In other words, from the beginning of this nation until its culmination in 1950 we built a tremendous manufacturing capacity. This has been doubled in 15 years. Since 1965 the rate of growth has continued.

Research, development, and engineering activities often require that they be located in an area zoned for industrial use. The reason is that the end product of such research, development, and engineering frequently is a prototype, or model. This activity may result in the manufacture of many prototypes, each differing slightly from the other, or being relatively similar; sometimes these may be tested to destruction. Many kinds of sophisticated machinery are required for some of these experiments, and often a machine shop is needed in the plant. Thus, while such structures have the appearance of office buildings, they may house a multiplicity of activity. They are usually not confined to thinking activities, but thinking and manufacturing. There are some, of course, connected with universities or large international companies which deal in matters of pure science, but these are the exception, rather than the rule.

In all of these R and D facilities, the elements of location which are the most important have to do with matters relating to the type of employee. Most of these people are well educated and they prefer the location of their plant to be near a residential area which has excellent schools. Many of them want to continue their studies and obtain higher ratings, engineering degrees, and doctorates. This means that they must be located in the proximity of some university offering night classes for advanced studies. Then, too, they are for the most part interested in music and the arts, and require the cultural sophistication of a nearby large city.

In the case of R and D facilities, it is well to set up criteria and weigh them according to the importance of the various elements.   Experience of personnel is very valuable to all research, and nothing is so wasteful of this talented type of personnel as turnover.   Once the personnel turnover becomes a prevalent thing, much of the value of previous experimentation is lost, because the unity of experience is thereby broken.

Of prime importance is the need for expansion without moving to another location.   However, there are limits to the practical size of research centers, and probably 5,000 employees in any one location is a maximum.   It has long been the experience of companies heavily committed to research that in an environment where there are many other firms similarly engaged and where there can be a cross-fertilization of ideas, there is an intellectual atmosphere which is conducive to better and better work.

Service-type business and professional.   These are the users of office space, and although a laboratory or servicing shop may be required, it usually is found as an adjunct to the office if the space is small or in another part of the city if the space required is substantial.   Cost of occupancy in office buildings is usually rent, light, and amortization of furnishings, partitions, and decorating over the period of the lease.   Heat, cleaning, and service are usually provided by the landlord.

Second-floor space for offices in the smaller cities is desirable use of real estate.   Such space in shopping centers in the periphery of larger cities is also desirable, but in either case care should be exercised to make sure that the approach to the space is attractive.   Too often the stairs are steep, dark, and narrow when they should be easy to climb, with landings, well lighted, and at least 5 feet wide.

Because the cost of occupancy must be a minor part of the total costs of professional practice for doctors, architects, engineers, and accountants, very efficient use of the space occupied tends to keep this portion of the cost to a minimum.   For reasons best known to themselves, this does not appear to be the case with lawyers.   Doctors, for example, usually have regular office hours, and therefore while one doctor is out, an associate may use his office, examining rooms, waiting room, and other facilities.   Often these doctors will rent the same space and thus use it for 60 or 70 hours a week instead of 40.   Architects, engineers, and accountants use facilities in common to a lesser extent, but they too achieve a flexibility by making use of the space of associates.   These factors tend to make the rent of professional space rather high on a square-foot basis, but low per individual, lawyer excepted.

The service-type business includes a great number of businesses.   The advertising firm, real-estate office, or insurance business is characteristic of others of the same type.   They are primarily sales offices out of which salesmen operate and in which policy meetings are held and detailed work prepared.   Any building in a central location adjacent to transportation lines may house such a business, but the more efficient the space the better it is.   Rent, or cost of occupancy, is usually a higher proportion of total cost than is the case with users of professional space.   A rule of thumb indicates that such users of office space pay from 3 to 8 percent of total costs for cost of occupancy.

In choosing a location for office space, certain considerations other than cost are important.   In the first place, a clean, neat building in a good setting will always be reasonably well filled at high rents, as compared with the same building in a declining section.   The physical characteristics of a building are important.   In order to be adaptable for the many uses to which office space may be put, flexibility in electric outlets, plumbing extensions, and other facilities is required.   A stock-exchange house, for example, may require 20,000 square feet of space, of which 19,000 square feet may be in two large open spaces and 1,000 square feet may be divided into 10 or more offices.   Law offices, on the other hand, require many small offices.

Office-building occupancy is a good index of business activity.   Here, more than in any other type of business space, the law of supply and demand works freely and the competitive demand for office space controls the cost of occupancy.

3. Public controls

State and local ordinances.   The law of supply and demand in free competition regulates the use of all business, including real estate, but in addition, real property is subject to public controls.   These controls are sometimes obvious, such as zoning regulations.   In some cases they are not so apparent, as in the case of state labor laws, which may permit one business to use a building, but would make it very costly for another.

Zoning is the police power of a political unit to enforce a master plan.   Most state laws provide that without a master plan zoning is not enforceable.

Zoning is a comprehensive mapping out of city land use and restrictions, in relation to the residential, commercial, and industrial areas.   Within each classification there are subsections detailing the type of residential use and its density; the various kinds of commercial and industrial use; parking requirements, landscaping, and other restrictions which may be its refinements.

Most cities have zoning acts, which to be effective must be flexible and change as the economy of the community changes.   Zoning is a device to enforce the planning concept of the city, town, or county.   There is an increasing tendency to coordinate local area plans into a master or regional system.   The plan is more important to a buyer or a business about to undertake a long-term lease than is the zoning ordinance, for if and when the long-term plan is implemented the character of the location may change and the zoning accordingly.   Zoning usually is limited to regulation of the use to which real estate may be put, of the height and area of buildings, and occasionally of population density.   As a rule, a business which exists in a district zoned for other use is there because it was in being prior to the zoning act and it may remain as a "nonconforming" use, but once it ceases to operate, zoning restrictions usually take over.

Building codes. Building codes are supposed to be based upon the concept of the community police power to ensure public safety. Specifications of the quality of construction and the strength of materials are primary considerations, as are plumbing and electrical codes. The importance of these regulations to a new business lies in the naïve assumption on the part of too many people that any building may be altered to be adapted to the use for which it is intended. Too often, the building code which permits a building to exist in a substandard condition will require that it be almost completely rebuilt if any attempt is made to alter it. Also many types of alteration are not possible under local codes.

There are about 2,500 building codes in this country and more spring up every day. Many of them are rudimentary and others are very detailed. Some communities have drawn their codes for aesthetic values, others for structural soundness. Many of them are flexible and recognize new materials and techniques, while others are completely rigid and out of date. In the fall of 1966, the Build America Better Committee started a large-scale attempt to set some nationwide standards in an attempt to correct archaic restrictions.

Health, labor, police, fire, and other regulations. There are all kinds of regulations, depending upon the complexity of the city. In some cities, there are no regulations about the number of persons who may be employed in a given space; in others, this is delineated. Many state laws control the number of employees per toilet fixture. Safety measures require sprinkler systems in buildings of certain types used for certain purposes. Still other regulations require special fire or police permits for certain types of manufacturing.

These regulations are particularly important in industrial operations. Some types of industrial buildings are built for the special use of their owners, and the buildings are not adaptable for general use. This is particularly true of the heavy-industry plants, which are usually of special design. This includes steel mills, building-material factories, glassworks, breweries, public utilities, chemical plants, and ice plants. When these appear on the market, it is only because they have become surplus property. The adaptation of such plants to other use is most unusual.

Other properties which are more adaptable to general use or industrial plants which were built for multiple industrial use are subject to an endless list of regulations, different in each city, ranging from elevator-load requirements to fire-door controls and from types of sprinklers to materials for stair treads.

The regulations for places of public assembly are particularly stiff. Department stores have to meet different rules from ordinary street-floor stores.

In New York City the regulations governing the use of occupancy of property are contained in four volumes, while in some cities only the state labor and health laws need be observed.

For a business seeking a location, a good local architect who understands the application of local laws and ground rules is essential.

With the increasing urbanization of our population and the spreading urban pattern air and water pollution has become a major problem. Except in a few of the largest and most polluted cities (Los Angeles and New York), little has been done to establish criteria for air pollution. Except where impure water has an economic impact upon other financial interests (the Gulf Coast shrimp and oyster business), little has been done to enforce the treatment of plant or community effluent. Lake Erie may be beyond redemption except by a major effort by three states and a province in Canada.

In the future, we may hopefully look forward to the establishment of criteria of both air and water cleanliness and the enforcement of the criteria. In many industries this may lead to technological changes, in others to expensive equipment, but in any event it will affect all of us.

4. Special considerations

Location in relation to customers. This is of primary importance to retailers and diminishes in importance to the extent that the business in question can go out to its customers.

Here the decision must be made whether the business should be located in a downtown core area or in a satellite location. In other words, will it rely upon the large volume of daily pedestrian traffic or upon the suburban vehicle-borne customers? Two considerations which have been previously discussed, the pattern of the metropolitan district and the character of the business, should be reviewed.

Chain stores, because of their excellent credit, large central purchasing, low overhead per sale, and diversification, are different from independent retail outlets, but they are an excellent illustration of location in relation to customers. Chain stores are as different from each other as are the independents, and the location needs are likewise different. Most chain stores want to be in the vicinity of the local 100 percent locations, except food stores.

Percentage Leases (see Leases, Percentage Rates, 1966 Percentage Lease Table, page 187). Percentage leases are based upon a basic minimum rent in fixed dollar amount against which may be compared a percentage factor applied to gross sales in a common device. The reasoning behind this is that if the retailer does not succeed in generating the business that he should, he is tied to a minimum base rent and neither he nor the landlord is particularly happy. If, however, he is successful and his sales generate enough volume to pay an "overage" by virtue of the percentage applied to gross sales, he pays more rent and both parties make more money.

Both the landlord and tenant entering into such a lease must take into consideration many factors. If it is a downtown location, pedestrian traffic, particularly women, is important. Stores selling to men or predominantly men are secondary, except in some of our larger sophisticated cities. Except for suits, hats, overcoats, and shoes, women buy 80 percent of men's clothing. Other considerations include night shopping and parking facilities.

The downtown chain store is usually the same chain store which also locates in a peripheral shopping center. Whatever the interior layout may be, it is interesting to note that each chain has evolved a pattern of its own. When a customer walks into store X at one shopping center or another, she knows where to go find what she is looking for. This is true for most chains except variety stores. Chain stores are the anchors for downtown as well as shopping centers and accordingly are the main users of percentage leases. It may take 3 to 5 years for a new store to really build up its sales to the overage level and in the meanwhile the base rent is all that is paid.

The importance of the chain stores to the success of the center as a whole and the local stores in particular cannot be stressed too strongly. Whether the chain be a large department store in a regional center or of the Grant, Penny, or Woolworth type in the smaller centers, the advertising output of the chain is so great as to attract customers.

This is equally true of the downtown established central business district (CBD). It is for this reason, primarily, that so much urban renewal effort since 1960 has been plowed into the core areas of our cities. Not only have office buildings, hotels, and civic centers been built, but so have attractive shopping malls. This has already begun to revitalize downtown in many of the cities which started early in the program. This has resulted in over 50 communities making plans for CBD revitalization in the 1964 to 1966 period alone.

Here again, careful planning has to take place to accommodate the merchant. It is the merchant who must eventually make the place pay. Architects and planners should think as a merchant does. Each should ask himself and others: Where is the key place for the department store; the fashionable dress shops; the variety shops; the household-goods stores; the theatre? Until and unless this is done, the drawings are just pretty drawings and the renewal sponsor is buying a pig in a poke.

Taking the existing residential pattern and blending it into the new mercantile facility, whether it be in the CBD or a new shopping center at the interchange of two arterial roads, requires careful evaluation. Then, too, the residential pattern must be tied to the retail district by some form of mass transportation as well as parking facilities for a substantial number of cars.

There are notable exceptions to this thesis. The grocery, drug, restaurants, tobacco, liquor stores, and others of local necessity may do as well or better in the core of a local residential area—a neighborhood environment. Plain clothing for business use, shoes, jewelry, expensive and luxury home furnishings, antiques, and other quality merchandise should be adjacent to, but not necessarily part of, the office building district.

On the other hand, air-line offices, travel agents of the better quality, and agents of foreign countries should be in the heart of the office-building district.

There are two aspects to the suburban or satellite business location. Most is heard about the one which has to do with the convenience to the customer, and it is not to be underestimated. The other factor is often overlooked in the enthusiasm of opening a business, and that is the occupational hazard of being a pioneer. All shopping-center developers have learned that even some of the most attractive older shopping centers would not be able to carry themselves on today's cost of construction. In competition with newer centers they often lose the stronger tenants, but because of lower rent, they can attract better local merchants. It is quite different for a well-established downtown business to open a suburban branch and for a new or unknown business to open up in a satellite location. There is obviously less risk for a drugstore than a specialty shop, but to the extent that there is a risk, there is the profit, if successful.

An aspect of business that is too often forgotten in good times when there is enough business for all is that extremely high profits breed ruinous competition. This is true in many cities where there is already an excess of peripheral retail outlets. There are more spectacular examples of this in Los Angeles than elsewhere, but still new ones are created and opened with the floodlights and fanfare of a new show.

Experienced real-estate firms, who keep the same customers and clients over a period of years, always advise the inexperienced or new ventures to start in a proven location.

Location in relation to materials or clients. Service business or professional services, which have contacts with all the walks of life of a large area, should seek a location near the theoretical center of population of the area served and then adjust it for zoning and other regulations and to fit into the transportation pattern.

Industrial firms must study their products to determine whether or not it is better that they be near their customers than that they be near their source of materials. The need to remain competitive in price and to furnish diversified products has resulted in diversification of many steel processes where there are very substantial markets to which components may be shipped by inexpensive water transportation. On the other hand, bakers have found it cheaper to serve a large area from a central bakery where materials can be handled in large quantities than to have numerous small manufacturing establishments. Fabricators of heavy metal products such as wire, alloy strip, tinplate, etc., generally find it better to be near the source of material and to ship the finished product to distant customers. This is especially true of plumbing fixtures, pipes, and cable. On the other hand, more complicated fabrications or those which may be made in a lesser number of units usually find that it is cheaper to locate close to customers and ship in the heavy raw materials.

Location as it affects employees. This consideration is of primary importance when continuity of service and low labor turnover are desirable, and it increases in importance as these factors become sufficiently important to outweigh inconvenience to customers, clients, or materials.

Many a large corporation has found it necessary to locate its research laboratory in pleasant surroundings where its employees can find the amenities of life to their liking. So it is that more and more business firms who specialize in research, analysis, design, or consultant service find that they can achieve the essential quality of performance only by retaining their employees long enough to train and take full advantage of their best ability, and for that reason they have located in suburban areas or college towns. The list of those firms which are finding this factor important is a long one and is being enlarged. Many investment-counsel firms, architects, engineers, and those who can have a separate technical and professional staff find it desirable to have a small office in a central location and large quarters for the rest of their staff elsewhere; the saving in rental overhead is important.

Publishing houses have sought such locations ever since Doubleday located its establishment in Garden City, Long Island, early in this century. Certified public accountants and insurance companies have followed this trend. Corporate headquarters have headed for the suburbs in mounting numbers in the last 5 years.

The importance of transportation facilities. It has been truly said that transportation is location. Nothing is more important to a business than transportation. All forms of transportation are of importance: land, air, and water, both public and private. Air transportation is as important to the home office of a national sales office as pedestrian transportation is to F. W. Woolworth. The former must locate in a city with good air service and the latter must be on well-paved Main Street. Grain shippers must be located on good rail or water transportation facilities and preferably both. Many industrialists to their sorrow have located on an otherwise good site for the manufacturing of a product which required either rail or highway transportation, only to find a few years later that they were forced to change their product and that such change required the use of the missing means of transportation as well as the other.

Employees who have to drive to work in their own cars must earn enough to pay for this expensive form of transportation. Dependable and cheap public transportation is essential for all general business locations. Time consumed in travel is nonproductive, and it is the time factor rather than the distance factor which is of importance.

The transportation aspect of a location is the primary reason for its rate of growth. In those cities where the growth is more rapid than the average, there is better transportation than the average. The 1940, 1950, and 1960 censuses all showed a slowing up of the rate of growth of our larger cities and an increase in the metropolitan regions outside of the cities. This trend has continued and while the growth of population has been numerically impressive, the rate of growth has continued to deaccelerate. The Bureau of the Census, in its report *The Growth of Metropolitan Districts in the United States,* shows that the large metropolitan districts grew faster than the central city in each year since 1900. Thus we see that "decentralizing" is taking place as between neighborhoods or industries, but not as between cities and their metropolitan areas.

This is caused largely by the modern rapid transportation systems of the American central cities and the extension of this transportation system to the metropolitan area as a whole. This system must be regarded as a vital, dynamic force having a direct bearing upon the use of real estate and its effect on every form of business.

Adequacy of space. The size and shape of the space required by a business is a matter of opinion and has to do with the manner in which a business is managed. It has to do with such things as inventory, off-premises work, ratio of office to shop areas, and other factors of a management type. There is adequate consulting management and engineering talent available to help in determining requirements, layout, and design. Graphs, forecasts, and market data help predict the future course of a business and determine probable future needs, but many a plant, warehouse, retail establishment, or other business real estate becomes economically and functionally obsolete because of lack of parking space, inadequate turning space for trucks, or an unsafe approach to the highway from the property. A good rule of thumb for manufacturers is to figure 250 square feet of off-street parking per car and to calculate one car for every three employees and one car for every visiting salesman or customer.

Retail stores outside downtown core areas would do well to provide a ratio of 4 or more square feet of parking space for every square foot of retail sales space. In many cases, it is well to double this ratio, as has been discussed earlier.

The same is true of building space. A manufacturer who made good-quality wooden radio cabinets turned to making modern furniture and immediately found that he needed one-third more shop space and double the storage space for the same number of employees and about the same dollar volume. A home-service store in a rural area had built up an excellent business selling and servicing stoves, washing machines, lawn mowers, and other house appliances; then along came television and the owner needed more space for display and repairs. Fortunately, he had consulted a good real-estate consultant prior to building his store and had excess height so that he could build a mezzanine.

In old buildings, one has to adjust to the limitations of the structure. There are features that are space savers and therefore make for efficiency. One feature of this kind is adequate loading space. Whether the business be a store, a manufacturer, or a distributor, a space where incoming goods can be placed for sorting and checking and then stored and where outgoing shipments may be assembled will save truck time, reduce costs, and make for efficient use of

space.   Floors that are of slightly different levels are to be avoided if possible;
if not, determine whether a conveyor can be installed to move goods.

Adequate space means usable space; avoid unusable space which you have to
heat and maintain.   Structural soundness is an important factor.   Always
remember that an architect or engineer can give you an impartial opinion
about the floor-load capacity and the characteristics of the building.   Additional bracing of floors can be costly and can so clutter up the space below as
to reduce its usefulness.

Economic stability of location.   This may be determined by a real-estate
market analysis.   The characteristics of the real-estate market are such that it
is an unorganized market based upon informal day-to-day transactions.   The
degree to which it may be accurately analyzed is in direct proportion to the
complexity of the city in which it is located.   Information is usually available
about the supply of space and the demand for it and the extent that population
pressure causes changes in the economic situation, thus creating new opportunities, but it takes an expert to properly analyze this information.   It takes
special training to list all the sales and leases in an area and to determine the
unit value of a property, the past trends, and the probable future direction.

Past experience in an area about mortgage foreclosures is not to be disregarded.   Another indication of stability or lack thereof is the number of vacancies as compared with the metropolitan district as a whole or as compared with
another similar section.   It is a full-time job to analyze this kind of information
and requires the type of expert who keeps his records up to date and who is
able to make an objective study.   Your local real-estate board will tell you
which of its members are members of the American Society of Real Estate
Counselors or the American Institute of Real Estate Appraisers.   If there are
no members of either in your community, the real-estate board will probably
recommend the best person to answer your particular problem.

Study the community pattern.   The community pattern is the result of the
habits of its people.   These habits cannot be changed, but the wise merchant
or manufacturer takes advantage of them and makes use of them.   The central
business district may appear to be a stationary fixed object held in place by the
weight of large buildings, but actually it is either growing or dying and seldom
static.   It grows with the development of the area served by it and diminishes
with the economic reduction of that area.   As the city or metropolitan area
grows to the extent that it can attract business from outside, so the downtown
business district grows.   Physical limitation may restrict the growth of the
business district and foster the establishment of outlying or peripheral business
districts, but if the outlying business district depends upon its local area for
support, it may not participate in the general economic growth or decline of
the city as a whole.   The ability to respond to the growth of a community is a
necessary characteristic of a good business district.   One factor to be considered in this respect is the ability of the district to be reached by auto, and the

parking capacity.   Another factor is the proximity of the business district to the
place of employment of the bulk of the people.   These and other factors make
a city pattern.

A careful study of the city pattern will locate the downtown core area, and
if it is drawn on a map it is well to locate the new stores or those that have
undergone modernization.   Then locate parking facilities, main routes to it,
and transportation facilities.   Surrounding this area is usually a twilight zone
of secondary business and light manufacturing.   Now locate the main freight
highway into the city and the rail lines; these locate the heavy industrial belt.
The next location to determine is the best established residential section and
the newest large-scale residential development.   The slums and other districts
now fall into the picture of themselves.   Once you have done this, you have a
picture of the city pattern.

Urban renewal has taken place on a large scale among the slum areas of
many of our cities.   Unfortunately, in destroying the slums the renewers have
brought about a relocation of the former slum dwellers, and have spread them
more or less over slum areas, thus intensifying the ghettolike qualities of those
slums.   If the former slums were replaced with residential structures, in all
probability they were beyond the economic means of those persons who were
displaced.   On the other hand, if they were displaced to create civic centers
or industrial parks, in all probability greater job opportunities have been
created.

In any event, the ethnic pattern of the city has been disturbed to a greater
or lesser degree, and very careful studies should be made of the effects of
planned or completed urban renewal projects.   They are indeed a mixed
blessing.

Trends—long-term and short-term.   Trends are caused by internal adjustments in the city growth or by basic economic changes which have a bearing
upon the life of a large segment of the population.   The advent or cessation
of a major industry in a small city is a matter of very considerable importance.
The impact upon a suburban community caused by the bankruptcy of a railroad and the removal of its service is very great.   Likewise, the economic
forces generated by the extension of an arterial highway or parkway to serve
a peripheral community have a great effect upon the area affected.   These are
fundamental forces and their influence upon real estate is expressed as trends.
These forces are slow to generate and of long-term type.   A railroad does not
fail overnight, nor does a responsible large industry move quickly.   The condition that brought about the change is one which may be anticipated if a thorough study of the subject is made.   The long-term trends are really the cumulative action of many shorter-term trends.   By short-term trends is meant the
sudden more violent movements that take place as a result of more localized
action.   An area may be donated by a wealthy citizen for a park and the effect
upon a neighborhood is immediately felt; new houses are built, bringing more

families; new stores result; and there is a need for new schools, better fire protection, churches, sewers, water—all this results in a relatively sudden increase
in land value. This is a short-term trend. The long-term trend commences
when these changes have taken place and the character of the area has been
established and the slow but inevitable decrease in value sets in.

These forces are many and often contradictory. Likewise, the short-term
trends are altered and the generating forces divert them from their course.
But the cumulative effect upon the long-term trends may be determined by the
skilled student of real-estate values.

5. Own or lease?

Having determined the location, the price that a business can afford, and the
adequacy of a property, it is well to determine whether it would be better to
own or lease. In general, the advantage gained by one method is a disadvantage to the other. The advantages of each may be stated thus:

Advantages of ownership—
    Cost of occupancy lower per year
    Interest on mortgage, maintenance, depreciation, deductible from income
        tax
    Permanence of address assured
    Possible income profit from tenants
    Alteration, demolition, or change of occupancy at own will
    Property may be security for loan
    Possible capital profit from sale
Advantages of leasing—
    Fixed and known cost of occupancy
    Rent deductible from income tax
    Limitation on period of commitment and extent of liability
    Lease salable as part of business
    No capital tied up in land, bricks, and mortar
    Less basic capital required

Both methods of occupancy require a great deal of paper work, legal forms,
and other technical work which should be handled by a lawyer. Both methods
also involve advance planning, but in the case of a lease the planning is of
shorter duration. This is the main reason why most tenants prefer to lease.
They feel that although it may cost more, there is a certain degree of flexibility
which cannot be otherwise obtained. These decisions, whether to own or
lease, have to do with the nature of the business and the degree of risk of the
business itself.

This problem, to lease or to buy, should be discussed with the real-estate consultant, the lawyer, and the income-tax adviser. All are important, and it
always pays to use the experienced services of all three. In the case of the

lawyer and the income-tax adviser, the fee is always paid by the business seeking space and so the services of an independent real-estate consultant should be used and a fee paid.   The broker in the transaction is paid by the lessor or the seller, and his advice may be colored by the commission involved.   Experienced and timely third-party advice for a fee is always worth its cost.   It is usually the best bargain that a young business can buy.

Section 7

AN INTRODUCTION TO ELECTRONIC DATA PROCESSING IN BUSINESS

BY

Lawrence L. Lipperman

AN INTRODUCTION TO ELECTRONIC DATA PROCESSING IN BUSINESS

Introduction

The necessity for keeping records has existed since men began to trade with each other. Any endeavor that resulted in a fact to be remembered had to be recorded in some form so that the details could be recalled later. At first, the process was relatively simple. The volume of transactions was small and the variety was limited. As business transactions grew in number and complexity, record-keeping methods were refined. Delineation of the different kinds of actions began to be made and the evolution of the account took place. Facts that were of a similar nature were recorded in the same place so that the data was related. An account was simply a storage place of related information. Thus, Accounts Payable were records of amounts to be paid to others, Accounts Receivable were sums owed to us, and so on. This is basically the accounting system as it is today. The important thing to remember is that basic principles have not changed. What has changed is the method of accomplishing the final objectives of the accounting system. As business procedures changed, record keeping changed to keep pace.

The steady increase in the volume of transactions and the growing need for more reports on which to base management decisions made manual methods too slow and expensive. Information on the ledgers was current, up to a point, but it was not easily summarized into the reports needed. Recapping was laborious and costly and the chance for error increased with each writing. Mass production in the factory is now possible only if the processing of business data keeps pace. The initial solution to this problem was to apply mass-production methods to the clerical work force. The typical clerical work force was organized into specialties, and the work flowed from large groups of clerks operating in each specialty.

Fortunately, the same forces that provided the techniques of mass production also furnished the climate in which mechanized data processing could grow. The first two decades of the twentieth century saw the slow growth of punched-card equipment and key-driven posting machines. Various typical business applications became quite common on these machines, especially in the larger companies. The processing of Payrolls, Accounts Receivable, Accounts Payable, and Billing applications in the larger companies were common by the end of the 1930s on so-called punched-card machines. The post-Second World War decades of the 1950s and 1960s saw these very same applications greatly expanded and a new technology introduced for the first time. The Second World War greatly developed our ability to use vacuum tubes for the design of rather complex pieces of equipment. This technology was applied to that of computation and we saw at the end of the Second World War the advent of the electronic computer.

Characteristics of electronic data processing systems. Today as then, the electronic computer is, to the layman, something of a mystery. I think that Jeremy Bernstein in *The Analytical Engine: Computers—Past, Present and Future* [1] characterized that mystery and described it succinctly in the following quotation:

> The electronic computer, young as it is, has come to play a role in modern life something like that played in other times by the oracles of Greece and Rome. There is a widespread belief that if one puts a question to, say the UNIVAC, it will perform a swarm of bizarre manipulations—comparable to the generating of the vapors in the Chasm of Adelphi—and come up, in oracular fashion, with the answer. It is more realistic, if less awe-inspiring, to look upon the electronic computer as an overgrown arithmetic machine. It can add, subtract, multiply, and divide, and it can perform long sequences of additions, subtractions, multiplications, and divisions, in highly complicated arrangements. It can also modify the course of a calculation as it goes along—that is choose which of several steps to take next in accordance with the way some previous step came out. Fundamentally, though, all this comes down to arithmetic, and, arithmetically speaking, the distinction between a schoolboy doing a multiplication a minute and a computer doing one hundred thousand multiplications a second is only one of degree.

I think that Bernstein in the above quotation has hit upon two of the major problems that we face today in understanding the essentials of electronic data processing in the business world. The first problem, of course, is that the layman looks upon the world of computers as one of mystery. This is probably because much science fiction has been passed as fact in too many reputable publications. In addition, the very complexity of these machines suggests that the application and use of the equipment is equally complex. One of the major objectives of this section is hopefully to dispel this feeling. Second, Bernstein very concisely explains the capability of an electronic computer, and this in itself is useful in that it delimits the abilities of the computing equipment itself.

Obviously, the use of electronic computers or electronic data processing equipment, as computers are commonly called today, must require intimate familiarity with the problem to which this equipment is addressed. Somehow, the computer equipment which can perform arithmetic operations and logical operations must be applied to common everyday business applications such as Payroll, Accounts Receivable, or perhaps Accounts Payable. To understand how electronic data processing is applied to common business problems such as

[1] Jeremy Bernstein, *The Analytical Engine Computers: Past, Present and Future,* Random House, Inc., New York, 1964.

these, one must first understand the basic capabilities of computing equipment and its associated input-output devices. Furthermore, one must understand the process of adapting this equipment to the common business applications. Such terms as flow charting, programming, programming languages, COBOL, Report Program Generator, must be used in describing the processes by which computing equipment is adapted for use in common business applications. Furthermore, another set of people-oriented terms become necessary when describing how these business applications are implemented for the computing equipment. We now begin to find that when implementing business applications, we need such people as systems analysts, electronic data processing managers, programmers, computer operators, and so on. It is important to understand the relation of these people to the computing equipment and the business applications of the computing equipment.

Objectives of this section. The first part of this section will deal with a description of the computer and its associated input and output devices.

The second will describe several typical applications of the use of electronic data processing equipment in business and the steps which must be taken in order to implement such systems. For the layman with experience in the business world, an understanding of the computer itself without an equivalent concept of its use in the business world is a rather sterile form of knowledge.

The third part will be devoted to the organization and personnel necessary for the implementation of electronic data processing systems.

1. Description of the electronic computer and its input and output devices

In the introduction, I described, in general terms, the capabilities of an electronic computer. I would now like to furnish a description of the various subsystems of a generalized electronic computer system and discuss the functions of each part of the computer system, i.e., subsystem. It should be pointed out that many different types of computers are manufactured today and each one differs in detail from the other. However, the basic capabilities of all of the systems are still very much similar to those described by Bernstein. Furthermore, the various functions that must be performed by the subsystems of the overall computer are also, at least in general terms, similar. The discussion in this section will speak in terms of a generalized computer.

Figure 1 portrays a generalized computer. The computer itself is made up of three basic sections. These are the channels, the core memory, and the arithmetic and control unit. All the devices that either bring data into the computer or print data out from the computer are pictured as going through the channels into the computer in Fig. 1. The arrows in the figure may indicate that data are flowing from the computer to the printer, for example, or from an input device such as the card reader into the computer, or in either direction in the case of devices such as disk storage. Where the data line is

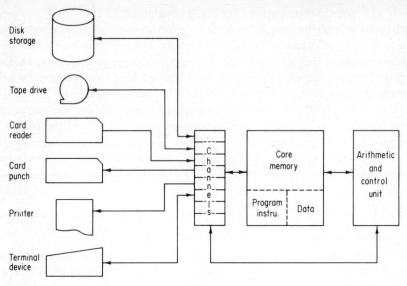

Fig. I.

shown as going both to and from a device, this simply means that this device may receive data from the computer or transmit data to the computer. Since the core memory is the central part of the computer, I will describe it first and the other parts in turn.

Core memory. A graphic representation of core memory is shown in Fig. 2. Each of the small circles at an intersection of two lines represents a memory core. This is known as a *bit.* In the particular coding scheme shown in Fig. 2, each position of core memory contains seven cores or bits.

In the majority of computers installed today, a core is a bit of magnetic material shaped like a tiny doughnut. The size of those cores is about the size of the head of a pin. The electrical conducting wires that go through each of these cores can cause them to be polarized magnetically, in either of two directions. One of these directions can be arbitrarily assigned, by the computer designer, to be the "off" direction. The other direction then can be assigned the "on" direction. The direction of magnetic polarization of each core can be controlled by the wires that pass through it.

Core organization. The core memory shown in Fig. 2 is organized so that the memory cores are grouped in sets of seven magnetic cores or bits, as I shall call them from this point on. Each bit position or row is uniquely assigned, by the computer designer, a specific value or meaning. In Fig. 3, you notice that we have positions A, B, 8, 4, 2, 1, and C. Any one of the numbers from 0 to 9 can be represented with one set of bits. Each memory location consists of one set of bits. The numbers 8, 4, 2, and 1 can be represented by turning

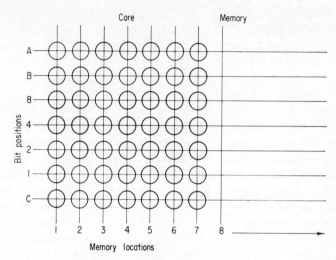

Fig. 2.

Letter or number	A	B	8	4	2	1	C
				Bit or code positions			
0		X			X		X
1						X	
2					X		
3					X	X	X
4				X			
5				X		X	X
6				X	X		X
7				X	X	X	
8			X				
9			X			X	X
A	X	X				X	
B	X	X			X		
C	X	X			X	X	X
D	X	X		X			
E	X	X		X		X	X
F	X	X		X	X		X
G	X	X		X	X	X	
H	X	X	X				
I	X	X	X			X	X
J		X				X	X
K		X			X		X
L		X			X	X	
M		X		X			X
N		X		X		X	
O		X		X	X		
P		X		X	X	X	X
Q		X	X				X
R		X	X			X	
S	X				X		X
T	X				X	X	
U	X			X			
V	X			X		X	
W	X			X	X		
X	X			X	X	X	X
Y	X		X				X
Z	X		X			X	

X Indicates bit on

Fig. 3.

212 J. K. LASSER'S BUSINESS MANAGEMENT HANDBOOK

on respectively each of those unique bits. The number 3 can be represented by turning on bit positions 2 and 1. The number 0 can be represented by turning on bits 8 and 2. As far as the letters of the alphabet are concerned, they can be represented by combinations of bits A and B with bits 8, 4, 2, and 1. Figure 3 represents one particular method of representing the numbers 0 to 9 and the alphabet in a coding scheme such as this.

You probably are wondering what the purpose of the C bit is. The C bit is commonly used in computers for checking to make sure that we have valid characters. Since electronic devices are subject to failure, and any one of these magnetic cores may fail, the computer designer arbitrarily sets forth as a rule in this particular case, that all characters must consist of an odd number of bits. For example, where a particular character may be coded by turning on an even number of bits, i.e., the number 3 would be coded by turning on bits 1 and 2, the computer will be designed to also turn on the check bit or C bit. In this way, the number of bits turned on in that particular position will be an odd number—that is, three bits. All characters moved through the computer will be automatically checked by the circuitry to see that they contain an odd number of bits. In those cases where one does not contain an odd number of bits, an appropriate signal will be given to the computer operator and he can then take corrective action.

Thus we see that Fig. 2 shows that a location in a computer's core memory will consist of seven bits. This set of seven bits can be made to represent any one of the letters of the alphabet or any one of the numbers, as well as a number of special characters not shown. Depending upon the size of the computer, the core memory can contain any number of such locations. Modern computers have recently been marketed which contain as many as a million such locations. It is more common to find among computers installed today anywhere from 4,000 locations of memory to 150,000 locations of memory—the latter in the larger installations.

The computer designer must now decide on a numbering scheme for the locations of memory. Typically, he will simply assign core memory locations numbers sequentially, from 1 through whatever number is needed to represent all the locations of memory. Later on when he designs the channels and the arithmetic and control unit, which will be described in the following sections, he will use these arbitrarily numbered memory location labels in order to fetch data in core memory or to put data into memory locations.

Storing data in core memory. The most obvious data that must be in core memory are those data upon which the computer must operate. These are the actual numbers which must be added, multiplied, or subtracted. If the computer is being used to calculate payroll, the man number of the person whose payroll is being calculated must be read into the computer memory. In addition, his rate of pay and the number of hours worked this period as well as his many deductions must also be brought into the computer memory. Further suppose the computer is to print, as a final product of the operation, a payroll-check statement.   Therefore, the man's name and address as well as other alphabetic data must also be brought into memory along with the numerical data previously mentioned.   Hence we begin to see the reason why each memory location must be capable of holding either numerical data or alphabetic data.

In summary then, the core memory will be used to hold all the alphabetic and numeric data necessary for the computer to perform a particular type of calculation or operation.   It is important to note at this point that it is not necessary for the core memory to simultaneously hold all the information, for example, 5,000 employees at the same point in time.   It must merely be capable of holding the information about one employee while it produces the payroll check for that employee, prints it out, and then goes on to get the information about the next employee.   The information about each of the employees may be in a punched card and read in through the card reader, or may be on a tape unit and read in from the tape unit, or may be in a disk-storage device and read in from that unit.

Storing program instructions in core memory.   Another use for core storage is to hold the program of instructions which the computer is to follow.   First, let us define what is meant by a program of instructions.   The computer, being a machine, must be instructed to perform a sequence of operations by its human user.   The person who actually writes this sequence of instructions, or program, for the computer is called a "programmer."

If we use the payroll example again, we can easily see that in order to process a payroll for a particular company, the computer must be instructed to perform the sequence of operations that are unique to this particular company.   A short, simple example of a program is shown in Fig. 4A.   Here the assumption is made that a punched card containing the employee's name in positions 1 through 9, his hours worked in positions 10 through 15, and his rate of pay in positions 22 through 26 is to be read into the computer from the card reader. In addition, two deductions are contained in positions 28 through 32 and 33 through 37 respectively.   The computer is to print out on the printer the man's name and net pay on the first line of the form and his deductions and rate of pay in the second line of his statement.

Therefore, the programmer must instruct the computer to read a card into positions 1 through 80.   He could, of course, have selected any core memory locations.   Next he must instruct the computer to multiply the number in positions 10 through 15 by the number in positions 22 through 26.   Here he is multiplying the man's hours worked by his rate of pay.   Next the programmer must instruct the computer to subtract from gross pay the deductions that are punched into the card in positions 28 through 32 and positions 33 through 37. Finally he must instruct the computer to print the data in positions 1 through 15, which now contains the man's name and net pay.   He must then instruct the computer to print the man's deductions and his rate of pay. Finally, he must tell the computer to return to Instruction 1 and read in the next card into positions 1 through 80. It is obvious that the computer would then continue the same process on the next card. This is a small example of a program. We will discuss programming in greater detail later in this part as well as in the next.

Fig. 4A.

Instruction number		Instruction description
1	READ CARD	INTO POSITIONS 1-80
2	MULTIPLY	POSITIONS 10-15 BY POSITIONS 22-26
3	SUBTRACT	POSITIONS 28-32 FROM POSITIONS 10-15
4	SUBTRACT	POSITIONS 33-37 FROM POSITIONS 10-15
5	PRINT	POSITIONS. 1-15
6	SKIP	TO NEXT PRINT LINE
7	PRINT	POSITIONS 28-32; 33-37; 22-26
8	SKIP	TO NEXT FORM
9	RETURN	TO INSTRUCTION 1

Fig. 4B.

Instruction number		Instruction description
1	R	001080✶
2	M	010015022026✶
3	S	010015028032✶
4	S	010015033037✶
5	P	001015✶
6	K	✶
7	P	028032033037022026✶
8	K	✶
9	B	100✶

The computer designer is therefore faced with the necessity of representing programs such as this one (see Fig. 4B) in such a manner that the instructions can be stored inside the computer memory. In this way the computer can reference its own memory, both for the instructions which it is to execute as well as the data which it is to act upon. Figure 4B represents a particular way of coding a set of computer instructions so that the operations described in Fig. 4A can be represented within the memory of the computer.

Note that Fig. 4B contains the coded representation of the respective program steps shown at the top of the page. Each of these steps are described respectively, as follows:

1. Read punched card from card reader into memory location numbers 001 through 080
2. Multiply contents of memory locations 010 through 015 by contents of memory locations 022 through 026, store result in memory locations 010 through 015.   This product is the gross pay
3. Subtract contents of memory locations 028 through 032 from the contents of 010 through 015
4. Subtract the contents of memory locations 033 through 037 from the contents of 010 through 015.   Steps 3 and 4 have now subtracted both deductions from gross pay
5. Print the contents of memory locations 001 through 015.   This prints employee's name and net pay on "Pay To" line of check form
6. Skip to statement line
7. Print contents of memory locations 028 through 032, 033 through 037 and 022 through 026.   This program step prints both deductions and hours worked on statement
8. Skip to print line on next check form
9. Return to instruction stored at core memory location 100.   The computer will return to instruction whose first letter is stored at memory location 100.   See Fig. 5 for chart of memory locations at which program instructions are stored

Asterisks following each computer instruction indicate the end of an instruction.

Summary.   The computer designer will specify a set of instructions that the computer must be capable of executing, and will arbitrarily assign a particular code to each of these instructions.   A representative example of a set of instructions is shown in Fig. 4.   These instructions in turn are stored within the core

Memory location	0 0 0 0 0 0 0 0 0 0 1 1 1 1 1 1 1 1 1 1 0 1 2 3 4 5 6 7 8 9 0 1 2 3 4 5 6 7 8 9
Contents	R 0 0 1 0 8 0 ∗ M 0 1 0 0 1 5 0 2 2 0 2
Memory location	2 2 2 2 2 2 2 2 2 2 3 3 3 3 3 3 3 3 3 3 0 1 2 3 4 5 6 7 8 9 0 1 2 3 4 5 6 7 8 9
Contents	6 ∗ S 0 1 0 0 1 5 0 2 8 0 3 2 ∗ S 0 1 0
Memory location	4 4 4 4 4 4 4 4 4 4 5 5 5 5 5 5 5 5 5 5 0 1 2 3 4 5 6 7 8 9 0 1 2 3 4 5 6 7 8 9
Contents	0 1 5 0 3 3 0 3 7 ∗ P 0 0 1 0 1 5 ∗ K ∗
Memory location	6 6 6 6 6 6 6 6 6 6 7 7 7 7 7 7 7 7 7 7 0 1 2 3 4 5 6 7 8 9 0 1 2 3 4 5 6 7 8 9
Contents	P 0 2 8 0 3 2 0 3 3 0 3 7 0 2 2 0 2 6 ∗
Memory location	8 8 8 8 8 8 8 8 8 8 9 9 9 9 9 9 9 9 9 9 0 1 2 3 4 5 6 7 8 9 0 1 2 3 4 5 6 7 8 9
Contents	K ∗ B 1 0 0 ∗

Fig. 5.

memory of the computer. This then is the first major function of core memory. That is to store the program of instructions which the computer itself is to execute. As you can see, the computer designer can easily design an alphabetically and numerically coded set of computer instructions. In addition, the memory locations, each of which can contain any letter or number, can also store data which the computer is to operate upon. This is the second major function of core memory. The arithmetic and control unit shown in Fig. 1 controls the sequence of operations of the computer.

Arithmetic and control unit. The purpose of the arithmetic and control unit shown in Fig. 1 is twofold. Its first function is to be capable of performing the arithmetic and logical functions necessary for computer operation. That is, it contains the electronic circuitry necessary to perform multiplication, addition, subtraction, and division. In a sense, it contains the circuitry found in the ordinary desk calculator which performs similar functions. It also contains circuitry which can compare one value in memory to another value in memory and determine which value is higher or lower, or find whether the two are equal. Second, the arithmetic and control unit will control the sequence of program instructions executed. By this I mean it will take the next program instruction from core memory, interpret the program instruction, and then execute the command on the data in core or on the input-output devices attached to the computer. Having executed this instruction, it will then go on to the next indicated instruction and interpret it, execute it, and then access the following instruction and so on.

Normally, the arithmetic and control unit works in two basic cycles. The first is the access and interpret cycle. In this cycle the unit will access the next instruction, i.e., get the next instruction. Normally, the next instruction simply follows the previous instruction in core memory. The arithmetic and control unit will then interpret this instruction and set up the necessary circuitry so that it may be executed. Lastly, it will actually execute the instruction. In some cases we may use a "go to an instruction which is out of sequence." In this case the arithmetic and control unit will simply fetch its next instruction from the indicated core memory location. The core memory location would not follow that of the instruction previously executed. Having accessed the instruction in this new core memory location, it will then execute these instructions in sequence until directed to go to an out-of-sequence memory location by an instruction.

A third function of the arithmetic and control unit is to control the channels which in turn are used to control the input and output devices shown in Fig. 1. In this way, the instructions stored in core memory which are designed to control the input or output devices will be interpreted by the arithmetic and control unit. It will then set up the channel which in turn will direct the input-output unit specified to perform the indicated operations.

Advances in arithmetic and control unit design. In the past, the electronic components of which the arithmetic and control unit are normally designed have been vacuum tubes and, more recently, transistors. Today, we see monolithic circuits being used in the design of arithmetic and control units. As the technology has advanced in this area, it has become more feasible to make faster arithmetic and control units and at the same time to make them more economically. The net result of this has been that computers in the near future will perform many more instructions in a given period of time than they have in the past, because the interpret and execute cycles, characteristic of arithmetic and control units, can take place in a shorter period of time. In addition, computers today have more instruction types available for use than they have in the past; the more economical circuitry possible in arithmetic and control units make it possible to provide a larger number of instructions for a given price.

In a similar fashion, core memories have evolved over a period of time so that they have become faster, and yet at the same time they have become more economical. Consequently more data and more program instructions can be stored in core memory for a given amount of money. More instructions and more data can be accessed from core memory in a given amount of time. Thus we see that both the power and the economic feasibility of computer configurations of various sizes has advanced; a computer configuration of a given capability has become economically feasible to a wider class of users.

Channels. The use of the term "channels" to describe the paths through which data must flow from the input-output device to memory or from memory to the input-output device is, I believe, very descriptive. A small computer system may contain only one channel. In today's systems, it is possible for larger configurations to contain more than one channel, sometimes as many as eight or ten. In the past, only the very largest computer systems contained as many as two channels. The same advances in technology that allowed core memory and the arithmetic and control units to develop and become more sophisticated have made it possible for less expensive computer systems to be provided with more channels. Their function is to channel data from an input-output device and convert it to the coded representation required for core memory.

The channel performs a number of functions. It must be capable of issuing commands to the input-output device. It must be capable of starting it, stopping it, causing it to read, or, in the case of a printer, causing it to print. It must also have a number of special capabilities. For instance, in the case of a tape drive, the channel must be capable of directing the tape drive to rewind itself; or, in the case of a printer, of causing it to skip a line. The channel must also be capable of providing a means of transfer of information on any one of the input-output devices to the core memory of the computer, or conversely, allowing information resident in the core memory to be directed to the appropriate input-output device. There are a large variety of input-output devices that may be connected to a computer. Each input-output device may code information on its particular medium in its own unique fashion. Therefore, the channel must be capable of converting the codes on the punched card, or on the magnetic tape, or on the punched-paper tape, to the code that is used to represent letters, numbers, and special characters in the core memory of the computer.

Channel operation as part of computer system. The first computers were designed in such a manner that only one of the subsystems of the overall computer system could be operating at one point in time. For example, if a card was being read into the memory of the computer, the arithmetic and control unit could not be executing a multiply instruction at the same time. Suppose the arithmetic and control unit was taking a program instruction from core memory in order to interpret it. At this same instant the channel could not be directing data from core memory to the printer. As computer designers became more sophisticated and as the cost of the basic circuitry decreased, it was found that it is economic to allow more than one component part of the total computer system to operate at the same period of time.

The computer designers quickly realized that the input-output units were the slowest parts of the entire computer system. To a large extent, with our first systems, the total rate at which data could be processed depended entirely upon the speed of the input-output units, since these were very slow in comparison to the speed of the core memory or the arithmetic and control unit. Computer designers decided to allow more than one input or output operation to take place at the same point in time. This required that data be read into the memory through a channel during the same period that data were being channeled to the printer or to a tape drive. Thus, at first channels were used to allow data to be read into memory while other data were being written from memory. This immediately resulted in virtually halving the time taken to process a particular group of data. This process time is the sum of the time required to read the data in, process the data, and then write the data out. The time taken to process data is negligible in business applications when compared to the time required to read or write data. Therefore this use of channels was a vast improvement over the previous method of reading and writing data.

Summary. Thus we see from Fig. 1 that the channels, the core memory and the arithmetic and control unit, in a sense, make up a rather self-sufficient group of subsystems which are designed to provide storage in core memory for program instructions and data; provide an arithmetic and control unit which interprets and executes program instructions; and finally provide through the channels a means of communicating with the outside world through input-output devices.

Input-output devices. The input-output devices available to computer systems today range from key-driven typewriter devices or terminals to punched-card readers or punches, to printers, to magnetic-tape readers or tape writers, to punched-paper-tape readers and punches and so-called disk-storage devices. The most commonly used input-output medium for computer systems today is probably punched cards. This is because computers have commonly evolved in companies which had punched-card equipment installed in the 1930s and 1940s. It was natural for the first users of computing equipment to attempt to use the machine-readable punched cards, which contained many of their business files, their computers and use them in conjunction with their existing equipment.

Punched-card input-output devices. The number of different types of punched-card input-output devices available on the market today precludes my discussing any particular device specifically. However, most of the devices in use today use the IBM punched card. An example of this particular type of card is shown in Fig. 6.

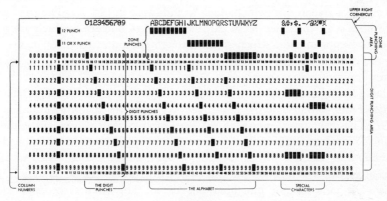

Fig. 6.

You will notice that there are 80 columns in which information can be punched. The information that can be punched in any one of these columns is any of the numbers 0 through 9; any of the letters of the alphabet; or any one of a number of special characters. The coding scheme is fairly simple in that there are nine rows in which numbers may be punched. These are rows 0 through row 9. The number of the row is the same as the number to be punched. In order to code letters, there are "12 and 11" row positions called "12" punches or "11" punches. These, in combination with the numbers punched below the 12 or 11 punch connotes a unique letter of the alphabet. You will notice that the letters A through I are all punched with the 12 punch, and the numbers 1 through 9 respectively. The letters J through R are punched with an 11 punch plus the number 1 through 9 respectively. The letters S through Z similarly use the "0" row as the zone punch and the numbers 2 through 9 respectively.

The information on these cards must be read into the computer and various types of card readers are furnished by the manufacturers for this purpose.   The main difference between the card readers manufactured is the speed at which they can read the cards.   These speeds range from as few as 50 cards per minute to as many as 2,000 cards per minute.

In addition to reading information from punched cards into core memory, it is also necessary to punch information residing in core memory into punched cards.   The card punches attached to a particular computer will punch information into the cards in accordance with the same coding scheme used by the card readers reading information into this particular computer system.   Figure 6 is also typical of the coding scheme used for many of the card punches installed today.   The main difference between card punches is the speed at which the cards may be punched.   The speed of card punching ranges from 50 cards per minute at the low end of the scale to as high as 250 or 300 cards per minute.

Card input-output equipment on computer systems is normally attached to the computer system through channels as indicated in Fig. 1.   The card reader will usually sense the holes in the cards by means of photocells which are placed to detect beams of light which shine through the punched holes in the card. The mechanism which moves the card past the photocells and to the input or output hoppers is mechanical.

Therefore, this equipment will run relatively slowly when compared to the speeds of the channel, of the core memory, or of the arithmetic and control units.   The mechanical nature of the card input-output equipment is the predominant factor in making this equipment slow in comparison with the central computer subsystems.   This makes the use of multiple channels tied to a computer attractive.   With multiple channels, card readers can be reading in cards while card punches are punching out data.   This allows the input-output equipment more nearly to balance with the speed of internal computation.

Printers.   The final output device of any computer system must be a printer. The results of computation cannot be used unless it is printed out and made available.

Normally, printing devices attached to computing equipment will have 132 print positions.   This means that anywhere up to 132 characters may be printed on one line.   Any one of these characters may represent any of the characters or numbers that may be stored in core memory.

The speeds of printing devices have increased tremendously in the last 10 years.   Output printers range in speed from 150 lines per minute to as much as 2,000 lines per minute.   Most printers used today are electromechanical in nature and are limited by the very fact that the print type must ultimately touch the paper.   The printers are attached to channels which in turn are attached to the core memory of the computer.   Those computer systems that have more than one channel may have more than one printer operating at the same time.

Magnetic-tape drives.   Very early in the development of computer systems, the designers realized it was necessary to increase the density of information on the input-output device so that the mechanical system that must be used to read the data could be as effective as possible. Magnetic-tape recording drives were used to read data into the system as well as to write data out for temporary storage. The fatc that data encoded similarly to that shown in Fig. 3 can be magnetically inscribed onto a small lightweight strip of magnetic tape without physical contact between the writing head and the magnetic tape itself is the basic advantage of magnetic-tape recorders. Furthermore, the tape can be read without the head actually touching the tape, and therefore the speed of reading or writing magnetic tape can be vastly greater than that of card input-output devices. Furthermore, where a 7.25-inch card can have 80 characters encoded on it, the increased density possible on the magnetic tape allows as many as 2,000 characters to be recorded on 1 inch of magnetic tape.

In this way, the speed of transfer of numeric and alphabetic information to and from a magnetic tape drive is as much as 500,000 characters per second on many systems installed today. On the other hand, the maximum speed at which data may be read into a computer device today from punched cards is approximately 1,000 characters per second. Consequently magnetic-tape drives are used for the storage of large, frequently used business files.

As can be seen in Fig. 1, magnetic-tape drives can also be attached to the channels of the computer. Therefore, in the larger computer systems, more than one magnetic-tape drive can be read from or written upon during the same period of time.

Disk-storage units. While the magnetic-tape drive represented a vast increase in speed over card input-output equipment, it lacked one valuable characteristic of card files. Even on the fastest magnetic tape drive it takes about 2 or 3 minutes to read a reel of magnetic tape completely. It also takes a minute to rewind the tape once it had been used. It is important to note that a magnetic tape is basically a serial device and it must read from beginning to end. On the other hand, a file of punched cards filed in storage cabinets is "randomly accessible." That is, any card can be taken from the file of drawers without reference to the other cards. The user need only know the sequence in which the cards are stored to go ahead to the particular card he wants, manualy pick it out, look at it, perhaps copy it, and put it back in its place.

There is no similar capability for the user of magnetic tape. He must read earlier records on the tape reel before he gets to the particular one he wants. Therefore, computer designers decided they required a device which would allow the system to randomly access any record stored on it. Disk-storage units are the most widely installed input-output devices that permit random access to magnetically inscribed records.

Figure 7 portrays the typical disk-storage device. The recording surfaces themselves are large disks mounted one on top of the other on a central shaft which is spinning. The recording heads or reading heads are also mounted on a shaft, one above the other, so that there is one recording and reading head over each disk surface. The data are recorded on the disks in circular tracks very similar to the recording on a phonograph record. The access mechanism or shaft upon which the recording heads are mounted can be moved so that the recording head can be placed over any one of the circular tracks upon which data are recorded on the disks. In this way, data from the computer can be

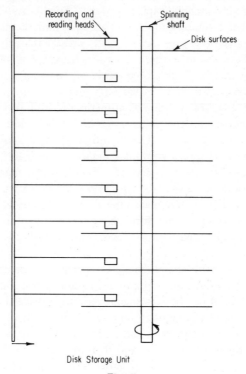

Disk Storage Unit

Fig. 7.

directed through the channel to any one of the recording heads. The recording head can be aligned over the particular track by the access mechanism and the data can be written onto any one of the tracks. The data that are already written on any one of these particular tracks may be read by the reading head.

The basic advantage of this type of system is that any one of the records stored on the disks may be accessed individually in any sequence. The computer need no longer get a particular record from the middle of a magnetic tape reel only after having read all of the records before the record desired. In this way, the disk-storage units provide for random access to any one of the records stored in them. This furnishes the computer system with the same ability that the chief clerk has in a business where records are kept on ledgers.

The computer can pick up any one of the records stored in the disk file and read it and perhaps alter it just as the chief clerk can handle a ledger card.

Terminal input-output devices. The geographically decentralized nature of the typical business operation today requires that the computer be accessible from geographically decentralized locations. In some cases, this means the direct transmission of information from terminals at remote locations over teletype lines or telephone lines to the computer at the home office. These terminal devices may consist of any one or a combination of the following: typewriter keyboards, typewriter printers, high-speed printers, card readers, card punches, tape readers, tape punches, as well as other devices.

Conceptually, these terminal devices are not different from the card input-output units and printer units described previously. The only difference is that they may be located at great distances from the computer installation and may transmit their information from the terminal device through various types of transmission lines to the central computer installation.

Much of the current design effort in large computer installations is directed toward allowing the geographically decentralized operations of a large business to use the centralized computer remotely. The distant locations can access the centralized files maintained by the central computer and also utilize the computing power available at the central computer installation through these devices.

Because of the relatively slow transmission speeds of publicly available transmission lines, terminal devices usually operate at much slower rates of speed than the directly connected input-output devices previously described. For instance, the typical terminal tape reader may operate at 7 to 15 characters per second. The card readers and punches operating from remote terminal devices may operate at speeds below 50 cards per minute. These devices are generally connected to the central computer through a channel especially designed to handle remote terminal devices.

2. Typical applications of electronic data processing equipment

Today electronic data processing equipment is widely used in business. The spectrum of applications ranges from those typical of the aerospace industries to such specialty applications as those typical of stock brokerage. Those common in most businesses will be described here.

The three steps to be taken in designing an application for use on electronic data processing equipment are systems analysis and design, flow charting, and programming.

Systems analysis and design. It would be difficult to exaggerate the crucial importance of the systems analysis and design phase of data processing applications development. Here, the real challenge of data processing is met. A systems design and analysis provides an opportunity for a comprehensive examination of an organization's application in a particular area, with the objective of making it more efficient.

The first step is to analyze and define completely the stated report requirements in this particular application. Reports should contain only necessary information. Detail in summary reports as well as exception reports should be analyzed in the same way.

It is possible that some reports could be eliminated and others combined. Perhaps some new reports should be added. Ingenuity and insight at this point should yield high dividends in the future. Data processing systems can generate information much faster and more accurately than any previous means. There is little point to this, however, unless the information generated can satisfy specific business uses.

Following are examples of questions which should be answered at this time:

What reports (format and information content specified) are necessary to operate this phase of the business?
What reports would improve the management of this phase of the business?
What data output will be used as input to other applications?
What policies and procedures will be affected by new reports or changed reporting methods?
What are the necessary or desired periods which reports should cover?

The second step is to determine what data, be they in files or flowing through business as transactions, are available as a base for generating reports and other output information. Ideally, all desired data will be available in the business today. If they are not available, a decision must be made whether the reports desired justify the additional data collection effort.

The results of the detailed analysis and a definition of the applications should be written up and supported with exhibits. It should also be approved and signed by the heads of the departments concerned. This is desirable because misunderstandings may easily occur in areas such as the following:

What are the estimated volumes?
What raw data will be available?
What input and output data format will be used?
What information is required in the input and the output data formats?
What codes will be used to identify the various input and output data fields, i.e., salaried or hourly employee?
How are the various transactions and exceptions to be handled?
What are the time cycles for collection and dissemination of input and output data?

A written document which has been reviewed, approved, and signed by all of the department managers concerned assures that the applications have been thoroughly investigated, documented, and agreed upon before flow charting and programming begin.   Under these conditions, there should be a minimum of changes required after the data processing system becomes operational.

Flow charting. Once the systems analyst has investigated the application as previously described, he must sufficiently define the application so that it can be broken down in terms of computer runs.   When defining the individual runs, the systems analyst must consider such things as the number of programming steps that can be accommodated in core storage, the number of input-output devices on the system and their type, the necessary sequence of operations, and lastly the frequency with which this particular run must be made.

An example of a run design is shown in Fig. 8, which represents a simple Accounts Receivable application.   Transactions are shown as entering the system as batches of punched cards.   These batches may have been made when the payments were received by mail.   First the cards are read into the computer by batch and are checked to see whether the batch totals are correct and whether the cards are punched in error.   At the same time, a tape copy of the cards is produced.   In order to post the payments or billings to the customer

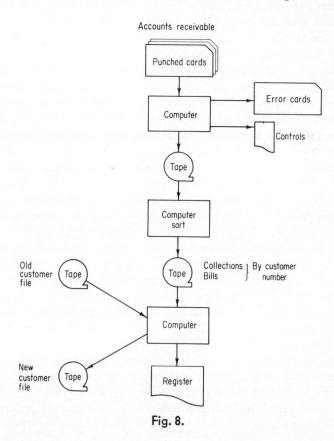

Fig. 8.

accounts, it is necessary to sort the cards recording these payments or bills into the same sequence as the customer file. The next computer run shown by the systems analyst in this case is a sort run where the input tape is the copy of the card images and the output tape is the same copy of these card images, now in customer number order. In the next run, the record of each payment or bill is read into the computer in turn. The matching customer account from the customer file is read in and the new receivable or payment is recorded on the matching customer record. At the same time a new updated customer file is written. This run also produces a register giving the latest version of all changed customer accounts.

Figure 8 in simplified form shows the type of activity the systems analyst will undertake during the systems analysis and design phase of the work. As you can see, a tape is connoted by a specific symbol, as are the punched cards and printed output from a computer. In this phase, the systems analyst will also design the layouts of the register shown and will design the makeup of each record kept in the customer file. He will also design the makeup of the punched cards recording the transactions as well as the types of controls that must be taken on each batch. He will specify the order in which the runs will take place and the way in which the customer file will be updated by the various types of transactions that may take place.

At the next level of detail the systems analyst will make up a detailed description of each of the so-called runs shown in Fig. 8. For example, when editing the transactions read into the first run of Fig. 8, he must specify each of the types of errors that must be searched for and each of the types of transactions that may enter the computer. Furthermore, he must specify the fields that must be checked to insure that the control totals for each batch are correct. The sort run is rather simple to specify in that he merely states the order in which he wishes the transactions to be sorted. In doing this, he must specify which field of the transactions must be scanned in order to put the transactions in proper sequence. In this case it would be the customer number field.

In the third run shown in Fig. 8, the systems analyst must specify the actions to be taken for each of the transaction types that may be fed in. Quite often in an application of this type, customers are given various complicated types of discount arrangements. The transactions read in must be examined by the computer for particular types of discount codes, in which case the customer file must then be updated in accordance with the particular types of discounts used in this particular business. The systems analyst at this phase of the design must specify each type of discount code applicable.

Furthermore, the systems analyst must specify the number of transactions that may take place on a given day. He must also specify the number of customers in the file. This is necessary in order for him to make sure that it is possible to process this particular application in a given day with this particular computer configuration.

Programming. Once the systems analysis work has been completed, the next step is to do the block diagramming of each program, and following that, the actual programming.

Quite often the person doing the systems-analysis work will be somebody who is very familiar with the particular applications being studied. After having written a specification of the particular application, he may turn over the specification to a programmer, who will do the block diagramming and programming. In this case, the programmer would be a person who is basically familiar with the computer equipment itself rather than with the applications.

However, in many installations the person who does the systems-analysis work will also do the block diagramming and final programming. The advantage is that changes that have to be made after the detailed programming is done can be tested for their effects upon the actual application by a person familiar with it. In this way the problem of communications between the systems analyst and the programmer is avoided. The difficulty here is that the person who knows the application must also be familiar with the computer. Unfortunately, the man or woman experienced with the application is generally a long-term employee of the company and perhaps not particularly suited to learning programming. In contrast, the young programmer has not been with the company very long and does not know the application. In these cases the separation of systems-analysis work and programming is perhaps the best method of implementation.

Once the systems-analysis work has been done, the next step is for the person doing the programming to plan how it will be designed. This planning must be done before actually writing the program. Figure 9 is an example of a general block diagram for a payroll program which gives the overall flow of computer processing necessary in the program. First, the employee's record is read. Then it is tested to see whether the employee is a salaried employee. If he is, the program will go to block 10, where his gross pay will be developed and stored. If he is not a salaried employee, the test will be made to see whether he is an hourly employee. If he is, the program will then go to block 20, where the gross pay will again be developed and stored. Next, the program will test to see whether he is on incentive pay. If he is, the program will develop the gross pay and store it. In all cases, the program will come from blocks 10, 20, and 30, and it will next make the calculations in block 40, where the deductions and the tax will be developed and the net pay will be calculated.

The so-called general block diagram in Fig. 9 is representative of the overall planning and design of a particular program. The so-called semidetailed block diagram which further defines block 40 in the general block diagram is shown in the middle of Fig. 9. Here, the sequence of calculations is specified for developing all the standard deductions, withholding tax, FICA, and finally net pay. In block 44 the new year-to-date balance is calculated.

The so-called detailed block diagram, block 41, at the right of Fig. 9 is sometimes used. Here, a block is set up for each computer instruction that must be programmed and we see where block 41.1 specifies the sequence of instructions necessary to calculate withholding tax.

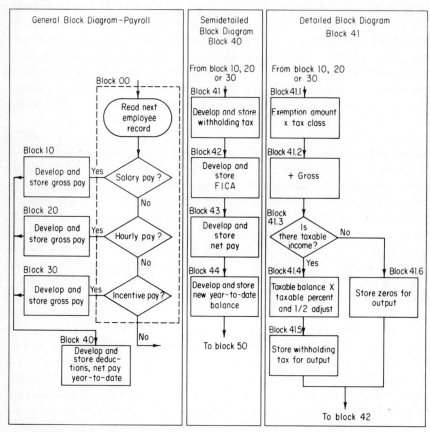

Fig. 9. (Adapted from "Planning for an IBM Data Processing System," F20-6088.)

Once the programmer has received the specifications from the systems analyst and made his block diagram, he can begin to program. Now he must use his knowledge of the computing equipment itself. He must translate the block diagram which specifies the sequence of calculations necessary to perform the business calculations required into the programming-instruction set which the computer itself must execute in order to perform the calculations. An example of a program was shown previously in Fig. 4. Here, each of the instructions that the computer must execute is signified by a code. The data upon which the instructions are to operate are signified by their location in core memory.

The program shown in Fig. 4B is an example of a machine-language program. In other words, this is the language representing the instructions which the particular computer can execute.   The computer can directly interpret the instructions and these instructions themselves can be stored in core memory.

The so-called machine-language programming instructions must be coded so that the computer itself can interpret the code.   Therefore, they are rather cumbersome as far as the human programmer is concerned.   The programmer is faced with the prospect of memorizing the individual instruction codes, which normally are either letters, single letters, or numbers.   In recent years, the use of programming languages to aid the programmer in writing his program has come into wide use.   Examples of programming languages are COBOL, Report Program Generator, FORTRAN, and many others.

Programming languages.   Computer manufacturers have developed a wide class of programming languages for use on their equipment.   The programmer, when using a programming language, can write his program in a format similar to English or, perhaps, in a mathematical representation for highly mathematical problems.   This makes it easier for him to write the program in the first place and to change it after he has written it.

Again referring to Fig. 4, we notice that the first instruction is to read a card into positions 1 through 80.   The machine language representation of the instruction read is the letter R.   Early in the use of computers, the programmer would have to memorize this fact and he would use the letter R in writing his program.   Languages such as COBOL, which are now in widespread use, will allow the programmer to write the word "read" or "write" or "multiply" or "subtract" in his program when issuing instructions to the computer.   He will write his program on special coding forms which will then be punched onto cards.   The punched cards will be read into the computer and the machine-language equivalent of the program will be punched out onto another set of cards.   The machine-language program will then be read into the computer and the programmer will test this form of his program.

The above procedure is given in Fig. 10 which shows the COBOL coding sheet where the programmer would write his program in the COBOL language, which is similar to written English.   The lines on this sheet are then punched onto cards and we now have a COBOL program.   The program is read into the computer and translated into a machine language, which can then be read into the computer and used by the programmer.

Program test.   The final step in the process of converting an application to a working set of programs is to test the programs written from two points of view.   First, the programmer must test to see that the program is processing the data as specified by the systems analyst in the original program specifications.   In doing so, he will find that in some cases he has not understood the specifications of the systems analyst.   In other cases, he will find that he has issued incorrect instructions to the computer.   He will make these tests by

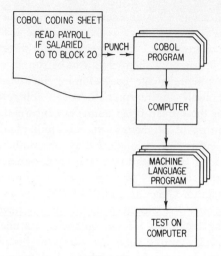

Fig. 10.

creating sample data which he will run into the computer and check the program output to see whether the output conforms to program specifications.

It is frequently desirable for the programmer, once he is satisfied that his program is working in accordance with specifications, to check his test data and test output with the systems analyst. With his deeper knowledge of the application, the systems analyst is in a better position to make sure that subtle errors regarding the application itself have not crept into the program inadvertently.

In summary, the process of creating working programs which will operate the computer so that normal business data processing can take place must proceed through these basic steps—

Systems analysis and design
Flow charting
Block diagramming, programming, and testing

3. Applications of electronic data processing equipment

Following the steps needed to implement a computer application, here are some typical basic electronic data processing applications. Figure 11 shows a flow chart of runs typical of a rather complicated payroll application which is being done on electronic computer equipped with a disk-storage input-output device.

Payroll and labor accounting. In this flow chart the disk-storage device is represented by the cylinder. As you can see, various records are stored in this cylinder and the computer will access these records when needed. Here the

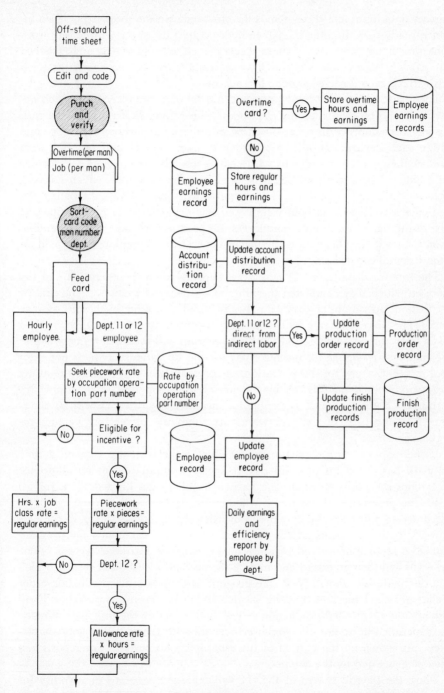

Fig. 11. (Adapted from "Payroll and Labor Accounting," IBM E30-8037.)

primary data input into the system is the off-standard time sheet.   The assumption is made that the only data recorded on the time sheet will be any work done that is not standard.   These sheets are edited and coded and punched into cards.   As a result, we now have overtime cards for each man and job cards which record each job done by each man.

These cards are sorted by department and by man number within each department and by card code for each man.   Therefore, as a result of the sort, the job cards and overtime cards will be in order by department sequence and within each department will be in order by man number and for each man number they will be in order by card code, each job card having a particular card code.   These cards will then be read into the computer, which happens to have a disk file attached.   The computer will first test to see whether the particular employee is an hourly employee or a department 11 or 12 employee. The distinction is that hourly employees are paid at a regular rate, depending upon their job classification, while department 11 or 12 employees are paid on a more complicated basis.

The rate for department 11 employees depends upon the operation and the piece on which they completed the job and on their occupation.   The rate by occupation, operation, and part number is stored in a table in the disk-storage unit.   The piecework rate by occupation, operation, and part number is then taken from the disk-storage unit and the program will then determine whether the employee is eligible for incentive pay for this operation.   If he is not eligible for incentive pay for this operation, the program will go ahead and multiply the hours worked on this job by the job classification rate to determine his earnings.   If the employee is eligible for incentive pay, the pay will be determined on the basis of the piecework rate times the pieces to give him his regular earnings.

If the employee is a department 12 employee, he is in this case on a time standard basis, and his pay will receive special computation at an allowance rate times the hours spent on the particular job to get his regular earnings. Next, the program will test to see whether this is an overtime card.   If it is, the program will store the employee's overtime hours and earnings in the employee's earnings records on the disk file.   If it is regular hours, the program will store regular hours and earnings on his employee-earnings records.   The program will then go ahead and update the account distribution record, which will distribute his labor.   Next, the program will update the production-order record to reflect the fact that this particular job has been completed and will also update the finished-production record, both stored in the disk file.   Finally, the program will update the employee's record with the record of job completion.   As shown on the bottom of this run chart, various types of reports can then be generated by the computer.

Thus, the payroll system in Fig. 11 will maintain a record of earnings for each employee on a daily basis.   It will also maintain a finished-production record and production-order record, as well as an account-distribution record.

When it is time to produce the weekly payroll, the employee's earnings record will be up-to-date as of the week. At that point, only the standard deductions need be taken from the gross pay to arrive at the net pay. Following this, the pay check itself must be printed, the reconciliation card issued, and a payroll register and earnings statement printed.

Thus, in addition to providing prompt and accurate pay check, the objectives of an electronic data processing payroll and labor accounting procedure are to—

Develop and maintain proper records of employee earnings

Record and report various taxes and other statistical data required by governmental agencies

Provide management with labor costs for general and cost accounting, budgets, and statistics

Provide operating management with up-to-date production order record and finished production record

Provide various operations control reports

Accounts Receivable. Figure 12 shows a layout of a typical customer-account record and flow chart of an Accounts Receivable application. The particular system upon which this application is shown is that of a tape system, that is, a computer system with magnetic tape as well as other input-output devices.

In this application, a master record is carried on the customer master tape for each customer. A customer-account number is assigned to each customer and the data shown in the customer master record layout are kept up-to-date on each customer. Notice that there is a "type of account" code, a "credit limit" code, a "status" code, and a "number of transactions in this month" field. Current month charges, current month payments, current month credits, and balances are kept up-to-date. In addition, aged balances over 30 days, 60 days, 90 days, and 120 days are also maintained. Lastly, various statistical data are kept on each account such as the year the account was opened, the year last active, and the highest balance owed.

On a daily basis, the sales, returns, payments, changes to existing accounts, and new accounts are punched into cards and read into the computer system. Before being read in, they are sorted by account number so that the transactions can be read in the same sequence as the customer master tape which is in account-number order.

On a daily basis then, the day's transactions are read into the computer along with the last version of the customer master tape. In this case, that would be yesterday's version. Each account is tested to see whether it has a transaction to be processed against it. In the event there is no activity for a particular account on that day, the next account is read in from the customer master tape.

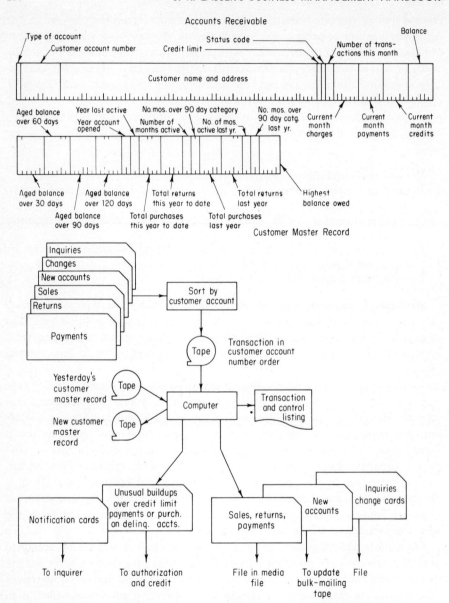

Fig. 12.　(Adapted from "Accounts Receivable," IBM E20-8035.)

When a customer account does have a transaction against it, the transaction is processed and the account is updated.　As a result of this run, a new customer master tape is written.　It will contain exact duplicates of those accounts which do not have any activity and the changed version of those accounts which do have activity. Various other outputs are produced as a result of this run.

A transaction and control listing is produced for auditing purposes. Those accounts which reflect unusual buildups of credit and delinquent accounts are punched out onto cards for further action. Various uses can be made of the transaction input cards. Sales returns and payments can be filed for various statistical studies. New accounts are filed for the future updating of bulk mailing tapes.

In summary, then, the use of data processing procedures in the Accounts Receivable application can result in many advantages, some of which are—

Increases in volume of transactions can be more easily absorbed by an electronic data processing system than by a manual system

Aged trial balances can be prepared whenever desired

Accurate account statements can be prepared when required

Automatic preparation of overdue notices can be built into the system

A flexible group of management reports can be produced as a by-product of such a system

Accounts Payable. In business, today as in the past, every purchase made creates a liability. Every liability must be paid. Every payment must be charged against the operation or process that made that liability necessary. In addition, complete records of each transaction must be kept if the business is to operate profitably and efficiently.

The bare requirements of an Accounts Payable procedure in business should produce accurate detailed records. However, efficient use of the basic information will result in various reports being made available to management. Careful analysis of liabilities history, payments, discounts, and statistical studies of vendors and their products usually constitute the data upon which management decisions are based.

The two basic classifications characteristic of Accounts Payable accounting are—

1. Disbursements, which are considered a record of liabilities from the time they are incurred until they are satisfied
2. Distributions, which are considered an accounting explanation of how much was spent and what the money was spent for

Figure 13 shows a very generalized form of an Accounts Payable procedure designed for electronic data processing equipment. We see that the purchase requisition is routed to the purchase department, where it is verified (Fig. 13A). The information on the requisition can then be keypunched onto an "on-order card."

The on-order card will contain all the information that is necessary in order to produce a purchase order from the computer. In many computerized sys-

Accounts Payable Procedure

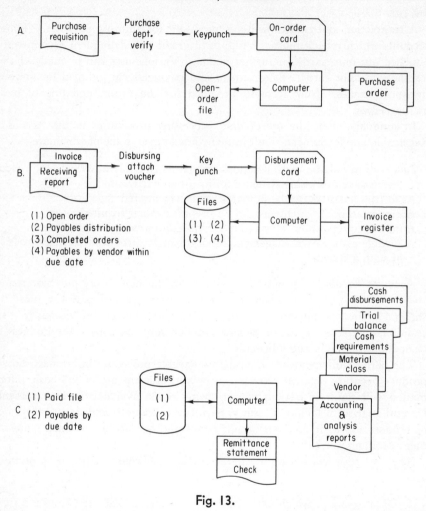

Fig. 13.

tems, a vendor file is kept on the disk file containing a record of all vendors by vendor number.   In these cases only the vendor number need be keypunched onto the card.   The vendor's address and other information can be then obtained from the vendor file.   In this first run the order is posted to the open order file and an order number is assigned to the purchase order.

When the material is received (Fig. 13B), the shipping and receiving department will fill out a receiving report indicating that the material has arrived in good condition.   Furthermore, the vendor will send an invoice and shipping notice to the purchasing department.   The purchasing department will inspect the forms and prepare a voucher for payment. As shown in Fig. 13B, a disbursement card will be punched from this voucher. The disbursement card will be read into the computer and the program will then accomplish a number of things—

The order will be removed from the open order file

The payment will be distributed to the payables distribution file

The order will be filed into the completed-order file

The order will be inserted by vendor within due date into the payables due-date file

Figure 13C shows the final run in the Accounts Payable procedure. The payables due-date file is scanned on a daily basis by another program, and each account payable is checked to determine whether its due date has come up. At the same time that the computer is scanning each account payable, it can summarize all the information required for a cash-requirements report over the next accounting period. In this way the business is able to insure that cash is available to cover checks that will be issued in the next period. For those accounts which the program determines must be paid, a remittance statement and check will be produced. Each account paid is added to the paid file.

The paid file can then be subsequently used to prepare various types of analytical reports such as—

An account-number report which furnishes, year-to-date, the payments made by type of expense account. These account numbers are assigned in order to spotlight critical areas of expense and this report can be used to see whether expense is staying within standards

A vendor report which analyzes all payments made year-to-date by vendor. This report has very obvious control uses

The material-class report which analyzes expenses by material class. This way a cross-check can be made to see whether expenses are remaining within standard by material class

A cash-disbursements register which lists all cash disbursements by vendor number. This is issued each run

The trial balance is a listing of all open Accounts Payable items. This balance will list all accounts payable by vendor number in vendor-number order. Summary totals will be made for gross Accounts Payable and net Accounts Payable by vendor

In summary then, the Accounts Payable procedure shown in Fig. 13 is intended to satisfy a number of objectives beyond that of merely producing the required checks and entries to accounts.

Among the many questions which a procedure of this type attempts to answer are—

What was the total volume of purchases from each vendor?

Who are our largest suppliers of merchandise?

How much of each class of merchandise have we bought this year?

Which vendors have the largest volumes of returns?

Are we receiving the maximum in anticipation discounts?

What cash discounts have we lost, and why?

What are the average daily cash requirements to meet payables?

What is our expense for each dollar of gross or net sales?

How much expense costs does each of our departments incur?

Summary comments on electronic data processing applications. The Accounts Payable, Accounts Receivable, and Payroll and Labor Accounting procedures described previously can be viewed as having certain common characteristics—

Pertinent files may be kept on disk-storage devices or on tape files

Daily transactions in the application are keypunched onto punched cards

The daily transactions are read, once only, into the electronic data processing system and are used to update the files and trigger the appropriate calculations and processing procedures

As a result of the entry of the transaction into the system, the required paper-work processing, whether it be payroll check, payment check, or recording of sale into proper account, is made

As a result of planning for and updating applicable or appropriate files, various types of analytical reports can be generated from this system. Since the basic data have been posted to the appropriate files in the daily processing, the analytical reports can be produced from these basic data files by a combination of sorts into proper sequence and selection of appropriate fields from records

These reports can then be utilized by management in controlling daily operations and in planning future operations. The unique factor in these systems is that the manual work required in order to process the daily transactions also results in the production of a wide variety of computer-produced reports for management purposes.

Therefore, the methodology of producing an electronic data processing application encompasses a number of activities—

The application must be analyzed and the overall flow charts must be designed

The files to be used in each computer run must be designed

A specification of required calculations and required data must be written for each computer program, i.e., run

Programs must be written for each run which will read in the input data and properly access the required files. The program will then make the necessary calculations as per specification. Lastly, the required outputs will be produced and the files will be updated

Finally, the program will be tested so that it will be free of all errors once it is put into operation

Before going on to a discussion of the implementation of electronic data processing systems, I feel I should discuss, at least on a summary basis, some of the newer applications now being implemented on such equipment. Many of the new applications have become possible today due to the development of such input-output devices as terminal equipment. In those applications where remote access to centrally stored records must be available at geographically scattered points, the advent of terminal input-output devices has made feasible the use of electronic data processing equipment. In these applications the terminal devices are connected by means of transmission lines to the central computer. The central computer will have connected to it a disk file containing the records to be accessed from the remote locations. In this way, applications in the industries listed below have recently been implemented on systems of this type—

The airlines-reservations application in the airlines industry
The demand-deposit application in the savings industry
The inventory and warehousing applications in the distribution industry

In addition, many entirely new applications have become possible due to the calculating characteristics or capabilities of electronic data processing equipment. The procedures for implementing these applications can generally be classified within the area of operations-research techniques. The implementation procedures for application of this type are similar to those described previously in this section. Here the people doing the systems-analysis work must be mathematically capable. The actual programming, flow charting, and systems analysis to be done are very similar to that previously described. Applications in common use today that fall within this area are summarized below:

Simulation. It is possible to write a program that will cause the computer to behave in a manner analogous to that of some particular industrial operation. In this way, computer programs have been written that will simulate the operations of airlines, shipping lines, or the shop floor of a manufacturing enterprise

The people studying the particular operation simulated can cause the simulation model to be varied. By varying the number of airplanes or types of airplanes in the airline or perhaps the different types of shipping routes for the shipping line, or the number of machine tools at the machine stations, the people using these programs can determine which is the best type of shop floor design, airliner design, or freighter design for their particular operation or for forecasted operations they expect to need in the future

Linear programming. This is a mathematical technique which allows a particular type of operation to be described in mathematical terms. The computer can then be programmed to solve the mathematical equations supplied by the analyst in such a way that the optimum value of all the variables in the operation can be determined by the computer program.

These techniques are used quite commonly today in various process industries such as oil refining and chemical manufacturing

Inventory management and control techniques. This technique is commonly used today in the retail and wholesale industries. In this type of application, an inventory file is maintained by the computer. The systems analyst installing this type of application will have to determine the rules by which the stock level of inventory will be scanned in order to determine reorder points. These rules can be rather complex, for they take into account such variables as sales forecast next period, purchase economic order quantity, production economic order quantity, level of service to customer, lead time for particular items, and finally effect upon manufacturing process of the various service levels

These and many other advanced techniques are commonly being programmed onto electronic computers today. However, the widest class of applications programmed today are implemented similarly to the so-called bread-and-butter applications, i.e., Accounts Receivable, Payroll, and Accounts Payable.

4. The organization for and the implementation of electronic data processing systems

In the popular literature today much is made of the idea that we are entering an era in which human beings will be replaced by computers and other types of automatic devices. I am sure it is obvious, even to laymen in this field, that electronic data processing systems must be implemented by large groups of people. Once in operation, they must be run on a day-to-day basis by human beings organized to function within a business.

Therefore, when considering electronic data processing in his organization, the business manager must answer the following questions:

How will it be organized within the organization?
How shall I staff the electronic data processing organization?
How shall I initially implement electronic data processing systems?

I will attempt to provide some of the answers to each question.

Where should electronic data processing be organized within the existing business organization? Figure 14A depicts the organization that is probably most prevalent within American industry today as far as electronic data processing is concerned. Here you will notice that EDP falls within the financial area and comes under the cognizance of the controller or assistant controller.

The reason is that quite often electronic data processing evolved within the organization as an outgrowth of punched-card data processing. This type of equipment is generally first used for accounting applications. It was therefore natural for the electronic data processing effort to fall within the

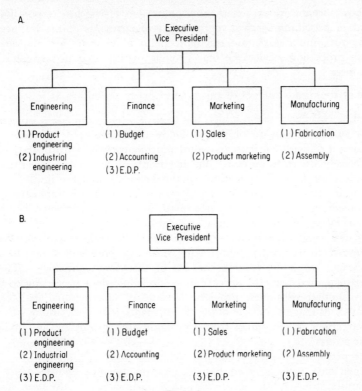

Fig. 14.

responsibility of the controller. In this type of organization, the engineering department, the marketing department, and the manufacturing department must come to the financial people for electronic data processing services. The advantages of this type of organization are as follows:

Electronic data processing is initially installed by those people within the business organization who are most knowledgeable in this area and who have the most sophisticated applications. It is typical in business organizations today to find that the accounting systems as represented by General Ledger Accounting, Accounts Receivable, Accounts Payable, and Payroll are those which are best developed. It is not unusual to see various types of ledger-posting machines and punched-card data processing equipment used in applications of this type

Planning for electronic data processing is done by one organization within the entire business. In this way, an overview of the requirements of engineering, marketing, and manufacturing can be maintained by the electronic data processing people. It is easy for them to do this since anybody requiring electronic data processing services within the organization must come to them for these services

In those organizations where the controller views his responsibility as that of providing services to the other departments of the business, it is easy for him to maintain the same point of view toward the electronic data processing services he may provide to the other departments of the business

Some of the disadvantages of this type of organization are as follows:

The financial department, which has control of electronic data processing, is not sufficiently aware of the problems of the other departments. This makes it difficult for it to give all departments their rightful share of these relatively scarce resources. The net result of this condition is that relatively unprofitable applications in the financial area are implemented on the computer. On the other hand, potentially profitable applications in the engineering, marketing, or manufacturing area are neglected because the financial people are ignorant of the problems

Since electronic data processing is within the jurisdiction of the financial department, the other departments do not become fully aware of the advantages available through the use of this new technology. These departments may be reluctant to allow electronic data processing to become too familiar with their problems because of jurisdictional jealousies and fears. Managers in the other departments may look upon systems investigations by personnel from electronic data processing as "prying into our affairs"

Quite often in this type of work, the most profitable application of electronic data processing equipment requires advance knowledge of future planning for activities in the various departments. In the type of organitional structure shown in Fig. 14A the controller might not be fully aware of plans in manufacturing, engineering, or marketing

Figure 14B represents an organizational structure that takes care of many of the weaknesses shown in Fig. 14A. However, the business can find itself faced with many difficulties if it is organized as shown in Fig. 14B. Some of the advantages of the organization structure shown are—

Each department has its own electronic data processing organization. Therefore, each manager of each department can implement the most profitable computer applications possible in his department

The systems-analysis work done for each of these computer applications is done by people fully familiar with the operation in each department. The systems-analysis people also report to the manager of the operation for each department and are therefore very much aware of the need for successful implementation in that department

Some of the disadvantages of this type of organizational setup are—

The independent and autonomous electronic data processing groups may find it difficult to produce applications that span departmental lines

The autonomous electronic data processing groups may find it difficult to cooperate on specifying a particular computer system and a standard method of operating this computer system.   This quite often results in each department procuring a small computer system for its own use.   The net result of this is that the costs of electronic data processing for the company as a whole are higher than they need be were a larger computer system to be procured.   A larger computer could be used for all computer applications in the business

Due to the autonomous and independent electronic data processing activities carried on in each of the departments, none of the departments are large enough to afford a truly able electronic data processing manager, and in addition none of the departments are capable of supporting a high-level electronic data processing technical group

The majority of electronic data processing systems installed are placed in the organization as shown in Figs. 14A and B.   However, in the recent past, a new type of organization has been recommended in the literature and in some cases adopted by some of the larger organizations.   This organization structure is that shown in Fig. 15.   Here a separate department is set up called manage-

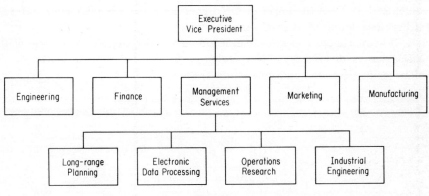

Fig. 15.

ment services.   This department reports at the same level as the other major departments of the business—engineering, finance, marketing, and manufacturing.   The function of this department is to provide management services to all the other departments of the business.   Specifically, these management services would include that of long-range business planning, electronic data processing, operations research, and industrial engineering.

By including this broad range of responsibility within one department organization, it is expected that computer applications can be designed with a full knowledge of long-range plans currently in effect as well as a complete knowledge of the manufacturing and other operations critical in this particular business.

It is expected that in this organizational scheme personnel from the various operating departments will be brought into the electronic data processing projects for limited periods of time in order to provide the intimate familiarity with the operations themselves that are required to install such systems successfully.

The top executive must decide where in the business the electronic data processing organization is best placed. His decision in all cases should be based upon the peculiarities of his business, his product, his existing organization, and the type of people working in it. In making his decision, he will have to consider where in the organization the applications most amenable to data processing currently exist and where in the organization he needs a complete overhaul of information handling. The way in which these two questions are answered for the individual business will largely determine which of the organizational setups described above is the proper one for the particular business.

How shall I staff the electronic data processing organization? To describe the typical electronic data processing staff, let us refer to Fig. 16. Here, we have a number of organization titles, or job titles, shown in an organization structure. Each of the boxes in the organization chart is numbered. Here is a short description of each of the positions shown.

1. The manager of electronic data processing may report to any one of the executives as described in the previous section. The responsibilities of the manager of electronic data processing are to—

Provide cost forecasts for all data processing activities

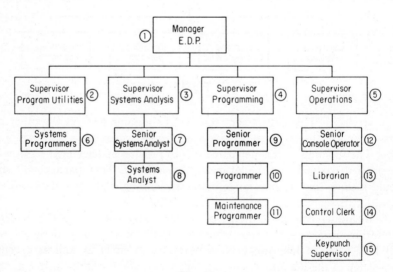

Fig. 16.

Recommend new uses for data processing equipment or abandonment of unprofitable present uses

Maintain and develop computer systems and use the equipment efficiently

Review performance of personnel and equipment in the electronic data processing organization

Direct professional development and training of staff

Evaluate applicability of new technical developments in computer equipment and in programming systems

Report to top management on the performance of data processing functions and the progress of data processing development and planning

The manager of data processing will also—

Review and approve computer systems and applications

Review and approve requests for additional data processing services

Evaluate new equipment and manufacturer's capabilities

Participate in management education in data processing concepts

Evaluate utilization of equipment and personnel

Normally we would expect that the manager of electronic data processing would be promoted from any one of the positions reporting to him. It is desirable, that depending upon the industry, he should have a Master's degree in business or some other suitable field.

2. The supervisor of programming utilities is responsible to the manager of electronic data processing for the upkeep of and use of programming systems provided to him by the computer manufacturer. It is his responsibility to insure that all programs commonly used by the working programmers in doing their daily work are in proper condition. Programs under the jurisdiction of the supervisor of utilities are generally sort programs, compilers, and operating systems. In addition, the supervisor of utilities will set programming standards and will provide the programmers with suitable means for testing their programs.

3. A supervisor of systems analysis will be in charge of all systems analysts and will plan their activities. He will provide technical and analytical assistance in the identification and solution of company systems problems. He will deal with management and other personnel throughout the company and is required to summarize problem characteristics, assign information requirements, describe procedural and operating improvements, and define data processing support.

He is responsible for the following activities:

Defining scope and tasks of systems study

Scheduling tasks and assigning systems personnel

Reviewing documentation prepared by systems personnel

Directing the design of new systems or systems improvements

Reviewing project progress and reporting status to management

Presenting systems recommendations to data processing and user department management

Reviewing systems performance and directing corrective action

Reviewing systems personnel performance for purpose of salary administration, training, and promotion

Among other technical duties the systems analysis supervisor must organize systems study schedules; estimate development cost, time, and personnel required; and evaluate the economic feasibility of proposed systems. Normally, he could be promoted from the position of senior systems analyst which reports to him. It is desirable that he have a degree in business administration or in some field applicable to the particular industry.

4. The supervisor of programming provides technical and administrative direction for the development of new programs and is responsible for the maintenance of existing programs.

The programming supervisor is responsible for the following:

He must assign personnel to programming projects

He must make estimates of programming costs and time requirements

He must schedule programming projects

He must review the performance of all people reporting to him

He must review program design with senior programmers and evaluate the operational performance of all programs

He must evaluate whether or not a program can be considered as operational and is fully tested. Usually the programming supervisor would have been promoted from the position of senior programmer or senior systems analyst. His education should be a college degree in business or in a field appropriate to the industry

5. The supervisor of operations is responsible for the operation of all digital computing equipment and the operation of the keypunching equipment. In this capacity he reviews equipment and personnel performance and develops techniques to improve performance. He reviews new applications and programs, and projects their effect on equipment operation and utilization for management evaluation. Basically, the supervisor of operations is responsible to management for the assurance of proper operational scheduling of the computer and proper operation of existing electronic data processing applications on the computer.

The necessary educational background for the supervisor of operations can be a high school diploma.

6. The systems programmer is the technical expert on all utility programs used in the data processing installation. It is the responsibility of the systems programmers to maintain and introduce new utility programs as necessary for the installation.

7. The senior systems analyst should be capable of undertaking the

initial specification and analysis necessary for the implementation of a computer application. He should be sufficiently familiar with the area of the business to which he is assigned to fully understand the data processing requirements of this area of the business. In addition, he should be capable of working as the lead analyst with a number of systems analysts.

8. The systems analyst should be capable of learning the facts about any given area of the business under the supervision of the senior systems analyst. He should be capable of working with the senior systems analyst in producing design specifications for computer applications.

9. The senior programmer is responsible for producing a working set of programs from the design specifications produced by the senior systems analyst. He should be capable of leading a group of programmers who produce a set of working programs in a particular application area.

10. A programmer should be capable of working under the leadership of a senior programmer in producing a system of programs. The programmer should be capable of planning and organizing his program and carrying it through test and final operation.

11. The maintenance programmer should be able to make changes, as necessary, to existing programs. These changes are usually the result of changes in business procedures. The maintenance programmer therefore must be capable of understanding existing programs and of changing these programs, of testing these programs and assuring that they are working properly.

12. The senior console operator is responsible for ensuring that a given system of programs currently in operation on the computer is being operated properly. He must assure that the proper tapes are mounted and that the proper cards are available at the time the program is being run.

13. The librarian is responsible for ensuring that all tape files are properly filed in the tape library and available to the operations people when they are required. The librarian is responsible for the proper cataloguing of files and for the replacement of tape files.

14. The control clerk is responsible for the maintenance of an accounting audit trail for each of the daily operations run on the computer. It is his responsibility to ensure that all necessary input is read into the computer and that all output control totals check with the expected totals.

15. The key-punch supervisor is responsible for managing the key-punch operators who punch into the cards the data necessary for input into the various computer applications.

How shall I initially implement electronic data processing systems? Since all of the larger companies in business today are already involved in electronic data processing to some extent, this section is mainly pertinent to the smaller businesses who are considering taking the step.

For the small business, the quickest and least risky method of starting down the path of electronic data processing is to procure the services of a data processing service company. These companies will, for a fee usually based upon volume of data processed, undertake to process on their own computers various types of applications. They will perform standard types of applications for most businesses, such as Payroll, Accounts Receivable, Accounts Payable, Sales Analysis, and other applications typical of the wide range of business enterprises.

When a company deals with a data processing service organization, the service organization will do whatever special programming is necessary for the user's application and will receive the data from the user on a regularly scheduled basis. These data will then be run by the data processing service organization with its own people on the service organization's own computer. The output of these applications will be returned to the user on a regularly scheduled basis. The advantage of utilizing this type of facility when first starting in electronic data processing is that the user can become fully aware of the advantages and costs of this method. In addition, many of the initial organizational problems can be surmounted when the work is done utilizing the data processing service organization personnel.

In many cases, it may be more economical, because of the volume of data to be processed, to begin to organize and run your own electronic data processing organization. In general, the larger the business, the more worthwhile it is for the business to install its own data processing equipment. In these cases, management must decide where in the organization the electronic data processing organization will be placed and in which of the existing departments will the most profitable applications be found. It is usually best to take people from these areas and use them as the core of the electronic data processing organization, giving them suitable training in computer programming and systems analysis. However, it is not always possible to find people within the organization who are capable of learning to work with computer equipment. In these cases, hire programming and systems analysis people, preferably within your own industry, who will then be the core of the new electronic data processing organization.

In any case, management will have to make critical decisions in each of the following areas:

Where will electronic data processing be organized within the business organization as it exists today? This question was discussed on page 240
What types of people are necessary in order to implement and operate electronic data processing system? See discussion on page 244
Which application areas do I first choose for conversion to electronic data processing? It is generally best to choose those areas of the business which are—
Presently operating with well-understood and well-documented manual systems
Traditional in the business and well accepted by all departments of the business. Applications such as Accounts Receivable, Accounts Pay-

able, Production Control, and Labor Distribution are of this type. Applications in the area of Business Simulation or Linear Programming would not be

Applications that can be measured to evaluate their economic feasibility when converted to computer equipment. The current manual method of processing can be judged against the computerized system and the economic advantages of the computerized system can be determined and agreed upon

Section 8

INSTALLING A PRODUCTIVE ACCOUNTING SYSTEM

BY

Maurice E. Peloubet

INSTALLING A PRODUCTIVE
ACCOUNTING SYSTEM

1. What accounting can do for management

How to run an accounting system and how to get the best results for the least expense and effort can be dealt with from two points of view: that of the executive, who is interested primarily in objectives and results, and that of the accountant, who is interested in the means and methods of attaining the objectives and getting the results required or needed by management.

No man can be a capable manager or executive and at the same time personally exercise any effective detail control of his accounting affairs. If this ever could have been done, in some simpler and faraway time, it is not possible now.

In a small business the executive must rely on his bookkeeper, his certified public accountant, and possibly some other advisors, such as specialists in machine accounting, appraisers, or industrial engineers, when the occasion demands.

In larger enterprises many of these functions are performed by members of his own organization, acting under his controller.

Other sections explain what we might call the "how" of an accounting system. They cover how to run a cost system, how to avoid business fraud, how to use budgets for the control of the business, how to design systems for internal control, and how electronic data processing methods are used in business today. This section is devoted to the "why" of an accounting system: why we use the elaborate and intricate forms and methods of modern accounting, with all of its burden of detail, its mechanical complexities, and its large number of employees engaged in producing masses of detailed statements. All accounting work must justify itself by results. The statements must either be useful to the management, or required by some outside body or agency, or required by some general business customs or regulations. Statements which have no internal use and which are not required for any external purpose should be discontinued as soon as discovered.

While management cannot devise or operate an accounting system, management is the only source from which we can discover what is expected of an accounting system and what its useful functions are. Accounting officials may suggest to management that there are certain accounting facilities which they are not using, but it is management's decision whether or not these should be installed.   To show what the properly organized accounting system can do —or, to put it in other words, what can be demanded from a properly organized accounting system—an oversimplified chart is presented showing functions under a controller and a financial vice-president.

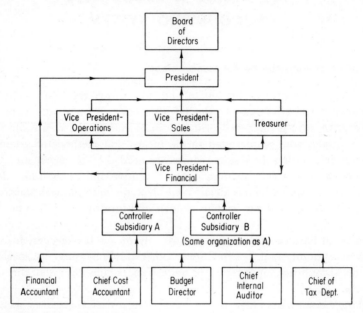

Fig. I.   Chart showing functions under a Controller and financial Vice President.

In many organizations, the controller and the financial vice-president will be the same person.   If there are a number of subsidiary companies and branches, there may be a man who fills the functions of controller in each branch or subsidiary.   In any event the functions under the controller will be the same.

In some organizations it will be advantageous to have functions such as the tax department and internal auditing under the controller of each branch or subsidiary.   In other types of organizations, it will be better for these functions to be centralized.   This depends largely on whether the problems in the different branches or subsidiaries are the same or different.   If, for example, state taxes are a very important feature, it might be advisable to have a tax division in each branch wherever it is located.   If the company has several branches in the same state, obviously it would be better to have the tax work concentrated.   These are questions for the individual organization, but the distribution of functions and what may be expected from the different accounting offices and officials are the same in any case.   Many variations in the distribution of functions might be required, but the functions themselves and the reports which management can expect are about the same.

A list of the reports and statements which management might expect from a modern accounting system follows on page 257. The list is neither inclusive nor exhaustive. Many reports with titles other than those in the list certainly will be required by the management of different corporations, although it is probable that few reports not covered in general in the list will be needed. The time classification of the reports is not at all rigid. Some of the "daily" reports may be required no more frequently than weekly, while some of the "weekly" reports may be necessary daily. With modern mechanical equipment, particularly with the use of electronic data processing, practically any of the "weekly" statements could be prepared on a daily basis, although this would be too expensive and complicated to be warranted except under special conditions. Some of the statements listed under the financial accountant might be prepared by the cost department; for instance, the statements on expenses. Some of the statements might be required only occasionally, and if this is so, provision should be made for discontinuance as soon as they are not required. What we are considering here is the use of the accounting system by management other than the accounting officers and staff. The collection and disbursement of cash, the preparation of sales and purchase orders, the mass of details involved in setting standard costs, and the collection of the voluminous details required to establish a budget are considered here only from the point of view of their final results. The sections following and a large literature cover these questions in detail. Our concern is with what the accounts can do for management.

In the last decade or a little longer, accounting has changed radically. Its purposes and principles have remained the same, but its scope and usefulness have grown almost beyond what could have been imagined, say in the 1920s or 1930s with the equipment and facilities then in existence.

Any thoughtful accountant knew, in those days, that many more extended daily reports would be useful. He also knew that physical and cost reasons made them impossible. In the same way, he knew that sales statistics, in greater depth and detail, were desirable; that money could be saved by tighter inventory and purchasing control; and that three, four, or five projections of a given policy on different bases or several alternative solutions to a business problem would be valuable, but he also knew the cost of such information would be prohibitive, and even though cost were disregarded, the results would not be available soon enough for them to be of practical value.

2. Applications of electronic data processing

The electronic computer was originally devised for scientific and engineering work, but its value for accounting and financial purposes was soon recognized by the pioneers in the management advisory service departments of accounting firms who developed the various methods and techniques for applying what is now called electronic data processing to business and accounting operations and problems.

This is, of course, a study in itself and no attempt will be made here to go into this in detail. This section is written primarily for the executive who uses the accounting records, be he the president of a national corporation or the head of a small local business. The technical aspects of electronic data processing are described in Sec. 7.

It is generally recognized that self-diagnosis or self-medication is a dangerous way to treat a disease, and that the man who is his own lawyer has a fool for a client. It is just as true that the businessman who is his own adviser on accounting, and particularly on electronic data processing matters, not only has a foolish client, but a dangerous and expensive one.

Every businessman should satisfy himself of the extent to which electronic data processing can be usefully applied to his own business. In arriving at this conclusion, there are several caveats he should bear constantly in mind. First, the equipment salesman performs a useful, indeed, indispensable function after the accounting adviser has defined the problems and indicated the solutions, but the businessman should not let the salesman act as a professional adviser.

Second, the businessman should not expect to see his present manually operated system transferred *in toto* to the computer. Nor should he expect his reports and information to be in exactly the form to which he is accustomed, although he should get the same and much more information in a much shorter time. Third, the average businessman does not realize what electronic data processing can do for him. He should have long meetings with his staff and accounting advisers to make sure that every reasonable need for information is supplied and, perhaps just as important, that any superfluous or obsolete reports are eliminated.

The areas to be explored might, for example, be—

Inventory control, particularly interplant transfers and unnecessary duplication of items

How much sales analysis is useful when an almost unlimited range is available?

What routine operations such as payroll, billing, or income-tax compliance reports are suitable for electronic data processing?

How can electronic data processing be applied to the selection of alternative and equivalent materials? This might be considered a segment of inventory control, but is of major importance in some industries

Fourthly, in some processing industries, the refining and smelting of non-ferrous metals and the fabrication of brass and copper, for example, process losses, properly analyzed, give a great deal of information about the efficiency of both machinery and management, and in some cases lead to the discovery of fraudulent diversion of valuable materials. Where this information can be drawn from an electronic memory quickly for comparison, or where the computer is programmed to call attention to anything abnormal, conditions can be corrected with a minimum loss of time.

These are only a few examples of what can be done by appropriate applications of electronic data processing. In general, the applications are specific and tailor-made. They are the result of cooperation between executives, accounting advisers, and electronic data processing technicians.

As the basic purposes of accounting have not changed, and as the applications of electronic data processing are changing almost daily, the best method for explaining to the executive the purposes and results of a modern accounting system is by comparison with the results of a manually operated system, but with the understanding that almost any of the information indicated can be secured more quickly, in greater depth, and with greater opportunities for comparison by the use of the electronic data processing, if this is needed.

With this in mind, the characteristics of a manually operated accounting system are described, but always with the understanding that more information can be obtained by electronic data processing. It is the duty of the executive and his accounting and technical advisers to decide what is necessary and useful.

Reports Usually Found Necessary in a Manufacturing Corporation

(It is unlikely that any one organization will require all the reports listed below and it is equally unlikely that an enterprise of any size will not require some reports which are additional or which differ in some way from those described. The check list is suggestive only, but it is hoped that everything of importance is covered.)

(Prepared by or under the Direction of the Financial Accountant)
Daily reports
    Cash position
    Sales (orders taken)
    Unfilled orders
    Purchase commitments
Weekly reports
    Payroll summary
    Payroll analysis, as between—
        Direct labor
        Indirect labor
        Construction labor
        Overtime worked

Number of employees
Average wage
Bonus or incentive wage
Shipments to customers (dollars or quantities or both)—perhaps analyzed
  as under "Sales"
Materials received
Collections on customers' accounts classified by age of accounts
Lists of overdue accounts receivable
Summary of accounts payable

Monthly reports
Balance sheet—comparative with beginning of year
Income account (month and year to date), comparative with same month
  of previous year
Sales, orders received analyzed by—
  Geographical distribution
  Products
  Size of orders
  Stock or special
  Salesmen or sales offices
Materials and supplies received and taken into account:
  Raw materials
  Parts
  Manufacturing supplies
  Other supplies
  Machinery and equipment
  Construction supplies
Expenses:
  Fixed
  Semivariable
  Variable
  Commercial
  Administrative
Cash receipts and disbursements agreed with income account
Inventory statements, estimated if perpetual inventories are impracticable
Construction program:
  Expenditures for year
  Expenditures or unfinished projects, in total
  Appropriations unexpended
Graphic presentation of reports for directors

Annual reports
Detailed comprehensive report to management on operations (this may
  sometimes be prepared by the independent CPA) including—
    Comparative balance sheet
    Comparative income account:
      Explanatory schedule for each balance-sheet and income-account
        item

Explanation of unusual or significant items

Cumulative surplus account

Statement of cash receipts and disbursements

Balance sheet and income account for stockholders or other security holders

Balance sheet and income account for credit grantors

Reports required by governmental bodies. (These are merely examples. There are many others and every corporate accounting officer should make certain what reports his company is responsible for)

Securities and Exchange Commission

Interstate Commerce Commission (if a manufacturing corporation has railway or utility subsidiaries)

Federal Power Commission

State Public Utility Commissions

Special statements

For security issues

For purposes of merger or acquisition or sale of subsidiaries

For management profit participation

For pension plans

For self-insurance of any type

Statements of current or appraised value of buildings, machinery, and equipment

Statements of current value of inventories, investments, or other assets not to be converted into cash in the ordinary course of business

(Prepared by or under the Direction of the Chief Cost Accountant)

Cost reports

Estimates of new work or products:

Full overhead basis

Differential basis

Standard or historical costs of products

Standard or historical costs of processes, cost centers or operations

Comparative statements of fixed, semivariable, and variable costs

Statements showing the nature of, and reasons for, variances of actual costs from standards

If job costs are used, progress reports on unfinished jobs

Statements showing comparative and cumulative processing losses

Comparative statements of any of the foregoing for different plants or subsidiaries

Production reports—daily, weekly, or monthly

(Prepared by or under the Direction of the Chief Cost Accountant)

Budgets

Preliminary budget

Agreed master budget

Monthly comparison of results and budget

Detailed monthly comparison of results and budget for departments, plants, or subsidiaries

Break-even point statements
Entire enterprise
Entire plant
Departments
Forecasts of—
Cash requirements
Effect of changes in sales volume
Effect of changes in wage rates
Effect of change in material prices
Effect of changing products, dropping some or taking on others
Effects of regulatory legislation other than tax legislation

(Prepared by or under the Direction of the Chief Internal Auditor)
Audit reports on plants and departments
Special investigations
Reports on system of internal check and control
Personnel reports

(Prepared by the Tax Department)
Tax returns
Federal income tax
State corporation taxes
Excise taxes, if these apply
Various reports on payments made to others, withholdings, and the like
Estimates of effect of proposed or current legislation
Estimates of effect of new decisions or regulations affecting the enterprise

Almost any of the reports or statements included in the foregoing checklist could be advanced in time or prepared in greater depth and detail by the use of electronic data processing. For example, the sales analysis indicated could be prepared weekly, or, to some extent, daily. It could be analyzed to show discounts allowed, returns, and allowances made for defective or damaged goods or other data.

As another example, unusual or excessive processing losses could be reported daily or weekly and inventory control and reports could be greatly extended and amplified.

The problem here is not so much what can be done as it is to decide what it is worthwhile to do.

One set of accounts to produce all statements. An accounting system should show the relations of the corporation or business to its individual creditors and debtors; it should give the management what it needs for operating and control purposes; it should make possible the preparation of statements for proprietors, security holders, and credit grantors; and it should provide for the preparation of statements to government departments, agencies, and other administrative bodies. All this should be done from one basic set of accounts. The accounting system should be designed in the beginning to produce the statements which are its final purpose and object.

There are many general principles and methods of devising and establishing an accounting system, all of which are fully covered in good technical works. Except, however, for the most simple and the smallest enterprises, there are no ready-made, complete systems. No properly devised system can be established until the accountant responsible for it understands fully the nature and the purposes of the business, the type of men who are the executives, and the type of men who will be operating this system. He must understand what is really in the mind of management and what its policies are before he can set up accounts which will produce statements that will express those policies or assist in carrying them out. He must be the careful and intelligent reporter and interpreter, always looking to the best interests of his client or employer, never deceiving him into thinking he has a temporary advantage, never letting him think that an easy way is necessarily the best way, but never restraining him from taking chances except by pointing out the nature of the chance that is being taken and the result if things go wrong.

Accountant's responsibility for management decisions. The accountant is not responsible for management's wrong decisions. He is, however, fully responsible for management's ignorant or uninformed decisions where the ignorance and lack of information is caused by statements which he has prepared improperly or inaccurately. No human mind can grasp the complexities of the operation of a large or even a moderate-sized enterprise without the use of accounting statements of some sort. If these statements are correct, if they give the proper impression, if they bring out the salient facts, then no management decision based on them is the fault or the responsibility of the accountant. But if the facts are incorrect, if the impression given is false, if the information is inadequate, then the responsibility is clearly and squarely on the accountant. Generally speaking, management must believe what its accounts tell it. It has neither competence nor time to examine into the accuracy of the statements which are presented to it. Management, security holders, creditors, customers, the government—all are entitled, if a proper modern accounting system is in effect, to rely on the statements produced by it.

If such statements can be readily prepared and are substantially accurate when they are prepared, then the system is functioning. If this is not the case, the system is not functioning. Management is entitled to have an accounting system which functions adequately, does as much as is required, but no more, and does this at a minimum cost.

Operating information. The list covers, primarily, the information which the management uses to operate the business from day to day. The management of a firm (say a manufacturing enterprise) generally must know its position in unfilled orders, purchase commitments, commitments under a program of capital expansion, and cash requirements for a considerable period in the future. Management must know, with more or less precision, what its various products cost it to produce, and frequently it must know the components of the costs of the different products which it makes or of the product which it might make.   Generally, the estimating function of cost accounting is more important than its historical function.

Electronic data processing will not only permit a cost estimate on any given basis to be prepared more quickly, but it will also permit the estimate to be prepared, at the same time or nearly so, on several bases; full cost, direct cost, or some type of differential or marginal cost.

Forecasts and projections.   These things all have to do with the future.   We are told that accountants should not prophesy, that it is their business to record and analyze and compare.   However, the ultimate value of all internal accounting information is as a basis for future action.   All management action which accounts and records can guide or affect is necessarily future action and all accounts designed for any management purpose must be looking to the future. As Patrick Henry said, "I know no way of judging the future but by the past," and it is the accountant's duty to provide the solid background of properly classified and analyzed past experience as a basis for future management action.

Requirements in integrated enterprises.   If all this information is necessary in one fairly large manufacturing organization, it is even more essential when one man or a small group of men are responsible for directing the operations of a group of manufacturing companies or of an integrated group as, for example, the United States Steel Corporation or one of the integrated nonferrous metal companies.   Management decisions in a single factory are difficult enough with adequate records and are, generally, impossible on the basis of personal observation and memory.   Without comprehensive accounts it is almost impossible to solve the problem of analyzing the conditions in a number of different plants and comparing these conditions as a basis for deciding when and where, for instance, to expand and contract, where to manufacture a new product, what manager is most capable, or what manager should be replaced. If such decisions are attempted without this accounting information, the result is almost certain to be chaos and failure.

Here again, the speed with which information can be prepared by electronic data processing and the capability of working out simultaneously several possible solutions to the same problem will make it possible for management to arrive at a sound and fully considered decision more easily and quickly.

3. Interaction of accountant and management

Policy decisions and the accountant.   No competent executive would attempt to operate a business of any magnitude without accounts which were, or which appeared to be, adequate and comprehensive.   While it is the duty and responsibility of management to make decisions, it is the responsibility and duty of the accountant to see that the information on which the decisions are made is accurate and that it conveys the correct impression.   While the accountant should not make decisions on matters of policy, it is nonetheless true that he cannot help influencing such decisions.

His statements must make an impression of some sort by their arrangement and emphasis as well as by the facts themselves. Management will act according to the impressions it receives from the statements.

A simple example of this is in cost accounting. If a company operates under a standard cost system, and if the costs are determined by operations, and if furthermore a new product is to be manufactured which will require no operations except those necessary for products already being made, the cost accountant can produce a cost for the new product by using costs for materials and operations similar to those now in effect. It will, to all appearances, be a proper cost for the new product and under some circumstances it might be. However, the cost accountant should not proceed with the compilation of such a cost until he knows more about what the management has in mind or about the purpose for which his cost is to be used. If it is intended to substitute the new product for an old one, it is probably correct to include in the costs, as he would have done if he used previous operation costs, all the overhead allocated on the usual basis. There would be no more production to absorb the overhead and the fixed charges would remain as they were. If, however, it were contemplated that the new product would represent an addition to the volume already manufactured, then the cost which he compiled might be quite misleading. The new cost either should show a new distribution of fixed charges or should show that the new product would not necessitate any increase in fixed charges and might be profitable on a differential or "out-of-pocket" basis.

Management must tell the accountant. Until he had some idea of the purposes and intentions of management, the accountant would not be able to give a proper statement of the cost of the new product no matter how carefully and accurately his figures were worked out. Management has a right to demand from its accountants and its accounting system correct answers to its questions on a correct basis. Mere technical and arithmetical accuracy is not enough. Management cannot, generally, look behind the figures presented to it. It must accept what its accounting department states as facts. Management itself may be at fault in not taking the accounting department sufficiently into its confidence, or in not giving the accounting department information which it may think is irrelevant or unnecessary but which, in fact, the accounting department needs. The real responsibility, however, lies primarily with the accountant. It is his statement that is being acted upon, and it is his duty to be certain that his statements are prepared on the basis and for the purpose which management has in mind. This in no way means that they should be warped to the desires of management; they should, however, be very carefully prepared according to the needs of management.

The accountant must understand the business. All this should make management realize that the accountant must now have a much broader and more comprehensive idea of the business than he ever had at any other time.   This does not mean that he must know the business in the sense of being able to operate or direct it.   He must, however, understand fully the processes, the purchasing policy, the sales policy, the general progress of mechanical or other invention in the industry, and its relation to other similar industries and the government.   He cannot arrive at any sound decisions on such matters as rates of depreciation, methods of depreciation, inventory methods, or costing methods without fully understanding these things.   Assuming that he must understand these things, and that he must prepare his statements with this in view, what in particular is the management of a modern, well-organized corporation entitled to receive from its accounting department in the way of statements of internal operation and control at the present time?

4. Statements required

First and foremost, correct and adequately detailed statements of past operations must be prepared.   In the early days of accounting it was often thought that these were enough and that management could, from a clear statement of the past, make its own decisions and reconstruct its own figures for the future.   That day has gone if, in fact, it ever existed.   Few men can be sufficiently versed in the technical and mechanical details of an industry and also be good enough accountants and analysts to arrive at sound conclusions from statements which merely show past transactions.

Management must have costs.   In addition to clear and adequately detailed statements of past transactions, management is entitled to costs on the basis most appropriate for the enterprise—standard, process, job, or whatever method really reflects the operations and the policy of the company.   The operation of a cost system and the selection of methods depend naturally on the purchasing policy of the company, the method of pricing, and the type of its customers, as well as on its more immediate cost factors.   As an example, in an industry where prices are fixed for a considerable period, the so-called administered-price industries, a different inventory and cost method is required than in industries where the price of the product varies almost directly with the price of the principal raw materials.   In the latter type of industry, the last-in–first-out inventory method is indicated.   In the former type, the first-in–first-out, or average method, may be better adapted to the needs of the enterprise.   Certainly it does not call imperatively for the last-in–first-out method where prices are not particularly sensitive to immediate changes in material prices and where commitments are made for many months or a season ahead.

Estimates and projections.   Once a reasonably satisfactory cost system is established, management is entitled to an estimating system based, of course, on the results of the cost system.   Another, and closely allied, statement to which management is entitled is a budget, annual or for shorter periods. In a sense, every standard cost or estimate based on a standard cost is a small budget, as it tells management what can be expected under given conditions in the future. The budgetary feature of the accountant's work is assuming more and more importance.

With the increasing requirements of government and with the increasing number of elements in our economic structure which make for rigidities of various sorts, the necessity for careful estimates of probable changes is even more pronounced than it was in earlier periods. A budget is in no way a forecast in the sense of the word which is used when accountants are told they should not make forecasts. A budget is merely a projection of what may be expected, given certain basic facts and assumptions. The accountant does not make the assumptions; he merely works out the results based on them.

Many accounting statements are called "forecasts"—for instance, forecasts of cash requirements—but all these statements are merely projections into the future based on the assumption that known facts and conditions will either continue or change in a given manner. The preparation of such statements requires great skill and judgment. Misunderstood or in the wrong hands, they are dangerous. Generally, they should not be permitted to go beyond the hands of management. Properly used, they are one of the most valuable tools which management has at its disposal. If certain given conditions and assumptions are presented to the accountant and he prepares from them a statement of projected operations which shows an undesirable result, management, if it is convinced that the accountant's statement is correct on the bases given, will probably change its plans and possibly its policies.

Internal check and control. Another feature which management is entitled to look for in any adequately designed accounting system is a proper, effective, and not too cumbersome system of internal check and control. Much has been written about this, and there are ample authorities to be consulted. The general principles are clear and well understood, but their application to an individual situation may be difficult and complicated. It is the duty of the principal accounting officer of any corporation to see that proper internal check and control is instituted and carried out. It is the duty of the public accountant to satisfy himself that this is the fact.

Accounting is a record of responsibility for money, property, and things. Internal control is a means of ensuring that this responsibility is actually discharged.

The means and methods of internal control are discussed in later sections and in a fairly large literature on the subject. It might, however, be useful to management to list what internal control might be expected to cover and establish:

Cash

Disbursements are for

Wages

Materials and supplies

Expenses

Dividends

Repayment of loans

Receipts are on account of

Goods sold to customers

Material and scrap sales

Sales of investments or property

Interest and dividends

Loans or sales of securities

Accounts Receivable

All trade accounts are for goods shipped or services rendered

No shipments are made which are not billed

No unauthorized credits or allowances are made

All accounts are collectible except those noted as bad or doubtful

All other accounts or notes receivable are for an authorized transaction for company account

Accounts Payable

All trade accounts payable are for materials received or services rendered

All purchases or expenditures are for company account and properly authorized

All accounts or notes payable for loans or advances are properly authorized and are for company account

Inventories and materials and supplies

All purchases are for company account and properly authorized

Physical receipt of all material is checked

Issues of materials to production departments are authorized and recorded

Process inventories are taken or estimated at least monthly

Scrap, waste, and spoilage is recorded, compared with past experience and analyzed as to cause and reasonableness

Proper physical inventories are taken and discrepancies between book and physical inventories are analyzed and reconciled

(In addition to the foregoing, properly developed statements of variances between standard costs and actual results are a valuable means of control)

Buildings, machinery, and equipment

All additions are properly authorized

All sales, retirements, or dismantlements of plant or equipment are authorized and recorded

Depreciation is calculated correctly on established bases

Taxes

All taxes, city, state, and Federal, are scheduled on return and payment dates and officer or employee responsible for preparing return is noted

Periodical statement of status of any disputed tax is made

Securities

A complete, up-to-date list is kept

Securities are with a trust company or other authorized depository or are kept in safe-deposit vault with proper control of access by officers

All securities said to be company property are so in fact

Title to securities is in the name of the company or in the name of a company representative properly indorsed

Securities, if not with a depository, are examined and counted periodically by company officials or independent certified public accountant or both

Income which should be received on securities has, in fact, been received

Current-value statements. There are statements of another type which, while not in universal use, are prepared by the accounting departments of many forward-looking corporations. These are statements of the present or market values of property as compared to book values. Many corporations which prepare such statements do not use them for any public purpose. They are, however, of great value to the management not only for their most obvious purpose, that of making certain that the property is adequately covered by insurance, but also for satisfying themselves that they are receiving from their customers, in their sales prices, enough to replace their plant at the prices at which it will probably need to be replaced when that takes place.

There are other advantages in having statements of values of assets on hand, particularly in states like New York where surplus is calculated on the basis of actual or current values rather than on book values. These records are not difficult to keep and maintain. If the company has a good engineering department, index numbers can be developed and applied which will bring the plant values to current values. If the inventory is carried on some method which produces other than current values, it is ordinarily a simple matter to apply current prices to the material in the inventories. Such figures would not necessarily constitute accounting figures for a financial adjustment of the books, but they are close enough to give management an idea of what it is dealing with and to give some idea of what a liquidation or replacement basis might be. Many corporations have a periodical or continuous appraisal made by an appraisal company, and this appraisal generally covers current or insurable values as well as cost values. In many corporations it would be dangerous to try to do business without some statements of this sort. A current-value statement has considerable usefulness, but like many other statements which are not directly taken from the financial books, it must be used with care, and as it is less subject to control it is more subject to abuse.

Statements to proprietors, security holders, credit grantors, and other third parties. There is another purpose in an accounting system which has been in existence almost as long as accounting, that is, the requirement to prepare statements for proprietors or for third parties who have some interest in the business as creditors, guarantors, and in some cases customers, and who have a right to statements of the position and results of the entire enterprise. These are usually statements of past transactions and at the present time are generally prepared on a basis of cost. Many businessmen and accountants think these statements should be modified to reflect current costs rather than past costs when the inventory method uses or produces a material cost other than one approximating current replacement cost (say first-in–first-out, or some similar method). These statements also show depreciation widely different from that which would be arrived at by depreciating on replacement values. The accounting profession and business in general have not yet come to any conclusion on these questions, but the seriousness of the problem is widely recognized. Some think the question should not be covered at all in published statements; others think that it should be covered in the income account and disregarded in the balance sheet; while others think the whole question should be covered by supplementary statements. In any event, the facts are of sufficient importance to be in the hands of management, and it is management's decision as to whether and how these shall be given to the public or to credit grantors. It is the accountant's duty, however, if he is making a statement which does not reflect current values, to make it perfectly clear that this is the case, that the properties are not stated at any current or realizable value, that this could be arrived at only by appraisal, and that the inventories are stated on a particular basis which is lower than cost, or lower than current market, or whatever description is appropriate. The accountant's duty in these statements is to present fairly the condition of the company on the basis indicated and to present the facts so that they will give a correct impression as well as being mathematically and technically correct.

Statements to Federal and state government agencies and departments. A function which a modern accounting system must exercise is the preparation of reports for different government departments and agencies, Federal and state, having jurisdiction over the enterprise. No business is too small or too large to escape this. Every business must report to at least one government department, the Internal Revenue Service. In addition, practically all businesses must report to one or more government departments. A manufacturing company listed on a registered securities exchange might easily have to report to the Securities and Exchange Commission, the Federal Trade Commission, the Internal Revenue Service, and its state taxation authorities. If it were a public utility, it would have to report to one or more state and Federal agencies. Its accounts would be subject to audit and review by representatives of all or any of these organizations. There are many other government departments and agencies to which a corporation might be required to report.

Frequently, these reports are to be certified by the corporation's independent auditors. The responsibility here, both that of the controller of the corporation and that of the independent auditor, is somewhat different from that of the auditor or controller when reporting to stockholders or credit grantors.

There is generally little flexibility in the form or content of reports to these administrative bodies. This is prescribed, and it is the duty of the accountant to fill out the report as nearly according to regulations or instructions as possible. He does not have any responsibility for the form, and he has no responsibility for the impression it may make on the government department, as the government department has exercised its authority in prescribing the form. Some government accounting forms give definitely false impressions under particular circumstances. The case of several railroads which are required to present their accounts in a certain manner by the Interstate Commerce Commission, where such accounts clearly and definitely misrepresent the income of these railroads, is a good example. However, if it can be established that the facts are correct and the form has been followed, everything which the accountant can or should do has been done, except possibly to append a disclaimer to his report and to protest the inapplicability of the form.

5. Use of mechanical equipment

Another general requirement of any accounting system, or perhaps something which any management is entitled to expect from its accounting advisors and officials, is the fullest and most economical use of the mechanical equipment best adapted to the company's business. There are few operations of an accounting system which cannot be improved and facilitated by mechanical means. The trouble generally is not to find a mechanical means of solving the problem, but to choose among the means offered.

The controller or office manager organizing a new office generally suffers from what might be called an "embarrassment of riches" in this respect. Every mechanical accounting device has its own place and its own advantages. There is probably none which does not fit admirably into some situation.

Among the mechanical devices available the most valuable and the most difficult on which to make a decision are the various types of computers and other electronic data processing equipment. Management should avoid making any decision until the best available advice is obtained. Choosing your own computer is on a par with a layman's diagnosing and prescribing for his own illness or acting as his own lawyer.

The salesmen for these machines and devices are intelligent men, often well trained in accounting and system work, and it is their business to exhibit the good points of their particular products. It is the duty of whoever is responsible for installing and improving the accounting system to weigh these various claims and to see how the devices can best be adapted to the business at hand. Some types of calculating and tabulating machinery are valuable where large volumes of work are to be taken care of but are impractical or uneconomical where the volume is small. Others are highly efficient with a small volume of work and fall down when the volume is increased. Some organizations require highly specialized machines for particular work, while others need a general machine which can be turned to a dozen different uses.   There is a fairly abundant literature in this field, and the claims of the companies manufacturing the machines are generally well founded from a positive point of view.   In other words, it is safe to assume that if something is not claimed for a machine, the machine will not have that characteristic or will not perform that particular operation.

It is, of course, well to standardize.   Generally speaking, it is better to use the same machine for the same purpose in every branch or department.   Maintenance and repair will be simplified and will be less costly, and operators will be interchangeable if it is necessary to concentrate on one department which temporarily has an extraordinary work load.   Here again the real answer is a good knowledge and careful analysis of the business and the operations.

One cautionary note might be sounded.   A machine which performs an operation efficiently but which leaves a record which cannot easily be audited is not so good as one which does a similar operation but which leaves a record which can readily be audited.   Every auditor has had experience with mechanical systems which worked fairly well as far as the operation (say getting out bills, recording accounts receivable, or writing payroll checks) was concerned but which left statements and summaries which could be proved only by doing a large part of the work over again.   This is seldom necessary and mechanical means can almost always be devised which will provide for proper detail checks and for adequate total and cross checks of mechanical work.   It sometimes requires a little extra effort in planning the system, but it is well worth the effort in the time saved by the company's internal auditors and by the company's independent accountants.   One of the purposes of records is to produce something that can be audited, and this purpose should never be lost sight of.

6. Background of accounting

Nature of the accounting process.   When we are deciding on what to expect from an accounting system, the fundamental nature of the accounting process must be considered.   Accounting is basically a descriptive art.   It is a method of presentation, a language, a method of description—what Santayana has so aptly termed "a universe of discourse."

We are describing one aspect of industrial, financial, trading, or governmental enterprises when we use accounting.   The aspect which we describe is the financial, the numerical side of the operations.   In all but the smallest enterprises this method of description is essential to operation.

Purpose of accounting.   As in all other organizational devices, the principal purpose of accounting is to permit one man to control and understand operations which would be incomprehensible to any single human mind without the aid of such a method of description.   It has been said with some reason that one of the causes of the disintegration of the Roman Empire was the difficulty, if not the impossibility, of maintaining contact and organization in all the different far-flung sections of the Empire when records had to be expressed in Roman numerals and when all calculations except those which could be made mentally had to be made on the bead frame or abacus. It is difficult to imagine the confusion which would result from attempting to operate the United States Steel Corporation or the American Telephone and Telegraph Company if such means of numerical expression and calculation had to be used. On the other hand, the mere provision of the means of proper accounting does not indicate that enterprises will be carried out on a basis of sound and satisfactory organization. The Mayas of ancient Guatemala and Yucatan had a highly advanced and efficient numerical system. This, however, was used almost entirely, so far as any records indicate, for astronomical and calendar purposes. There is no record of its use for commercial or organizational purposes.

Slow development before twentieth century. Every student of the history of calculating machines knows Blaise Pascal built, around 1640, a number of calculating and adding machines, basically similar in principle to most wheel-driven machines of the present day. With the exception of the electronic data processing equipment, the changes made since Pascal's day are not matters of principle but merely increased speed of operation and modifications such as the negative total and printing devices. Practical calculating machines were not on the market until the eighties or nineties of the nineteenth century. Since then, as we all know, the development of machines of this type and of other calculating and adding machines has been phenomenal.

What is the reason for this slow development? Is it because some new principles were discovered? None were necessary. If there had been a sufficient demand, if there had been a great enough necessity for a calculating machine, Pascal's machine could, in all probability, have been developed in less than a hundred years after its invention. It required no new discovery, such as steam or electricity, to make his machine practical. It required merely a working out in detail of what was already known and understood. The development, say, of the chronometer in the eighteenth century, which made exact long-distance navigation possible, was no more difficult than would have been the development of a speedy and practical adding and calculating machine from the beginning made by Pascal. The real reason no such development took place was that commerce did not imperatively demand such a machine. Commercial enterprises were comparatively small, comparatively simple. Even great organizations, such as the British East India Company, the Dutch East India Company, or the Hudson's Bay Company, were trading companies and did not require elaborately organized cost accounts or budgets. Their traders did the best they could with the natives, made large profits, in many cases appropriated substantial parts of these profits for themselves, but still turned enough over to the parent company to make a good showing.

Manufacturing processes were not complicated. Textiles were probably the most highly mechanized industry. We all remember Adam Smith's famous illustration of the making of pins as an example of what he called the "division of labor" or what we would now call mass production. Of course, the pin manufacture now seems to us very simple, very easily controlled. Another condition which delayed the introduction of accounting systems which were efficient in detail was the fact that clerical labor was abundant and quite poorly paid. All these things tended to work together to make it unnecessary to develop anything like our present accounting systems.

Utilitarian character of accounting. While accounting is undeniably an art, it is an art which does not and should not exist in and of itself. The mathematical elegance of the basic concept of double entry has fascinated many minds, including that of Goethe, who once said that double entry was one of the "fairest inventions of the human mind." Nevertheless it is still true that a detailed description of unimportant facts by means of double entry is of little value except possibly as an example for teaching.

In literature or painting we may have a description of something quite unimportant in itself which, by the mere description and by the implications which the author or artist brings into it, is of the utmost human importance. Accounting, however, cannot accomplish this. Accounting is a strictly and purely utilitarian art. Its only value is in its results. The only way in which it develops is in response to the needs of business, government, and individuals. It is the basic means by which single human minds, or a group of human minds, transcend some of their fundamental physical limitations when they come to deal with matters beyond what we might call the "verbal" or "pictorial" scope of any mind.

It is the conditions and necessities which call forth the developments in accounting. Developments in accounting have taken place step by step with developments in industry, commerce, and government. The first large and well-organized business operations in modern or medieval Europe were those directed by the Church. We find, therefore, some of the earliest examples of accounting, and double-entry accounting at that, in the accounts of the monasteries. We find that the first well-organized public debt, the securities of which were sold to the public, was instituted by the Vatican.[1] Next we find that accounting was applied to the results of commerce in the great trading republics of Italy, Florence, Genoa, and Venice, for example. Accounting was applied in a smaller way to manufacturing and on quite an extensive scale to banking. This is because these were the activities which were of importance in the Middle Ages and in the days of the Renaissance. Such cost accounting as then existed was rudimentary in the extreme, because small enterprises gen-

[1] Leopold von Ranke, *History of the Popes,* G. Bell & Sons, Ltd., London, 1913, vol. 1, book IV, p. 319.

erally had no need for more cost accounts than the proprietor could carry under his hat.

Accounting develops with industry.   As Great Britain was the first country to feel the full impact of the Industrial Revolution, so it was the country where accountancy developed first and developed to the greatest extent.   Professional accountancy was recognized in Scotland in the middle of the nineteenth century, about 30 years later in England, and about 20 years later in this country.   It is now, of course, a well-recognized profession here, with several important specialties.   It has developed so much that no accountant can pretend to be a master of all features of his profession.   No man can at once be an expert in accounting for corporate financing, in income-tax accounting, in cost accounting, in public-utility accounting, in accounting for consolidations and holding companies, in budgeting, and in the giving of expert testimony and the representation of clients before administrative bodies (generally called "forensic accounting"), to name only some of the specialized accounting fields.

All these activities have developed, not as a result of the initiative or inventiveness of accountants, but as a result of conditions in business and government and in the lives of individuals which required accounts and which required such services.   The profession has, so far, never failed business and government when new conditions arose.   Whether present conditions—changing value of currency, and unsettled political and economic conditions—are presenting problems the profession will not be able to solve is still an open question.

What is expected of accountants.   Having established, then, that accounting is an art, that it is an art which is nothing in and of itself, and that it is a servant of business and government, let us examine what those who employ these servants called accountants expect from them.

Some accountants may not relish being called servants.   A little thought, however, should make everyone see that there is nothing derogatory in that title.   Probably no one ever has lived to and for himself alone, and certainly no one at the present time can do so.   He must constantly serve others.   We are all familiar with the phrase "civil servant" as applied to a member of the civil service of Great Britain.   The title of servant to management, to the public, to government, is a proud rather than a demeaning one.   The accountant records what has happened.   He classifies the information in such a way that management can make its decisions, so that the proprietors of a business can understand what is going on, and so that those who wish to extend credit to the business will know whether they are justified in doing so.   He classifies the information so that the government will know whether the client or the corporation by which he is employed is carrying out its duties and obligations toward the government.   He also will tell the management, or any other legitimately interested party, the result of any course of action under any given set of circumstances.   He will make this projection not as his employers wish it would work out, but as he sees the facts.

There is nothing incompatible in the idea of professional or personal dignity and the rendering of the service which the client or employer requires.   The accountant, in his constructive capacity as a recorder of facts or in his critical or analytical capacity as an auditor, should not at the same time have executive responsibility for that which he records or criticizes.   Although the service of the controller or any accountant performing similar functions for a corporation is primarily to prepare an impartial record and to make an impartial critical review of the facts which he records, it is nevertheless impossible and undesirable for a man of such position to have no voice whatever in executive policies or decisions.   So far as his own department is concerned, the controller has, or should have, full executive responsibility.   When decisions of general policy are discussed, for example, questions having to do with production, technical changes, expansion of business, advertising, promotion, or the like, the controller often takes part in the discussion but should naturally confine himself to the financial aspects of such questions.   His statements and opinions on the financial, tax, cost, and accounting features of the questions under discussion should be made available to management.   The controller should not, of course, have executive responsibility for technical, operating, or sales decisions.

Many accountants have become capable executives, and it is frequently greatly to the advantage of an enterprise to choose an accountant for such a position, but the fact remains that once he becomes an executive he ceases to be an accountant or auditor.

Division of work between public and private accountant.   In all the foregoing, little distinction has been made between the accountant in public practice and the accountant in private or corporate employment.   Most of the operations and functions described would be carried out, in a large and well-organized corporation, by the controller and his staff.   At the other extreme, in a small organization, say, where only one bookkeeper was employed, most of the work beyond the mere original recording would probably be done by the professional public accountant.   Between these two extremes we might have almost any division of work and circumstances.   This would have to be considered when deciding on the propriety and necessity of work to be done by the professional accountant.   Questions of independence and responsibility would arise, but this is not the place to discuss them.   The opinions of the Accounting Principles Board of the American Institute of Certified Public Accountants, the rules of the Securities and Exchange Commission, and numerous individual writers have covered this field.

Accounting as a tool of management.   In this section, accounting in all its forms has been described and illustrated from the point of view of the man who makes use of it, not from the point of view of the man who produces the accounting results.   The position of the man who uses the results of an accounting system is not unlike that of the man or woman who may be a skillful driver but who has practically no idea of what goes on inside the engine or under the hood of his automobile. In these days of highly complex and highly efficient and reliable cars, few of us really understand the operations of our automobiles. But we all know what we expect from a car and we know what it will do. True, we are all somewhat helpless when it breaks down, but there is almost always a friendly and capable expert available to help us out of our troubles. If everyone who drove a car understood his vehicle, we would have a nation of good automobile mechanics, but no one would have much time for anything else. So it is with modern accounting. Modern accounting is a useful and indispensable tool to modern business and industry, but no one but an expert can understand or operate the details of an accounting or cost system.

There are two tests for an accounting system: (1) whether it produces the statements desired as promptly as it should, (2) whether it produces them as economically and efficiently as possible. Management generally has a good idea of whether the system produces the results desired, but no one but an expert can tell whether the system is actually operating efficiently and economically. There are few places in an enterprise where waste and leaks can be more serious and more difficult to detect than in the accounting and record keeping. The fact that every employee works hard and conscientiously may be entirely irrelevant to the question of the proper operation of the system. The fact that the most modern equipment is used may have nothing to do with its effectiveness, and the excellence of the statements may give little indication of the efficiency of the system. The real indications of economy and efficiency are (1) whether the system is designed to produce the statements with the least effort and the least amount of duplication, (2) whether the mechanical equipment most suited to the operation is used (not whether mechanical equipment of the best and most modern type is used). This caveat is especially important with electronic data processing equipment. The first question is whether the enterprise generates a large enough volume of work to make any use of such equipment desirable; the second question is whether to rely on a service bureau. There are many reliable, well-organized service bureaus, and the cost, under some circumstances, may be far less than the rental or purchase of a computer.

Another source of invisible leaks is requiring employees to do work which could be done by an employee of a lower grade or a lower salary. Unnecessary work done in the most capable and industrious manner is wasted. Necessary work, even if it is not done perfectly, is of value.

The question of whether a given accounting system is designed to operate efficiently and is operating efficiently is one which can be answered only after much study by a well-qualified expert. This expert may be an accounting official of the enterprise, or he may be a public accountant. He will never be an operating man, a technical man, or a salesman. Furthermore, examining into whether an accounting system is operating with maximum efficiency is not a thing which can be done quickly or easily. While an experienced accountant can, almost as soon as he enters a strange office, get a general feeling of whether the office is well run or badly run, it will take him a long time, first, to prove that it is badly run, and second, to institute the necessary changes and improvements.   There are certain general tendencies familiar to all accountants who have any breadth of experience.   One of these is that uniformity is something from which everything tends to depart.   Another is that familiarity with work, if it does not breed contempt, at least has a tendency to breed carelessness.   Most employees whose work is not periodically checked have a tendency to take what seem to them well-justified shortcuts.   These generally result in incomplete records, which cannot be used for the purposes for which they were intended. In an integrated enterprise, uniformity, in some features of the accounts, is of the utmost importance.   This uniformity is never attained except by continual check and inspection.

The way for management to get the best results out of its accounting system is to have a competent man responsible for the operation of the system, whether this man be the chief accounting officer of the enterprise or whether, as happens in smaller enterprises, he is the public accountant.   Management should hold such a man strictly accountable, but give him great freedom of action.   Management must also give such a man its complete confidence and give him all the information it possibly can about the business.   Management should be demanding as to the results it requires, it should be keenly alive to the possibilities of accounting as a useful tool to management, but it should not concern itself about the details or about the means by which the information is collected and summarized.   Modern accounting is a complicated and highly technical service to industry, and few men can be really fully effective as accounting executives and still be able to perform any other important business functions. If management and the accounting department each performs its own function and neither tries to encroach on the other, a smoothly running organization will result.   If the place and function of each are not well defined and understood, waste, inefficiency, and lost motion are sure to result.

Section 9

HOW TO INCREASE YOUR MARKETING PRODUCTIVITY

BY

CHARLES H. SEVIN

HOW TO INCREASE YOUR MARKETING PRODUCTIVITY

This section shows how any business firm can increase its sales volume or its net profits very substantially, and more than once, by obtaining and using (1) marketing-cost and profitability information and (2) marketing experimentation to do a better job of allocating its marketing efforts to the various segments of its business.

Using the definition of marketing productivity as the sales or profit output per unit of marketing effort, the section thus suggests that any firm can achieve a continuous series of increases in the productivity of its marketing operations. We are concerned with quantitative factors affecting marketing productivity, such as the allocation of marketing efforts to different segments of a firm's markets, rather than with qualitative factors such as "better" selling or advertising.

1. Marketing decisions in an information void

Most business organizations are multiproduct firms; the typical business, whether that of a manufacturer, wholesaler, or retailer, markets a fairly large number (sometimes several thousands) of differentiated products. In fact, it is hard to think of a firm which markets only one product. Each one of these numerous products of a single firm shares a different market with competing products of other firms. Also, each one of these products requires more than one type of marketing effort; a marketing "mix" of several types of effort is expended on each product. Additionally, business firms generally sell to several different types and size classes of customers, and (except for single-unit retailers) they generally market in a number of different sales territories.

But that part of the total marketing effort of the firm which was expended during any given time period on each product or customer class or sales territory is generally not known. For example, single-product marketing-cost figures now generally available in most firms are patently inaccurate and misleading. Correct and useful determinations of marketing costs and net-profit contributions for individual products in the multiproduct firm require sophisticated analytical techniques which are not generally used.

In only a relatively limited number of firms does management know its single-product marketing costs and profits, even at past sales levels. An even smaller number of firms can predict with reasonable accuracy how sales volume and net profits of a single product would vary with changes in the total level or composition of the marketing efforts expended on the product. (This same lack of information also generally prevails with regard to the marketing costs and profits of other segments of the total business, such as individual customer classes and sales territories.)

If the marketing expenditures for any single product of a manufacturing firm were to be increased over time from one period to the next, two separate but related phenomena (see Fig. 1) would generally be encountered:

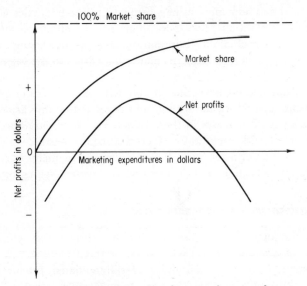

Fig. 1.   A product's market share and net profits as functions of its marketing expenditures.

1. Sales volume sooner or later would tend to increase at a decreasing rate —flattening out and approaching (but never reaching) 100 percent of market share as its upper limit
2. Net-profit contributions sooner or later would reach a maximum, then decrease, then become negative

Together, these two relationships pose an obvious dilemma for marketing management:

1. High sales volume (market share) for a differentiated product may require such a high level of marketing effort that net profits may be much lower than they potentially could be
2. High net profits may involve a relatively low level of marketing effort. Consequently, the differentiated product may have a low and unstable

sales volume (market share) exceedingly vulnerable to competitive pressures

In reality, of course, marketing planning and decision making proceed in a manner quite different from that suggested by both these oversimplified alternatives. This is not only because the actual market situations are much more complex, but also because none of the seemingly rudimentary information involved in the two functional relationships illustrated in Fig. 1 is generally available to marketing management. In fact, it is reasonable to say that the following errors usually occur in marketing operations because of the lack of necessary information:

The marketing budget for a single product is too large. The present level of expenditure results in such sharply diminishing returns that substantial gains would be obtainable through shifting efforts to other products (where the rate of diminishing returns is not so great)

The marketing budget for a single product is too small. Either added expenditures would bring increasing returns, or the rate of diminishing returns is still low as compared with that for other products

The marketing mix is inefficient. Either not enough or (more likely) too much is being spent, for example, on advertising a product as compared with personal efforts to sell it. Changes in the marketing mix would increase the product's sales or profit contribution dollars

Marketing efforts are grossly misallocated as among products, customers, and territories. If the allocations among products were changed, even though the total level of expenditure remained the same, total sales or net profits would be increased

This listing is critical of the generally existing kinds (or lack) of marketing information rather than being a criticism of marketing management. Even the fact that a particular decision was followed by a much less than achievable increase in sales or profits is not generally known to marketing management because of the limitations on available information. Conversely, management undoubtedly would make better decisions if better information were available.

2. Concentration of markets

Our economy is still a highly concentrated one, in spite of all movements toward decentralization. More than half the persons in this country live in fewer than 150 metropolitan areas, which constitute but a very small fraction of the total land area of the continental United States (maybe 4 percent). Retail and wholesale sales and manufacturing activity are even more geographically concentrated. In 1963, it was found that nearly half of all retail sales and nearly two-thirds of all wholesale sales were made in only 50 metropolitan areas—pinpoints on the map. In manufacturing approximately 60 percent of all factory employees were located in about 50 metropolitan industrial areas.

The bulk of all markets was found in a relatively few business establishments as well as in a few geographic areas. Less than 9 percent of the retail stores accounted for almost half the retail business. Similarly, less than 9 percent of the wholesalers did almost 60 percent of the wholesale business. A relatively small number of factories produced the bulk of the goods manufactured. Ten percent of the factories turned out more than 75 percent of the total value added by manufactures.

The markets and sales of the individual business firm show a pattern of concentration which parallels the above pattern of concentration in the economy as a whole. For example, one manufacturer found that 78 percent of his customers produced only slightly more than 2 percent of the sales volume. In another business, 48 percent of the orders accounted for only 5 percent of the sales. In yet another case, 76 percent of the number of products manufactured accounted for only 3 percent of the sales volume. In another business, 59 percent of the salesmen's calls were made on accounts from whom only 12 percent of the sales were obtained.

In a wholesale grocery firm, it was found that more than 50 percent of the total number of customers brought in less than 2 percent of the total sales volume. Similarly, 40 percent of the total number of items carried in stock accounted for less than 2 percent of the total sales volume. Finally, the consumption of many products appears to be concentrated in a relatively small percentage of households. Thus, for example, it appears that only 17 percent of the households consume 88 percent of the beer.

One result of these patterns of concentration in the markets of the individual firm, as will be shown below, is that no company makes all its sales at equal profit. There is some sales volume in every business which is much more profitable than would be indicated by the company-wide net-profit ratio. Likewise, there is a sizable proportion of sales transactions in almost every business which are much less profitable than average—or even definitely unprofitable. Where grossly unprofitable segments of the business are revealed, there is an opportunity for significantly improving the overall productivity of marketing expenditures.

Achievement of one or more of the five kinds of increase in marketing productivity which are outlined in the following section is facilitated by two types of information. The first is the matching of the marketing costs and revenues of segments of the business, such as individual products. This reveals the generally numerous unprofitable segments. Often, this profit (or loss) information by segments is alone sufficient.

Frequently, however, it is also necessary to know what would happen to sales and/or profits if marketing efforts were shifted from one segment to another, as from an unprofitable to a profitable segment. There appears to be only one reliable way of obtaining this second type of information, namely, by means of market experimentation.

3. The concept of marketing productivity

The concept of productivity or efficiency is borrowed from the subject of mechanics in the science of physics and is defined there as the ratio of effect produced to energy expended. In the present context, marketing productivity refers to the ratio of sales or net profits (effect produced) to marketing costs (energy expended) for a specific segment of the business. Thus, the productivity of marketing operations can be increased in any one of the following five ways:

1. An increase in sales or net profits proportionately greater than a corresponding increase in marketing costs
2. An increase in sales or net profits, with the same marketing costs
3. An increase in sales or net profits, with a decrease in marketing costs
4. The same sales or net profits, with a decrease in marketing costs
5. A decrease in sales or net profits proportionately less than a corresponding decrease in marketing costs

In brief, it appears to be inefficient to run a marketing organization to generate sales and profits only. The marketing operation should also be run so as to generate information that will facilitate increases in marketing productivity.

The businessman is not—or rather he should not be—basically interested in limiting his overall marketing expenditures to a certain number of dollars, or in attempting to force each of these expenses within the mold of some arbitrarily arrived-at ratio of expenses to dollar sales. The actual experiences of a number of businesses which have successfully achieved striking increases in their marketing productivity show that an entirely different line of attack is necessary. Basically, this different approach involves a fresh and objective look at fundamental marketing policies, such as—

How many and what kinds of customers to sell
What channels of distribution to use
What territories to cover
What products to sell, and at what price

To get this fresh look at fundamentals, and thereby accomplish a reduction in their distribution costs, many of these businessmen are using a management tool derived from their internal records. This tool, distribution-cost analysis, is used to determine which sales are most profitable and which segments of sales are unprofitable.

Examples of the actual results achieved and methods actually used by some businesses, which are described in the following pages, show how marketing productivity can be increased.[1]

4. Customers

Long-standing policies or philosophies, such as "Customers are the lifeblood of business," or "Get the volume and the profit will take care of itself," or the widespread belief that "100 percent coverage of the market" is necessary in all cases to "support" the national advertising of consumer convenience goods, help to explain why most businesses continue to sell to a large number of unprofitable customers. A further explanation can be found in the reluctance to adopt any action or policy that disturbs the *status quo,* such as doing something about unprofitable customers. Finally, of course, there is the fact that most businesses do not have sufficient knowledge of their marketing costs to enable them to uncover, with exactitude, their unprofitable customers.

But the experiences of some businesses show conclusively that knowledge of unprofitable customers, and wise action based on this knowledge, can lead to increased selling effectiveness and substantial reductions in marketing costs as a result of greater efficiency, lower prices, and important increases in profits. This even applies, perhaps especially so, to manufacturers of consumer-convenience goods with national advertising campaigns. To increase their profits, the businesses in the cases discussed below reallocated their selling and advertising effort to selected customers and prospects to bring these efforts into closer relation with sales and profit potentialities.

Case 1. Customers were classified on the basis of the amount of their annual purchases, and marketing costs were allocated to each size group. Of the total number of accounts, 41 percent, bringing in only 7 percent of the sales, were found to be unprofitable. Over a period of years, most of these unprofitable customers were dropped. In a period of 4 years, sales increased 76 percent, marketing expenses were cut in half from 22.8 to 11.5 percent of sales, and a net loss of 2.9 percent of sales was changed into a net profit of 15.0 percent.

Case 2. This business changed a policy of 100 percent coverage to a policy of selective selling. The number of stores contacted by salesmen was reduced by almost one-third. In the first year after the change, the company operated with half the number of salesmen, while sales increased after 45 percent. Since then sales have increased 82 percent, marketing expenses have been reduced from 31.8 to 18.2 percent, and operating profit has risen from 4.7 to 14.8 percent of sales.

Case 3. Although this businessman sold through exclusive distributors and franchised dealers, he found that he had too many outlets. Poor merchandisers and those unprofitable to the company were eliminated; the number of dealers

---

[1] The actual cases described in the following sections are taken from Charles H. Sevin, *Marketing Productivity Analysis,* McGraw-Hill Book Company, New York, 1965.

was reduced from 12,000 to 5,000 in round numbers, while 93 wholesalers were also dropped. Sales volume doubled, and the company's marketing expenses were cut in a period of 2 years from over 13 to 7.32 percent of sales.

Case 4. A distinction was made between fixed and variable marketing costs, and the latter were allocated to customers to find the relatively unprofitable ones. It was realized that not even all the variable expenses would be automatically saved or reduced if unprofitable customers were dropped, so management drew up a definite plan of cost reduction in each case where a group of unprofitable customers was to be eliminated. Sales executives were at first reluctant to drop customers, even though they were unprofitable, because advertised products would not be available in all possible outlets. In spite of dropping customers, however, sales volume increased, while over a period of years the ratio of distribution expenses to sales declined more than 50 percent.

5. Channels

A determination of what is the "best" channel of distribution for any business involves an appraisal of a large number of specific factors. Many of these factors have broad applicability to all businesses; they relate to sales volume, the costs involved in obtaining that volume, and the resultant profit.

It is axiomatic that any business should use those trade channels which will produce that combination of sales volume and cost which will yield the maximum amount of profit. However, the most profitable sales volume is not the greatest attainable sales volume, whereas, on the other hand, the "best" cost is not necessarily the lowest possible cost. Moreover, both the short-run and the long-run points of view must be taken into consideration. Consequently, the determination of the most profitable channels of distribution is not a simple job.

When analyzing the comparative advantages of different channels, many businessmen give primary consideration to the factors related to sales volume, without giving sufficient consideration to the relative marketing costs involved in obtaining that volume or to the comparative net profits. One likely explanation for the difficulty in making sound decisions regarding problems in connection with channels is the lack of adequate cost information.

When a business is already using several different channels, a customer-cost analysis (with customers grouped by class of trade instead of by size) will show the relative costs and profits by channels. More often, however, the problem is to compare actual costs and profits of present classes of trade with estimated costs and profits of alternative channels under consideration. In this case, the problem is not so simple, and it may not always be possible to determine what the results will be until an experiment has been tried.

The cost analyses and experiments of the businesses whose experiences are described in this section show that the choice of the most profitable channels is a problem to be solved individually by each business. A channel that is the most profitable for one firm may not be so for another competitive firm. These cases do show, however, that there is considerable opportunity generally to reduce costs and increase profits through analyses of relative costs and profits by channels.

Case 1. This company distributed through three major channels—route sales, direct shipments, and sales through wholesalers. A test study was made of marketing costs for one of these channels—route sales—subdivided by class of trade and by size of customer. The results showed that 87 percent of the route customers were probably handled at a loss. It is planned to extend this study to cover all channels of distribution, and if the results are the same, the company intends to revamp its entire distribution system.

Case 2. A distribution-cost analysis showed that 95 percent of all the customers sold direct in one small area were unprofitable. By applying the results of this analysis to the overall company picture, two-thirds of the direct customers were estimated to be unprofitable. As a result of these studies, the company is in the process of changing its channels of distribution by transferring unprofitable small accounts, served direct, to its dealer organization. On the basis of accomplishments so far, the company expects to achieve lower inventory, overhead, and break-even points, a 15 to 30 percent net reduction in marketing costs, and a 20 percent increase in net profits.

Case 3. In direct contrast to the preceding case, a cost analysis showed that industrial users sold direct were more profitable to this company than dealers. However, variations in cost and profit by size of customer were more significant than variations by channel of distribution. Salesmen were instructed to stop calling on small dealers and to spend more time with large industrials. Distribution costs were reduced by 38 percent in one year.

Case 4. A unique graphic method of cost analysis was used to separate the variable from the fixed element of each category of marketing cost and for getting costs at different levels of sales volume. Variable costs were allocated to four different channels of distribution. As a result of these analyses, one entire channel of distribution was discontinued, as were small customers in another channel, while sales pressure on the remaining profitable customers was increased. In one year, net profits doubled from $150,000 to $300,000.

Case 5. Three comparable test areas were chosen, in each of which a different channel of distribution was used for a trial period of one year. This was thought to be the only sure way to find out what would happen to sales, costs, and profits if new sales channels should be adopted. As a result of these tests, far-reaching changes in marketing methods are being made by this company. Distribution costs are being cut by approximately 50 percent, and profits are rising correspondingly, while prices have been reduced.

6. Orders

Small orders have long been an obvious cause of high distribution costs and unprofitable sales. Most businesses have a small-order problem, but many of them are prone to accept it as one of the basic conditions of distribution for which there is no real solution. Most businessmen have long suspected that small orders are a source of losses, but very few of them have any accurate facts on the dividing point between profitable and unprofitable orders or on the exact extent of the losses caused by unprofitably small orders in their own business.

Of course, no business can do away entirely with small-order losses. But the experiences of the companies which have made attempts to do something about the small-order problem show that many lines of action are possible, and that the problem is susceptible to control. The first step is to make an analysis of distribution costs and profits—or losses—by size of order. The problems of dealing with unprofitable orders are, of course, closely related to cost control and cost-reduction methods as they relate to unprofitable customers. Likewise, the techniques of cost analysis by orders are similar to the process of customer costing, involving merely a different classification of sales.

Case 1. Most of the orders received from 57.5 percent of the number of customers, comprising 2.7 percent of total sales, were found to be unprofitable. This unprofitable business was dropped, and sales effort concentrated on the remaining profitable volume. Salesmen were thereby relieved of 50 percent of calls formerly made. This enabled them to do a better job by increasing their volume of profitable orders, while reducing their traveling expenses.

Case 2. This businessman made a cost analysis to determine the minimum size of order which could be handled at a profit; over 50 percent of all orders received were found to be unprofitable. As a result of this analysis, the company changed to a plan of selective distribution, so that the proportion of unprofitable orders has been cut from over 50 to less than 10 percent.

Case 3. This company also made a cost analysis to find the minimum size below which an order could not be filled at a profit. After a careful study of all the possible effects, it was decided not to accept any orders below this minimum. Not one customer was lost due to this policy, and unit distribution costs were reduced by one-third.

Case 4. A pilot study of the cost of handling various-sized orders showed a range in marketing cost from 4.24 to 21.52 percent of sales. The results were so revealing that it was decided to make a more extended analysis. This analysis revealed that the total marketing costs for orders of less than $3.75 were 21.52 percent of sales, whereas the cost of handling the largest orders was only 4.24 percent. Needless to say, orders in the smallest size-classes were handled at a loss. Most of the unprofitable orders were eliminated, as a result of a change in marketing policy, and the ratio of distribution costs to sales was reduced by one-third.

7. Territories

Analysis usually reveals wide variations in the ratios of sales to regional potentials as between the different territories of a company's market. Businesses covering a large market often get strikingly different results from territory to territory, judged against any measure of the potential business available. These irregularities in sales are usually the result of at least a partial disregard of regional sales possibilities in the distribution of salesmen and advertising to territories. Many firms reduced their distribution costs by reapportioning their selling effort, after analyzing these regional differences in the ratios of sales to potential.

Analysis also reveals wide differences in distribution cost and relative profit ratios between different territories. Distribution-cost analysis pointed the way to greater profits by enabling some companies to realign their selling effort and to concentrate their resources against the more responsive segments of their market. Other steps taken to correct the faults disclosed by these cost analyses, such as the reorganization of territories, also resulted in substantial cost reductions as well as in increased selling effectiveness.

Coverage of more than a profitable amount of territory is common. Although a continued high level of production and employment requires an expanded volume of overall sales, unprofitable market coverage will in the long run benefit no one. Several firms reduced their costs and increased their profits by eliminating unprofitable territories. Furthermore, potential demand in a new market is only one important factor affecting a decision of market expansion. Distribution-cost considerations also enter into a decision to establish new sales territories on a profitable basis.

Case 1. An index of actual sales in relation to potential sales for each product in each territory enables this company to find, diagnose, and correct sales "soft spots." As a result, sales have increased 366 percent and there has been a 45 percent reduction in the ratio of field sales costs compared with the average for the period 1939 to 1941.

Case 2. Towns with the lowest "net yield" (gross profit minus direct costs) have been identified by this company, and it has been determined how much travel costs could be saved if they were eliminated. This has enabled the management to form a judgment whether or not a town should be visited and how often. On this basis, approximately 28 percent of the total number of towns covered were found to be unprofitable, and they were either eliminated or the number of calls was reduced. During a 15-year prewar period, the total number of salesmen was cut from 334 to 189, while sales rose from $10,000,000 to $22,000,000.

Case 3. A large number of towns and trading areas was found by this company to be unprofitable, and over a period of years the number of markets covered by salesmen was reduced from 15,000 to 5,800. A need for continuous analysis and weeding out of unprofitable markets was shown by the fact that a large proportion of the markets retained was still unprofitable. As a result of shifting effort to more profitable markets, there has been a 78 percent increase in average sales per salesman and a 36 percent reduction in the ratio of field selling and advertising expense.

Case 4. An analysis of marketing costs by territories and by individual sales routes showed wide variations in costs and profits and revealed wastefulness in the organization of territories. Territories and routes were completely reorganized. As an example of the results, one salesman increased his average number of calls per week and increased his sales volume, while he saved 2,000 miles of travel per month and reduced his expense by 38 percent within a period of 3 months.

Case 5. Big-city business was thought to be more profitable than that from small towns. A cost analysis, however, showed that 84 percent of all unprofitable accounts were in big cities, whereas a large proportion of profitable customers was in smaller towns. The company is now shifting selling and advertising effort from unprofitable accounts in big cities to profitable customers in smaller towns. In three towns the distribution-cost ratio has been reduced by one-third, while the ratio of net profits to sales has doubled.

8. Salesmen

The average businessman is keenly aware of the necessity for controlling the cost of his sales force. But the typical businessman apparently views the control or reduction of his selling costs as a process of arbitrarily reducing specific elements of expense which appear "out of line" as compared with a budget, or else he asks himself the question, "What can we eliminate—do without—do more cheaply?" This approach, however, has been viewed by some as a destructive approach and as a method of attack which does not really get at the heart of the problem of reducing selling costs.

Others have taken what may be regarded as a positive and constructive approach to the problem. These firms concentrate on getting increases in sales volume from the same or even smaller selling expenditures by apportioning selling effort in closer relation to potential volume, thereby reducing unit costs.

Analyses of the relative costs and profits of individual salesmen, comparisons of sales with regional sales potentials, and routing and scheduling of salesmen are some of the management tools used to reduce selling costs through this positive approach. The first two of these management tools, as well as actual experiments in changing the number of salesmen in a specific territory, have been used to settle the ever-present problem of determining the most profitable number of salesmen to be assigned to each territory. Setting up a detailed route and a definite schedule of calls for each salesman proved to be a most effective way for achieving substantial cost reductions by increasing the proportion of actual selling time spent in the presence of customers.

Case 1. Regional sales potentials, territorial cost analyses, and actual experiments in changing the number of salesmen are used by this company as guides in the territorial apportionment of selling effort. Other factors, such as a tendency toward diminishing returns from selling effort, are also taken into consideration. More efficient apportionment of selling effort by territories was one of the factors responsible for a decline of more than 50 percent in the ratio of variable selling expenses to sales during the 4 years preceding the Second World War.

Case 2. Under their old system, this company's salesmen spent much time and money in unnecessary travel. Under the new, definite routes were laid out for each salesman which provided the best coverage with the fewest miles of travel. Rerouting increased average selling time spent with customers by 19 percent, saved 1.5 million miles of travel per year for 105 salesmen, and net travel savings totaled more than $65,000 per year.

Case 3. The basis of organization of this company's salesmen's territories was found to be a serious cause of inefficiency and high costs, especially after unprofitable towns and customers were dropped from salesmen's territories. Sales calls were routed and scheduled to reduce costs and to ensure the proper frequency of calls on customers. As a result, within a period of 4 years, sales increased 76 percent while the number of salesmen was reduced 20 percent and travel expense was cut 53 percent.

Case 4. Since travel and waiting were found to take up as much as 80 percent of the salesmen's time, an extensive routing and scheduling system was set up to increase the proportion of actual selling time spent in the presence of the customers. As a result, selling time was increased from a low of 20 percent to as much as 50 percent of total salesmen's time. The number of salesmen was reduced from 334 to 189 over a period of 15 years, while sales rose from 10 million dollars to 22 million dollars.

9. Products

The urge to increase volume so as to utilize plant, marketing facilities, and personnel more economically has caused many firms to add new products to those already handled. How far the combined selling of products may be extended economically depends on several factors. If these new products appeal to similar consumer groups, sell through the same channels, move to the same markets, and require equal amounts and similar kinds of selling efforts, adding them may be profitable.

On the other hand, lack of uniformity in these and other respects often creates many managerial problems. The manufacturer may find the advantage of more complete utilization of facilities and personnel offset by such difficulties as the training of salesmen to sell a multitude of products and the managing of distribution for dissimilar products.

Where products are marketed in combination with others, their individual sales rates depend to a considerable extent upon their "family" relationships. That is, a product's sale may depend not only on its own characteristics in relation to the market, but also on the degree to which its distribution fits in with that of other products. Where perfect conformation takes place, the selling of an additional product may, within limits, bring about substantial economies.

However, the selling of different products involves the use of facilities and

personnel in varying degree because of differences in their physical characteristics, handling requirements, sale in varying amounts, and distribution to different classes of customers. As a consequence, the distribution expense for
some products is very much greater than for others sold by the same firm, and
the different products earn varying rates of net profit.

As in the case of customers and territories, product-cost analysis and comparison of actual sales with potentials reveal that many companies have expanded their product lines unprofitably. Shifting efforts from less profitable
to more profitable products, or eliminating unprofitable products entirely,
resulted in more efficient selling efforts, lower costs and prices, and higher
profits.

Case 1. Actual and potential sales volume and other factors were the basis
on which 18 unprofitable products out of a line of 39 products were discontinued. Besides eliminating the losses for which these unprofitable products
were directly responsible, other cost savings and advantages were achieved.
Sales increased 366 percent, while distribution expenses were reduced 55 percent.

Case 2. A new product was added and promoted vigorously because of its
high gross-margin rate over factory costs and because of the theory held by
some of this company's sales executives that a new product added to a family of
products costs almost nothing to distribute. However, analysis showed that the
expenses of distributing this company's family of products were not true joint
costs, even though many of these costs were incurred in common. Allocation
of costs to product lines showed the new line to be relatively less profitable than
others, and effort was shifted. As a result, total distribution costs per unit of
product declined from 65 to 59 cents, whereas net profits rose from 9 to 17
cents.

Case 3. Annual profit-and-loss statements are prepared for each line in this
multiple-line business; product lines are regarded as independently operating
subsidiaries making use of certain common distribution facilities. These profit-
and-loss statements are used by management in connection with product development, apportionment of selling effort, pricing, and other marketing problems.
A "forecast" profit-and-loss statement for each product line is used to reduce
operating data to their corresponding amounts at any level of general business
activity. As a result of this system, marketing-cost ratios have been reduced
by almost 50 percent.

Case 4. Standard unit order-filling (office and warehousing) costs are allocated to each of approximately 175 commodity classes. These standard unit
order-filling costs have helped the company accomplish a more efficient order-
filling job, while relative profits by product classes have helped to concentrate
selling efforts on the most profitable products.

10. Physical distribution

An additional course of action for reducing marketing costs—and one which

292   J. K. LASSER'S BUSINESS MANAGEMENT HANDBOOK

might well precede those described above—is to make cost studies of the performance of internal or physical distributive functions, such as storage, inventory control of finished goods, order assembly, billing, receiving, shipping, and delivery. Many firms have found that there are important opportunities for eliminating inefficiencies in the performance of these distributive functions.

Some companies have benefited from the experiences of progressive wholesalers in improving their physical distributive operations. For instance, the modern, one-story, streamlined warehouse building in the wholesale grocery trade is an outstanding example of how efficiency can be improved and costs reduced. Here orders are made up according to the assembly-line principle and mechanical tabulating equipment is used for preparing invoices, for making sales analyses, and for perpetual inventory control.

The experiences described in this section show that there are many practical possibilities for reducing costs by eliminating inefficiencies in the physical distributive functions.

Case 1. A study by this company revealed that it cost more than twice as much to handle the same amount of the same kind of merchandise in one company warehouse as in another. Remedial actions resulted in net annual savings of $70,000.

Case 2. In this company's highest cost warehouse, the cost per case of merchandise handled was more than eight times that of the lowest cost warehouse. A typical case of merchandise was physicaly handled 14 times before it was delivered to a customer. By using pallets and fork trucks, this was reduced to three handlings, with a warehouse-labor saving of 9 cents per case. These and other savings added up to $100,000 in 1 year, and when several new warehouses have been constructed, annual savings in excess of $250,000 are expected.

Case 3. A detailed analysis of delivery operations was made by this company, including the placing of time-study men on delivery trucks. For each truck studied, various cost factors were computed, such as the cost of deliveries for any size and any distance. These cost factors were the basis for far-reaching charges which resulted in reductions in delivery costs, as well as in other cost savings, such as in warehousing. Over a 10-year period there was a 50.4 percent reduction in unit marketing costs, amounting to savings of over $2,000,000 per year.

11. Evaluation of cost-reduction experiences

Several questions are likely to arise just because the experiences of the companies which have been highlighted in the preceding sections are so striking. These questions are discussed below.

Are the above cases extreme examples, or could others expect similar results? It is probable that when time-and-motion studies, cost accounting, and the principles of scientific management were first being developed in the factory, skepticism greeted the announced results of increased output and reduced unit costs. Now, however, hardly anyone would question the very great achieve-ments in the way of increased output per man-hour and reduced unit factory costs since the 1880s when Frederick Taylor developed certain principles of scientific production management; yet production men would be the first to admit that unit production costs are still very far from their irreducible mini-mum. It should not be too surprising, therefore, to find cases where striking achievements have been made in the reduction of unit distribution costs.[2]

Even in the more efficiently managed companies there is much misdirected marketing effort and, therefore, important opportunities are present for re-ducing distribution costs. Furthermore, disproportionate spreading of market-ing efforts appears to be common throughout our distribution system. Rather than the above cases being extreme examples, therefore, it is probable that others, if they took similar action, could expect to achieve improvements in their efficiency and reductions in their distribution costs at least as striking as those which were highlighted in the preceding pages.

Is the use of management tools such as marketing-cost analysis and market experiments solely responsible for the results achieved? Some firms have greatly reduced their costs and increased their profits by abandoning "indiscriminate distribution," or a policy of "100 percent coverage" in favor of a policy of "selective distribution." The actual experiences outlined above clearly demon-strate that the use of distribution-cost analysis and market potentials as manage-ment tools for eliminating misdirected marketing efforts offers to most businesses an important opportunity for reducing distribution costs, increasing net profits, and lowering prices.

Of course, other types of marketing research in addition to distribution-cost analysis and market potentials need to be brought into play in connection with a policy of selective distribution. For example, in product selection, while distribution-cost analysis is most useful in discovering unprofitable products already being sold, additional market analysis is needed to find out in advance what new product fields should be entered, and how the entry into the new market should be made for maximum profit.

Also, there are other very important marketing policies which have a bearing on the control and reduction of distribution costs. For example, the proper selection, training, and compensation of salesmen; the correct organization of the sales department; the use of sales forecasting and budgetary control; the careful formulation of the advertising plan and the selection of advertising media—all these play important and familiar roles in distribution-cost control which should not be minimized.

---

[2] It is not to be inferred from the above that what is suggested is an application of so-called "engineering thinking" to the problems of distribution. Rather, the parallel to be drawn is between the very large reductions in unit production costs, which actually have been achieved, and the possibly equally great (if not greater) opportunities for reducing unit distribution costs by the development and use of management principles and techniques peculiarly adapted to the more difficult problems in the field of distribution.

In many of the cases, increases in sales and reductions in costs following various changes in distribution policies have been due in large part to rises in price levels and to generally favorable business conditions. However, allowance for these extraneous influences does not detract from the validity of the cases as a whole as examples of the cost reductions which can be achieved by the use of distribution-cost analysis and market potentials.

What caused increased sales volume in spite of the fact that, in some cases, selling and merchandising efforts were reduced to an even greater extent than the reduction in the number of unprofitable customers, towns, and so forth? A policy of selective distribution led to increased profits by one or the other of the following routes:

Where the total expense that was saved exceeded the gross margin that was given up as the result of dropping a segment of unprofitable sales

Where the marketing efforts and total expense were reduced, while sales were maintained, as the result of better apportionment of effort

Where the marketing effort and total expense were maintained, while sales were increased, as the result of better apportionment of merchandising activities

Where, although marketing effort and total expense were reduced, sales were actually increased—also as the result of apportioning effort in the closest possible relation to potential sales results

While some companies reached greater profits by all of these routes, it is the last one, of course, which calls for an explanation. In some companies, the misdirection of marketing effort was of large proportions; that is, a distribution-cost analysis showed that a very large part of the distribution efforts and costs was matched up with a small but very unprofitable segment of the company's total sales. When these unprofitable sales were dropped, the diversion of some effort to profitable areas increased sales at the same time that cost per unit fell and net profits rose.

Will the elimination of unprofitable sales cut off small business from sources of supply? Some have objected to the general adoption of a policy of selective selling on the ground that many small businesses would be cut off from a source of supply. Such an objection, however, appears to be groundless.

In the first place, selective selling does not mean that all small-volume sales fall in the unprofitable category, or, conversely, that only small-volume sales may be unprofitable; nor, as will be discussed below, does it follow that all unprofitable sales should be eliminated. In some cases, a very large business may be an unprofitable customer to a particular supplier because of its small orders and requirements from that supplier, whereas a small business may be a profitable customer.

One wholesaler who has been following a policy of selective selling for the past 15 years through the operations of his voluntary group explained as follows why this policy does not cut off retailers from a source of supply:

It is a fallacy to assume that selective selling would cut off many food outlets from a source of supply if generally adopted. If each retailer concentrated his purchases with a relatively few sources of supply, then, instead of retailers buying from many wholesalers, and instead of wholesalers selling a large number of retailers, each retailer would have a few sources, each wholesaler would have fewer customers, and there would be closer relationships between wholesalers and retailers—and lower operating costs—to the benefit of all concerned.

Finally, some suppliers, such as wholesalers, have found it profitable to organize their entire operations so as to handle efficiently the business of relatively small-volume dealers. Surrounded by other wholesalers who were competing vigorously for the business of the largest retailers in the area, they have concentrated on selling a segment of the market in which they could, and did, operate profitably.

12. Converting loss sales to profitable volume

Although the cases highlighted in preceding pages place apparent emphasis on dropping unprofitable products, customers, and territories, it should be stressed that there are many practical possibilities for converting losses into profits other than by the elimination of unprofitable sales. For example, the following list, by no means exhaustive, shows some of the policies that can be adopted for converting relatively unprofitable commodities into sources of profit:

Simplify the line. Reduce the number of sizes, styles, qualities, and price lines. Simplification may result not only in reducing distribution costs, but also in increasing sales, by permitting concentration of advertising, selling, styling, and design on a smaller number of items. One knitting mill, for example, sharply reduced its storage costs and inventory losses by restricting the variety of articles offered for sale and attributed a rapid increase in sales to this policy

Repackage the product. A change in the package may reduce the direct costs of packing, and the new container may make possible reductions in transportation, storage, and handling costs. A new package may also influence the volume of sales

Increase—or decrease—the amount of advertising and promotion work. Whether it would be profitable to increase or decrease advertising depends on such factors as the effect of advertising on volume of sales and the effect of the volume of sales on unit production and distribution costs

Decrease the price. Sometimes, it may actually pay to reduce the price of unprofitable commodities. When consumer demand is so elastic that a small reduction in price leads to a substantial increase in sales, the result may be a greater excess of dollar gross margin over distribution costs than the net contribution of the commodity at the old price. This may come about as the result of both an increase in the unit of order, with a reduction in costs, and an increase in total sales sufficient to at least counterbalance the loss of gross margin per unit of sale that follows the price reduction

Increase the price. Where an increase in price may lead to only a small reduction in sales, it may be possible to raise the price in order to recover the loss on unprofitable products. This would be true if the increase in dollar gross margin would exceed the increase in per-unit cost of production and distribution that might result from the lower volume or the smaller unit orders

Many possibilities also exist for minimizing the losses resulting from orders that are relatively unprofitable because of their small size. Some of these are outlined as follows:

Devise special routing for handling small orders. An electrical manufacturer, for example, uses only about 25 percent of the usual clerical routine in handling small orders

Reduce services offered on small orders, such as special storage, free acceptance of returns, and repair services

Minimize broken-package sales by reducing the original package unit, by employing package units of several different sizes, or by developing special-assortment packages for filling small orders

Make a special handling charge for all orders below a minimum size

Employ quantity discounts or increase present quantity discounts with the size of the order. Quantity discounts must, of course, be in line with cost differentials

Establish a minimum-size order that will be handled

Offer bonus to salesmen for orders above a certain size, or penalize salesmen for orders below a certain size

Turn small orders over to jobbers, brokers, or agents

In short, it was only after the companies whose experiences were described previously were convinced their unprofitable sales could not be turned into a source of profit by any alternative course of action (such as those outlined above) that, as a last resort, they dropped them. Of course, these companies first made sure that their profits would actually be increased before they dropped the unprofitable sales. However, once they decided that this was the most profitable course to follow, they did not shrink from the seemingly drastic action of eliminating the unprofitable sales.

13. Marketing-cost analysis techniques

The usefulness of marketing-cost analysis is emphasized by the fact that all the companies whose experiences were highlighted in preceding pages were able to accomplish striking cost reduction despite reliance by some of them on relatively crude and simple methods of analysis. The cost reductions were accomplished because the misdirection of marketing efforts was of such large proportions and, therefore, the opportunities for improvement were so great. It is probable that any company, if it has been operating for many years on a program based on drift plus intuition, likewise has a marketing operation which can be improved substantially by the adoption of policies based on even relatively simple techniques of distribution cost analysis.

An extended discussion of the principles and methods of distribution cost analysis is beyond the scope of this section. However, the basic procedures or steps involved, which will be discussed later, are outlined here:

1. The separable, or direct, expenses are measured and assigned direct to customers or commodities
2. The common, or indirect, expenses are allocated or assigned to functional-cost groups
3. The factors which measure the variable activity of the various functions are identified, and the amounts of these factors, in the aggregate, are determined
4. A measurement is made of the share of the variable activity of each of these functional-cost groups which is utilized by the segment of sales whose cost is being measured
5. The ratio of the share of the activity of the function that is being utilized by a segment of sales (Step 4) to the total quantity of the activity of that function (Step 3) indicates the portion of the cost of that function which is allocated to that segment of sales
6. The excess of dollar gross margin over the sum of the direct expenses and the shares of the various functional-cost groups allocated to a commodity or customer or other segment of sales indicate its relative profitability or unprofitability

Functional classification.[3]   Although the proportion of direct marketing costs may frequently be significant, the greater part of a firm's distribution costs is likely to be indirect.   To facilitate their allocation, as well as for purposes of expense control, these indirect expenses are classified into functional groups.

The basis of the functional classification which would be used by any given firm is a study of the marketing activities performed by that company.   It is important that the functional classification be sufficiently detailed so that the work performed in any one function will be of the same general kind.   Such homogeneity facilitates the assignment of an entire functional-cost group by the use of a single factor of allocation, as will be described hereafter.

Assignment of natural expenses to functions.   It is usually necessary to apportion many natural-expense items among several functional-cost groups, since they relate to more than one functional activity.   They are distributed by means of time study, space measurements, counts, managerial estimates, and other methods.   The increased cost and effort of preparing functional-cost classifications may be much more than offset by the advantages of improved cost control, as well as by the advantages of cost analysis.

[3] A functional classification puts together all the expense items that have been incurred for the same activity. A functional classification, therefore, permits the allocation of an entire cost group by means of a single factor.

Illustrative functional classification.   Most companies, especially those serving wide markets and producing and selling a number of products, have complex organizations and engage in a wide range of marketing activities. Consequently, it is difficult to set forth a widely representative functional classification of marketing expenses. Each company would have to set up its own classification to reflect its own marketing activities. For illustrative purposes, however, a functional classification of marketing expenses is shown below:

Functional-cost group for a pharmaceutical manufacturer

Warehousing
Order filling and inventory control
Transportation
Invoicing and order processing
Accounts Receivable
   Credit and collection
Product planning
Product programming
Trade size packaging
Medical investigation
Pricing
Detailing (personal selling)
Medical journal advertising
Medical direct mail
Professional sales promotion
Drug-trade advertising, direct mail, promotion, and trade relations
Hospital advertising, direct mail, and sales promotion
Samples, free trade, visual selling aids
Market research

Allocation procedures.   After the indirect costs have been classified by functions, they are allocated on the basis of utilization by products, customers, and so forth of the variable activities giving rise to these costs. The principle followed is to charge the product or customer (or other segment of sales) with the cost of its share of the variable activity of each functional-cost group, that is, the cost of the portion of the variable marketing and administrative effort for which it is responsible.

Variable functional activity.   The identification of the variable activity which is involved in each functional-cost group and the broad relationship between the functional costs and the characteristics of products and customers are often evident merely from study. Some functional activities vary according to certain characteristics of the commodity and are not greatly affected by customer characteristics. Others vary primarily according to certain customer characteristics regardless of what product is being purchased.

For example, the variable activity involved in the storage and investment functions depends almost solely on the bulk, weight, perishability, and inventory value of the product stored, and is affected but little by the customer who buys the product. Similarly, the credit function will vary according to the financial integrity and other credit characteristics of customers with little regard to the nature of the commodity on which credit was extended.

As regards still other functional-cost groups, the broad relationship between these costs and product and customer characteristics is more complicated. For there is every shade of combination of customer responsibility and commodity responsibility for the variable activity, and therefore for the amount of expense, within the different functional-cost groups.

Partial allocation. It is the considered opinion of this author that it is neither feasible nor useful to attempt a full allocation of all marketing costs in most businesses, although there are many who make such an attempt. That is, those functional activities which vary entirely with customer characteristics should not be allocated to commodities, and conversely, those related solely to commodity characteristics should not be allocated to customers. However, some functional-cost groups would usually be allocated to both customers and commodities.

Partial allocation and pricing. In addition to the difficulty of tracing a direct connection between the variable activity of some functions and product or customer characteristics, there is another reason for not making a full allocation of distribution costs. For the control uses of these cost data which we are discussing—namely, to discover the unprofitable parts of the business, to determine the appropriate action to be taken in regard to these unprofitable sales, and to set profitable prices—little would be gained by making a full allocation.

A full allocation may involve the assignment of some indirect expenses which represent functions not being used to capacity,[4] on the basis of an arbitrary factor such as sales volume. This may have the effect of making some commodities, customers, etc., with large sales volume and low percentages of gross margin appear to be relatively unprofitable. Actually, since these functions are not being used to capacity, these indirect expenses would not be affected by substitution, elimination, or an increase of sales in the short run.

For example, storage and investment costs usually would not be allocated to customers, because these activities are not usually related to customer characteristics and because they would not be affected by short-run changes in the number of customers. Likewise, credit costs usually would not be allocated to commodities, since they would not be affected by addition or elimination of products "at the margin."

A desire for a full cost allocation may involve an erroneous conception of the use of distribution-cost analysis in connection with pricing policy. It ap-

---

[4] Such evidence as is available indicates that important distribution facilities or functions may, in normal times, be rather consistently underutilized in the typical business.

pears to some that if they know the total or "real" unit distribution cost, plus the total unit production cost, they can then arrive at the proper price merely by adding the desired unit net profit. If, however, such a pricing procedure gives insufficient recognition to demand, it may be worse than one which is not based on any knowledge of unit costs at all.   If prices determined on this total unit cost-plus basis are too high, in the light of demand and competition, sales volume may be lower than before, so that total costs per unit will be higher than calculated and may not be covered even at the higher prices.   Or if cost-plus prices are too low, then profits are sacrificed.

Summary of procedure. Chart 1 summarizes the preceding discussion of distribution cost analysis techniques, showing some illustrative functional cost groups and bases of allocation to commodities and to customers.

Chart I. Functional-cost Groups and Bases of Allocation

Functional-cost groups	Bases of allocation		
	To product groups	To account-size classes	To sales territories
1. Selling—direct costs ...	Selling time devoted to each product, as shown by special sales-call reports or other special studies	Number of sales calls times average time per call, as shown by special sales-call reports or other special studies	Direct
2. Selling—indirect costs ..	In proportion to direct selling time, or time records by projects	In proportion to direct selling time, or time records by projects	Equal charge for each salesman
3. Advertising	Direct; or analysis of space and time by media; other costs in proportion to media costs	Equal charge to each account; or number of ultimate consumers and prospects in each account's trading area	Direct; or analysis of media circulation records
4. Sales promotion	Direct; or analysis of source records	Direct; or analysis of source records	Direct; or analysis of source records
5. Transportation	Applicable rates times tonnages	Analysis of sampling of bills of lading	Applicable rates times tonnages
6. Storage and shipping ..	Warehouse space occupied by average inventory. Number of shipping units	Number of shipping units	Number of shipping units
7. Order processing	Number of order lines	Number of order lines	Number of order lines

14. Cost analysis as a basis for sales policy

Sometimes, as a last resort and after investigating all other alternatives, the decision is made by the executives to eliminate the unprofitable sales which have been revealed by a distribution cost analysis.

A decision to eliminate unprofitable sales is far-reaching, affecting every aspect of the business. A decision to eliminate an unprofitable segment of sales because its "savable" distribution costs exceeds its net revenue, for example, would need to be reviewed in the light of the fact that smaller production runs and a reduced scale of production with the same amount of fixed costs might increase the unit manufacturing cost. Thus, controlled marketing experiments and/or further cost analyses are necessary if the business executive, after studying all the alternative courses of action, seeks to determine the effects of eliminating those unprofitable segments of sales that cannot be turned into source of profit. These further analyses involve the following steps:

Make a forecast of just what will happen to sales volume over a period of time, after the business changes from a policy of indiscriminately covering the entire market to a policy of selective distribution. This, of course, is an analysis to be made by the marketing executives

Estimate the decrease in total expense that would result from eliminating the unprofitable sales. This is not an easy matter, since the distribution costs which were allocated to sales to discover the unprofitable segments would not provide the answer, for some of these costs could not be saved and would continue after the sales were dropped. Therefore, it is necessary to separate the nonsavable (or fixed) costs from the savable costs. The total savable costs less the net revenue that will be given up show, of course, the net savings, or the addition to the net profits of the business that will result from dropping the unprofitable sales (Of course, if the net revenue that will be given up exceeds the expenses that will be saved, the net profits in the short run will be greater with the relatively unprofitable sales than without them)

Make definite plants to get expenses down when unprofitable sales are to be cut off. The experiences of several businesses have shown that projected savings in distribution costs often are never realized because of failure to make and execute definite plans for expense reduction

As is true of cost accounting in the factory, although there are certain general principles or basic techniques, there is no one "right" method of analysis which can be used by all businesses. Rather, these basic techniques of analysis must be applied by each company individually and adapted to the individual circumstances of the business.

Despite the fact that businessmen are left to make their own choice among an array of possible procedures, however, it is hoped that they will be encouraged to use the same basic management tools of marketing-cost analysis and controlled marketing experimentation, to improve their marketing productivity.

Section 10

COST ACCOUNTING SYSTEMS

BY

William E. Weber

COST ACCOUNTING SYSTEMS

Introduction

Every business, whether large or small, employs cost accounting to some extent in its accounting procedures. Cost accounting is often considered as being different from general accounting, although it is really an extension of general and financial accounting. While general accounting is used to report on the profit-and-loss status of an enterprise on a monthly, quarterly, or annual basis, it does not provide a detailed breakdown of the cost incurred. It is cost accounting that provides this additional necessary detail.

Cost accounting defined. Cost accounting might be defined as a process of ascertaining, analyzing, and interpreting the cost of manufacturing a product, rendering a service, or of performing any function or operation in an enterprise. Breakdown of these costs may be by department, processes, products, or units of products, lines, sales, territories, selling or distribution divisions, services, and functions in the administrative division.

The cost system. The usefulness of this cost breakdown depends on the reliability and degree of accuracy of the cost data, and upon the distribution and allocation of these costs. Just any cost-accounting system will not produce the desired breakdowns in an enterprise. The cost system that is employed must fit the particular enterprise; and cost accounting is not strictly limited to a manufacturing concern.

The system that is adopted can be only as good as the ability and experience of the person in charge of the accounting system. Necessary cooperation must be given by all employees having any part in the accumulation and reporting of cost information. The system cannot be expected to operate efficiently if the information given is not reliable or is slanted to favor one department over another. The system also cannot operate efficiently if the cost of it is not justified in the particular enterprise.

Accuracy of reporting costs becomes one of the major parts of an efficiently functioning cost-accounting system. These costs are dependent on the degree of systemization in reporting costs of labor and materials. Along with these costs the determination of an overhead rate makes up the basis for all cost-accounting systems. Unless the method used for determining overhead is fairly accurate, large variances will result, which will cause a serious distortion of all costs in any statement and will make difficult the establishment of prices, which must be based on accurately determined costs. This determination of over-head costs to be applied becomes simpler when it is possible to classify departments, or cost centers, making it possible to apply different and more realistic rates to these departments, rather than to the enterprise as a whole.

The comparative presentation of items in the balance sheet, the profit-and-loss statement, or schedules of operating costs is desirable for observing dollar amounts in their historical perspective. However, it is impossible to control each kind of cost or expense by taking note of the trend of the expense. Controlling costs through this type of analysis is not an effective way to run an enterprise.

Effective financial management. Effective financial management of a business is dependent largely upon an efficient system of cost and budgetary control. It is virtually impossible to make more than a few decisions in the broader financial area regarding the growth of an enterprise, unless the decisions are supported by as complete a report of internal operating conditions as it is possible to secure.

The only effective way to run any enterprise is through the operating budget. Forecasts derived from informed and intelligent planning set the control limits at the outset of the accounting period, and variances at the end of the period report the efficiencies and inefficiencies which actual operations produce.

Effective budgetary control should be the main concern of all enterprises. But effective control can be accomplished only by following the objectives of cost accounting to the letter. There are many different ways to adapt a cost-accounting system, but in general they all conform to the same objectives.

All accounts must be classified in order to provide costs by departments, processes, products, and units in the manufacturing divisions. Any form of cost accounting, whether job-order cost, process cost, or standard cost, depending on the suitability to the particular enterprise, will accomplish the necessary allocation of costs. This alone is not sufficient, and further breakdowns must be provided by services and functions in the administrative divisions. It is also necessary to include sales divisions, territories, and different products according to sales for a complete breakdown in order to organize an efficient budget.

Effective breakdown and budgetary control in the manufacturing divisions provide control of materials and supplies in order to reduce to a minimum waste due to misappropriation, deterioration, obsolescence, scraps, spoilage, and defective units of output. This in turn provides information on the real cost of materials and supplies used on specific jobs, processes, and by departments allowing more accurate selling-price determination.

Variances in materials and supplies accruing during the period are relatively easy to control with the use of almost any cost system, and the reasons for the variances can be found easily when an accurate budget is prepared.

The second main area of breakdown in budgetary control is labor. Direct and indirect labor must be allocated accurately to processes, departments, products, and services. Classifying costs as direct and indirect and assigning them to the job or product at each stage of production must be done with extreme care and accuracy. Separating the costs is not always easy, and the criteria for separating them must be thought up and worked out well in advance of any budgetary planning. Variances due to efficiencies and inefficiencies are more vital in this area than in materials and supplies. Union-wage rates and incentive-pay raises must be considered if an effective budget is to be worked out.

Administrative costs and service-department costs are the major part of the indirect labor and the most difficult to distribute effectively. Controversies between departments about the appropriate charges to be made for these costs always arise and must be dealt with effectively so as not to hinder the effectiveness of the allocation of direct-labor costs. This applies to any system of cost accounting that the enterprise adopts.

These areas can be considered the minor part of budgetary control through cost accounting. The major area lies in overhead rates to be applied to the different processes, departments, and units of output. It is in the application of an effective overhead rate that determination of the ultimate profit or loss of a manufacturing enterprise lies.

There is no set way to determine the overhead rate that is to be applied, whether the enterprise is a manufacturing concern or any other type of enterprise. When determining a rate, machine hours, direct-labor hours, direct material cost, or any reasonable system can be applied. The important thing is not the system, but the accuracy of the costs that are applied.

The budget. Budgets must be used to predict expenses and costs must be analyzed to determine the feasibility of the system employed. Control of overhead costs is the main factor in increasing profit. No selling price can be determined without taking into consideration an estimation of overhead. The greater the diversification of products, the more important it is for a manufacturer to have an accurate assignment of all overhead costs of the enterprise to each product manufactured.

Taking all these factors into consideration, the budget is the main control tool. Budgets should be provided for every department and every operation; administrative, selling, and manufacturing. Budgetary procedures must be set up whereby predetermined costs can be obtained rather than having this information available only after the close of the accounting period.

Effective budgets provide detailed reports of complete costs regarding operations of the enterprise for purposes of comparing such data with other periods of operation and with other concerns in the industry, and for analysis of the nature of any variances that occur.

The compilation of all the data regarding actual costs as compared with the budget should be something built into the cost system so that it can be done on a moment's notice, to aid management in guiding the enterprise to a greater profitable period.

1. Cost aspects of income determination

Recognition and classification. The recognition, classification, and expiration of costs, and their assignment to revenue for purposes of income determination, involve some of the most difficult problems in accounting and should be discussed before the operations of the various cost systems. Before we begin to view these various cost aspects, it is necessary to acquire an understanding of the cost principle as described by the executive committee of the American Accounting Association:

> Cost incurred is measured by cash outlay or by fair market value of considerations other than cash. For each accounting period there must be a determination of the amount of cost which has been absorbed in producing revenue or has otherwise expired, and also the amount of cost which is reasonably applicable to future operations.

The cost principle represents a well-established concept in accounting. It is not, however, so inflexible that it automatically produces uniformity of results. Costs vary usually subject to current market conditions. There is also a large variety of cost alternatives, some of which will be discussed. Each of these alternatives viewed separately has a definite effect on income for the period. The selection of a particular cost alternative involves many technical considerations in an effort to determine the most profitable under existing circumstances. Some of the many alternatives include costs which arise out of external acquisition or internal construction of property, costs which may be actual or imputed, cost based upon displacement or replacement value, product cost or period costs, and historical or predetermined costs.

Constructed property. All applicable charges should be incorporated into the cost of the property, but it is possible that these charges include expenditures of a wasteful and avoidable nature. The property was, however, constructed to provide a source of revenue and each revenue increment produced by the use of the asset should absorb its share of the actual cost. In regard to allocation of factory overhead charges on constructed property, there are two distinct views: (1) that the assets being constructed should bear their proportionate share of normal factory overhead, and (2) that property costs should include only overhead which can be directly ascribed to the asset under construction and is in excess of overhead which would normally be incurred in connection with the fabrication of company's products.

Those who favor the second viewpoint think that allocation of a portion of the overhead cost to the construction job will cause an improper reduction in product costs. In other words, these proponents think that there is excess plant capacity when costs are allocated to the construction itself. But accountants must report the feasibility of such excess plant capacity, and that is why the allocation of cost to the assets being constructed in an equitable manner is the proper treatment.

The deterioration and ultimate dispossession of fixed property is evident to all accountants. The problem, however, lies in the prediction of life expectancy. Even under the most controlled operation and advanced techniques the anticipated life-span of property may deviate sharply from the actual useful life. Regardless of the uncertainties involved, adherence to the principle of matching cost against revenue compels the accountant to allocate the proportional share to each period, most often the period being a year.

The most frequently used method of cost write-off is done on the straight-line basis, which uses as its basis, time and equal periodic apportionment of the net cost of the property. Most often the straight-line method is very satisfactory, but adherence to it does tend to overstate income during periods of accelerated output and understate it during years of declining production. The straight-line method neglects at least three important facts: (1) the amount charged to operation, if placed on interest, will accumulate to more than the amount to be distributed; (2) the asset will usually require heavier repairs in later periods, and therefore the method will not result in uniform operating charges, including maintenance; (3) the product may vary from year to year and season to season with resulting relatively high cost per unit of output when production is low. Nevertheless, it is the most common method and its simplicity is deemed to offset its theoretical weaknesses.

Inventory costs. Inventories have been classified as those items of tangible personal property which (1) are held for sale in the ordinary course of business, or (2) are in process of production of goods or services to be available for sale. By associating costs with products or inventory, the cost accountant has devised an excellent method for measuring period income.

Clearly, if a product and the cost attached to it can be traced from its inception to its ultimate disposition, you have an accurate and valid measurement of income. Despite the progress which has been made by the cost accountant, product costing has not been sufficiently refined so that it is always a reliable determinant of income. Products do not always lend themselves to precise cost calculations. Certain costs because of a definite pattern should be treated as period costs (i.e., considered as expenses of the period regardless of whether related products have been sold) rather than product costs. Often the apportionment of costs between products is very technical and complex, which is still another factor which limits the accuracy of product costing. The difficulty of product costing can be summarized as follows: The actual cost of inventories is generally not readily ascertainable. Determining costs is a difficult task, fraught with technical difficulties and requiring the use of judgment all along the line. At the worst the reported cost is little more than an arbitrary guess; at the best it is a careful esimate made by competent people familiar with the circumstances.

From an accounting standpoint, the cost of a manufactured product comprises material, labor, and factory overhead.   These costs can be classified into three distinct categories: (1) direct costs, (2) indirect costs, and (3) unassignable costs.

1. Direct product costs represent charges that can visibly be identified with particular products.   The cost and quantity of products flowing into the production of the products, along with the cost of laborers directly engaged in this production, are included in the direct-cost category,
2. Indirect product costs are those costs that cannot be readily identified with particular products but are assigned on a reasonable basis
3. Unassignable product costs consist of charges for which no reasonable product allocation exists

Purchase discounts.   Discounts given on purchases when payments are made within a specific time period are regarded by many accountants as representing a source of income similar to interest or dividends earned on securities.   This approach seems a little unrealistic, since accounting is concerned with transactions actually occurring, not mere possibilities.   Furthermore, since discounts are generally standardized throughout an industry, the seller in establishing prices for his commodities anticipates their deduction and adjusts his price accordingly.   The intent of the purchase discount is to penalize the slow payer rather than to reward those who are punctual.   The disposition of purchase discount can have a significant effect on income.   However, there is little justification for treating it other than as an initial reduction in cost.

Intangible costs.   Intangible costs have been classified by the committee on accounting as (1) those having a term of existence limited by law, regulation, or agreement or by their nature (such as patents, goodwill, copyrights, or leases), and (2) those having no such limited term of existence and as to which there is, at the time of acquisition, no indication of limited life.

Since there are time limitations inherent in intangible costs of type (1) nature, a basis is available for distributing their costs to revenue.   However, if their legal life, as predetermined, does not coincide with their economic life, then an adjustment is to be made in the amortization basis to allow for the correction.

Probably the most difficult aspects of intangible costs arise from particularly goodwill as seen in type 2.   It represents a capitalization of the excess of the actual earnings rate over the normal rate of return for the business.   The difficulty arises because the factors entering into its determination cannot be readily isolated or agreed upon.   Some accountants feel that goodwill should be written off against future earnings as soon as possible.   However, this procedure is objectionable since it does not provide for the disposition of goodwill in periods of financial loss.   Usually goodwill is restricted to the excess earning power for a limited number of future years and its write-off is accomplished by amortizing it against income according to the number of years it was originally based on.

It is the cost accountant's job to analyze the different alternatives and to arrive at that one which will be most profitable for the given concern.

2. Controlling overhead costs

The costs themselves.   Overhead is not a miscellaneous item which must be allocated to satisfy the organization's chief accountant.   It is an item which can consist of as much as one-third of the total cost of the product.   Many small plants and businesses have failed because the executives directly charged with their operation did not understand what the overhead costs consisted of and how to control them.

Overhead costs or indirect costs have increased because of the decrease of production workers (through automation, improved technology, etc.) and the increase of nonproduction workers (through the demands of the economy for more services rather than products).   Where production workers have not significantly decreased in certain industries, nonproduction workers have increased from 20 to 50 percent.

Again, the mere allocation of overhead costs is not enough.   These costs have to be religiously and periodically evaluated.   A tendency exists to ignore control of overhead in prosperous times.   This can be extremely dangerous in competitive markets.   Overhead expenses become highly variable in periods of growth and fixed in periods of slack or decline.   Therefore, cutting costs in the latter periods may prove to be quite difficult.

What is overhead?   One definition reads: "The essential cost that is necessary in your plant operations and represents expenditures that do not often add value to the product."

Examples of overhead costs are (1) management and supervision, (2) purchasing activities and material handling, (3) supplementary costs of labor— those items related to employee services, such as vacations, pensions, etc., (4) personnel activities, (5) indirect factory labor, (6) equipment and building maintenance, (7) tools and supplies, (8) plant protection, (9) quality control, (10) utilities, (11) staff services, (12) selling, marketing, and distribution costs, (13) clerical and paper-work expenses, (14) communications, (15) outside professional aid, (16) asset ownership and rental, and (17) taxes.

Certain items are selected to illustrate the various controls applicable to them.

The most formidable problem related to material handling is excessive inventories.   Not only do they decrease working capital, but they also take up costly space.   If space is at a premium, then palletized unit loads are economic.   This also minimizes excessive hauling.   The idea is to reduce the many operations associated with the same materials.   The seemingly minor problem of controlling the storage of scrap should not be overlooked.   If it proves to be uncontrollable, unnecessary overtime costs will have to be incurred for cleaning up this scrap.

Operations can be reduced by making picking, checking, and packing of materials one operation. Conveyor belts can be useful here as well as adequate space for forklift equipment. These suggestions are easy enough to implement, but are often not considered.

The supplementary costs of labor are the fringe benefits, such as insurance, payroll taxes, vacations, holiday pay, feeding and rest periods, pensions, and employee recreational activities. These fringe benefits consume from 18 to 25 percent of the total payroll cost. These costs must be incurred to maintain the employee's confidence in the company. One cannot ignore them, but they can be reasonably controlled. For example, the employee-benefit programs of life insurance and pension plans do not have to be provided for by sinking funds, which can consume vast quantities of working capital; they can be adequately provided for by buying these programs from companies dealing in such a business. An employee contributory program is desirable.

Perhaps the most irritating of all items to control are the customary washup and rest periods and the coffee-break programs. Some police effort should be executed to control them, since they can be well abused. The use of vending machines for the lunchroom should be considered.

One of the larger costs is maintenance. It can amount to as much as one-third of the total overhead cost. The most uncontrollable factor here is idle employee time. All work of the mechanics and janitors should be preplanned. Enormous costs can be incurred if the mechanics and janitors are unsystematically performing their duties. Therefore, it is necessary to have standards of work measurement. For example, if the repair of equipment is exceeding 15 percent of the equipment's book value, the equipment should be considered for overhauling or replacement, or the men might be retrained, since poor training might be the cause of the excessive maintenance costs.

Tools and supplies are a good subject for cost reduction. Furthermore, most cost-control programs in this area are very responsive to the efforts of management to obtain results. Responsibility to the individual mechanic or porter is best. Also special tools should be rented and not bought.

A safety program is the best answer to plant protection. With regard to insurance of the plant for casualty, your insurance rating can be reduced by demonstrating to the insurer the effectiveness of your safety program. A company's insurance rates are too often taken for granted. Management should check to see whether a lower rating can be obtained. There is no harm in merely asking the insuring company whether or not a reduced rate can be obtained. In some risks self-insurance is the best answer. Sears, Roebuck and Co. uses this method.

Utilities include heating, electric power, gas, water, telephone, and steam. Costs can be cut without impairing the utilization of these facilities. Office personnel will still be kept warm. As much as one-half of the heating cost can be eliminated by just seeing that working areas are heated and not merely empty space. In addition to this, electricity costs can be reduced by adjusting the work hours to minimum power-load periods of the day. Furthermore, a better power rating can be obtained from the power company through this control.

Fewer and better records are indicative of good management control. Payroll checks, their related records, and bills of lading should never be kept longer than 4 years. The idea is to eliminate useless records, but nevertheless protect historical and vital ones. There should also be regular schedules for the retirement and destruction of certain types of records. Since office space is at a premium, excessive file cabinets should be stored. It costs $6 to store a four-drawer file cabinet versus $145 per year to retain the cabinet uselessly in the office.

If an overhead problem exists, it is sometimes advisable to hire professionals, such as management services and certified public accountants, to deal with these problems; they are especially useful for specific engagements. Whatever the overhead problem is, an effort must be made to control these costs, and the costs are inevitably reflected in the company's pricing structure.

Reporting the costs. Corporations have devised the best cost-accounting systems through experience and careful planning. It can employ the most elaborate, reasonably accurate system, and yet, due to improper reports, still fail in one of its primary purposes—to help management make decisions.

Periodic and simple reports are necessary for comparison with the budgeted figures; if this is not done, the department head will lose interest in his responsibilities. Standardized forms should be used since they are economical and accurate and they also make comparisons with prior periods easier. Naturally, consistency in reporting must be maintained, if the other precautions are to be effective.

The reports should be made monthly. They should include a profit-and-loss statement and a listing of actual overhead expenses for the month by type of expense and by department or function. Before the type of report is established, it is necessary to have a chart of accounts for good financial accounting and internal management control. The expenses should be clearly identified by their nature, be related to the proper departments, and be compared with the data of prior years.

The expenses should be classified into controllable and semicontrollable expenses (preferably never use noncontrollable as a category). The first category can be allocated by relation to specific factors, e.g., packing and crating expenses increase with sales. The second category is determined by higher management, e.g., insurance, retirement plans, and building rentals. A basic control of these expenses would consist of the total amount of each expense along with its ratio to sales or direct labor, and a comparison with planned results or actual prior expenses.

The expenses can be controlled in either of two ways: major control by account and minor control by organization, or major control by organization and minor control by account. With the first method the different departments can vary widely in their expenses while the account total remains the same. Consequently weak control might result, especially if one department head knows the other is underspending. The second method exerts greater control, since the department head is authorized to spend a specific sum; however, a danger exists here, since the department head might be hindered from doing a good managing job with the limited amount.

For income-measurement purposes, a fixed and variable cost segregation is best. It should also be provided that unit costs do not vary with volume. These assumptions are necessary for manufacturing-overhead accounting. These expenses should not be incurred without asking some basic questions. Is the expense warranted? Is it providing the service at a reasonable cost? What would be the impact of a reduction of the expense? Is an increase in expenses necessary with an increase in activity or prices?

Budgeting the costs. The most effective budget provides for essential records, timely reports to management, realistic analysis before fixed assets are bought, income and expense budgets, special studies on out-of-line expense items, and an active cost reduction committee. Its effectiveness is increased when the budget forecasts not only expenses but also sales figures and profits. In measuring, overhead ratios or statistics should be used since the sales volume is constantly changing.

The functions of the budget plan are establishing the budget and forecasts, supplying guidelines, and furnishing overhead performance data. In establishing the overhead budget, the plan must first of all have management's full support and be compatible with the company's financial plans. It must begin high enough in the organization so that there is enough authority to carry out the budget. Also, the controllable part of the budget should be assigned to specific individuals with authority. The type of budget is affected by the size and structure of the company. In larger companies, for example, detailed control is too expensive; therefore penny accuracy is ignored.

The budget should be related to the accounting function so that the different items are accumulated in parallel with the actual expenses. The maximum limit of the budget can be changed or discussed at regularly scheduled meetings rather than at just one or two meetings. This is desirable since it preserves the department head's interest in his responsibilities. There are also partial budgetary controls which can assist management. For instance, an index can be constructed of personnel requirements at the different levels of activity. Delivery or trucking activity can also be segregated in the regular budget.

Although the precautions presented can be followed, all too often no follow-up of the measures is executed. This is to suggest that overhead costs must be watched just as carefully as the inventory is and just as carefully as the financing of working capital is.

3. Job-order cost system

Cost accounting is an expanded phase of the general or financial accounting of a business concern which provides management promptly with the cost of producing or selling each article or of rendering a particular service. There are two major classifications of cost-accounting systems: the job-order cost system, under which costs are accumulated by specific jobs or lots; and the continuous process or departmental cost system, under which production is more or less continuous and costs are accumulated by departments for a definite period of time.

A job-order cost system can be defined as one that collects separately each element of cost for each job or order worked on by the plant. The system is widely used in many industries, such as job printing, manufacture of special types of machinery, building and public works, construction work for the complete job and for portions subcontracted, and by producers of differentiated lots of goods. It is also widely used as incidental to some other system of cost accounting. Even a continuous-process plant operating under a process cost system may well use a job-order cost system for ascertaining the cost of factory maintenance and repair, the cost of special research projects, and the cost of construction machinery and equipment for use in the plant.

Setting up the system. In establishing a job-order cost system, one of the most important steps is to make a complete survey of the production methods, procedures, and practices of a firm. This is regularly done by preparing a flow chart which shows the movement of raw materials through the various processing departments. A simplified flow chart would show the cost of materials accumulated in the stores or materials account. The cost of materials applicable to the various jobs are charged to a Jobs-in-Process Account. The cost of labor is accumulated in a Payroll Account. This account is closed when the expenses are analyzed into direct labor—which is charged to work in process—and manufacturing overhead expenses (which are charged to the manufacturing overhead control account).

The cost of indirect manufacturing expenses (such as indirect materials and labor, applicable depreciation charges, etc.) is charged to a Manufacturing Overhead Control Account. The manufacturing overhead expenses are usually estimated and applied to a Work-in-Process Account at a predetermined rate. The balancing credit is credited to a Manufacturing Overhead Applied Account, and this account is closed out to the Manufacturing Control Account. The balance in the account—if any—can be closed out in two ways. It can be applied to a Cost of Sales Account or it can be applied to a cost of sales, finished-goods inventory, and work-in-process inventory on a pro rata basis.

When you have analyzed the operations, you should then establish cost centers for the important activities in the manufacturing cycle—in other words, establish various departments. After establishing departments, you can draw up a chart of accounts. These sundry accounts will separate the accumulated costs for each of the cost centers.

The design of the job-order cost sheet is the next and most important step. The heart of the system of the cost accounting for specific jobs is the cost sheet. The three main elements of cost (direct materials and direct labor and manufacturing overhead) are recorded thereon. Columns are provided for the date, explanation, and amount of each element of cost. If desired, a summary section may be used to recapitulate the totals of the cost elements. To identify each job, a job-order number is assigned to each job-order cost sheet and this number is used to identify the materials and labor costs for that specific job. In addition, job cost sheets for jobs in process at the end of the account period act as the subsidiary ledger for the work-in-process controlling account. This account provides a book inventory suitable for checking against the physical inventory.

Once the job-order cost sheet is set up, management must begin to set standards. This is usually done with the aid of the industrial engineer and the cost accountant. Material standards can be set by ascertaining the amount or quantity of materials needed and their price. In addition, an allowance for waste and spoilage must be taken into consideration. Where production is on a custom basis, standards are more difficult to apply. They can be applied by preparing a standard cost card for each job.

Labor standards are set with the aid of time and motion studies. The total labor cost of the article produced is the accumulated cost of the standard operations for the article. The efficiency of the individual operator is determined by comparing the standard time allowed for the quantity of work which the operator has produced with the actual time which he spent. In addition to being used as selling price and cost determinants, these standards are sometimes used for incentive-pay systems and manpower planning.

An overhead rate (based on various levels of production) is multiplied by direct-labor hours or machine hours. Determining this rate raises the question whether or not all overhead is to be applied to this volume of production. Where idle capacity exists, its costs cannot be added to the product without pricing inventory too high relative to sales price.

There are various methods of allocating costs of burden: material cost, direct-labor cost, direct-labor hours, and machine hours. Material cost is seldom used as a basis, because no relationship between material cost and indirect manufacturing costs exists. The direct-labor cost method of distribution is not widely used either. It is based on the assumption that there is a relationship between the dollar cost of direct labor and the amount of indirect manufacturing cost incurred. The direct-labor hours method is based on the assumption that there is a relationship between the number of direct-labor hours and the indirect manufacturing cost incurred, and the machine hours method is based on a similar assumption, but in regard to machine hours.

Therefore, in summary, the basic steps in setting up a job order or specific order cost system are: to survey production methods; to establish cost centers; to establish a chart of accounts; to design a job-order cost sheet; to set standards for materials, labor, and overhead. These steps must be followed in order to assure the accuracy and dependability of the system. How well these steps are followed will determine how well the system will operate.

Operating the system. The primary objective of a job-order cost system is to charge correctly the three cost elements of direct materials, direct labor, and manufacturing overhead to the individual job orders.

In dealing with material charges, a definition of direct materials is necessary. A direct material is one which (1) is identified with a particular product, and (2) is feasible to measure and charge to the cost sheet for particular production orders. Indirect material is identified with particular units of product which it is not considered feasible to measure and charge to the cost sheet of specific production orders.

Although bills of materials may be the media through which required materials are issued to jobs, there are times when additional materials are needed. When these materials are issued, a material requisition is prepared. This form is also used to record issues of operating supplies. If the wrong type of material is delivered to a job, it must be returned to the stores. Record of the return is made on a material credit slip which is similar to the material requisition.

Besides materials which are returned, there are other materials which are not incorporated into finished goods and have been issued. This is due to spoilage and scrap. Most spoilage occurs as the result of defects in workmanship in the factory. When this occurs, the credit to the job and the debit to departmental overhead may include not only the cost of the materials, but the cost of labor and overhead as well.

Scrap is seldom credited to individual jobs because it is extremely difficult to trace scrap to the particular job in which it originated. Scrap is often less usable for further production than the materials from which it came. Thus material costs do not provide a valid basis for evaluating scrap recovery. Scrap is usually priced at its current market value.

Bills of material and material requisitions are sent from the storeroom to the stores clerk. The clerk inserts unit costs on both bills and requisitions, makes extensions, and credits the stores card for the cost of materials issued. Bills of material, material requisitions, and material credit slips are analyzed and totaled daily, weekly, or monthly and are entered on the specific job-order cost sheet. The monthly total in this journal is posted to the general ledger.

In any cost system, payroll accounting falls into two distinct parts. The first involves computation of gross pay earned by each employee and the subsequent payment. The second involves analysis of the total payroll in order to distribute labor costs to the appropriate accounts. In a job-order cost system, cost distribution involves considerable detail and numerous problems. The timekeeping department is really the control center of good accounting for labor cost.

Only the portion of manufacturing labor cost which is classified as direct is charged to job cost sheets. The remainder, indirect labor, is charged to manufacturing overhead. The principle underlying this division into two classes is the same as the one that was cited earlier in connection with materials. Care is necessary to avoid misunderstandings in the use of the words *direct* and *indirect* labor. Some employees, such as power-plant workmen, material handlers, maintenance, and clerical personnel, work in only one cost center. Since the cost of their labor cannot be identified with a specific job or lot of production, it is classified as indirect labor. Although the cost is charged to manufacturing overhead, it is identifiable with a specific cost center and consequently is a direct cost of that service center.

Distribution of labor cost is accomplished by various methods, depending on the work performed and the organization position of the employee. The salaries and wages of supervisory and other employees whose work is entirely of an indirect nature, that is, not traceable to specific jobs, are assigned in advance to specific manufacturing overhead cost accounts, and the time card provides the only basis for cost distribution. In a job-order cost system the time ticket is the basis of determining the hours worked by the employee for each job he works on during the day. Labor in process is charged for the dollar amount of work that was put in on the job and Payroll Account is credited.

The term *manufacturing overhead* refers to those manufacturing costs which cannot be directly identified with specific jobs. Manufacturing overhead costs are accumulated by departments, both in detailed expense accounts and in departmental summary or control accounts. Each department should have a summary account to accumulate the amount of burden absorbed in production. As work goes along, work-in-process accounts are debited for the burden absorbed or burden applied. At the end of the reporting period, the difference between the balance in the cost summary and burden absorbed accounts represents the aggregate burden variance for the period.

Manufacturing costs are usually classified as fixed costs, variable costs, and semivariable costs. Fixed costs are those which do not fluctuate in response to fluctuations in volume. These are for a particular period of time, and include items such as the factory fire insurance on buildings, real-estate taxes, and rent. Variable costs fluctuate with the volume of production in a more or less direct ratio. Variable costs are best exemplified by charges for power and indirect materials. Semivariable costs are similar to variable in the sense that they fluctuate in the same direction as changes in volume, but not in the same ratio.

The relationship between this estimated manufacturing overhead and estimated volume or production must be established in order to allocate a proportionate part of the overhead cost to each unit of product. This relationship is known as the predetermined manufacturing overhead rate. When this rate is applied to the base selected for this purpose to measure volume produced, estimated manufacturing overhead is available to complete the cost of production. When direct-material cost and direct-labor costs are recorded on the job cost sheets, the job costing is completed by the addition of estimated manufacturing overhead. When the various jobs have been completed, the cost sheets are summarized to ascertain the total cost and the unit cost of the goods manufactured.

The three inventory accounts, raw materials, job in process, and finished goods, appear in the company's general leger or main file of accounts and are known as summary accounts. This means that these accounts show the total cost relating to each category of inventory. The balance in these control accounts corresponds to the amounts shown in more detailed subsidiary ledgers.

The financial statements under a job-order cost system are no different from statements prepared under other cost systems. Special reports are frequently prepared and take the form of summaries of completed jobs and jobs still in process, and detailed analysis to show variations of actual cost from estimates.

A report showing gross profit on each job finished and shipped provides a desirable analysis of the totals taken from the job cost sheets. A similar summary can be prepared showing the total cost for materials, labor, and manufacturing overhead and comparing these totals with the estimates for each of these elements of cost. Management's attention is focused on those jobs showing significant cost variances from estimates, and detailed analysis of material and labor elements may be made to identify the cause for variance and suggesting corrective action.

The advantages of job-order costing may be summarized as follows: ability to detect which jobs are profitable, which unprofitable; use of job costs as a basis for estimating similar work in the future; use of job costs as a basis for controlling efficiency of operations (This is done by comparing actual costs against estimates that are prepared when making quotations to a customer.); use of job costs on government contracts and other contracts where cost determines selling price (In such contracts the manufacturer is allowed to charge cost plus a fixed fee or cost plus a reasonable profit. Such cost must be kept on a specific order basis.).

However, it should be noted that job cost information as a basis for estimating similar work in the future can be used only within limits. There may be considerable discrepancies in the cost of production because of differences in time between the completed order and the one being estimated, and also differences in the size of the order. It is possible, of course, that when compiled in useful form, job-order costs may furnish serviceable data for estimating purposes.

In general, the cost of operating a job-order system is considerable. The volume of detail that must be kept is large and the question often arises of the justification for the heavy clerical expenses necessary to find out what an order actually costs.

4. Process cost system

The process cost system, which is employed primarily by a firm that manufactures in a more or less continuous flow, has the cost broken down over various time periods. It may be based on the day, week, or month, the emphasis being placed on the period of time involved and the number of units completed. The continuity of production in process costing gives rise to the problem of estimating the most profitable output at any particular time. Since production is geared for warehouse stocks instead of specific jobs, it is necessary to estimate sales in advance.

A process costing system may be applied to any type of mining, manufacturing, or public utility company. The main prerequisite is that the firm have a homogeneous product or products. This is because the costs must be distributed evenly as they occur, and on a daily, weekly, or monthly average basis. Total materials, labor, and manufacturing overhead are calculated for a given period, then divided by the number of units in arriving at a unit cost. The number of units worked on in each department is then used in calculating the cost to be attributed to each department.

In many instances, even though a single product is being produced, several departments, each with its own individual function, may be involved in the manufacturing process. Sometimes materials may be added in other departments, at other times this may not be necessary, and the initial department is the only one in which materials are put into production. In some cases, as a product passes from department to department, it increases in units due to added materials, in other cases the number of units is decreased due to the loss of units through the production process or other causes. When units are lost, it is more difficult to come up with an accurate unit cost to be allocated to each department. It may also happen that there will be a work-in-process inventory in some department and not in others at the end of the period. All the aforementioned circumstances add to the difficulty of accounting for costs through the process costing method.

When a company utilizes a process cost-accounting system, it is possible for management to apply average costs to each department involved in the manufacturing process. It is also possible to assign these costs to each product within each of these departments. Once the unit average costs are determined, the company may set up predetermined estimates or standards of probable costs over a specific period. This is helpful in preparing budgets for each of the departments, and in tracing deficiencies to the one responsible.

Installation and operation. Before embarking on installing a process cost system, one should obtain two basic foundations of such a system: a set of objectives to serve one as a guide in the installation of all procedures, and an accounting philosophy to underlie policies and practices and to help one work out answers to questions on which expert opinion differs. A set of objectives might encompass and try to (1) determine how much money is being made or lost before Federal taxes, by product, product group, or service rendered, (2) provide adequate control over all inventories to ensure their accuracy, (3) provide for the control of fixed assets for cost insurance and tax purposes and to determine rates of depreciation which will represent the estimated useful life of the equipment for cost purposes, and (4) determine the relative performance in each department or plant comparing actual money spent with the standards set up. After having adopted a set of objectives, one is ready to install the system.

The person installing the system should—

Get proper introduction by top company officials to all concerned in the work of setting up the system

Take a walk through the plants with the top official in order to get a bird's-eye view of operations

Request the preparation of flow charts of the operations in each processing department showing the major pieces of equipment through which the company product passes

Get a complete list of finished products

Determine whether or not the fixed-asset record is by individual piece of equipment. If not, have such a list made showing the cost value of each piece, its date of acquisition, and its remaining useful life

Prepare a list of cost centers which are centers making the product or servicing it, and an accounting device for the collection of expenses

Obtain floor plans of each building and assign all floor space to specific cost centers

Classify each piece of equipment by cost center, and note the cost value and the monthly depreciation charge. Prescribe a routine for reporting additions to, retirement from, and transfers between each center's roster of equipment, if one is not already in use

Arrange for an engineer to make a study of the usage of each utility, such as steam, electricity, gas, water, compressed air, or refrigeration and derive factors for the usage of each per unit of production or per machine hour, where products are involved, and on a monthly or other basis, where they are not

Determine the type of cost system applicable to each department of the plant —whether a process cost system or a job cost system (The use of standards must be treated separately.)

Adopt a code of accounts for both general and expense ledgers which will fit the contemplated cost procedures and which will be suitable for financial statements

Get samples of all current factory forms used either for accounting or for production. Determine whether each contributes to the system which you plan, or whether revisions are necessary

Examine the established duties of the factory and accounting clerks and supervisors to determine how they fit in with what you propose

Set up a timetable for the collection of all expenses by cost center and by accounting code

Determine the method for recording receipt of each class of raw materials and supplies, and coordinate production planning and purchasing. Provide for a numerical code for each class and decide whether the accounting is to be done manually or by machine. Determine the frequency of physical inventories for verification of book figures

Determine how labor will be reported. Prepare labor codes by operation and product or job for cost requirements and for the measurement of factory performance. Set a timetable

Make up bases for distributing all expenses collected by cost center (excluding direct labor, which will be reported and summarized by operation or production): service centers to operating centers, and operating centers to products, or operations, or jobs

Make a schedule of all data needed from factory reports and decide whether to use available reports or create new ones. For the process cost system, decide how data ought to be assembled for cost calculations and for verifying inventories. Arrange for assembling data on scrap, wastages, and degradings for use in both costs and performance reports

Obtain a set of formulas, yields, and so forth, for use in both cost determinations and performance reports for a process system

Arrange for the determination, by the methods of industrial engineering, of standards for direct labor, yields, wastages, scrap, and degradings for use in measuring performance. Include also standards for indirect labor, repairs and maintenance, and other items of overhead for which standards are applicable

Arrange for the determination of standards for each item of shipping, distribution, selling, advertisement and promotion, research and development, and general and administrative expense for use in the preparation of profitability statements by product or product group

Set up a system for research and development for the accumulation of money spent by project. This system will be coordinated with the division of profitability statements and for the use of management in deciding on a budget for research and development

Set up timetables and procedures for the forecasting of sales, profits and expenses for the entire company for the coming year

Settle on and get approval for the regular and special report with which management is to be provided

Under the process cost system, the costs of material, labor, and manufacturing are usually accumulated in individual expense accounts until the close of the accounting period, when they are summarized and the unit cost of the articles produced during the period ascertained by dividing the total cost by the total number of units produced. Sometimes the costs of materials, labor, and manufacturing expenses are charged to processes or departments. This is a control and a means of promoting efficiency within the factory. The primary objective is to ascertain the unit cost of the products manufactured during the accounting period. Process costs are in reality daily, weekly, or monthly average costs.

Material, labor, and overhead costs are accumulated and recorded by department or processes. An efficient stores control is vital. Through this control several advantages are obtained: (1) It provides the information necessary for the preparations of periodic accounts and also ensures that the charges included therein are in respect of actual usages and not necessarily purchases during the accounting period; (2) waste due to carelessness, stealing, and faulty handling are quickly revealed and immediate steps are taken to eliminate or at least reduce them; (3) physical stores can be compared regularly with book inventories and the differences investigated.

During the accounting period the materials received may be accounted for in much the same manner as under the job cost system. Material requisitions may be used, but consumption reports can facilitate the accounting, since the same materials are used in the same department time after time. No distinction is made for direct and indirect materials and since all materials used in manufacturing are to be placed in the initial department, the procedure for handling material costs will be controlled by this department. It is necessary to ascertain only the total amount requisitioned or consumed. The entry is:

Work in process department X
Stores control

For labor during the accounting period, payroll vouchers may be issued each payday and be recorded in the same manner as under the job cost system. Job time tickets are not necessary. At the end of each accounting period a labor-cost summary should be prepared which will serve as a basis for recording the labor cost in the general ledger accounts. No classification needs to be made on a basis of direct or indirect labor. The entry is:

Work in process department X
    Accrued payroll payable

All manufacturing expenses may be accumulated in individual accounts during the accounting period. These accounts may be kept in the general ledger or subsidiary manufacturing expense ledger with a control account in the general ledger. If the factory is departmentalized, expense analysis ledger sheets may be substituted for ordinary ledger accounts, or work sheets may be used in summarizing the department costs at the end of each period.

Instead of distributing manufacturing expenses to jobs on a basis of predetermined rates as in a job cost system, it is necessary to accumulate expenses by department or process. Certain expenses may be charged directly to the department or process, while others may have to be apportioned over several departments or processes on some appropriate basis such as floor space, etc. If the expenses are accumulated by department, service-department expenses should be distributed over productive departments on some basis. The primary objective is to determine the amount of manufacturing expense to be borne by the product as it passes through each department or process. The use of a predetermined rate for process cost has increased in popularity because it permits more satisfactory comparisons of unit costs from period to period. The entry is:

Work in process department X
    Manufacturing overhead control or applied overhead

When the materials, labor, and overhead have been accumulated, these costs are charged to work in process by one of several arrangements—

    A single work-in-process account might be used by a company that has only one production department or produces a single product

    Department work-in-process accounts would be more suitable if production flows through several cost centers and separate costs for each process may be desirable

    A separate work-in-process account for each of the three cost elements would allow more accurate costing if the enterprise produces multiple products. Costs can later be analyzed for definite identification with each production run

A work-in-process account for each product would be used if several products are processed in the same department. Costs are charged against production as follows:

    Materials are charged to work in process and manufacturing overhead through posting from material-requisition journals

    Labor charges are picked up from monthly summaries of payroll by processes

    Manufacturing overhead costs that have been accumulated and classified in departmental overhead analysis sheets during the period are allocated to production departments (processes) either directly or by predetermined rate or by some combination plan

Output data from each department are summarized in periodic production reports. Then the average costs, which are characteristic or process costs, are computed and presented in the cost of production summary report

Costs are transferred from one process to the other as the product flows toward completion

In a process cost system, presentation of unit-cost figures must be made available to assist management in determining prices and to control costs and direct operations. The variation in the total costs of producing a product in two different periods is meaningless. It is only when the cost per unit has been determined that any real comparison can be made, because the only common factor between periods is the unit of product. Since any one of the three factors of cost can vary in such a way as to result in the same or lower total costs than the prior period, yet not disclose inefficiencies that should be corrected, a report must be made on the unit costs per product by each of the three factors of cost.

This characteristic of the unit cost is the concept of the process cost system. The development of these unit costs is accomplished through the use of the summary cost of production report.

The form of the summary cost of production reports for process cost systems is not standardized. The form depends upon the type and number of products bieng manufactured and the number of departments through which the materials must pass in the course of production. In general, the report will consist of five major components:

1. Equivalent units of production
2. Prior department costs
3. Beginning work in process costs
4. Current department costs
5. A summary of costs of units transferred to subsequent department and the current work in process

The summary cost of production report does not change with the method of process cost used, and therefore it remains the same regardless of the method of costing, i.e., the first-in–first-out method and the average cost method.

Average cost method. In the manufacturing process, the function of gathering accumulated costs with the units produced is important. In process costing, one of the methods of allocating cost to units produced, on a per-unit basis, is to average the cost during a given period of time into the total goods manufactured or in process for that period. This method is the more widely used of the process costing methods because of its simplicity and its ability to adapt to most situations. It is the only practical method of costing for goods made in a large multidepartment manufacturing process.

The averaging method of process costing is based on an equivalent production concept, whereby all work done on a production run is estimated in whole units. The equivalent production quantity would therefore include all the goods finished during the period plus the work still in process, totaled in order to account for the number of units they would have equaled had they been finished. The average unit cost is determined by dividing the total cost by the units of equivalent production.

The procedure given above was for a simple one-department process. However, there are more complex processes, which require two or more departments to produce a finished product. There will also be units lost in production and units added to work in process by the addition of materials.

For a multidepartment process, costs are accumulated as the materials are brought through the process. The cumulative cost in the first department is divided by the equivalent production of the first department to get the unit cost. Then the work transferred from this department to the second department has only the cost associated with the units transferred and the unit cost identified with these units. The total cost transferred is the basis for the materials used in the subsequent departments, unless there are further materials in the manufacturing process in those departments.

The cumulative cost for each in-process department is the cost transferred in from the previous department plus the cost added in the current department. The cumulative cost for the final product transferred to the finished goods center is the cost of units worked on in the final department less the ending work-in-process inventory from that department. The average cost is built up as the units are brought through the various manufacturing departments or cost centers.

Each cost center takes the work transferred to it and adds its own labor and manufacturing cost to the total cost of production (or, in the case of the first department, the initial costs are put into production). In each cost center the cost added by these departments is divided by the equivalent production for the department to attain an average unit cost of the work done in that department. This average unit cost, based on the estimated production of complete units, is added to the average unit cost accumulated in the previous departments to give the cumulative per-unit cost through that department.

An important adjustment which must be made in figuring the average unit cost is the adjustment for lost units. In the department where spoilage occurs there is no need to adjust the unit cost for goods produced in that department. However, it is necessary to adjust the unit cost of units transferred into the department. This is in order to get full value for the remaining units. A cost is assigned to the lost units and a lost unit is allocated over remaining units to arrive at a per-unit cost for lost units. This is added to the unit cost of goods from the previous department to obtain an adjusted unit cost for the work done in the previous department.

The averaging method of process costing has the advantage of a simple calculation of equivalent units of production and the opening inventory does not have to be separately treated as in the first-in–first-out method. The makeup of cost is also simplified by having only one cost basis for each department. However, it has the disadvantage of obscuring any change in unit cost arising during the period, because it permits opening inventory costs which were worked on in a previous period to affect that of the current period.

First-in–first-out method. This method is based on the assumption that the first goods purchased are the first to be sold, and that the goods which remain are of the last purchases. FIFO assumes a procession of costs that are assignable to revenue in exactly the same order in which they were incurred. When the initial work-in-process inventory is treated under the FIFO method, the costs expended in any department for materials, labor, and manufacturing overhead must first be applied to the completion of the accounting period, and then to the new production. Therefore, the final work-in-process inventory in any department will consist of the unit cost of the latest production. The costs of the initial work-in-process inventory will be reflected in the first transfer out of any department.

Various methods are used by firms using the FIFO method of costing the initial work-in-process inventory. Under one method the initial work-in-process inventory keeps separate its lots of production throughout the manufacturing operations. It is almost like job-lot costing applied to a process industry. This method is in use by some pharmaceutical product manufacturers. This method is quite possibly the most expensive to install and operate, but it is also the most accurate in performance. Also, it becomes increasingly complicated when there are many producing departments, each having work in process at the beginning. For example, if there were three operating departments in a firm, the finished goods produced would show separate costs for the following, in the final department:

Work in process, department I, at the beginning of the period
New production, department I, carried through departments II and III
Work in process, department II, at the beginning of the period
Work in process, department III, at the beginning of the period

If there were no added materials or lost units in any departments after the first, this method would be practical. Often this method is termed "pure FIFO," since each work-in-process inventory keeps its cost of production separate.

Because of the fact that it becomes increasingly complicated to keep track of the various lots of production under the pure FIFO method, very often the modified FIFO method is used by those firms planning to use the FIFO method of costing the initial work-in-process inventories. Also, where there are lost units in any department after the first, the modified procedure must be followed. In this procedure, the costs of the preceding department, though separately stated for the initial work-in-process inventory and the new production received into the department, must be averaged before computing the lost unit cost adjustment. From then on, when the total cost of goods transferred out of a department is computed, the final work-in-process inventory in that department must be computed at the latest unit costs for that department, then deducted from the cumulative cost total of that department. This is the cost of work transferred to the next department. Dividing this total by the number of units transferred results in the unit cost of the transfer. This figure is the average cost figure.

The procedure just described is similar to the one used when there are added materials in the department after the first, increasing the number of units in production. In this procedure we use the average cost of the transfer into a department before computing the adjusted unit cost resulting from the added materials. Thus, here again, when materials are added in a department after the first, increasing the volume of production, the computation of unit costs adjusted and corrected for added materials and lost units, if any, for the preceding departments is on the average basis not FIFO.

The FIFO principle requires that the costs of production for the current period must first be used to complete the initial work-in-process inventory and then be applied toward the new production. It should be stated that to obtain the cost of the production completed in any department, the final work-in-process inventory must be computed at the latest unit costs. The work-in-process inventory is then deducted from the total cumulative manufacturing costs to obtain the cost of the completed production. From this cost of completed production it is possible to compute the amount of the completed production transferred to the next department and unit cost thereof by dividing the number of units transferred.

When there are both added materials increasing the number of units in production and lost units, the mathematical computations become so involved as to practically eliminate the use of any modifications of the FIFO method. Under such circumstances the use of the average method of treating the initial work in process inventories is recommended as being most practical.

5. Estimated cost system

Estimated costs are a form of predetermined costs set up by a firm in advance of production or construction. The types of companies which usually use estimated costs are—

Shoe manufacturers
Furniture manufacturers
Clothing manufacturers

Construction companies
Bottling companies

Most of these companies do not use a full or complete estimated cost system. However, they do utilize a system that fulfills these three conditions:

1. The system does not cost too much
2. It provides management with some degree of comparative costs
3. Management can compare actual with predetermined costs

Installation and operation.   Before firms decide to establish a standard cost system, it would be advisable to implement an estimated cost system, since the latter produces averages, is not too expensive, and responds very well to good estimates.   In order to start such an estimated cost system, there are certain problems which small manufacturers must solve—

How to set prices and what prices to set
How to forecast orders
What would the costs be at various volume levels?
What is normal operating capacity?
What are the labor charges at normal operating capacity?
Can we make employees more productive?

After these basic problems have been answered, it must be determined what the estimated cost system will be used for.   The following are legitimate objectives of such a system:

Determination of income and financial position
Control and reduction of costs
Decision making and planning

The predetermined estimated costs calculated by a firm can be used in several ways—

Cost estimating.   The estimated cost figures are not used in the accounts, but are merely compared with the actual costs recorded in the accounts
Statistical costs.   Again these are also not incorporated in the accounts
Estimated and standard costs

These three methods of using estimated costs are not merely printed in textbooks and never followed in practical business situations.   It is customary in some companies to use the estimated and statistical data, and yet not enter the data on their books and records.   Periodically, however, the data actually recorded in the records are compared.   In addition, an estimated cost system gives management a chance to revise its plans and a cost of sales figure without the use of an expensive perpetual inventory system.

Before any cost system is installed, the management should face certain questions and plan accordingly—

The management staff should be efficient, adequate, and progressive enough to allow the firm to grow. Are more people needed? Fewer?

Look over the plant layout. Is the firm ahead of, even with, or behind its competitors in the area of technology? Does the firm have to expand?

What procedures should be followed for production and scheduling?

It is also necessary to determine the size of the system to be used commensurate with the firm's size, the amount of working capital readily available, and any restrictions that the type of industry may impose on the firm. It would be a mistake to burden the company with a system that costs too much or cannot expand with the company. It should be apparent that the system should be tailored to the needs of the company, in the present and in the future.

An estimated cost system should also provide certain additional information—

Determination of how much money is being made or lost by products, product groups, or services rendered

Determination of the relative performance in each department or plant and for the plant as a whole in each classification of expense

In addition to all the aids that could be used in the establishment of an estimated cost system, there is a checklist of items to be considered. These items cannot be overlooked—

Know the people who will be involved in the change; if this is not possible, at least inform them of the change

Know the plant layout

Know the finished products and all that is necessary to make them

Study the firm's flow and processing charts

Know what your assets are and the way they are depreciated

Find out where the cost centers are

Floor space should be distributed to cost centers so as to have some basis of allocation for overhead

Classify equipment by cost center

Adopt a chart of accounts which will be applicable to the cost centers and the systems and procedures devised

Utilize time and motion studies

The use of production formulas may be necessary

Types of management reports that should exist: budget forecasts, evaluation of free assets, and evaluation of research and development

Preferably the firm should have a good basic accounting system as a start. The estimator for the new cost system should possess, naturally, a knowledge of cost accounting and some engineering ability. He must also have a thorough knowledge of the plant layout, the production methods, and the machinery and tools available and required for the various jobs. Estimates of labor are more involved than material.   Labor operations should be known in detail; this also pertains to wages paid and time estimates on operations performed.   Time and motion studies or random tests are a prerequisite.

Material standards may be established on a variety of bases, on an average year or on an average of a number of years reflecting good, bad, and average conditions.   Once established, it is best not to change the basis unless the product or the processing method changes.   In preparing estimated standards for materials, the estimator should allow for losses such as shrinkage and spoilage in processing.   Material standards do affect the allocation of labor charges. The labor costs on the materials must be assembled on those materials requiring further processing or fabricating and on the assembly work of the completed product.

Any variances resulting from studying the allocations of the labor charges to the material used and in process can be explained, and the extent of these explanations will depend only on the amount of money the firm is willing to spend.   If the firm is not willing to spend a substantial amount of money to explain the variances, then only the variance in the work-in-process account is dealt with.   This variance is prorated to the various inventories or charged to the cost of goods sold.

Following is a suggested procedure for determination of a variance:

Materials should be put into the materials inventory at actual cost.   Materials, labor, and manufacturing overhead are debited to the work-in-process accounts at actual cost.   Units are put into finishing goods at estimated cost by crediting the work-in-process accounts and debiting the finished-goods account for this total.   The balance in the work-in-process accounts then represents the ending work-in-process inventory at the end of the period at estimated cost.   This is compared with the estimated ending work-in-process inventory for the month.   Adjustments are then made to an adjustment account.   If the actual ending work-in-process inventory is under the estimated figure, a debit would be made to this account and a credit would be applied to the adjustment account.   Thus, a credit to the latter account is favorable and a debit is unfavorable for the reverse situation.

The same situation applies to the manufacturing-expense accounts.

A diagram, Fig. 1 on page 332, will illustrate the previously mentioned procedures.

Every item incorporated into the product must be enumerated and carefully measured.   Provisions must be made for scrap material.

Methods of estimating materials' quantity—
Engineering specifications
Chemical formulas
Pilot runs
Records of past performance
Measurement of finished product

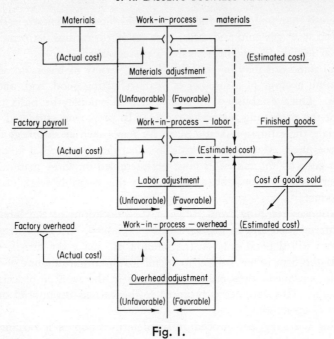

Fig. I.

Methods of estimating labor expended—

Time and motion studies
Pilot runs
Records of past performance

In this instance materials are not so troublesome as wages because materials do not vary with union contracts.

There are certain guidelines which must be followed—
Estimates should be carefully prepared for inclusion in the company's system and be based on normal capacity
Work-in-process for materials, labor, and overhead applied are the accounts used
Actual costs are debits in the work-in-process accounts; estimated costs are credits in the same accounts
When goods are sold, the charge is to cost of goods sold and the credit is to finished goods based on estimated costs
The quantity of work still in process is determined through a physical count or analysis of materials consumed and production completed

An estimated cost-accounting system for more than one department is more complex but basically the same. The system involves—

Determine the value of the work-in-process inventory

Determine the quantity balances in the various work-in-process accounts

Use the amount transferred to the next department as the adjustment account balance for the first department

Set up an adjustment account for the first department

Prorate the variances on an equivalent production basis to the cost of sales, finished goods, and the work-in-process inventories

There are various way to dispose of the variances—

Allocate the variances to the various inventories and cost of goods sold and finished goods.   The variances result from the estimated costs of production for the period—
    Based upon revision of the estimated cost records
    Based upon units produced and equivalent units in process

Charge off the variance to the cost of goods sold and profit and loss.   This is considered the better of the two, because it saves the cost of revising the inventory records

With the proration of the adjustment account completed, the final work in process consists of (1) the original work-in-process value, and (2) the amount allocated by the adjustment.   The adjustment indicates the extent to which the original estimates differ from the actual costs.   For the next fiscal period or for a similar job, it will be necessary to decide on new estimates according to the adjustments arrived at in the previous period.

Expansion may cause unit costs to decline, remain the same, or rise.   For example, a new office added to a plant will cause the unit cost of materials produced to increase while production remains the same.   An analyst should ferret out incremental and decremental costs when contemplating change.

In order to operate an estimated cost system, it is necessary to—

Prepare cost cards for each product showing its estimated unit cost

Charge work in process with actual costs incurred.   In the case of overhead, charge the work-in-process account with applied overhead for the period

Credit the work-in-process account with the cost of the product made and transferred by multiplying the number of units by estimated cost as shown on the estimated unit cost card

Dispose of the variances

Precomputed costs overcome the limitation of historical costs and they permit economies in bookkeeping.

But the estimated cost system has its limitations.   It indicates that actual costs were higher or lower than expected, but does not disclose where the variations are.   To obtain more information and more details, more work must be performed, and this defeats the purpose of the system.

Advantages of an estimated cost system.

It is economical in use because of the elimination of clerical detail

There is easy availability of needed cost information
Estimates can be used for purposes other than cost accounting
It can act as a basis for the establishment of a standard cost system

Disadvantages of an estimated cost system.
Estimates are often not too reliable
Valuation of inventories is rather unstable
Useful information is often sacrificed
Specific application is limited

In order to make such a system effective, formulas can be used correlating the relationships between the costs and the characteristics of the product. Formula cost estimation requires formula recording and weighing of the most important relationships between cost and product characteristics and also requires that these be stated numerically. These formulas must be kept up-to-date. Electronic or mechanical solution of formulas greatly increases the experienced estimator's productivity.

To set up these formulas, a step-by-step analysis of all the components of a product is needed in order to find useful relationships. The first step would be to list all the phases in the manufacturing of the product. For example, how many turns does a coil of wire have and how much wire is there to a turn, by weight, depth, width, and height? Then it is beneficial to plot the data and the formula can be developed from such data. This will result in more effective estimates.

Perhaps an estimated cost accounting system would never have been devised if it could not have been sold to some private firm. Why are cost accounting systems not sold? The foreman of a plant may reject the system for several reasons—

Reports and figures puzzle him
Most of these reports seemed unnecessary to him; also in most cases these
    reports did not assist him in doing the job better
He was not allowed to participate in the planning

These deficiencies can be corrected by—

Making the foreman a part of the team
Establishing a method of measurement of his performance with his assistance
Encouraging his criticism
Using his terminology
Giving him results promptly
Giving him responsibility over the management of his own costs
Reducing his clerical work to a minimum

6. Standard cost system

A standard cost system is a system wherein predetermined standards are used in computing the standard cost of production, the standard costs being charged to the work-in-process account and compared with the actual costs previously recorded in other cost accounts, which results in variances that are used to measure the efficiency of production. The expenses per hour of running each production center are predetermined and are applied against all units produced in the center. The elements that enter into the costs of each section of the factory are studied, and rates are set representing all expenses that are likely to be incurred when the factory is operating at normal capacity.

Thus under such a system the cost assigned to each product does not vary, regardless of whether the factory is working at partial capacity or more than capacity. The rate is set as already stated for the factory to run at normal capacity. With this type of system it is easy to realize the cost of producing an article beforehand, so that a contract is not underbid or overbid. Such a system is developed with painstaking care after careful study and observation of past and present production activities.

Because of the inefficient nature of actual costs and the need for a system in which a definite, reliable unit cost of operation can be applied to production at all times, standard costs have been developed. In a system of standard costs, manufacturing expenses are broken down, as they are in actual cost systems, into material costs and operating costs. Standards are set for each of these and are rigidly adhered to, and all units produced are charged with the standard rates no matter what conditions may have developed since the standards were set.

The chief foundations on which standard costs are set are—

The cost center. A section of the plant in which a particular kind of work is done, so that every unit entering receives the same type of treatment as every other unit

Normal capacity. The basis for standard cost is a volume of production that is a fair average output based upon sales expectancy for a typical year and adjusted to the mechanical capacity of the plant

Material cost standards. The most obvious factor to be used in arriving at the cost of producing a unit of output is the material cost, the cost of the raw material of which the finished article is made. The effect of materials on cost of production is executed in two ways: (1) through prices; and (2) through quantity. In a system of standard costs, there is only one material price—a price that is predetermined and that is used throughout a period covering at least 6 months of production. In other words, fluctuations in market price are not reflected in the unit costs of material used. The material price that seems to be nearest to the normal price is the one selected, and every unit produced is charged with this standard predetermined cost.

In regard to the influence of the quantity element, it is found that in a system of standard costs, the quantity of materials to be charged in producing each unit is determined before a single unit is manufactured. As in the case of material prices, it is possible to come to a conclusion about what is the average amount of material needed to produce an article, and to set that average amount as a standard which will be used. In fact, this standard is probably easier set than any of the others.

Since in a standard cost system both the amount of material and the cost of material that will enter each unit is predetermined, it is possible to know definitely the material cost of each article that is to be produced.

A standard cost system provides for management a measurement of the operating efficiency of the plant through the accumulation of cost variances. The variances are either unfavorable or favorable; that is, the actual costs are either higher or lower than the standard costs. Unfavorable variances are signals of trouble in the cost of production; favorable variances indicate operating efficiency. Unfavorable variances appear as debits in the accounts and favorable as credits. The unfavorable variances call attention to off-standard conditions or losses which should be speedily remedied, since the longer the losses are allowed to continue the smaller will be the profit. Of course, all this assumes that the standards are accurate in the first place.

Direct-labor cost standards. Just as it is necessary in setting standards for materials to fix upon a unit cost that may be used in all cases, regardless of fluctuations both in prices and in the amount of material used, it is necessary, in setting direct-labor standards, likewise to determine a unit labor cost which will remain fixed in spite of different rates of pay and different periods of time required to do the task. Scientific methods and job studies must be used in order to determine the amount of time needed to perform a single operation of any particular type. This clearly shows why a production department must be divided into cost centers, in each of which only one kind of work is done. As long as only one kind of work is done in each cost center, it is possible to measure the amount of time required by each unit for these operations. Job studies must be made to discover how much direct labor is required on a product from the time it enters a cost center until it leaves.

Overhead cost standards. The material cost can be directly determined because the amount of material is measurable. The labor cost can be directly determined because the amount of time needed to finish an article can likewise be measured. But overhead costs require different treatment. They must be calculated in total and then spread over production in the form of an overhead rate per standard labor hour or machine hour or percentage of labor cost.

In the treatment of overhead expenses, the first thing to be remembered is that direct overhead and general overhead must be sharply differentiated. Because of this, two overhead rates must be determined, one for each of the two types of overhead. The reasons for this distinction are not hard to understand. The direct overhead expenses are those which are incurred directly and entirely in the cost center to which they pertain. In order to hold the supervision of that center responsible for the costs incurred, it is essential that this direct expense be separated from the prorated or general expense items, for which the supervision is not responsible. The schedule of direct overhead expenses must, therefore, be drawn up for each individual department or cost center because the nature of the costs in each will vary. The schedule of general overhead expense, however, is drawn up only for the factory at large, since it consists of those expenses which cannot be definitely allocated to one center. After the general schedule is compiled, the total expenses are apportioned among the cost centers in whatever manner is thought to reflect best the way in which the expenses arose.

Two methods to control overhead expenses are (1) budgets adjusted to sales volumes, and (2) budgets adjusted to the standard production hour volume. In either case, the budgets are based on the experience of the company in the past as to the level that should be considered normal capacity. Some of the preliminaries to installment of a standard cost system are—

The plant must be correctly organized and the code of accounts fitted to the organization plan

Supervising responsibility must be definitely placed

Layout of department and operating or cost centers must be determined

Overhead budgets must be built not only for normal capacity, but also for other capacities above and below normal (flexible budgets)

Standard cost rates, comprising all expense for direct labor and for direct and general overhead as well as standard cost rates for materials, must be compiled

A simple method of calculating the cost of units must be developed

Provision must be made to set forth the variances in the off-standard conditions

Some of the outstanding advantages of a standard cost system are as follows: The details that accompany the operation of the older types of actual cost systems are largely dispensed with; the costs are predetermined before production takes place rather than having to wait until after production is completed to obtain the actual costs; the analyses of the cost variances are invaluable in disclosing to the management the details of operating efficiency or inefficiency.

In the historical cost system, production costs are not known until after production is completed, and hence many production operations which are wasteful, inefficient, and unprofitable cannot be disclosed until after the jobs are completed, or until the production cost report is prepared. Historical costs are of real value for statistical purposes only. In an actual process cost system where a production cost report is not available until after the end of the month, 5 to 10 days may elapse before some unfavorable operating condition is discovered.   Under such circumstances the actual cost report is obviously of small value for control purposes.

The use of cost variances in a standard cost system enables the cost accountant to present to the management detailed analyses of off-standard conditions. Production cost reports can be prepared daily for any cost center if off-standard conditions are found to be present.   This possibility of being informed of the unfavorable variance at the time of its occurrence enables the management to take immediate steps to correct the conditions.

How can the standard cost plan be attuned so perfectly that it will yield this information speedily and effectively?   There are several methods: The stores requisition calling for more direct materials than the standard quantity originally specified is an index to excessive material costs; comparison of the actual labor costs shown on the time tickets for various operations bares an unfavorable labor variance; the use of overhead expense budgets for each cost center discloses in which cost center these expenses are not being controlled.   Where a sizable unfavorable overhead variance appears, the monthly overhead budget is then broken down to a weekly, semiweekly, or daily basis for the purpose of closer supervision and control.   The variances are then seen to be the gauges in production cost control.

The original records in a standard cost system are the same as in any other cost system; only their form varies in accordance with the manner of handling the details for the stores inventory, the labor, and the overhead expenses.

The first step in setting up standard costs in a company is to establish a standard cost for every type of material that is purchased.   This is done by adjusting the current market price for any irregularities that might be expected to continue for the following year.   Having established standard costs for all materials, the accountants next calculate standard rates for direct labor and manufacturing overhead.   This is done on a departmental basis and the rates are set up to be applied according to the number of standard direct-labor hours incurred in the production of each product.

From each department data are obtained for the past few years on the actual direct-labor payroll and the number of direct-labor hours worked.   On the basis of these data and from estimates of future conditions and labor union contracts, the accountants select a figure of hours worked under normal conditions of activity in each department.   By dividing this payroll figure by the normal number of hours, a standard direct-labor hour for each department is obtained.

The same calculations are made to determine standard manufacturing overhead rates for each department.   The procedure may become complicated by the necessity of allocating all service-department costs to the producing departments.

Various methods are used to allocate the service-department costs to the producing departments.   For example, the total cost of the boiler room might be allocated to the producing departments according to the number of square feet of floor space taken up by each. The maintenance-department expense is allocated on the basis of the number of hours the maintenance men normally work for each producing department. This continues until all the cost of the service departments has been allocated proportionately to the producing departments. The final result is that their cost is reflected in the final overall cost of production even though they are not directly part of the actual cost of production.

The budgeted or estimated cost for the forthcoming period is another concept of standard costs. The budget figures serve as good standards with which to compare the subsequent actual performance. The real purpose for cost standards is—

To assist in planning the input quantities necessary to create a given set of outputs

To provide a basis for comparing actual input quantities consumed in producing a given output

Basic elements in the development of standard costs are—

The manufacturing operation
The bill of materials

Major elements in any standard costs are—

Physical input required to produce a given physical output
Unit prices of input factors

The fixed or bogey standard is seldom if ever changed. It serves largely as a base from which to measure changes over a long period of time. Quantity standards for material yield and labor performance are changed less frequently than price and wage-rate standards.

The objectives underlying comparisons of actual with standard costs are—

To indicate whether costs are being kept under control
To locate any apparent deficiency in cost-control efforts
To facilitate the identification of the probable causes of deviations from standard
To assign responsibility for deviations that may have occurred

Some common features of standard systems are—

The cost accumulation unit is the department or cost center which is the direct responsibility of a single supervisor
Each such cost center is charged with the actual costs of production and credited with the standard cost of production
The difference between actual and standard cost is known as a "variance" and represents the aggregate departure of the cost center's performance from standard

Deviations from standard cost can arise from differences between actual and standard input quantities (quantity variance) or from differences between actual and standard input prices (price variance) or both.

Standard costing generates quantity variations by charging a cost center for the actual quantity of input to be used and crediting it for the standard input equivalent to the cost center's actual output. The difference represents the quantity variance, expressed in physical input units. When these are multiplied by standard input prices, the result is the dollar quantity variation that appears in the accounting records.

Some types of standard costing are—

Single plan. All work-in-process and finished-goods inventory accounts are carried continually at standard quantities and standard prices. This means that debits to work in process are for standard quantities of labor and material, multiplied by standard prices for these items

Partial plan. The work-in-process accounts are charged with actual costs of the input of labor and materials and credited with the standard cost of finished output. The in-process balances under a partial plan system, therefore, consist of price variances, quantity variances, and actual quantity of goods remaining in process, priced at the standard cost of operations performed to date

Modified partial plan. This differs from the partial plan only in that the debits to work in process represent the actual quantities of labor and material input priced at standard prices instead of actual prices

Dual plan. This consists of a two-way recording of inventory charges and credits, one recording for actual costs and actual quantities of both input and output and one for standard cost of input and output. Only the actual cost accounts are a part of the formal accounting records; the parallel standard cost accounts are memorandum accounts used for the purpose of establishing variances

Flexible budgets. Flexible budgets reflect the amount of cost that is reasonably necessary to achieve each of several specified volumes of activity. More specifically, flexible budgets allowances express standards of what costs should be at each level of volume, on the assumption that production is stabilized at this production.

Various types of standards. Some types of standards are—

Ideal. Established without reference to changes in conditions and represent the level of performance which would be achieved under the best possible combination of factors (Utopia)

Normal. Cost predicated upon normal operating conditions for a company over the period of a complete business cycle

Current or expected actual. Based on current business conditions, and representing the achievement level at which management aims for the ensuing accounting period

Basic or "bogey" standards. Representing a special class of standard of a statistical nature, prepared for some base year, and used in much the same way as the statistician uses commodity price indices. These standards serve merely as a yardstick with which to compare actual performance and are not revised unless the products or the manufacturing operations or processes are changed

7. Direct costing

Direct costing is a method of costing where only those costs that vary directly with products or sales volumes are charged to the cost of the product. Those costs would be direct labor, direct material, and factory overhead expenses, such as supplies, some indirect labor, and power. The cost of the product would not include fixed or nonvariable expenses such as depreciation, factory insurance, taxes, and supervisory salaries. Thus, direct costing is distinguished from absorption costing, the common cost-accounting method in which the product is charged with all manufacturing cost, both fixed and variable.

In direct costing the product is charged only with those costs that are directly affected by changes in volume, while under the absorption costing method, period costs or those that are a function of time and are not affected by volume changes are also charged to the cost of the product.

Under the absorption costing method, inventories will normally be reported at a higher figure than under the direct costing method. This is due to the fact that fixed costs, under the absorption method, are deferred by being included in the cost of the goods inventory. This element of fixed cost will not be reported as a deduction from revenue until the goods are sold and then becomes an expense in the cost of goods sold section of the income statement. Under the direct cost method, no fixed costs are deferred; they are charged against revenue in the period in which they are incurred.

Neither the Internal Revenue Service nor the Securities and Exchange Commission accepts direct costing methods in determining inventory values as reported on tax returns or annual reports. It is reasonable to assume that they will continue to maintain this position at least as long as the AICPA does. Nevertheless, many accountants feel that direct costing is a most useful tool in assisting management in controlling costs and planning operations.

8. Joint product and by-product costing

Many interesting and perplexing cost-accounting problems arise in situations in which two or more products are made from a single raw material. The same or similar problems also arise when two or more products from different materials are made jointly with the same labor and production facilities and are administered and sold by the same administrative and sales departments.

One approach to the problem is to adopt the viewpoint that no allocation of joint costs to joint products should be attempted. This viewpoint is based in part on the argument that all allocations are arbitrary and therefore presumably inaccurate or at least not worth the cost of calculation. More important grounds are that such allocations do not aid the decision-making process or the efficient conduct of a business and may in fact be misleading in this connection. This approach takes the viewpoint that a business should be regarded as a whole and should not be separated into parts. Material, labor, and other joint costs should be compared to the total revenue from joint products in determining the net profit.

This first approach to the problem, however, is usable only in a limited number of cases. For example, just the difference between the timing of the processes and the timing of financial reports make some form of cost allocation necessary. Raw materials from which joint products are produced are subjected to processes and are separated into various parts which take varying amounts of time for further processing and disposal. By the close of an accounting period some of the products from the various parts will have been completed and sold, some will have been completed and not yet sold, and some will still be in process. It is necessary, therefore, to split the raw material cost on some reasonable basis in order to compute the cost of goods sold for the period, and to place inventory values on material in process and finished goods still on hand.

There are many different bases which can be used to allocate these costs. The first and a very simple method of allocation is based on area or weight. Under this method the cost of a certain amount or quantity of raw material and the cost of processing this material is distributed to the various products manufactured from the material at an equal amount per unit. This method is satisfactory in cases where two or more products are made from the same type of raw material and when the material used in these products is exactly the same in each individual case and differs only in size or weight.

The second basis of allocation then is one which takes market value into consideration as well as area or weight. The clearest cases for which this approach is appropriate are those in which the market values are available for the various segments of raw material at the point of separation and prior to further processing. In meat-packing, for example, hides, hoofs, and other parts of the cattle are bought and sold in their green state in sufficient quantities to provide the packer with acceptable market values as a basis for allocating live cattle costs, whether he wishes to sell these parts as they are or subject them to further processing. More difficult problems are faced in situations in which no market values exist for some of or all the various parts at the point of separation, since they are not commonly sold in this condition. One approach here is to allocate costs on an area or weight basis even though it is believed that the different parts would probably show some differences in value if their market values could be established.   Another approach would be to use a form of by-product costing under which those parts having known market values would be assigned these values, the total of which would be subtracted from the cost of the given raw material, and the balance of the cost would be charged to the remaining parts on an area or weight basis.   A third method is to start with the market values of the end products produced from each of the parts and subtract estimated selling, administrative, and conversion costs, to arrive at an approximation of their market values at the point of separation. The market values would then be used to establish the proportions in which raw material cost would be allocated to the various parts.

This third method should be approached with caution, however, since quite apart from all the clerical work involved, differences in the market value of end products alone are not enough to justify its use.   The key to the problem lies in the question whether or not it is really believed that if these parts were to be bought and sold commonly in their condition at the point of separation, they would in fact be exchanged at different unit values and if so, whether or not the relative values at which they would be exchanged would correspond with the relative values arrived at by subtracting estimated selling, administrative, and conversion costs from the market value of the end products to which they are converted.

There are also different methods of treating main product and by-product costing.   Under one theory of main-product–by-product costing, all profits or losses for the company are recorded only on its main products.   Moreover, the by-products are charged nothing for the raw materials furnished to them.   The cost of raw material and all processing costs up to the point where materials are separated are charged to the main products; by-products are charged only for their own costs from this point on, and all revenues above these costs from the sale of by-products are treated as reductions in the cost of the main products.   Another way to view this accounting treatment is that by-products are charged indirectly for material at an amount which shows them as breaking even, and the profit and loss on all operations appears as the profit or loss on the main product.

A second approach to main-product–by-product costing is to charge the by-product divisions for the material parts furnished to them at the market values of these parts.   Corresponding credits for these charges are used to reduce the raw material cost and operating cost up to the point of separation, and the net of these costs is allocated to the main products on an area or weight basis or on a market value basis, whichever seems appropriate in the given case. In this way the by-product divisions are held accountable for showing a profit on their operations, and those handling the main products are held accountable for their skill in purchasing raw materials and processing them up to the point of separation as well as for showing a profit on the further processing and sale of their products.

A third approach is to treat the by-products simply as joint products and to allocate raw material costs to them, as to the other joint products, in proportion to area or weight, or in proportion to their relative market values at the point of separation.

9. PERT and CPM

Known collectively as critical path analysis, PERT and CPM have been around for about nine years. CPM, or critical path method, developed out of a joint attempt by the DuPont Company and Univac Division of Sperry Rand in 1957 to find a dependable way to schedule the fantastically complicated business of building a chemical plant.

CPM served the purpose very well, and has since been used in millions of dollars of chemical plant construction, not only by DuPont, but by Monsanto, Olin Mathieson, and others.

PERT, or program evaluation review technique, is essentially a variation of CPM. It was formally announced in 1959 by the United States Navy as a scheduling technique used in the Polaris weapons program. It was jointly devised by the Navy Special Projects Office, the consulting firm of Booz, Allen and Hamilton, and Lockheed's Missile and Space Division.

PERT is a system of network analysis that makes it possible to predict with accuracy the outcome of inherently uncertain activities, such as the development of an entirely new weapons system. It has been given much of the credit for the completion of the first Polaris missile 2 years ahead of schedule.

During the 1960s CPM and PERT really arrived. More than 30 variations of the techniques have found their way into commercial applications in research engineering and manufacturing.

PERT and CPM have been defined as the science of using networks, formulas, statistics, and data processing in planning, scheduling, and controlling work. PERT and CPM's greatest asset is that it makes a complex job easier to understand and handle.

At the heart of PERT and CPM is the network, which shows graphically all the tasks that must be performed to complete a project from start to finish. The network consists of the activities and events that make up the project and shows how one is related to the other.

An activity is a specific task or effort applied over a period of time and is bounded by two events. An event, then, marks the end of one activity and the beginning of another. In the PERT diagram, activities are represented by arrows, events by circles. The completion or end of the job is called the "objective event."

The network shows the order in which activities must be performed. A new activity cannot begin unless the scheduled preceding event has taken place. Some activities are dependent on one another, others are not. The manufac-

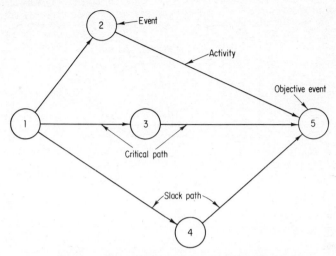

Fig. 2.   Components of a typical network.

ture of one machine component and the subcontracting of another are not, for example, dependent on one another; they can therefore take place concurrently. Assembly of the machine, however, depends on completion of both components, and is therefore dependent on both foregoing activities.

Because of these varied relationships, the network ends up with several parallel paths, some of which may be interlinked at critical event points. One of these paths will take longer to complete than any of the others. It is therefore called the critical path. It cannot be defined, however, until the time each activity will take has been determined.

It is in this time-estimating procedure that PERT and CPM differ most markedly. PERT uses a statistical method to approximate the time an activity will take. By a simple mathematical formula, the expected time is calculated from three estimates times; an optimistic or shortest possible time, a pessimistic or the longest time that assumes everything will go wrong, and a most likely time that is based on normal progress. Because CPM was devised to deal with more precise activities, it uses only one time estimate, normal time.

Once the time estimates have been made, either by PERT or CPM method, you can calculate the total time it will take to complete each path of the network and determine the longest, or critical path. The critical path indicates how long it will take to complete the project. By definition, the other paths will take less time to complete, and so the activities along them will contain slack or free time. These activities are therefore noncritical and will not have to be performed in the estimated time.

By monitoring each activity as it takes place, a manager is able to see readily whether it is moving on schedule or not. When there are delays on the critical

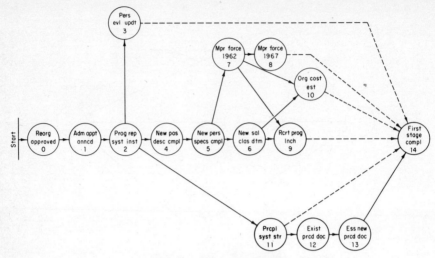

Fig. 3.   The critical path.

path, he can draw manpower or other resources from the noncritical activities which have time to spare. The fact that PERT and CPM provide for consistent monitoring is a distinct advantage over other systems. If a program is in trouble, PERT and CPM pinpoint the activities at fault. A manager then needs to concentrate only on the critical activities that are behind schedule.

When used in the planning stages, PERT and CPM can predict when a project will be completed. But they can go further. If the predicted time is not satisfactory, the network can be redrawn to give the desired result. But a program cannot be speeded up by simply reducing the time estimates.

There are only three ways to shorten a schedule—

1. Eliminate part of the work. In an electronics system, for instance, it may be better to eliminate the breadboard assembly and move directly to a pilot model.
2. Run concurrently activities normally scheduled to run consecutively. Instead of waiting for test results on a new product, it may be worth taking the risk of buying raw materials while testing is still going on, and thus cut purchasing lead time.
3. Apply additional resources, manpower, facilities, etc.

The big advantage of PERT and CPM is that they help control costs. You can estimate the cost of each activity on the network, then compare this figure with actual costs as work progresses. But whether or not cost figures are made an integral part of PERT or CPM, the network will show precisely where extra money must be put to achieve the desired schedule. It will show where to borrow resources needed for a critical area. It can predict performance and provide continuous control over an activity.

A new language has emerged with **PERT**:

Activity. A time-consuming element in any project, usually represented on a network by an arrow

Activity time. Time for completion of an activity. In PERT there are three activity times for each event—

1. Optimistic time. Assuming unusually favorable conditions, the shortest time required to perform a given task. It is given the symbol a

2. Most likely time. The most realistic estimate for the completion of a given project. It is given the symbol m

3. Pessimistic time. Assuming the most unfavorable conditions for the completion of a project, the longest time that the activity should take. It is given the symbol b

Network. A diagram of events, activities, and time estimates, which constitutes a pictorial representation of a project

Event. A specified part of a project, which is represented on the PERT diagram or network by a circle

Critical path. The sequence of interrelated events between the beginning of a project and its completion date that will require the longest time to complete

Expected completion time for an event. A weighted mean of its three estimated activity times: optimistic, most likely, and pessimistic

$$t_e = \frac{a + 4m + b}{6}$$

Preceding event. An event that must be completed before the following activity can begin

Succeeding event. An event that cannot be started until the preceding event is completed

Latest allowable time. The time equal to the latest allowable time of the succeeding event, less the expected event time of the activity joining these two events. It is given the symbol T_L

Earliest expected time. The time equal to the sum of the expected times of the preceding events, beginning with the start event. It is given the symbol T_E

Slack. The difference between the latest and expected completion times for an event. It is positive when the expected date is less than the latest completion date, and it is negative when the expected date is greater than the latest date

Case study. PERT network for the installation of a new organizational structure for a company had to be installed. Management wanted to know how long it it would take for them to install their new organization. Since a reorganization can cause a great many personnel problems if it is not installed properly, it was decided to use PERT to insure a smooth installation of reorganization.

The first step was to appoint an analyst to (1) coordinate the development of the PERT network; (2) keep all concerned fully informed; and (3) prepare and issue revised networks and plans as often as necessary.

Listing of events

0. Reorganization approved
1. Administrator's appointment announced
2. Progress reporting system installed
3. Personnel evaluations updated
4. New position descriptions completed
5. New personnel specifications completed
6. New salary classifications determined
7. Manpower forecasts completed to 1962
8. Manpower forecasts completed to 1967
9. Recruitment program launched
10. Organization costs estimated
11. Procedural system started
12. Existing procedures documented
13. Essential new procedures documented
14. First stage completed

Calculation Sheet

Event	Pre-ceding event	Optimistic time a	Most likely time m	Pessi-mistic time b	Expected time te	Earliest expected time T_E	Latest allow-able time T_L	Slack T_L-T_E
1	0	0.1	1.0	2.0	1.0	1.0	1.0	0*
2	1	1.0	3.0	4.0	2.8	3.8	3.8	0*
3	2	4.0	6.0	12.0	6.7	10.5	35.8	25.3
4	2	0.1	2.0	4.0	2.0	5.8	28.7	22.9
5	4	1.0	1.5	3.0	1.7	7.5	30.4	22.9
6	5	1.0	4.0	8.0	4.2	11.7	34.6	22.9
7	5	1.0	3.0	4.0	2.8	10.3	34.8	24.5
8	7	1.0	2.0	4.0	2.2	12.5	35.8	23.3
9	6	0.1	1.0	4.0	1.3	13.0	35.8	22.8
9	7	0.1	2.0	3.0	1.9	12.2	35.8	23.7
10	6	0.1	1.0	3.0	1.2	12.9	35.8	22.9
10	7	0.1	1.0	2.0	1.0	11.3	35.8	24.5
11	2	0.1	1.0	2.0	1.0	4.8	4.8	0*
12	11	6.0	13.0	30.0	14.7	19.5	19.5	0*
13	12	10.0	12.0	40.0	16.3	35.8	35.8	0*
14	9	0	0	0	0	12.2	35.8	23.6
14	10	0	0	0	0	12.9	35.8	22.9
14	11	0	0	0	0	4.8	35.8	31.0
14	13	0	0	0	0	35.8	35.8	0*
14	3	0	0	0	0	10.5	35.8	25.3
14	8	0	0	0	0	12.5	35.8	23.3

Notes: Time is given in days.
       Events on critical path are starred (*) in Slack column.

Advantages of PERT.

A concept inherent in the new technique, which was not a part of earlier planning and control systems, is the definition of the "critical path," and the consequent degree of control that can be concentrated on the activities associated with it

A more carefully defined understanding of a given project than would ordinarily be available is provided by PERT, because of the amount of detail necessary to define the PERT network in the planning stage

Ability to reschedule manpower and resources in the most efficient way is provided

Early warning of potential trouble spots in meeting scheduled completion dates and costs is given

Because of the computerization of networks, management has the ability to simulate different networks and on the basis of these simulations to select the network of optimum effectiveness

Limitations of PERT.

Reliance on subjective estimates. PERT relies upon the same subjective judgments necessary in earlier scheduling techniques. Consequently, the computer can check only the consistency of the network; it cannot indicate to management when improper and inaccurate judgments are part of the input to the network

A tendency to incur high operating costs because of—

The amount of planning necessary to implement the program

The necessity of training, or possibility of hiring a specialist to direct the establishment of the scheduling system

The computerization of the system

The necessity for frequent updating

But the application of PERT and CPM is far-reaching. Computer manufacturers offer package programs for the solution of PERT networks. PERT cost is now mandatory for all government contractors doing research and development work for the Defense Department and NASA. Defense contractors are demanding that subcontractors submit PERT networks with their bids. Several major construction contractors are using PERT or CPM on all major projects. PERT has recently found its way into marketing and advertising.

PERT and CPM do not require huge programs to be effective. The Polaris weapons program involved 23 separate networks and over 3,000 events. A computer was needed. But the Ortho Pharmaceutical Corporation uses a PERT system of 100 events in product development work, and does all the calculations manually.

Conclusion

Modern business is highly competitive and complex. Management must always endeavor to find savings in every possible way and to eliminate unneces-

sary costs and inefficient operation.   A complete knowledge of costs is necessary.
An effective cost-accounting system will provide the necessary information to
assist management in—

Planning and controlling current operation
Making decisions and formulating long-range plans
Making decisions and formulating short-range plans
Making the necessary plans to achieve the above goals
Evaluating the results and discovering where current operations are deviat-
    ing from the plans

Cost reports—contents of reports.   The most important factor in all cost
reporting is the need for promptness in reporting.   If management is to have
effective control of costs, it must be able to act swiftly when costs get out of
line.   This means that cost-accounting procedures must be set up in such a
way that information can be recorded and reported swiftly.   In most cases,
complete accuracy must be sacrificed for promptness in reporting.   Most managers would prefer to have 90 to 95 percent accurate information today rather
than 100 percent accurate information in 5 or 10 days.

The reports should be prepared in such a way that management can quickly
compare the current operating results with the planned budget or program for
the current period and the year to date, with the results of similar operations
for the immediately preceding period, and with similar operations during the
same period last year.   The reports should pinpoint trouble spots and unusual
trends.   All data must be presented in terms that are clearly and easily understood by all concerned.   The reports should be broken down by areas of responsibility, so that the operations of departments or individuals involved will
be clearly reflected.

One of the most frequently used cost reports is the detailed analysis of production.   This report quite frequently is prepared daily so that management
can quickly spot the unusual trends or danger signals.

The following items are normally found in this report:

Quantity of direct material used
Direct-labor hours and cost
Indirect-labor hours and cost
Indirect material and supplies used
Overhead applied to production
Actual overhead incurred
Idle time report
Overtime premium payments
Spoiled or defective work
Maintenance hours and cost
Scrap

Other reports useful to management are—

Interim income statement
Inventory status report
Reports of orders received and shipped
Report of material price variances
Sales forecast

Beyond the above cost reports and analyses which form an integral part of the cost-accounting system, many special cost reports and analyses are prepared as the need arises. A few of the many special cost studies are listed below:

Ranking of capital acquisition proposals—
    When investment is identical
    When investment is not identical
Standard after-tax rate of returns on investments
Reports on leasing versus ownership
Plant location
Plant construction
Plant layout
Distribution channels
Territorial coverage
Economic unit of production
Manufacture or purchase of parts
Product design or redesign
Waste control
Employees efficiency reports

The preceding discussion of cost accounting for cost control has been directed toward industrial situations. However, today businesses "both large and small" require coordinated management effort in which the services of each individual specialist and technician and each functional operating division are integrated with the aims of the business as a whole. Working closely with all other members of the team, the cost accountant must determine and analyze the facts which will assist in timely, current operating control and form the basis for proper planning and sound judgments for all types of business enterprises.

Section 11

HOW TO PREPARE AND UTILIZE BUDGETS AS A MANAGERIAL DECISION–MAKING TOOL

BY

JOHN H. McMICHAEL
AND
CARL A. POLSKY

HOW TO PREPARE AND UTILIZE BUDGETS
AS A MANAGERIAL DECISION–MAKING TOOL

1. Introduction and objectives of budgetary control

Budgeting is planning. Whether it be husband and wife planning the purchase of a home, the small entrepreneur planning to open a new business, a large business planning to expand or change product lines, or the President of the United States planning future action, budgets are a necessary part of the thinking process. These budgets may be as formalized as the hundreds of pages in the presidential budget submitted to Congress, or may be simply the thinking process of the individuals concerned.

This section will deal mainly with the formalizing of the budgetary process which will serve as a future reference for executive action. The budget is the forecast or anticipation of future revenue and of related costs and expenses needed to produce such revenue. In dealing with the coordination process necessary to prepare a budget, one must consider a number of assumptions, such as the nature of costs, cost-volume-profit relationships, and the competitive market in general.

A review of the formalized budget at periodic intervals provides management with an opportunity to appraise the results of present activity and to make amendments to the budget for future activity. This review of past relationships, current budgets, and current activities will provide a major aspect of the budgetary process, that is, control. Basically then, the budgetary process consists of planning, coordination, and control. All budgets, including a family's informal budgets and the President's annual budget message to the Congress, provide for these three factors: planning, coordination, and control.

The budgetary needs of management involve proper planning in the projection of sales, which will eventually be an aid for the projection of purchases of material, labor needs, and overhead. The overhead will cover the everyday needs of operation, plus the costs of capital assets.

Preparation of the budget on a formal basis forces the entrepreneur to forecast cash flows, including cash in and out of the business as a result of collection of revenues and receivables and the disbursement of funds for all related costs, expenses, and payables. This aids management in the determination of future cash needs.

An examination of the planned revenues and the projected related costs and expenses and related changes in assets and liabilities through the receipt of cash or receivables, inventory changes, purchase, sale, or retirement of plant or equipment, and changes in other assets, as well as the payment or incurring of other liabilities, will enable management to obtain a profit plan for the budget period. This budget plan will consist of a proposed income statement and a projected balance sheet at the end of the budget period.

On the basis of these proposed statements management will be able to calculate a rate of return on invested capital. This rate of return on the invested capital with the related risks involved will be used by management to determine whether or not the projected activities should be continued, revised, or dropped entirely. Assuming there are alternative revenue-producing activities or related cost applications, new budgets will be prepared to determine whether the rate of return can be sufficiently improved to provide an acceptable rate of return. Management can then make a decision to proceed with alternative action.

The need for proper planning, which to a large extent will aid management in making alternative decisions, has been indicated. However, once the decision to proceed is made, the formalized budget is an important aid to management in coordinating the entire management operational activity. The cooperation of all division supervisors in the preparation and use of all the budgets outlined above will enable management to coordinate activities toward the common profit-making goal.

Adherence to the budget will avoid bottlenecks in sales and production that would thwart achievement of the forecast profit. Absence of a formalized budget could result in each division supervisor acting in his own capacity to achieve what he believes to be the goals of overall management. Thinking to benefit the company, he would act without due and proper consideration of the effect of his actions upon the related phases of operation. For example, the purchasing expediter might take advantage of an excellent buy, which he thinks he would not be able to get at any other time. Later he might find out that these goods will not be used by other divisions. If the personnel department hired or fired individual employees without regard to the future personnel needs of the various departments as disclosed by the budget, the consequent shortage or oversupply of labor could result in a bottleneck of production.

The control achieved over operations through the preparation of the operational budgets is a further aid to management. The various budgets will project the sales and related costs and immediately establish a control measuring stick over these activities. The periodic review of actual results enables management to obtain some degree of control over the individual operations of the operational supervisors. However, to be most effective this control should only be exercised when individuals who are being supervised through a budget actually participate in its preparation. It is then agreed that the forecast figures will be reasonable and achievable.

The differences between actual results and budgetary figures should not necessarily be construed as favorable or unfavorable, but may simply indicate further analysis is needed to determine the cause for the differences. They may be the result of unavoidable changes of cost or volume factors.

2. Nature of costs

The preparation of a budget or plan for any future undertaking must be based upon an as accurate as possible forecast of the costs to be incurred. This projection must, of course, include a listing or itemization of the specific (natural) costs or expenses to be incurred and certainly a classification of these costs on some functional basis, i.e., selling and administrative or manufacturing, selling and administrative. These cost classifications and their use will be discussed briefly in a subsequent section. This section is concerned with a more basic, underlying facet of the behavior of costs and/or expenses. The classification of costs into categories reflecting the manner in which they react to changes in volume (of sales or of production or both) is an absolute essential to planning, coordination, and control—the three phases of the budgetary process.

The concept of a unit cost resulting from the division of the total cost of a "lot," or the total cost of production for a given period, by the units produced in the lot, or during the given period, is quite simple and well understood by most individuals. Yet, the behavior of certain costs in total and per unit is subject to considerable misunderstanding and misinterpretation, not only by those untrained in accounting or budgetary procedures, but by operating personnel as well. Generally, the behavior of costs with respect to changes in volume is reflected by classifying costs as fixed, variable, and semivariable or semifixed. At the outset, it should be clearly understood that these classifications are somewhat arbitrary and are not universally accepted by accountants, economists, statisticians, and engineers. Rather, the reader and user of these concepts should immediately recognize the artificiality of the classification, and interpret results in light of the restrictions imposed by the narrow classifications and the definitions thereof. It may well be argued that no costs are "fixed," as they shall subsequently be defined, and such a position is entirely tenable within its framework. All costs may be described as variable in the long run, but while "variable," they are not variable as defined in the framework to be presently outlined. However, the classification of costs into these categories with the restricted definitions that follow are not only useful but essential to the establishment and operation of a successful budgetary system.

A "fixed" cost is one that does not change in absolute amount as the result of a change in volume. Rent paid for premises occupied by a retail establishment, depreciation (on a straight-line basis) of machinery used by a manufacturing company, and the property taxes of an individual's residence are examples of costs which do not change in absolute amount as a result of a change in sales volume, units produced, and/or sold, or in the number of individuals residing in the home. Obviously, these costs are fixed in the short run or for limited changes in volume, and would change to provide for volume changes of sufficient magnitude that might occur in the long run. The definition, therefore, is restricted to volume changes that fall within a given range; this is customarily referred to as "the relevant range." Limitation of this concept to those changes that fall within the relevant range enables the definition to remain effective and the concept to be utilized for many purposes in planning, coordinating, and controlling cost.

"Variable" costs are those which will change in absolute amount, *in direct proportion* to changes in volume. Commissions paid to sales personnel as a flat percentage of sales dollars, raw material costs of a standard product, and the cost of admission to the opera are examples of variable costs. The amount of commissions paid to salesmen will be directly proportional to dollar sales (if dollar sales double, commissions payable will also double), the raw material cost of units produced in a given period will be 10 percent less than the raw material costs of goods produced in a prior period if the volume of goods produced in the given period is 10 percent less than that of the prior period. The total cost of going to the opera for a family of six will be double that for a family of three. It should be noted that this definition of a variable cost considers only changes due to a change in volume and ignores any possible change in price. Obviously, if the percentage rate of commissions to salesmen was increased, the total increase in commissions might be due to the increased rate only (sales dollars remaining unchanged) or to the effect of both a volume and the rate change. Similarly, the cost of raw materials to the manufacturer may change, or the price of admission to the opera may change, but these changes cannot be regarded as reflecting change due to volume. In using this concept of variable cost, it must be emphasized that change due to volume is the only behavior pattern of costs being considered.

The description and definition of fixed and variable costs given above stress *the change in the absolute amount* of such costs, which may be associated with a change in volume, but it is equally, if not more, important to recognize the effect of volume change upon fixed and variable costs *per unit*. If the retail establishment rents its business premises for $1,500 per month, the total rent cost per month will be $1,500 regardless of the dollar volume of sales in any given month. However, if sales in October amount to $300,000 and increase to $600,000 in November, and to $750,000 in December, the cost of rent per dollar of sales (the unit of volume assumed) has changed from $0.0050 in October to $0.0025 in November, and to $0.0020 in December. Thus, an increase in volume resulted in a decrease in the fixed cost of rent per unit. Furthermore, the decrease in the per-unit fixed cost was inversely proportional to the increase in volume. A 100 percent increase in sales from October to November resulted in a 50 percent decrease in unit fixed cost, the 20 percent decrease in unit fixed cost from November to December was associated with a 25 percent increase in sales.   To summarize, fixed costs per unit vary inversely with changes in volume.   *Note that unit fixed costs are variable.*

Conversely, if a manufacturer's raw material costs amount to $350,000 when 10,000 units of product are produced, and total $525,000 when 15,000 units are produced, the unit variable material cost is $35 at each of the volume levels.   *Thus, it can be seen that unit variable costs are fixed, or constant.* This characteristic of variable costs to remain unchanged *per unit* irrespective of volume changes is a basic building block for budgeting, cost-profit-volume analyses, standard costs, and many other cost studies.   The remainder of this chapter will make frequent reference either directly or by inference to this basic concept.

In the business world and its realities one can find only a few examples of costs which meet the above rigid definitions and can therefore be referred to as either fixed or variable.   Most costs or expenses will not remain fixed in absolute amount with changes in volume, but will vary with volume *but not in direct proportion*.   These costs are usually referred to as semivariable costs.   A semivariable cost is one which does change with volume, but not in direct proportion.   In addition, semivariable costs do not all assume a similar pattern of change.   Some may remain fixed or constant for volume changes up to a given amount and then increase abruptly to a new level where they will remain for a further range of volume change and beyond that again increase abruptly to another new level.   Such costs (wages of foremen, for example) are depicted on a graph as a series of steps with each step parallel to the base of the graph. These are sometimes referred to as semifixed costs to distinguish them from other semivariable items.   Other semivariable costs vary with production but not in direct proportion, because they contain a fixed amount which will be incurred at every volume level without change in absolute amount.   The cost of electricity for lighting or lighting and power is a good example of such a cost.   The electric bill is computed by starting with a fixed charge of, let us say, $3 per month for the first 10,000 kilowatt hours used, and then a charge is made for each additional 1,000 kilowatt hours.   Other semivariable costs will increase with increases in volume, but may increase at an increasing or at a decreasing rate.   When plotted on a graph, these costs take a curvilinear rather than linear form as variable costs varying in direct proportion take.

For budgetary and other analysis purposes, these semivariable or semifixed costs must be divided into fixed and variable components and be included in the fixed and variable framework.   Costs which increase in a step fashion, such as the foremen's wages mentioned above, are simply classified as fixed, and the analysis is thereby restricted to the range of volume change indicated by the step range.   Budgets or cost projections below or above the given step range must be recalculated, using the lower or upper step for the step semivariable cost.   Costs such as the electricity cost mentioned above can readily be separated into the fixed and variable components by simple recognition of the flat charge for kilowatt hours of use below 10,000 hours as the fixed component and a variable rate per kilowatt hour for all hours over 10,000. Semivariable costs which are curvilinear in form present a more difficult problem, but several methods are available to the analyst *to approximate* the fixed and variable components of such costs. Perhaps the simplest of these methods (and possibly the least accurate) is called the "scattergraph" method. Historical data with respect to various volume levels and the corresponding costs at those levels are plotted on a graph with volume plotted on the *x* axis and dollars of cost plotted on the *y* axis. The plotted points will not fall on a straight line, but a line is drawn so that the plotted points fall equidistant above and below a line drawn by visual observation. This line of "best fit" is extended to the *y* axis and the fixed component is determined at this intersection point. The slope of the line of best fit provides the variable component of the cost.

Another method of approximating the components of a semivariable cost is sometimes referred to as the "high-low method." Again, historical data reflecting the amounts of such a cost at varying volume levels are used. Assume the following costs of inspection were incurred for the related volumes of production:

Production in units	Inspection cost
80,000	$13,900
50,000	11,000
120,000	18,000
70,000	13,200
100,000	15,900

Determine the volume which exhibited the highest inspection cost and the volume level which exhibited the lowest inspection cost.

120,000	$18,000
50,000	11,000
70,000	$ 7,000

Subtract the lowest volume level from the highest and the lowest cost from the highest. Divide the volume difference into the cost difference and the resulting rate will be the variable rate component per unit of volume.

$$\frac{0.10}{70,000 / \$7,000.00} \text{ or } \$0.10 \text{ per unit}$$

Multiply the variable rate per unit times the units at the highest or the lowest volume level. The result will be an approximation of the variable cost at that level. Subtract this figure from the total cost at the higher or lower level, whichever was used, and the resultant figure will be the approximation of the fixed component of the total cost.

120,000 × 0.10 = $12,000. $18,000 − 12,000 = $6,000 (fixed cost)
50,000 × 0.10 = $ 5,000. $11,000 − 5,000 = $6,000 (fixed cost)

Note that the $6,000 and the $0.10 per unit are only approximations and not exact, as may be observed when they are tested with any one of the intermediate volumes assumed in this example:

100,000 × 0.10 = $10,000. $15,900 − 10,000 = $5,900.
 70,000 × 0.10 =   7,000. $13,200 − 7,000 = 6,200.
 80,000 × 0.10 =   8,000. $13,900 − 8,000 = 5,900.

If the data observed had not included the volume level of 120,000 units and its related cost of $18,000, the highest volume would have been the 100,000 level and the highest cost, $15,900. The following computations would then have resulted:

$$
\begin{array}{ll}
100,000 & \$15,900 \\
\underline{50,000} & \underline{11,000} \\
50,000 & \$\ 4,900
\end{array}
$$

$$0.098$$

50,000/$4,900 or $0.098 per unit
100,000 × 0.098 = $9,800. $15,900 − 9,800 = $6,100.

or

50,000 × 0.098 = $4,900. $11,000 − 4,900 = $6,100.

Thus the fixed component might have been approximated at $6,100 and the variable rate at $0.098 per unit.

The third method is the method of least squares and may be found in any statistical reference book. This method is the most accurate of the three mentioned, but because the semivariable cost involved is curvilinear, its results will also be only approximations of the fixed and variable components and will not be discussed in detail here.

Although it has been indicated that most costs in actuality are of a semivariable nature and the fixed and variable components of such costs can only be approximated, the advantages of classifying all costs as either fixed or variable by such methods cannot be overemphasized. Continuous reference to this classification of costs will be made throughout the remainder of this discussion of the budgetary process. In the following section on cost-profit-volume relationships as manifested in break-even analysis, this classification is mandatory.

3. Cost-profit-volume relationships

A complete understanding of the interaction of volume and costs upon profits is a basic prerequisite for the budget executive. A brief, concise picture of these factors is simply portrayed in a break-even chart. This chart, when properly constructed and interpreted, will provide the executive with an idea of the amount of fixed costs which will be incurred over a given relevant range of volume, the rate at which variable costs will increase with volume, and the probable profits to be expected with operations at a given level. Thus, the executive can see at a glance the overall effects of a change in volume upon costs and profits. A number of variations of the break-even chart may be found in the literature reflecting slight preferences in the mode of construction, but one commonly used is illustrated in Fig. 1.

It must be emphasized, at the outset, that this chart assumes all expenses of the company have been classified as being either fixed or variable, so that these costs may be plotted on the graph accordingly. The horizontal or x axis is used to measure sales in terms of units or percentages of some capacity level previously established as 100 percent. The vertical or y axis is used to measure dollars of sales and dollars of expenses. The fixed-cost line is drawn

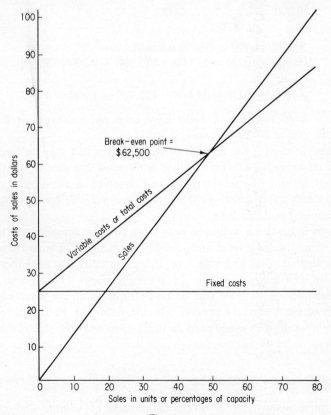

Fig. I.

parallel to the base at the level determined by the summation of all those expense items which were classified as fixed. The variable-cost line is then drawn starting at the y axis at the level established by the fixed costs already plotted and with a slope determined by the summation of the unit variable expense rates for each such cost previously established by analysis. In lieu of the above, a second point may be established by multiplying the sales dollars at any volume level by the total variable expenses per dollar of sales and drawing a straight line connecting this point to intersection of the y axis and the fixed-cost line. This line is also referred to as the total-cost line since the distance from it at any point on the line to the x axis represents the total cost which should be incurred at that volume. The sales line is then drawn starting at the origin with a slope equal to the ratio of the unit sales price over one. The sales line can also be drawn by determining the total sales dollars at any given percentage of capacity and plotting that point on the chart and connecting it with the origin. The point of intersection of the sales line and the total-cost line is referred to as the break-even point. The area between the total-cost line and the sales line below the break-even point is the loss area and the anticipated loss at any volume less than that at break-even may be estimated by determining the dollar value of the segment between the total-cost line and the sales line at the desired volume level. Similarly, the area between the total-cost line and the sales line above the break-even point is the profit area and the profit to be attained may be forecast by measuring the length of the line segment between the sales and total-cost line at volumes above break-even.

The break-even point may be calculated mathematically by use of the simple formula: Sales (at break-even) = fixed costs + variable costs.

Since unit variable costs are fixed, it follows that variable costs expressed as a percentage of sales is also fixed at all volume levels. Therefore, variable costs may be determined as a percentage of sales at any observed volume and this percentage will also apply at break-even or any other volume. Therefore, the formula becomes:

Sales (at break-even) = fixed costs + % sales (variable costs)

Using the information shown in Fig. 1, variable costs may be seen to be 60 percent of sales at any volume level and fixed costs are \$25,000. Substituting in the formula, we have:

$$\text{Sales (at break-even)} = \$25,000 + 0.60 \text{ sales}$$
$$0.40 \text{ sales} = \$25,000$$
$$\text{Sales} = \$62,500$$

Frequently, this calculation may be made on a unit basis rather than on a total dollar basis. Using the data in Fig. 1, the unit sales price is \$1.25 and variable costs are \$0.75 per unit. The marginal income (\$1.25 − \$0.75) is

$0.50. The marginal income figure indicates that the sales of each unit provides $0.50 towards fixed costs and profit. Dividing the total fixed cost of $25,000.00 by the marginal income per unit of $0.50 yields the number of units (50,000) which must be sold in order to fully cover the fixed costs and therefore is the number of units which must be sold to break even. Sales in dollars to break even is determined by multiplying the unit sales price of $1.25 by the units required to break even. The marginal income concept is also quite useful in determining the amount of profit to be expected at any volume in excess of the break-even volume since each additional unit sold will add $0.50 to total profit. The variable cost figure per unit is also a useful concept since it represents the out-of-pocket costs which will be incurred in the sale of each unit. It, therefore, represents the minimum sales price which could be used without resulting in out-of-pocket loss.

Before the reader draws any conclusions with respect to the accuracy of or the desirability of the break-even chart, it is essential that he be acquainted with the assumptions which have been made in its construction, and the limitations these assumptions place upon its usefulness and interpretation. These assumptions may be stated as follows:

The chart assumes that *only one product is being sold* or that *the same mix of products is going to be sold* at each volume level. If more than one product is sold, the costs per unit of product (variable and fixed) will undoubtedly vary and the unit sales price will also probably differ for the various products. Therefore, the assumption of linear total cost and linear sales functions would hold true only if it was assumed that at each volume level the proportion of each product sold to the total remained constant. If it was possible to accurately determine the fixed and variable costs applicable to each product, separate charts might be prepared for each product sold. These charts could then be combined to estimate profits at any combined sales volume for the individual products

The chart assumes that fixed costs remain constant throughout the range of volumes depicted on the base line. The relevant range for the fixed-cost assumption may be far less than the entire volume range and any accurate forecast of future profits would have to be based upon the expected fixed costs for the projected volume rather than upon the fixed costs depicted on the break-even chart. Stated in other terms, it may be necessary to prepare a number of break-even charts which accurately depict the fixed costs and corresponding variable costs which will be incurred for several relevant ranges of volume rather than to combine all ranges of volume in one chart

The chart assumes that the variable costs will vary in direct proportion to changes in volume or will remain constant per unit. As was previously explained, some semivariable costs may increase at increasing rates or at decreasing rates and the assumption of a constant variable rate per unit may not be valid over a wide range of volume change. Again, this problem could be solved by resorting to the preparation of a series of charts covering relatively small changes in volume

A constant unit sales price is another assumption which is reflected in the chart in Fig. 1. If the unit sales price must be reduced to obtain sales volume beyond a given point or additional advertising costs must be incurred to stimulate additional sales volume, the chart must be revised to reflect these facts

If the break-even chart is prepared for a manufacturing company rather than for a merchandising concern, another assumption must be clearly understood. The costs or expenses which are plotted for any given volume level are the expenses associated with the sale of that given volume level, or conversely the sales dollars shown are the value of the goods sold at a given capacity and not the value of the goods produced at that productive capacity level. If the quantity of goods produced in a given year differs from the quantity sold, the profit of the company will not be that which the chart would have reflected for the sales volume attained. The cost of goods produced will not be equal to that for the goods sold and, consequently, the net income will be more or less than the chart would indicate for the attained sales volume. If the budget executive wishes to forecast profit for a year in which inventories are expected to increase, he must increase the profit as depicted in the chart by the increase in the value of the inventories anticipated for the year

The costs or expenses included in the total cost line of a merchandising firm will be limited to the costs associated with each sales volume and, consequently, will not consider any increase in inventory levels of merchandise available for sale. If a decline in inventory stocks is anticipated by the merchandiser, the total cost line will again include the cost of the merchandise sold, which includes the cost of the inventory decline

Increase in costs (fixed or variable) due to increases in price rather than volume is not reflected in the chart, and estimated or budgeted figures for costs and profits must be adjusted for such increases or decreases when it can be forecast that they will occur during the budget period. Revision of the chart is required for any major price change in costs as well as for any change in physical facilities which cause a change in the cost structure

The above list should not be considered as being all-inclusive, since many corollary assumptions are inherent in the above itemized assumptions. For example, efficiency and productivity are assumed to remain unchanged, otherwise the cost relationships would change. All costs have been included on a going-concern basis and consistent accounting procedures are assumed to be used throughout the entire volume range.

Although the assumptions stated above are quite restrictive to general use of break-even analysis in all situations, they should not be construed as voiding or negating the usefulness of the break-even chart in the budgeting process. Rather, when used with appropriate awareness of the inherent assumptions, break-even analysis gives the executive keen insight into cost-profit-volume relationships.

Other forms of the break-even chart.   Figures 2 and 3 are variations of the break-even chart which are sometimes used to stress the point that the variable or "direct" costs should be fully recovered in the sales price of each unit at any level, and that each unit sold provides some margin for fixed costs and profit.   Note that in each of these charts the variable costs are plotted first and then the fixed costs are plotted as lines parallel to the variable cost line previously plotted.

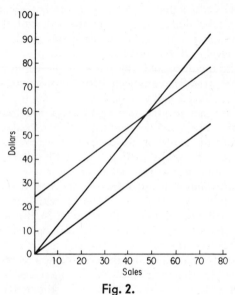

Fig. 2.

The "profitgraphs," illustrated in Figs. 4 and 5, are forms of cost-profit-volume analysis which omit the sales, fixed-cost, and variable-cost lines from their construction.   As was the case with the break-even chart, the horizontal or *x* axis in Fig. 4 measures changes in volume (in dollars or percentages of capacity).   However, the vertical axis measures dollars of profit or loss from a "0" vertical line parallel to the *x* axis.   The single line on the graph depicts the amount of profit or loss which should be incurred at each volume level.   The line is drawn by plotting on the *y* axis the amount of the fixed costs below the "0" vertical or in the loss area and then plotting as a second point the profit or loss which would be anticipated at any observed volume level and connecting the two points.   The break-even point is represented by the intersection of the profit line and the "0" vertical.

Figure 5 is a linear representation of the same information shown in Fig. 4 and has the advantage of enabling the reader to determine expected profit at any given sales level directly without resorting to measuring the length of a line segment, as in Figs. 1, 2, or 3, or to measure along both axes, as in Fig. 4.

The assumptions of a single product and a constant sales mix which were listed above may be ameliorated by multiple use of the profitgraph as depicted

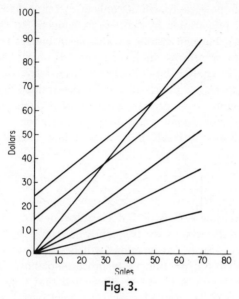

Fig. 3.

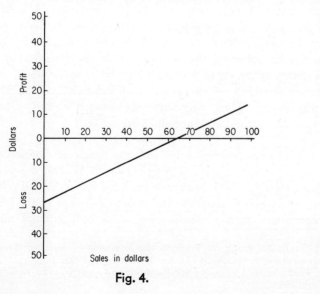

Fig. 4.

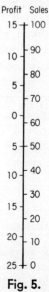

Fig. 5.

in Fig. 5.   This multiple use of linear profitgraphs is called a profit polygraph.[1]
The profit polygraph enables the user to observe break-even relationships, and
in addition, enables a forecast of the total company profit to be determined
with varied assumptions of the product mix and fixed costs.

The cost-profit-volume relationships depicted on the break-even charts,
profitgraph, or profit polygraphs will not only be a great aid to the budget executive in the original preparation of the various budgets (to be discussed in the
subsequent sections), but will also be invaluable in budget revisions to achieve
desired profit goals or returns on investment.   It must be emphasized that
although this type of analysis has historically been referred to as "break-even
analysis," the preparation of the chart and the determination of the break-even
point is only incidental to its primary purpose of depicting cost-profit-volume
relationships.   No businessman plans to break even or is interested in the
break-even point as an end result, but complete knowledge of its determinants
is invaluable.

4. Types of costs

The budget executive will find that classifications of costs into categories
other than fixed and variable are frequently not only desirable but in many
respects mandatory.   Such classifications will be found to be extremely valuable in all three phases of the budgetary process—planning, coordinating, and
control.   In some instances, it will be discovered that these classifications are
mutually exclusive, while other classifications may overlap or even coincide.
The degree of completeness with which each of the classifications is maintained
and/or used can and will vary with individual companies.   Usually, the
determinant of the need for a particular classification or its detail will be
predicated upon the usefulness of the resulting information and the cost or
expense associated with obtaining the information in the classification categories.   A total-system approach to such classification of costs would require
a complete, detailed recording of all pertinent information upon its original
recognition in the system.   Thus, with sufficient detailed coding, costs may
be retrieved from the system and accumulated according to any desired
classification.[2]

The classification of costs usually begins with the simple recognition of the
nature of the cost incurred into natural categories such as rent, depreciation,
power, etc.   Such a classification is ordinarily provided for in the basic chart of
accounts of any organization to recognize the initial incurrence of the cost factor.   In some companies, such a classification is the only attempt made to

---

[1] Paul A. May, "Profit Polygraph for Product Mix Evaluation," *National Association of (Cost) Accountants Bulletin,* vol. XXXVII, no. 3, November, 1955.
[2] Robert Beyer, *Profitability Accounting for Planning and Control,* The Ronald Press Company, New York, 1963.

categorize costs for purposes of planning, coordination, and control, and may be all that is necessary or feasible in a small commercial business establishment. However, it will usually be found that an analysis of such natural cost classifications into categories of fixed and variable is extremely desirable under almost all circumstances. The fixed and variable analysis may not be given formal recognition in the accounts and records, but the budget executive will find forecasting and control of these costs facilitated by the analysis.

For a manufacturing company, an additional classification of costs into functional groups such as manufacturing, selling, and administrative is mandatory. The merchandiser may also find it highly desirable to classify his operating costs into selling and administrative categories for purposes of budget preparation and responsibility. The manufacturer must isolate costs incurred in the production of his products from those required to market the products and from those of a general administrative nature. Manufacturing costs are inventoriable or included in the inventory or asset value, and the distribution and administrative costs are charged off to "expense and revenue" or "profit and loss" in total amount each financial period. Thus, manufacturing costs are sometimes referred to as "product cost," while selling and administrative costs are called "period costs."

Departmentalization of costs or the classification of costs into departmental or cost center groups is utilized by both manufacturers and merchandisers in the budgetary process. The collection of budget data, the coordination of departmental activities, and the fixing of responsibility for the incurring of costs are immeasurably enhanced by a departmental classification of costs. In a manufacturing company, this departmentalization usually includes a differentiation between producing and service departments for purposes of allocating manufacturing overhead costs to the products.

Frequently costs are referred to as either "direct" or "indirect." It is imperative that the base of reference which is utilized in a particular classification (direct or indirect) be understood by all persons involved in its use. Costs may be referred to as direct or indirect with respect to their assignment to a product, i.e., direct materials, direct labor, or manufacturing overhead (indirect). Direct costs may also be considered as those which are directly assignable to a particular department (within manufacturing or commercial). It should be noted that a specific cost, such as the depreciation of the machinery in the foundry department, may be classified as indirect (with respect to the various products produced in the department) or direct (with respect to its assignment to the foundry department). In general, direct costs are those which can be determined exactly and without allocation; indirect costs are those which must be estimated by allocation to products or departments, etc., on some equitable allocation base. Direct costs will normally not be incurred if the product or department is eliminated, whereas indirect costs will continue if a particular product or department is eliminated. Although the terms are not always interchangeable, direct costs are sometimes referred to as "escapable" and indirect costs as "inescapable." The cost of electricity for a department store is ordinarily considered to be indirect with respect to departments, since usage is not metered by individual departments and the cost must be assigned departmentally on a floor space or other equitable basis. Yet, the elimination of a department on the top floor of the building without replacing it or in any way utilizing the space may result in a reduction in the total electricity cost. Thus, some indirect cost has proved to be escapable.[3]

The control of costs is frequently facilitated by reporting costs as being either "controllable" or "noncontrollable." This classification of costs takes cognizance of the fact that costs incurred are under the direct control of some individual or group of individuals within an organization at some time or other in the inevitable cycle from incurrence to utilization or exhaustion of use potential. All costs are controllable by someone or some group at some instant of time. Depreciation of the factory building is certainly uncontrollable by any given departmental foreman, by the plant superintendent, or by even the company president. Yet, it was controllable by the board of directors or other group which originally made the decision to construct or purchase a given building at a specific cost.

The above classifications should not be construed as being all-inclusive, but rather as illustrative of those which will be used in subsequent parts of this section. Classifications such as capital or revenue expenditures, historical or budgeted or standard, relevant or sunk costs, and many others should also be recognized.

5. Budgets in general

The size and complexity of business necessitates breaking down the budget period into short-range budget planning and long-range budget planning. Short-range budgets cover the period of a year or shorter. Many companies will prepare budgets for sales, overhead, cash, etc., for the year. These budgets will then be broken down to shorter periods of 3 months, 6 months, and possibly even each month. It has been said that the shorter the period the more flexibility management has. It is important to review the budgets from time to time to compare actual figures with budgeted figures. If the budgets are found to be out of line, they will have to be readjusted for future periods. The key is constant review and updating of short-term budgets.

With the growth of industry and competition, management has also to go beyond the short-range plan to look ahead 1, 5, and 10 years. The long-range budget covers generalities and is not so detailed and specific as the short-range budget. For example, budgeters are interested in the general projected in-

[3] Rufus Wixon and Robert G. Cox, *Principles of Accounting,* The Ronald Press Company, New York, 1961.

crease in sales volume. Stemming from the projected sales volume would be capital budgeting, that is, planning expenditures for capital improvements. This would give management an idea of what new types of equipment, new plants, etc., the company should be planning on acquiring. Stemming from capital budgeting and sales budgeting, management will find the cash budget as an integral part of long-range planning. Management cannot overnight plan on issuing additional stock or arranging for long-term financing through the bond market. Financing will be helped considerably if planned many years ahead of time based on long-range budget forecasting. It is very important, in addition to reviewing the short-term budget, periodically to review the long-term budget to see whether there are any changes in the economy or industry that will affect the overall long-range plan.

The responsibility for preparation of the short-range budget generally rests with department heads. Top-level management will receive the departmental reports to coordinate the final budget. There should be a great deal of inter-action between the departments in the preparation of the budgets.

Long-range budgeting is initially made up by top-level management. At that level, they are thinking of the long-range plans of the company and are basing their managerial decisions not only on internal factors but external factors, such as competition, the economy today, and what it is expected to be in the future, the stock market, world conditions, etc.

Two common classifications used in the preparation of budgets are fixed or static and flexible budgets. The term "fixed budget" is probably a misnomer. The fixed budget is generally thought of as predetermined costs projected at a particular capacity level. That is, once capacity is projected at a particular level, the individual departments gather and classify their costs at that level. The budget thus prepared will be known as a fixed budget. This is a mis-nomer mainly because the fixed budget really is never fixed. Conditions change and management will review and change the budgets. It merely is a budget of costs at a projected capacity level.

The flexible budget consists of budgets set up at various levels of capacity. Capacity levels are set at percentages of capacity or at the production of a speci-fied number of units at set levels of capacity. Under these various levels costs —fixed, variable, semifixed, semivariable—are broken down.

Budgets are usually based on projected but predictable situations. Given the hypothesis, a fixed budget could be prepared at the projected capacity level or at the normal capacity level. However, actual operations rarely fol-low the original projection of operations. The results of comparing actual activities with a fixed budget would sometimes be misleading because different capacity levels may be involved. It would be much better to have a budget at various capacities so that management could compare actual figures with budgeted figures at the actual capacity level. Management could also com-pare actual capacity with projected normal capacity.

In the actual preparation of the flexible budget, each department would project its costs at the various capacity levels. Each department would consider the fixed, variable, and semivariable elements of each cost item. The departmental budgets would be combined in one master budget. Proper planning, coordination, and control are important. An example of a flexible budget is set forth in the following table:

Flexible budget

Capacity level	70%	80%	90%	100%
Budgeted costs:				
Rent	$ 8,000	$ 8,000	$ 8,000	$ 8,000
Depreciation	3,000	3,000	3,000	3,000
Insurance	800	800	800	800
Maintenance	1,000	1,200	1,200	1,400
Power	1,400	1,600	1,800	2,000
Supplies	900	1,100	1,300	1,500
Miscellaneous	400	500	600	700
Total budget costs	$15,500	$16,200	$16,700	$17,400

In preparing a fixed budget, the capacity would be predetermined. For instance, normal capacity may be 90 percent. Departments would prepare their budgets at that predetermined level.

In the table above, production level was set as a percentage of capacity. It could be set at units of production, direct labor hours, or other basis which would relate to a level of capacity.

In the preparation of the budget, fixed or flexible, the natural costs (such as heat, light, rent, etc.) could be broken down into functional classifications (selling, administrative, etc.). In addition, the fixed and variable elements could be segregated.

The key to the preparation of a budget is successful forecasting. Without forecasting, there would be very little need for budgets. In forecasting, one must consider one's own operations, including one's capacity and ability to change under changing conditions. The forecasting not only takes into consideration one's own operation, but also the industry as a whole and the competitive market. Probably most important is an accurate forecast of general business conditions. It is very important to relate general business conditions to a particular company.

Proper forecasting includes external factors which cannot be controlled by management, and internal factors which can be controlled.

In considering the external factors, the economic and political conditions of the country are important. It is important to relate these conditions and their effect on consumers and competitors. Other external factors are new products, technological changes, and labor disputes. Weather conditions may also be a factor. This is not an all-inclusive list, but enough to indicate consideration to be weighed in forecasting.

Internal factors could be such items as capacity, quality, promotional activities, suppliers, storage and warehousing facilities, production, and distribution factors.

Some of these items are difficult to project accurately, if at all. At that point, it becomes an issue of whether the possible error in planning is greater than if there were no projection at all. Many of these factors can be projected from past activities, with the government providing many sources of raw information upon which budget forecasting might be based. It is much better to attempt to forecast based on the above factors, even with a known chance of error, than not to forecast at all.

In the control aspect of budgeting discussed later, constant review and comparison with actual results will be an aid in improving future budgets.

6. Merchandise budgets

A company that sells a product in substantially the same form as it was purchased, such as a retailer or wholesaler, is described as a merchandising company. The term is used to distinguish it from a manufacturing company, which substantially changes the raw materials it acquires by converting them into a new product. Although some of the budget problems are similar, the major differences are in the area of the cost of the product. Here, the manufacturer must consider labor and overhead factors.

The key budget which leads to the preparation of all other budgets is the *sales budget*. A company will have some sort of sales projection, which will be made on a periodic basis, and the sales budget will be prepared based on both internal and external factors. As discussed earlier, the internal factors to be considered are such items as past activity, present and projected capacity, size of sales force, advertising program, etc. This budget is not based only on the staff's or divisions' projection. There would also be an interaction of various departments, including the advertising department, packaging department, and also top-level management in relationship to capacity, price, etc. External factors include such things as competition, present and future economic condition of the country, legal matters, etc.

When this information is compiled, the budget can be prepared. Basically, the budget consists of a projection of sales on a periodic basis such as monthly, quarterly, and annually. This is the short-range budget. Long-range budgets consist of yearly figures on a 5- and 10-year basis. The sales budget is broken down by product lines or by departments. The budget is prepared both in units and in dollar amounts.

The sales budget, much more than any other budget, must be under constant review based both on internal and external factors. If the sales budget changes, all other budgets—purchase, production, overhead, cash, among others—have to be revised.

Sales changes in units affect variable costs in total and unit fixed costs. Price changes may affect volume with its corresponding effect on costs. Changes in other budgets would not necessarily affect all budgets.

The *purchase budget* is based on the sales budget. It also is stated in units and dollar amounts. This budget is more thoroughly discussed under the manufacturing budget. Basically, it consists of considering the units needed to meet projected sales. This item is increased by minimum requirements for ending inventory and decreased by beginning inventory.

Management also budgets selling and administrative costs. Personnel budgets are also prepared.

The *cash budget* as well as other budgets will be based on the budgets set forth earlier. Cash receipts are primarily based on sales adjusted for collections. The amount of collections is projected from past receivables as well as current receivables. A payment schedule is prepared which includes the payments for merchandise and overhead acquired or incurred for the current month as well as for payables on past months. Special items must be considered, such as increases in cash from the sale of equipment, issuance of stock, borrowing, etc., and from this are deducted some special expenditures like capital improvements, retirement of debt or stock. Cash on hand at the beginning of the month is added to the figures above. The result will be a cash overage or shortage. If a shortage exists, the company will have to arrange for raising the cash through bank loans or other financing methods.

After preparation of the budgets set forth earlier and those under the manufacturing section dealt with in the next part, a *master budget* can be prepared. The master budget consists of all the earlier budgets combined into one to project the revenue and expenses and resultant net income for the projected period. Management can project revenue from the sales budget. Expenses are set forth through cost of goods sold based on the units sold, the cost of the material, and if a manufacturing concern, the cost of labor and overhead that is applicable. From this figure, operating costs are deducted; that is, selling and administrative costs to determine a projected net income. A projected balance sheet may also be prepared.

As was set forth in the introduction, if management finds that the projected net income is not within proper limits, projections, budgets or alternatives have to be reestablished. It may be necessary to set an adjusted projected sales volume and adjust overhead accordingly, especially in the area of fixed costs. A major advantage of budgets is the opportunity given to management to consider alternatives to projected results.

7. Manufacturing budgets

The budgetary process for a manufacturing company, like that for a merchandise firm, begins with the preparation of the sales budget. The techniques discussed in the preceding part for the preparation of a sales budget for a merchandising firm will be duplicated to a large extent by the manufacturer in estimating sales for established products. Reliance upon market-research techniques or research organizations may be utilized more frequently for new products or products which are going to be produced by the specific manufacturer for the first time in an attempt to secure a portion of an already established market for a product. Since the preparation of the sales budget will not differ too greatly for the manufacturer, this part will presuppose that a sales budget has been established for each product for the budget period.

When the sales budget has been agreed upon, the budget executive for the manufacturer turns his attention to the problem of preparing a *production budget*. In broadest terms, a production budget is an estimate of the number of units of each product which will be produced in the coming budget period. For each product this estimate must consider the quantity which is now on hand in inventory, the quantity required to meet projected sales, and the quantity which it is desired to have in inventory at the end of the budget period. The desired-ending-inventory quantity plus the quantity required to meet projected sales yields the quantity which must be made available for sale during the budget period. The quantity to be made available for sale during the budget period less the quantity on hand in the inventory at the beginning of the budget period yields the quantity to be produced during the budget period or the production budget in terms of units for that product.

It should be noted that this budget is in terms of units only and that no dollar costs are involved. Other than the projected sales, the most critical figure in its computation is the desired inventory at the end of the budget period. This quantity will have to consider such factors as the projected sales for the first few days, weeks, or months of the following budget period; the production time required to produce a unit of product; the storage facilities which are available; the amount of investment required to carry such an inventory; the "cost" of unfilled or out-of-stock orders; and perhaps even the perishability of the product.

The production budget as determined by the above calculations must be reviewed by the plant superintendent or budget committee with a view to determining whether or not the projected units can be produced with existing facilities. The time schedule for production of these units must also be reviewed so that it will result in a balanced operation without creating bottlenecks or shortages, or necessitating layoffs and/or overtime operations. This review of the production budget may result in plans to acquire additional productive capacity, in curtailing operations and reduction in work force or scrapping of obsolete facilities, revision of the sales budgets to keep them in line with productive capabilities, revision of the desired inventories at the end of the budget period, or recruitment and training of new personnel who will be required to meet increased capacity operations.

When the production budget has been agreed upon with respect to the quantities of each product which can be produced and the scheduling of production during the budget period has been worked out, the budget committee or executive must turn attention to the preparation of *the budgets of the costs of production*. These are the direct-materials budget, the direct-labor budget and the manufacturing overhead budget. Each of these budgets must consider the quantities to be produced as reflected in the production budget and the prices of the factors which it is expected will prevail during the budget period.

The direct-materials cost budget will also provide a budget for the purchases of raw materials, since the materials to be used will usually consist of those on hand at the beginning of the budget period and others which will be purchased during the period. A schedule of material requirements is prepared, indicating for each product the unit quantities of each material required per unit of finished product. Multiplying these raw material requirements per unit of product times the projected production of each product will yield the total production requirements, which then may be combined by type of raw material. The resultant material requirement may be increased by some predetermined percentage to allow for waste and spoilage. Again, a desired inventory at the end of the budget period must be established which will consider such factors as available storage, cost of storage, cost of ordering, delivery time, and daily usage requirements. The sum of the material requirements for production and the desired ending inventory will equal the quantities of each material which will have to be available during the budget period. The quantities of each material which must be available, less the inventories at the beginning of the budget period, will yield the quantities of each material to be purchased during the budget period. The materials to be purchased and those to be used in production will then be given dollar values by using unit costs for materials to be purchased, which will reflect the costs expected to prevail during the budget period. The direct-materials cost budget and the materials purchases budget will usually be prepared for shorter time periods than for the complete budget period, to provide for fluctuations in the production volume due to seasonal sales or fluctuating production schedules or both.

The direct-labor budget will be prepared by use of standard or estimated labor hours per unit of each finished product multiplied by the units forecast in the production budget.[4] To be of maximum value in planning coordination and control this budget will have to be in sufficient detail to indicate the amount of each specific labor operation required to produce each product. By examination of this budget, the personnel department can

---

[4] In some industries, i.e., aircraft, space, etc., where the quantities produced are relatively small and design change is customary, the number of labor hours required for a specified amount of production may not be assumed to be constant per unit and some other means of estimating the total hours required for production must be used. See learning curve applications, Charles T. Horngren, *Cost Accounting, a Managerial Emphasis*, Prentice-Hall, Inc., Englewood Cliffs, N.J., 1962, pp. 156–157.

make the necessary provisions for the hiring, firing, and training of qualified personnel. The budget is then converted into dollar terms by use of the pay scales expected to be in effect during the coming budget period.

The manufacturing overhead budget will usually be a flexible budget even though the other production budgets may have been prepared in a static form. The flexible budget form should be used since it is assumed that some method of applying a predetermined overhead rate to production will be used and it will therefore be desirable to analyze the over- or underapplied overhead at the end of the period. The preparation of a flexible budget would be desirable even in those cases where the actual costs are to be charged to production at the end of the month or at year end. Any meaningful comparison of budgeted and actual overhead figures must be made at the level of capacity actually attained, and since the actual level is not known until year end, the advance preparation of budgets at various levels aids in such analyses. Assuming that some predetermined rate is to be used in applying overhead costs to production, the particular rate to be used must then be established and budgets prepared for overhead costs estimated at meaningful capacity levels in the framework of the system to be used.

Some of the factors affecting the selection of the rate and therefore the overhead budget are—

Base to be used—
  Direct-labor dollars
  Direct-labor hours
  Machine hours
  Others
Activity level to be used—
  Normal capacity
  Expected actual capacity
Inclusion or exclusion of fixed overhead items—
  Absorption costing
  Direct costing
The use of a single rate or several rates—
  Plant-wide or blanket rate
  Departmental rate
  Cost center rates
  Operational rates
The use of separate rates for service activities [5]

The following presentation will assume the use of a direct-labor hour rate established at expected actual capacity for the plant as a whole. This will be done primarily to aid in illustration and keep the discussion within space limitations. The use of normal capacity rates on a departmental basis has many

[5] Adolph Matz, Othel J. Curry, and George W. Frank, *Cost Accounting*, 3d ed., South-Western Publishing Company, Cincinnati, Ohio, 1962, pp. 285–286.

merits and should be thoroughly investigated, as should some base other than direct-labor hours or the possible use of direct costing.

A flexible manufacturing overhead budget will then be prepared at the expected actual capacity level and in intervals of, perhaps, 10 percent above and below the expected actual level. The classification of each of the manufacturing overhead cost items into fixed and variable groups will be a great aid in the preparation of this budget. Some knowledge of the cost-volume relationships for these costs is required to prepare the budgeted costs as accurately as possible. Capacities in 10 percent intervals will be stated in terms of direct-labor hours as well as to aid in estimating the costs to be incurred. Those costs which have been previously determined to be fixed will simply be estimated at the amount previously determined. Those which vary in a steplike manner will be considered fixed for each level, but may increase to a new level at an increased capacity (fixed at a new level). Those costs which are strictly variable will be estimated by multiplying the variable rate per direct-labor hour times the number of direct-labor hours at the varying percentages of expected actual capacity. Finally, those which are semivariable should be estimated in two portions—a fixed amount for each capacity level as determined by some analysis method and a variable portion using the approximate variable rate per hour. Dividing the total budgeted overhead costs by the expected hours at actual capacity will yield the predetermined rate to be used during the budget period.

The manufacturing budgets described in the preceding discussion have forced management to plan and coordinate its manufacturing activities with its established sales budget. These same budgets may later be used to aid in the control of these costs as they are incurred and to aid in future budget preparation. When overhead rates are established for each production department, it is advisable to prepare budgets for each service department as well. This procedure not only aids in the control of the service-department overhead costs, but also enables a better estimate to be prepared for the producing departments, since service-department estimated costs must first be prorated to production departments before the predetermined rates are finally established.

In the discussion of the production budget the possibility of the need for expanding productive capacity was indicated. Such expenditures must also be included in the budgetary process and in the master budget. Acquisitions of plant equipment to replace existing equipment, to expand production, or to produce a new product will be considered along with all other capital expenditures in the subsequent section.

8. Capital budgeting

A capital expenditure may be defined as one which results in the acquisition of an asset which will render some sort of service over several accounting periods. Capital budgeting is the planning, coordination, and control of the acquisition of such assets. The investment in such assets is usually of substantial magnitude, and the benefits or services received from their acquisition usually extend over a fairly long period of time. Obviously, the budgeting of such expenditures must be handled with as much care as possible. Extensive research and analysis are required to aid management in making a decision to commit these large sums, which it is assumed will be returned in greatly reduced installments over many accounting periods.

Probabilities of future returns, risk, present value of future returns, cost of capital, and long-range company objectives must be evaluated in each such decision. In addition, the Federal income-tax implications and the amount and source of funds for such projects must also be a part of the capital budgeting process. The ultimate authority for approval of capital expenditures is ordinarily retained by the board of directors, who may delegate responsibility for approval of such expenditures below a given sum per project and in total amount to a capital improvements committee. The committee, in turn, may delegate responsibility to the company president to approve projects calling for expenditures less than some sum and less than a specific amount in total for a budget period. Thus, the authority to commit the company to such expenditures may be a pyramid with the board of directors, the final authority at the apex. It may be necessary to obtain the consent of the stockholders before a project can be undertaken if funds needed are to be obtained in the capital market.

Most capital expenditures involve alternative decisions—this may simply be a decision to make the investment or not to make it. It may be a choice between one particular machine or a similar one; it may involve a decision to introduce laborsaving equipment or to expand the present work force to increase production; it may be concerned with a decision to continue to use present equipment or to purchase new, improved equipment; but it will almost invariably involve a choice between a specific investment proposal and one or a number of other proposed projects. Funds required to make such investments are limited, and the profit motive dictates that those which indicate the most profitable returns, in line with company long-range objectives, should be selected. The capital budget process is then deeply involved in the determination of the relative profitability of various investment proposals.

Some capital expenditures may be classified in a "must" category. These expenditures may be required by local, state, or Federal authorities and normally are not income-producing. They may be mandatory upon the company because of a contract with the labor union representing the employees or because of an insurance company's condition precedent to issuing a policy. They may result from the inability of a labor force to handle a voluminous work load, e.g., acquisition of a computer. In most cases, these investments cannot be justified on an income-producing or profit basis, but must be included in the capital-improvement program. Some may be postponed until adequate funds are available, others will have to be undertaken with new capital funds. Proposals or investments of these types will not be given further consideration here. Attention will now be turned to determining the merits of the many income-producing proposals which may be advanced.

Funds for capital investments may be obtained from a number of sources. Most companies would prefer to finance these expenditures from funds provided by operations through depreciation charges and through retained earnings. Financing may also be obtained through the issuance of bonds or new equity securities. Leasing of long-term assets is also a source of such financing which is very popular today. Each of these sources of funds for capital expenditures has a cost associated with its use. This cost may be an actual legal obligation, such as the interest on bonds, or it may be simply the "opportunity cost." This cost is frequently referred to as the "cost of capital." The cost of capital may be defined as the weighted-average cost of the estimated cost of the future funds to be invested in the company.[6] Some concept of the cost of funds or capital will ordinarily be used to establish a minimum required return on any investment project.

Income-producing projects will generate additional income through increased revenues less associated expenses or through the reduction of existing expenses or "savings." The investment required by the capital expenditure must be justified by the "earnings" (additional income) created over its life. These two elements of the capital expenditure—the amount of the investment and the earnings—are utilized to calculate a rate of return to evaluate the profitability of investment proposals. Rates of return on investments may be determined by several different methods yielding somewhat different results. Some variation may also be found in the application of these methods, but basically they may be itemized as follows:

Rate of return on original investment
Rate of return on average investment
Payback period
Time-adjusted rate of return (discounted cash-flow rate)

The use of the rate of return on the original investment as an evaluation of capital proposals is perhaps the simplest and most common method used by individuals in estimating returns on personal investments. This rate is simply calculated by dividing the yearly return by the amount of the original investment. If an investment of $100 returns $120 at the end of the year, the rate of return is calculated to be 20 percent as follows:

$$\frac{\$20}{\$100} = 20 \text{ percent.}$$

It should be noted that the return of the original investment is ignored in the

[6] Robert N. Anthony, *Management Accounting*, rev. ed., Richard D. Irwin, Inc., Homewood, Ill., 1960, p. 546.

determination of this rate of return. If an investment were made in depreciable property with an original cost of $1,000, an estimated life of 10 years, and an assumed return of $120 per year for 10 years before considering depreciation, the rate of return on the original investment would be 2 percent yearly or 20 percent over the life of the project. This rate of return does not consider that 10 percent of the investment is recovered yearly and that the investment is thereby reduced yearly. The average annual return for the 10-year period is divided by the original investment regardless of timing or pattern of return. If $1,200 were received in a lump sum at the end of this period, the rate of return on the investment of $1,000 would be 2 percent yearly or 20 percent over the life of the project. A flow of $150 yearly for 5 years and $90 yearly for the next 5 years; or $110 for the first 6 years, and $135 per year for the last 4 years would also yield an annual return of 2 percent on an original investment of $1,000. Thus, this method is acceptable for evaluating proposals which are all of 1-year duration, but falls short of accurately evaluating proposals of longer duration or which have different income-flow patterns.

The rate of return on average investment takes into consideration the return of the original investment in installments over the life of the project by utilizing the average rather than the original investment. The previous example of the $1,000 investment in a project with a 10-year life and an annual return of $120 per year for the 10 years would have an average investment of $500 and an annual rate of return of 4 percent.

$$\frac{\$20 \ (\text{average annual earnings})}{\$500 \ (\text{average investment})}$$

However, this rate also fails to take into consideration the timing and pattern of the income flows over the project life. A rate of 4 percent on the average investment would also be obtained if the total project return of $1,200 were received in a lump sum at the end of the 10 years; $150 per year for 5 years and $90 per year for the next 5 years; or $110 for 6 years and $135 for the remaining 4 years. Yet a project promising $150 for the first 5 years and $90 a year for the second 5 years would be more desirable than any of the other alternatives if we consider *the present value of money*.

Although the computation of the payback period is not actually a method of determining a rate of return on investment, it is used very frequently by companies in evaluating alternative proposals. This computation emphasizes the period of time which will be required to fully recover the original investment through the income flows generated by it. Using the previous example of a $1,000 investment and an annual return of $120 per year for 10 years, the payback period would be $8\frac{1}{3}$ years, calculated as follows:

$$\frac{\$1,000 \ (\text{original investment})}{\$120 \ (\text{annual earnings})} = 8.33 \text{ years}$$

If the entire $1,200 of income was expected to be received in the tenth year, the payback period would be 10.   An income flow of $150 for 5 years, and $90 for the second 5 years would yield a payback period of 7⅔ years, and one of $110 for 6 years and $135 for the next 4 years, a payback period of 8¹⁴⁄₂₇ years. A company interested in a quick return to a liquid position would, therefore, select those projects with the shortest payback periods.   However, the procedure does not evaluate the profitability of the proposals, does not consider the entire length of the economic life of each project, and does not consider *the present value of money.*

The time-adjusted rate of return or discounted cash-flow rate is the most scientific method of those mentioned here, but is actually only an application of the use of compound interest.   It is the only method illustrated here that does take into consideration that a dollar received during the current year is more valuable than one received next year or 10 years from now—*the present value of money.*   The rate which is determined is that rate of discount which when applied to the future income stream will exactly equate the present value of that stream to the present value of the investment.   In the previous examples, the discounted cash-flow rates would be as follows:

Original investment	Income stream	Rate of return, %
$1,000	$120 per year	3.37
$1,000	$1,200 at end of tenth year	1.72
$1,000	$150 for 5 years and $90 for 5 years	3.98
$1,000	$110 for 6 years and $135 for 4 years	3.60

SOURCE: Robert N. Anthony, *Management Accounting,* Richard D. Irwin, Inc., Homewood, Ill., 1960, pp. 531–545.

From the above tabulation it may be clearly seen that the discounted cashflow rate of return measures the profitability of each proposal in terms of its present value and distinguishes between proposals having the same amount of original investment and the same total cash flow over the entire economic life but with different timing or pattern of cash flows.

When the rate of return on a capital expenditure has been established to the satisfaction of the budget executive, and a decision has been reached to undertake a given proposal, its effects must be incorporated into each of the budgets which it will affect.   It is also very desirable to follow up the actual results of the investment and compare realized earnings with those budgeted, and estimated economic life with that actually attained, to evaluate the effectiveness of the capital budgeting procedures and to aid in future estimates.

9. Responsibility

The budget is a very important tool of management.   It is so important that in large organizations there is a separate budget officer. In smaller organizations, there may be a budget committee made up of various officers or a budget group under the authority of the controller.

The initial planning of the budget will be put in motion by executive policy action. This initial general policy, concerning product lines, research, new products, elimination of some product lines and emphasis, deemphasis of various products, advertising policy, etc., must first be set by executive policy before the budget committee can begin working. It will then be up to the budget committee to initiate and coordinate the various departmental budgets. Coordination is important so that all departments act as a unit rather than individually.

Budget control will then be achieved largely through continuous review of the budgets and through continuous comparison of actual results with projections. Since the budget is a tool of management, it must be flexible. Management must be ready to meet actual demands and changing circumstances, notwithstanding the budget.

Differences between actual results and the budget figures do not necessarily mean that the company was more or less efficient than projected. Results could differ because of a change in projected volume which would affect the cost-volume factors mentioned earlier in the chapter.

Review, however, is important to indicate possible inefficiency, errors in budgets, price differentials, etc. Review will be important in controlling costs and in the preparation of more accurate budgets in the future.

An important consideration in the preparation of budgets is management's goals. Do not set impossible goals. This could discourage department heads and other employees. If realistic goals are set, budgets will be an aid in establishing efficiency and maximizing profits.

Section 12

HOW TO CONTROL BUSINESS
PAPER WORK

BY

G<small>EORGE</small> S. V<small>ANDERWENDE</small>

HOW TO CONTROL BUSINESS
PAPER WORK

Introduction

The importance of forms management and control has not been lessened by constant improvement and change in office machines. Rather, the importance of such programs has increased. Many systems previously in use have been replaced by electronic data processing equipment, but the results produced by that equipment are only as good as the information fed to it. That information comes from forms.

Proper layout and sequence of information on the forms in use take on substantially increased importance, as does the number of forms from which the information must be obtained. The program outlined in this chapter for establishing forms management and control, the authority and responsibility for keeping the program in operation, and the basic steps for forms improvement are applicable to new mechanized equipment.

1. Convert your paper work to working papers

Why do forms need to be controlled?

Forms are the beginning of records. Records are the beginning of files. Files cost money and take up space. Space means more money added to the cost of doing business. Control your forms and you control costs. What is more, you make a start toward converting paper work to working papers

Forms take clerical work to fill in, handle, process, and file. Clerical costs are a real expense in business. Simplify your office work through forms control, and you take another stride toward the conversion of paper work to working papers

Forms help to shape customer attitudes. Good customer relations—including public acceptance of your business practices—is good business. Advertise your good business methods through good easy-to-use forms, and you complete the jump from paper work to working papers

Conversion from paper work to working papers means lower cost; faster, simpler service to your customers; more repeat business; better profits

How, you may ask, do I go about putting forms control to work? What if my business is a small one—perhaps just getting started? Or perhaps a good-sized concern using many kinds of forms? How does the problem differ?

A form is a form, whether the company using it is a one-man concern or a giant corporation. Certain principles apply in any event. For example, no matter how small or large the organization, some responsible person or group needs to give careful study to each and every form that is to be used. As businesses grow, so do the needs for forms and the number of new ones. If you do not start early to control your forms, the forms will control you. Business forms should not be permitted to grow like Topsy, if they are to be real working papers.

The basic elements of forms design and arrangement, and the analysis of the working procedures to which the forms relate, remain essentially the same in a firm of any size. So do the requirements for readability and clarity in the captions and instructions included in forms. So also the need to avoid "overlapping" forms and uneconomical practices in the purchasing or printing, as well as in the storage and distribution.

It is chiefly in organizing and assigning responsibility to meet those needs that the forms control problem grows more complex in the larger enterprise. So, while the forms problem may be well handled as a part-time chore of the proprietor himself in a small concern, a full-scale forms control program with clearly defined divisions of responsibility among many people may be necessary in the large firm.

In order to avoid unnecessary repetition, the subject is dealt with here in a manner suitable to small or large business. The various topics are organized and identified, however, so that the small-business operator can readily identify the parts that are most pertinent to his problem. If your business is one that uses a large variety or a large quantity of forms, you will probably be concerned with every topic. If your business is a small one, using only a few forms, you may want to skip the topics that deal with organizing a forms control program and concentrate on those that deal with forms themselves and their procedural analysis. To simplify selective reading, the outline below provides a handy checklist and reference guide to the main body of the chapter:

Steps in establishing and maintaining a forms control program

1. *Establishing the program.* The success of a forms control program is largely dependent upon its effectiveness at the start. For an effective program the following steps should be undertaken before any attempt is made to operate the program:

a. *Get top-management support.* The program should not be undertaken without topside support. To ensure cooperation of all parts of the organization, the program should be sponsored by the president, a vice-president, the comptroller, or some similar official (see page 397).

b. Assign responsibility for operation of program. Control over the program should be vested in an office operating across departmental lines, preferably in a company-wide methods-and-procedures group—never in a purchasing department (see page 394).

c. Define organizational scope of program. A decision should be made whether the program will be limited to the parent organization or home office or will be extended to other units such as branches and subsidiaries (see page 392).

d. Recruit qualified personnel. Results of the program will depend upon careful selection of personnel with experience in forms control and methods work and with a knowledge of printing production. The staff should include personnel qualified in forms analysis, forms design, drafting, varityping, and filing. The number needed depends on the size of the operation. Forms control is a technical process and should not be assigned to pensioners, clerks, misfits, and inexperienced personnel (see page 395).

e. Announce establishment of program. An official statement should announce the establishment of the program, review its purpose and aims, indicate the organizational unit responsible for its operation, and request full cooperation (see page 392).

f. Collect samples of all forms, together with usage and cost data. All parts of the organization, including stockrooms, should be asked to furnish a minimum of two samples of every form, regardless of how produced, plus estimated annual usage and cost during the past year (see page 399).

g. Establish numeric and functional files. One set of samples should be filed in folders by function. Another set should be filed numerically, a separate folder for each form number (see page 400).

h. Establish file of usage and cost data. The annual usage and cost should be entered on a separate card for each form (see page 401).

i. Establish standards of design and construction, including form numbering system. Standards for type, rules, margins, sizes, paper stock, finishing operations, and methods of reproduction should be established, and a form numbering system should be developed (see page 401).

j. Coordinate program with other operations. An adequate inventory control of stock forms, realistic minimum stock balances, a procedure for prompt issuance of low-stock notices, and a schedule for requisitioning to equalize stockroom work load should be developed. Arrangements should also be made to develop a schedule for the procurement of printing on routine and emergency basis, and to provide for the purchase office or the printing plant to refer to the forms control office any suggestions for changes in specifications and any requisitions received direct from ordering departments. A determination should be made of the commercial printers best qualified to produce forms of various types and quantities on the most economical basis (see page 422).

2. *Operating the program.* Once the machinery described above has been established, the following steps can be taken to operate the program:

a. Review all forms requested. A forms contact representative should review each form requested to determine necessity, to consolidate like or similar forms, and to determine adherence to standards. Subsequent review of these points should be made by the central forms control office if necessary.

b. Apply standards to forms. Forms control representatives should apply approved standards currently to new forms and to revisions and reprints of existing forms. The central forms control office should apply such standards to the forms it handles currently if the work has not been done previously. Either the forms control representatives or the central forms control office, or both, should also undertake as time permits the application of standards to groups of forms by function or department.

c. Prepare specifications for reproduction of forms standardized. For each form standardized, printing or reproduction specifications should be prepared to include form number and title, method of reproduction, finished size, number of pages, number of sides, margins, paper and other materials, construction, special operations such as numbering and perforating, padding if any, and wrapping and labeling.

d. Maintain forms control files. The numeric and functional files of forms should be maintained on a current basis by adding new forms, replacing revised forms, and eliminating superseded and obsolete forms. The cost data files should be maintained on a current basis. This is achieved by entering immediately the quantity ordered and, as soon as available, the costs for each order.

e. Issue list or catalogue of forms. Periodically a list of forms should be issued, with the forms listed in (1) numeric sequence, (2) alphabetic sequence by title, and (3) functional sequence. If the list is included in a catalogue, a reproduction of each form should be shown on a separate sheet together with pertinent information.

f. Review forms periodically for currency. The functional and numeric forms files should be reviewed periodically to eliminate deadwood. Forms not ordered in a specified period should be referred to their sponsor to determine whether they are obsolete.

3. *What will it cost?* No fixed figure of cost can be stated. The size of your business, the number of forms used, the number of clerical, sales, or shop employees required to fill out forms as part of their day's activity, the type of business you operate—all have a direct bearing on the extent to which you may invest in savings through better forms. Commercial forms manufacturers having recognized forms-design representatives can offer smaller companies excellent means of savings. The more progressive printers are also available for advice and assistance. The larger the demands because of the number, type, or uniqueness of the forms or because of business problems, the greater the need for personnel on your own staff or the use of consulting forms engineers. The cost of printing forms is not the starting point of savings, although reductions in printing costs are possible in a forms control program.

2. Objectives of forms control

It takes a lot of forms to keep the wheels of industry turning. In industry as in government, it is a rare transaction or procedure which does not require the use of at least one form.

It has been estimated that in industry for each dollar spent in the purchase of printed forms, from $10 to $100 is spent in the clerical processes accompanying the use of the forms, not to mention the cost of the total procedures in which the forms play a part, or the cost of space and equipment required in the filing of them, or the storage space required to house the supplies of blank forms.

Thus, a question often more pertinent than the merits of the form itself is the necessity for or the efficiency of the procedure which requires its use. This section accordingly stresses control over the substance, design, and utilization of forms as a means of uncovering and solving problems of procedure.

The step-by-step techniques for devising forms are not treated fully. The problems of developing a forms control program are treated in some detail, the accent being on forms work as a single gear, meshing smoothly with all the other gears in the management mechanism to increase the efficiency of the whole machine.

The forms control function. From the procedural viewpoint, forms are something more than their dictionary definition as "printed or typed documents with blank spaces for the insertion of . . . information." They are pieces of paper predesigned to facilitate work. More specifically, they are devices by which management seeks *uniformity* and *simplicity* in the recording, transmitting, reporting, and data-processing elements of a company's operations.

A working definition. From the same point of view, then, *forms control* may be thought of as the management function which gives four broad assurances:

1. The assurance that unneeded forms do not exist
2. The assurance that needed forms are so designed that they actually accomplish the uniformity and simplicity specified in their definition
3. The assurance that forms are produced and distributed economically
4. The assurance that old forms are periodically reviewed, and proposals for new or revised forms studied to identify and solve problems of organization and procedure

Objectives. While accomplishing the elimination, consolidation, and simplification of forms, *forms control* should contribute to the same result in procedures and should help to improve relations between company activities and with the public if activities are in this direction. Three broad objectives may be separately recognized, though they are not separately achieved in practice.

1. *Savings through better procedures and work methods.* Since forms are used for performing work, they frequently dictate the way work is laid out. By their very design, forms often determine how work flows through a department, an office, or a number of offices. Well-designed forms should help increase production, promote accuracy, and develop smooth work flow, with a minimum of duplication, backtracking, and overlapping. When a form is studied in the light of related forms and procedures, possibilities arise for improvement that go beyond the specific actions of entering information on the form or taking data from it in some prescribed sequence. The very nature of the information called for by a form may tell much about work load, work flow, and work content that is far more significant than the immediate act of making entries.

2. *Savings through standardization and printing.* Standards of design, paper stock, printing, or duplicating, along with improved methods of estimating, stocking, controlling inventory, and distributing, offer quick and obvious returns. Not only do analyzing forms and applying standards usually result in lower paper and printing costs for a given number of forms, but also, by revealing possibilities for eliminating or combining forms, these steps should help to cut down the number of different forms needed and the accompanying stocking problems.

3. *Better service and public relations.* Combination and simplification, better work methods, greater accuracy, and faster production all have an important bearing on getting the work done. An adequate forms control program, besides improving service internally, should assure that forms required for use outside company activities reflect the logic, simplicity, and clarity of purpose that are necessary to outside acceptance and cooperation.

Scope. Coming properly under control are not only the major activity forms of an organization but also many such incidental working tools as tabulating sheets, tally cards, route slips, transmittal forms, telephone memorandums, tags, checks, and labels.

Characteristics—not names—determine coverage. The fact that a printed instrument may be called something other than a form—such as a contract, a lease, or a form letter—does not exclude it from forms control.

Form letters seem to be especially subject to misunderstanding in this connection. While the presence of the word "form" in the term "form letter" does not make it so, the fact is that many form letters are also forms. Quite a few would serve their purpose more efficiently if converted completely from letter style to regular form layout, for there is little to be gained by farfetched attempts to preserve an illusion of the personal letter in obviously routine work papers.

Regardless of what it may be called, if a form is used in quantity and is primarily a working paper requiring significant entries on it, transcriptions from it, or procedural handling of it for either internal or external company use, it should be subject to forms control. It probably will benefit by the application of forms design standards and at the same time throw light on procedural problems.

A seven-point forms control program. While all companies need some type of forms control, and while certain basic elements are common to every forms control program, questions of organizing such a program vary as the programs of individual companies vary. The number of forms in use, although an important item of consideration, should not be the sole criterion of determination.

Elements of the program. Primarily forms control should supplement the practical knowledge of line operations with the objective approach and questioning attitude of industrial analysis and the technical know-how of forms design, production, and distribution. These several elements may be translated into the following essential activities in what might be called a seven-point program:

1. Recording or registering the form
2. Analyzing its purpose, content, and related procedures
3. Applying design standards
4. Assigning identification
5. Determining specifications for reproducing the form
6. Developing specifications for storing and distributing the supply produced
7. Evaluating the control program itself

Whatever the specific assignment of responsibilities, these seven points should work out somewhat as below.

Registration. Each request for a new or reprint form is channeled to a central point to be recorded and assigned for analysis. Essential data on numbering and identification, previous or proposed form revisions, volume, use, and production are available at this registration point, along with copies of all the forms used by the company.

Analysis, purpose, content, procedures. Every request for a new or reprint form is analyzed, its necessity questioned. The purpose and content of the form are evaluated, its effect upon work methods and procedures studied. By close cooperation between operating people and industrial engineers, new forms and procedures are developed or old ones improved. As procedural and organizational problems going beyond forms usage are revealed, they are scheduled for further attention.

Design, standardization. Staff with special knowledge of forms design assists in laying out the form. Content is transformed into items which are spaced and arranged to accommodate desired entries, meet the needs of the writing method to be used, mesh properly with procedures, and assure readability. Determination of size, typography, color, and paper stock is made accordingly.

Identification. Title, number, approval date (and expiration date, if any) are assigned as positive identification, linking the form to its function, operating unit or program, and showing that the form has been authorized for use. Forms can be identified as those that must be retained and those of short or temporary life.

Production specification, printing, duplicating, binding. Efficient and economical production methods are determined. Appropriate evaluation is placed upon the use of specialty forms and special bindery operations such as punching, stapling, perforating, folding, collating, carbon interleaving, etc., as against individual cut forms in relation to savings in preparation and use.

Distribution determination. Specifications for effective storage and distribution are developed. Methods of determining current supplies, establishing minimum stock levels, purging obsolete forms, and setting distribution patterns and controls are essential elements at this stage.

Evaluation, measuring results. A running record of results is accumulated as forms control work progresses. Before-and-after data (showing clerical, printing, and other savings) are gathered as changes in forms and procedures are made. These facts, with recommendations, are reported to top management for use in appraising the forms control program and in shaping future policy on it.

Responsibility. The forms control program branches out; it merges with, and depends on, many other company activities. Varying degrees or kinds of responsibility for the different elements of forms control, therefore, must be carefully defined and carefully placed, so as to be clearly understood by all concerned at each level.

Center of responsibility. Experience has shown that the forms control program is likely to be most effective if primary responsibility for it is centered in a specific individual or unit of the office-methods staff or of a similar office, whatever it may be called, having responsibility for organizational and procedural problems. This is true regardless of the organization level involved— headquarters office, department, office or factory, or branch establishment. The responsibility should cover the preparation of directives and control procedures, the establishment of standards, the recording of requests for new or revised forms, the searching of files for duplications, the recommendation of procedural studies involving forms, and consultation with other units on such matters.

Since the office-methods staff is bound to encounter many forms problems in dealing with the procedures of which forms are a part, to assign forms control to that office is to add a major tool to its procedural working kit. Conversely, both forms work and organization and methods work will suffer if an attempt is made to separate the improvement of procedures through forms analysis from its corollary, the improvement of forms through procedures analysis.

Fixing primary responsibility for the forms control process in an office-methods unit, however, does not alter the staff status of that unit; in forms control, as in its other activities, its job is to serve the line operators. Nor does fixing forms control responsibility in the office-methods unit minimize the contribution that files, statistical, drafting, printing, and duplicating personnel, outside the unit, must give in the design and production of forms.

Level of responsibility. The problem of determining at what level or levels to centralize forms responsibility is a very real one in many large concerns. Decision will always depend on such factors as the size of the concern, location of its offices, and diversity of its operations.

Two balancing principles should be kept in mind—

Control should be centered at a level high enough to give the broad perspective needed for review, coordination, and across-the-board improvement

Control should remain close enough to program (either in the headquarters office or at points in the field) so that forms can be planned, designed, or revised in the light of actual program needs and with an intimate understanding of operating problems

In a large company, forms control programs may be required at two or more levels—headquarters, departmental, office or factory, and, under certain circumstances, in the field. Assuming that responsibility for office-methods work has been placed at the appropriate level, similar responsibility for forms control would ordinarily be appropriate at the same level.

If the program is established at the departmental level, responsibility should still be maintained at the company level for—

Control of company and interoffice, factory, or branch forms

Stimulation, coordination, and evaluation of the control activity within the office, factory, or branch

Staff resources. Staff requirements for the forms control program are determined by the amount of forms control work to be done, the relationship of this program to the total office-methods program, the availability of the needed knowledge and skills within the various units concerned with forms development or use, and the volume of other work claiming office-methods staff time.

In the absence of an adequate forms control program, a frequent problem is that of overparticipation in forms development by operating personnel. To the extent that they use time and energy in those tasks of forms development which can be more efficiently performed by technical specialists, they do so at the unnecessary expense of their primary responsibilities. On the other hand, it would be no less a mistake to assume that the whole burden of forms development can be shifted to the forms control staff. There can scarcely be a substitute for the first-hand knowledge of operating personnel in determining forms content.

Sources of technical aid. In addition to constant collaboration with program-developing and line-operating people, participation in forms problems should come as needed from any of several points in the company.

Statistical personnel may need to be consulted frequently concerning statistical reporting, sampling, and tabulating standards which many forms must meet.

Editorial or information specialists, if available, may help make forms more readable and understandable, especially if for outside-company use.

Drafting staff may be called upon to do the final drawing of many forms and may be a source of advance suggestions on layout.

The office responsible for printing or duplicating should be a source of technical information needed in advance for making design specifications consistent with economical printing or duplicating practices.

Other persons outside the forms control staff may need to be consulted on questions of intercompany relations, which may require consideration before final decisions are made on certain forms.

Thus, no company can expect to have at hand in any single unit all the knowledge and all the services needed in developing, producing, and controlling forms. If the volume of forms is great enough, it may be feasible to provide for certain of those needs within the forms control unit itself. For example, a draftsman might be assigned to specialize in drawing forms. The need for drafting service, however, is not peculiar to forms work. The same is true of most other supporting services. Short of very exceptional volume and stability in the flow of forms work, therefore, it is rarely profitable to add technicians directly to a forms control unit or even to an overall office-methods unit, to provide those services.

It is in these same staff services that some of the savings of forms control should be realized. Advance attention to design problems and printing limitations, for example, should simplify the work of drafting and duplicating staffs, when forms come to them for processing, just as the time of operating personnel is saved by relieving them of technical details in developing forms. In addition, duplicating work load is reduced by the elimination of nonessential forms and the consolidation of others.

Control staff. Certain activities, however, do accompany the primary control responsibility. The recording or registration of forms, the analysis of forms content for procedural implications, the development and application of standards of design, the relating of forms design to appropriate printing or reproduction processes, and the control of storage and distribution practices impose staffing (or training) considerations upon whatever unit is given primary responsibility for forms control.

These activities may call merely for special attention to forms by office-methods staff already working on other administrative problems. Such existing staff, possibly supplemented (on a full-time or part-time basis) by a design technician, may well suffice if the forms control program is to be developed gradually and is to depend for its intake upon requests for new forms and reorders for old ones. On the other hand, if the company is large, if its control plan is new, and if complete long-range coverage is anticipated, a separate compact working unit may be feasible. This arrangement has paid dividends in several large companies.

The job of designing forms and preparing them for printing or duplicating may require only the part-time attention of an office-methods engineer or it too may be the full-time responsibility of an individual or a unit, again depending on whether the volume of forms work justifies that degree of specialization.

To the extent that necessary abilities may be lacking in an organization, they will have to be provided either by training or recruitment; or, if needed only occasionally, by getting temporary assistance from outside the company. Any office-methods engineer should already have at least the basic qualifications for forms work, and should be able to absorb any forms design training needed in a relatively short time by tapping all available pertinent published sources. Other companies and private engineering firms offer possibilities to be explored, also, in seeking short training periods to familiarize employees with sound practices of forms design.

Top-management participation. No matter how well conceived the forms control plan may be in other respects, the plan will not become a reality—or will not remain so—without a certain minimum of top-management support. Forms control authority, like that for any other program cutting across all segments of a company, should stem from the top. Not only must top management make the decision calling for such a program; it must take certain steps as a basis for that decision and certain continuing steps to see that the resulting program is effectively carried out.

Among other things, it is up to top management to—

Call for, and weigh the results of, such preliminary survey and analysis as may be necessary to determine the nature and extent of the forms problems within the company

Formulate and issue a policy directive which will—

Clearly specify the scope of the forms control program in terms of organizational units and classes of forms included (with any necessary exemptions expressly designated)

Clearly fix responsibility for participation in the program (both the centralized primary responsibility and all aspects of collaboration)

Make its positive endorsement and vigorous backing clearly understood throughout the organization

Require, review, and act upon periodic reports of the program's results as a basis for any needed correction in forms control policy

A preliminary survey within the organization discloses the volume and variety of forms involved, and brings to light some of the more obvious cases of overlapping, duplication, and procedural discrepancy. Ordinarily this is enough to show the need for a forms control program, as well as to suggest its initial scope and direction. In addition to internal facts and figures on potential savings and improvements, experience in other companies can be drawn upon as needed to reach a decision. From such facts, a clear statement or simple visualization can be developed to help get the story across all along the line.

The sheer volume of forms in some companies may be so great that it may be wise to confine the program at first to those forms offering the more obvious and immediate savings in paper, printing, and processing. This does not mean, however, that benefits even in the beginning should be limited to the production aspect of the forms problem. It means only that the number of forms dealt with may have to be arbitrarily limited in getting the program started. Every form that is brought under control should be considered in conjunction with the procedures involved in its use.

3. Establishing the program

Once top-management policy and backing have been clearly established, the cornerstone for a forms control program has been laid. With responsibilities firmly fixed, the framework has been raised. A structure exists in which to carry out the regular processes of (1) registration, (2) analysis, (3) design standardization, (4) identification, (5) production specifications, (6) distribution determination, and (7) evaluation—processes found necessary to any fully useful forms control program.

But before production can begin, the machinery must be installed. The staff member or unit made primarily responsible must do certain nonrecurring setup work before the regular processes can be set in motion to make the program a going concern.

The machinery required by forms control need not be elaborate. Many of the common tools of management can profitably be applied to this activity. The basic equipment peculiar to forms control, however, consists of—

A collection of all the company's forms, made available for use in—
  A functional file
  A numerical file
A set of company forms-design standards
A forms-identification plan
A forms control procedure
A set of forms control records

If staff members need training in the methods of forms design or forms production to prepare them for responsibilities newly assigned under the program, such training can be started while the preliminary collection and classification of existing forms is under way. In fact, this work may well be a part of the training process.

In any event, the development of suitable design and production standards, or the adaptation of standards developed elsewhere, is a delicate task. Because many persons in an organization have a rightful interest in the design, typography, and general appearance of forms, and because frequent changes of standards are costly and confusing, staff members made responsible for establishing the standards must be familiar with the necessary technical considerations before attempting to do the job (at least sufficiently familiar to evaluate the advice offered by specialists in related activities).

Similarly the adoption of an identification plan and control procedure should not be attempted until thorough familiarity with the problem and any necessary training in technique have been provided. The process of collecting and classifying the forms should contribute much to such familiarity and training.

Collecting forms. If not done in the initial directive establishing forms control policy and responsibility, a follow-up instruction should request all forms-using and forms-originating units to submit copies of all their forms. If the volume is large, it may be necessary to schedule the submittal of forms by different units at different times.

The units should supply not only samples of all forms in current use but also copies of any obsolete forms which have not been officially rescinded. All temporary and all permanent forms, numbered and unnumbered, regardless of origin or method of reproduction, should be included.

It is important not to omit copies of such predesigned working papers as—

Tabulating cards and paper, including ruled-stock forms
Preprinted duplicating masters, tags, labels, and checks
Memorandum sheets, routing slips, and other communication forms
All formlike form letters

Although some of the papers submitted may not meet the forms definition, any doubt should be met by submitting them for determination.

General forms used by many or all units of an organization, however, may not need to be submitted by each unit. Unless the method of use varies significantly in the different units, it should be sufficient to get copies only from the highest organization level using them or from the office that controls the manner of use.

Standardizing the method of submitting forms facilitates handling, classification, and filing. Accordingly, with respect to all forms included in the call, the using units should be requested initially to—

Furnish two copies of each form, if the form is a single sheet
Furnish two complete sets, if the form is part of a set

Furnish two complete books, if the form is padded or bound

Identify each form by number or title, if identification is not printed on the form

Show name of unit or units which use each form

Show approximate quantity of each form used—daily, annually, or otherwise—and the quantity on hand

Identify the instruction which prescribes or authorizes the form, and indicate any change expected or needed in such regulation or directive

Include or refer to instructions for use, if they are not contained in full on the form itself

Show distribution of the form (in its blank state)

Explain writing method used for fill-in (hand or machine), number of copies prepared at one writing, and routing of completed copies (specifying those who use or act on the information recorded)

Show relationships to other forms (those used in conjunction, those to or from which data must be transcribed, and those known to call for some of the same information from another source or similar information from the same source)

Specify any mechanical equipment in which the form must be used (for posting, tabulating, counting, or special filing)

Explain any recognized need for change or revision in design or use

Submit forms unfastened and unstapled

Cancel or void any negotiable forms or other prenumbered forms, or else submit photostats instead of actual forms

Include name of using unit on package

In many instances operating manuals or other instructional materials will include much of the information required to show the complete purpose and use of the forms to be submitted. Submittal of, or reference to, appropriate pages of such materials, therefore, may often minimize the amount of information to be especially prepared in submitting samples of forms.

Classifying the forms. As the forms are collected they must be sorted, classified, and filed to make further reference and analysis as orderly and time-saving as possible. Two files are needed, the functional and the numerical.

The functional file. The functional classification helps in collating forms which serve similar working purposes and which, by reason of similarity of content or purpose, may be susceptible of consolidation and standardization.

In establishing the functional files, the first broad division might well be that between administrative and operating forms. Beyond that grouping, varying degrees of analysis are required to determine appropriate subgroups.

The extent and nature of such classes and subclasses depend upon the size of the organization covered, the degree of administrative specialization, and the number of forms involved within the various possible classifications.

Once established, however, the functional file permits comparison of existing or proposed forms with all other forms employed in the same or related activities.   The file brings together in one place data which the office-methods staff can use in simplifying, combining, eliminating, or evaluating forms.   The functional grouping tends especially to show up duplications.

Only one master copy of each form should be kept in the functional file; but care should be taken to see that notations have been made on the form to show the names of all units using it, the procedural purpose, the quantity used by each unit, and other pertinent information available at the time the form is received.

The numerical file.   The numerical file should include a separate folder for each form.   These folders, arranged in form-number sequence, should serve as a cross reference to or from the functional file and as a repository for explanatory material accompanying each form.   It may be sufficient to establish this file gradually, setting up the individual folders as the forms are taken up for detailed analysis and procedural study, or as requests for revision or reprinting are received.   In any event, forms cannot be given regular places in the numerical file until they have been assigned form numbers.

In order to provide a complete picture of each form, its evolution and work setting, each numerical file folder, as soon as possible, should contain—

A copy of the form itself and of any previous editions

Notes on the form's history, with any rough drafts or work papers that show significant stages of development

A copy of, or reference to, the instructions or other issuance upon which the form is based

A copy of the request for approval, including such data as the name of the originating or using unit, manner and rate of use, suggestions for improvement, or notices of pending changes in procedure

A copy of the requisition for duplicating, including available data on cost, process, and specifications

Complete documentation relating to official approvals of copy, and pertinent correspondence or conference proceedings

Any available information on contemplated revisions

Establishing standards.   Efficiency in the procedure of which a form may be a part can hardly be guaranteed by anything so pat as a set of standards. Certain yardsticks are necessary, however, as means of assuring that all forms have the physical or graphic features required for—

Simplicity and efficiency in those fill-in and routing procedures that may be influenced by the arrangement of items on the forms

Visual efficiency in reading, using, filing, and finding

Uniformity and general adequacy in appearance

Economy in reproduction

Before the forms control program can become operative, therefore, the staff primarily responsible should work closely with operating units and the company's reproduction or printing services to develop a set of standards which will be realistic in terms of program responsibilities, staff limitations, and forms volume.

Because of the many variables among companies, few general standards are possible. It is possible, however, to point out some of the factors which must be considered in determining a company's individual standards and to touch upon some of the practices which other companies now operating successful control programs have found effective. For purposes of illustration, a skeleton set of hypothetical standards is shown starting on page 427.

The review of forms in the functional file serves as a base from which to work in considering the applicability of various possible standards. While forms are being compared for classification or other purposes, notes applicable to paper or design specifications should be made on the file copies.

The standards selected should be applicable to as many of the company's forms as possible and should anticipate future requirements.

Once they have been determined, the standards should be circulated throughout the company to guide all those who initiate forms or participate in their development.

Factors to consider. The physical aspects of forms most readily standardized are—

Size and shape
Weight and grade of paper
Colors of paper and ink
Typography and format
Mechanical characteristics (such as punching, binding, perforating, carbon interleaving)
Methods of reproduction

Considerations in the selection of standards for each of those features are outlined below.

SIZE AND SHAPE. Company standards for form sizes should be such that all forms can be cut without waste from a minimum number of standard paper sizes. In limiting permissible form sizes, however, consideration must be given to requirements imposed by office machines, files, binders, envelopes, or other equipment and supplies commonly involved in the use of forms.

WEIGHTS AND GRADES OF PAPER. Similarly, the weights, grades, and finishes of paper should be reduced to a reasonable minimum. Factors to be considered include—

Suitability of paper surface
    For duplicating processes involved
    For writing methods used in making entries
    For erasures which may be necessary
    For safety (protection against unauthorized alterations in entries made on certain forms)
Visual efficiency (considering volume and conditions of use)

Suitability of weight, thickness, and durability
    For number of carbon copies required
    For handling required in use
    For any office machines in which used
    For relative permanence of record required
    For filing methods and space required in storage (for both unused forms
       and completed records)
Cost as related to other factors

All existing forms should be sorted according to the approximate grades and weights of the paper on which they are printed. By application of the above factors, all unsuitable and unnecessary varieties should be excluded, with substitutions made as appropriate.

COLORS. The use of colored paper in existing forms should be analyzed to determine if color is necessary in each instance. All colored forms in use should be sorted and examined individually to see whether color (1) increases efficiency in distribution, or (2) makes handling easier for the person filing, referring to, or filling in the form. If color is found advisable, variations should be reduced to a few basic shades.

A similar routine should be followed in selecting standards for ink colors. The use of color, either in paper or more especially in ink, is justifiable only if the additional cost is balanced by improved performance and efficiency. Technical advice again may be needed in selecting color standards, for some color combinations in paper and ink reduce legibility critically. Poor color selection can thus increase inaccuracies and waste in clerical processes.

TYPOGRAPHY AND FORMAT. It is important to avoid hard-and-fast criteria for the arrangement of forms content. The sequence and arrangement of items on a form must be determined by individual analysis of the working procedures involved. Standards of layout, therefore, become (1) general principles to be followed in analysis and (2) statements of alternative locations permissible for certain mandatory items such as title and form number.

Matters of type face and spacing, on the other hand, can be more precisely treated.

A review should be made of the type faces available on typewriters and any composing machines (such as the Vari-Typer) in the company, along with the letterpress faces recommended for various uses by a competent printer. On the basis of this review, a standard selection can be made which will—

Make for visual efficiency in forms use by assuring legibility and permitting ample variety in type size and weight for purposes of differentiation and emphasis among various copy elements

Promote uniform appearance among company forms, by limiting the styles of type to be used

Reduce direct costs, by excluding hand-set or other special composition, by prohibiting purely ornamental all-around borders and typographic nonessentials, and by simplifying the task of specifying type when requisitioning forms

Similarly, uniform spacing provisions can be established in accordance with the different writing methods to be used for fill-in; and relative locations of item numbers, captions, check boxes, and instructional notes within the individual blanks on a form can, within limits, be predesignated.

MECHANICAL CHARACTERISTICS. Extra make-ready, press time, and bindery work can add materially to form costs. Although such extra operations often pay off in the more efficient use of forms, the forms-control staff should be alert to eliminate frills.

In order to keep these extra expenses at a minimum, the company should develop standard instructions on such details as these:

Prenumbering ....Permissible only if sequence control or strict accounting for each copy is required.
Punching ....To fit standard binders or special filing equipment used in the company.
Stapling ....Standard number and location, varying by class or size of form.
Perforating, folding, carbon interleaving, collating, and padding ....Only on individual justification based on economy in use.

REPRODUCTION METHODS. One of the biggest sources of unnecessary cost commonly found in forms production is the use of reproduction processes not suited to the *quantity* of forms required. Similarly, one of the major causes of inefficiency in forms is the production of forms by processes not capable of a *quality* suited to the conditions under which the finished forms have to be used. Often, for example, forms are run off by stencil duplicator when the quantity would have justified the letterpress process and the legibility, usability, and appearance would have been improved by it. Quite often many hours at the drafting table are devoted to drawing the finished version of a ruled form for office offset reproduction when skilled compositors could have set up the form from a rough sketch in a fraction of the time and with better results. Conversely, forms are sometimes sent to the printer for costly composition and presswork when, with a few minor paste-up alterations of an existing printed form, the quantity needed could have been run by the offset method at a fraction of letterpress cost.

Here, especially, should the advice of the company's reproduction staff or a competent printer be sought in determining company standards. Although general standards are available for use in selecting reproduction processes for varying quantities and conditions, these need to be considered in the light of the equipment available to the specific company and with special reference to the writing surfaces needed in forms use.

Adopting an identification plan. Every form should bear a title, a number, and an issuance or revision date, in addition to company name and location.

The title should identify the form clearly for the user. Number and date should identify the form positively for control purposes. Titles are originated as a rule by operating units, subject to review and possible improvement by the forms control staff. Numbers are assigned schematically by the forms control staff itself.

A plan for the assignment of titles and numbers should be established, like design standards, before the forms control program goes into operation. Once the plan is formulated, each form-using unit should be given an explanation of it, preferably along with a copy of the design standards.

Titles. Although a definite system of form titles cannot be determined in advance as can a numbering scheme, certain criteria can be predesignated to aid units in suggesting acceptable titles at the time they request forms. Titles should be brief and yet specific. Words used should be few; yet they should show the precise subject (usually first) and precise function by careful choice of words. The subject designation in the title should be as specific as the subject-matter limits of the form itself.

In the titles "Materials Receipt," "Purchase Order," and "Sales Invoice" there is not much room for doubt about either subject matter or purpose.

Additional guidance may be provided in advance by preparing a glossary of terms having general acceptance for use in titling common types of forms. One such glossary is included on page 432.

Numbers. The numbering system should be simple, logical, and uniform to help form users understand the plan as a whole and remember individual form numbers.

A complete form number (including any affixes) should serve as—

A symbol of the authority under which the form is issued
A control symbol showing that before issuance the form has been checked against
    Existing forms for possible duplication or overlapping
    Design and production standards for economy and suitability in use
A positive identification code logically indicating—
    The originating unit
    The activity or function served
    The relationship to other forms in the same activity, process, or procedural series

The steps to be taken in establishing or overhauling a numbering system include (1) determining the adequacy of present numbering practices within the company, (2) identifying any changes needed to assure a sound basic numbering pattern, and (3) gearing the numbering system into the total forms control procedure.

DETERMINING ADEQUACY OF PRESENT NUMBERING. Certain observations concerning the adequacy of existing form numbers will have been made during the original assembly and classification of forms for the functional and numerical files.   Further review and comparison may be necessary, however, to assure the spotting of any duplications in existing numbers and to evaluate the pattern of numbers as a whole.

Special effort should be made to determine the extent to which form-number sequences correspond to procedural sequences and tie into instruction manuals and inventory or other records.

DETERMINING DESIRED BASIC PATTERN.   Although there is room for considerable discretion, the determination of a specific numbering scheme may depend to a large extent upon such factors as—

The quantity and variety of forms coming within the program
The nature and scope of control authorized
The frequency of activity and organizational changes within the company
The extent to which key form numbers are already firmly and favorably rooted, especially in major procedural uses
The nature of related control and accounting codes already existing in the company
The need for consistency with the numbering system for standard company-wide forms

Whatever scheme is selected, the two basic elements, numbers and affixes, are subject to certain common considerations.

Base numbers assigned in sequence are the foundation for any forms-numbering system.

Assignment of form numbers in blocks is not recommended.   In starting a register, it is impossible to predict how many different forms will be printed for each group or block set up; and when a block of numbers has been used it may be necessary to set up a new block of numbers for the same class of forms, increasing the possibility of confusion and error.   Forms for large organizational groups can be identified by descriptive affixes for each division and still have the basic numbers assigned in sequence.

Affixes may be used to differentiate company-wide forms from those used within subordinate units of the company, such as departments, branches, divisions, or field offices, or to designate specific functions, such as *personnel, accounting, sales, or purchasing.*

Such affixes may be made up of the initials of the company or organizational unit, abbreviations, code letters, or code numbers.   Although usually used as prefixes, decimal or other number codes are frequently added as suffixes to denote function, program, or procedural series.

INTEGRATING NUMBERING PATTERN INTO FORMS CONTROL PROCEDURE.   If major numbering changes in a variety of long-established forms are found necessary, it usually is wise to convert on a gradual basis by assigning new numbers as stocks of the various forms are replenished and as program and procedural changes within the agency provide convenient opportunities.   Allowances for such necessary expediencies will have to be made in setting up the forms control procedure. When revising form numbers, it is often desirable to show the old number with the new number, placing the old number in a subordinate position. After the new number has become known, the old number may be dropped completely. It is important, however, to make the transition as rapidly and as uniformly as such necessary considerations will permit.

Dates. Though it is the simplest element in forms identification, issuance and revision dating is nevertheless important. For example, the current version of a form may be quite different from its earlier counterpart, though title and number may be identical. Without the revision date, positive identification may be difficult and operating complications serious.

The forms control staff should be responsible for supplying the appropriate date before any form goes to press. Ordinarily it should follow the form number, preferably below it. Enclosing the date in parentheses avoids confusion with the form number. Abbreviations to conserve space may be desirable, as "(5–70)" rather than "(May 1970)." Revision may be indicated by the abbreviation "Rev." The date then would become "(Rev. 5–70)."

Developing a control procedure. The numerous procedural steps into which the seven basic forms control activities (page 393) may be divided are much the same in substance wherever the complete program is in effect. Yet these detail steps vary among companies in terms of who performs the specific tasks, how certain steps are combined, and the order in which they occur. Whatever the individual variations, the procedure should be clearly outlined and thoroughly understood throughout the company before any attempt is made to put the program into effect.

The order of steps in such a procedure may be approximately as follows:

Initiation procedure
> Each request for the initiation and approval of any new form or the revision or renewal of any old one is made in writing, preferably on some standard form such as the *form design and approval request* shown in Fig. 1. Each request is accompanied by—
>> Any information (in addition to that called for by the request form) needed to show content, purpose, and use of the proposed form
>> A sketch of the proposed form

Registration and review
> Receipt of each request is entered in the *forms control log* (Fig. 2, page 409)
> If the request is for revision or renewal of an existing form, the numerical file is checked to see if recommendations have been received for changes in the form
> Numerical and functional files (together with any available file of other-company or commercial samples) are checked for—

FORM BSC -1000 June, 1970 BEST SELLING COMPANY FORM DESIGN AND APPROVAL REQUEST	THIS BOX FOR USE OF FORMS CONTROL UNIT APPROVED FORM TITLE

	FUNCTIONAL FILE CODE	FORM NO.	DATE OF FORM
FROM:		DATE	

TO: Forms Control Unit: Office Methods Division

PROPOSED FORM TITLE	PROPOSED FORM NO.	OLD FORM NO.

EXPLAIN BRIEFLY THE PURPOSE AND NEED FOR FORM. *(Attach two copies of proposed new or revised procedures with which form will be used.)*

WHAT PUBLISHED AUTHORITY DIRECTS USE OF FORM. | WILL INSTRUCTIONS FOR USE OF FORM BE ISSUED.
NO ☐   YES ☐   *(If "yes" attach two copies of instructions.)*

LIST BY FORM NUMBER ANY FORMS SUPERSEDED, REVISED, OR ELIMINATED BY THIS FORM. *(Attach two copies of each.)*

NAME OTHER UNITS OF THE COMPANY CONCERNED WITH SUBJECT MATTER OF FORM AND NOTE CONCURRENCES OBTAINED.

LIST BY FORM NUMBER ALL FORMS TO OR FROM WHICH INFORMATION WILL BE TRANSCRIBED TO OR FROM THIS FORM.

NUMBER OF COPIES PREPARED AT ONE WRITING	ENTRIES WILL BE MADE BY

ENTRIES WILL BE MADE BY ☐ PENCIL   ☐ INK   ☐ TYPEWRITER   ☐ OTHER *(Specify)*

COPY	ROUTING TO	USE
1		
2		
3		
4		
5		
6		
7		
8		
9		
10		

HANDLING OF FORM WILL BE ☐ LIGHT   ☐ MEDIUM   ☐ SEVERE

TO BE FILED IN: FOLDER   RING BINDER   OTHER
☐ *(Press type fastener in top center margin.)* ☐ *(Three holes in left margin.)* ☐ *(Specify)*

RETENTION PERIOD OF RECORD OR FILE COPIES
|YEARS| ACTIVE FILES |YEARS| INACTIVE FILES |YEARS| AFTER WHICH FORM MAY BE DESTROYED

SIZE OF FORM		PAPER		
HORIZONTAL	VERTICAL	TYPE	WEIGHT	COLOR
INCHES	INCHES			

QUANTITY OF FORMS REQUESTED						QUANTITY ON HAND *(Outside of stockroom)*		
INITIAL DISTRIBUTION	NOT OVER 6 MONTHS STOCK	ESTIMATED 1 MO. SUPPLY	TOTAL REQUESTED	BASIS	QUANTITY	NO. OF MONTHS SUPPLY	METHOD OF DISPOSAL	
				SHEETS SETS ☐ ☐			☐ DESTROY ☐ EXHAUST ☐ USE UNTIL REVISED FORM IS AVAILABLE	

REMARKS:

NOTE: 1. For initial distribution to offices outside of Home Office furnish shipping addresses and quantities to each. 2. Attach a sketch of the proposed form to this request, or the old form with revisions indicated. Furnish detailed specifications for location, type, size, style, color, etc. of paper, ink, binding, stitching, padding, punching, perforation, preprint numbers, overprinting, machine registration and spacing, etc.

REQUESTING OFFICER'S SIGNATURE	DATE	FORMS CONTROL APPROVAL BY	DATE

Fig. I.

FORM BSC 1001 NOV.1970			FORMS CONTROL LOG (Requests for New, Revised and Reprint Forms)							DIVISION *Service*	PAGE *1*
DATE RECEIVED *1971*	REQUESTING OFFICE	FORM TITLE AND NUMBER	ASSIGNED FOR REVIEW TO	TYPE OF FORM			ACTION TAKEN			FORM NUMBER ASSIGNED	
				NEW	REV.	RE-PRINT	REJECTED	APPROVED AS SUBMITTED	APPROVED WITH REVISION		
1/2	*Personnel office*	*Interview blank No. 614*	*Smith*		✓				2/12	*OS-202*	
1/2	*File room*	*Cross index sheet*	*Smith*	✓				1/4		*OSA-101*	
1/3	*Service section*	*Request to install telephone No.207*	*Brown*			✓		1/5			
1/8	*Duplicating*	*Requisition*	*Smith*	✓							

Fig. 2.

Any existing form that may serve the purpose of the requested form
Any related forms to be displaced, revised, or consolidated

Analysis

Consultation is held with units which would use the form or be affected by it as to handling, retention requirements, and content

Work involved in using the form is analyzed to determine the need for further study of procedures or methods; a checklist (Fig. 3) is one method of assuring that all the problems have been considered

Determination is made of the need for issuance or revision of procedural instructions to accompany the form

Development

Those responsible for records and files are consulted for advice on questions of form size, paper weight, and quality

Standards of design, paper stock, and reproduction method are checked and any necessary design changes made

Preliminary copies may be reproduced for clearance or pretesting

Clearance

To assure compliance with reporting standards and to see that concurrence is obtained from any other office or department that may be concerned, clearance is carried out as appropriate with units concerned with the use and the policy or procedural effects of the form

After final approval, the form is prepared for reproduction or printing

Issuance procedure

A number is assigned the form, along with issuance and approval dates, and entered in the form number register

The quantity and delivery specifications are checked against the estimated rate of use

The distribution pattern is checked

Specifications for printing or reproduction are made out

CHECK LIST

For_____ Date _____
          (Name)

Address_____

Person Interviewed _____ Position _____

Using Department _____ Manager _____

         Prepared By_____

Sales Dept.	Invoices Credit Memo Orders Acknowledgements	Shipping Dept.	Bills of Lading Express Receipts Delivery Receipts Packing Slips Shipping Notices	Administrative	Interoffice Memo Check Vouchers Tabulating Forms Teletype Forms Addressograph Forms Statements
Purch. Dept.	Inquiry for Price Purchase Orders Receiving Records	Production Dept.	Manufacturing Order Requisitions Stock Records		Ledger Sheets Loose Leaf Equip. Visible Records

1. No. and Name of form covered in this survey_____

2. How many transactions or what quantity of this form is used per day_____ Month_____ Year_____

3. How is form now written: Hand Typewriter Billing Machine Tabulator Teletype Addressograph

4. Name of machine_____ Spacing Vertical_____ Feed Front Pull Out _____

                            Horizontal_____ Back Feed_____

                                                Front Feed_____

5. Number of parts in form now used _____ Average number lines per set _____

6. Number of parts needed_____

7. Is form completed at one writing_____ If not, when, and by whom _____

8. How is form filed: Numerically, Alphabetically, Post Binder, Vertical File_____

9. Can this form be combined with any other form _____

10. Are shipments made complete_____What is percentage back-ordered_____

11. Is composition arranged for minimum of typing lines_____

12. Are most important items prominently placed_____

13. Is the information shown in comparable sequence with preceding and/or succeeding form_____

14. Is all recurring information PRINTED, leaving only variables to be filled in_____

15. Is colored paper used to facilitate distribution _____

16. Does form have Code No_____

17. Can form be re-designed for combination with other forms or for economy_____

18. How many persons required in writing this form _____ Do they have other duties_____

19. Is order writing and invoicing done in same Dept._____By same persons_____

20. Can items be extended before billing_____

21. Is work evenly distributed throughout day_____Or come in peak loads_____

22. Can any copies be eliminated _____Or used for more than one purpose_____

23. Have we checked with actual user of form for suggestions_____

24. Have we obtained samples of the form now in use_____

Fig. 3.

Final recording procedure

After reproduction, stocking, and distribution, the form is included in the company forms catalogue.

Record is made in the functional and numerical files

The minimum stock level (reorder point) is established

When the forms control staff receives notification from the stock-control point that the minimum stock level has been reached and reorder is necessary (see Fig. 4), a number of simple steps should be carried out.

The numerical file should be checked to see if any suggestions for revision have been received

Determination should be made on whether any changes are pending in procedure, program, or organization, which might affect the form

If revisions are required, appropriate steps, among those outlined above, should be taken before an order to replenish stock is approved

Selecting necessary tools. In addition to the major equipment—the forms classification, standards, identification plan, and control procedure—a few essential working tools are to be selected before regular processing begins. These tools are certain forms and records designed to simplify performance of the steps in the control process.

Two general classes of forms are used in carrying out the forms control program: (1) those which flow to or from the forms control staff, either to request action or to report facts relating to the program; and (2) those used only by the forms control staff, either as work sheets or as continuing control and progress records.

In the first category are such forms as the Form Design and Approval Request, Fig. 1, and Forms Minimum Stock Level Notice, Fig. 4. The request form is initiated by form-using units when they want a new form developed or an old one revised. The stock-level notice is initiated by the stockroom or supply unit when the supply of any form reaches a predesignated level. Like the request form, the stock-level notice is a signal for review and action by the forms control staff, so that any appropriate design or procedural changes can be made before additional forms are printed. This is further discussed on page 415.

In the second category are such work sheets as the Forms Analysis Chart of Recurring Data, illustrated in Fig. 5, a form to simplify the cross comparison and simple item analysis of related forms; and the Form Design Layout Sheet, Fig. 6, a form to simplify the spacing and sketching of form layouts. Then, as a separate group in this category, there are the internal records for control purposes. Aside from the files, these include such records as the Forms Control Log, Fig. 2; and (not illustrated here) a form-number register and a forms catalogue.

The Forms Control Log (Fig. 2) is a chronological record of incoming and

FORM NO. BSC-1235
   REV. 3-70   BEST SELLING COMPANY
DEPARTMENT OF ABC   FORMS MINIMUM STOCK LEVEL NOTICE

1 FROM Forms Stockroom   Date

       TO   Forms Control Unit.   Office Methods Division

        THE MINIMUM STOCK LEVEL HAS BEEN REACHED ON THE FOLLOWING FORM.

                                            SUPERVISOR OF STOCKROOM

FORM NO.	FORM TITLE			
QUANTITY ON HAND	QUANTITY OF UNFILLED ORDERS	NO. OF DAYS SUPPLY WILL LAST	QUANTITY LAST ORDERED	DATE LAST ORDER DELIVERED

2 FROM Forms Control Unit.   Office Methods Division   Date

       TO

        BASED UPON THE ABOVE INFORMATION FURNISHED BY THE FORMS STOCKROOM, ACTION MUST BE
TAKEN TO REPLENISH THE SUPPLY. IN ORDER THAT REPRODUCTION OR PROCUREMENT CAN BE INITI-
ATED, COMPLETE AND RETURN THIS NOTICE NOT LATER THAN_____19___.
COMMENT:-

                                            FORMS CONTROL UNIT

3 FROM   Date

       TO   Forms Control Unit.   Office Methods Division

ACTION RECOMMENDED:

   1.   THE FORM IS TO BE CONTINUED IN USE.
        [ ] a. REPRINT WITHOUT CHANGE.   REPRINT QUANTITY
        [ ] b. TEMPORARY REPRINT PENDING REVISION.

   2.   THE FORM SHOULD NOT BE REPRINTED.
        [ ] a. PRESENT STOCK MAY BE ISSUED UNTIL EXHAUSTED.
        [ ] b. PRESENT STOCK MAY BE ISSUED ONLY UNTIL REVISION IS AVAILABLE.
        [ ] c. DRAFT OF REVISION AND "FORM DESIGN AND APPROVAL REQUEST"
                (Form No. BSC 1000) ATTACHED.
        [ ] d. REVISION TO BE SUBMITTED LATER.

   3.   THE FORM IS OBSOLETE. DISCONTINUE ALL DISTRIBUTION.
        [ ] a. SUPERSEDED BY FORM NO._____.
        [ ] b. CONSOLIDATED WITH FORM NO._____.
        [ ] c. NOT SUPERSEDED BY ANY OTHER FORM.

REMARKS:

        ACTION RECOMMENDED BY   DATE   PHONE

Fig. 4.

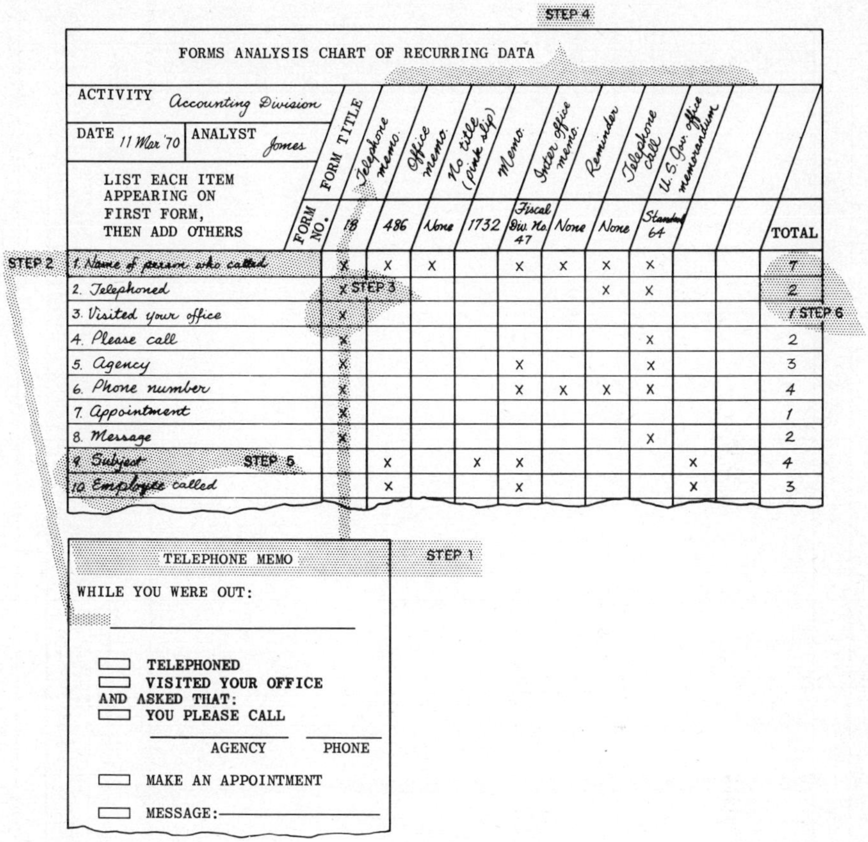

STEP 4

	FORM TITLE	Telephone memo	Office memo	No title (pink slip)	Memo	Inter office memo	Reminder	Telephone call	U.S. Gov office memorandum		TOTAL
FORMS ANALYSIS CHART OF RECURRING DATA											
ACTIVITY *Accounting Division*											
DATE *11 Mar '70* ANALYST *Jones*											
LIST EACH ITEM APPEARING ON FIRST FORM, THEN ADD OTHERS	FORM NO.	18	486	None	1732	Fiscal Div No 47	None	None	Standard 64		TOTAL
1. Name of person who called		X	X	X		X	X	X	X		7
2. Telephoned		X					X	X			2
3. Visited your office		X									1
4. Please call		X						X			2
5. Agency		X				X		X			3
6. Phone number		X				X	X	X	X		4
7. Appointment		X									1
8. Message		X						X			2
9. Subject			X		X	X			X		4
10. Employee called			X			X			X		3

STEP 2 — STEP 3 — STEP 5 — STEP 6

TELEPHONE MEMO	STEP 1
WHILE YOU WERE OUT:	

_____

☐ TELEPHONED
☐ VISITED YOUR OFFICE
AND ASKED THAT:
☐ YOU PLEASE CALL

_____
AGENCY   PHONE

☐ MAKE AN APPOINTMENT
☐ MESSAGE:—————————

Fig. 5.

outgoing forms, their assignment for analysis, and the action taken on them. The log serves as a basis for compiling a monthly report of work load and progress, and shows the status of any form under consideration. Date-stamping the written request from the initiating office serves to identify the form in question so that reference can be made readily to the corresponding entry in the log.

When the volume of forms to be controlled is large, greater flexibility and easier reference may be achieved by maintaining a log on individual vertical or visible file cards. This method has the advantage of permitting records of completed forms to be pulled, with only records of forms being worked upon retained, and may be of assistance in the development of a forms catalogue.

The Form Number Register is a record of form titles and numbers assigned. A simple notebook or ledger will serve the purpose. The form title, date, and

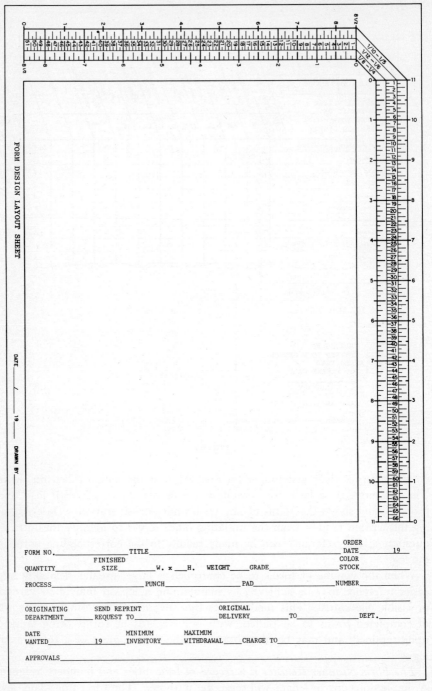

Fig. 6.

name of the initiating office are entered opposite the assigned form numbers as forms are approved.   The number register and catalogue can be consolidated when straight numerical sequence of form number assignment is followed.

A *Forms Catalogue* completes the list of forms control tools.   This usually is of loose-leaf construction.   Supplied to the operating units for reference in planning and requisitioning forms, such catalogues have been found to reduce duplication and the use of nonstandard forms.   This catalogue can be one of several types: numerical and alphabetical by form-title listing; or a reduced-size facsimile of each form, arranged numerically by form number; or a combination of these types.

4. Administering the program

With the structure up, "machinery" in place, and tools at hand, it takes administrative teamwork to make the forms control program pay the limit in operating dividends.

As has been already pointed out, a written procedure tailored to the needs of the individual company is a *must* in every instance.   To regard the procedure as a complete blueprint, however, would be a dangerous oversimplification.   The written procedure can be a blueprint only for the simpler parts of the process.   As such, it can help make bothersome details less bothersome, help clear the way for the more critical tasks, and in doing so, help promote the teamwork necessary to bring the right knowledge and analytical skills to bear upon form problems at the right times.   To expect more would be unrealistic.

In actual practice the necessary analytical processes tend to telescope into each other.   The degree to which they do so depends on the complexity of the specific problem and the experience of the person dealing with it.   Various aspects of a form—its design, its tie-in with work methods, the duplicating specifications it imposes, its distribution requirements—may all actually be in process of analysis at the same time, with standards being applied throughout the process.   These critical activities, therefore, are not discussed here in terms of any precise procedural sequence, though for convenience they are discussed separately.

Registering and reviewing forms.   Among the simpler yet usually quite rewarding stages of analysis is the review carried out in conjunction with the registration of each request for either the approval of a new form or the renewal or revision of an old one.   This stage, before intensive effort is made to refine the design of a form, brings to light possibilities of combination and elimination.

Cross comparison of forms.   In the initial review a critical cross comparison, or simple item analysis, of related forms may be made.   The principal tools for the purpose are a questioning attitude and a chart, such as the forms-analysis chart of recurring data already shown.   Because it spreads out on a single sheet in simple cross classification the individual items of information sought on any two or more forms, it aids in quickly visualizing possible deletions and combinations.

Thus, in Fig. 5 it appears that three of the eight forms listed—the telephone memo, the reminder, and the telephone-call form—might well be consolidated. More detailed analysis may be necessary, however, before a final determination is made on such possibilities—particularly in dealing with complex forms.

Purge of obsolete forms. Not only should the work of eliminating or combining some activity forms make others obsolete and subject to disposal, but stock inventory reports, routed to the forms control staff and reviewed in connection with the registration and cross comparison of active requests, should provide a fertile source of information on slow-moving, obsolete, or inactive forms.

It is advisable, in addition, to set up a system whereby the using units regularly submit information concerning forms which they have ceased using, so that prompt action may be taken to discontinue stocking them. Conversely the forms control staff should notify using units when forms are officially declared obsolete, and all such changes should be reflected immediately in the forms catalogue and in any procedural manuals or other instructions affected.

This process of review and comparison should not only reduce the number of forms by logical consolidations but should quickly identify those which lapse into disuse as a result of policy or operating changes.

Analyzing forms and their functions. If the major values of forms control are to be realized, however, it is important that forms be approached from a viewpoint broader than the mere analysis of recurring or duplicate data. If a form guides or regulates the way work flows through an office, or between offices, it is important to ask how well the form is designed to give this guidance. If economical work methods are to be followed in filling in or using the form at the various way points in its journeys, it is important that its construction make such economical work methods possible, and that it be as nearly self-explanatory as possible.

In order for design to contribute to efficiency of method, forms must be subject to functional analysis. They must be examined in relation to the specific working purposes they serve (or fail to serve) and in relation to the specific working methods by which those purposes are sought. Once this process has carried the analysis properly into the area of methods and procedures, opportunities inevitably appear for procedural study and improvement beyond the point of forms usage itself.

Such analysis requires a thorough knowledge of the flow of each form, the writing method, and types and sources of information either drawn from or added to the form as it moves from desk to desk. On the basis of such facts, the content, layout, and design can be adjusted so that they serve the form's purpose efficiently and economically. Forms with similar purposes can be related and the procedures to which they apply can themselves be standardized or simplified.   This analysis should be carried out with an attitude which asks—

Does the form help to get the job done promptly, at a minimum cost in man-hours and with a maximum of service, accuracy, and utility in terms of the completed record or transaction?

In asking and getting answers to such questions, the office-methods engineer can look at a form profitably from four viewpoints: (1) the writing method, (2) the procedure, (3) the design, and (4) the copy.

Certainly these are not mutually exclusive.   The conditions under which a form must be used may arbitrarily govern the writing method or means of fill-in.   The writing method in turn may govern many aspects of procedure and design.   Thus, the fill-in process is itself a part of procedure (either within the company or outside), and the first three viewpoints mentioned—writing method, procedure, and design—are merely different approaches to the same problem.   The value of each is in double-checking the others.

Writing method (fill-in).   The end use, the quantity used, the number of copies filled in at once, the number and complexity of required entries, the work steps involved, as well as the working conditions under which the form is used, are primary considerations in evaluating writing method.

Such tasks as entering data, copying, computing, or tabulating may be handled by different persons or may be combined in a single job.   The decision to separate or combine tasks frequently depends upon the writing methods available.

If handwriting is selected, special considerations may apply.   Should cut or loose forms, padded forms, unit sets with interleaved carbon, or continuous autographic-register forms be adopted to facilitate the handwriting method?

Likewise, if machine-writing is selected, questions must be answered concerning size, mechanical specifications, and limitations of the specific machines involved.   Specified grades and weights of paper may be required.   Arbitrary spacing may be imposed.

All such questions must be settled before final determinations on either procedure or design can be made.

Procedures.   In addition to the procedural aspects of making entries on a form are all the activities leading up to and growing out of the act of making entries.   Usually these are less routinized and hence even more in the need of simplification than are the immediate tasks of making out the form.   These are the "nine-tenths of the iceberg below the surface."   They are among the *operating implications* which staff people may tend to overlook in developing forms.

Among these additional procedural and work-load aspects are (1) the processes of tallying, searching, assorting, assembling, and computing which may be necessary before required data can be entered on the form; (2) the

making and routing of extra copies; (3) the excerpting or transcribing of selected data from the completed form for any collateral records involved; and
(4) the ultimate review, interpretation, and end action without which the
form and all the activity generated by it would be meaningless.

Process charts can be used for following forms in their procedural movements and for analyzing the activity engendered at their various stopping
points, just as they can be used to trace and analyze the movement of workers,
materials, and components in a manufacturing process. Many types of
charts are in use. Selected types, including a forms-distribution chart, are
illustrated in Fig. 7. It is not the purpose here to introduce new tools for the
procedural analysis that should accompany forms control, but rather to stress the
more apt and economical application of existing tools as part of the hand-in-
glove relationship of forms control to total office-methods activity.

Presupposing the use of existing office-methods tools consistent with the
nature and importance of the procedural problems met, the approach is the
same whether the work is handled by personnel who specialize in forms work
or turned over to other office-methods staff.

Answers to such questions as these must be found:

What work is done, and *why*? Is all of it necessary? Does each step serve
a recognized purpose and produce a desired result?

Who performs each step, and *why*? Organizationally and occupationally,
are these the appropriate persons? Can tasks be rearranged, simplified,
or combined for more efficient staff assignments?

Where is the work performed, and *why* there? Can it be combined with
similar work at another point to produce a greater volume and a more
stable work load?

When is the work done, and *why* then? Why are the steps done in that
particular order? Can peak loads be leveled off by better scheduling, to
permit better staffing, more effective control, better quality, and higher
average production?

How is the work done, and *why* that way? Can the method be improved?
How about layout, setup, motion sequence, mechanical aids?

By finding answers to these questions, the office methods staff is able to determine whether the form helps in the performance of a necessary function of
the company. It is able to see more clearly how unnecessary copies of forms
can be eliminated; how different forms can be combined so that they can be
written in one operation; how the amount of information required—and hence
the work of obtaining it—can be curtailed.

By identifying or arranging common work steps in different procedures
and then combining them, it is often possible to assure a more even work flow
and to level off peaks and valleys in work load.

Design. The design of a form should evolve primarily from the methods and
procedures of its use. To that extent design and layout considerations are

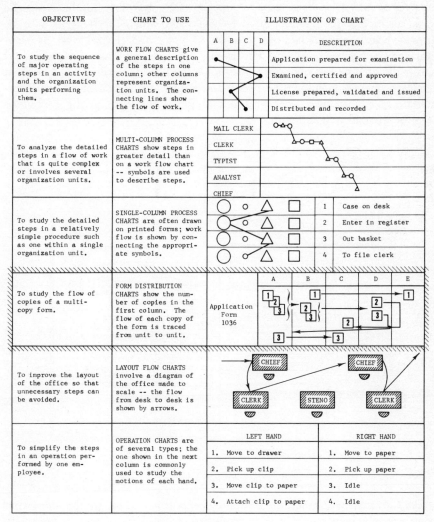

OBJECTIVE	CHART TO USE	ILLUSTRATION OF CHART

Fig. 7.

products of procedural and writing-method analysis, or in fact, a continuation of such analysis.

Similarly, copy determinations—the wording used for item headings and for explanatory and instructional notes embodied in the form—should be made in the light of the uses and users of the form.

It is predominantly in the design development, proceeding from the functional design analysis, that standards are applied. In terms of function, the following questions may help to evaluate the effectiveness of design:

Is the sequence of items easy to follow?   Does the order of items on the form correspond to that of source records from which information is to be drawn?   Are the items laid out to make reference and clerical work as accurate and as fast as possible?   Hit-or-miss arrangement invites mistakes and lowers the quality and quantity of clerical output in transcribing or recording. Logical sequence, including the planned grouping and boxing of related information, speeds up such work and also simplifies reference to the completed form by the end user.   See Fig. 8.

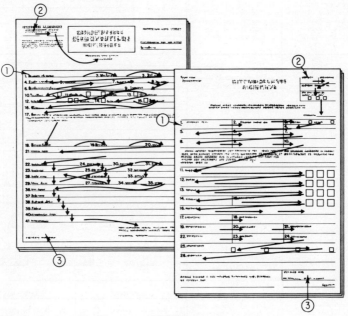

Fig. 8.

Does arrangement make for continuous execution?   Has the line-flow concept been observed (will hand or typewriter proceed from item to item with a minimum of travel)?   By whom, and in what order, will data be entered? If by different persons, will they each have to hop, skip, and jump all over the form, or are the items grouped as nearly as possible to avoid searching, backtracking, and eyestrain?

Does the design reduce the amount of writing to a minimum?   Writing, either by hand or by machine, takes time.   Is maximum use made of such devices as check boxes and preprinted alternatives?

Does the design take advantage of writing-machine characteristics?   Is the form designed for use in types of machines known to be available where the form is to be used?   Would a slight change make it equally usable in a wider range of equipment? Do vertical and lateral spacing on the form match spacing of the machine? Is the bottom margin ample to permit use in the machine without slipping?

Is the design consistent with the files or binders to be used? Will identifying data be readily visible in the file? Are adequate margins allowed for binding?

Does the design simplify identification, distribution, and control? Will titles, numbers, or colors facilitate routing, dispatching, handling, and checking? Will such devices assist in locating misplaced or delayed forms in the work process? Will arrows, pointers, fists, leaders, or other visual guides draw attention to points of special importance? Or are such devices misused or overused, serving only to clutter up the form and distract the user?

Is space used economically? Are unneeded borders eliminated to allow continuation of writing into margins? Has an analysis of completed forms been made over a period of time to verify space requirements for individual items? Have unneeded sections been eliminated in favor of either a smaller form or more space at those points where actually needed? Is there a simple and logical provision for the overflow or continuation of information to a designated space if regular spaces prove inadequate in certain instances?

Does layout achieve proper visual effect? Will all copy be legible under conditions of use? Are logical relationships among subject headings borne out by correspondingly related type sizes and positions? Has recognition been given to visual habit patterns in determining sequence and position of items? Have pointers, guide lines, leaders, and type variations been judiciously used to facilitate eye movement?

Copy. Even if the use of a form must be based on detailed instructions in a separate sheet or procedural manual, the form itself should be made as nearly self-explanatory as possible without overburdening it with detail. This need is met partly by the layout and arrangement of elements on the form, as already mentioned, but chiefly by the literal content of the copy itself.

"Copy" placed on the form to aid the user is of importance increasing with the complexity of the form. Even in very simple forms, however, wording can be a stumbling block. In fact, the time consumed in filling out forms—especially forms not used repetitiously—may be multiplied over and over by omissions, complexities, and ambiguities of wording. When hundreds of thousands of persons use a form, even a few lost minutes by each can total weeks and months of lost time—not to mention losses in worker morale and public good will.

Applying form standards and getting results. It has been pointed out that standards for the design and reproduction of forms should be developed before any attempt is made to put a forms control program into operation. Once developed and circulated among all form-using units, the standards should find continuing use within those units as the need arises for new forms or the revision of old ones and as the first rough sketches take shape preparatory to any formal request to the forms control staff. In the forms control unit, the standards are applied throughout review and analysis, but especially in the final stages as design and copy are made ready for duplicating or printing.

Specific needs of an operation or procedure, such as the use of a window envelope, will frequently dictate many aspects of design. Certainly the relationship of form to procedure should have been agreed upon by the forms control staff and the using units, and a list of all required items determined, before any final application of standards is attempted.

The sketching out of completed forms is simplified by the use of design guide sheets (Fig. 6). There are many types of design guide sheets, generally preprinted so that they can be photographically reduced or enlarged to various standard form sizes. The sheets are calibrated in sixths and tenths of an inch, vertically and horizontally, so that spaces on the form can be ruled off quickly and with assurance that they will conform to standard typewriter line and letter spacing. Forms to be used for tabulating, bookkeeping, or special equipment should be designed on special guide sheets obtainable from manufacturers' representatives.

Controlling storage and distribution. Sound storage and distribution practices applicable to forms will assure that—

Operating units are supplied with forms when, where, and in the amounts necessary

Storage space is conserved (1) by limiting the supply of forms on hand to feasible time-period requirements; and (2) by disposing promptly of obsolete forms

Production costs are minimized by ordering in economical quantities

Coordinated approach. Storage and distribution of forms normally are the job of an office services, publication and distribution, or similar service unit. The primary responsibility for formulating the storage and distribution pattern and the stocking and reordering procedure, however, may well be centered in the forms control program. In any event, that work, like most other work in the development and control of forms, requires close coordination among the units concerned.

In all cases, the general pattern of storage and distribution must be considered along with design and reproduction specifications, for the factors are largely the same.

Taking inventory of existing forms and reducing working stocks within individual using units are the first steps in bringing form supplies under control. A directive instructing operating units to return to a central location all forms in excess of actual needs for a given period should clean out desks and bring supplies into the open. Except for current working requirements, the supply of forms should always be stocked at central locations in order that inventories can be kept at a reasonable operating minimum. Initial quantities of new forms can be estimated in the usual way, by the initiating units, and reviewed by the forms control staff. After this initial supply has been determined, an account of actual usage should be maintained by the stockroom, along with current inventory records of all other forms. Such inventory and rate-of-use information then provides the basis for establishing realistic minimum stock levels, distribution patterns, and reorder procedures.

Determining quantities to stock. The factors to be considered in deciding how many of any given form to order and store at any one time are perhaps obvious. It is essential, however, that none of the more important factors be overlooked. Included among them are—

Volume and rate of use
Place of use
Physical characteristics (size, shape, weight)
Method of reproduction or printing
Place of reproduction or printing
Economical production quantity
Economical shipping quantity
Probable deterioration
Possible obsolescence
Availability and cost of storage space

The chief problem is to take advantage of the low unit cost of volume production while at the same time avoiding undue use of storage space and undue risk of loss through obsolescence or deterioration. Forms are seldom as "permanent" as they are expected to be. Changes in activities or methods, requiring changes in forms, cannot be anticipated long in advance. The obsolescence of forms in storage and in distribution pipe lines often wipe out savings expected from volume purchases.

Establishing minimum stock levels. Aside from determining economical quantities for ordering or reordering purposes is the problem of assuring that reorders are placed at the right time to prevent any lapse in supply to using units. This is the problem of determining the "minimum stock level" for each form—the inventory balance which denotes the reorder point. Factors entering into such determinations include—

Volume of use
Rate of use
Place of use
Time of use (one-time, periodic, or continuous)
Time required for reproduction or printing and delivery

The time required for reproduction or printing is particularly important and quite likely to be underestimated if controls are lax. This time will differ according to the method of reproduction, place of reproduction, and complexity of specifications. Printed forms ordinarily require more time than forms produced by office duplicator. Forms ordered from another location usually require more time than those produced locally. Multipage, padded, or specialty forms normally require more time than single-sheet forms (cut forms). Forms that call for an extra color of ink or for extra bindery operations require more time than those that do not.

Alternative reproduction processes, as well as decentralized production facilities, should be considered when appropriate, as means of reducing delay in stock replenishment and permitting the establishment of stock and reorder points at levels which are reasonably low but still safe.

As soon as issuances from stock bring the supply down to the designated reorder point for any form, the stockroom should notify the forms control staff (see forms minimum stock level notice, Fig. 3) so that any possibility of revising or discontinuing the form can be considered and a reorder placed if appropriate.

Establishing distribution pattern and procedures. In the local distribution of forms, it is common for the using units to requisition initial quantities from the stockroom. Alternatives are for either the stockroom or the reproduction plant to make the initial distribution on advice of the forms control staff. The choice of the procedure to be followed will depend on what operating units are concerned with the form, their locations, and their individual requirements, as well as the distribution facilities available to the duplicating plant or stockroom. After the initial working supply is distributed, subsequent distribution is by requisition from the using units to the stockroom.

On those forms which have been standardized for company-wide use, a company headquarters can maintain bulk stock of forms and fill field-office requisitions on a monthly, quarterly, or semiannual basis. (In the case of forms peculiar to such an office, or of forms used in small quantities, it may be advisable to ship in annual quantities.)

On the other hand, if quantities used in the field are large, it may often be more economical to have forms produced with distribution handled on a decentralized basis, rather than pay shipping charges from headquarters. This practice bears consideration particularly if field or local changes must be made in forms or if volume use of certain forms is concentrated in a few areas remote from the headquarters office. In any event, the cost of shipping should be added to the cost of centralized production before comparing the total cost with that for decentralized production. The reproduction or printing method desired and the availability of facilities for such reproduction in the field, as well as the availability and relative cost of storage space in the field, are not to be overlooked either.

Companies using many forms often follow a combination of these two patterns. Some customarily have all printed forms centrally produced and distributed, while duplicator-processed forms may or may not be, depending upon their complexity of design, the volume and extent of their use, and other factors.

Before coming to a decision on such questions, however, all possibilities should be reviewed. For example, if facilities for the desired reproduction or printing process are economically available in the field, but the complexity of design or the composition costs make it undesirable to decentralize the total production job for certain forms, it is possible to retain the advantage of centralized composition and at the same time the shipping advantage of decentralized press work and distribution by having printing plates or mats, offset plates, or negatives, or preprinted or die-cut master stencils prepared at a central point and sent to field locations to be reproduced or printed locally.

Still a third pattern may be advisable in certain instances. A form which may have to be widely used, but only for a brief period, may be advantageously printed at a central point and distributed directly to all using offices.

Whatever distribution pattern is adopted, however, the procedure should be such as to assure accountability in terms of such considerations as have been outlined here. If field production, storage, and distribution are involved, the procedure for such accountability must necessarily provide for regular reporting of form supplies and usage to the central control unit, and for occasional redistribution and balancing of stocks. In fact, the more decentralized the storage and distribution activity, the stronger the central reporting system should be.

Evaluating the program. A plan for evaluating results of the forms control program should be developed at the time the program is begun. Probable benefits should be identified and a procedure established for estimating, recording, and reporting such results.

Among the many units of measurement which may be used for the purpose are money, man-hours, and storage space.

Among the areas susceptible of such measurement and reporting are—

Improvements in procedures which reduce backlogs, shorten total processing time, or reduce spoilage

Improvements in writing methods that save time in typing or writing, clerical processing, tabulating, filing, and finding (particularly where such tasks are done in great volume)

Improvements in design that mean savings in paper, printing, storage, and distribution costs

Many of the more valuable results will be intangible and amenable only to subjective appraisal. This fact alone, however, makes it all the more important that those results which can be measured should be and that reports of such measurement be reviewed regularly by management in estimating the total dividends, spotting the inadequacies, and charting the future course of the forms control program.

Figure 9 shows a simple form as an example of the type of information which can be used for the monthly reporting of forms control progress.

Keeping perspective.   There is no escaping the fact that forms are necessary, often in large numbers.   Without them, paper work would be many times its present volume.   Yet there are forms that are not necessary, and these too may exist in large numbers.   *They should be eliminated.*

BSC FORM NO.1234 (4-70) DEPARTMENT OF ABC OFFICE METHODS DIVISION	BEST SELLING COMPANY FORMS CONTROL PROGRAM _____ PROGRESS REPORT (MONTH)		
1.*FORMS SUBJECT TO FORMS CONTROL PROGRAM		LAST MONTH	THIS MONTH
2. FORMS REVIEWED (ACTION COMPLETED)		LAST MONTH	THIS MONTH
3. ANALYSIS OF WORK LOAD: A. NUMBER OF FORMS ON HAND PENDING REVIEW		START OF MONTH	END OF MONTH
B. ACTION TAKEN ON REQUESTS	REJECTED	APPROVED WITH REVISIONS	APPROVED AS SUBMITTED
C. FORMS CONSOLIDATED		NUMBER OF OLD FORMS	RESULTING NEW FORMS
D. FORMS ELIMINATED		BY CONSOLIDATION	NOT REPLACED
E. FORMS STANDARDIZED		AT TIME OF REPRINT	BY SURVEY,REQUEST,ETC.
4. NUMBER OF MANHOURS EXPENDED			MANHOURS
* INDICATE BELOW OFFICES OR REGIONS UNDER THE FORMS CONTROL PROGRAM.			
5. REMARKS: (REPORT SAVINGS EFFECTED IN PRODUCTION OR DISTRIBUTION COST, MANHOURS, ETC.)			

CHIEF OF FORMS CONTROL SECTION

Fig. 9.

Among those that are necessary, many are unnecessarily expensive, in terms of either their production cost or their procedural use—if not both.   In addition, many forms may be found expensive from the using standpoint because of attempted economies in the printing.   *These should be "procedurized," simplified, and standardized.*

Savings to be realized by these means are considerable indeed.   In general, however, forms are a reflection of the work methods, operating procedures, and management know-how which give rise to their use.   If a company's forms constitute a simple, orderly plan showing clear and related purposes, there is reason to believe that its personnel—knowing what they are doing and why—may be giving fairly efficient service.   If, on the other hand, its forms constitute an unintelligible tangle of red tape, it is pretty safe to assume that its methods and procedures—its service or relationships to the public—are in much the same shape.

Therefore, great as may be the savings from eliminating unnecessary forms and getting all necessary ones properly related to existing procedures, *forms control offers a still greater value as a means of detecting the need to treat the procedures themselves.*

Here, then, are the orientation and the challenge to which it is hoped this material has held in outlining some of the principal considerations necessary to the establishment of a forms control program.

There are limitations, to be sure. The ideal of standardizing all forms and bringing them all under strict production and distribution controls, to avoid the waste, confusion, and inefficiency that are bound to attend uncontrolled practices, is a worthy goal. Yet, if well grounded, the staff having reponsibility for bringing such controls into practical application will not, in its zeal, forget that forms control, like any other staff function, exists only to serve major operating objectives. *It is no end in itself.*

There are times when forms that are essential to major operating obligations must be developed, produced, and widely distributed almost overnight. The intrinsic value of the forms in question—though representing many dollars—may be insignificant compared to the overriding values of the operating objectives at stake. In such a contingency the risk of not having enough forms may so far outweigh the calculated risk of having too many that ordinary standards of production, storage, and distribution may have to go by the board. Any unused forms resulting may be a cheap premium for the operating insurance bought.

On the other hand, without the effective balancing of a strong forms control program, pressures to justify exceptions on such grounds usually get out of hand. Certainly, therefore, complete consideration to all aspects (function, design, identification, production, storage, and distribution) and all their procedural and public relations implications must be given on the basis of regularized review and analysis, with a minimum of exceptions.

With vigorous topside support, clear placement of responsibility for each step in a well-defined procedure, and close coordination to utilize the scattered talents that must be drawn upon, the centralized review and analysis of company forms will pay off in double dividends.

5. Common standards for forms design

As an aid to companies in developing their own standards for the physical aspects of forms, the following pages contain standards that have been selected from those now followed by many industrial activities. The list covers 17 characteristics found adaptable to standardization. A large company may wish to develop more explicit criteria in the light of its own circumstances and to expand the number of different items covered as it gets under way, so that specialized classes of forms—form-type form letters, accounting forms, and others—may have specific criteria for their design.

Such standards should be applied by the initiating unit when drawing a rough sketch of the form to be submitted with the forms requisition, and by the forms control staff in reviewing the request and sketch or in making up a new design, as well as in making any necessary adjustment of specifications before forwarding the requisition for duplicating or printing.

Cut form sizes
   Any size that can be cut from 34 by 44 inches without waste, particularly sizes 4¼ by 5½, 8½ by 11, 17 by 11, 17 by 22, 22 by 34
   Normal file-card sizes: 3 by 5, 4 by 6, 5 by 8
   Postcard size: 3¼ by 5½
   Considerations:
      Avoid crowded content
      Conform to dimensions of storage and filing facilities (i.e., legal size, letter size, etc.)
      Fit to standard office machines for fill-in (i.e., typewriter, bookkeeping machine, etc.)
      Fit to standard-size envelopes
Paper weight and grade
   Operating unit ordinarily should specify one of the following four:
      Mimeograph, 16- or 20-pound (basis 17 by 22) [1]
      Card, 180-pound (basis 25½ by 30½)
      Sulfite, 16-pound (basis 17 by 22)
      Bond (25 percent rag), 16-pound (basis 17 by 22)
   More precise specifications may be made by forms control office
   Variations permitted on special justification
   Selection should be based upon—
      Handling requirements
      Writing method
      Number of copies to be made at one writing
      Length of time the form will be retained
      Printing requirements (i.e., printing on two sides, by a given process, etc.)
      Filing and storage space requirements (affected by thickness of paper)
   The above considerations may be required to apply on each copy of multiple copy forms
Color of paper
   Specify color only when needed for emphasis or for more efficient filing, routing, or sorting
   Reduce the need for colored paper by use of sorting symbols, bold headings, heavy ruled lines, or other devices when possible
   Exceptions permissible for specific organization or operating requirements.
Color of ink

   [1] Dimensions refer to sizes on which weights are based; not necessarily to sizes stocked by the printer (see "Cut form sizes," above).

Specify other than black ink only when fully justified by volume and increased efficiency in use of the form and when the more economical possibilities of colored paper are inadequate

Two-color printing should be avoided except under extreme justification

Identification and heading

Heading may be centered across entire top of form, or centered in space to the left of any entry boxes placed in upper right.   (Upper right should be designed for file or other ready-reference entries if needed)

Within space decided upon, arrange generally as follows:

Form number and issuance or revision date—upper left corner

Company name and location—upper left (under form number) or top center (depending on its importance in use of form)

Form title—center of top (under company name and location, if that item is centered).   Use conspicuous type

Exception: Run identification across bottom of vertical-file card forms unless needed for file-reference purposes

Instructions

Well-designed forms require few instructions other than captions and item headings.   When required, instructions usually should be—

Set in two or more narrow columns rather than full-width lines

Listed as numbered items rather than in paragraph style

Placed as near items to which they apply as possible (unless length would detract from effective layout)

When instructions are segregated on form, they should be placed—

At top right or top center, if concise and applicable to the whole form

At bottom, if that will make possible more economical use of space

On reverse, if no space available on face

Address

If name and address are inserted prior to mailing, position of name and address should be suitable for window-envelope use

Forms requiring return should be properly identified as provided above

Forms intended for use in window envelopes must conform to postal regulations, which in general provide that nothing other than name and address, and possibly mailing symbol, shall appear in the window.   The form must fit the envelope to avoid shifting of the address.   Standard-size envelopes only should be used

Preprinted names or facsimile signatures

If form is to be stocked for continuing use, personal names or signatures of officials should be preprinted only on special justification, to avoid having large numbers of forms made obsolete by change of officials

Preprinting of titles only, and the use of rubber stamps or automatic signature inscribers, are alternatives to be considered.

Form arrangement

Align beginning of each writing space on form vertically for minimum number of tabular stops

If box design is used—

Serially number each box in its upper left-hand corner

Start caption in upper left-hand corner, to right of number, leaving fill-in space below caption

Draw box size to provide sufficient space for fill-in

Place essential information where it will not be obscured by stamps, punches, or staples, or be torn off with detachable stubs

Group related items

Include "to" and "from" spaces for any necessary routing

Provide for use of window envelopes, when appropriate, to save additional addressing

To the extent practicable, provide same sequence of items as on other forms from which or to which information is to be transferred

Arrange information for ease in tabulating or transferring to machine punch cards, if those are involved

Check boxes

Use check boxes when practicable

Place check boxes either before or after items, but all in the corresponding positions within any line series

Avoid columnar grouping of check boxes if possible, because of poor registration when carbon copies are required. Place check boxes before first column and after the second column when there are two adjacent columns of questions

Margins

Printing margin

Printed all-around borders usually should not be used, since they tend to increase production problems and costs

In any event an extra margin of $\frac{3}{8}$ inch, or not less than $\frac{3}{10}$ inch, from edge of paper should be allowed on all four sides for gripping requirements in printing and as a safety margin for cutting

No printing—neither border nor text—should be permitted in that space

Binding margin (printing permitted, but no fill-in items should be within these margins)

For press-type fastener, side or top, 1 inch

For ring binder, 1 inch

Fill-in margin

Top typewriting line, at least $1\frac{1}{3}$ inch from top of paper if possible

Bottom typewriting line, not less than $\frac{3}{4}$ inch from bottom

Hand fill-in permissible above or below these lines

Space requirements for fill-in

Typewritten

Ten characters to the horizontal inch, to accommodate both elite and pica typewriters

Three fill-in spaces to the vertical inch, each space being double typewriter space

Handwritten

One-third more space horizontally than for typewritten fill-in

Three spaces to the vertical inch, each space double that of typewriter space

Rulings

Use heavy 1½-point or parallel ½-point rulings as first and last horizontal lines, between major divisions, and across column headings

Use ¾-point rulings across bottom of column headings, and above a total or balance at the foot of a column

Use hairline rulings for regular lines and box lines when no emphasis required

Use ¾-point rulings for vertical subdivision of major sections or columns

Use leaders as needed to guide eye in tabular or semitabular items

Signature and approval date

Single handwritten signature usually goes at bottom right of last page.

Allow ½ inch (three single typewriter spaces) vertically and 3 inches horizontally

Two handwritten signatures normally go left and right at bottom of last page

Space below the ¾-inch bottom typewriter margin generally reserved for handwritten signatures and dates

Two-sided forms

Two-sided forms ordinarily should be printed head to foot (top of front to bottom of back), especially if top-punched for binder use

If punched in left margin for binder use, two-sided forms should be head-to-head

Three- or four-page forms (one sheet folded once) should be head to head throughout if open-side style, and head to foot if open-end (so that, when opened for use, head of third page follows foot of second page)

Head-to-foot open-end forms are preferable for machine fill-in

For multipage forms, separate sheets of proper page size should be used instead of larger sheets folded to page size, unless the larger sheets can be cut economically from standard paper sizes and run on standard printing or duplicating equipment

Prenumbering

Use prenumbered forms only if accounting or control is required for each form or document

Place number in extreme upper right corner

Punching

For standard press-type and three-hole ring binders:

Distance from edge of paper to center of hole should measure ⅜ inch

If two holes are punched, for press-type fastener, the distance between centers should be 2¾ inches

If three holes are punched, distance from center to center of adjacent holes should be 4¼ inches

Consult printer for slotted, square, or other unusual punching, if necessary

Common terms used in titling forms

In selecting a combination of words for the title of a form it is important to indicate clearly and briefly the subject to be dealt with by the form (e.g., "office materials") and the function or purpose of the form (e.g., "receipt"). One way to avoid misunderstanding is to rely on words known to have commonly accepted meanings among the group that will use the forms. Certain "function words" recur frequently in the titles of the more common types of administrative forms, and thus tend to become more or less standardized. Some of these are listed below, each with a brief notation on the purpose which a form would be expected to serve if its title included the word indicated. It will be observed that these notations are in no sense definitions; they merely show purpose or function in terms or forms usage.

Terms	*Purpose of form*
Acknowledgment	To make known the receipt of
Agreement	To offer and accept in writing
Application	To request something
Authorization	To permit an action
Checklist	To verify, or to remind of action or data to be considered
Claim	To demand as due
Contract	See "Agreement"
Estimate	To forecast or calculate approximately
Follow up	To remind of uncompleted action (tickler file or follow-up letter)
Identification	To name
Instruction	To explain how (not to order or direct)
Inventory	To report or record a periodic count of stock on hand on a certain date
Invoice	To bill or charge for
Itinerary	To list places to be visited, showing arrival dates or times
Notice	To transmit an unsolicited statement of action or status
Order	To order (procure) purchased materials, work, etc., or to order (command) to travel, duty, etc.
Pass	To permit or license to pass, or to go and come
Permit	To permit or license to perform a specific act
Receipt	To acknowledge delivery or payment given by recipient
Record	To retain an account of facts or data
Report	To transmit an account of action or status
Request	To ask for
Requisition	To formally request
Routing slip	To send an attachment along a circuit of persons or places
Schedule	To outline regularly recurring events or write a plan of future events
Stock record	To record stock on hand
Transmittal	To send an attachment to another person or place

Section 13

DESIGNING SYSTEMS FOR INTERNAL CONTROL OF A BUSINESS

BY

Joнn J. W. Neuner

DESIGNING SYSTEMS FOR INTERNAL CONTROL OF A BUSINESS

Today, more than ever before, business firms in the United States are growing in size, either by increasing the volume of production and sales or by means of diversified acquisition of other firms. The larger the business organization in terms of the number of employees, departments, or branches, the more difficult becomes the problem of managerial control and the greater the need for delegating authority and responsibility to subordinates for the care and preservation of the assets and property of the firm, as well as for the increase of the profits of the business.

Internal control of a business takes on two aspects: (1) internal control or internal checks to prevent errors, fraud, or theft in the accounting records, or wrongful conversion of the property of the firm; and (2) internal control through a system of reports of the business operations to measure the accountability of the subordinates to whom responsibilities were delegated.

Every business executive is interested in this problem of internal control for two reasons—

1. To understand just what his responsibilities are in the functional and administrative organization of the business
2. To note how the work under his supervision relates to the profit and operating results of the firm

Both of these must be further implemented by a knowledge of how the work under his supervision may be properly organized and supervised to prevent errors, fraud, and theft.

Internal control system for prevention of errors, fraud, and theft

1. Why the protective phase of internal control is a necessity

A rather complete system of internal checks to prevent errors, fraud, or theft will result in reasonably accurate accounting and financial business records. Such a system is necessary because (1) the large number of employees who must be hired to maintain the business records increases the possibility of error and fraud, (2) the work of a large number of individuals is so interrelated that errors or fraud of one seriously interferes with the work of another group; and (3) the ultimate result of the lack of internal control is such that a business not only may suffer business reverses from errors and fraud, but may actually fail. For the sake of illustration, let us take several cases which in recent years have caused business firms serious financial difficulties and problems because of inadequate or faulty internal checks—

In one large brokerage firm in New York City, the office manager was able to steal more than $25,000 through the improper internal control of the expenditures for postage, even though the postage meters were in use

In another large brokerage firm, one of the partners familiar with the punched-card accounting procedures was able to falsify the margin-account records and embezzle more than $250,000

In an electronics firm, the losses from small tools taken by the employees caused the firm to close down, relocate, and hire only workers who brought their own tools. The first closedown was due to faulty internal control of tools

A large manufacturing concern with more than 10,000 employees on three shifts found out too late that some employees were checking in and immediately going out with the employees who had completed their shift work. They returned in time to punch out, thus being paid for not working—again faulty internal control of factory payrolls

It has been estimated that because of improper internal checks, the losses to business firms through errors and fraud amount to more than $3 billion a year. To have a 100 percent perfect system of internal control is too costly for any business firm to maintain. Therefore, the best that can be hoped for is a practical system to protect the more important assets and phases of the business operations.

2. What elements of business operations require internal control?

Business records are based upon a series of transactions. These transactions involve the handling of cash, merchandise, accounts receivable, payrolls, other assets, and the operating expenses. These transactions must be appropriately recorded and physically safeguarded in storing, transferring, and receiving. Errors in recording may occur without any fraudulent intent, but nevertheless must be detected with a minimum of delay. Fraudulent conversion of these assets may be concealed by manipulating the accounting records. The system of forms, the separation of personnel making the records, and mechanical and accounting controls must be so designed and operated that errors will be eliminated, or at least reduced to a minimum, and that fraud will be prevented or easily detected before it assumes major proportions. It should be emphasized, however, that because the cost of a 100 percent foolproof system is too great to be practical, additional protection must be achieved through the use of fidelity insurance covering the essential employees of the business.

The following lists the items that need internal control and checking through an appropriate system of records and protective handling procedures of the physical properties:

Inventories
   In a trading business firm, merchandise and supplies inventories
   In a manufacturing business, raw materials, finished parts, supplies, finished goods
   In all firms, the storage facilities, whether they be warehouses, branches, or consignee's facilities

Cash
   Cash receipts and deposits
   Cash disbursements
   Petty-cash disbursements
   Branch office cash receipts and disbursements
   Bank reconciliations

Special assets
   Securities and investments
   Notes receivable
   Capital stock certificates—unissued or treasury

Payrolls
   Factory payrolls
   Office payrolls
   Sales payrolls and commissions
   Branch office payrolls

Expenses
   Manufacturing expenses
   Selling expenses
   Office and administrative expenses
   Financial expenses
   Branch houses expenses
   (It should be noted that most of these involve the payment of cash, and are listed separately primarily because of the high risk of fraud and embezzlement in this area.)

Analyzing this list further, it will be noted that in one form or another internal control is primarily concerned with the protection of the physical assets of cash, inventories, securities, equipment, receivables, and that many of these overlap since they involve the receipt or expenditure of cash.

3. Phases of internal control

Internal control of business operations is based upon an integrated co-ordinated plan which results in low cost and high profits—termed *managerial efficiency*. This plan achieves a minimum of loss from errors, fraud, and embezzlements, and a maximum of control through prompt reports of operating results. This plan standardizes carefully developed procedures. Such a plan encompasses the following segments properly balanced and coordinated:

Element of the system	*Description*
Organization charts	To indicate the functional organization of the various business activities. These will indicate the line of authority and responsibility. They are also the basis of administrative accountability. These may be supplemented by job analyses and descriptions.
Forms and records	The use of carefully designed forms and records so that all transactions may be promptly and accurately recorded and controlled. When these are used with up-to-date, efficient mechanical devices, the paper work of the business will be performed more quickly and accurately and will provide built-in mechanical "proofs."
Standard operating routines	A series of flow charts, manuals of procedures, supplemented by scientifically prepared job analyses and descriptions will insure that the office and administrative work will be completed promptly, correctly, and at a minimum of cost.
Managerial reports	To establish accountability, as contrasted to the procedures used to prevent fraud, errors, and theft, top management must have a minimum number of necessary informational reports. The more extensive the business organization, the greater the need for reports of basic operations.
Auditing procedures	No matter how complete and thorough the foregoing internal controls are, management must decide to what extent the records will be audited to detect errors, fraud, and embezzlement. Two types of audits must be considered—the internal auditing procedures, and the extent of the external auditing by the public accounting firms.

An analysis of this outline will emphasize that there are two phases of the internal control of business operations—that which will verify the accuracy of the routine transactions and prevent fraud and embezzlement, and that which top management needs to be able to create a business firm whose growth in profitability and expansion are measured by the achievements and accountability of its intermediate management team. Each of these phases of internal control system will now be expanded in detail.

Organization as a phase of internal managerial control. Organization of business activities for internal control is best indicated by means of organization charts because these establish the lines of authority, the lines of responsibility, and perhaps the accountability for operating results. Organization charts may be of several lines of responsibility, e.g., (1) the *entire organization,* which is more condensed than the others; (2) *top management only,* which is also condensed, but more limited, and (3) *divisional,* which applies to branch offices, separate factories, or more diversified organizations. But do not forget, these charts are much more effective than the illustrative reaction may indicate. They *illustrate what is what* without any questions of dispute or discussion. These charts may be *functionalized,* that is, they may show the lines of functional responsibility; they may show the interdepartmental relationships; or they may show merely the flow of work and authority.   Some firms use (rarely, however) the old military line and staff arrangements; others follow a functional accountability arrangement.   Whatever the organizational arrangement is, the following organizational *principles* should be remembered to maintain the best internal control system to prevent fraud and errors—

If possible, have more than one person involved in the completion of every business transaction—one to *handle* the physical asset such as cash or merchandise, and one to *record* the transaction.   Thus one checks the other

Have as much of the work as possible performed with the use of self-checking machines or mechanical devices.   These provide automatic verification of the recording as the transactions are recorded.

Institute some form of auditing program to regularly or continuously verify the accuracy of the accounting records.   In some organizations, such as chain stores, or multibranch factories, it may be desirable to maintain an internal auditing staff whose main function is to audit the accounting records; in other firms, it may be satisfactory to have regular periodic audits performed by independent certified public accountants.

In the following pages the various aspects of internal control and lines of responsibility established through the use of organization charts are illustrated. Four charts are given for this purpose:

Chart 1 illustrates the complete administrative and operating organization of a manufacturing concern.   Emphasis in this illustration is on the top-management personnel.   Brief statements indicate the type of work or the duties of each of the major executives, and the activities under his supervision

Chart 2 illustrates in detail the organization and the activities which pertain to the chief accounting officer, namely, the controller.   The larger the organization, the greater the responsibilities of the controller, and the higher his status in the management team, up to the title of vice-president

Chart 3 illustrates the organization of the financial manager of the business firm, namely, the treasurer.   In many ways his duties or functions must dovetail with those of the controller

Chart 4 illustrates the division of the administrative duties of a firm engaged in the retail men's furnishings business

The use of printed forms as a phase of internal control.   To fix responsibility, to reduce the possibility of error, to standardize the procedures in recording business transactions, and to standardize the location on the forms of important

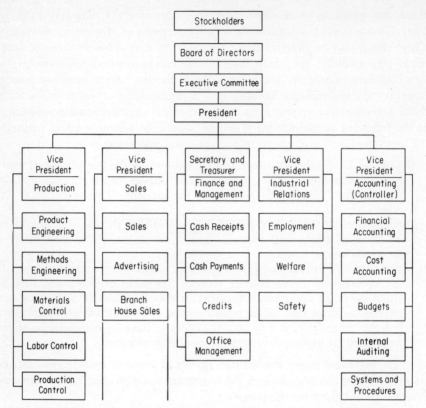

Chart I.   Complete organization chart of a manufacturing firm illustrating
the functional activities of the top management personnel.

business information relating to business transactions—these are the reasons why
business forms are such an important part of office procedures and are known
as the silent partners of a business.   Forms are used to either *request action*
or *record action taken*.   Both of these are phases of internal control—both
protective and managerial supervisory.   Internal control through the use of
forms is therefore established by means of the following:

Information which must be recorded repeatedly on each form may be printed,
thus saving the time of recording it

Numbering the forms consecutively establishes a certain amount of control
over the number of transactions or omissions

Provision by descriptions, boxes, and numbers will be made so that no necessary information will be omitted

Provision for signatures, dates, and listing of items fixes responsibility; measures efficiency; and prevents the error of omissions

By having manifold forms prepared in sets, the proper number of copies will

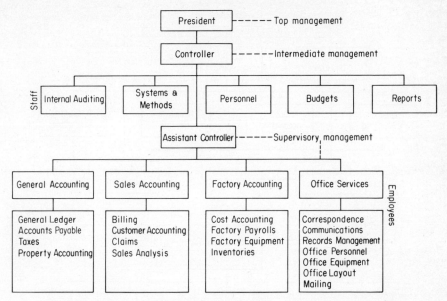

Chart 2.   A line and staff organization chart of a Controller's office.

always be prepared; by descriptive directional printing these will be properly directed and transported; and manifold copies reduces the cost of preparation of the forms by avoiding the duplication of work

By the use of differently colored paper for each copy, it is possible to indicate to which department or person the form is to be sent

Flow charts are used to indicate the various operations and departments through which each form must travel.   These charts serve as guides of the proper internal procedures; the places at which the physical handling of the asset or property is to take place—thus setting up the basic principle of internal control—*segregating* the handling of the asset, and *recording* the accounting aspects of the transaction

Standardized operating routines. The basic principle of management is *control*—control of income, expenses, and net profit.   There are many facets of this control function.   Since in most offices the most wasteful aspect of the management is too many forms, too many employees, and too much duplication of effort, forms, and records, therefore management must examine the operating routines to eliminate these inefficiencies.   These operating routines may be variously listed and classified.   In one firm, they may be listed as covering the following transactions: purchase of merchandise, sale of merchandise; maybe the manufacture of the finished product instead of purchasing it; preparation of payrolls; cost accounting of goods manufactured; and the expenses of maintenance of plant and equipment.

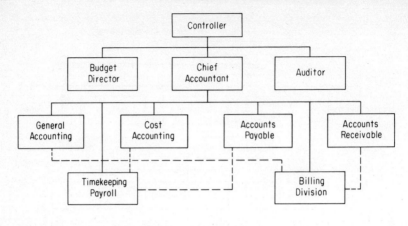

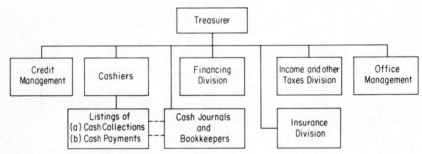

Chart 3.   Organization chart of the Treasurer's office.

To obtain the maximum of efficiency in the systems in a business organization, three procedures are possible—

1. Employ a firm of management consultants or engineers to make a special or overall survey of the procedures presently being used, or planned to be used.   For example, a firm of specialists may be employed to determine whether or not an electronic computer should be used, and what type of computing service or installation would be most economical

2. Develop an internal staff organization of systems and procedures analysts. One large department store established a staff of four highly paid individuals to constantly study all the systems and procedures throughout the organization and to make changes and improvements.   Considering that the annual payroll of these four was in excess of $75,000, you can estimate what the results should or must have been to justify such an expenditure —and it did pay off in a more efficient control of operations and increased profits.   Another large mail-order firm has a large staff of systems and procedures analysts who are constantly making improvements to justify their salaries

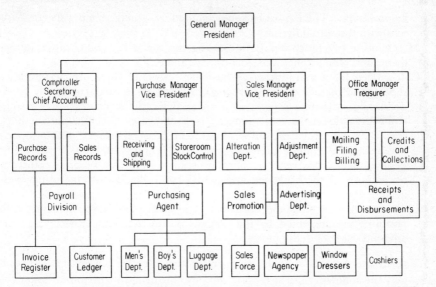

Chart 4.   Organization Chart—division of administrative duties in a retail men's furnishing business.

3. Have the office manager or controller direct and supervise system and procedure changes, improvements, and economies

Whatever method is used, it must be remembered that improvements in systems and procedures require a study of the forms used; the flow of work with these forms; and finally time-and-motion studies to be sure that the employees are producing the maximum volume of work.

Internal control through the use of managerial reports.   As the size of a business organization increases, the number of employees will also increase accordingly.   Top and intermediate management gets further away from the actual business operations, and it therefore becomes necessary to have some form of reports or information *summarizing* what is happening or what is being done, and also a series of reports which indirectly indicate whether an implied system of *internal control* is operating to prevent errors and fraud.   Reports have been variously classified.   One such classification groups reports for internal control as either *informational* or *performance*.   Informational reports are part of the communication system in business and are also a measure of performance.   For example, the income statement is an informational report and also measures the achievement.   However, for internal control, more attention is given to the performance or accountability of departments or individuals.   Some of the basic reports required by business firms are—

Budgets, both short-term and long-term, of sales forecasts by territories and

by products.   These must be supplemented by weekly or monthly comparisons with the actual figures

Merchandise inventory reports indicating the turnover; comparative investment; and obsolescence and slow-moving materials

Cost reports for a manufacturing business.   Most of these are performance
reports and include efficiency reports of labor, either departmentally or individually; idle-time reports with an analysis of the causes, such as machine breakdown, lack of material, lack of proper machine instructions;
report of departmental ratios of indirect labor to direct labor; reports
measuring the volume of work produced by individuals or departments.
Besides these labor reports, there are spoiled-materials reports; comparative reports of the budgeted and actual controllable manufacturing overhead

Cash reports of receipts and deposits for the week; cash disbursements; cash
position; supplemented by the analysis of the Accounts Receivable—the
amounts, state of delinquency

To indicate the nature of the reporting system used by a large textile manufacturer, the following list of reports used by this firm and prepared under the
direction of the controller is given:

Statement of operations, the first section indicating the sales income and cost
of sales plus selling expenses to produce the trading profit; the second section presenting the manufacturing division results which include the price
variation from the standards set for materials and supplies; cost variations
from standard for labor and manufacturing overhead, and spoilage

Sales analysis by products, presenting comparatively the budget and actual
figures

Returns and allowances indicating the causes, the frequency of the causes,
and the amounts involved

Gross profit analysis, first by method of sale such as retail, wholesale, and
catalog, and under each of these headings by product line.   The net sales
and the gross profit and the ratios are shown for each product under each
grouping

Selling expense analysis grouped under the headings of salesmen, sales office,
advertising, and management

Selling expense analysis of the New York sales office

Price variations of materials purchased, showing the variations from the
standard or budget figure

Material usage variation report, actually a report on waste in material usage

Analysis of budgeted and actual operating costs of the various departments or
operating units

Auditing procedures for internal control.   The size of the firm, the physical
organization of the activities, and the nature of the business operations will
influence the auditing procedures necessary for proper internal managerial
control.   A manufacturer with a single plant location will have less of an audit-

ing problem than a firm with 2,000 retail outlets, or 50 branch offices. Because it is dealing in cash, a small-loan company with numerous offices has a more important auditing problem than a retail dress chain which deals in merchandise. The business characteristics will determine whether or not a regular internal-auditing department is necessary, or whether periodic audits by an outside firm of public accountants is sufficient. Whenever it is possible, the use of a regular internal-auditing division should be encouraged as an efficient phase of modern business management, because errors, fraud, and embezzlements will be discovered with a minimum of delay. Furthermore, reports to management by the internal-auditing division showing the work done, the errors discovered, and the recommended changes in the system and procedures should justify the expenditure for this service.

Applied internal control procedures

In the preceding discussion, it was pointed out that management of business operations requires a properly *coordinated system* of organization charts, forms and records, operating routines, reports, and internal auditing. It was also brought out that internal managerial control covers two phases: accountability of the employees, and the prevention of errors, fraud, and embezzlement. The accountability phase has been indicated in the previous discussion, but it overlaps the preventive or corrective phase of the work. This preventive or corrective phase of internal control is to a large extent accomplished by a system of double-checking—that is, by having one person handle the physical properties, and another the recording of the business transaction involved. If this is not possible, it is possible to have mechanical devices used with built-in checking mechanism, or to have certain summaries or control accounts set up. In examining the following descriptions of applied internal control to the more common business transactions, these points must be kept in mind:

A carefully coordinated system covering the entire business operations
Segregation of the work so that more than one person is involved in the handling and recording of each business transaction
Use of built-in mechanical checks, or controlling accounts

The most common types of business transactions or items which should be considered and illustrated to emphasize internal control procedures are (1) inventories, (2) cash, (3) special assets, (4) payrolls, and (5) expenses.

4. Internal control of inventories

The internal control of inventories ranks second only to cash in management's responsibility. Losses from pilferage and stealing by the public as well as employees is tremendous. In a recent newspaper article it was indicated that such losses for the modern supermarket average 1 percent of sales, in an industry in which the net profit on sales averages only about 2 percent. Inventories may be variously classified. The nature of the inventory determines the departmental procedures and personnel to properly control it. For example, in wholesaling and retailing, there are *merchandise* inventories; for a manufacturing concern, there are *raw materials, work-in-process, finished-goods,* and *supplies* inventories. Sometimes inventories are described by location, such as *branch house* or *warehouse* inventories. In a retail, wholesale, or department store, the following departments are involved in the handling of the merchandise and supplies:

Purchasing department
Receiving department
Selling and shipping department
Accounting department
    Accounts payable for purchases
    Accounts receivable for sales

These departments are closely interrelated. Errors or fraud in any one may affect the work in the others. Therefore, they should check each other through proper organization, forms, and routines.

Although the system of internal control for the various types of merchandising is influenced by the size and organization, certain basic internal checks are common to them all and might be described as follows:

Purchasing department procedure. The size of the business organization and the type of material handled determine the complexity and elaborateness of the purchasing function. In very small businesses, the owner or manager personally makes and approves all purchases. As the organization grows in size, it becomes necessary to establish a centralized purchasing function with established forms and routines. To prevent overordering, some form of inventory control must be established. If the supervisor of a centralized purchasing department in a large organization is not too familiar with the needs of the various departments, he may require proof of the need for the material. This can be supplied by means of a list of the materials required and the list of the materials on hand. If the merchandise is valuable enough, some firms maintain a perpetual book inventory showing at all times the amount received, the amount issued or sold, and the balance on hand, in addition to the maximum and minimum of material that should be on hand. By comparing the balance on hand with the maximum and minimum quantities set up, the supervisor of the department will know when to reorder and how much. The use of electronic data processing equipment, properly programmed, has enabled many of the larger firms to maintain careful control over their inventories by constantly keeping the records up-to-date, supplying information about any or all stock instantly, and by having built into the program warnings when the stock gets below a certain set minimum.

To prevent errors in ordering, many of the larger firms use a purchase requisition form to notify the purchasing department that certain material should be ordered. In a competitive commodity, the purchasing department may send out requests for price quotations, delivery dates, etc., before placing an order. When the vendor has been selected, the purchasing department authorizes the placing of the order. However, the important principle of managerial control involved in the purchasing function is *that nothing should be ordered unless the purchase is authorized by a responsible executive.*

Receiving department procedure. This department is responsible for the physical handling of the merchandise ordered when it is received. The receiving clerks are responsible for—

Checking the quantity of goods received
Examining the quality and condition of goods received
Preparation of receiving reports in sufficient number to meet the system of
    internal control. On this report will be recorded—
        Date of receipt
        Shipper's name
        Method of shipment or delivery
        Freight or delivery charges
        Order number
        Quantity and description of material received
        Any other pertinent information

The number of copies of the receiving report that must be prepared will depend upon the internal control routines set up. The minimum number of copies should be four: one kept by receiving department; one sent with the goods to the storeroom; one sent to the purchasing department for comparison with the purchase order; and one to the accounting department for checking against the invoice approved by the purchasing department. In order to be sure that the receiving department actually inspects and counts or weighs the material received, many firms do not permit the receiving department access to the purchase order unless the quantities have been deleted or omitted on this form. To reduce the possibility of fraud to a minimum, it is necessary that a copy of the receiving report be sent with the goods to the storeroom, so that the stores clerk can verify what is being received. In one large chain of retail dress shops, there always were shortages between the time the goods were received on the first floor by the receiving department and the time they were entered in the stockroom on the sixth floor. To eliminate these shortages, the procedures were revised so that when the goods reached the sixth floor, they were verified again and signed for by the stores clerk.

Accounting department procedure for the Accounts Payable. Most modern business firms use a voucher system to record their payments because the receipt nature of an endorsed check acts partially as a form of internal control. To further improve the internal control of payments for materials purchased, the following procedures may be adopted:

The vendor's invoice is sent to the purchasing department (A duplicate copy may be sent to the accounting department)

The purchasing department compares the invoice with the purchase order and the copy of the receiving report

To be sure that this invoice is properly checked in the purchasing department, all invoices are "Approved Stamped," showing the following:

Approval Stamp

Pur. Order Number NY-406	Invoice Date 11-5-19___
Quantity O.K.	J.K. Allen
Price O.K.	G. Mills
Extensions checked by	LKM
Date paid	11-12-19___
Check No.	401-720
Amount-gross	$4,350.00
Discount	87.00
Net amount	$4,263.00

Although this arrangement may seem a little cumbersome, it is absolutely necessary for a system of proper internal control, particularly when the amount of purchases is large, or where the merchandise is of high value. The approved invoice is sent to the accounting department for their entry and payment.

The basic rule to follow in maintaining a reliable system of internal check within the accounts-payable division of the accounting department and the purchasing department is that no invoice should be approved for payment unless management has first made sure that the merchandise has actually been received in good condition. The use of the approval stamp helps to fix responsibility for all errors and omissions.

Selling and shipping department procedures for maintaining internal control over merchandise inventories. Internal control of the purchasing activities is only half the work of preventing errors and fraud and improper conversion in handling merchandise or materials inventories. The merchandise must be stored and issued when sales orders or material requisitions are received. In establishing a system of internal control for all merchandise sold, every precaution must be taken so that

The merchandise actually billed is the merchandise that is packed and shipped

The proper prices are charged for the merchandise sold

The accounting records contain entries for all sales, whether for cash or on account

When listed in this fashion, internal control of sales or issuance of merchandise or materials does not seem to be a very difficult problem. However, this problem becomes much more serious and important when the following illustrations of losses in inventory due to lack of control are considered. All occurred in recent years.

Over a period of 2 years, more than $50,000 worth of liquor was shipped from the company warehouse to its retail store without any entries or charges being recorded because of the lack of internal control. Obviously, the liquor never reached the retail store, but was disposed of en route.

In a high-class department store, over a period of 3 months, employees were able to take home without detection merchandise worth more than $20,000. Only when a physical inventory was completed did the firm learn of this shortage.

Due to improper control of the issuance of materials to be used in manufacturing operations, one large motor-manufacturing company suffered a $250,000 inventory loss, because employees were placing valuable parts in plastic bags and putting them in garbage cans. In collusion with the garbage collectors, they split the profits. When the garbage collecting racket was eliminated, the employees were discovered making many visits to their cars in the parking lot during the lunch hours—thus removing the parts directly to their cars. The firms then relocated the parking lot outside the factory premises, and no employees were allowed to visit it except when leaving for the day.

In each of these illustrations (and there are many more that could be cited) management should have been more careful in providing internal control and procedures.

Sales may be classified as *cash* and *on account; retail* and *wholesale.* Retail sales for cash are best controlled by using cash registers and, if possible, having the work divided among three persons: the sales clerk who makes the sales, a cashier who handles the cash receipt and makes the change, and a separate packer who checks the sales slip with the merchandise before packaging and delivery of goods to the customer. Separating the work may seem more expensive in clerical costs, but results in the better-managed retail chains and discount houses have indicated that the reduction in losses from errors and theft have more than offset this additional cost.

Retail sales on account require verification of credit standing of the customer. The use of electronic computers in the large department stores for this purpose has simplified and expedited this work greatly. Use of the more or less standard sales-slip procedure and detachable perforated price tags has in recent years improved the internal control of these sales. The standard sales slip is usually composed of four parts: (1) the customer *receipt* of the sale, (2) a properly prepared *label* to be used where the package is sent to the packing and shipping department for delivery. If to be taken instead of delivered, this can be destroyed or enclosed with the merchandise; (3) a third copy for the *accounting* department, and (4) a copy to be retained by the sales clerk for the daily *sales recapitulation report*.

Sales by *wholesalers, jobbers,* and *manufacturers* usually involve larger amounts and a more complicated procedure. The procedure of forms, routines, and entries will require the services of an order department, a credit department, a billing department, and the shipping department.

Most of these sales will be on account. The orders may be received by telephone, in writing, or from salesmen. Where received by telephone, a standardized form should be used to prevent error and to be sure that all the required information is recorded. Where orders are taken by sales representatives, multicopies of the order blank should be prepared, with one copy provided for signing by the customers approving the items, quantities, and prices. When written orders are received through the mails, the customer usually has a specially printed form which serves the same purpose as the form used by the salesmen. Before authorizing the shipment, approval of the credit department is necessary. This may be achieved by having multicopies of the order blank prepared, one copy of which can be used for obtaining the written approval of the credit department.

If the merchandise is usually in stock, it is possible to use a billing procedure whereby the multicopies of the sales invoices are prepared before the goods are shipped. In that case, one copy of the sales invoice is sent to the customer; one copy to the storeroom authorizing the issuance of the material; and one copy to the shipping department authorizing the packing and shipping. In the shipping department, a report is made detailing the shipping instructions and listing the merchandise sent. One copy of this report should go to the billing department authorizing the mailing of the invoice to the customer; one copy should go to the accounting department for authorizing the entry in the sales journal and accounts receivable ledger. This system of having the work of one department check the work of another is basic in a good system of internal control and may be modified to fit varying conditions. The following two checklists serve to illustrate and emphasize the internal control procedures:

Checklist Outline of Forms and Departments for Internal Control of Inventory for a Merchandising Type of Business

Forms to be used	*Departments affected*
Merchandise stock cards or inventory sheets. On these cards a maximum and minimum quantity to be kept on hand is indicated. When quantity approaches the minimum, the stock-control clerk prepares a purchase requisition in duplicate. If merchandise has not previously been bought, the manager of the department in which it is to be sold authorizes the preparation of the requisition.	Inventory or stock-control department.

Forms to be used	*Departments affected*
Purchase requisitions (two copies). One copy is kept in file in stock-control department and the second is sent to the purchasing department for its action.	Stock-control and purchasing departments.
Request for price quotations (two copies). One copy is kept by the purchasing department and the second is sent to each prospective vendor.	Purchasing department.
Purchase order (at least four copies). One copy is kept by purchasing department, one is sent to the vendor, one goes to the receiving department so that it may know what merchandise to expect, and one is sent to the stock-control department so that it may know the merchandise has been ordered.	Purchasing, receiving, and stock-control departments.
Receiving list or report (at least three copies). One copy is kept in the receiving department, one is sent with the merchandise to the stock-control department, and one is sent to the purchasing department for comparison with the purchase order and the invoice when it is received.	Receiving, stock-control, and purchasing departments.
Vendor's invoice (one copy). First sent to the purchasing department for their O.K. of the type, quantity, and price of merchandise, and then forwarded to the voucher clerk in the accounting department.	Purchasing and accounting departments.
Voucher check (one copy). Prepared in the cashier's department in the treasurer's office and sent to the vendor.	Cashier's department.

A second phase of the internal control of inventory for a merchandising type of business relates to the issuance or sale of the merchandise. A checklist for this second phase follows:

Forms to be used	*Departments affected*
Sales orders. If the firm sells merchandise in large volume, these are prepared in at least four copies: one is kept by the order department, one is sent to the inventory-control department authorizing the release of merchandise to the shipping department, one is sent to the shipping department, and one goes to the accounting department so that it may prepare the customer's invoice.	Order, inventory-control, shipping, and accounting departments.
Cash sales, charge sales, and COD sales slips. If the merchandise is in smaller volume, either taken by customer or delivered to him, four copies are prepared: One goes with goods to packing and shipping department, one is sent to the inventory-control department, one goes to the accounting department, and one is kept by the salesclerk.	Sales, packing and shipping, accounting, and inventory-control departments.
Customer's invoice or monthly statement. If the sales slip is not treated as an invoice, then a separate invoice is made out at time of sale or a monthly statement is sent out. The former is prepared in the billing department: One copy goes to the accounting department for sales record, and one is mailed to the customer. The latter is prepared in the accounting department, which retains one copy.	Billing and accounting departments.

Forms to be used	*Departments affected*
Customer's credit memorandum. This is used when merchandise is returned by a customer. One copy is sent to the customer, one is sent to the accounting department, one goes to the inventory-control department for its record on the stock cards, and one is kept in the billing department, where the credit memo is prepared.	Billing, accounting, and inventory-control departments.

In using both of these checklists, it should be noted that the handling, the recording, and eventually the payment for merchandise are segregated so that no one person is in complete charge of all the work, preventing loss except by collusion.

Internal control of inventories for a manufacturing concern. In manufacturing concerns, there are raw materials, work-in-process, and finished-goods inventories. The internal control for the *purchase* of raw materials is the same as that of a nonmanufacturing concern. The treatment of the finished-goods inventory is the same for *sales* as for a nonmanufacturing concern. However, between these two extremes of purchasing and sales, there are internal control problems. The major problems relate to maintaining an accurate control of the inventories of raw materials and of finished goods, and the withdrawal of goods from the storeroom for use in manufacturing.

A checklist to be used in examining the system of internal control of stores in a manufacturing concern would provide answers to the following questions:

Stores-control Checklist of a Manufacturing Concern

Is the stores keeper responsible for the raw materials and supplies inventory investments?

Is there a perpetual inventory record of every important item carried in stock in the storeroom?

Has provision been made so that nothing but regular stock items are ordered, unless properly designated major executives have given authority for special purchases, including tools and equipment?

Are all purchase requisitions sent to the purchasing department in a uniform manner?

Are all raw materials and supplies received, itemized carefully by the receiving department—that is, by stores item name and quantity—in order that no invoice may be paid unless there is a record that the materials actually were received?

Has procedure been established so that nothing will be issued from the storeroom without first having a properly prepared and authorized requisition?

Has procedure been established so that each stores item issued on the stores requisition is properly priced and accurately extended?

Work-in-process inventory control and checklist. To set up a properly controlled work-in-process inventory, attention must be centered on the work and records of the manufacturing department on the one hand and the cost-accounting department on the other.   The work-in-process inventory is made up of the cost of the materials, labor, and manufacturing overhead used in producing the various products, which as yet are still incomplete.   The cost-accounting department is responsible for the accumulation of the costs of these unfinished products.   It is the function of the cost-accounting department to devise a system so that the materials actually issued and used, the payroll costs applicable to specific production, and the proportionate share of the manufacturing over-head are properly allocated, recorded, and summarized by the cost-accounting department even though the work is still incomplete.   A checklist of the factors which must be considered in the control of the work-in-process inventories would include the following:

Work-in-process Control Checklist for the Manufacturing Department

Have all the stores requisitions prepared by the shop foremen or the plan-ning department been charged to the work-in-process inventory accounts?

Have proper time tickets for charging the workers' earnings to the various items being manufactured been prepared and recorded in the work-in-process inventory accounts?

Has a charge for the manufacturing expense or overhead been made for the work not yet completed?

Has the manufacturing-expense charge been recorded or deferred?

Is this charge a reasonable amount considering the fact that the work is still incomplete?

The cost-accounting department is responsible for recording and summariz-ing the charges made in the manufacturing department.   It is the function of this department, as part of the internal control program, to compute and sum-marize the material requisitions, the labor-time tickets, and the manufacturing overhead charges, and record these on the cost summary sheets—*job-order* cost sheets for a job-order cost system, and *cost of production reports,* if it is a con-tinuous process or departmental cost system.   A checklist of the work of this department must consider answers to the following questions:

Work-in-process Control Checklist for the Cost-accounting Department

Have proper job-order or process-cost-of-production summary sheets been used to summarize the work-in-process costs?

Have all entries thereon recorded been verified before being recorded to be sure they are in agreement with the work in the manufacturing depart-ment?

Are the entries up-to-date?

Finished-goods inventory checklist for internal control.   A third type of in-ventory of a manufacturing firm requiring some form of internal control is the *finished goods.*   The objective of the internal control system is to be sure that all the units completed are actually transferred to the stockroom, and that all the issues are properly accounted for. The following represents a series of questions which should be checked in setting up a system of internal control for the finished-goods inventories:

Have all the units completed been transferred to the stockroom?

If these units are to be sent out to salesrooms or warehouses, have daily or weekly reports been made of the units thus shipped out?

Have the unit costs been computed and recorded for all units placed in the stockroom? Are these unit costs reasonable?

Have the proper unit costs been used in charging the shipments of finished units to the salesrooms or warehouses?

Has a detailed finished-goods ledger been established and used in maintaining the quantity and value control over the finished goods on hand?

Is the finished-goods inventory verified regularly by physical count of the quantity on hand?

Are finished-goods control accounts used to check on the subsidiary perpetual finished-goods inventory records?

Internal control checklist for branch house inventory control. In a number of studies made, it was discovered that the greatest number of frauds and thefts occur in branches or warehouses. Where large amounts and valuable inventories are maintained at such locations, the problem of internal control becomes important to management. While branch house management and procedures vary with the different firms, nevertheless the answers to the following questions should provide a guide to the internal control system to be used:

If the branch does its own purchasing, are copies of the purchase orders sent to the home office?

Under such conditions is a copy of the receiving report of all merchandise thus ordered sent to the home office?

Does the home office make careful comparisons of the orders and the receiving reports?

Does the home office periodically check the physical and book inventory records of the branch or warehouse?

Are systematized sales tickets or invoices prepared for each shipment of merchandise? Does the home office receive copies of these, and reconcile the shipments with the inventory on hand?

Are perpetual or book inventory records maintained at the branch for all merchandise received? Is this a quantity only, or a quantity-and-price inventory?

Merchandise frauds that should be guarded against through internal control. The purpose of internal control is the prevention of loss through errors, fraud, and theft. Errors can be forgiven if unavoidable and not repeated; fraud and theft must be detected and prosecuted without delay. Some of the frauds and thefts which have occurred and could have been detected through a good system of internal control are—

Having frauds caused by failure to investigate the character and experience references of prospective employees. As a double checkup, bonding employees is a desirable protective device, since the bonding company will investigate character and experience. One large retail store in leather goods suffered a loss of $30,000 by failing to investigate the past experience of a newly hired bookkeeper. If the owner had, he would have learned that she had committed a similar embezzlement in her last position in another city

Having frauds arising from the manipulation of the accounts, especially true when one person has sole charge of the records and the handling of the merchandise

Having fake purchases entered on the books, and, when paid, having the cash or part of it returned to the employees involved

Having the invoices overpriced for purchases authorized by certain employees, and when the invoice is paid, having the employee receive a kickback from the vendor

Having the merchandise received, counted, checked, and *acknowledged* and then immediately taken back by the shipper or his truckman

Having inferior quality material received, but paid for at prices of the higher quality, and then having the employees receive a kickback (restaurant department of a large hotel)

Having material recorded on the receiving report even though never received

Having incorrect or overstated freight bills paid for from petty cash and pocketing the difference

Maintaining fictitious inventory records (McKesson & Robbins case)

Making payments for purchase returns, even though never received. One large department store paid out more than $60,000 in one year in its electrical-goods department

Having employees steal from the warehouses due to improper supervision

Shipping merchandise without charging or recording it in any customer's account

Having thefts of manufactured goods before they have been placed in the stockroom

Having branch managers convert stock to their own use

5. Internal control of cash

Merchandise and cash are the two business properties that require the greatest amount of internal control and checking. Internal control of cash must be subdivided into two distinct yet closely related phases, namely, (1) cash receipts, and (2) cash disbursements. Because of its tempting nature and the ease with which it can oftentimes be taken, cash must be most carefully guarded by a thorough, foolproof system of internal control. Such a system will tend to discourage unauthorized taking of cash.

Internal control for cash receipts. *From cash sales and COD sales.* The basic principle involved in this form of internal control is the *segregation of*

the handling of the goods from the handling of the money. The steps to be followed in achieving this might be tabulated as follows:

Internal Control for Cash Receipts from Cash and COD Sales

Selling department	Cashier's department	Bookkeeping and accounting departments
All cash sales must be recorded on prenumbered sales slips.	Cash with copy of slip sent to central cashier's department. Deposit slip is prepared daily and a copy is sent to the bookkeeper.	Total of cash-sales slips received from cashier's department must be compared with bank deposits made. If in agreement, entries are made in cash-receipts journal.
If sales slips are not in use, then all cash sales must be recorded on cash-register machine.	If a central cashier is in charge of the cash-register machine, a formal cash-register receipt must be given to each customer.	Again, cash in the register must be checked against totals recorded and locked in machine totalizer, and then compared with bank deposits before being entered in cash-receipts journal. Definite procedure should be established as to who is to make bank deposits and when they are to be made.
On COD sales, special sales slips are prepared, one copy going to the cashier's department and the other to the shipping department. The shipping department prepares the drivers' daily COD delivery report from the COD sales slips. Daily, either the cash or the merchandise must be checked. Cash is delivered to the cashier's department where it is checked against copies of COD sales slips.	Daily cash turned in by drivers for COD sales is checked against COD sales slips or report from selling department. Deposit slip is prepared regularly and a copy of it is sent to bookkeeping or accounting department. Where feasible, rotation of personnel in the cashier's department and the accounting department may be a means of internal check.	Compares deposit slip with COD sales reported before entering in cash-receipts journal. It may be that this comparison is made simultaneously with that of the cash sales.

From customers making on-account payments. The procedure followed varies because many of the payments are received in the mails. If the customers pay their accounts in cash and in person, a formal receipt must be given to each customer, the duplicate of which must be so controlled as to prevent alteration or substitution. This is done by having prenumbered receipts, and using special carbon paper and special paper to discourage erasures or alterations.

The procedure to follow where most payments are received in the mails should cover the following:

Where possible, mail-opening operations should be performed by two or more individuals, one opening, and one counting and listing the cash receipts

Persons handling this kind of work should be bonded, if the firm does not have a blanket bond covering all employees

Listing of cash, money orders, checks, etc., received should be on a duplicate record, one copy with cash being sent to the cashier's department, and the duplicate to the bookkeeping and accounting department.   On this listing should be shown date of receipt, name of sender, amount, and nature of receipt such as cash, money order, check

The bookkeeping and accounting department uses its copy of the list as the source of entries in the cash-receipts journal and for posting to the customers' ledger.   It is also used as a means of checking on the deposits made by the cashier

Internal control for cash disbursements.   Internal control for cash disbursements is just as important as that for cash receipts.   Unauthorized conversion of cash is just as possible through false payments or through recording the incorrect amounts as through the immediate conversion of cash receipts before they are actually recorded.   Cash disbursements for payrolls are discussed on page 459.   Internal control for the disbursements for other transactions may be established as follows:

All purchases of equipment or inventory, as well as the payroll, must be attested to by a responsible executive before the accounting department uses the invoices, or bills, or payrolls in the preparation of the voucher

A good system of internal control of cash payments presupposes the use of a voucher system, and the making of all payments except petty cash by check

In addition to the proper approval of the purchase or payroll, a definite routine of making the payments must be followed.   This approval should not be given by the same person who authorized the purchase originally

Where possible, all checks should be mailed to the creditor named in the payment

All paid invoices and canceled checks must be kept for future reference

Use cash reconciliation of bank balance monthly as means of internal check. By having this made either by the external auditors, or by someone in the controller's office, it is possible to establish some degree of internal control over cash and confirm the accuracy of the balances in the cash records

Cash frauds that can be eliminated by internal control.   A good system of internal control can eliminate the following cash frauds:

"Lapping" accounts. (This is discussed separately on page 458)

Juggling accounts receivable by not crediting a customer for a payment, and pocketing the amount involved

Fake cash payments for sales returns and allowances

Incorrect or false payments of freight and cartage bills

Payment of wages to nonexistent employees

Overpayment of wages to employees because of improper calculations, whether intentional or not

Payment to nonexistent creditors for merchandise never received

Payment to existing creditors for merchandise never received

Payment to creditors for incorrect invoices

Payment to creditors for full amount of invoice, although a purchase discount should have been taken

Theft of cash received by mail from customers

Theft of cash received by mail for cash purchases

Paying for false petty-cash expenditures

Discounting the firm's notes without recording cash received

Selling capital stock without making any entries

Inflating payments for various expenses

Falsifying various cash expenditures

6. Internal control of special assets

The procedures described above summarize the internal control methods set up by many firms to promote accuracy and honesty in the accounting records and in the handling of the physical assets and liabilities. There are, however, a few special problems which require attention if this outline of internal control is to be complete.

In some firms, embezzlement of cash received from customers covered up by a practice known as "lapping"—converting cash received from a customer to personal use, and covering this up later by crediting the account of the customer by using the cash received later from another customer. This is a continuous process and while it may ultimately be discovered, it has been known to extend over a long period of time. For example, in one large building-and-loan association, by manipulating 17 depositors' accounts in this manner, a clerk was able to cover up more than $100,000 of illegally converted cash. As a precaution in this matter, internal controls may be set up as follows:

In a merchandising business, have one person record the sales charges to the customers' accounts, and another the credits for cash received. The cash should be handled by the cashier but the entries by the bookkeeping department. This has already been indicated

In banks, duplicate deposit slips have been widely used, with the handling of cash and depositors' accounts segregated. More recently, recording commercial deposits by means of locked machines in which control or audit sheets are used, together with a printed receipt of deposit given the depositor, has proved effective

In smaller business firms which cannot afford the subdivision of activities indicated above, the use of an accounts-receivable ledger control account, and the issuance of detailed monthly statements to all customers, acts as a means of safeguarding cash received from customers and reduces the possibility of "lapping"

In some firms it is necessary to prevent the discounting of *customers' notes* to obtain unrecorded cash.   To achieve this, the handling of the notes should be centered in the treasurer's office, with a memorandum of the receipt of all notes being sent to the customers' ledger clerk for his entry.   Thus any internal or external audit must reveal the presence of the notes or the cash received therefor.

Internal checks for *securities owned* must be carefully set up.   This is especially true if they are in the nature of temporary investments.   A detailed procedure for internal control of securities owned might include the following:

Authority to purchase any securities must be set forth in the minutes of the board of directors

The voucher prepared in payment of these securities must clearly indicate the reference to the minutes of the board of directors under which it is authorized

Records should be set up counterchecking each other: in the accounting department, a posting to the securities account from the voucher register; in the treasurer's office, a record of securities owned

Securities should be deposited in the firm's safe-deposit box kept in a bank. If possible, access to the box should always require the presence of two executives of the firm, whose names should be recorded in the minutes of the board of directors, a copy of which has been transmitted to the bank's safe-deposit staff

7. Internal control of payrolls

The internal control of payrolls is a variation or application of one phase of the internal control of cash.   The main purpose of the internal control of payrolls is the prevention of the overpayment of the salaries or wages of the employees, or the improper conversion of cash by employees for the payroll charges of nonexisting, deceased, or discharged workers.   Although payrolls may be divided into types such as factory payrolls, office payrolls, sales payrolls, administrative payrolls, part-time workers payrolls, and sales commissions, the basic problems of internal control are essentially the same for each type.   The departments in a business organization affected in the payroll preparation and with the reasons for their importance.

disbursement, and the internal controls to be used are given below, together

Departments Affected in Internal Control for Payrolls

Department	Nature and importance of department's work
Timekeeping	Because of the requirements of the wages and hours laws, the work of this department has taken on added importance. Unless timekeeping is carefully controlled, workers who are paid on an hourly basis may be paid for work not done. Control of the work of this department should prevent payment of wages to persons not even employed.

Department   *Nature and importance of department's work*

Payroll ....Checks or verifies the work of the timekeeping department. Computes and checks accuracy of work of timekeeping department, and computes earnings and payroll-tax deductions of workers. Controls must be set up to ensure that the workman actually receives the amount of money shown as earnings on the records.

Accounting ......Segregated into the vouchers-payable division and the cash-payments division. Controls cost and managerial analyses of payrolls. Maintains income-tax records for employee earnings.

How a system of internal control is set up for the timekeeping department. The following table gives a comprehensive list of the procedures used to establish a system of internal control so that the workers will not be fraudulently overpaid, and so that nonexisting employees will not be added to the payroll and their earnings taken by other employees.

Procedure followed	*Internal control established*
1. Selection of efficient time-recording devices, which include individual time-clock cards, dial time recorders, continental time clocks.	Avoids crowding at checking-in-and-out gates. Sufficient number permits more careful supervision of time-clock punching.
2. Each factory worker is given an identification number and badge.	Facilitates supervision at checking-in-and-out gates. Serves as identification within the factory when presence of workers is verified.
3. Each morning and each afternoon, a time clerk must check the presence of each worker in the factory and record the necessary information in a time book.	This prevents one worker from punching the time card for another who may be absent. It also verifies the departmental location of each worker. This is important if different departments have varying wage rates. It acts as a check against time cards or time sheets.
4. The timekeeping department must be sure that there are enough time clocks, located so that workers will be admitted with a minimum of delay. This department must also provide watchmen at each gate.	Prevents errors in handing out cards. No one should be able to punch more than one card.
5. It may be desirable to have the office workers sign a time book, thus keeping a record which may be used in the event that any questions are raised under the wages and hours laws.	Provides written record of time actually worked. Psychologically encourages workers to be on time and not leave early.

Internal control through the payroll department. One of the simplest methods of defrauding a firm is through the payroll. Falsifying the time records and later, through collusion, improper payroll records may cost a firm thousands of dollars. How then may a form of internal control be set up? An outline of the procedure which may be followed to create this internal check is listed:

Internal-check Procedure for the Payroll Department

Procedure to be followed	*Internal control established*
1. Comparison of time tickets received daily from each worker with the timekeeper's time records and with time-clock records.	Check and verification of each report to assure reliability of information and proof of worker's presence.
2. Verification of earnings of each worker.	Double check on accuracy of computations.
3. Checking and approval of payroll sheet by paymaster.	Fixes responsibility for payroll of factory workers.
4. Preparation of payroll analysis—bills and coins required for payroll.	Facilitates the preparation of pay envelopes, and acts as a check on accuracy of the payroll.
5. Preparation of receipts of payment to be turned in by worker receiving payment.	Usually a stub attached to the envelope must be signed and turned in upon receiving payroll. It is one of the best forms of internal check unless there is collusion between worker and payroll department.
6. Distribution of pay envelopes by persons other than those responsible for preparation of the payroll.	A form of internal check by having the accounting record and the physical handling of the cash segregated.
7. Use of bank checks wherever possible in making payment to workers. This is particularly true of office workers, and should be extended to the other workers if possible.	A check is a better form of receipt of payment than the actual cash. The indorsement offers some chance for tracing payment, particularly if cashing of checks is made through the bank offices rather than a check-cashing firm or some local bar or store.
8. All increases in pay rates must be in writing by a special officer.	This avoids inflating payrolls.

Internal control of payrolls through the accounting department. Internal control of payrolls is achieved in part through the segregation of the preparation of the payrolls, the distribution of the cash or checks, and the recording of the payrolls. It is with the third of these, namely, recording the payrolls, that some degree of internal control is established. The accounting phase of the payroll work is composed of (1) preparation of payroll sheets from time cards, (2) computation of tax and other deductions, (3) preparation of voucher for total payroll, (4) recording of the voucher in the voucher register, and of the check in the check register, (5) posting to the employees' earnings records, and (6) annual preparation of the income-tax reports of earnings and deductions, whether this be on Form W-2 or Form 1099. Erroneous reports will quickly come to light when the employee complains or the governmental income-tax department checks on the information shown on tax returns. To outline the internal control achieved in the matter of payrolls through the *accounting department,* the following schedule is given:

Internal Control of Payrolls through the Accounting Department

Procedure used in the accounting department	*Internal control effected*
1. Receipt in the payroll department from the employment department of employment notice and rate-of-pay authorization.	Prevents anyone being put on payroll without official notice. Approves the rate of pay.
2. Withholding-tax deduction form is sent to payroll department.	Authorizes withholding-tax status.
3. Other deductions authorized on special forms sent to payroll department.	Puts in writing and fixes responsibility for all other deductions.
4. Compares payroll sheets with time-clock cards or records.	A form of internal check to assure presence of workers.
5. Compares time-clock cards with timekeeper's morning and afternoon check of presence of workers.	Additional check on presence of workers.
6. Makes analysis of denominations to be used in preparing payroll.	Ensures reliable filling of pay envelopes.
7. Have pay envelopes prepared and filled by others than those who prepare time records.	Segregation of payroll functions.
8. If possible have workers paid by checks.	Easier to verify payment through indorsement.
9. Whether paid by cash or by check some form of receipt must be obtained. Pay envelope stubs may be used or a detailed statement on face of check.	This acts as receipt of payment.
10. Occasional payoffs to be made by auditors or others in rotation of personnel, especially if unannounced.	This provides a form of internal check and has a psychological effect on employees responsible for preparation and distribution of payrolls.

Payroll frauds that can be eliminated by internal control. A good system of internal control can eliminate the following payroll frauds:

Paying wages for nonexistent employees placed on payroll by dishonest managers or employees, who pocket the money

Having employees "kick back" part of the wages which have been paid to them but which have not been earned by them

Overpaying employees for time not actually worked

Errors in computing payrolls so that workers get more than their earnings

Pocketing unauthorized deductions from employees' pay

Deducting more than the necessary amount of taxes from the payroll and pocketing the difference

Overstating the tax deductions in the records and pocketing the differences

8. Internal control of expenses

Business expenses may be grouped under a number of headings. A common but simple grouping for a manufacturing concern would be (1) manufacturing expenses, (2) selling expenses, (3) office or administrative expenses, and (4) financial management expenses. For a large department store, a longer list is used as follows: (1) direct selling expenses, (2) advertising and sales promotion expenses, (3) buying expenses, (4) stock-control expenses, stores and warehousing, (5) delivery expenses, (6) administrative expenses, (7) credit and collection expenses, and (8) financial expenses.

Internal control of expenses is established in several ways: (1) by the use of budgets; (2) by the proper recording of the actual expenses incurred and then comparing these with the budgeted figures, (3) by the control of the cash disbursements for the various expenses to be sure that they are genuine, and not inflated, and (4) by supervisory accountability for the expenses incurred in each department. To understand how each of these is achieved, the procedures used for each of the four types of expenses listed above will be outlined.

Internal control of manufacturing expenses. One of the first methods of setting up internal check or control of expenses in a factory is the preparation by each department of a budget of its manufacturing expenses. The purpose of this budget is (1) to focus the attention of each department on the estimated amount of the expenses for that department, and (2) to make some comparison of the actual expenses with the estimated. The control is established in the comparison. By making each department estimate its expenses and then checking on each department's performance by comparison with the actual, a definite control is established because the department must account for the variation or difference. The most effective control is established by means of monthly comparisons of estimated expenses with the actual expenses. To illustrate this control, see the actual and the budgeted manufacturing expenses of a department on page 464.

The second method of setting up a control of the expenses of a manufacturing concern is a system which will result in a proper record of actual expenses incurred. For the manufacturing department, this is achieved by the following suggested procedures:

Toolroom expenses: All small tools such as chisels, hammers, etc., not in constant use should be kept in a central toolroom. When a tool is issued, the workman must leave a metal check with his number printed thereon, which is substituted for the tool until it is returned to the toolroom. For tools in constant use, the workman is given one issue, and before additional issues are made, the worn-out tools must be returned. A new issue for a worn-out tool is usually approved by the departmental foreman

Freight and delivery charges: These should usually be charged to the account

CONTROLLABLE EXPENSE REPORT
Drill Press Department
90% Operating Capacity

For the Month of March, 19___

C. J. Norman   Foreman

Expense	Actual this month	Budget this month	Difference for month between actual & budget	Actual year to date	Budget year to date
Light & Power	$150.00	$160.00	−$10.00	$550.00	$610.00
Indirect Labor	210.00	230.00	− 20.00	700.00	600.00
Supplies	85.00	100.00	− 15.00	200.00	240.00
Repairs	90.00	100.00	− 10.00	300.00	160.00
Spoilage	50.00	70.00	− 20.00	220.00	150.00
Total	$585.00	$660.00	−$75.00	$1,970.00	$1,760.00

for which incurred. Copies of incoming freight bills should be attached to the invoices for supplies for which incurred

Shop and factory supplies: These are controlled through the inventory records and are issued only upon properly approved requisitions

Indirect-labor charges: All employees placed in this category should be identified by number, and their presence in the factory verified by time-clock-card records, and a foreman

Expenses involving cash payments: All such expenses should be approved by the superintendent or some departmental executive. Invoices for such payments must be given by the superintendent to the voucher payments clerk

For the selling expenses, it is necessary to set up an internal control as follows:

Salesmen's salaries must be approved by the sales manager before being forwarded to the payroll department

Salesmen's commissions must be computed and verified from the sales records

Traveling expenses: To avoid too much padding, many firms either allow a flat rate or a maximum amount for expenses each day or week. It is not expected that this item be controlled too minutely or it will destroy the morale of the employees. However, if no flat rate or maximum limit is set on the expenses, some control can be established by comparing the amounts submitted as charges each week with those of the previous weeks

Subscriptions to trade publications and dues to trade and professional organizations. Although these are legitimate business expenses, they should be scrutinized or approved by the sales manager or controller before the voucher is prepared for them. In many concerns, definite rules are laid down as to what organizations may be paid for by the firm, and the procedure to be followed in joining and approving the payment of dues therefor

Office expenses. Certain of these expenses also require a method of internal control. Among these would be—

> *Telephone and telegraph expenses.* Many firms place little or no restriction on the local calls. If it is desired to control these, the operator may keep periodic checks on departmental calls, but since firms for the most part use the automatic dial switchboard for local calls, this control is not only unnecessary but quite unreasonable. For long-distance calls, control seems more important. In many concerns, all long-distance calls are recorded by the switchboard operator by departments. Monthly, these departmental charges are submitted to the departmental head for his approval. He must indicate that each call was a "business" and not a "personal" call. The psychological effect seems desirable, especially in large organizations. For example, in a large bank, where there are 4,500 employees in the main office, telephone and telegraph expenses, unless controlled, may become a large item
>
> *Postage and stamped envelopes.* This expense item should receive only minor or indirect control. Although the cost may loom large because of the possibility of theft, the cost of the control may be larger than the savings effected. Therefore, control may best be established by using metered mail and having all other postage and stamped envelopes issued by the office manager

Financial and other expenses. A third group of expenses requiring control appears under this heading. These expenses and the method of their control are shown in the accompanying table.

Control of Financial and Other Expenses

Expenses	Method of control
Customers' accounts charged off	All credit sales above a certain amount should be approved by the credit manager.
	No customers' accounts should be written off until all efforts, including legal, have been used to effect collection.
	All actual accounting entries made to write off the uncollectible customers' accounts must be made only upon written instructions from the treasurer.
Sales discounts	Rates must be approved by the treasurer in cooperation with the sales manager.
	Periodic reviews or test checks should be made by the internal-auditing department to be sure the amounts and the realization of the discounts are correct and not used to cover up the conversion of cash by employees.
Bank interest and discount	All loans or discounting of customers' notes must be authorized in writing by the treasurer.
	Payment of loans and notes payable must be approved by the treasurer.
	All interest and discount computations must be verified.

Expense frauds that can be eliminated by internal control.   A good system of internal control can eliminate the following expense frauds:

Paying unreasonable amounts for traveling expenses

Faking factory expenses paid from the petty-cash fund or by check

Padding factory payrolls for indirect factory workers who are not actually employed or are treated as part-time employees

Improper or incorrect amounts for salesmen's salaries or salesmen's commissions

Computing salesmen's commissions on sales which were not made or on which no commissions are to be paid

Charging personal telephone and telegraph expenses to the business firm

Theft of postage stamps (in one business concern during a national radio campaign, two employees were caught stealing $500 worth of stamps a week—caught after 10 weeks of success)

Fake postage payments—stamps not actually bought

Recording sales discounts on past-due accounts and pocketing the difference

Recording interest charges which were not incurred

Recording payments of charges not actually incurred, for freight and delivery

9. Special phases of internal control

In the preceding discussion of the applied internal control, specific methods and procedures were presented for the handling and recording of merchandise, cash, and other assets.   Nevertheless, there is always the possibility of fraud through the collusion of two or more employees.   Although these frauds may be discovered by the annual audit by the firm of public accountants, the long delay between audits may be damaging to the business operations.   Therefore in some firms, where there are many branches, or departments, such as chain stores, banks, insurance companies, it has proven worthwhile to have the firm's own auditing staff constantly check the work and records of the employees.   Such an internal-auditing staff is an important phase of internal control.

In spite of the best systems of internal control, frauds and theft will occur. If the amounts are not large, they may not seem important enough to control. However, for the one case in maybe a hundred where the amount of loss may be excessively large, some protection should be provided.   For this reason, many firms take out fidelity bonds on some or all of their employees to protect the firm against losses from dishonest employees.   Bonding is no substitute for a good system of internal control, since losses may accumulate over a long period of time before being discovered.   A good system of internal control should point out these losses at the earliest possible moment.   Bonding is merely a supplemental protection should any phase of the internal control system be inadequate.

One additional phase of internal control is sometimes overlooked.   That is the use of mechanical appliances or methods in accounting and business procedures. Most of these devices have built-in mechanical "proofs" or checks, and when supplemented by a double-checking set of forms and procedures, are an important aspect of internal control. For example, in preparing punched cards for use with the punch-card accounting system, all source data on the cards must be checked before being processed. This is accomplished by means of a verifying punch. Similarly, in the modern electronic computers, accuracy checks are built into the equipment to verify the input or output at very rapid speed. For example, by means of duplicate circuitry, arithmetic computations are verified; by means of reread and read-back units, it is possible to check the input and output. When these mechanical proofs are supplemented by definite routines and procedures, the internal control system is improved noticeably.

10. Limitations of the internal control procedures

When Mr. Costa, president of the McKessons & Robbins firm at the time of the $10 million inventory shortage, committed suicide in his office, he had placed opened on his desk a book on accounting in which were underscored these words: "No firm can have a foolproof system of internal control, because the cost would be so prohibitive that it could not remain in business." It was on the basis of this statement that he decided to perpetrate his fraud. Since no foolproof system exists, the best that can be hoped for is a reasonable system of forms, reports, mechanical devices, and established routines, supplemented by internal and external auditing, and fidelity insurance. It must be remembered that most frauds and thefts are committed by skillful and at times brilliant personnel, who can conceal their crimes, so that discovery in most cases is accidental. Furthermore, most employees are reasonably honest until "baited into dishonesty" by a loose, inefficient system of supervision and control.

Section 14

HOW TO AVOID BUSINESS FRAUD

BY

ELMER I. ELLENTUCK

HOW TO AVOID BUSINESS FRAUD

The problem of fraud

Fraud has been defined as the use of deception to deprive a victim of something of value. More specifically, the act of fraud may involve the commission of crimes such as larceny, embezzlement, or forgery. It may also arise from acts of trickery or cunning which, though immoral, are not necessarily punishable under the criminal law.

To most businesses, the problem of fraud is twofold: It threatens them from within through disloyal employees; it can hit them from outside through unscrupulous customers.

No precise figures exist to provide a grand total for the losses sustained annually by American business because of fraud. In many areas, law enforcement agencies do not compile or transmit meaningful records of local "business crimes." Moreover, it is not unusual for such crimes to be hushed up by the victims themselves to avoid embarrassing publicity. However, a study published by *Fortune Magazine* estimates that the annual loss to business from embezzlement alone is between $500,000,000 and $1,000,000,000.

1. Employees

It will never be possible to cite all the methods which human ingenuity can devise for committing on-the-job fraud. A writer in the *Saturday Evening Post* listed 210 ways in which crooked personnel had robbed banks, including an official who, after looting his bank's entire cash assets, also mortgaged its real and personal property and pocketed the proceeds!

Here are a number of the more frequent techniques used by dishonest employees.

Stealing loose cash. In companies which do a large amount of their business in cash, it is very difficult to avoid exposing currency to the eyes of employees—and so tempting them. In a retail store, a clerk may pocket the proceeds from cash sales before the sales can be recorded. Where a company does a considerable mail-order business, envelopes may be surreptitiously rifled of their contents. Anywhere, an open and unguarded cash drawer or box may invite a quick theft.

Creating false bills. Bills are paid to nonexistent companies and checks are cashed through a dummy. A typical example of how this can be done was

471

provided by a chief accountant employed by a food-processing company. He prepared bills on the printed forms of a fictitious company for nonexistent shipments of glass containers. He forged the initials of the purchasing agent and presented the bill together with a check to be signed by the treasurer. The signed check went to the address on the bill, which was nothing more than a mail drop used by the accountant. When he picked up the check, he deposited it in a bank account he had opened for the imaginary supplier. Later, he withdrew the funds for personal use. By the time he was caught, the accountant had embezzled $25,000 over a 3-year period.

Stealing merchandise and equipment. "During the past year," said Robert T. Wood, manager of the American Surety Company, "we have received employee-theft claims for the loss of aspirins, automobiles, barley, cod-liver oil, face powder, feed, shaving cream, toothpaste, and typewriters. Why, we even had a building superintendent who defrauded his boss by selling the radiators and washbasins of a vacant building."

Rigged invoices. Through collusion with unscrupulous customers, an employee invoices goods at prices below those established by the company. Part of the illicit saving is rebated to the employee by the customer.

A variation on this technique is for the employee to give the customer allowances on the bill for imaginary defects in the merchandise shipped him. The allowance is then split between the employee and the customer.

Forging checks. According to W. E. Rose, an authority on crimes involving checks, there are 800 ways of defrauding by check. A frequent method is for a dishonest employee to forge a company check to his own order and then to destroy the check when it is returned by the bank. He then conceals the transaction by raising the amounts on legitimate checks. Another trick is to change the name of a payee or to increase the face amount of a check after it has been signed.

In one case, a bookkeeper forged a number of checks to his own order. After each forgery, he wrote a check for the identical amount payable to a company creditor and presented it to the company's signing officer with the creditor's invoice. The bill had already been paid, but the bookkeeper so changed it that the signer did not recognize it. The bookkeeper kept the signed check, faked an endorsement, bank stamps, and a perforation and held onto it until the monthly bank statement reached the company. Now, he substituted the prepared check for the one he had forged to his own order. The bookkeeper was successful until the bank got one of his forged checks on which the amount in words and the figures did not match. When the bank called the company treasurer to ascertain which numbers were intended, the officer said he had never heard of the check. The jig was soon up for the bookkeeper.

Collecting "uncollectible bills." Every business has its share of delinquent accounts receivable, some of which inevitably turn out to be hopeless and have to be written off as bad debts. Others are marginal and may pay under pressure. If the employee assigned to handle overdue collections is dishonest, he will pocket funds obtained from delinquent debtors while reporting the account to the company as "uncollectible."

Padding payrolls. In a large company, a crooked paymaster, usually in collusion with a bookkeeper, may add some fictitious names to the payroll. The paychecks will be cashed by the pair and the proceeds split between them.

"Lapping." The employee steals from incoming payments and then applies subsequent remittances on other items to cover the amounts stolen. The shortage is always there, but not in the same amount. Should an audit be made, the employee will typically try to conceal the shortage by having a check drawn to transfer funds from one bank to another. The check is deposited on the last day of the year, but he carries it on the books as a credit to the short account. The check does not clear until the year is over—and when it does, the employee offsets it by "borrowing" again from a customer's account.

Other frauds

Paying creditors' invoices twice and appropriating the second check

Failing to record purchasers' returns, allowances, and discounts and appropriating the check or the cash payment therefor

Making fictitious advances to employees and neglecting to deduct them from subsequent payrolls

Burying improper disbursements in the personal accounts of partners and officers

Mingling cashier's funds with company funds and withdrawing company funds after the cashier's are exhausted

Misappropriating coupons, bonds, or dividends

Illegitimately removing merchandise covered by misstatement of lists of physical inventory

Reporting as received items not received, in collusion with suppliers

Allowing other employees free services or merchandise when not entitled to them

Manipulating financial data to secure excessive commissions, bonuses, or dividends

Raising amounts of petty-cash vouchers

Stealing postage stamps

Misappropriating the proceeds from the sale of scrap

Ordering items for the company's use and then diverting them to personal use

Manipulating time cards

Padding expense accounts

Illegally using extra sales books

2. Executive fraud

The press often carries news stories concerning executives arrested for robbing their companies. Their otherwise alert employers forgot that high-echelon personnel are just as vulnerable to temptation as workers in humbler capacities.

Managerial, technical, and professional employees are likely to be *trusted*. Their activities are rarely checked closely, and they are given almost carte blanche access to company property.

Their superior education, intelligence, and experience can lead them to apply ingenious and subtle twists to the types of fraud discussed above. In addition, they are capable of inventing an original trick or two. Not all of these strategems run afoul of the criminal law, but all are immoral and destructive of their employer's interests. Here are some of the most frequently used methods.

Bribes and kickbacks. Many companies suffer at the hands of dishonest officials who steer business to favored suppliers and contractors in return for outright bribes.

An example was provided some years ago by a buyer of women's dresses and coats for one of the world's largest mail-order firms. During a period of 7 years, he bought $6,000,000 worth of merchandise for his employer, for which he received $250,000 in kickbacks from suppliers. His regular salary during the period was $12,000 a year, plus a $5,500 bonus. The firm was tipped off about the buyer's crookedness and he was arrested for violating a state law against kickbacks. He received 6 months in prison and a $1,000 fine. Undoubtedly, the buyer's worst drubbing came at the hands of the Internal Revenue Service, which demanded $185,000 in back taxes, interest, and penalties.

Self-serving. The employer is led into buying goods or services from a company secretly controlled by one of its own executives. The executive keeps business flowing to his own enterprise and pockets the profits.

A local manager, an accountant, and a manager of a dairy company secretly acquired three local farms that supplied their company with milk. Milk was then purchased from the farms at excessive prices. What is more, dairy company funds were advanced to the farms and concealed through write-off accounts to bad-debts reserve. Fraudulent statements covering dealings with the three farms were prepared and certified to by the dairy company. These statements were used to secure loans from a lending institution. As a result of this treachery, the dairy company lost over $100,000. Discovery came when a company auditor became suspicious of the bad-debt write-offs and, delving further, stumbled on the outside interests of the disloyal trio.

Betraying company secrets. There are executives who steal confidential business data about industrial processes from their employers and sell them to competitors or use them in setting up their own businesses. Norman Jaspan, head of an agency of "managerial engineers," estimates that several hundred high-echelon employees are caught and convicted of stealing company secrets each year and that five times that number are not tried because management prefers to avoid the publicity which prosecution would stir up.

3. The average embezzler

The following is a composite picture of the average dishonest employee (without distinction by job status) developed by the Continental Casualty Company of Chicago, Ill.:

Age	Oldest	—62 years
	Youngest	—17 years
	Average	—35 years
Sex	Male	—93 percent
	Female	— 7 percent
Term of employment	Longest	—36 years
	Shortest	— 3 days
	Average	— 9 years, 3 months
Term before starting to steal	Longest	—29 years
	Shortest	— 3 days
	Average	— 6 years, 5 months
Term of stealing before discovery	Longest	—20 years
	Shortest	— 3 days
	Average	— 3 years, 2 months

The Surety Association of America describes the "average" embezzler as about 36 years of age, married with two children, having served his present employer for about 5 years with apparent honesty. There is nothing about the average embezzler to set him apart from the average man or woman.

4. Why they do it

Various agencies involved in coping with employee fraud have made analyses of the motives which impel the culprits to commit their crimes. Studies made by the Chicago Crime Commission, the Surety Association of America, and the United States Fidelity and Guaranty Company have been of particular interest.

While the reports vary somewhat as to the prominence they give each of the various motives, seven stand out for the frequency with which they crop up.

1. Extravagant living standards. Every company has its share of employees who are constantly being dunned by creditors. Some are simply bad financial managers. In one way or another, they manage to scrape through without recourse to dishonesty.

Others, however, have expensive tastes in cars, homes, furniture, clothes, and vacations, which can never be satisfied by their earnings. Even while bills pile up and they are under intense pressure from creditors to make payment, they entertain lavishly and continue to make more and more purchases.

An office manager in a commodity brokerage firm earned $6,000 a year. Nevertheless, he spent huge sums for social entertainment. Once he threw an elaborate party for 600 guests. He got his money by using the firm's funds to speculate in cotton futures; when there was a loss, it was the firm's loss; when there was a profit, it was his.   He embezzled a total of $63,075.79.

Sometimes, the employee's own tastes are modest and inexpensive.   His problems derive from a wife who craves and nags him mercilessly for luxuries which cannot be purchased on his salary.   To find the money to meet his wife's demands, the desperate husband turns to stealing from his employer.

Ironically, the employer himself is sometimes responsible for the employee's extravagance.   A typical example is the salesman who, while on a meager expense allowance from the company, must cultivate the society of affluent customers to obtain orders.   Inevitably, his finances are strained to the breaking point in the struggle to keep up appearances.

2. Gambling.   For many people, gambling is a disease.   Among the causes are rebellion, a drive for self-destruction, or a plunge into the frenzied excitement furnished by gambling as a means of escaping from what to the gambler are the unbearable encounters of real life.   The disease requires a constant supply of cash.   To obtain it, many an otherwise honest white-collar employee will turn into a thief.   He ultimately reaches the point where he steals to meet his gambling debts or to be able to continue to gamble.

3. Drinking.   Even a solitary drinker's liquor bill can be high.   Once under the influence of alcohol, many drinkers feel an uncontrollable urge to act out a role of importance and wealth.   In this they are cheerfully encouraged by the many spongers and hangers-on who frequent taverns and cocktail lounges.

It is just not possible for many problem drinkers to cover their home and family expenses together with the costs of drinking.   The next step is to augment their salaries with some quiet embezzlements.

A clerk employed by a large company gradually became a problem drinker. His wife persuaded company officials to send his paycheck directly to her. She, in turn, gave her husband a $3 a day allowance for lunch, cigarettes, and car expenses.   But the clerk continued to drink.   Now he borrowed from fellow employees and bartenders.   Eventually, his credit vanished because he could not repay his borrowings.   He then started to steal merchandise from the company and sold his thefts to tavern customers.   Two years later he was caught.   By this time, he had stolen $45,000 worth of goods.

4. Criminal character.   Every society suffers from the presence of a hard core of psychopathic personalities.   Devoid of conscience or remorse, without thought of the harm they inflict on their victims, they snatch whatever property opportunity places within their grasps.   From childhood on their names are familiar to truant officers, policemen, courts, and prisons.

Because many employers neglect to check carefully into the backgrounds of job applicants, criminals are often able to slip into honest employment—for what are usually transient periods.   While so employed, the criminal's basic interest in the job is what, if any, opportunity it provides for stealing.

The United States Fidelity and Guaranty Company reports the case of a 32-

year-old man who had a criminal record which he was apparently able to conceal through his military service.   After his service discharge, he worked for 5 months as an accountant for a commission merchant, being empowered to sign checks.   In those 5 months, he used his employer's current cash for his own purposes by drawing checks to the order of fictitious payees.   When his employer's cash was exhausted, the accountant fled to California, where he was apprehended a few months later.   Only a few hundred dollars were left in his possession.   The total amount embezzled was $35,293.

5. Bad business management.   Oddly enough, not all embezzlers profit financially from their peculations.   There are department heads and managers who, through carelessness and inefficiency, cause considerable wastage of company assets.   To conceal their failings, they resort to stealing and the juggling of records.

An example is furnished by the branch manager of a food company who had carelessly sold merchandise to patently poor credit risks.   In fear of being fired if he were found out, he started making entries in the accounts receivable ledger showing payments for a number of delinquent or bad accounts where no payments had actually been made.   The branch manager never profited by receiving any remuneration on any of these accounts, but his poor business methods and his false records cost his employer $29,000.

6. Women.   An employee with "women trouble" is invariably beset with financial difficulties.   If he has been divorced and rewed, he often finds himself obligated to support at least two families—on a single income.

If the employee is a married man committing adultery on the sly, he too is hit by staggering expenses.   If his lady loves cannot achieve marriage, they in any event expect a good time.   The cost of trips to night clubs and motels and the buying of jewels and furs overwhelm the employee and soon he is tempted to take company funds to support his style of living.

7. Unusual family expense.   A frequently pitiable cause of employee fraud is the sudden catastrophe of a family or personal emergency.   A wife, mother, child, or brother—or the employee himself—is hit by a serious illness.   There are huge medical and hospital bills.   In desperation, the employee "borrows" from the company.

A hitherto honest, hardworking truck driver worked for a manufacturing company.   He was 30, married, and had one child.   The child was stricken with rheumatic fever and hospitalized for a prolonged period.   During this time, his wife gave birth to another child and there was an expensive operation.   To meet the emergency, the driver sold some of his company's goods.   The amount of the embezzlement was $2,500.

In its study of defalcations in business entitled *1001 Embezzlers,* the United States Fidelity and Guaranty Company analyzes the causative factors behind the frauds committed by 845 men and 156 women embezzlers.   Here is what this analysis produced:

Men

Motivation	Number	Percent
Grudge against employer	23	2.72
Saving for rainy day	1	0.12
Domestic trouble—extravagant wife	33	3.91
Operation of another business	17	2.0
Irresponsible	34	4.0
Inadequate income	40	4.73
Family illness	24	2.84
Own illness	20	2.37
Speculation	4	0.47
Women	56	6.63
Poor business manager	25	2.96
Accumulation of debts	24	2.84
Living above means	170	20.12
Gambling and/or drink	195	23.08
Criminal character	114	13.49
Bad associates—dupe	24	2.84
Reduced income	6	0.71
Mental cases	2	0.24
To replace lost money	2	0.24
Aftermath of war	5	0.59
To finance marriage	6	0.71
To start elsewhere	6	0.71
To finance political candidacy	2	0.24
Spent on hobby	2	0.24
To help friends	1	0.12
Juvenile delinquents	3	0.36
Got woman "in trouble"	3	0.36
To pay alimony	1	0.12
To pay for motor accident	1	0.12
Mother-in-law	1	0.12
Total	845	100

Women

Motivation	Number	Percent
Family expenses	18	11.5
Husband unemployed	1	0.6
Living above means	31	19.8
Husband responsible	3	1.9
Family illness	8	5.1
Own illness	6	3.8
Clothes—extravagance	16	10.3
Influenced by man who shared proceeds	14	9.0
Lost in business venture	2	1.3
Gambling	1	0.6
Drink and dissipation	7	4.5
Criminal background	16	10.3
Weak character or dupe	5	3.2
Drug addict	1	0.6
Mental cases	4	2.7
Pregnancy	4	2.7
To finance wedding	4	2.7

Women

Motivation	Number	Percent
Grudge against employer	3	1.9
To start elsewhere	8	5.1
Regarded money as earned	1	0.6
Juvenile delinquent	1	0.6
To save cash	1	0.6
Unknown	1	0.6
Total	156	100

5. Where they work

Studies show that no type of business is immune from embezzling employees. They work everywhere; for manufacturers, wholesalers and retailers, small enterprises and large, publishers, laundries and banks, governmental agencies as well as private industry. Embezzlers turn up in small rural villages as well as large cities. They occupy every kind of position from janitor to corporate president.

Here is the occupational distribution of the *1001 Embezzlers.*

Men

Positions	Number
Agent and representative	18
Armed Forces—P.X., theatre, hospital, QM personnel	20
Auditor and accountant	11
Bartender	5
Bookkeeper	42
Branch manager—groceries, clothing, shoe, liquor, candy, cigar, accessories, optical stores, loan company, insurance, bank, etc.	155
Buyer	4
Cashier	21
City, county official	3
Clerk	43
Club steward	13
Collector	25
Department head—credit, traffic, sales, etc.	7
Driver and delivery man	53
Executive	35
Federal government department employee	8
Foreman, laborer	24
Hotel manager and clerk	8
Letter carrier and postal clerk	15
Newspaper reporter	1
Office, errand, and bellboy	9
Paymaster, payroll clerk	13
Plant guard	5
Postmaster	6
Route salesman—soft drinks, bakeries, dairies, breweries, laundries, cleaners, tobacco, etc.	30
Salesman—products and services of all kinds	117
Service man—pinball machines, burglar alarms, automobile, watch repair	8
Ship captain, purser, steward	5
Superintendent of apartments, hospital, lumberyards, oil depot	10
Ticket seller—railroad, bus, travel agent	6
Timekeeper	2
Treasurer or secretary—building-and-loan companies, credit unions, cooperatives, and social organizations	20
Warehouseman, stock and shipping clerk	32
Watchman, porter, handyman	21
Union official—national and state	3
Union official—local	47
Total	845

Women

Positions	Number	Positions	Number
Branch manager	12	Ticket sellers	2
Office manager	6	Collector	3
Auditor	1	Union and fraternity treasurer	8
Bookkeeper	25	Postmistress	7
Cashier	31	Waitress	1
Stenographer	3	Seamstress	1
Office clerk	10	Bus girl	1
Building-and-loan secretary	2	Maid	1
Store clerk	34	Charwoman	1
Apartment manager	7	Total	156

6. Steps for preventing employee fraud

Here are methods and guidelines which experience has shown to be particularly effective in protecting a company from employee frauds.

Hiring procedures. Too many employers are casual or even impulsive in their manner of hiring or promoting personnel. Often decisions are made on nothing more than an applicant's pleasing appearance or glibness in describing his qualifications.

A thorough reference check should be conducted on all new employees. Business and personal references should be contacted. A complete history should be obtained of the applicant's education and every period of employment and unemployment after he reached working age.

A number of employers now give polygraph (lie detector) examinations to prospective employees for high-risk departments.

The independent audit. An exhaustive, independent audit of the business should be made at least once a year by outside certified public accountants. Each audit should include a complete inventory of merchandise, equipment and supplies, cash, securities account, accounts receivable and payable.

In conjunction with the independent audit, all outstanding accounts receivable and payable should be confirmed by mail to all customers and creditors for verification of the account. This procedure should be conducted by persons outside the departments regularly handling such accounts.

Using the internal auditor. The internal auditor should be responsible for seeing that the assets of the business are properly controlled and accounted for, that expenditures are authorized, that procedures are followed, that organizational responsibilities are fulfilled as assigned, and that accounts and reports portray a fair picture of operations.

Internal control. This medium of control establishes and defines the limits within which the internal routines of a business must be conducted and beyond which a violation exists. Internal control has the following requirements:

To separate operating responsibility and accountability so that no person has sole control over any transaction, assets, or the records established to account therefor

To keep individual employees constantly but unobtrusively aware of the controls and boundaries and the procedures applied by the employer, because this knowledge will act as a deterrent against violation

To verify the continued maintenance of established controls and to remedy violations through prompt and effective action. The knowledge that violations are promptly and rigorously dealt with is also an effective deterrent to any prospective embezzler

Signing checks. Except in individually owned businesses, all checks should be signed and countersigned by two or more responsible officials.

All checks should be prenumbered and a record kept of those issued. All unissued checks should be accounted for and a file maintained of all canceled checks. Voided checks should be filed with canceled checks.

Checks should be printed on paper designed to prevent alteration, and the amount for which a check is drawn should be stamped by a checkwriter machine to prevent alteration.

Enforced vacations. Every employee in a position of trust should be required to take an annual vacation. Many frauds have been discovered when an embezzler has suddenly been forced away from the office by illness or accident.

The refusal or extreme reluctance of an employee to take any vacation whatsoever often alerts an employer to the possibility that the employee is concealing some dubious activities.

Working conditions. Employees who feel they are abused by their employers are often ready to steal with an easy conscience, especially if they are already under financial pressure. Employees who are underpaid, overworked, or abused will justify their embezzlements on the ground that the money they took was "coming to them."

The employee's personal life. It is a good idea for management to take a genuine interest in the personal and family problems of employees. By trying to become familiar with such problems and helping the employee to solve them, morale is improved and in many instances a tragic violation of trust can be forestalled.

Bonding or insurance. While a carefully developed program of fraud prevention will make stealing difficult, it will not make stealing impossible. Vigilance will discourage many potential embezzlers, but the company will still be in danger due to collusion or "steal-and-run" fraud. This is where bonding or insurance comes into the picture.

The fidelity bond is a guarantee up to a stipulated amount against financial loss caused by employee dishonesty. The purpose of the bond is to indemnify the firm for the loss of money or other property occasioned by dishonest acts of its bonded employees. The bond covers all fraudulent or dishonest acts including larceny, theft, embezzlement, forgery, misappropriation, wrongful abstraction, or willful misapplication committed by employees acting alone or in collusion.

There are various forms of fidelity insurance available to meet the requirements of any business. Any good fidelity insurance company will be glad to recommend the bonding coverage appropriate for the company's needs.

7. Checklist

The following is a list of suggested precautions which can assist businessmen in plugging their internal security loopholes. Even where many of the pointers have already been applied, an occasional review of the list can serve as a reminder to check their effectiveness.

General
Shift clerks from job to job to reduce opportunities for collusion
All employees *must* take their annual vacations
All personnel in high-risk jobs are bonded
The company books are checked regularly by outside accountants
The company gets comparative financial statements which are carefully scrutinized by a responsible officer
A roster is kept of all employees who are permitted to have keys
Keys are held only by carefully selected employees and are recalled when the holders leave the company
The ledger keeper is forbidden to handle cash transactions
Trial balances are checked to general and subsidiary ledgers by employees other than the ledger keeper
The bank is instructed to address all bank statements *personally* to an executive who is not connected with the bookkeeping section

Cash in general
A mail-room employee (not connected with the bookkeeping department) lists all the checks contained in the mail with name of the maker, bank, and amount. A copy of this list is kept separately from these checks and money orders
The receiving and disbursing of money is not performed by the same department that handles the accounting therefor
Monthly bank reconciliations are made by an employee who does not handle the receipt and disbursement of cash
Transfers between bank accounts are carefully audited

Cash disbursements
The company pays all bills by check
Authorizations for payment should be canceled at the time of payment so that they will not be reused to support a second (fraudulent) disbursement
All blank checks are prenumbered

Endorsements on returned checks are scrutinized

Checks are prepared with the use of checkwriter machines

Checks in any significant amount must be countersigned

Presigning of checks is strictly forbidden

Personal delivery of checks or cash by employees to creditors is forbidden

No checks are made payable to "bearer" or to "cash" except under special circumstances

Signed checks are not returned for mailing to the person who prepared them

Blank checks are kept under lock and key

Canceled checks are compared with vouchers for names of payees, dates, and amounts

Notice is taken of all outstanding checks and those which remain outstanding over 60 days are referred to a responsible executive

All canceled checks are scrutinized for unfamiliar payees, irregular endorsements, lack of bank cancellation, strangeness of perforation or stamping, alteration in date, amount or payee, or improper signature, endorsements which show variations from the past, and endorsements by check-cashing agencies

All branch or local office bank accounts are on an imprest basis and properly controlled through regular auditing or other routine

Employees who sign checks and cashiers are forbidden to prepare or approve vouchers for payment

The number of stamps used by the mail department is checked against purchases

All stamp purchases are made directly from the post office and paid for by check

Cash receipts

Sales slips are always prenumbered

Daily receipts are deposited promptly and none are used to pay bills or cash checks

The deposit slip is checked to ascertain whether all the day's receipts have been deposited

Records of cash receipts are checked against duplicate deposit slips

The bank deposit is prepared by someone other than the bookkeeper

The employee who balances the day's cash against sales slips or cash register tape does not himself handle sales

A responsible officer makes certain that the receipts are credited to the correct account every day

All checks and money orders are immediately endorsed "For Deposit Only"

Cashiers, salesmen, deliverymen, or others responsible for receiving money are denied access to ledgers or statements covering customers' accounts

The cashier's working space is physically enclosed and is off limits to all other personnel

Cash and records are never left unguarded

Accounting between the home office and branches is reviewed regularly

Petty cash

Petty-cash slips are prenumbered, written in ink, never in pencil, and are dated

Amounts on petty-cash slips are written in words as on a check

Slips are checked before reimbursement and stamped "paid" to prevent reuse

As soon as he is paid, the petty-cash recipient signs the slip

Checks are never cashed out of the petty-cash fund

Daily collections are never intermingled with the petty-cash fund

Petty-cash funds are on an imprest basis

Reimbursement checks are made payable to the petty-cash custodian (never "petty cash," "bearer," or "cash")

The petty-cash fund is balanced daily

The petty-cash fund is never used for making advances or loans to anyone

Petty-cash and stamp funds are audited frequently, preferably on a surprise basis

Sales and accounts receivable

Billing to customers is handled outside the accounting unit

Salesmen are forbidden to keep money for sales made

Customers are asked to confirm their balances to someone other than the bookkeeper

Items are priced by machine or rubber stamp, not by handwriting

Only authorized employees are permitted to set prices and to mark merchandise

Unannounced spot checks are made to be sure that actual prices agree with authorized prices and price-change records

Customers' questions about their accounts are handled by a person other than the one who posts Accounts Receivable

Sales registers with totals controlled by special locks are used and locked totals kept inaccessible to the opener of the register

Invoices for credit sales are serially numbered

The shipping department gives the accounting department a copy of the shipping order after shipment and the order is checked to the sales invoice

New accounts can be opened only after approval by the credit department. Schedules of overdue accounts receivable are drawn by someone other than the ledger clerk. Copies of the schedules are furnished the credit department

Defaulting accounts receivable are referred to an employee not a member of the bookkeeping department for collection

If employee efforts to obtain collection are unavailing, defaulting accounts are forwarded to company attorneys for legal action

The writing off of a bad debt must be approved by the treasurer or other responsible official

Monthly statements of account are mailed to all customers

All correspondence related to Accounts Receivable are handled by an employee other than the one who sent the monthly statements

Purchases

Competitive bids are secured whenever practicable

Cost-plus contracts must provide for inspection and supervision by company executives

Requisitions are approved by responsible executives

The company is alert to any hints of favoritism in the placing of business

Separate inspections for quality and quantity are made by employees not concerned with purchasing

Report of receipt of merchandise goes directly to the voucher unit

Close control is exercised over the issuance of purchase orders

Invoices go directly to the voucher unit, there to be matched with orders and receiving reports

Checks to pay for invoices are mailed directly to vendors after the check signer has examined and approved the invoice

Receiving is a function separate from purchasing

When bulk commodities are purchased and the company is unable to check specifications, arrangements are made for independent laboratory analysis on a lot or spot-check basis

Purchase orders should be in sequence and each number accounted for. Blank forms are kept under lock and key

Bills are compared with requisitions or purchase orders

Materials purchased are reconciled with inventory and materials used in production

Requisitions require approval by a responsible employee other than the purchasing agents

Receiving reports are checked to purchase orders

Separate records are maintained of items purchased by employees for personal use

Creditors' invoices are reviewed carefully to avoid duplicate payments

All invoices and supporting documents are marked "paid" immediately after payment is completed

Returned purchases are recorded

Payrolls

Cash payrolls

Cash payrolls are not made up from current receipts

Cash payrolls are delivered by the bank or picked up by a responsible messenger. If the amount is large, the messenger is accompanied by an armed guard

Employees paid in cash must sign the payroll or give a receipt

Check payrolls

The payroll is prepared by someone other than the person who will prepare the checks

Like other checks, payroll checks are signed by at least two responsible officers. If they are signed mechanically, the operation should be supervised by a responsible officer

The amount of each check is carefully scrutinized and the actual existence of the employee is verified

All payrolls are supported by time sheets or cards signed by the department heads for their own departments

Employees who quit the employ of the company must clear through an official outside of their own department

Unclaimed salaries are deposited with a responsible executive other than the paymaster

All pay increases must be confirmed in writing and approved by a responsible officer

Inventory

Physical inventories are taken regularly and are reconciled with perpetual-inventory records

Supplies are kept apart from other inventories

Inventories are covered by casualty and theft insurance

Nothing may be removed from inventories except on requisition

A card record is kept of all merchandise in the inventory

All warehouse stock is in the charge of a responsible custodian who is responsible for moving goods in and out of the warehouse or storeroom

No driver or deliveryman is allowed to put goods in storage or stock or to remove goods from storage or stock without the supervisor's or the custodian's presence

Valuable merchandise is never left unattended while on the docks or platforms of the receiving or shipping room

Scrap

The grade and quantity of scrap is measured as soon as it is created

The responsibility for checking and measuring scrap is separated from the responsibility for disposal and accounting

Every possibility of using the scrap elsewhere in the company is checked

All avenues of scrap sale are covered and rechecked periodically to guard against collusion or favoritism

8. Customers

Dishonest customers fall into two types. The first is that of the hardened criminal whose very purpose in going into business is to fulfil a crooked design. The other is that of the once honest businessman who allows circumstances to turn him into a thief.

To the hardened criminal, apprehension and imprisonment are mere interludes in a life of thievery, to which he returns as soon as he leaves jail. The "victim of circumstances" is generally so profoundly shaken by his punishment that he rarely resumes his career of fraud.

Career thief or occasional offender, here are some of their principal techniques.

Insolvency. A Dun & Bradstreet study reveals that in 1965 there were 13,514 business failures involving total liabilities of $1,321,666,000. However, these figures are only the visible portion of the insolvency iceberg. They do not include a vaster number of business collapses which are rarely noted on bankruptcy-court records. Thus, Dun & Bradstreet notes that in recent years over 400,000 concerns have been started annually, of which between 350,000 and 400,000 have been discontinued. The losses *their* creditors have sustained are incalculable.

Most business mortalities do not involve fraud. They die from such causes as their founders' inexperience, ineptitude, lack of capital, or plain hard luck. There is usually very little a creditor can do about the uncollectible bills this group leaves behind it other than to chalk them up to "experience" and the bad-debt reserve.

However, as creditors well know, a significant proportion of the failures are tainted by fraud and trickery.

Planned bankruptcy. This is a merchandising swindle based on the abuse of credit either legitimately or fraudulently established. In the argot of the underworld, this type of operation is called "scamming." It consists of five steps.

1. There is an overpurchase of inventory on credit
2. The merchandise is sold or otherwise disposed of quickly
3. The proceeds are concealed
4. No creditors are paid
5. Some of the creditors file an involuntary petition of bankruptcy against the business

In past years, this type of bankruptcy was almost exclusively a province of the lone, cunning entrepreneur. Now, according to FBI Director J. Edgar Hoover, hoodlums, racketeers, and Mafia elements have invaded this area of business.

Scam operators look for each scheme to produce a quick "profit" of at least a quarter of a million dollars or more. It is estimated that in the Chicago area alone organized crime's gross annual income from scam operations is over $5,000,000.

An example of a typical scam is described by N. E. Kossack, Chief of the Fraud Section, Criminal Division, U.S. Department of Justice.

This scheme centers around the Christmas buying rush. The swindle starts in October or November, and by New Year's Day the operator is out of business. The rush of the Christmas season, the eagerness of suppliers to sell, the prospective loss of a large order if a long-credit check is taken, the seeming opportunity to clinch a big sale—all these prompt quick delivery. When Christmas is over, the sellers discover they have been taken.

The creditors also discover that the "customer" had little interest in maintaining genuine books and records. What few are left behind in the wreckage of the scam operation are confused and inaccurate.

Bankruptcy as an "afterthought." This occurs among businessmen who start out with the intention of conducting an honest business but later turn to fraud. The time when the line between honesty and dishonesty is crossed can vary widely. The decision may be abrupt or take a long time to form.

One day, the hitherto honest businessman applies for substantial credit from suppliers. By furnishing false balance sheets he lulls their suspicions about his ability to pay. When the business collapses, the defaulter may claim he did not really intend to practice fraud. He simply wanted to preserve or expand his business and thereafter pay his bills. But this type of debtor frequently winds up in jail because he obtained credit through false representations.

Though the distinction may offer small comfort to cheated creditors, "the bankrupt by afterthought" differs markedly from the "scam" operator, in that he is recklessly (and criminally) optimistic. The scam operator is coldly deliberate.

The professional debtor. This type of customer rarely winds up in jail; he doesn't "steal." He merely takes advantage of the easy credit afforded by many sellers. Thereafter, he balks at paying bills. He makes collection so difficult that he does indeed avoid paying many a debt in all or part. Unfortunately, this class of debtors is so numerous that the total losses it inflicts on businessmen are relatively high. Here are some characteristic professional debtor types:

The judgment proof. He rolls up bills with impunity. Everything the debtor owns is held in another's name, such as that of his wife, mother, child, or brother. Legal action to recover unpaid bills is generally fruitless because the debtor has stripped himself of any assets from which a judgment obtained against him can be satisfied. If he is employed, the chances are that most creditors cannot attach his wages because a senior creditor already has hit him with a garnishee which will have priority for perhaps a decade before another claim can be levied against the debtor's pay. (Most states rigidly limit the percentage of a debtor's wages which may be garnisheed.)

The mover. After a buying spree, he (or very often she) changes his address. All bills mailed by creditors are returned by the post office for lack of a forwarding address. After the dust settles, the mover, now ensconced at a new location, ventures forth into the market again. To make life even more difficult for their victims, many of these debtors change their names as frequently as their addresses.

The charge-account operator. He is a byproduct of the modern charge and credit card age. The operator accumulates as many cards as sellers and credit clubs will allow him. He will not relinquish a card when requested, but keeps presenting it, raising his balances to enormous—and unrepayable —figures.

Check frauds. Retail businesses in particular are victimized by customers who obtain cash or pay for merchandise with bad checks. While acts of this nature are generally punishable as crimes, apprehension and punishment of offenders are difficult because of their high mobility. Here are the methods most commonly used by check swindlers:

Checks are drawn on nonexistent bank accounts
They forge the signature of the maker or endorser on a legitimate check
The amount on a legitimate check is raised
Checks are drawn on accounts with insufficient funds

Cautious businessmen take their time in cashing checks of persons unknown to them. They will ask such a person to endorse his check in their presence. They compel him to make identification by producing something with handwriting which corresponds with the check's signature. Remember, it cannot be claimed that a check is fraudulent until it has been returned by a bank and so marked.

Shoplifting. While retail store owners are the business group hardest hit by this form of crime, they are by no means the only victims. Shoplifting occurs wherever there is internal traffic, as in factories, showrooms, and warehouses. Besides store shoppers, culprits include vendors, buyers, servicemen, and deliverymen.

Types of shoplifters. Here are descriptions of some of the leading practitioners of the shoplifting "craft":

THE PROFESSIONALS. Crime like other human pursuits has its specialists. Among them are career shoplifters. They typically dress inconspicuously and are polite and deliberate in manner. They take considerable pride in their skill and varied techniques. Working closely with these "pros" is an underworld of fences who dispose of their loot.

It is not unusual for career shoplifters to continue working until late in life. The Boston police arrested a 78-year-old woman for shoplifting. She had $111 worth of stolen retail merchandise on her person. It was her seventy-seventh arrest for shoplifting.

THE AMATEURS. These are once-in-a-while shoplifters who are often driven by a sudden impulse to seize some attractive merchandise within easy reach. Unlike the poised professionals, the amateurs are self-consciously furtive and nervous.

They come from all stations of life. Some steal because of economic need. But others are men and women in comfortable circumstances who suffer from compulsions to steal traditionally described as "kleptomania." When they are captured, long-suffering relatives generally appear to pay for the stolen goods.

JUVENILE DELINQUENTS. Police and newspaper accounts indicate that the number of youthful shoplifters has increased sharply in recent years. Like the amateur adult shoplifters, the juveniles come from both sides of the railroad tracks. The poor ones steal to acquire glamorous clothes and jewelry; the well-to-do shoplift only for "kicks" to relieve the ennui of an overindulged home life.

DRUG ADDICTS. This is another group which has grown to be particularly menacing in the last few years. In constant and invariably pressing need for money to support their vice, addicts will frequently wander into places of business, grab merchandise—and run. Desperation frequently makes them vicious and violent when efforts are made to apprehend them.

How shoplifters work. The methods practiced by shoplifters are more varied than can possibly be detailed in these pages, but here are some of the more frequently used techniques:

"PALMING." The thief waits until the view of the clerk behind the counter is obstructed by shoppers or an accomplice. He then snatches and makes off with some merchandise the clerk cannot see.

A variation of this strategem is for a thief to provoke a dispute with a sales clerk and to keep him distracted until an accomplice has a chance to walk away with some goods.

INSPECTING. The shoplifter handles various items as though inspecting them. She acts out the role of a fussy customer. But when she leaves, only part of the merchandise is returned to the counter; the remainder stays with her.

CARRYING AWAY. This form of shoplifting is specially popular with unscrupulous deliverymen and servicemen. Items such as furniture, tools, and appliances are carried or wheeled out of a store ostensibly for delivery or repair. It is not unusual for some of the more brazen practitioners of this art to enlist the aid of store employees to convey the loot to waiting vehicles. The employees suppose that they are merely assisting a legitimate freight handler or repairman.

CONCEALMENT. Merchandise is slyly transferred from a counter or show case to a man's trouser or coat pockets or to a woman's clothing—or even underclothing. The shoplifter has, of course, mastered the art of showing little or no bulge.

Other customer frauds
Burglaries
Counterfeit money
Fraudulent accident claims
False claims concerning goods or services rendered

9. Steps for preventing customer fraud

As in the case of employee fraud, no list of suggested precautions can anticipate every trick and device which dishonest customers will spring on their sellers. Moreover, each industry has fraud problems which are peculiar to it. That is why every businessman should consult his trade association—and his own experience—for protective measures most appropriate to his type of business.

Nevertheless, there are a number of countermeasures which have been found to be universally practicable in warding off customer fraud.

The threat of insolvency. The consistent application of sound and prudent credit policies will prevent or at least cut losses due to insolvency. A business must draw credit interchange and mercantile agency reports on all unsolicited first orders. Here are some of the danger signals credit reports can disclose:

Current judgments and prior bankruptcies and defaults
Overly high officer salaries and expense accounts
Sudden repayments of loans by corporate officers and their families
Big, sudden reductions in inventories
Big increases in inventories out of line with sales
Customer refusal to supply data which credit agencies and suppliers have a
   right to demand

If these insolvency symptoms turn up on the reports, do not sell. If sales have already been made, do not wait any longer than you absolutely must before pressing for full payment of any money due.

When bankruptcy occurs. A fraudulent debtor rarely voluntarily allows a creditor to inspect his books. When a court forces him to reveal his records, here are a number of vital subjects worth checking carefully for evidence of possible fraud:

See whether the debtor has transferred any money or other assets to members
   of his family
Check his accounts receivable
Examine the bankrupt's checking accounts for evidence of preference to
   particular creditors
Check whether he withdrew large amounts from business checking accounts
   for personal use
Compare bankrupt's most recent financial statements with his general ledger
   records
See whether there are any shortages in assets
Go over past tax reports for possible tax refund or carryback claims
Check for fictitious sales
Have an audit made of all of the debtor's assets and liabilities
Scrutinize the debtor's past and current operating statements and balance
   sheets to learn why he went bankrupt

If it turns out the debtor committed fraud, his discharge from bankruptcy can be blocked. This in turn may force him to disgorge concealed assets. It may thereupon become possible for creditors to retrieve all or a substantial part

of their losses.   As is well known, in ordinary, "uneventful" bankruptcies, creditors collect either nothing or token amounts.

Credit insurance.   One method used by a significant number of businessmen
to ease their losses from debtor insolvencies is to obtain credit insurance.   There
are companies which will insure part, most, or all of a creditor's accounts receivable.   These insurers, however, do not cover retail accounts, and they
reserve the right to deny coverage to accounts whose solvency or stability they
have reason to doubt.   Another limitation is that premiums are relatively expensive, a fact which makes it difficult or impossible for businesses which operate on low price markups to buy credit insurance.

Safeguards against check frauds.   Here are some pointers frequently recommended by cautious businessmen:

Do not cash out-of-town checks
Demand better identification than a Social Security card
Do not cash checks for juveniles
Do not cash checks written in pencil or which show signs of alterations or
    erasures
Do not cash postdated checks
Be on guard when customers pay for merchandise with personal checks larger
    than their bills, so that a certain amount of money has to be returned to
    them in change
The most dangerous times to cash checks are evenings, weekends, and holi-
    days when banks are closed

What to do about shoplifters.   There are a number of protective measures
that businesses which are particularly vulnerable to the shoplifting problem
have learned to apply.

Watch customers who are holding merchandise.   Shoplifters often carry
    merchandise openly to make it appear that they are examining it or waiting
    for a clerk.   Actually, they are waiting for an opportunity to conceal the
    article
Crowded and deserted areas are both popular with shoplifters.   These areas
    should be under frequent observation
Expensive items should be displayed in a pattern, if possible, making it pos-
    sible for the clerk to tell at a glance whether everything is there
Sales clerks should glance frequently toward those customers waiting to be
    served and remind them they will be served as soon as possible.   This tends
    to discourage those who are there for the purpose of shoplifting
If the business is large enough to warrant it, hire some internal-security per-
    sonnel such as store detectives
Doors near display or merchandise counters should be locked or guarded
Set up mirrors and peepholes in areas where customer "self-service" is per-
    mitted.   You should also consider installing mirrors through which trusted
    employees can see without being observed

If you can afford it, consider the advantages of using closed-circuit TV monitoring, placing your "transmitters" at the particularly vulnerable regions of the business

Carry theft insurance

Do not jump to hasty conclusions. Seizing a suspicious-looking customer who turns out to be innocent can lead to lawsuits against the business for false arrest and the like.

Section 15

HOW TO MARKET YOUR PRODUCTS AND SERVICES

BY

G. Dryver Henderson
AND
J. Richard Schneider

HOW TO MARKET YOUR PRODUCTS
AND SERVICES

Introduction

Marketing is the development, promotion, and distribution of a product or service at a profit to the company. It consists of those business activities which direct the flow of goods and services from producer to consumer. Marketing activities often take place even before a product is made—as when a market study is made to determine the potential for a new product or service, or when new consumer-pleasing features are added to a product's design. The concept that marketing only begins when a product leaves the factory has been outmoded.

The purpose of marketing is to satisfy a particular group of consumers with a product or service. In a competitive economy, all firms have to succeed in this purpose in some manner. Today, more and more successful firms operate within this *marketing concept:* The activities of their entire businesses are directed toward *satisfying consumer needs at a profit.*

This chapter will show how products are usually marketed, and will enable you to apply your judgment to the application of specific marketing activities to your business. While marketing is usually thought of in terms of manufactured *products,* it is equally important to the commercial offering of *services,* such as insurance policies, bank loans, haircuts, or automobile repairs. For convenience, the term "product" will be used in its broadest sense to refer to a firm's output, whether in tangible or intangible form.

Three cautions about marketing. Three cautions about marketing should be kept in mind, particularly by those lacking prior experience in the area. These cautions may seem obvious, but the high mortality rates for small businesses and new ones indicate they are too often overlooked.

First, marketing is critically important to the firm. Managers may become too internally oriented to their business, especially when complex manufacturing problems or internal finances make constant demands on their time and effort. Under such conditions, the firm's marketing strategy and activities may receive too little managerial attention. The old saw, "If you have a better mousetrap, the world will beat a path to your door," no longer holds true. You will not sell many mousetraps if they are improperly priced or unattractively packaged; if people are not particularly interested in eliminating mice; if people do not want to travel to your door, or if they do not even know where to find your door. It has been estimated conservatively that 80 percent of all products introduced do not succeed. Many of this 80 percent can be considered better mousetraps which fail because they are not properly marketed.

Second, marketing is not so easy as it looks. As consumers we are exposed to marketing efforts all our life. We see and hear numerous advertisements, are presented with promotional offers, and are invited to try new products. Being on the receiving end of such activities, it is easy for businessmen to develop a false sense of marketing expertise. Marketing problems may appear simple, and their solutions may seem a mere matter of common sense. This can be deceptive. Marketing *is* easy in one respect—it is easy to make a wrong and costly decision.

Marketing problems are as complex as any in other areas of business, and are seldom easily quantified. Often there is no one best solution. The advertisement you read in your favorite magazines may have involved as much planning and effort as would a decision to increase plant production capacity or float a capital-stock issue. For example, a single advertisement represents decisions on what the copy should say, what the art should depict, to whom the advertisement should appeal, what medium would best present the message, how much should be spent on running the advertisement, whether or not a coupon should be used, and which specific magazines could deliver the most prospects at an efficient cost. A wrong decision on any of these considerations could cause the advertisement to miss its objective and result in largely wasted effort. Just as specialized engineering skills are required in designing a plant and accounting skills are needed for financial control, a highly developed understanding of the marketing function must be possessed by company management to ensure the firm's ability to satisfy consumer needs in a profitable way.

Finally, the marketing field is so varied and complex that some outside counsel and assistance are almost always necessary to carry out the function properly. Even the largest and most successful companies continually avail themselves of outside counsel. Some examples of specialized organizations in the marketing area are advertising agencies, marketing-research firms, packaging specialists, sales-promotion agencies, and sales-management consultants. These organizations can relieve your firm of much of the burden of marketing planning and performance. If used properly, their contributions should far outweigh their costs. Today's manager must be sufficiently skilled in marketing to properly direct and make effective use of these outside organizations.

The complete marketing program. This section covers all aspects of a complete marketing program. First the role of marketing strategy and planning is explored. This is followed by an examination of the major marketing activities and how they are used. Finally, considerations for making a firm's marketing efforts effective are covered.

1. Develop your marketing strategy

Marketing strategy means directing the firm's planning and activities toward the attainment of consumer acceptance of its products and services in order to reach a profit objective. There are two elements of a marketing strategy—

1. *Define the market target.* This involves determining the scope and extent of the market in which the product or service will be offered. The firm must select the primary group of consumers—the market segment—for whom the product is intended
2. *Develop a marketing mix.* A marketing mix is a combination of marketing activities chosen to appeal to and satisfy a consumer target group

The selection of a consumer target or segment can be based on a wide range of criteria. Furthermore, the marketing mix can be composed from a broad selection of marketing tools and techniques. Since both the market target criteria and the universe of marketing activities contain many possible variations, the number of possible marketing strategies which could be considered in any given business is almost endless.

It is not feasible for the manager to exhaustively evaluate all of the possible marketing strategies for his product. A list of possible strategies can be reduced to manageable proportions, however, by the progressive elimination of those which are obviously the least desirable or those which lie beyond the resources of the firm. Although ideally there will exist one "best" strategy, for practical purposes a number of strategies, each with quite different elements, might be suitable to achieve the marketing goals. Since consumer behavior and preferences are always changing, and since the marketing environment is normally in a state of flux, even the best strategy might be in a state of constant change and revision.

While selection of the best strategy or of any well-targeted strategy that will adequately achieve the firm's growth and profit objectives is essential for marketing success, having the right plan is not in itself a guarantee of success. Strategies are only as successful as the manner in which they are implemented. The best marketing plans in the world cannot succeed if they are not implemented and executed with enthusiasm and drive. Conversely, an aggressive attitude on the part of the marketer may somewhat make up for deficiencies in the basic strategy. As with successful athletic teams, there should exist a marketing spirit founded on the basic desires to compete, grow, and succeed.

Define the market target. To define the market target, a detailed analysis of potential customers should be made in the light of what the firm has to offer in its product line, particularly with regard to the firm's objectives and capacities. In the first place, a market is essentially a combination of people with both the willingness and ability to buy a given product or service. These people will not all have the same financial means. They will most likely be unevenly distributed over a designated geographical area, and even people in a given area with similar means will possess differing individual preferences and willingness to buy any given product.

The ability of people to buy provides the basis of any given market. Shepherds in the Saudi Arabian desert might desire a color television set even more greatly than the American suburban housewife. However, they do not possess the economic ability to buy this kind of item, and hence do not constitute a market for it.

The basic selection factor in determining most markets, then, is income. Many demographic characteristics often correlate with income. These include education, age, and occupation. All these factors are indicators of the level of quality in the market.

Some products, such as the basic items of food and clothing, are not wholly dependent on income in seeking suitable markets. However, the level of a consumer's buying power is an important determinant on what *kinds* and *qualities* of food or clothing are sought by different market segments.

Willingness to buy a product or service is as important as the ability to buy in itself. Variations in taste, social class, or physical living conditions will affect people with identical incomes to spend in different consumption patterns. Given any one level of income, any of the following nine characteristics may prove important in determining the willingness of final consumers to buy your product:

1. Age
2. Sex
3. Environment
4. Education
5. Occupation
6. Religion
7. Ethnic origin
8. Marital status
9. Family size

It is important to note that willingness to buy is an attitude of consumers, and hence subject to frequent change. One of the primary objectives of marketing is to effect favorable changes in consumers' willingness to buy the products or services of your particular firm.

The definition of a market target should be based on as concrete and specific factual data as possible. Once such information has been compiled, it is then possible to estimate the market potential for a new product and to set specific sales objectives and goals for its introduction.

Information relating to the size of various markets can be found in government reports and available published sales statistics. A wide range of market data is available from a number of different creditable sources. In addition to numerous government sources, data about different industries are available from many trade associations and the trade publications which cover those fields. The latter are of particular use to industrial marketers. The following list is intended to suggest sources of a wide variety of data which should prove useful in determining the extent of many markets:

Publications of the U.S. Department of Commerce—

Selected Trade Associations of the United States
Survey of Current Business (monthly)
Marketing Information Guide
Publications for Use in Marketing and Distribution
Catalog of U.S. Census Publications (quarterly)
Sources of Information on American Firms
Industrial Statistic Guide and Finder Catalogue
Guide to Foreign Business Directories
State, Regional and Local Market Indicators
Directory of National Associations of Businessmen
Facts for Marketers (9 regional editions)

Other government publications—

Decennial Census of the United States
Census of American Business
United States Census of Manufacturers
Quarterly Survey of Consumer Buying Intentions
Basic Library Reference Sources for Business Use
Directories for Use in Marketing

Other sources—

Business publications
Consumer magazines and newspapers
Survey of Buying Power, published annually by *Sales Management Magazine*
Sourcebook of Specialized Markets, published by National Business Publications, Inc.
Consumer Markets, published monthly and annually by Standard Rate and Data Service, Inc.
Annual Market Data Issue, Advertising Age magazine
Industrial Marketing: Market Data and Directory (annually)

This list is merely intended to suggest the kind of basic market data that are easily available. A comprehensive compilation of source material on national and regional markets, and on specific industries and marketing institutions, is contained in Robert N. Carpenter's *Guidelist for Marketing Research and Economic Forecasting,* published by the American Management Association.

In addition to the kind of basic data sources listed above, more specific and contemporary information is available from several marketing-research organizations. Perhaps the best known of these is the A. C. Nielsen Company, Chicago, which supplies periodic reports based on purchase and inventory records from representative groups of food and drugstores. The Nielsen store panels are sufficiently large to be useful for most geographical markets. Several other firms can also set up retail store panels for various product classifications upon request.

Additional basic information about a market may be learned from consumer panels. Consumer panels are made up of representative groups of families who report their purchases of certain products weekly or monthly along with pertinent information relating to price and retail outlet. These panels can be used to study the purchasing and usage habits of consumers over long periods. Useful data can be derived on brand loyalty, frequency of purchase, buying rate per family, and brand switching. Since the demographic characteristics of each participating family are known, the data may be broken out by income, employment status, race, and size of the families. There are a number of permanent consumer panels available to the marketer, perhaps the largest of which is the National Consumer Panel of the Market Research Corporation of America, New York. Many newspapers in major cities maintain consumer panels as a service to advertisers, and these may be of particular interest to the local or regional firm.

In identifying the consumer target, it can be valuable to have other kinds of information over and above the standard demographic and statistical data. In order to understand the buying motivation of consumers, behavioral or motivational research may be employed. This kind of information may prove useful in the development of your advertising copy strategy.

Develop your market mix. Once the critical task of choosing the target consumers has been accomplished, the firm must combine all of the marketing tools at its command in order to reach this target. Many manufacturers, preoccupied with problems of finance and production, often back into this part of strategy development. A product might be developed, for instance, and only then, almost as an afterthought, does the manufacturer set off in search of a market. Even when the consumer has been carefully identified and analyzed, it is not a simple task to complete the development of an effective marketing strategy. The number of possible elements of a marketing mix is infinite. A product might have many appearances, flavors, sizes, colors, brand names, and other attributes. It might be advertised on television, radio, newspapers, magazines, billboards, and so on. The company may apply its own salesmen, brokers, or various kinds of wholesale distributors. There may exist a wide range of possible prices which could be charged. For each of these marketing variables, many different options may be chosen. From this endless range of possibilities, managers are expected to select the most effective combination or mix to obtain the desired sales response from the market target. While a number of effective approaches may be used to develop the best possible mix for your firm, we recommend that the new firm develop its strategy in the following manner.

First, the firm should examine the various marketing activities it can engage in. These should be taken in the sequence in which they would normally be executed. These activities, which are discussed in detail in the next part, are marketing research, product development, packaging, pricing, sales and distribution, advertising, other promotion, and results measurement.

In reviewing how each of these activities may be profitably employed in the total marketing effort, the manager can develop a sense of perspective on the relative importance of each of these tools to his business. The amount of effort each activity requires should be proportional to the degree of contribution it offers to the fulfillment of your firm's marketing objectives.

The advantages of following the above order stem from its sequential approach. First, the consumers are analyzed and a product is developed and packaged to meet their needs and wants. Having developed a product, the manager then sets the price in the light of expected consumer reaction to the product and in line with the profit objectives of the firm. Next, a way is determined for obtaining and maintaining effective distribution to our consumers. Advertising is developed to tell the consumers about the availability and desirability of the product. Other suitable measures of demand stimulation may then be employed to promote the product. Finally, these marketing efforts should be kept under constant review in order to ensure their effectiveness.

The marketing plan. When the marketing strategy has been finally formulated, it is useful to embody it in a written marketing plan. The written plan should contain a clear statement of the product's marketing and profit objectives for a given period (usually one year). The critical data and background information required to execute the strategy should be summarized. The marketing plan should make clear how the various marketing activities are to be used to meet the product's marketing objectives.

A marketing plan should be a useful, actionable document. Periodic reviews and updating should be carried out throughout the year. A good marketing plan will provide the manager with a continually workable blueprint for his marketing action. It should also be used to inform and indoctrinate all personnel who play a significant part in its execution.

2. Using marketing activities

Marketing strategy is carried out through a number of different but related activities. While marketing activities represent different approaches and perform separate functions, they are related in their purpose of achieving the firm's marketing goals. For example, a single marketing effort to improve consumer recognition of a product's brand name might involve such diverse actions as writing a research survey questionnaire to determine consumer awareness; designing a new package label to improve the brand name's visibility; and filming a television commercial to highlight the brand name to the public.

Marketing activities often overlap one another. Suppose a soap company decides to run a reduced price *promotion* on a dishwashing liquid. Such a decision would probably be based on some *marketing research* indicating the sensitivity of the product to price promotion. *Pricing* analysis would determine how much the reduction should be. *Packaging* may be involved if the reduction is to be highlighted by a "cents-off" label. It may be decided to support the promotion with special *advertising* to inform consumers of the price savings. *Selling* effort is required to see that retailers have the product on their shelves at the time when the advertising will run. After the promotion has been run, *results measurement* would be performed to evaluate the promotion's performance.

As in this example, marketing activities are usually interrelated. To meet specific marketing objectives, the manager must select the particular combination of activities which will best do the job. The task of making these choices is far from simple. Depending on the situation and objectives, the suitability of any marketing activity may vary. In considering the activities available to implement his marketing strategy, the marketing manager must view their application in the light of the nature of his product, the desires of the consumers, and the prevalent marketing environment.

Marketing research. Marketing research is the activity of gathering and evaluating information on which marketing decisions are based. It seeks to answer questions about the consumer and the market environment. Such questions may be fairly basic, such as: Who are the consumers of portable radios? What is the size of the market for structural steel? What are consumer wants concerning frozen dinners? On the other hand, research is used to answer narrower and more specific questions such as: What is the per capita consumption of soft drinks by Negroes living in Chicago? What is the effect of page position for a newspaper coupon on the number of coupons redeemed?

Marketing research fulfills the *intelligence* function in marketing. The effectiveness of a firm's marketing strategy and tactics is largely determined by the quality of the intelligence on which they are based. The availability of accurate and actionable information can be vital to the making of sound marketing decisions.

The performance of other marketing activities can be improved through marketing research of various kinds—

Performance research. Measurement of customer satisfaction or attitude toward an already existing product, service or company

Product-development research. Determination of product and features best liked or wanted by the consuming public

Pricing research. Research determining price guidelines relative to competition and relative to consumers' opinion of value for specific products or services

Advertising research. Study of method and message content used in communicating with the consumers

Distribution research. Research directed to determining optimum or improved channels of distribution from producer or supplier to the consumer

While personal judgment plays an important part in every phase of marketing research, it is important to know and understand the sequence of steps which make up the usual "scientific" approach to marketing questions. For convenience, this methodology can be broken into the following nine sequential steps:

1. Problem definition
2. Internal analysis or situation evaluation
3. External analysis or informal investigation
4. Final planning
5. Data gathering
6. Data tabulation and processing
7. Analysis and interpretation of results
8. Presentation of findings and recommendations
9. Follow-up

Problem definition. The definition of the problem is the most important and, depending on the problem, sometimes the most difficult job for the marketing researcher. Correct identification of the problem is vital, because research based on the wrong problem will pay off in inconclusive or impracticable results.

It is rarely an easy task to get at the major underlying considerations of a problem; symptoms of problems are often mistaken for the problems themselves. One of the best ways of targeting in on the more important considerations is called *exploding the problem.* In a sales problem, it is almost meaningless to ask: How do we stop our sales decline? While this may be the general problem, it is equivalent to asking how a sick man can be cured before knowing what kind of sickness he has. Instead, the problem should be exploded or broken up into more manageable parts. The sales decline should be viewed in terms of its possible causes: Are prices out of line? Are there product deficiencies? Has competitive promotional activity intensified? Is the advertising campaign effective? This kind of examination enables the marketer to understand his current situation more clearly and to pinpoint his problem.

Internal analysis or situation evaluation. When the problem has been identified and defined, it is useful to first undertake an internal analysis of the firm's own record, recent history, operating assumptions, and any research previously done in the problem area. This step provides an opportunity to examine the components of the problem explosion and thus further sharpen the problem definition.

The internal analysis will often reveal the existence of much pertinent information of which the manager may not have been aware. Sometimes sufficient data are found at hand so that no new data gathering will be required.   More often the internal search gives the researcher a better idea of what additional information must be obtained.

Internal analysis may include focused interviews with company personnel who might have insight on some part of the problem.   These additional viewpoints can shed light on little-known or overlooked aspects, and can provide useful avenues for the researcher to follow.

External analysis or informal investigation.   As part of the planning phase of marketing research, an informal investigation should be made of information sources outside the firm.   This step is somewhat of a scouting expedition, and might involve informal interviewing of contacts within the industry and with others doing business with the company.   This is the time to determine what published and public data are pertinent to the problem before making final plans to undertake the gathering of new information.

Final planning.   This is the step where the final research course of action is chosen, and commitment is made for the necessary expenditures.   At this point the researcher (1) makes the final choice of data-gathering method; (2) creates the final instrument (usually a questionnaire for recording the data; (3) selects the sample; (4) conducts one or more pretests of the method; and (5) reviews the cost-and-time estimates to complete the research.

During this planning phase it is useful to develop and test hypotheses.   A hypothesis is a statement, based on the best judgment of the moment, of the expected or probable conclusion of the research.   Development of a hypothesis requires the identification of the variables involved in the problem, and exacts prejudgments from the decision maker.   Then the hypothesis, or statement of expectation, is tested for accuracy in the light of the known facts.   If a hypothesis is tested and determined to be off target, an improved statement must be developed and tested.   During the final planning of the research project, the questionnaire, sample, and data-gathering method should be reviewed against the hypothesis in order to determine their adequacy to prove or disprove it.

Data gathering.   In marketing research there are three basic methodologies for gathering data: (1) survey, (2) observation, and (3) experiment.   For almost every problem, any one of the three methods would produce valid results.   Choice among them is made purely on the basis of costs involved, depending on the type of information to be determined.

Survey data gathering is perhaps the most commonly used method.   A survey is used to ask questions of fact, such as, "How often does a housewife shop at a certain shopping center?," or to gather opinions.   The majority of surveys will be a combination of fact and opinion gathering.   Some surveys ask just a few questions of a large sample, while others go into great-depth interviewing of only a small sample of people.

Observation data gathering usually requires a large sample and normally employs a relatively simple questionnaire.   The observation method comes closest to being a "nose-counting" technique, such as determining how many cars on a highway pass a certain point at a certain time. As a rule, the object is to record the frequency of a particular phenomenon. In all instances, the aim is to record factual data.

For determining some kinds of information, a survey or extended observation would be too difficult or costly. These are situations, such as package testing or price testing, which usually lend themselves best to experimental data gathering. In an experiment, the number of variables or interference factors can often be controlled.

Sampling is always an issue in data gathering. Naturally, the need for sampling arises in marketing research because limitations of time and money rarely permit study of all the members of a population. With a need for data or information and limited funds available, the question always arises, "What size of sample is needed to provide reliable information?" The answer to this question depends on the degree of accuracy and reliability required and the size of the *population universe* in question. There is no standard answer.

Data tabulation and processing. The raw data collected during the data-gathering step are usually not immediately usable in the analysis and interpretation step which follows. In most cases the data must be tabulated, and in a variety of ways, before the various quantities of information make any sense. The results of tabulation may also indicate that certain data need to be validated or verified. This is indicated whenever certain parts of the data appear to be out of line with the majority of similar information collected.

Analysis and interpretation of results. Analysis may be described as breaking data into small pieces, examining each carefully, and then putting the pieces back together again in a meaningful pattern. For simple "black-and-white" problems, analysis may only entail describing or presenting the figures and commenting on them. More often, analysis is more difficult, demanding logical thought and a full working understanding of the business involved. How and what to analyze depends on the nature of the study and the type of data gathered. Some analyses must be solely dependent upon statistical or mathematical techniques, while others are relatively subjective in nature.

There are several pitfalls to be avoided in preparing research analysis. One is the making of unwarranted generalizations; the urge to generalize is understandably great, for the value of a set of findings often increases with their scope. Another problem involved in analyzing data is the danger of extrapolating or extending the conclusions beyond the range of the observations.

Another pitfall is the tendency to identify correlation with causation. This fallacy in logic is sometimes missed (for example: Tom swims; fish swim; therefore, Tom is a fish). While a lack of correlation invariably proves absence of causation, the presence of correlation does not by itself prove causation.

Presentation of findings and recommendations. A well-executed marketing-research project is presented in a clear and meaningful way, and should include action-oriented recommendations suitable for implementation. The researcher must not assume that the factual analysis of the results has marketing meaning just as it stands. It is the researcher's job to translate the analysis and communicate the action steps to be taken as clearly as possible. If the results of the research substantially diverge from what was expected, the researcher should include the full rationale which led to the unexpected results. A lack of understanding of the basic reasons behind a conclusion or recommendation may result in no action being taken on the report. When results are presented in a simple, persuasive, and believable manner, the recommendation's chances for implementation improve substantially. When research turns up surprising results, there may be a tendency on the part of the manager to disbelieve it. This makes it essential that the researcher explicitly communicate the reasons behind the conclusions.

Follow-up. Marketing research should not end with the presentation of the results. The effective researcher should audit or follow up on the implementation of his recommendations at a reasonable time after presentation of his report. If the recommendations are not being translated into action, it may be due to insufficient understanding which the researcher can clarify.

In summary, marketing decisions are often difficult to make because of vaguely defined goals, lack of time, inadequate information, the number of variables in question, and uncontrollable external conditions. Marketing research is a primary tool of decision making because it helps to remove these roadblocks. It helps to clarify marketing goals and objective; it saves decision-making time in the long run; it provides necessary information; it identifies the key variables of the situation; and it provides the manager with more accurate knowledge of those conditions affecting the market which lie beyond his control.

Product development. In the face of constant change on the part of both the consumer and the marketing environment, the importance of developing new and better products must not be overlooked by the firm. Many products which were leaders in their fields yesterday have become obsolete, and some of the shining stars of today's business economy are products that did not even exist a few years ago. Some of the products we take very much for granted—television, air travel, instant coffee, and so forth—were in but the crudest stages of development before World War II. In a dynamic economy the importance of careful product planning is clearly evident.

First, it must be understood what is meant by "product." Does a consumer buy a bar of soap, an automobile, or a life-insurance policy? While the consumer receives these things in physical form in return for his money, he has not intended to buy a compound of chemicals and animal fats, a complex rendering of well-tooled metals and glass, or a sheet of paper covered with small print. Instead, the consumer has purchased a convenient way to wash his hands, the ability to ride from one place to another in comfortable fashion, and the assurance that his family will be financially protected in the event of personal tragedy.   In short, it is not enough to offer the consumer the output of your firm in physical form.   The consumer is primarily concerned with the satisfaction derived or expected from the purchase of the product.   The marketing-oriented firm, whether engaged in manufacturing or in providing services, is aware that what it sells is *consumer satisfaction*.   It is possible for business executives who have come from a different area of the business to be overly concerned with the speed of a production line, the size of the payroll, or the care with which an invoice is made out.   While these are all important to the firm, they have little bearing on how the consumer perceives the product. Consumers are only concerned with the finished product or service and what it does for them.   This applies as much to the industrial buyer of nuts and bolts as it does to the housewife shopping in a supermarket.

Product-planning strategies can usually be described as involving *diversification, simplification,* or *expansion*.   It is possible for a firm to employ different product strategies to its different product lines, if the product categories are sufficiently different in nature.   Within diversification there are two different approaches, both of which seek to appeal to specific groups of target consumers and to carve out for themselves special markets within larger markets.   These approaches are product differentiation and market segmentation.   Their primary difference is one of emphasis.

A *product-differentiation* policy attempts to create new consumer demand for an existing or slightly modified product.   This policy is followed heavily in product categories where there are few significant differences between competing brands.   Usually firms following a product-differentiation policy will employ heavy advertising and promotional efforts to try to convince the consumer of the superiority and advantages of their product, when the product is actually closely similar to competitive products.   Whatever differences there are, even though only psychological or minor, are heavily emphasized.   Despite the functional unimportance of such product differences, consumers are very often responsive to them if effectively presented.   Since much of the satisfaction a consumer derives from a product may be psychological, psychological product advantages then become important.

By contrast, a *market-segmentation* strategy attempts to change or adapt the product itself to consumer demand as perceived by research.   Whereas product differentiation promotes products to as large a market as possible, market segmentation not only recognizes the existence of many district submarkets, but further tries to appeal to the submarkets by adjusting or adapting the product or service to the particular needs of these markets.

A disadvantage of market segmentation is that the necessity of producing a multiplicity of products may sacrifice some mass-production economies.   It may also increase the cost of advertising and selling as the number of different products to be promoted increases.   On the other hand, tailoring the products to the needs of various submarkets can enable a firm to penetrate those markets more deeply, thereby increasing the total output of the firm.

Simplification strategies, on the other hand, call for reducing the number of product variations offered. When competitively possible, this strategy works to minimize the higher costs which may accompany the firm's efforts to satisfy as many consumer-demand variations as possible. A further refinement of the simplification concept is standardization, in which specifications or grades to which goods must conform are established and which allow for a specific categorization of products. This strategy is most applicable to industries where there are few essential product differences, such as with agricultural commodities. While this will often increase the production efficiencies of the firm, and hopefully the price to the consumer, it also results in narrowing the field of choice available to the consumer.

Line expansion usually involves the development of a line of related items to a product or product line which has already achieved a measure of success. Since the new products are somewhat similar to the existing products, new production facilities are not necessarily required. The good name or image that has been built up for the existing product will serve to benefit the new product in its introduction to the consumer. Considerable marketing economies can result from the sale and promotion of a number of items under one overall brand name.

The advantages of line expansion ordinarily do not apply if the added products belong to a unrelated market field. New equipment may be required to manufacture the new addition, and the consumer may find it hard to perceive the logic of the application of one brand name in two unrelated product categories. Furthermore, the new product may have a wider potential than the product to whose line it is being added; consequently, the sales limitations of the existing product may inhibit the broader acceptance of the new item.

In order to guide the firm in the choice of the number and kinds of products it will produce and sell, a clearly defined *product policy* should be established. The product policy should be developed in the light of the resources and capabilities of the firm. Every company has its own different strengths and weaknesses. A good product policy will capitalize on these strengths and avoid product development which is incompatible with its weak points. A thorough enumeration of factors to be assessed in this regard is contained in Table 1 below:

Inventory of Company Resources *

Financial strength ....Money available or obtainable for financing research and development, plant construction, inventory, receivables, working capital, and operating losses in the early stages of commercial operation.

* Charles H. Kline, "The Strategy of Product Policy," *Harvard Business Review*, pp. 91–100, July-August, 1955.

Inventory of Company Resources

Raw material reserves .....Ownership of, or preferential access to, natural resources such as minerals and ores, brine deposits, natural gas, forests.

Physical plant ....Manufacturing plant, research and testing facilities, warehouses, branch offices, trucks, tankers, etc.

Location ....Situation of plant or other physical facilities with relation to markets, raw materials, or utilities.

Patents ....Ownership or control of a technical monopoly through patents.

Public acceptance ....Brand preference, market contracts, and other public support built up by successful performance in the past.

Specialized experience ....Unique or uncommon knowledge of manufacturing, distribution, scientific fields, or managerial techniques.

Personnel ....Payroll of skilled labor, salesmen, engineers, or other workers with definite specialized abilities.

Management ....Professional skill, experience, ambition, and will for growth of the company's leadership.

Having established a basic policy for the selection of new products, three steps should precede the actual design:

1. *Develop a list.* Efforts should be made on a periodic basis to utilize every possible source to build a list of ideas for possible new products. In the firm that is properly geared toward the satisfaction of its consumers, the atmosphere should be ripe for soliciting encouraging ideas and suggestions from field salesmen, suppliers, research-development personnel, market researchers, advertising agencies, and, of course, those entrusted to the new product function itself.

2. *Screen the ideas.* It is useful to establish a new product acceptance scale which would permit consistent and objective ratings of new product ideas. If the product policy is well matched to the resources of the firm, such a scale is easily contrived. This should prove quite useful in the initial task of sorting out ideas that are well geared to the potential of the firm.

3. *Evaluate and implement.* After the screening process has narrowed down the field of product candidates to a fairly selective list, evaluation judgment must be brought to bear. The potential product must be viewed in the light of all operating costs it would add to the firm and what profit potential it might possess under a wide range of environmental conditions. It is often helpful to undertake original research to provide a clearer picture of consumer reaction to the product concept.

Once the product concept has been shown to have sufficient potential to warrant implementation, it is ready for the product-design stage. Product design can be a major factor in the degree of marketing acceptance that a product can gain. The design of the product should be undertaken with three objectives in mind.

First, a design should maximize the overall utility of the product. Where competing products offer relatively the same basic utility, consumer preferences for one or the other may relate to the presence of some additional utility in one of the products. In attempting to incorporate supplementary utilities into a product, manufacturers often add a feature to the design which is of insignificant consequence and does not increase the service of the product to the user. Sometimes features of this sort do add the element of novelty, which may temporarily add appeal to the product, but which usually soon wears off. On the other hand, some design elements have been devised to offer some supplementary utility, but have become so widely accepted that all the producers in the field have been compelled to adopt it, and have thus become essential ingredients in the basic products themselves.

The second objective is the incorporation into the product of selling design. Selling design is not intended to increase the product's service to the user once it has been purchased, but does add to the sales appeal at the point of purchase. Thus, the consumer, when faced with relatively similar products, often prefers to make his decision on the basis of appearance and style. Selling design has been an important factor in the market success of many individual items in fields where the utility appeals of various products are relatively equal.

The third basic objective of product design is minimizing cost. While it is important to maximize the efficiency of product manufacture or service application, it is equally important to resist altering a good design in order to substitute less expensive material or to avoid an expensive step in the production process. The manufacturer who develops a winning product, and then proceeds to strip it of its basic consumer-satisfying qualities through indiscriminate cost reduction, quickly finds that consumer acceptance often fades as swiftly as the satisfaction-producing qualities of a product are diminished.

Packaging. Packaging should be an integral part of a firm's marketing efforts. Not all businesses recognize this. Some firms are content to stuff their product in a box; others, while careful to produce packages which are technically perfect in containing and protecting the product, nevertheless overlook the role of the package as salesman, communicator, and promoter.

The concept of packaging should not be limited to boxes, cans, and jars. A package may be anything which contains a product or service at the point of sale or use. For example, when a bank gives plaid checkbook covers to its customers, the covers serve as packages for the bank's checking services. Shea Stadium may be considered an extremely successful package for the New York Mets.

Packaging has two equally important functions, the *physical* and *promotional*. The physical packaging job includes the following:

The package is a *container*. Many kinds of goods are sold by weight or size. A package thus holds a given *measure* of the product

The package makes products easier to *handle*. Consumers find it more convenient to buy cookies in packages, instead of loose from a barrel as once was the custom. The six-pack carton makes larger beer and soda purchases practical. Pins and tacks are usually offered in easy-to-handle packages instead of loose

The handling consideration also applies to the transportation and storage of the product. The design must be practical enough to ensure that the package is compatible with the material handling and storing ability of all distributors, warehousers, and shippers

The package provides *protection* to the product from spoilage and contamination. For instance, the process of vacuum-packing not only protects food products, but extends their usable life almost indefinitely

Another physical function of packaging is *ease in dispensing* the product. Utility is added to the product itself by such dispensing features as the squeezable toothpaste or hair tonic tube, the pour-spout on paper milk containers, and even the disposable baby nurser which comes complete with rubber nipple

Finally, a package may have the quality of *reusability*. Jars of jam and peanut butter are often designed for reuse as drinking glasses. The empty coffee can with its plastic lid is perhaps the most widely used household container in the country

The promotion function of packaging concerns how the package is used to help sell and satisfy the consumer. The following qualities are important to packaging in the marketing sense:

The package should *identify* the product. Even if the package only contains the brand name, it serves as a reminder to buy the product every time a consumer sees it

The package should incorporate *selling design*. It should be visually attractive and appealing to the consumer. Usually, until the consumer actually uses the product, all she will see is the package. If the package lacks appeal, the consumer will be less interested in the product itself

The package should convey all necessary product *information* to the purchaser. This may include usage information, directions, recipes, weight and measure, servings, contents, and storage suggestions

The package is also an excellent vehicle for *advertising copy* in addition to the product information. This helps to sell the product off the shelf, and also serves to reinforce the consumer's satisfaction after the purchase

The package should project a favorable *image* for the product. The product should look its worth. The package appearance should build confidence that the product is of good value

While large companies often have their own packaging design departments, most firms make use of industrial designers to execute their packaging development requirements. The marketing executive will normally state the physical and promotional objectives for the package. The designer will submit alternative design executions in line with the objectives. Samples will be made of the most promising designs, and usually some consumer research is done to test their relative appeal.

The opinions of several departments should be sought. The sales manager is consulted on the package's sales potential. The advertising agency may be consulted on the package's appearance and promotion potential. The traffic manager must determine whether the package meets existing shipping requirements. The production engineer must determine whether the package is feasible to use in terms of production and packing capability.

While the consultation of several departments is usually required, the manager must make sure that the design remains faithful to the objectives set for it. Otherwise there is risk that too many pet ideas will be added to the design by the various departments, thus resulting in a complicated and confusing package.

Pricing your product or service.   Pricing is of utmost importance to the marketing executive because of its close association with profit and profitability. Profitability—the rate of return on money invested times turnover—is usually the most important measure of a company's success.

Since profitability is determined by the combination of margin and turnover, it is possible for firms to sell similar kinds of products with totally different pricing structures and still have a similar net profitability result. This can be seen in retailing, where a discounter might work on low margin with high turnover, while a regular department store might have the same profitability as the result of higher margins and lower turnover. For each kind of store, pricing is an important part of its marketing approach.

As a practical matter, successful pricing is but one of several actions a firm takes to reach its profit goal. Pricing should not be established without full consideration of its probable impact on other aspects of the business. Specifically, all price decisions should be related to such factors as production capacity, advertising requirements, selling methods, channels of distribution, and probable competitive reaction. At certain times it may be wise to reduce price in order to offset an expected sales decline due to a reduced advertising budget. Under certain conditions a price rise may be an effective strategy when coupled with a campaign to upgrade the image of a company or product. If a firm is expanding its production capacity, perhaps a temporary price reduction will help to fill the additional plant up to an economic operating capacity more quickly. It is essential, however, to guard against the kind of price cutting which results in the establishment of new reduced industry-wide price levels which are harmful to the longer-range profits of the company, as well as the industry in general.

When introducing a new product, or when beginning to operate in a new market area free from competitive pressures, the first pricing consideration should be "What price is necessary to cover production and selling costs?" and second, "Above this point what price will the customer be willing to pay?"

Assuming the latter is higher than the former, the next consideration should be to evaluate whether there is sufficient margin to make it profitable for one or more distributors to handle the product between the manufacturer and the final customer. If the "product" is a service, the fundamental questions are very much the same: First, "What price is necessary to cover all costs of supply?" and then, "Are there enough customers who will be attracted to the service at a price somewhere above the former?"

When it has been established that there is an adequate market which will support a product or service with a price range which allows for an acceptable profit, there is next the challenge of positioning the product's price in such a way as to maximize the probability of meeting the profit objectives. To do this the firm must make appropriate choices among basic pricing policies and key pricing strategies. *Pricing policies* are established as a guide for members of the organization in deciding specific pricing questions. Price policies are particularly vital in a competitive situation, since such rules often make it possible for a subordinate in an organization to make decisions on specific questions without having to place the questions before higher authority. *Pricing strategies* are pricing plans designed to meet certain competitive situations or to convey certain psychological impressions.

One-price policy. A one-price policy means the firm will offer the same price to all customers who purchase under essentially the same conditions and in the same quantity. A one-price policy does not preclude a seller from changing the price as frequently as he desires; however, the price is usually fixed for a reasonable length of time. A long-established one-price policy sometimes results in what are called *customary prices.*

Flexible-price policy. A flexible or variable price policy is one under which the same products and quantities are offered to different customers at different prices depending upon the bargaining ability, personal relationships to the seller, and possibly some other irrational factors. Although the one-price policy is more common in the United States today, the flexible-price policies still exist in most foreign countries. The flexible-price policy generally can work only where products are not standardized and where advertising has not educated the customer to expect a certain price.

Price-level policies. It is quite common for a company to adopt a policy of *meeting competition* or taking a position *under the market.* Typically in highly competitive categories such as milk, bread, or gasoline, producers must meet competition or lose out to the lower-price competitor. Companies which have the policy of pricing their products under the market are usually those whose business depends on large volumes and high turnover, such as discount retailers.

Loss-leader pricing. Loss-leader pricing is a strategy normally employed by retailers for the purpose of building store traffic. Certain products are selected for their promotional value and offered at very low prices. Typically advertised as "specials," loss-leader items are usually bona fide bargains. The hope is to attract people who might otherwise shop or patronize a competitor, and to attract new customers for an introductory trial. In the latter case, the object is to induce this customer to return regularly to make future purchases at regular prices.

Bait pricing. Like loss-leader pricing, bait pricing is used to attract business. The difference, however, is that under bait pricing the seller really does not expect to sell any merchandise at this price. Bait pricing is occasionally used by some retail furniture or appliance stores. The expectation is that once the customer is in the store, he will be traded up to a higher priced item which serves the same utility as the advertised bait. Customers are actually able to buy the bait item, but only after a great deal of sales assurance by the salesman that they are buying the wrong product.

Full-line pricing. Full-line pricing establishes a profit-margin objective for a whole number of products supplied through a given outlet, or with the same brand name. It does not establish a profit margin consistent with the costs of each separate product involved. Full-line pricing is intended to maximize overall or total profit, not just profit on each specific item. For example, a major television set manufacturer will probably have a low-price model with a low margin which he can use as a "fighting" brand to be in competition with lesser-known brands for the purposes of satisfying price-conscious or lower-income customers. The same manufacturer will probably have a top-of-the-line "prestige" model which has a fat profit margain. The net result is an averaged profit margin across the entire line. The same principle is used in loss-leader pricing in a food store. While the supermarket will make little or no profit on the special items, the manager expects to maintain overall profit through the normal margins on other products likely to be picked up at the same time by the average customer.

Price lining. Price lining is the practice of setting prices for a given category of products all at the same price, even if there is slight variation in the cost to produce those products. For example, this is typically done with neckties: These are often sold at only four prices, $1.50, $2.50, $3.50, and $5.00, although there are probably many more variations in the actual cost of the ties. The advantage of price lining is that it helps avoid confusion on both the part of the salespeople and the consumers. There is no problem with price lining so long as there is a wide enough price range to allow sufficient choice to satisfy most customers.

New-product pricing. There is no consistent strategy for pricing a new product. Some prices may be lower than the long-range expected price for the purpose of gaining early consumer acceptance and quickly filling production capacity. Other products might be introduced at a high price in an attempt to take the cream of the market before catering to the more price-sensitive sections of the market. The latter strategy maximizes profits for a new product and follows the thinking that a price can more easily be lowered than raised.

Starting with a high price has other advantages. It may establish something of a prestige image for the new product or service. A high price will probably hold down demand while production capacity is being built. Starting with a high price and then working down is more likely to lead to maximized profit margin as indication of the product's demand elasticity is uncovered.

Psychological pricing. Psychological pricing is based on the premise that certain prices have more consumer appeal than others. Common examples are decile pricing, just below a rounded ten-cent increment (69 cents instead of 70 cents), and odd pricing, just below an even dollar increment ($5.95 instead of $6.00).

Prestige pricing is another psychological price stratagem. Such pricing aims to connote prestige in the consumer's mind, and thus encourages him to buy it for its associated value. For instance, an $11.00 Scotch whisky may be no better than another brand selling at $6.25, but under the belief that "You get what you pay for," the $11.00 Scotch will undoubtedly taste much better.

Pricing should be viewed in relation to the other marketing activities. In the consumer-package-goods field, for instance, the price of most products is set sufficiently high to allow for a measure of promotional activity. If a product is priced high in its category, it may be mandatory for the advertising to stress the product's premium quality. If a price is set so as to yield a more profitable margin to the retail trade, the product may benefit from increased trade merchandising support. By integrating pricing strategy with other elements of the marketing plan, a firm can employ greater leverage in realizing its aims of building a consumer franchise and maximizing profitability.

Selling, sales coverage, and distribution. Sales can be defined as a combination of activities which satisfactorily brings about the delivery of product or service into the hands of a customer. Sales activities include personal selling, arranging for a product to move through the various channels of distribution, and providing for ongoing personal servicing required for customers to whom a product or service has been delivered. Usually these activities are supervised by the traditional position of sales manager.

Sales is the culmination toward which the marketing effort is usually pointed. Without sales there would be no revenue, no ongoing production, no fulfillment of customer needs—in short, no business enterprise.

Sales includes both personal and nonpersonal selling. Personal selling includes—

Customer-comes-to-you selling, as in a retail outlet
You-go-to-the-customer selling, for which salesmen are employed
Telephone selling

By contrast, nonpersonal selling is just what the term implies, and includes mail-order selling and vending-machine selling.

Personal selling. Personal selling is the most complicated, costly, and commonly used form of selling. It requires a thorough understanding of the product, an ability to perceive the customer's viewpoint, and an ability to communicate the product story in terms of the customer's needs. Personal selling is challenging, as one must deal directly with people who are often quite knowledgeable. As no two sales situations are exactly alike, selling requires continuous adaptation to changing circumstances.

There are basic steps involved which repeat themselves in most selling situations. While they may appear self-evident, they are not always easy to accomplish in practice. They include—

Search out and meet prospective buyers
Select appeals especially adapted to the particular buyer
Help him to make a selection—that is, help him to "buy"
Give him advice
Answer individual questions and objections
Assure him when he has doubt about a particular point
Show samples and demonstrate the use of the product
Help indecisive buyers to make up their minds
Close the sale—that is, ask for the order
Make suggestions for additional or complementary items
Follow up buyer after sales to assure satisfaction

While these steps may seem all too obvious, the absence of any one of them could seriously interfere with a selling transaction.

Obtaining repeat business from present customers for many companies is dependent on servicing the customer after the initial sale. Assuming that the product is up to the customer's expectations, the salesman must look after other considerations such as providing technical service and assuring a satisfactory method of distribution. The salesman who provides good service expects to gain goodwill, customer understanding, and, hopefully, repeat business.

Bringing the product and customer together. For a retailer or a service organization, bringing the product and the customer together is almost taken for granted. Such a business establishment need only be placed in a convenient location for easy customer access to the products. Beyond that, the retailer need only make sure that his store is clearly marked; once inside the store it is usually clear to the customer where to find the product and where to pay for it.

For the manufacturer who does not sell his product directly to the final consumer, bringing the product and customer together in the most efficient way can be challenging. The alternative routes from manufacturer to consumer through one or more distributors to one or more types of retail outlets are called *channels of distribution.* Sometimes channels are direct and simple, but often they are quite complex.

Consider, for example, the variety of distribution channels required for a maker of electric batteries. Large batteries may go directly to original equipment manufacturers, such as electronic and automobile producers, who are their final users.   Other batteries may go through a complex maze of intermediate wholesalers or jobbers to reach different kinds of retail outlets, such as grocery stores, drugstores, electronic repair shops, gas stations, hearing-aid specialists, and so forth.

Suppose further that this battery manufacturer has only one plant. He must arrange to channel his products to the desired geographical extent of distribution, whether national, regional, or local. He must arrange for warehousing and storage of his inventories. He must choose whether to employ outside distribution organizations or to perform this function with his own personnel.

Intermediary wholesalers and distributors are usually specialists catering to specific markets, specific kinds of retail outlets, or specific kinds of transportation situations. In selecting among alternative channels, the marketer must consider such aspects as product life, product handling requirements, and allowance for profit margin for the intermediaries.

Before distribution can be achieved, sales coverage must be established. Inadequate sales coverage creates the risk that distribution channels will be dominated by competitors. The firm must determine whether it can cover its desired channels adequately with its own personnel, or whether its products can be more effectively handled by brokers, jobbers, or other intermediate selling organizations.

It is recommended that the new business firm begin and expand its distribution selectively with regard to both geography and channels. It is important that the firm not allow its ambition to spread its resources too thin. Concentrating sales efforts on a limited number of markets, distributors, wholesalers, and kinds of retail outlets can provide substantial sales and distribution economies. By selling intensively, it is possible for even a small firm to achieve a measure of dominance within a distribution channel.

Advertising.   Advertising is the most evident form of promoting a product or service. Basically, it is mass selling. Advertising encompasses *any paid form of nonpersonal presentation or promotion of ideas, goods, or services by an identified sponsor.*[1]

The content of advertising is some form of selling *message* which will reach consumers through a communication *medium,* such as the following:

Television
Radio
Newspapers
Magazines
Billboards
Posters and signs
Transit cards (trains, buses, taxicabs)
Direct mail

[1] "Report of the Definitions Committee," *Journal of Marketing,* p. 205, October, 1948.

Motion pictures
Novelties (pens, calendars, matchbooks, etc.)
Programs and menus
Circulars
Catalogs, directories, and references
Skywriting
Recorded telephone messages
Point-of-sale materials

The effectiveness of advertising may well have a large bearing on a firm's profits. In most fields consumers have shown willingness to pay substantial price premiums for advertised brands. In the dry-grocery field, for instance, manufacturers' advertised brands accounted for only 18 percent of all brands in 1965, but accounted for 74 percent of the consumer sales. The influence of advertising is obviously felt despite the fact that powerful food chains almost without exception are careful to price their own nonadvertised brands significantly below comparable manufacturers' advertised brands.

In some business categories the importance of advertising is so critical that large portions of net sales income are invested in advertising expenditures. One leading health and beauty-aid firm turned as much as 40 percent of its sales dollars into advertising in 1965. While this is an exception (a more balanced picture is given in Table 1), it serves to point out the potential importance of advertising dollars in generating and sustaining sales.

How to develop your advertising. Good advertising should be properly targeted in both message and media. Sound research should underlie your efforts. This research should cover three areas—

1. *Consumer research.* What are consumer needs, wants, and preferences with regard to the product category?
2. *Product analysis.* What are the want-satisfying qualities of the product in the light of consumer desires? What features of the product or service appeal most to consumers?
3. *Market analysis.* What are the characteristics of the market for which the product is intended, and how should the presentation of advertising be influenced by them?

The planning stage comes next. Having used the results of marketing research to define the possibilities of your advertising opportunity, you should next examine the opportunity within the context of your overall marketing strategy. This may be accomplished in four steps—

1. Setting objectives for your advertising
2. Media strategy
3. Copy strategy
4. Allocating advertising funds

Setting objectives for your advertising. Consider the role advertising is to

Table I

Advertising Expenditures as a Percent of Sales Dollar among Largest National Advertisers in Their Fields in 1965 *

Industry	Advertising as percent of sales
Drugs and cosmetics	27.6
Gum and candy	16.3
Shaving goods	15.3
Soft drinks	12.3
Latex products	12.1
Soaps and cleaners	10.9
Beer	10.8
Toys	10.4
Food	8.7
Liquor	5.9
Tobacco	5.8
Paper products	5.0
Photographic equipment	4.4
Floor covering	4.3
Broadcasting	3.2
Airlines	2.7
Chemicals	2.1
Tires	1.8
Retailing	1.3
Appliances	1.2
Metals	1.1
Containers	1.0
Automotive	0.8
Oil	0.8
Communication	0.6

* Taken from "125 Leaders' Advertising as Percent of Sales," *Advertising Age,* p. 44, Aug. 29, 1966.

play in the overall marketing mix. Objectives should be established to specify the kind of consumer reaction the advertising should produce.

Here are a number of specific objectives an advertisement or advertising campaign might be geared to attain:

Announce the introduction of a new product into the market
Encourage consumers to try a product for the first time
Continue to remind and convince current users of the product's merits
Inform consumers of ways in which the product can be used, such as with a recipe illustration
Influence wholesalers and retailers to stock products
Presell potential direct-trade customers on the desirability of using, distributing, or promoting a product before the salesman calls
Obtain direct-consumer response, such as having a housewife cut out a coupon to redeem on a purchase of the product
Influence the public on a matter of concern to the company

Create a favorable "brand image" for the product
Develop goodwill toward the company

It is essential that your objectives be well defined if the advertising is success-fully to do its job of mass selling within your marketing strategy. Any given advertisement or campaign may be run to accomplish only a single marketing objective or several objectives. The advertising execution must be well tar-geted to be effective. No matter how clever or creative the ad, if it does not focus on the intended objectives, it cannot do the job you want. Keeping ad-vertising efforts in proper relation to their marketing purpose will help to avoid the predicament of the corporate executive who said, "I know that half of my advertising dollars are wasted, but I don't know which half."

The second stage of your advertising planning should be the development of media strategy. You have already identified your consumer target or targets; now you must determine how to reach them most effectively.

Media effectiveness has two important aspects. An obvious goal is to reach the most target consumers at the most efficient costs. This is reasonably quanti-fiable. An equally important consideration, however, is the suitability of the medium as a vehicle for the execution of the advertising message.

Determining whether the medium provides a good environment in which your selling message can accomplish its objectives is a matter for careful judg-ment. For example, an outdoor billboard is not a good place to deliver a complex message requiring long copy, but is suitable for a quick visual impres-sion or a slogan. Television is usually unsurpassed for product demonstrations involving action. Magazines are often used for recipe advertising because of the power of color illustration in stimulating appetite appeal. Direct mail is uniquely suited to obtaining immediate consumer response, such as the redemp-tion of coupons.

Having identified your target consumers earlier, you must choose media which are seen, heard, or read by them. Audience profiles have been developed for most major media. These often break down their audience by age, sex, in-come, occupation, and other demographic data. Many media have developed fairly sophisticated research which can provide such information as automobile and home ownership, travel intentions, and product usage for many categories among their audience.

Evaluating media cost efficiency requires reasonably extensive knowledge of the field. With few exceptions, only the larger advertisers have the resources to become proficient in this area, and most firms rely upon their advertising agencies to handle the evaluating function as well as the task of media buying.

There are useful yardsticks for use in evaluating the cost efficiency of any given medium. Most media costs can be equated, for instance, on a basis of "cost per thousand." This term refers to the expenditure necessary to reach 1,000 consumers via the medium. Such measurements of efficiency are best used when comparing different advertising vehicles within the same category, such as two magazines or two television time periods. The selling effectiveness of your advertising may vary from medium to medium, and skilled judgment must be employed to properly interpret this kind of comparative data.

The concepts of reach and frequency are useful in determining the kind of market penetration through television and radio a media plan can give. *Reach* means the percentage of households exposed to an advertising campaign in a market within a given time period. For example, an announcement on a local radio program might have a reach of 12; that is, 12 percent of all households in the area will have been exposed to the advertisement.

Frequency refers to the average number of times in a 4-week period the households reached have been exposed to the campaign. If the radio commercial mentioned above is repeated once weekly for four weeks, it is said to have a frequency of four among the households listening.

You can get a good idea of the total weight of your campaign in a market by multiplying the total households reached by the average frequency. This reach times frequency figure—sometimes referred to as "gross rating points" when referring to broadcast media—is useful in comparing your market coverage from period to period, or in comparing your advertising weight with that of competitors. Table 2 shows how different media can be combined to produce an extremely heavy media weight penetration.

Table 2

Medium	Schedule	Reach	Average frequency	Reach × frequency
Network TV	8 commercials/week	86	5.4	464
Local spot TV	6 commercials/week	64	3.2	205
Combined TV		88	7.6	669
Local spot radio	90 to 100 spots/week	54	7.9	428
Combined radio and TV		93	11.8	1097
Consumer magazines	Full pages in 5 magazines	64	1.9	122
Combined media		95	12.8	1219

Note that the reach figures are not additive. The network television schedule, for instance, has a broad reach, and the reach of the local spot-television schedule largely duplicates it. In this example spot television and radio are being used primarily to increase the frequency of consumer exposure to the campaign.

The choice of using specific media should be made in the light of four factors: (1) the objectives of your advertising campaign, (2) the effectiveness of the media in reaching your target consumers, (3) the size of your advertising budget, and (4) the ability of the media, alone or in combination, to achieve your target reach and frequency levels. Normally newspapers, television, radio, and consumer magazines attempt to reach a broad public, while direct mail, specialized magazines, and trade publications have more specific market targets. For example, if you wish to advertise only to medical doctors, you can usually reach them most efficiently through professional medical journals or by a direct-mail campaign directed to doctors' offices.

The development of copy strategy is usually the most critical stage in planning your advertising. Some even feel that copy strategy should be developed before media strategy is considered, and that media should be largely selected for their compatibility with the planned copy executions. Copy strategy is the approach an advertiser takes to communicate his message to the consumer. Depending on the media to be used, the message may be communicated in words, illustrations, or sounds. Most often the objective of copy is to motivate a consumer to buy the offered product or service.

To attain the copy objective it is useful to develop a general approach grounded on continued consumer research. It must be keyed to constantly changing consumer preferences, desires, and outlooks.

It must be remembered that the consumer is constantly bombarded by many selling messages and stimuli. It has been estimated that the urban male on the average day is exposed to 1,500 different messages, all of which seek to influence his future buying behavior. Since both the consumer and his environment are in a constant state of change, it is difficult to formulate hard-and-fast rules that will apply to all situations. The successful campaign which ran last year may be a dud this year. Or a campaign which is attuned to urban tastes may fall flat on its face in the more rural areas. Because peoples' wants and tastes differ widely, it is practically impossible to appeal to all of them. It is therefore necessary that your consumer targets be identified with care. Only by developing a sound knowledge of their attitudes, thinking, and reactions can you hope to effectively communicate your message to them.

Four elements of communication are common to most effective advertisements. First, you must attract your audience's *attention.* Just because a consumer happens to be looking at the television set when your commercial runs, or leafing through a magazine which contains your illustrated advertisement, you have no guarantee that he is going to notice your message. Your first task, therefore, is to become noticed, and in such a way as to make a consumer tune in.

Second, the advertisement must be interesting to the consumer. There are many different ways in which you can attract attention, but in order to hold the consumer's *interest,* you must communicate something which substantially appeals to him. By effective presentation you should make the product itself of primary interest to him.

The third step in successful advertising is to awaken in the consumer a *desire* for your product. The consumer's attention should be directed to thinking about the product and what it can do for him. Your message may be an appeal primarily to his reason or to his emotion. Ideally, a desire for a product already exists within him; by effectively keying your message to his wants and aspirations, you can arouse his desire and convert it into buying action.

Action is the fourth element of a good advertisement. The consumer must be induced to bridge the gap between desiring the product and taking the active step of acquiring it. Influencing the consumer's behavior in a positive manner is the payoff of the advertising job. A good advertisement may be defined as one which results in buying action.

To every generality which is offered as a rule of advertising there are many exceptions. Nevertheless there are some general rules which can be useful in producing good advertising much of the time. The following list of suggestions is intended as a broad guide for use in directing those who must create the advertising for your firm:

The product should be the star of your advertisement

Avoid including matter which is extraneous or distracting from your advertising message

Content is important. What you say is more important than how you say it

Give the facts. Factual information *does* sell the product

Structure your advertisement around a central selling idea

In your enthusiasm to convince the consumer, do not become obnoxious

Be sure your content is centered about the consumer's interest. You cannot afford the luxury of talking to yourself in an advertisement

Humor demands careful handling. Never hold the product itself up to ridicule

Do not get caught out-of-date. Keep your advertising contemporary and fashionable

Maintain consistent good taste. Vulgarity does not sell

View every advertisement as a single step in a long-term journey. Each ad you run helps to build a long-term image of your product or company in the consumer's mind

If you find that your advertisement *does* result in buying action, continue it. If the consumer is not tired of your ad, you should not be either

Do not imitate. Imitation implies inferiority

People want to know how to live a better life. Show how your product can help them

Do not be afraid to be different. Your consumers will prefer your product because it offers them a difference from other products

Use entertainment to attract, not distract. If you want people to listen to you, do not stand on your head. People will only remember how you looked, and not what you said

The copy strategy should be subjected to continuous scrutiny by research. If your advertisement does not communicate your selling message, even the most prolonged repetition of it will not influence the consumer to buy your product.

How to determine your advertising budget. There is no perfect formula to determine how much of a firm's resources should be devoted to the advertising budget. The size of the advertising budget should depend on the firm's marketing objectives. Ideally, once a firm has defined the job it expects its advertising to do, sufficient funds should be allocated to ensure that the job will be done. Here are five methods which are commonly used in determining advertising expenditures:

1. Set the budget at a percentage of sales. The percentage normally depends on the relative importance of advertising in any particular industry
2. Key the expenditures to those of major competitors
3. Key the budget to the product as it is sold; set the allocation as so many dollars or cents per unit of sales
4. Investment spend. Plow all available funds into advertising and other promotion forms. This method is usually only practical early in the life cycle of a product with high growth potential
5. Predetermine the product's sales goals, whether in terms of new customers or increased sales volume. Then determine the advertising program necessary to achieve this goal. Finally, allocate sufficient funds for the program

Whatever the method of budget allocation used to determine advertising expenditures, efforts should be made to determine just how effective your program has been. Advertising should be viewed as an investment in the future business of your firm. Dollars alone will not result in a competent advertising job. It should be pursued with the same diligence as any other major business function.

The advertising agency. It should be evident that considerable creative and technical know-how is required to do the advertising job. For this reason almost all firms which advertise (other than small retail businesses) retain the services of advertising agencies. Advertising agencies are specialists in planning and executing the work of the advertising function. They usually bring broad experience to bear on the advertising needs of a client and can be of utmost value if they are considered a marketing partner. Those firms which involve their advertising agencies deeply in their business can benefit more from the agency's understanding, independent viewpoint, and sense of participation in the progress of the firm.

The two marketing functions common to all advertising agencies are the creation of advertising copy and the placing of such advertising through media. Nearly all advertising agencies, however, offer a range of services which go far beyond this (see Table 3 for a complete listing). While every advertising agency has its own preferred organization and way of servicing the clients, they are normally set up to perform four areas of client service—

1. *Research.* Nearly all agencies are equipped to offer marketing research services to their clients. Since the nature of their business involves effective communication with the consumer, it is only natural that the agency

possess a research capacity for analyzing and interpreting consumer motivations, attitudes, preferences, opinions, and buying behavior

Table 3

Services Performed by Advertising Agencies in Addition to Planning, Creating, and Placing Advertising *

Marketing	*Sales Training*
Pricing policies	Sales meetings
Distribution policies	Sales portfolios
Sales policies	Visual sales aids
Sampling	Slide films
	Demonstrations
Research	*Direct Mail*
Consumer panels	Letters
Audience and readership analysis	Folders
Market research	Booklets
Copy research	Envelope stuffers
Pretesting	Return cards
Motivational studies	Brochures
Recipe testing	Couponing and sampling
Trade Promotion	*Product Analysis*
Dealer promotions	New-product development
Dealer contacts	Product design and styling
Convention exhibits	Brand name development
Catalogs	Trademark design
Sales literature	Labeling
Bulletins	Packaging
Broadsides	
Publicity	*Public Relations*
News stories	Employee-employer relations
Product promotion	Consumer relations
General	
Merchandising Pieces	*Miscellaneous*
Wall banners	Annual reports
Package inserts	Testimonials
Counter, floor, and window displays	Contests
Shelf tape	Recipes
Talking displays	Reminders—calendars, desk gifts, etc.
Counter giveaways	Instruction booklets
Sampling cards	House organs
Dispensers	Premiums
	Cookbooks

* "Growth of Advertising Agency Services," *Printers' Ink,* pp. 21–30, Jan. 27, 1956.

2. *Creative Services.* The basic creative service of an advertising agency is to assist in the formulation of copy strategy and to produce advertisements which effectively carry out that strategy. Considerable expertise is required in the preparation and production of the advertisement itself. This

requires highly specialized skills in art and design, layout, copy writing, recording, photography, printing, and the production of television commercials.

3. *Media.* The job of the media department is to place the client's advertising so as to reach the largest number of target consumers the maximum amount of times that the client's advertising budget will permit. The advertising agency usually recommends the media strategy and selection. Media departments possess detailed knowledge on media costs and capacities to deliver consumers. Expertise is required in making specific media purchases in such a way as to maximize consumers reached for each advertising dollar.

4. *Account Management.* The fourth basic area of client service is that of account management. Unlike research, copy, and media, account management is not in itself a function, but is the path through which client service is directed and the other functions are carried out. The account-management system is fairly universal among advertising agencies. The responsibility for liaison between agency and client is usually vested in one man—the account executive. He maintains contact with the individual in the firm directly responsible for the firm's advertising. It is through the account executive that the agency's services and capacities are brought to bear on the problems and requirements of the client. Account executives are normally generalists who are sufficiently familiar with all areas of the agency's services to enable the client to make the best use of them.

Agency compensation. The most common method by which advertising agencies receive compensation for their services is the "commission plan." Under this system the advertising media will discount from 15 to 18 percent of the total of advertising billings to the agency. These discounts are not available to advertisers, so in effect this aspect of agency compensation does not directly cost a client anything. Since agencies perform other services which are not billed through media, other methods of payment are used in compensating them for such work. For some materials and services the advertiser is charged the cost to the agency in preparing them. For other services the charge is cost plus 15 percent, which also compensates the agency for their service. For still other services a flat fee, mutually agreeable to advertiser and agency, is charged.

There is a growing trend for agencies to be compensated for *all* services by various fee systems, in which the charge to the client is negotiated and determined according to various formulas. While this practice is not too widespread, it is usually designed to guarantee the agency a minimum profit on the client's account, while allowing refunds to the client if the account profitability exceeds a maximum level.

Advertising requires highly specialized skill and talents, and agencies are able to retain these capacities more efficiently and economically than could most firms which advertise. Agencies can do a better job for clients who have well-defined advertising and promotional objectives, and who are willing to involve them fully in carrying out these objectives.

Other promotion. Promotion in the broad sense is any method of nonpersonal stimulation of demand for a product or service or retail institution. Promotion efforts should be aimed at ultimate users of your product, although they may be indirectly channeled through the wholesale or retail trade. In its broader aspect, promotion includes advertising, publicity, and sales promotion.

In advertising, as we have seen, an identified sponsor attempts to stimulate demand for his product by the communication of the selling message to potential consumers. Advertising is paid for, and usually consists of claims that the product will satisfy some consumer need or want.

Publicity consists in getting favorable mention of the product in media that reach the public other than through paid-for advertising. It is not openly sponsored. It includes getting newspapers and magazines and broadcasting media to carry news items and photographs about an identified product or manufacturer. Often journalistic in approach, publicity is valuable because it is not openly sponsored. A consumer is more likely to perceive it as an item of news, and is likely to accept it with less resistance than he would an identifiable advertisement.

Publicity is a relatively sales-oriented function of public relations. Public relations is a broader field which evaluates public attitude, and seeks to identify the policies of an individual or firm with the public interest. Public-relations programs seek to earn public understanding and acceptance for the sponsor.

The term *sales promotion* has a narrower meaning than the general concept of promotion. It refers to various activities which support the advertising and sales functions. Their objective is to produce an intensified short-term stimulation of demand for the product. These activities very often overlap with advertising and selling. The sales-promotion device of couponing, for instance, usually requires the use of an advertising medium to distribute the coupons. Likewise a sales promotion which seeks to obtain product displays in retail stores must be executed through personal selling.

Sales-promotion activities fall into two general classes—consumer promotion and dealer or trade promotion. There are five major classifications of trade promotion—

1. *Buying allowances* consist of payments made to the trade based on the number of units of product they purchase. These payments may be deducted in advance from the customer's invoice. Buying allowances provide a strong stimulus for the trade to take on distribution of your products, or to build their inventories of products already in distribution
2. *Performance allowances* require that the trade undertake some sort of merchandising activity in order to qualify for a payment. Payments are normally based on amount of product purchased, the amount of product

moved to retail outlets, or the amount of product displayed during the period of the offer. The two types of performance usually most sought by manufacturers are advertising in which the trade includes your product in their own retail advertisement (often at a special reduced price), and display activity in which a retailer prominently features a significant amount of your product in a special position in his store

3. *Trade premiums* consist of merchandise gifts offered to the trade to secure their cooperation, usually in providing displays or as purchase incentives

4. *PMs* (an abbreviated term for "premium merchandise" or "push money") are special allowances sometimes given to retailers to pass on to their retail salesmen in order to obtain more aggressive effort on particular items or lines. *PMs* are usually used only for new merchandise or higher margin items

5. *Merchandising to the trade* consists of presenting your marketing program to your customers with the object of securing their support of your program. This usually consists of a presentation, aided by high-powered selling material, which seeks to convince the customer of the benefits of tying in with your overall consumer program. These efforts are often accompanied by buying allowances or performance allowances. If a heavy new advertising campaign is about to break in a market, you might merchandise your program to the trade in a presentation designed to secure mass displays using point-of-sale material which ties in with the advertising copy

The number of sales promotion activities targeted at a consumer is endless. By and large they fall into three broad categories: *Price promotion, sampling and couponing,* and *extra-value promotions.*

Price promotions consist of several forms of temporary price reductions, using price savings as the primary incentive for increased consumer sales. Common variations of price promotion include cents-off deals, prepriced sale merchandise, and 1-cent sales. Also included in this category are promotions which offer a consumer an additional product with his purchase of a normal amount of product. Examples of this would be bonus product packs ("2 ounces free"), and "buy-one, get-one-free" promotions. The danger of such price promotions is that if they are repeated with regularity, they tend to cheapen the image of the brand which uses them. In many product categories, they appeal primarily to current users of products, while providing only a marginal incentive to prospective new users. However, their effectiveness in price-sensitive undifferentiated categories cannot be denied.

The second category of sales promotion to consumers consists of the trial-oriented promotional tools. Foremost among these is *sampling.* When affordable, sampling is probably the best method of obtaining consumer trial, and is especially effective in new-product introductions. The best possible way to assure yourself that your product is getting trial is to put the sample into the hands of consumers free of charge. Samples are usually distributed by mail, by door-to-door delivery, in retail outlets, and occasionally by packaging them with established products.

Couponing is on the whole the most effective technique in obtaining immediate consumer response. Coupons are normally distributed via direct mail, in packages, on packages, and in magazine and newspaper advertisements. It is the manufacturer's invitation to the consumer to try the product partly or completely at the maker's expense. Couponing is extremely effective when used as an integral part of a total merchandising program. Because of its swift and immediate consumer attraction, the coupons often provide a brand with excellent trade leverage. One drawback of couponing as a promotional vehicle is the factor of faulty redemption. Due to the laxity or neglect of retailers, in several areas of the country a significant portion of all coupons redeemed by consumers does not result in a concurrent product purchase. In such areas a sales-promotion device known as the *cash-refund offer* is often employed. A cash-refund offer promises the consumer a sum of money in return for his buying the product and sending in a proof of the purchase, such as a label. Since cash-refund offers do not offer the consumer an immediate saving, as do coupons, their appeal is much more limited. However, the manufacturer at least has the satisfaction of knowing that the consumers who did participate in the offer actually did purchase his product.

All the above offer some sort of direct compensation (lower price or free product) to the consumer in order to induce her to try the product. Sampling and couponing are particularly useful in the introduction of a new product when the marketer is attempting to communicate product identity and availability. This kind of offer keeps the eye of the consumer trained on the qualities of the product itself.

Extra-value consumer promotions consist of trying to stimulate a product purchase by offering the consumer something other than the product itself. Sometimes this added incentive is offered free; at other times the consumer is required to pay all or part of the cost of the offering. This kind of promotion is more applicable to a product that has been in the market for some time. If used in conjunction with a new-product introduction, it would tend to distract the consumer from basic consideration of the product itself. Consequently, these promotions should not be used until the product has reached a sales plateau, and a specific effort is required to spur a new sales increase.

Premium promotions are used quite broadly and in many different fields. A premium is simply some kind of merchandise offered to your consumer either free or at a bargain value as a bonus for purchasing your product. When premium merchandise is too costly to be given away free, it is usually offered at the manufacturer's cost plus handling and shipping. Successful premiums should be compatible with the image of your product, and should be perceived by the consumer as having high value or utility. Premium promotions can be very effective if the appeal of the premium is broader than the appeal of the product.

Sweepstakes and contests provide extra value to consumers by offering them the possibility of winning valuable prizes for their participation and accompanying product purchase. If they are designed simply and interestingly, and are easy for the consumer to enter, they can invoke consumer involvement on a massive scale. They can be fully integrated into the marketing program if their theme is relevant to the product or to the product's advertising. As with premiums, most sweepstakes and contests do not lend themselves compatibly to a new-product introduction. They do, however, draw consumers to the store or showroom and are useful in obtaining trade cooperation and display.

Trading stamps have long been used primarily as a device to build traffic and loyalty for retail establishments. Trading stamps or product premium coupons have been shown to be effective for some products in building consumer loyalty. A well-known example of this are Raleigh Cigarettes coupons, which the consumer may save for ultimate conversion into valuable premiums.

Another kind of extra-value promotion offering is the *reusable container*. The package in which the product comes then itself becomes a premium having a value of its own to the consumer. An outstanding illustration of the reusable container is the Instant Maxwell House Coffee Carafe, in which 10 ounces of instant coffee are offered to the consumer packed in a heat-proof coffee maker.

The effects of sales promotion should be measured as carefully as any other major business expenditure. They should be viewed as marketing investments and should pay back in increased sales, at least in the short run. To insure their effectiveness, they should be tested in limited areas whenever possible before being expanded to all your markets. While sales increases stemming from sales promotion are usually evident in the short run, this is only one factor in determining the promotion's success. The most effective promotions usually have long-term effects also. Specifically, sales promotions should result in an increased share of the market even after the promotional period has expired. If no long-term business is gained, the short-term sales increase may not be sufficient to pay for the cost of the promotion.

Measuring marketing results. Rounding out a good marketing program is an adequate system of records, reports, and control documents. It is difficult to achieve continually effective and well-directed execution of marketing activities if the firm is unable to measure its results in the light of previous experience, or in comparison with those of competitors.

Marketing's contribution to a company is not fully understood if its function is looked upon as merely the performance of several related activities. In the ongoing business concept, marketing activities are the tools or techniques employed to achieve the profit aim of the enterprise. Records serve the purpose of determining whether the aim has been met and should form the basis for redirection of efforts if marketing results are off target.

Budget.   In budget preparation, the recorded results (or anticipated results) of the last accounting period become a prime input source for building and projecting results for the next period and beyond.   For the budgeting activity, both marketing records and the accounting and control records should be brought together and reviewed in light of one another.   It should be understood that the budget is much more than an accounting device.   It is an action plan. The significance of the marketing projects becomes apparent when brought together with the profit and investment payback expected in return for the time and money put into them.

The budget is perhaps the major part of the marketing plan.   The budget establishes financial constraints and relates specific expenditures to specific periods of time.   It relates action steps to both cost and calendar.   It tells management what is being paid to promote and support the movement of the product into the customers' hands.

External comparisons.   Internal analysis, particularly profit analysis, is very important; however, this often gives an incomplete picture of overall results. The marketer also wants to know where his particular product or company stands in comparison with direct competitors and other companies in the same industry or type of business.

Market and share analysis is perhaps the most meaningful of the external indicators of marketing results.   This kind of evaluation not only shows the growth, decline, or stagnation of the total market, but is also the best indicator of consumer favor shown among alternative sources for a product.   A company, for instance, may be quite self-satisfied with a sales growth of 5 percent per year, but would be motivated to more aggressive action if it knew that its competitors, as indicated by the market growth in general, were growing at a rate of 20 percent per year.   In the absence of competition, or in an unusual market area, it is wise to make comparisons with national trends for the industry as a whole.   Government publications have data available on almost every industry, with information breakdowns by significant product or service categories within most industries.   A success index which falls below the national or local average is always cause for investigation, unless there has been an intentional holdback.   If a company is doing its marketing job, it should be growing at a rate equal to or greater than the industry as a whole.

Economic indicators available from various published sources are another good results measurement index.   Some industries are so highly fragmented that it is difficult to make direct product comparisons against competitors.   Usually in such cases the next best thing is to compare against national or local trends for the industry or consumer group which uses the product.   For example, roofing materials, window glass, and water pipe, or any of their associated products, closely follow the economic trends in housing starts. New housing construction data are available from several sources, such as the U.S. Department of Commerce *Construction Review,* F. W. Dodge *Reports,* the Bureau of Labor Statistics *Housing Starts,* and various mortgage lending activity reports.

Cost control. There is no reason to be less cost conscious in the area of marketing activity than in any other area of a company's business. In fact, in some major companies, cost control originated in the marketing area under the subject of distribution-cost analysis.

Distribution-cost analysis is the application of the "sharp pencil" to the cost of each item that goes into the distribution and promotion of the product from the producer or manufacturer into the hands of the customers. Distribution-cost analysis can be done on either a marginal contribution or net cost per item basis. By either method, all direct or indirect costs related to the marketing of products are allocated to one or more of the several marketing activities. The application of the distribution-cost accounting procedure has resulted in closer scrutiny of such things as advertising-media selection, freight-equalization analysis, marketing-profit center determination, and recently, the fee basis for advertising-agency compensation.

Although the distribution-cost analysis has most commonly been applied to the study of middleman costs and profit margins, it is also a tool which has received wide use in the analysis of retail operations. In a food store, for instance, distribution-cost analysis has been used to determine such things as profit per cubic foot, net sales per square foot of shelf space, direct-product profit, feature and display profitability, and overall profit contribution of individual retail outlets as in a chain-store operation.

Customer-service records. Motivated by the marketing desire to provide better service to customers, many companies have found application for record keeping and measurement of certain customer-service activities. For example, depending on the industry, it would be good to know such things as the length of time the average customer waits in line; the length of time from receipt of a customer's request to the time the acknowledgement is returned via the mail; the average number of telephone rings the customer must wait before being answered; the frequency of product failure under normal use; the lead time required from receipt of an order to delivery of product; the measurement of peak and slack periods of customer traffic for purposes of reducing staff during slack periods and perhaps increasing staff during time of peak demand; the frequency of billing errors, and so forth.

Service and treatment are influencing factors in obtaining repeat business from customers. They also influence the word-of-mouth image that is projected from current or former customers. In some industries, the service received is the only product differentiation customers can perceive between one supplier and another. An example of such a situation might be two filling stations competing with one another on the same street corner. Likewise with only slightly noticeable differences between products, supermarkets and banks also depend on their services as customer attractions. Customer-service measurement provides a good way to look at your services as they are perceived by your customers.

3. Make your marketing effective

Effective marketing requires effective people with a motivation to compete. Good marketing is not done by robots and it is not performed in a vacuum. Good marketing not only requires good execution of customer-oriented activities, it also requires overall ability to remain flexible in order to move with the changing desires of the customer and the changing pressures and tactics of competitors.

In an organization of any size, the marketing responsibilities are typically assigned to an individual or individuals other than the chief executive. As organizations grow in size, entire marketing departments are often established. In nearly all of the largest corporations of the country, marketing is a divisional function. At Procter & Gamble, marketing personnel number several hundred, filling many floors of a large office building. If the sales organization were to be included, it would add still another thousand marketing employees.

Corporations, regardless of size, sometimes find it convenient to call on outside specialized marketing assistance. Most large companies have a relatively permanent advertising agency affiliation. Advertising agencies typically can provide public relations assistance in addition to their normal activities of ad placement, copy writing, and graphics preparation. Management consultants, market researchers, promotion consultants, and still other organizations can provide help in other areas.

Good marketing performed by a company is to a large extent built upon employee *esprit de corps*. Fundamentally established on high confidence in the ability of the company's products to fill the customers' needs, *esprit de corps* combines a spirit of competition with high personal and "team" self-confidence in such a way as to develop a momentum of success. Related to these conditions of attitude are the subjects of image and merchandising.

Image is the customer's perception of a product's or company's quality, ability to serve, and stature in the community. The favorable image is a strong advantage. An image helps to presell a product even before it is used the first time. A good image becomes "something to be associated with" and therefore, a favorable preconditioning of customers toward the acceptance of anything bearing the company's or brand's name.

Merchandising is the special efforts and selling techniques by which products are presented in the final form to the consumer. Merchandising is a combination last-step technique used for attention getting, enticement, motivation to buy, and finalization of sale. When done by people, merchandising is hustle, confidence, persistence, and ability to close the sale. Merchandising, viewed as something which must move products without the direct aid of a salesman (as in a supermarket), is the way a product is set up on the shelf, the point-of-purchase material which draws attention to it, and the combination of packaging and price which a customer cannot resist. The merchandising concept is that last effort which clinches the sale. It provides all the answers and rebuttals to last-minute questions and is not completed until it provides the pat on the back in reassurance to the customer as he walks away with your product tucked securely under his arm.

Marketing organization in your firm. The first and most important step in organizing for the marketing concept is to recognize the importance of consumer orientation. If a company does not recognize the importance of the consumer in his business, selling the company on the need for the marketing concept and a marketing organization is very difficult. When the marketing concept is initially introduced to an organization, others in the company frequently see this as an encroachment upon their own "empire." A development of the marketing concept and the marketing organization must be fostered on the understanding and foundation of a team situation. In most enterprises, marketing is a combination of line management and staff function. Marketing is line management with regard to the company's sales force. The staff aspects come to play in the assistance and direction given to other departments of the organization in order that the other parts represent themselves to the customers in a favorable and coordinated way. In a similar way, direct support of the sales organization is provided.

As in other sections of business, marketing can have a functional organization, geographic organization, product organization, or organization by customer classification. In each case, the full range of marketing activities is usually grouped in the following manner: advertising, sales, marketing research, public relations, and product planning and development. Depending on the nature of the business, additional suborganizations of marketing may be delineated: sales service, promotion planning, retail outlet site analysis and development, distribution management, packaging services, and so forth.

A geographic organization means all the functions are performed to serve just a certain specific geographic territory. Product organization implies functions are performed in support of one particular product or group of products. Organization by customer classification means that the marketing functions are grouped together in an organization which is established to serve a certain category of direct customers, usually with the same characteristics and needs. The type of organization selected by a company is usually based on management's judgment of the most important variable about which all the marketing activities should be pivoted.

As a company grows and additional marketing staff is required, management must evaluate the expected gains in comparison to the additional cost involved.

Staff additions may be necessary for many reasons, such as to reduce the workload pressures of top executive, to fulfill the communication requirements of an expanding number of personnel and offices, or to husband the activities required to study, develop, and introduce a new product or service.

Use of outside assistance. Every major city in the country now seems to have business organizations which specialize in providing marketing research or general marketing consulting assistance. The primary reasons for companies to seek outside help for marketing assistance are to—

Obtain specific experience or knowledge
Overcome manpower shortages or temporary absences
Obtain an outsider's objective viewpoint
Provide a source outside the company for securing information
Minimize the time requirement to complete a project
Improve the likelihood of management acceptance of the recommendation
Draw upon the outsider's ability to make specific contacts for information-gathering purposes

Marketing researchers and consultants range from single individuals to "full-service" management consultants with technical knowledge in depth in a number of functional areas. The latter might even include executive research work in the field of marketing.

It is important to select a qualified organization to provide the outside help. It is said the best source in obtaining a consultant is the recommendation of another satisfied customer. Other sources of contact include the Association of Consulting Management Engineers, professional directories and journals, trade publications, and suggestions from industry associations.

Before interviewing prospective consultants, the manager should clearly define and delineate the area for consultation. The client's ability to articulate the problem will largely determine the aptness of the consultant or research organization's response. In common practice, this response comes in the form of a letter of intent called a "proposal letter." The proposal letter outlines the consultant's understanding of the problem, the approach the consultant will probably follow, and identification of the individuals involved who will be working on the assignment. It is typically concluded with an estimate of the time and cost required to do the assignment in the proposed manner.

A variety of compensation methods are used by consultants and research organizations. Some work on a flat contract, fixed-fee basis; more often, consultants calculate charges on a per diem or per hour basis; others use a cost plus a certain percentage fee for the period; still another form of compensation is that of a retainer arrangement. Regardless of the compensation method, in most cases the consultant is additionally reimbursed for out-of-pocket direct costs incurred during the conduct of an assignment.

Working with a management or marketing-research consultant, it is important to insure complete understanding and agreement of costs and approach before beginning. To facilitate smooth consultant-client workings together, it is a good idea for both the consultant and the client to designate individuals who will be the primary contact and liaison persons between organizations. As the outside work is carried out, it is a good idea to have progress meetings at significant stages of investigation prior to presentation of a final report. The steps involved in a consulting assignment follow closely those outlined earlier under the subject of marketing research.

After the consultant or research organization has presented its conclusions and recommendations, the acceptance and implementation, or rejection, of the report is up to the management which hired them. The consultant's commitment usually ends with the presentation of a clearly presented final report.

In addition to advertising agencies, management consultants, and marketing-research organizations, other institutional marketing specialists include sales-training organizations, promotions consultants, public-relations counsels, and special-market (i.e., local or ethnic group) consultants. There are also specialty item suppliers who supply such things as contest premiums, mailing lists, ready prepared artwork, printing, and tabulated market data.

Commitment to flexibility. Business firms which focus on the consumer as key to their marketing approach should commit themselves to the process of continuing change. Thus can they develop the flexibility which is so vital in today's business arena. Marketing is not the one-shot application of the several marketing activities. Marketing is a dynamic business system which not just once but continuously tracks and follows the consumer and his wishes. The most common reason for a once-established company to fail (or decline in relative standing) is its inability to comprehend or take action in a changing situation. Modern business competition requires both agility and flexibility to get ahead and stay ahead.

A consumer changes his wants and buying habits not because he is collectively fickle, but because he is continually seeking improvements and a higher level of satisfaction. In the long run, the "winning" business organization is one which continuously searches to initiate an improvement, or responds most quickly to an advantage of new development. An example of such a winning business is the duPont Chemical Company. Ten years ago it had not known of the products which now account for more than half of its volume and profit today. Ten years ago duPont was the nation's leading supplier of nylon. They have since sold most of their interest in nylon, and now products like Teflon, Mylar, Dacron, and Corfam have taken its place in importance in duPont's continuing process of change.

Small or single-product companies in particular must always be on the alert to change. Companies having an already established market, outlets, and channels of distribution should look at change as an opportunity instead of a threat.

The reasons for change can be classified as coming from one of three categories: (1) expanding market opportunities, (2) technological change, and (3) competitive pressures. The marketing-oriented businessman should be alert to all three.

Expanding market opportunities present themselves in numerous ways. One such opportunity comes as the result of consumers' finding new uses for the same product. Expansion opportunities present themselves when new trading areas, such as new suburbs, are opened. Still another common form of expanding market potential is the recognition of a secondary market opportunity, such as that provided by the institutional field for food products originally developed for home consumption.

Technological change is the change most difficult for a small business to adjust to. Technological change comes as a result of scientific discovery which replaces or improves existing products, or replaces existing product ingredients with better quality or less expensive materials.

Although technological changes have brought about some of the most significant changes in history for the small businessman, these changes need not be for the worse. For instance, he might alter his primary role to that of new-product distributor if he does not possess his own scientific development capability. While most smaller firms cannot match the scientific development resources of the giants, many have successfully adapted themselves to distributive roles, or have incorporated the improvements of others into their own products.

Competitive pressures bring change because of either competitors' technological developments or new ways which competition has found to distribute, advertise, or price their products. In the absence of a technological advantage, competitive pressures can be viewed as something of a game which one company is playing against others. Competing companies keep score by indicators of profit, volume, number of customers, market share, and "firsts" which are brought to the customers.

In the light of competition a company must decide whether it is going to be a pricing and promotion leader or a follower. In terms of seizing expanding market opportunities, a company must decide whether it is going to be offensive or defensive. An offensive company will try to be first into a new market situation and try to present new approaches or methods of gaining customers. A defensive company is one which takes action primarily to defend its market share or market position. A defensive company typically acts in rebuttal to a competitor's offensive move, or in anticipation of what it believes will be an imminent competitive move.

The opportunities to be either offensive or defensive will vary by company, product, and trading area. There are times when a company should be offensive, and others when it should be defensive. In any case, for each situation a separate analysis of probable costs and profit consequences should be made in evaluating possible competitive reactions before deciding the appropriate posture of marketing action.

Common marketing errors.   The need for the manager to fashion his marketing judgment on a basis of solid research has been stressed. Such executive judgment may be founded on exhaustive market research or simply on a thorough "desk-top" analysis from readily available internal data. The marketer's need to understand the actionable facts of his business is well illustrated in the following list of common marketing errors recorded over a 3-year period by the A. C. Nielsen Company: [2]

The average executive overestimates his company's percentage of the total market.   Perhaps it is natural to belittle one's competitors

The average executive greatly overestimates the percentage of prospects who—
   Have heard of his product
   Understand its virtues
   Believe the claims made for it
   Are using the product
   Have found the product satisfactory

The average executive overestimates the importance of his competitors as a sales obstacle and underestimates the opportunity for creating new business

The average executive thinks his product suffers a good deal more from price resistance than it actually does

The average executive underestimates the virtues of his competitors' sales policies. We usually find that competitors are using methods which get results, but which our client has assumed are "all wrong." There is a strong tendency to credit the competitor with less brainpower than he actually possesses

The average client has an exaggerated conception of his standing with the trade. He is usually surprised at his low percentage of displays and special sales

The average executive fails to gauge accurately the relative values of various sales and advertising appeals. This results in the frequent use of weak appeals and the overlooking of appeals that have power to increase sales

The average executive overestimates the success of a deal

He overestimates the success of a new product or size

He makes an unsound distribution of effort—
   By city sizes (e.g., neglect of small cities)
   By seasons

He is unwilling to allow sufficient time to really complete a testing operation. Feeling that it is necessary to meet promptly some competitive campaign, but realizing that the best method has not yet been determined by testing,

[2] F. K. Leisch, A. C. Nielsen Company, address before American Management Association (American Management Association Consumer and Industrial Marketing Series C. M. 24).

the management often proceeds halfheartedly on too small a scale to produce satisfactory sales results. We recognize that there are some situations that really demand prompt action, but there is a solution for this problem. Start testing in advance, before the need for a new campaign becomes acute

The average executive makes the mistake of testing the effect of displays or other merchandising operations by measuring sales only in the cooperating stores. These stores may make their gains at the expense of neighboring stores, in which case the manufacturer gains nothing

The average executive places too much reliance on his own observations, failing to realize that these observations may not be wide enough in scope to be representative. A good example is the average price to the consumer, which is almost always estimated too low, because the average executive has more contact with the chains and the price-cutting independents than with the average store

The average executive refuses to face the facts promptly when sales decline

He is unwilling to study and dig—to analyze complex statistics. The head of one large business asked us to summarize the results of a $20,000 survey in two or three sentences. It takes an average of 4 hours for a group of executives to absorb the important facts in each bimonthly index report. Some companies have 15 executives present at each such meeting, including the president and four vice-presidents. Attempts to oversimplify are often fatal. *Marketing is no longer simple.* While one simple idea (e.g., halitosis or BO) may sweep all before it and win big success regardless of attention to details, these occurrences are rare. The executive who counts on finding such a cure-all is likely to find himself face to face with the sheriff

There is a tendency for each department or function to claim all the credit for sales gains and blame the others for declines. Our data show that making a profitable sales volume is a cooperative job to which many factors contribute. It pays to spend less time protecting your own position and concentrate on getting the facts and applying them to increase profits

There is a failure to meet competitive increases in advertising. Maintenance of your percentage of the total market requires maintenance of your percentage of the total promotion expenditure—barring some definite improvement in the effectiveness of your work. To protect against this danger, measure the expenditures of competitors and calculate every month your percentage of the total expenditure

There is a refusal to admit the high percentage of error in executive judgment on marketing questions. Our records, based on tests made over a period of years, have proved that the average executive is right, or substantially so, in only 58 percent of the cases. The lowest record made by any company is 42 percent and the highest is 72 percent. The 42 percent erroneous decisions place a staggering financial burden on any business. No wonder there is so much complaint about low profit margins!

There is a refusal to spend enough money for marketing research. Authorities state that business spends $200,000,000 annually for production research but only $5,000,000 for marketing research, in spite of the fact that marketing is further from perfection and hence might justify more research

Summary. Marketing is the ongoing system of activities which promotes, develops, and distributes products or services desired by consumers at a profit to the supplying company. Basic to the marketing approach is a sound set of profit and sales objectives and criteria which translate themselves into a marketing plan. The plan is an organized, step-by-step outline of strategy and tactics required to reach the desired results.

Marketing strategy and tactics require familiarization with each of the various marketing activities, what they can do, how they operate, and their general relationship to one another. A well-executed marketing plan will be centered around an understanding of the consumers for whom the product and its promotion are targeted.

Marketing research is extremely helpful in determining the consumer group for which a product should be targeted, and in determining how the price, promotion, package, and method of distribution should best reach the intended consumers. Research can be used both in the development of the marketing plan and in the follow-up to determine customer reaction and market impact produced by your marketing actions.

The firm must therefore be dedicated to a position of flexibility in order to maintain a progressive business position, as well as to meet both present and future profit objectives. The marketer must understand the volatility of his industry in a rapidly changing consumer environment if his firm is to successfully generate opportunities from expanding markets, technological development, competitive actions, and dynamic shifts in customer wants and preferences.

While providing consumers the products and services they want, and in the way they want them, marketing makes its basic contribution to the firm in terms of that important dollars-and-cents denominator—profit.

Section 16

CONSIDERATIONS CONCERNING CORPORATE HOUSE COUNSEL

BY

HOWARD SCHWARTZBERG

CONSIDERATIONS CONCERNING
CORPORATE HOUSE COUNSEL

There was a time when relatively few business corporations could afford the luxury of a full-time salaried attorney. What was once a luxury has now developed into a practical necessity. Today's business organizations operate under numerous and complex regulations, generating legal problems that must be handled quickly and correctly. In response to this need for "on-the-spot" legal advice, corporate law departments were formed.

A corporate law department may consist of one attorney or "house counsel," as he is commonly called, or it may consist of a staff of attorneys, specializing in different fields. The size of the corporation and the type of business in which it is engaged will generally determine the composition and function of its law department. Many corporate law departments employ a much larger number of attorneys than average-size private law firms. Moreover, since many large corporations maintain numerous branches or divisions throughout the country, it is not uncommon to find a miniature decentralized law department located at these branches or divisions, with coordinating authority vested in the general counsel located at the corporation's main headquarters. In such cases, the general counsel is usually an officer of the corporation and often a member of the board of directors, participating in the formulation of corporate policy and plans.

1. Advantages of house counsel

To most corporations of any appreciable size, the question of whether or not to establish a law department is an academic one, since many large corporations already employ at least one attorney on a full-time basis. However, those corporations or business organizations that do not employ house counsel and are weighing the possibility of doing so will be influenced in all likelihood by one or more of the following considerations.

Economies. In order for business corporations to realize maximum profits they must minimize business costs, including fees paid to outside law firms. Most corporations produce a large mass of routine legal work, much of which is of a repetitive nature, such as standard purchase or sales contracts, leases, licenses, corporate minutes, employment contracts, government reports, etc. Since law firms usually compute their fees on the basis of the time spent in the performance of their services, their fees for handling this time-consuming work, albeit routine and repetitive, must necessarily exceed that proportion of the house counsel's salary corresponding to the amount of his time spent in taking care of these matters. This is not to say that the house counsel's time is of less value than that of an outside attorney. It simply means that the house counsel's time is at the exclusive disposal of his only client, whereas his counterpart in an outside law firm must allocate his time among his various clients. Understandably, the outside attorney cannot afford to devote an excessive amount of time to one client's routine problems without charging that client for the lost time that could have been allocated to another client's work that might have been more rewarding financially.

Not only can the house counsel handle the large quantity of routine corporate legal matters at less cost than an outside law firm, but he can also afford to devote more time to a specific problem than can the outside law firm. The house counsel is solely concerned with completing the project at hand, and he is not influenced by such extraneous factors as the cost of his time and the distracting demands of other clients.

Since the house counsel's salary is a factor that remains fixed, regardless of the time he spends on a particular matter or the difficult or complex nature of the problem involved, corporate personnel are not reluctant to call upon him, because they know that his services will not add to the cost of the project. Thus there are occasions when the house counsel is afforded an opportunity to come to grips with a potential legal sore spot before it develops into a festering lawsuit, whereas had his services not been available, the corporate personnel might not have engaged outside counsel for fear that the legal fees would have exceeded budgeted expenses. This point touches upon the second advantage associated with the employment of house counsel and the establishment of a corporate law department.

Preventive law. As in the case of the patient who does not call the doctor until his illness has veritably descended upon him, many business men are loath to recognize a legal pitfall until they have stumbled onto the brink of litigation. Outside law firms are limited in their ability to prevent the aggravation of current legal problems in that they must first know of the existence of the legal malaise. Not only is it unprofessional for an outside lawyer to stroll about his client's premises for the purpose of discovering potential legal problems, but additionally, such solicitation of business violates the legal canons of ethics, for which the attorney is subject to disciplinary action. Needless to say, apart from the aforesaid restrictions, the corporate personnel generally would not warmly accept such outside legal policing.

The house counsel on the other hand encounters fewer restrictions in ferreting out legal risks and preventing them from developing into court actions. As an employee of the corporation he can raise questions concerning his employer's activities without fear of being guilty of soliciting legal work. He has access to facts through his normal channels of corporate communications, and he can establish a meaningful working relationship with the corporate personnel through his understanding of the personalities involved. This relationship can be conducive to their consulting the house counsel and seeking his advice at an early planning stage so as to enable him to anticipate and prevent the development of legal difficulties.

Knowledge of the facts. In addition to his knowledge of the personalities and capabilities of his corporation's personnel, the house counsel has another distinct advantage over his counterpart in an outside law firm in that the house counsel is usually thoroughly familiar with his company's products and customers. He is also to some extent familiar with the products and operations of his company's competitors. Thus, a suggestion or idea that may appear to an outside attorney to be perfectly sound and correct from a legal standpoint may be rejected out of hand by the house counsel on the ground that the idea or approach would not be in keeping with his corporation's business operations. For example, an outside trial attorney, who was thoroughly familiar with the rules of evidence and the substantive rules of law pertaining to the subject of express and implied warranties affecting the sale of manufactured products, recommended that his client in the future adopt a certain procedure so as to avoid the thrust of one of several arguments that had been raised previously by his opponent in a lawsuit. This point was immediately rejected by the client's house counsel, who knew that not only would this procedure adversely affect the marketability of his corporation's products, but also that the procedure was economically impracticable and that it was not employed by any of his corporation's competitors. The house counsel also believed that from a legal standpoint, the removal of one of the contentions raised in the past by an opposing trial attorney might only result in its being replaced by a different argument in another lawsuit and that the number of potential allegations was limited only by the imagination of opposing counsel.

Because of his close association with his exclusive client, the house counsel not only understands his corporation's business operations, but he also knows where and how to go about obtaining facts and details that may be necessary for the attempted solution of a specific problem. He is aware that certain questions can be resolved only if information of a definite nature is made available, and that this information is readily obtainable from certain corporate departments or areas of business operation. There is no doubt that an outside attorney will also recognize the need for this information and will make an effort to secure it. However, his recognition of the complete problem and his ultimate decision with respect to the appropriate avenue to follow to a satisfactory solution will involve a time-consuming effort to obtain all of the necessary supporting facts. Since time is usually an essential aspect of a business decision, the house counsel is in a better position to recognize all of the ramifications of a particular problem and gather the pertinent facts faster than can the outside attorney, with the result that the house counsel can render his decision sooner than his outside counterpart.

The advent of the computer age has heralded a quickening of the business pace, so that decisions must be made at an acceleratingly faster rate. The house counsel's knowledge of the intricacies of his corporation's operations enables him to keep up with its need for prompt and accurate legal opinions. Generally speaking, lower-echelon executives are the greatest beneficiaries of on-the-spot legal advice. They are frequently confronted with legal problems that require an immediate answer, but because of the urgency of the moment, they cannot afford the time it would take to clear through higher level management before outside counsel may be consulted. The availability of the house counsel's services for prompt consultation regarding such urgent lower-level legal problems redounds to the benefit not only of the immediate personnel involved but also of the corporation as a whole, since resolved lower-level legal problems never develop into top-level headaches.

Knowledge of the law. One of the most important functions of the house counsel is to keep himself and interested corporate personnel informed on current and proposed rules and regulations as well as recent court decisions affecting his corporation and its business. Since the house counsel's field of endeavor is necessarily limited by the scope of his corporation's sphere of activity, his concentrated knowledge of the law affecting this circumscribed area will qualify him as a specialist in his field. Therefore, the house counsel is in a position to apply promptly this specialized knowledge to a given problem, whereas an outside attorney may be required to spend valuable time researching the applicable law before he can properly render a decision.

In the case of a law department composed of one or several attorneys, the specialized legal knowledge acquired by the house counsel as a result of his narrow area of concentration is not necessarily the same type of specialization that may be found in outside law firms, where attorneys will specialize in depth with respect to specific subjects, such as taxation, real estate, labor relations, trade regulations, patents, etc. The house counsel's specialty may cut across one or more of these topics, since his major concern is the corporation's business involvement, which may include several specialized areas of law. Thus, the house counsel is a specialist in the laws affecting his corporation's business and his concentrated knowledge may include only a portion of one or several specific fields of law.

Where a corporation employs a large staff of attorneys, with separate departments set up to handle specific subjects, as in the case of a patent department or a real-estate department, the attorneys in these departments are equally as expert as outside attorneys who also specialize in the given field. In such case, factors other than the house counsel's specialized legal knowledge will be considered in determining whether or not he will handle a particular problem. Consideration may therefore be given to the probability of trial involvement or the desire to obtain an objective or detached legal approach.

2. Limitations of house counsel

Although most large corporations have adopted the practice of employing full-time salaried attorneys, there are, nevertheless, certain limitations inherent in reliance upon the advice of house counsel as opposed to consulting outside counsel. It is, therefore, important that these limitations be recognized by those who intend to avail themselves of the house counsel's services.

Objectivity. Since the house counsel's services are available from the inception of a project on through to its ultimate fruition and subsequent application, he may tend to become too involved with the intricacies of the subject matter. Consequently, it may be difficult for him to render an objective and detached opinion regarding some phase of the project. He may be so desirous of its success that he may not take the sufficiently critical approach which may be called for under the circumstances. It is not a case of failing to see the forest for the trees, but rather a reluctance to see the forest at all. While it is true that in certain situations it may be good business to risk following a specific course of action, the business decision should be made by the appropriate corporate personnel with full knowledge of all of the possible legal consequences. An overly optimistic house counsel may not be sufficiently impartial to apprise fully the corporate personnel of all of the legal aspects, including those that, although unlikely to occur, are nevertheless possible drawbacks.

Influence by management. Unlike an outside law firm whose income is derived from its various clients, the house counsel's eggs are all in one basket. He is financially dependent upon one source, his employer. This factor has been the basis for derisive references to the salaried corporate attorney as "kept counsel." The house counsel, as an employee of the corporation, is cognizant of the fact that management does not expect him to sit back and in a judicious fashion merely play the part of the corporate umpire who declares which action is legally proper and which is not permissible. His concern is not with isolated legal questions, but rather with the accomplishment of the corporation's overall objectives and policies. Therefore, the house counsel must take an affirmative position and cannot simply say that certain action is improper. He must offer constructive advice on how the desired end can be achieved in a proper and correct manner. He cannot give the impression to the corporate personnel that he is a negative factor or an obstacle that must be overcome before certain action can be taken.

The requirement for constructive and affirmative action on the part of the house counsel does not prevent him from maintaining his professional standing. He is not expected to say only what management would like to hear. However, since his income is derived solely from one source, he is not usually afforded the luxury of independence that may be enjoyed by outside attorneys, whose practice may be sufficiently large to be impervious to the risk of incurring management's displeasure. While the house counsel may not be a captive of management, neither is he a free spirit.

Business decisions. Since the house counsel may often be an officer and director of his corporation, his involvement in corporate affairs is not exclusively limited to dispensing legal advice. He is frequently confronted with problems of a nonlegal nature as well as matters that involve mixed questions of law and business policy. To the extent that the house counsel has acquired a knowledge of his corporation's business operations as a result of his participation in legal work affecting these operations, he is in a position to offer his advice with regard to nonlegal business problems. It is, therefore, not uncommon for the house counsel to be called upon for his business judgment, in which case the corporate personnel should not accord to his decision the same weight that they would to a legal pronouncement. By stepping into the arena of nonlegal business affairs, the house counsel doffs his professional garb and dons the mantle of a business layman. His decision should be accepted or rejected for what it is worth, unlike his legal conclusions, which are to be accepted as correct declarations of the applicable law. Nevertheless, it is very difficult for corporate personnel to determine when the house counsel is acting as a businessman and when he is speaking as a lawyer. Indeed, it is often difficult for the house counsel himself to distinguish clearly between the two areas.

As was previously noted, the house counsel's knowledge of his corporation's business affairs is a distinct advantage that he possesses over an outside attorney. However, it does not follow that an outstanding lawyer is also an outstanding businessman. There are quite a few successful attorneys whose incursions into the business world through the means of various ventures resulted in ultimate failure. It is, therefore, important that the corporate personnel attempt to recognize the distinction between the house counsel's legal advice and his business judgment, and since this differentiation is most difficult, the failure to do so may be costly.

Restricted experience. The outside corporate attorney is exposed to a broad scope of problems that confront his various corporate clients engaged in diversified activities. An idea or solution affecting one client may prove helpful or useful to another when faced with a similar problem. Indeed, a point that appears peculiar to one industry may be equally applicable to another, or may be adaptable with some modifications. Hence, in addition to his fresh or objective viewpoint, an outside attorney may possess a wealth of experience in different areas which cannot be matched by the house counsel. As a corollary to the proposition that the house counsel is equipped with a depth of knowledge as to his own corporation's business and personnel, it also follows that his restricted legal exposure deprives him of the broader outlook and experience of the outside attorney. No matter how imaginative the house counsel may be, his limited experience may prove to be a distinct handicap in the introduction of fresh ideas or new methods of approach.

3. Conclusion

It does not follow from a consideration of the advantages and limitations involved in the employment of house counsel as compared with the retention of an outside law firm that one is mutually exclusive of the other. As a rule, those corporations that do maintain law departments also retain outside law firms either on a general retainer basis or for specific legal problems. Although there is an increasing tendency for corporate law departments to engage in litigation, usually involving collection matters, trial work is more commonly in the domain of the outside law firm. The house counsel's advice is sought in this connection for the purpose of recommending the outside law firm to handle the case and assisting in its preparation and trial.

Since the services of a corporate law department complement those of an outside law firm, a corporation can derive maximum benefit from its house counsel's services only through a clear understanding and recognition of the limitations as well as the advantages inherent in such use.

Section 17

THE ORGANIZATION OF GOOD EMPLOYEE RELATIONS

BY

LEE H. HILL

THE ORGANIZATION OF GOOD
EMPLOYEE RELATIONS

Introduction

Labor relations are often considered the sum and substance of employee relations.

Happily, that is not true. Labor relations cover the relatively limited area of contact between management and the labor unions representing some or all of its employees. Employee relations cover *all* the myriad contacts between the company and its employees.

Although the relationship between management and individual employees is often forgotten when public attention is focused on management-versus-union conflict, management cannot afford to overlook the broader, more fundamental relationship.

Unfortunately, some managements themselves have been misled by the assumption that their chief concern is with *union* relations, overlooking the far more significant and basic factor of *employee* relations.

Management-employee contacts. When an employee is hired, there is no labor-relations aspect to his selection as an employee and his assignment to a specific occupation or department. The employer selects from among those available the worker best qualified for the specific job. Subsequently, the employee may be subjected to an orientation program, during which he learns of the history of the company and something about its products or services. He is advised of company employee policies, is given some preliminary instructions concerning safety on the job, and is told something about the benefits to which he becomes entitled as an employee of the company. Then he is introduced to his foreman. He is assigned to a particular job. A foreman or instructor may show him how his machine operates or how the job is to be performed, or may tell him from whom he is to take orders, when and where he is to have lunch, where and how he may get needed tools, what to do in case he feels sick or gets hurt, when and how he will be paid, and all the other details of the starting routine. After the new employee goes to work, probably the most important single factor in his mind is the attitude of his foreman and the care that his foreman takes in helping him to bridge that difficult adjustment period until the new employee becomes "one of the gang."

During this period the union steward may approach him with reference to union membership, but the employee's main concern is whether or not he is making the grade, whether the foreman approves of his work and actions, and whether the other employees accept him as one of them.

When he receives his paycheck at the end of the pay period, that paycheck comes not from the union, but from the paymaster of the company. It is true the union may have negotiated the wage rates and therefore may bear some responsibility for the amount of the check, but the connection is an indirect one and the employee very properly regards his check as coming from the company and the amount of the check as being determined by the company. If the employee has some question in his mind, the natural person to whom he turns is his immediate supervisor. It is only when the employee does not get a satisfactory solution to his problem and feels it necessary to call in a union steward that *labor relations enter the picture.*

In addition to these points of contact, there are such important factors as safety on the job, availability of machine safeguards and personal protective devices, adequacy of the machines that he works on, the flow of material, the making of time studies and the setting of incentive rates, the provision of lockers and sanitary facilities, organized recreation, group insurance, employee-benefit associations, and communications to and from the company. All these are but some of the points of contact between employee and management which go to make up the complete entity of employer-employee training, counseling, welfare activities, requests for transfers, individual wage increases, promotions, the suggestion system, and use and issuance of personal protective equipment and tools. Only a very small proportion of these are ordinarily included in the term "labor relations."

1. Evidence of poor employee relations

Poor employee relations manifest themselves in a variety of ways.

Absenteeism. A rising rate of absenteeism is one reliable index of growing employee discontent. Sometimes the employee stays home because of a slight indisposition that he would normally take in his stride. Sometimes he may find other pretexts, for the average worker hates to admit, even to himself, that his job has become so distasteful that he prefers to stay home and watch TV rather than go to work.

In themselves, absenteeism figures may be considered a fair rule-of-thumb index of employee morale. They assume even greater significance, however, if each absence is investigated to determine the real underlying cause, and if the various causes are then tabulated, analyzed, and interpreted, and brought to the attention of top management. Absentee figures have an important story to tell, if management will but take the pains to evaluate their significance. Both from the viewpoint of interrupted production and the viewpoint of employee relations, absenteeism deserves more study than it normally receives.

Requests for transfers. Similarly, a request for a transfer may be a sign of discontent with work, supervisor, environment, or fellow employees. Normal human inertia tends to make people prefer to remain on the same job and a part of the same informal group. Changing jobs requires effort and adjustment to a new environment, new people, and usually somewhat different work. When an employee requests a transfer, it is well to look into the situation to determine the root of any possible discontent that might be sufficient to make him overcome this normal inertia.

High turnover. A high rate of turnover is an even more urgent danger signal for alert management, and particularly so when it affects the long-service employee. He prefers the environment he knows, with all its imperfections, to the turmoil and readjustment involved in finding and fitting into another job with a different company. And he is likely to think twice before he sacrifices the seniority "rights" associated with most jobs. He has a stake in his present job.

Therefore, when he is so upset and dissatisfied with his present job that he decides to change, there is likely to be a serious underlying cause.

Disciplinary difficulties. Poor employee relations are likely to lead to deterioration of plant discipline. If an employee believes that management has no interest in him or, what is even worse, that management has no use for him, he is not likely to respond to the normal disciplinary requirements of any civilized group. Disciplinary action is necessarily based on regard for others and on respect for authority. If employee relations have reached such a state that employees disregard management's authority, discipline goes out the window. Loss of control within an organization may result from loss of respect for that authority which is necessary to the smooth, orderly operation of an industrial plant.

Cleavages. Militant unionism or other direct action by employees may be caused by the nature and political inclination of the union's leadership. On the other hand, continued and increasing demands on the part of unions, an excessive number of grievances, evidence of restricted production, short work stoppages, and many other manifestations of cleavage between management and employees may be the outcome of poor employee relations within the organization.

Work stoppages. The final and well-nigh inevitable climax of poor employee relations, if not corrected, is a complete interruption of the business by strike, slowdowns, or "work holiday." While it is well known that "unauthorized" strikes, "spontaneous" walkouts, and the like are not always what they are claimed to be, many work stoppages are the end result of poor employee relations. In many cases a strike is an explosion resulting when long-smoldering dissatisfactions are suddenly touched off by what may appear to be a trivial incident. Unfortunately, some managements are unaware of the dangerous status of their employee relations until the explosion of a strike brings it dramatically to their attention. And even then, management is likely to lay misplaced emphasis on *labor* relations rather than undertake the less glamorous but more fundamental job of building sound employee relations.

Summary. Where good employee relations do not exist, it is easy to blame many things for the condition. Some point to the employees and say that they are lazy, unreasonable, or uncooperative. Some point to the union and say that it fights management and prevents management from doing the right thing by its employees. Some point to the union leaders and say that they are trying to undermine management or invade the sphere of management. Some point to union-biased legislation and say that management's hands are tied. Some point to the national administration and say that it appeases organized labor and is opposed to progress in enterprise. Others point to the critical times in which we live and say that in these days we cannot do what we want to, anyway.

There may be some element of truth in all these explanations. But the fact remains that, after making due allowance for all these factors beyond the control of management, the most decisive factor in creating a sound employer-employee relationship is a management that is alert, sound, enlightened, and appreciative of the critical importance of sound employee relations.

2. Employee wants

Many surveys have been made in an effort to determine what employees want and which of their wants are the most important to them. It is not surprising to find no unanimity about the results of these surveys and opinions. Americans are a heterogeneous people, composed of segments of different backgrounds and cultures. There can normally be no unanimity on such questions as opportunity versus security, shorter hours versus more pay, etc.

Moreover, the relative importance of various employee wants changes with time and economic conditions.

Security, an important employee want, includes job security and personal security—meaning that the employee can trust his employer, that he can count on being accepted as "one of the gang" in his work group, and that he will not be discriminated against. It is in large measure the search for security that accounts for employees joining with others to form unions, since the very act of doing things in concert lends an aura of security and approval to employees' acts.

The employee's feeling of security may be enhanced by good management in many ways. In the first place, management's complete assumption of its responsibility for adequate planning can result in greatly increased regularization of employment, minimizing the peaks and valleys that characterize many company employment charts. Second, a considerable part of the employee's lack of security may be due to the fact that he knows little about the company or about his status in it. Adequate information can help in this respect, together with an indication from the supervisor that he knows the type of work the employee is doing and the problems he is meeting and that his progress is being noted. And, finally, it is up to management to sell the employee the conviction that he will be fairly treated. In this connection it is deeds, rather than words, that count.

Another vital employee need is the knowledge that complaints will be fairly and promptly heard and appropriate action taken. If the employee has a valid complaint, it is up to management to do something about it—and do it promptly. If the employee's complaint is based on misunderstanding or imagination, he deserves an explanation.

Working conditions are important. Working conditions refer not only to the physical working environment, but also to the relationship between the employee and his supervisor, and other psychological factors. Many employers have gone to great lengths to provide excellent physical working conditions for their employees and have been surprised that better relationships have not automatically resulted. Employee goodwill cannot be bought by lush expenditures. It has to be earned by proving to employees that they are being treated like the human beings that they are.

Rates of pay and working conditions are high on practically every list of union demands. Entire industries have ceased to function and national crises have arisen over the question of an hourly wage increase. But the individual employee is also concerned with the question whether his rate of pay is fair as compared with others in his department (and, to a lesser extent, in comparison with others in his plant and community). His relative pay keenly affects his pride and dignity, and these are of most concern to him. Accordingly, wise managements are concerned with job evaluation, merit-rating systems, and other techniques for attaining and maintaining a just and fair rate schedule, and positioning employees appropriately within the rate ranges. It is quite probable, however, that wages might come very close to the top of the list in times of rapidly rising prices.

Employees are interested in receiving pay increases when deserved. A pay increase means more than increased earnings; it is a symbol of progress and of recognition of the employee's work. Accordingly, a pay increase based on merit is far more significant to the employee than one based on length of service.

Employees are also concerned with fringe-benefit plans, pensions, medical service, and group insurance. Promotions should be made fairly, with due recognition for merit and ability as well as for length of service. Employees properly consider it to be management's responsibility to provide a safe place to work, with appropriate machinery safeguards and personal protective devices. Failure on the part of management to provide these is regarded as evidence of management's disregard of employee welfare.

Job instruction represents the employee's desire to be told what is expected of him and how he may best perform it. Many employee-training programs are helpful in this respect, but in the great majority of cases, job instruction is left to the employee's immediate foreman or instructor.

Employees are human. Regardless of temporary variations in direction, regardless of passing catchwords and slogans, one thing seems unalterable and fixed in the catechism of employee wants: *Every employee wants to be treated like a human being.*

That is a simple statement to make, but its implications are profound. Every slight to his personal importance, every wound to his pride, every insult to his dignity will find some way to express itself. The slight may be unintentional, the wound purely accidental, the insult mere carelessness; but the effect on the employee will be felt and will seek to make itself heard.

Being a human being, the employee wants his pride and dignity respected. For that reason alone, a public reprimand can wreak havoc.

Pride in work. Every self-respecting man takes pride in his work. While it may be true that the creative pride of the artisan has been reduced because mass production has resulted in skill dilution, it is too often overlooked that the man whose job it is to tighten nut No. 3,467 as the cars go by on the conveyer takes real pride in his work. He needs to feel the significance of his contribution.

Pride in one's work is not only a basic expression of individual dignity; it is one of the most useful characteristics for management to cultivate and develop.

A man's just pride in his work is a good thing for a man to have. It is a good thing for management to encourage. Given pride in his work, the employee will give it his best. Take away his pride, and the work loses significance.

Much has been said about the workers' loss of pride because work simplification and mass production have led to less need for skill and judgment. While it is true that there are now relatively few workers who take a single operation all the way through to make a complete product, nevertheless it is not to be overlooked that each worker's self-respect requires that he attribute significance to his particular part of the operation.

Acceptance by fellow employees. Every employee wants to be treated like a human being. He wants and needs the acceptance and approval of his fellow employees. And to get it he will cut his income, if necessary, or help out a fellow employee, or badger his foreman. If the group, with or without union intervention, has agreed to restrict production to an agreed level, most employees will participate in controlling output, even though it may result in loss in take-home pay, in order to retain the approval of fellow employees. Other employees have sought to gain the admiration of fellow employees by egging on the foreman, by pretending to misunderstand instructions, or by getting the foreman to "blow his top." These are cases in which a regard for approbation by fellow employees is more important to the individual employee's pride than his chances of promotion or his acceptance by representatives of management.

Evidence of management interest. It is the need for self-respect that makes management interest in employee suggestions so effective. Sometimes the mere fact that the supervisor has taken the trouble to get the facts makes the employee realize that management is interested in him. For example, one employee submitted a safety suggestion involving the application of a lift that he had seen in operation in a railroad shop. A thorough investigation was made, including a visit to the railroad shop to see the lift in operation, and the matter was fully discussed with the suggester. Despite the fact that the suggestion was not adopted, the employee expressed his appreciation for the thorough consideration that had been given his suggestion. He knew and management knew that the decision was sound, and both learned something in the process. The obvious consideration of the suggestion and the explanation for its nonacceptance did more to build a sound relationship than if the employee had received a $50 suggestion award, for the employee knew that his suggestion had been treated with all the respect it deserved.

Fair play. Despite the normal desire for progress and advancement, not every employee wants to be president of the company. Many employees do not want promotion and the responsibilities that go with it. But it makes a great difference to every employee, regardless of his ambition, whether promotion in the company is based on merit or on favoritism. Promotion by whim or favoritism not only hurts the employee who should have been promoted, but arouses resentment in most other employees.

A consideration of the fundamental importance of the employee's desire to be recognized as a human being inevitably leads to the conclusion that the most important relationship in which the employee is involved is that between him and his immediate supervisor.

If management is sincere in pursuing the goal of ideal employee relations, it will give primary importance to the problem of selection and training of the first level of supervision. Training, of course, includes not only formal training but the examples set and instructions issued by higher levels of management.

No one has yet been able to write a contract specifying the content of "treatment like a human being." The union cannot supplant management in assuring the employee that he will be treated like a human being. That treatment must come from management. Management selects and trains the foremen; management determines the policies and organization for putting them into effect; management determines the working conditions. Management and management alone can determine how much effort it will devote to the problem of showing the employee that it recognizes him as a human being.

3. Employee morale

The employer who is truly and vitally concerned about employee relations finds the root of that concern not only in the knowledge that it is good business to have good employee relations, but also in his personal interest in and attitude toward his employees.

While high morale and good employee relations are not identical, it is clear that the establishment of good employee relations is the major factor in high employee morale. Whether morale be measured in the employee's attitude toward the company or in the degree of his satisfaction with his work environment, good employee relations inevitably lead to high morale.

"Morale" is a much abused word. Not only is it the pretext for all kinds of nonsense, from questionable motion pictures to the fanfare of "pin-up" publicity, but it has resulted in all kinds of mistaken ventures on the theory that high morale can be created by the fluff of high-pressure propaganda exemplified by parties, inspirational programs, rallies, shopping services, beauty parlors in the plant, door prizes, and beauty contests. Some or all of these may have their place in specific situations. But they cannot safely be substituted for the basic factors that determine morale in the employer-employee relationship.

Employee "morale" may be defined as the attitude of the employee toward his work environment, and more specifically toward the employer as represented by the foreman and higher supervision.

In a sense, the state of the employee's morale may be dependent upon the degree to which the employee's deep-rooted wants are affected by his work situation. That is, morale is likely to be high if the employee is convinced that—

His job is secure so long as he continues to do satisfactory work
His supervisor recognizes him as an individual human being and treats him as such
He is being treated fairly by the employer—and has an adequate opportunity to be heard if he is not being treated fairly
His company is interested in his welfare and progress
His work is important and significant
He knows his company and its products, and when changes are made, he is notified in advance and is told why
The company recognizes when he does outstanding work (and, conversely, the company is alert to condemn shoddy work by those who try to get away with it)
There is a fair opportunity for advancement
The company is willing to listen to his suggestions and consider them on their merits
His company is well thought of in the community

4. Organizing for good employee relations

How, then, does a management that is really concerned about good employee relations go about achieving them?

There is an unfortunate belief that all that is required to establish good employee relations is to "do a selling job." Some people believe that the employees can be sold on the company as one would promote a new brand of tooth paste. Good employee relations can be achieved, but not that simply. Good employee relations are like any other commodity: they cannot be "sold" for long unless the product to be sold is good. In the case of employee relations, that "product" is a vital interest in employee welfare, buttressed by sound, fair, definite employee policies, administered by a competent, carefully selected, and thoroughly trained management group. Neither good intentions nor good policies alone can result in good employee relations. But both of these can bring about good employee relations if administered by sound management.

In the first place, the interest in good employee relations must start at the top. It has been well said that an organization is but the lengthened shadow of the chief executive. If the chief operating executive (whether he has the title of chairman of the board, president, executive vice-president, or general manager) is vitally interested in good employee relations, he will infuse that interest throughout the organization. If he has no real concern in sound employee relations, anyone else in the organization, whether he is in charge of production or head of the employee-relations department, will have an uphill battle, with the odds against him.

Within limitations, every business management carries its own employee-relations destiny in its own hands.

Good employee relations do not come into existence simply by wishing for them. The first step to implement such a desire is to *organize* for good employee relations.

Management knows that production requires a manufacturing organization, and marketing requires a sales organization. Similarly, in order to achieve sound employee relations, management must be prepared to maintain in its organization an employee-relations organization or its equivalent (sometimes referred to as the industrial-relations, or the human-relations, or the personnel organization).

But the employee-relations function differs from every other management function. It touches every employee in the entire organization from president to sweeper. The employee-relations department is an arm of management, and at the same time a confidant of the worker who has a gripe against management. It originates and interprets company policies in order to achieve uniformity, and at the same time is alert to human reactions that may make it desirable to make exceptions in specific cases. It has no line authority, yet advises all members of management in their relations with their subordinates. It is the source of specialized and technical information, and yet it must keep its feet on the ground, and appreciate the importance of the very practical work environment and human reaction of every employee in the organization.

Because it is in intimate contact with every element of the organization, the operations of the employee-relations department are doomed to failure unless its functions are clearly understood by top management and have its backing. It is not enough for top management to set up an elaborate employee-relations department and say, "That takes care of our employee relations. Now we can forget that phase of the business and devote our attention to production, sales, and finance." By setting up an employee-relations department, top management simply provides additional help in getting its employee relations on a sound basis; but employee relations remain a major function of every supervisor, from the assistant foreman to the president. By their very nature, employee relations are not a separate segment or function that can be delegated to a specialist for handling. Employee-relations department specialists can assist, evaluate, investigate, interpret, recommend, advise, and carry out a few specialized functions, but they cannot replace the supervisor in his role as management representative in the employer-employee relationship.

Fundamentally, employee relations are the living relationship between every employee and his immediate supervisor. The cultivation of that relationship cannot be delegated to anyone else. The employee-relations department cannot segregate and take over the complete task of building sound employee relations.

Staff. It is this characteristic of inseparability between the supervisor as an operating link of the organization and as the core of the management-employee relationship that is responsible for the employee-relations department's being designated a *staff* department. As a staff department, it replaces the operating or line department only as to certain specialized functions. It does not replace the line supervisor as the major representative of company authority and source of company decisions with respect to individual employees. It is available for advising the supervisor with respect to personnel or labor-relations matters when he is in doubt. It collects necessary personnel and labor-relations information to help the supervisor in his relations with his subordinates (and sometimes in his relations with his associates and superiors). It interprets and defines company policies in their application to specific situations. It forecasts and anticipates future problems and prepares appropriate company policies to cope with such problems when they arise. It reports to top management concerning the effectiveness of existing policies and practices. It is the *staff* on which the line supervisor and top management lean in employee-relations matters.

The full importance of the employee-relations department's role in the company organization can best be understood if consideration is given to its major functions.

Major organizational functions. These major functions of the employee-relations department may be grouped under three main classifications:

1. To evaluate employee policies in operation, and report to top management on the operation of existing policies, suggesting desirable changes and forecasting trends
2. To formulate, codify, and interpret company policies
3. To carry out specialized functions, such as recruitment and selection of new employees; technical assistance in safety matters; training; admin-

istration of group health and group life insurance and other welfare plans; initiation and supervision of job-evaluation plans; advice on merit ratings; provision of special employee services (such as canteens and cafeterias); assistance in labor negotiations; maintenance of channels of communication, etc.

While the last two major functions are fairly well understood, the significance of the employee-relations department as controller of the employee-relations account is not generally understood. Even those managements that appreciate the vital importance of the human element seldom look to the employee-relations department to keep them advised of the current overall status of their employee relations.

Employee policies. Especially in the older, larger companies, "company policy" is a phrase to conjure with. There is the supervisor whose stock reason for not complying with any and every employee request is, "It's against company policy." On the other hand, there is the staid, routine mind which rejects every suggestion of change with the standard roadblock: "It's against company policy." To these people, company policy is a convenient subterfuge.

In the very same company, conscientious supervisors may be having a hard time trying to determine what *is* the company policy applicable, let us say, in the case of a requested transfer on the part of an employee who is doing satisfactory work in his present department. In all too many cases, the applicable company policy may be buried in the memory of the oldest living supervisor, or contained in some circular letter, long lost in somebody's files.

Written policies. Since employee relations are the everyday business of every supervisor, each with a different degree of training and understanding, company employee policies must be reduced to writing and made available to every supervisor, in order that employee policies may be known and may be uniform. Besides these obvious reasons for reducing employee policies to writing, there is another reason not so apparent. In any specific employee-problem situation, a decision may be made which is suitable for that specific situation but entirely unsuitable for other situations of the same class. Yet that decision may be followed as a precedent in these other situations because no one with sufficient authority has taken the time to think it through. When, however, an employee policy is reduced to writing, someone at the policy-making level must think it through, and the resultant policy is likely to be far sounder than one arrived at as an expedient to meet a specific situation and thereafter blindly followed.

It is sometimes objected that reducing employee policies to writing ties the hands of the line supervision and limits their discretion. It is true that dependence on written policy limits supervisory discretion. That is one of the purposes of written policies. Unlimited supervisory discretion necessarily results in departmental and even individual discrimination. If the elimination of such discrimination requires limitation of supervisory discretion, then it must be limited. But even a written policy leaves a great deal of discretion in the hands of the supervisor. There is no way in which top management can get its policies known to and carried out by first-line supervision unless such policies are reduced to writing. In fact, as has been well said, "A policy is not a policy unless it is in writing."

In order that written policies may be easily available to first-line supervision, it is obvious that in an organization of any magnitude it would be wise to develop a policy manual, preferably loose-leaf, for easy amendment, and indexed for easy reference.

The policy manual, while desirable, should not be relied upon as the sole instrument for disseminating information concerning employee policies. Discussion meetings, oral explanations, and policy-training classes are all helpful. But the best training that any supervisor can get with respect to employee polices is to have *his* superior practice those policies, especially in relation to the supervisor himself.

"That's the company policy." It is a fine thing for management to develop and apply enlightened employee policies. It is an even finer thing to know when to make exceptions in the application of policies.

It is the easiest thing in the world to apply every policy inflexibly. But mankind is too various, human situations and their effects are too different to ensure fairness by following rules or policies, no matter how wisely prepared. Even judges find it necessary to temper justice with mercy. In the field of employee relations, policy application must be tempered with a liberal dose of judgment. In fact, while supervisors should be guided by company policies, the reason for any action should be explained on its own merits, and the trite explanation, "Sorry—that's company policy," should be forbidden. Passing the buck to company policy is just as bad as passing the buck to higher supervision. Not only should "company policy" be avoided as an excuse or pretext for any action or decision, but foremen should be alert to cases warranting exceptions being made in the application of company policies, and management should provide an easy way for approving exceptions in meritorious cases.

Policy development. Before a policy can be written, it must be developed. An employee policy cannot be prepared by a policy formulator in an ivory tower. It must be the result of intimate knowledge of the company's operations and practices, and their effects on employees in all departments. If a policy is formulated to meet a situation in one department, it must not be adopted until its application to other departments and classes of employees has been evaluated.

If a complaint results in a decision to furnish rotary-furnace operators in the gear department with special face shields, what should be done about the furnace operators in the carburizing department? And what should be done about the cupola tenders in the foundry and the electrolytic-furnace operators in the metallurgical laboratory?

If exempt salaried employees in the home office are to be paid for authorized overtime, consideration must be given to the application of the same policy to the regional offices where the degree of supervision is likely to be much less. If overtime is to be paid for, will the policy be equally applicable to the employee who is called upon to be on the road for weeks at a time, when he alone can determine how much time per day his mission requires? The extension of the policy to salaried personnel on the shop payroll must also be considered.

Some considerations of a similar nature are involved in every policy decision. No one man can make a sound decision unless (1) he knows a great deal about the organization and operations involved, and (2) he has the benefit of recommendations from those who are intimately familiar with the many applications which that policy will receive in practice.

The development of employee policies takes time and patience. It is more important that they be right than that they be developed to meet a specified schedule. Time is of the essence—plenty of time.

5. Specialized employee-relations functions

In addition to its policy-forming and human-auditing functions, the employee-relations department is usually charged with the performance of certain specialized functions to assist the line organization and to help provide, maintain, and train the manpower through which the line organization operates.

Because certain specialized employee functions are delegated to the employee-relations department, it is easy to reach the fallacious conclusion that the employee-relations department handles all employee-relations problems. Whether employee relations are good, bad, or indifferent depends primarily upon the interaction of line supervisors and the workers under their supervision. The employee-relations department can help, advise, observe, recommend, and perform some specialized employee functions; but it cannot and should not try to replace line supervisors as *the* representatives of management in the eyes of the employees. In performing its specialized employee functions, the employee-relations department acts in a staff capacity, an arm of operating management.

Industrial experience has shown that there are specific formal techniques of personnel administration which can be delegated to specialists in an employee-relations department, and particularly in companies which are large enough to warrant a fully staffed employee-relations department. Even in companies which are so small that a separate employee-relations department cannot be justified, it is necessary to delegate these functions to some group or individual, even if only on a part-time basis. The important thing is to recognize the need for the use of these various techniques and to make sure that responsibility for their performance is specifically designated and generally understood.

Employment. The central employment office is usually the first element of an employee-relations department to be created. At first the employment manager's job may be limited to recruitment, selection, and placement of new employees. But before long the employment manager finds that employees whom he has hired come back to him for advice and look to him as a source of information about the company and about their place in it. He finds his activities expanding considerably beyond the mere matter of hiring new employees. He begins to receive complaints, requests for transfers, questions about safety, etc. Every employment office finds itself called upon to do far more than merely recruit, select, and place new employees.

While an employment office may thus acquire additional personnel functions by default—because no other agency is available to discharge these functions— it cannot discharge them properly unless it is specifically organized to do so. And if it is organized to discharge a wide variety of personnel functions, it becomes a personnel department rather than an employment department. No personnel function should be permitted to remain unassigned. If a personnel function needs to be performed, it should be specifically assigned to a given person or department, and the entire organization should be informed that such person or department is responsible for handling all problems involving that function.

It is now generally understood that an employee-relations department performs specific personnel and labor-relations functions. As a minimum, the employment section of the employee-relations department should be responsible for recruitment, interviewing, selection, and placement of new employees, and termination of employment of employees leaving the organization. Usually the employment section also has the responsibility for maintaining personnel records and identifications, administering leave-of-absence and absenteeism policies, conducting special investigations, and clearing transfers. In some cases the employment section also participates in recommending promotions and administering centralized discipline.

The primary functions of an employment office in an industrial plant are to procure, select, investigate, classify, and place as many workers as are needed in the shops and offices of the plant.

In a "tight labor market," when labor is scarce for the many jobs available, the main problem of the employment office is to get enough people to satisfy the growing demands of the company. At such times, employment interviews may be shortened, and every effort made to expedite hiring available applicants and putting them on the job. On the other hand, when there are more applicants than jobs, the employment office may be justified in spending more time with each applicant in order to make sure that the company hires the best of those available. However, whether the labor market is tight or plentiful, any management which is vitally interested in its employees will take pains to set up desirable standards which must be met by applicants for employment. The kind of people who will make up the organization is determined at the employment office. As labor leaders are fond of saying, "After all, if you complain about the acts of our members, remember that you hired them."

Many problems may arise in connection with the primary function of the employment office—the recruitment, selection, and placement of a working force. Adequate sources of desirable applicants for employment need to be developed. One of the most important factors in the development of an adequate source of desirable applicants is good employee relations and community public relations on the part of the company.

A company's reputation in the community may very well determine the caliber and composition of its working force. The opinion of its employees is a most important factor in determining its standing in the community.

In that connection, it is most interesting to note the experience of one long-established factory. Being hard pressed for additional employees at a time of serious labor shortage, the company carried on an intensive advertising campaign by means of local newspapers, radio announcements, billboards, motion-picture appeals in the local theaters, churches, etc. At the same time, the company urged its own employees to invite their friends to come to work for their company.

During a 3-month period, while recruitment was at its peak, records were kept of the sources that brought new employees to the company. The results were startling. Of all the employees hired by this company, 61 percent applied for employment either because they had friends or relatives there, or because they were former employees themselves. The remaining 39 percent applied for a variety of reasons, such as referred by the U.S. Employment Service (10 percent); by nearby residents (2 percent); referred by local school (2 percent); radio advertising (2 percent); billboard advertising (1 percent); referred by local draft board (1.5 percent); and newspaper advertising (3 percent). It is also interesting to note that only 6 percent of all the employees who came could ascribe no reason for having picked this particular company as the one in which they wanted to work.

Obviously, the employees must have been sold on the company, or they would not have urged their friends to come to work there. It is quite clear that satisfied employees are an asset to the employer in many ways that are not obvious at first blush.

Employees do not, however, automatically act as recruiting agents for their companies, even if they are proud of them. But they can be encouraged to do so by bulletin-board notices or appeals in employee publications. In the specific case discussed, a portion of the employees were circularized weekly by individual letters addressed by the employment manager to their homes.

A company that considers itself a permanent element in its community should develop as many points of contact with the community as possible. The employment section can play an important role in this contact with the community. The employment manager (or an assistant) should be available for active participation in business groups, parent-teacher groups, school programs, vocational-guidance clinics, nationality organizations, veterans' organizations, and social-service organizations. He should be prepared to explain his company's place in the community, the opportunity it offers for permanent, useful employment, and the kinds of skills that are most likely to be in demand 1, 2, and 3 years ahead. He should cooperate with local vocational schools, encouraging their full utilization by present and prospective company employees, and bringing the benefit of his practical knowledge to the assistance of local school boards and directors.

The employment manager can do much to make his company a respected member of the community.

The development of adequate sources of applicants for employment, essential as it is, is only the beginning of an employment program. Even when sources of applicants have been carefully developed, the efficiency of a company's working force may depend largely on proper techniques of selection and placement. It is being increasingly recognized that attitudes toward reasonable authority and cooperativeness may be as important as technical ability in the development of a proper body of employees. Successful selection and placement, in turn, depend upon adequate knowledge of the jobs for which the employees are being selected. The absence of job analyses and job descriptions frequently contributes to employee maladjustment and may result in high turnover.

Placement. Getting the right man on the right job is no easy task. Many employees come to industrial plants offering specific skills or services. Unless employees are utilized at their highest skill, they will be dissatisfied and will show their dissatisfaction in any number of ways. The best safeguard for getting the right employee on the right job is to have an adequate, trained staff in the employment office, utilizing a standardized and tested interview procedure, to the end that all the available information regarding the applicant will lead to placing the employee on a suitable job.

Placing the employee on a suitable job does not necessarily mean hiring the best available employee and putting him on an available job. An employee with a great deal of initiative assigned to a monotonously repetitive job not only would be unhappy on the job, but would not perform the job as satisfactorily as would another employee with less initiative. An important consideration in placement is to place the employee so that he will be utilized at his highest skill, to assure best performance, satisfactory adjustment, and maximum development of human resources.

Applicants for jobs do not ordinarily resent being asked a large number of questions. However, interviews can be so conducted as to arouse antagonism and give the company an unfavorable reputation. A series of essential questions can be developed into a standardized interview procedure which will give the employer all the information he needs in determining the experience or training of the applicant, his adjustment to his work and fellow workers, and his motivation for desiring a job in that plant, without seeming to pry into the applicant's private life. Information about the applicant's background gives the employer some protection against unscrupulous job seekers who have little or nothing to offer the productive effort or who are getting jobs for reasons not in accord with the company program.

Another adjunct to the placement procedure is personality and aptitude testing, a technique that has received fulsome praise as well as severe condemnation.

If tests are administered by people who have adequate training in the interpretation of the test results, and if they are used to supplement other types of information rather than as the basic information on which to make final decisions of job placement, they can be very valuable.

If a testing program is to be undertaken with respect to employees already on the payroll, great care needs to be taken because employees may be led to believe that the testing program may be used as a device to avoid promoting those who deserve it, or otherwise as a pretext for discrimination. It is preferable to start a testing program on a voluntary basis, as an additional service to those employees who want to find out where they are likely to make most rapid progress. It may also be used in the case of "problem children," to help them orient themselves.

Employment section as a screen. In its relationship to the line departments, the employment office, being a staff department, should not definitely hire an applicant for a specific job. It interviews all applicants and screens out those considered undesirable. Then it recommends suitable applicants for specific openings, subject to acceptance or rejection by the head of the department concerned. It is the line department that actually hires the applicant.

After an applicant is hired, it is desirable that he be put through an induction, or orientation, process, which can conveniently be a function of the employment section. This induction procedure may take 15 minutes or a whole day, depending on the size of the company and the stage of development of its employee relations.

Those companies which devote appreciable time and effort to the induction procedure find that it pays dividends in helping the employee to feel more at home, more welcome on the job. It shortens the period of instability and insecurity that usually accompanies immersion in a new environment. It gives the employee the necessary preliminary information that makes him feel at ease. It helps the employee get off to a good start, and it may permanently affect his attitude toward the company.

Since placement is still far from being a scientific process, even when all available devices are utilized, it is good practice for the employment section to maintain contact with the new employee for a brief period of time, by means of postemployment interviews on the job with the new employee and with his immediate foreman. Such interviews may take place a week or 10 days after the employee starts on his job, and again 5 or 6 weeks later, or in any event before the employee has completed his probationary period.

These interviews are designed to determine whether the employee is adjusting properly to his new environment, whether any special questions or problems have arisen, and whether his work and attitude are satisfactory. These adjustment interviews help the employee to feel the company has maintained its interest in him, and may also disclose whether the employee should remain on his current job or should be transferred. It requires care and tact to conduct these interviews in such a way that the immediate foreman's prestige is fully protected and increased, rather than minimized.

Arranging such an adjustment interview with the new employee and his foreman just before the employee completes his probationary period constitutes an excellent method of determining whether the employee is the kind who is likely to be a permanent asset to the company, or whether his employment should be terminated. All too often, the probationary period, designed to be a period of testing, is allowed to lapse by default, and no action is taken until too late. An employee who is retained beyond the probation period is justified in believing that he has made good, and that he will be retained so long as he continues to render the same kind of service and so long as business conditions permit his continued employment.

Records. Records are the history upon which present action is based in an effort to determine the future. In order that they may be of real assistance, records should be scrupulously fair, adequate, and centralized in one place.

Usually, the place where employee records are centralized is the employment office, which contains not only the records of present employees, but also all records of applicants and of former employees.

Employee records are of many kinds and of various degrees of complexity. The larger the company, the more it is likely to rely upon records. Accordingly, a larger company would be likely to have more detailed records, to compensate in some measure for the widening gap between upper management and rank-and-file employees.

As a minimum, every employee record should have the information necessary to identify the employee fully, and to identify his occupation, classification, and department. It is highly desirable that his rate of pay and history of changes in rate of pay and occupations be included, as well as a record of his correspondence with the company, promotions or demotions, transfers, health records, accidents, absenteeism, length of service, discipline record, and suggestions.

Many of the larger companies have found it convenient and economical to incorporate all of these data and other available information about an employee in some form of data processing system. This enables them to determine rapidly any pertinent information about a group of employees, for example, how many will retire in the next five years, how many have graduated from high school, etc. Before installing such equipment, the economics of the move must be carefully considered. Data processing systems vary from very simple forms involving low costs, up to very sophisticated computers of high cost.

Transfers. Transfers between jobs or departments are an important aspect of employee relations. An employee who is a detriment to one department may be a positive asset in another. Transfers are a mechanism for better matching employee wants and skills with job demands. Transfers may be used to alleviate situations due to incompatible personalities. Transfers are required to give selected individuals varied work experience. Incorrectly used, transfers may be a source of great employee discontent.

Since it usually contains the central employee files, the employment section properly serves as a clearinghouse for all transfers. It is the exchange to which notices of surplus manpower or vacancies are sent. It is the one place, aside from his foreman, where a disgruntled employee may go to announce that he wants a change, or is ready to quit.

Every request for a transfer deserves a careful investigation to determine the real reasons. If the request comes from a supervisor, the employment office should ascertain whether the supervisor is merely trying to foist an undesirable employee on another supervisor, or whether there is a personality or other problem involved, or whether there is a sound reason for making the transfer requested. If the request comes from the employee, there is very likely to be an unsatisfactory situation at the bottom of it, since ordinary human inertia would make the employee desire to remain on a job he knows and remain a member of his informal group. It is the duty of the employment office to ascertain the facts and to make recommendations that will remove the cause of any dissatisfaction that exists. Here again the services of a liaison representative of the line organization or an employment advisory committee can be extremely helpful.

Each time a man is moved from one machine to another or from one department to another, a whole chain of new reactions is set up. Does the employee understand why he is being moved, or is he left to suspect that he may not have been doing his job properly, or that he made some important mistake, or that his foreman "has it in for him"? How does the transfer affect the employee's prestige and self-esteem? Is he being taken away from a job in which he takes real pride to another which he knows little about? What may be to the superintendent merely efficient allocation of the working force is to the employee an intensely human problem.

Transfers made at the request of the employee have just as much capacity for error as those made at the instance of management.

Despite the cost of transfers, management has an obligaiton to make transfers whenever a transfer will enable an employee to be used at his highest skill or maximum ability. Even a well-organized placement service in the employment office will not make the correct placement in every case; or a more suitable opening may develop after the employee has been hired on an available job;

or the employee may develop new skills or learn additional techniques or acquire other interests after he has been hired. Continuous efforts to place employees at their highest skills is good management and makes for good employee relations.

Exit interviews. The employment section is the gate through which an employee enters the organization and through which he leaves it.

Every employee who is about to leave an enterprise offers management at least three significant opportunities: (1) He may be able to point out something wrong in the organization or its policies, for when he is on the point of leaving he is likely to speak very frankly; (2) He may be saved as an employee, preventing loss of his experience and skill, and avoiding the time and expense of recruiting and training a new employee to take his place; and (3) The manner of his leaving may improve or damage the company's standing in the community.

All these factors justify the increasing utilization of the exit interview for all employees leaving the company, whether the termination be voluntary or by way of discharge. Some companies also provide for an exit interview in every case of layoff, at which time employees are told about their rights to unemployment compensation, and what are the prospects of their being called back to work, and when.

Where the employee is leaving the company of his own volition, the exit interviewer at the employment office attempts to determine the real causes, and if the employee is worth saving (and the presumption is that he is), the exit interviewer does what he can to retain the employee. In this task, the exit interviewer must maintain a delicate balance. On the one hand, he should not show any special favors to a quitting employee, as this would not be fair to other employees and would simply encourage threats to quit over any minor complaint. On the other hand, if the employee has a legitimate grievance that is within the company's control and employee policy to straighten out, the exit interviewer should take steps to do so.

In any event, if the employee finally decides to quit, it is a function of the exit interviewer to "sell" the employee on the reasons for the company's action, if possible, so the employee will remain an asset to the company even after he terminates his employment relationship.

The valuable information gathered from exit interviews should be transmitted to some centralized point, which evaluates all employee reactions. At the same time, any unhealthy situations discovered as a result of exit interviews should be promptly corrected, again preferably with the aid of the line-organization liaison representative or employment advisory committee. It is frequently desirable to have members of line supervision sit in on exit interviews.

Job evaluation. The correct determination of wage rates is obviously of great importance to the employee and an essential in a sound employee-relations program. To the employee, the rate of pay is important not only because it determines his standard of living, but also because it determines the employee's relative standing in the department in which he works.   If the employee finds another worker doing the same work but getting more money, he will immediately suspect favoritism, with all the demoralizing effect of such suspicion. Similarly, if employees receive the same pay for work of varying degrees of skill and effort, there will be no incentive for greater effort and self-improvement.

The setting of wage rates "by gosh and by guess" is responsible for many of the inequitable and unjustifiable wage rates that may be found in industry today.   Such wages have been responsible for a great deal of friction and for some of the charges of favoritism brought against management.

Some wage structures "just growed," like Topsy, with no logical relationship between wages paid for various jobs.   Some wages have been set by superficial comparison with other jobs.

Job evaluation, based on accurate job descriptions and an analysis of the factors required to perform the job satisfactorily, is an art compounded of intimate knowledge of the job and its requirements, an understanding of the factors into which all jobs can be broken down (such as education, physical exertion, responsibility, mental effort, and experience), and judgment.

Once the jobs have been properly analyzed and evaluated, it is a relatively simple matter to convert job ratings into wage rates.

Obviously the line supervisor cannot be expected to be an expert on rate setting.   Nor can the line supervisor alone achieve uniformity in rates throughout the organization.   This is a job for the specialist, and such special service may well be rendered by a job-analysis section of the employee-relations department.

The job-analysis section may have the functions of working with the line organization to obtain accurate job descriptions for each occupation, preparing job evaluations, advising on merit ratings, incentive systems, etc.   In brief, it renders a technical service relating to wage rates and promotions.

In performing its wage-evaluation functions, the job-analysis section also has an auditing function.   Frequently it is used as a central control in wage matters, so that every increase in wages or salaries, and every initial wage or salary for new employees, becomes subject to screening by the job-analysis section.   In times of plentiful manpower, and under pressure to cut costs, some supervisors may attempt to pay less than the minimum rate for certain occupations, while in times of manpower shortage, and pressure for higher production, rates higher than the maximum may be resorted to.   There may also be differences of opinion when it comes to setting rates for new occupations.

Here again the services of a liaison representative with the line organization or committee may be very helpful in getting good results.

Likewise, the job-analysis section can be very helpful in explaining wage rates to employees who believe their jobs should receive a higher rating.   It can also play an important part in the handling of wage grievances and complaints.

Management should be on guard lest its reliance on scientific wage evaluation make it blind or insensitive to employee wage complaints. While sound job analysis should reduce legitimate employee complaints on this score, no technique is so perfect as to avoid all errors. Job content may change, or may have been wrongly evaluated. Moreover, whether or not the employee's complaint be factually justified, if he believes his wage is wrong or unfair, he deserves sympathetic consideration and a full explanation. It may be that the employee's wage complaint has its root in some other maladjustment that can easily be corrected.

Being intimately familiar with wage rates and the basis underlying these rates, the job-analysis section should be called upon in all wage negotiations, either to participate actively or to furnish the necessary information.

The job-analysis section should be responsible for making accurate wage surveys in the area and industry, to serve as a guide to management and as a corrective for false information that comes by the grapevine. No company is ever entirely free of the rumor that someone else nearby is paying 10 (or 20, or 30) percent more for the same job. The job-analysis section should be able to state authoritatively whether the rumor is true, or what the facts of the case really are. Sometimes such wage surveys are conducted by a local trade association.

The job-analysis section should also be in position to advise management concerning the operation and relative merits of various incentive systems, and their applicability to the company's specific situation.

While job analysis is a valuable tool to assure equitable wage rates in the shop, a modified job-analysis technique is equally essential for the salaried occupations. There is just as much need for equitable salary administration as there is for equitable hourly wage administration.

Merit rating. Just as job evaluation is a technique for the evaluation of jobs, so merit rating is a device for fair and impartial evaluation of people as workers.

Every time a foreman makes a decision with respect to job assignment, transfer, discipline, promotion, wage increase, or demotion, he must evaluate the person he is dealing with and judge his capacity as compared with that of others in the department. Merit rating was developed in an effort to substitute calm analysis in place of prejudice on the one hand and favoritism on the other, and to get away from the injustice of snap decisions.

Merit ratings are periodic evaluations of employees in relation to their performance on the job. Their primary function is to determine the relative ranking of employees in the order of their effectiveness on the job, to assist the foreman in making decisions on promotion, demotion, work assignments, and transfer. Another important function of merit rating is its influence upon the employee's supervisor, since it forces him to evaluate the employee's work with a considerable degree of objectivity. A third important function of merit rating is that it provides the supervisor an opportunity to discuss the employee's record with the employee, thus giving the employee some idea of where he stands and why, and how he can improve his record.

Merit-rating programs are of various kinds. The most common variety of merit-rating program is based upon supervisory evaluation of separate characteristics, such as quantity and quality of work performed, initiative, dependability, cooperativeness, etc., of each employee. The total rating is supposed to determine the employee's effectiveness on the job, at the same time highlighting his shortcomings.

A simpler method of merit rating is for the supervisor merely to list the employees in his department in the order of their relative overall effectiveness, from best to poorest. This method may also be utilized with reference to various specific employee characteristics, combining such specific rankings to obtain a general rating of each employee. It eliminates the need to give an absolute (and artificial) rating to each employee characteristic, since it merely requires the supervisor to consider each employee in relation to other employees.

A more theoretical approach to merit rating is the "forced-distribution" system, in which the supervisor is required to separate his employees (on paper) into five groups, the best employees being put in group A, the second best in group B, and so on. Furthermore, he is required to locate a given percentage of the employees into each group, as for example, 10 percent in group A, 20 percent in group B, 40 percent in group C, etc. Each supervisor is required to allocate the same proportion of his employees in each of the various groups, thereby eliminating to some extent the tendency of some supervisors to rate all their employees on the high side, and of others to rate their employees low.

Whichever method of merit rating is selected, supervisors must be trained in its correct usage, in its limitations, and in the best ways to make the most of a merit-rating system. It cannot simply be installed and then forgotten. It needs the continuing observation, follow-up, and control of a staff specialist or group, although its actual administration must be a line responsibility. It is logical to assign the staff function with respect to merit-rating plans to the job-analysis section of the employee-relations department.

The staff assistants of the job-analysis section should be limited to recommending an appropriate merit-rating program, gaining its acceptance by the line organization, being prepared to advise in its administration, and checking to see that it is operated properly.

A merit-rating program, properly administered, can be extremely valuable in focusing supervisory attention on employee performance and development. Sometimes the effect of personalities is further minimized by having each employee rated by two or three supervisors. It is easy, however, to reach the point of diminishing returns.

Merit rating is far from foolproof. There is always a tendency to misuse it by "working backward from the answer"—i.e., filling out a merit-rating form

in such a way as to come out with the rating the foreman has previously concluded is right.   For this reason, no merit-rating plan can be successful unless
supervision is thoroughly sold on its advantages and is determined to make it
work.

Properly introduced and used, merit rating can be a definite asset.   Improperly introduced or administered, it may do more harm than good.

Promotions.   Promotion policies very largely determine the composition of
management itself.   From the viewpoint of the employees, promotion is both
the road to bigger and better things and a reward for loyalty, application to the
job, skill, and experience.

Promotion not only builds the management group, but constitutes a force for
good or bad employee relations.   Even those employees who do not want the
responsibility of promotion for themselves are very much affected by the criteria
used in making promotions.   All employees understand the justice of promotion on the basis of merit, while promotion on the basis of favoritism or "pull" is
universally condemned.

Accordingly, management tends to be more and more careful about promotion policies.   But just what constitutes merit?   Does a superior mechanic necessarily make a good supervisor?   So varied and diversified are the duties and
qualifications of a good foreman that, were he to excel in them all, he would
deserve the level of salary usually reserved for the president of the company.
But it is clear that the human-relations aspect of the foreman's job is second to
none in importance, for his success is measured by his ability to weld his subordinates into a loyal, cooperative team.

Accordingly, selection of men for promotion is not a simple procedure of
pinning a badge on Joe and saying, "O.K., Joe, now you're the foreman of
department X."   It is a matter that requires the most careful consideration of
(1) the characteristics required of a good foreman, and (2) the capacities and
qualifications of the available candidates.

It is expecting the impossible to expect each foreman and superintendent to
be able to make such a selection unaided.   Merit rating helps, but more than
that is needed.   The characteristics required of a good foreman may very well
be defined by the job-analysis section, with the closest cooperation of the line
organization.   The selection of candidates for promotion might very well be
done by a central committee of high-level supervisors, with a representative of
the job-analysis section sitting with such a committee as a consultant.

The very existence of such a committee might well serve to offset charges of
favoritism in promotion and gain fuller employee acceptance of the company's
promotion policies.

Training.   Employee training may be as far-ranging and versatile as industry
itself.   It ranges from the induction program and on-the-job training to apprentice training, university-level classes, broad-gauge training in economics
and company policies, and executive development.

On-the-job training given by a foreman or instructor to a new employee or a newly advanced employee is an important element of employee training, and no amount of staff assistance from the training section of the employee-relations department can replace the valuable relationship created by a foreman teaching a subordinate the proper or safest way to do a job and the best way to get along with the gang.

But there are many useful ways in which the training section can supplement the foreman's training and provide additional training in other fields.

For example, the training section can offer classes in shop mathematics, micrometer reading, basic electricity, shop sketching, etc., all of which are directly helpful to the employees on their jobs and help them to prepare themselves for progress and advancement. Such courses should preferably be offered to the employees without charge, on their own time. If the demand is great, special booklets may be prepared for use in such classes, using the company's own products, familiar to the employees, as examples to illustrate the various courses. The more closely these courses are related to the employees' work, the more effective they are likely to be.

Courses of this kind can be organized most effectively by means of a training committee consisting of representatives of upper levels of shop supervision. The training committee may request the training section to offer certain desired courses, or may pass on suggestions made by the training section.

The advantages derived from this type of employee training are greater than those that meet the eye. Not only does such training result in greater skill and ability on the part of the employees, but it gives employees a sense of accomplishment and progress that cannot be obtained from their daily work. Employees who feel that their progress on the job is inadequate may feel that after all they are not wasting their time, since they are preparing themselves for better jobs. And they are, for the interest resulting from scholastic progress may make promotable material out of employees who would otherwise stay where they are.

The training section does not necessarily need to include on its staff the instructors or discussion leaders for these various subjects. It is far better, and arouses greater participation and interest, if the classes are conducted by employees or members of supervision, and often unsuspected teaching talent may be thus uncovered. Resort may also be had to part-time teaching by local vocational-school, technical-school, or other adult-group teachers. Where classes in these subjects are available in the community, many companies encourage their employees to take these courses by paying part of the tuition.

There is another type of employee training that is receiving increasing attention from management. This relates to general training, which may not help the employee directly on his job, but teaches him more about his company, its products, and its place in industry. This may consist of classes, open to all employees, describing the company's products, achievements, contributions to industry and consumers, famous machines or other products, inventions, etc.

Courses may also be given on the company's organization and policies, describing the work of the various departments and how they mesh together to produce the company's products or services. It makes the work of most employees, both shop and office, far more significant when they understand the contributions made by the various departments, many of which are but vague names to most employees.

If at all possible, these classes should be led by the heads or other responsible executives of the departments concerned, with a discussion period following the presentation. This type of class offers a channel of communication between employees and management that is seldom appreciated.

Some companies have done a splendid job of using classes on company organization to illustrate problems of basic economics, providing the best possible basic education concerning the nature of our economy and how it is affected by taxes, wages, profits, prices, etc. Such classes probably constitute the best possible form of adult education, especially if active employee participation can be obtained. In many cases, local school facilities may be available for such courses.

A still different field of employee training relates to subject matter which may be unrelated to the employees' work or company, but which improves employee morale by directing their interest and increasing leisure time into constructive channels. For example, the training section may offer classes in foreign languages, current events, labor relations, etc. How much the company may want to do in this direction may well depend upon the ready availability of similar instruction at extension courses and vocational schools.

The training section should directly supervise any apprentices the company may be training. It takes time and development to make a journeyman—a skilled craftsman. Apprenticeship programs have a definite place in industry, and their usefulness has not been reduced by the advent of mass-production techniques. The need for skilled craftsmen will probably always exist, despite the pronouncements of those who believe that mechanization will invalidate human skills.

If the apprenticeship program involves any appreciable number of apprentices, they should preferably be supervised by full-time apprentice supervisors reporting to the line organization. These apprentice supervisors should, however, consult periodically and frequently with the training-section staff to discuss progress, receive suggestions, and keep the training section fully advised of the development of each apprentice. The training section should be responsible for the classwork for the apprentices, either directly or through local vocational schools, and it should be responsible for routing apprentices through the various job assignments necessary to complete a full schedule of craft training.

In the larger companies, the training section is also responsible for advanced scholastic work, such as that for graduate engineers, and in some cases companies have undertaken to provide a complete educational program leading to postgraduate degrees.

One of the most fundamental training needs in any company is the training of foremen and other supervisors. As employee relations become ever more important, the training of foremen in the human-relations aspect of their work needs more and more emphasis. No sound training program for foremen is possible unless management has (1) determined what are a foreman's functions; (2) determined who are foremen and who are not; and (3) clearly identified those who are foremen.

Foremen need to know how to be effective supervisors above all else. The best way to learn is the conference method, with a limited group and plenty of opportunity for discussion. Courses in leadership, in grievance handling, in employee policies are essential. Also necessary are courses in forms and procedures, how the payroll is figured, production control, etc.

But foremen's courses cannot be effective unless thoroughly endorsed and backed up by higher line supervision. Nor is it much use to teach a foreman good human-relations techniques if he himself does not receive that kind of treatment from his own superior. So the best way to begin foreman training is to start at the top with the plant managers and superintendents, and not until they have been through the entire course and approved or modified should it be given to the foremen, preferably using line supervisors as conference leaders. The role of the training section in this field is to help develop the course and to provide the facilities for organizing conference groups. The greatest possible participation from the line organization in all aspects of foreman training should be cultivated.

The training section is the natural department to maintain the closest possible liaison with local vocational schools, university extension courses, colleges, etc. It should always be prepared to advise employees about available local educational facilities and courses, help employees register for such courses, and advise with them on progress from time to time. The training section should make it a point to advise employees' superiors that their employees have registered for special studies, either within the company or at outside schools.

It becomes apparent, then, that the role of the training section is that of a catalytic agent in the employee-training process, rather than that of a school or university. It requires but a limited staff, but can perform unlimited miracles in employee advancement, morale, and communication, and it can do much to strengthen the very fiber of the supervisory group. It multiplies the human assets of the organization.

Health and safety. Promotion of safety on the job is good business and good employee relations. Safety is an integral part of each employee's job and each foreman's responsibility. But the foreman can get a great deal of help from the safety section.

A good safety program depends on safety engineering, the development of safeguards on all equipment used, whether it is a loading platform or a punch press. It is the employer's legal and moral obligation to provide a safe place to work and to have all machinery appropriately guarded. Safety engineering enables the employer to do so. While safety engineering can be done by the line organization, there is less likelihood of compromise with production demands if safety engineering is carried on as a staff function of the safety section.

Closely allied to safety engineering is the provision of personal protective devices—safety goggles, safety shoes, respirators, masks, leg guards, asbestos gloves, etc. Some of these, such as safety goggles and safety shoes, may be worn by all employees. Others, such as respirators, gloves, and masks, may be necessary only for employees doing special jobs such as painting, tending open furnaces, etc.

The utilization and selection of machinery safeguards and personal protective devices require highly specialized knowledge, including intimate knowledge of the requirements of state laws and codes, familiarity with plant operations, safety devices available, safety practices elsewhere, available safety literature, and contact with safety and health organizations.

The line foreman or superintendent can hardly be expected to have such information at his finger tips. But he should always be able to call on the safety section to provide him with the answers to any health or safety problems that may arise.

In addition to recommending suitable personal protective devices, the safety section is frequently delegated the job of maintaining all personal protective devices in good repair and of distributing and fitting them to individual employees.

The safety section frequently has the responsibility of supervising a health program. This involves solving problems of plant ventilation and heating, noxious gases, toxic materials, allergies, excessive heat or dust, etc. To be fully effective in this field, the safety section should be called to sit in whenever new materials, equipment, or plant layout are under consideration. Many of the problems can be solved far more easily if the safety experts are called in on the initial planning, rather than by trying to effectuate changes in an existing layout.

The safety section cannot operate effectively unless it has complete information available on all safety matters. This requires (1) continual periodic inspection of safety conditions by trained safety inspectors, and (2) detailed reports, followed by analyses, of all accidents. With this information, the safety section can submit periodic reports to top managements and superintendents, and can determine what phase of safety work is in most urgent need of attention. Accident analysis is a sound basis for safety-program development.

The effectiveness of safety work depends in great measure upon the employees themselves—upon their interest and concern about safety matters and upon their having adequate knowledge. A perpetual educational campaign is an integral part of every safety program. The safety section should carry on such a campaign with the assistance of the staffs of the advertising and public-relations departments, directing its educational program at supervisors as well as rank-and-file employees. Safety classes for foremen, safety classes for employee-safety committeemen, posters, letters to employees at their homes, safety items in employee publications—all have their place and are helpful. The foremen are the key to a successful safety program. No amount of "education" about the need for safety glasses will be effective if the foreman himself neglects to wear them in the shop. Top management has an obligation to impress on the foreman that he is no less responsible for safety than he is for protection.

From the employee standpoint, a company that is callous about employee safety is obviously selfishly interested in nothing but profits, regardless of its official pronouncements, while a company actively engaged in promoting safety thereby proves its interest in employee welfare.

The close coordination required between the safety section and shop supervision can be promoted by the organization of a safety council of top-level shop supervisors, meeting periodically to discuss safety progress and special safety problems.

Full utilization of the safety section may well include having the safety section pass on new product design from the viewpoint of customer safety. This may not only improve the product but provide the sales department with an excellent selling advantage.

Medical facilities. The extent of medical facilities necessary in any plant may obviously depend on (1) the size of the plant, (2) the types of operations involved, and (3) availability of nearby medical assistance.

Whenever possible, a doctor should be available to examine applicants for employment before they are hired.

A doctor should also be available to provide physical examinations for employees working on dangerous occupations; those who work with poisonous or toxic materials; crane operators and others who must climb to high elevations; those who work under conditions of extreme heat; etc. Such periodic examinations are desirable from the viewpoint of both employees and management, and may result in a transfer from a harmful occupation before the condition becomes serious.

Some companies provide periodic physical examinations for all employees, and there is much to recommend such a program.

Liberality should be used in making medical and first-aid facilities available to employees, for it is far better to spend some time unnecessarily than to run the risk of infection or injury. Many companies encourage their employees to come to the plant hospital for minor nonindustrial illnesses or first-aid assistance, on the theory that it makes them better workers while they are on the job. Liberality in medical and first-aid matters pays off in good employee relations.

Responsibility for supervising the medical staff and medical policies may be assigned to the safety section.

Discipline. The word "discipline" has a rather horrendous sound, evoking visions of courts, jails, and arbitrary defense of arbitrary authority. It is even possible that callous enforcement of discipline in some companies has given some semblance of fact to such a concept. At any rate, such a concept is far removed from enlightened, genuine industrial discipline.

Industrial discipline is the maintenance of orderly operation. Shop rules are merely one guide for the maintenance of discipline. Penalties are but one way—one of the least effective ways—of maintaining industrial discipline. The provision of a fixed penalty for a given violation of shop rules is probably the worst possible approach to the problem of industrial discipline.

The very existence of industrial organizations depends upon the *voluntary* cooperation of the people who make up the organization. Voluntary cooperation is not brought about by rigid rules and penalties.

On the other hand, employees are entitled to an orderly place in which to work. The operation of any organization depends upon each individual doing his particular job, in order that raw material may be received, processed, assembled, and shipped. Obstacles anywhere along the line may affect many employees, since the work of each depends upon that of others. Interdependence is as real as it is in the case of a group of mountain climbers fastened to each other by a rope.

Those who look upon discipline as a question of meting out punishment to fit the crime have an entirely erroneous conception. Industrial discipline is the maintenance of orderly voluntary cooperation.

The enlightened view of discipline means that whenever there is a failure in orderly, voluntary cooperation, management must determine the real causes and take whatever action may be appropriate to prevent recurrence of such failures. The real causes are seldom apparent. It may require careful consultation, inquiry, investigation, and judgment to determine the causes and to provide appropriate measures to prevent repetition.

For this reason, some companies have developed a central board to consider all disciplinary cases which, in the opinion of the foreman, require more than a simple warning. The board, which may be located in the employment section where all employee records are available, may utilize the services of investigators in order to obtain complete information on any case coming before it. The board considers each case on its own merits, determines the causes of discipline failures, and takes appropriate measures acting through the line organization. These may include transfer, demotion, correction of company policy, suggestions for correction of an employee's domestic situation, reprimand or transfer of a supervisor, or layoff or termination of employment of an employee.

Employee services. Industrial history is studded with shining examples of employers who took great interest in their employees, provided extensive services for them—and came to grief. In some of these cases, managements have felt that their employees were ungrateful, or did not know what was good for them, or were being led astray by outside agitators.

The fault may have been attributable to management. The manner of rendering services is fully as important as the content.

Employees do not want to be made to feel that they are objects of managerial charity. Many of the paternalistic schemes of bygone days made them feel that they were recipients of charity. They did not like it. Paternalistic employee services got a bad name.

These unfortunate experiences should not deter employers from providing all the employee services that are reasonably possible. But they should be furnished by an appropriate organization, in a manner to make employees feel that they are really helping themselves, rather than being objects of employer charity.

The employee-service section can be of inestimable value in promoting employee morale and in cultivating the desire to cooperate.

Employee counseling, whether used only when employees want someone to help them out of their troubles or as a major continued activity, can do much to assist employees to help themselves. The undirected employee interview, in which the employee is led to recite the whole situation that troubles him, and encouraged to think through his own solution, has much to recommend it. In other cases, the counselor may be able to explain the misunderstanding on which the employee's unhappiness is based, or direct him to someone, in or out of the company, who can help him. Not all types of employee problems are amenable to the same treatment.

If the employee-service section has skilled counselors available, the entire organization should be advised to refer troubled employees to the section, since well-meaning but amateur counselors can sometimes do more harm than good. It is fundamental that counselors, to be effective, must respect employee confidences.

While the company should not put itself in the position of giving legal advice to its employees, it can frequently assist them with quasi-legal advice in cases of evictions, income-tax problems, garnishments, leases, etc. Sometimes the mere advice to take his case to a lawyer may be helpful. The employee-service section should be prepared to render such quasi-legal assistance.

Another field of activity for the employee-service section is that of employee recreation. Good healthy participation in such employee activities as sports, amateur dramatics, musical activities, debating clubs, airplane clubs, women's groups, folk dancing, etc., can draw employees into active, sociable participation that can do wonders for individual happiness and creation of plant friendships.

Healthful recreation becomes ever more important as the work week grows shorter and leisure time increases.

In order to encourage maximum participation, such activities should be so planned as to leave the major work of organizing, planning, and operating them to the employees themselves. The amount of unsuspected talent discoverable through such activities is amazing, and the human development it brings about is well worth the tactful supervision it requires from the employee-service section. The section should be prepared to see that all activities fall within the broad outlines of company employee policies, recommend appropriate financial support, where necessary, for the various activities, and be in position to make contact with all outside recreation personnel and facilities.

While employee housing is usually left to the employees themselves, the employee-service section should be prepared to find housing facilities when the situation is tight, and should assist employees facing eviction or other unusual housing problems. The section should also maintain close contact with local housing officials and organizations.

Employee cafeterias, restaurants, and commissaries, which can be a fruitful source of employee problems, are also frequently a responsibility of the employee-service section. So are transportation problems, including group riding. Other miscellaneous employee services may include contact with retired employees, correspondence with employees on military leave of absence (and welcoming such employees when they return for a visit), supervision and training of matrons, and a wide variety of personal services designed to relieve employees of unnecessary worries and keep them on the job.

Many plants have a welfare fund to relieve needy cases among employees. This is appropriately administered by the employee-service section. If there is an employee credit union, it may be a function of the employee-service section to maintain close contact with its operation. Similarly, the employee-service section may supervise or advise on the operation of a suggestion-award system.

Not the least important of the employee-service functions is the administration of such employee-benefit functions as group life insurance and retirement pensions, which are too often handled as mere accounting problems in the accounting or controller's department.

Another important function that may be assigned to the employee-service section is the supervision of employee publications and the servicing of bulletin boards. Employee publications are an extremely important channel of communication. Properly used, employee publications may not only sell the company's story and employee policies to the employees, but may also be used as a medium to express employee reaction to management. The greatest possible employee participation is desirable.

In publishing employee bulletins, plant papers, and booklets, the employee-service section should work very closely with the advertising and public-relations departments, and utilize all the technical, writing, and artistic facilities of those departments.

Thus, the employee-service section seems to be a catchall of many unrelated activities. But they all lead to one purposeful goal—give the employee room for individual development, relieve him of unnecessary worries, and make him feel an integral part of "the company."

Employee communications. If it is assumed (1) that the chief operating executive is vitally interested in good employee relations, (2) that sound employee policies have been developed and reduced to writing, and (3) that all levels of supervision have been informed of these policies and have been trained in applying them, there still remains the basic problem of getting management policies thoroughly understood by employees.

Management must tell its story to its employees. It must do a thorough, careful selling job, evaluating its "prospects" (employees) as carefully as an advertising executive seeks to evaluate the field to which he hopes to appeal. The language must be simple, the approach sincere, and the intentions inherent in actions, rather than limited to words. Employees resent insincerity as much as they resent being talked down to. And they are quick to detect inconsistencies between act and deed.

In order for management to sell its story to its employees, it must establish channels of communication. "Channels of communication" is a cold, technical-sounding phrase. One way to make it meaningful is to think of it as a private line between the president's office and Rudy, the sweeper in department Z. How can the president show Rudy that he is interested in him? Even more important, how can the president find out what Rudy thinks of him and of the company?

President to Rudy. The president can demonstrate his interest in Rudy by seeing that Rudy is provided with an employee manual, a booklet in which company employee policies are reduced to informal, clearly understandable language.

Some companies, having developed their employee policies with exactitude and appropriate legal reservations, publish these policies word for word in their employee manuals. The wording essential to employee understanding is usually quite different from the wording of a board of directors' resolution or a legal document. Much is to be gained by making the employee manual an informal, human document, written from the employee's rather than the company's viewpoint. The policy may be:

> The corporation shall grant every employee who has completed 1 full year of continuous employment a vacation period of 1 week with pay for 40 hours at his base hourly rate. Vacations shall be scheduled in such manner as not to interfere with operations or require the hiring of additional personnel.

The employee manual may cover the subject thus:

> If you have been with us for a full year, you are entitled to a full week's vacation with pay during the vacation season. When you are eligible for a vacation, tell your foreman when you'd like to take it, and he will do his best to meet your wishes, provided it doesn't conflict with vacation schedules of other employees or with production requirements.

One way in which the president can talk to Rudy is by bulletin-board notices. Some companies reserve bulletin-board notices for stiff, formal announcements that make Rudy feel that he ought to hire a lawyer to tell him just what they mean. Such notices serve to emphasize that the factory involves the formal, nonhuman regimentation of masses of people in an artificial environment. On the other hand, the notice can be clear but friendly, with a personal touch that makes Rudy feel that there must be a real guy rather than a legal automaton in the president's office.

Note, for example, the difference in tone between the following two bulletin-board notices:

BULLETIN-BOARD NOTICE

September 6 being Labor Day, the shops and offices of the corporation will be closed.

*   *   *

HOLIDAY NOTICE

My very best wishes to all my fellow workers for a happy holiday weekend. Since all shops and offices will be closed Saturday, Sunday, and Monday, September 4, 5, and 6, a big weekend is ahead of us.

If your weekend plans include driving on the road, let us remember that Labor Day weekend brings all too many fatal accidents. Let us drive so that we can all be back in one piece next week.

Those who are back on the job on Tuesday, September 7, will be paid at their base rate as though they had put in their regular 8 hours on Monday. Those who are requested to work (on special rush work or emergency maintenance) on Monday, September 6, will be paid at double their straight-time earnings for work done on that day.

(signed)   G. H. Fraser
President

Bulletin-board notices need not be limited to notices of holidays, layoffs, and changed schedules. Rudy would be very much interested in reading on the bulletin board (before he sees it in the paper) that the company has just received a big order, or marketed a new product, or declared a dividend. Many of the things that require executive attention also deserve a place on the bulletin board at the appropriate time—and that time is *before* the public at large learns about it. One of the best ways to establish confidence in management is for employees to get the facts from management before they hear about them from their friends and neighbors.

Another frequently utilized medium of communication with employees is the poster. Some companies believe they improve employee morale greatly by exhibiting series of colorful posters on bulletin boards throughout the plant. Such a "morale campaign" has the advantage of simplicity and ease of operation, since, once the selection is made, it is only necessary to change posters every week or two.

The poster does have a definite place among the media of communication, especially in the fields of safety, health, and plant housekeeping. But it is quite probable that the advantages of posters as a means of communication have been oversold. In some few cases, poster campaigns have done more harm than good because managements have relied upon such a campaign, believing that the poster campaign would perform the miracles claimed for it, when they would have done better to take more specific corrective measures. While suitable posters have a place in a rounded program of communication with employees, they should not be relied upon as an exclusive medium.

If "the company" is to be more than a vague, impersonal entity, more than the "soulless corporation" he reads about occasionally, Rudy should be brought face to face with some of the facts about his company. Too often managements feel that Rudy would not understand anything about that, and that, moreover, Rudy just does not care.

Rudy wants to know about his company. And he has some awfully mistaken ideas about how much profit the company makes, and how much of the sales dollar goes to him. The more alert managements tell Rudy about it by means of special annual reports for employees—employee yearbooks that tell him about employee activities and company sales, employee benefits and company profits, how much went to the stockholders and how much went into reserves to make his company stronger, and how annual employee earnings have risen steadily from year to year. It makes Rudy proud to be able to talk about his company's activities and sales and prospects. He will talk about it to his wife and children at dinner, and all of them will acquire more interest in their company.

Some managements make their regular annual stockholders' reports available to their employees. That is better than nothing, but it is far better to prepare a special annual report to employees. It goes without saying that the financial information in the employee report must be as simple as it is possible to make it. At the same time, its preparation must avoid "writing down" to the employee. It takes time and no little imagination to prepare an annual employee report. In addition to showing the share of total outgo that goes for materials purchased, salaries and wages, and dividends and reserves, the annual employee report offers management an opportunity to show employees how much its taxes amount to per employee, how the number of stockholders compares with the number of employees, how much investment is required to make one job in the company, etc. The employee yearbook is also an excellent medium for reviewing the operation of various employee-benefit plans, the suggestion system, recognition given the company during the past year, and the role of the company in the community.

Annual statements come only once a year. The president talks to Rudy more often than that. The president may talk to Rudy monthly, or semimonthly, or weekly, by means of an employee publication—a publication that tells him about fellow employees returning from military service, about employee recreation, about employee safety and promotions, about employee suggestions and what was done about them, about the products the company makes, about distinctions or awards the company has won, and about the contributions the company has made to the community or the nation.   It lends dignity and interest to Rudy's job to know about these things.   And he likes to know about them in advance, so that he can tell his friends about them rather than have them tell him.

Occasionally the president writes a special letter to Rudy (and Rudy's fellow employees) telling him of something especially interesting and timely.   If these letters are reserved for the annual Community Chest and Red Cross drives, the president is missing a bet.   He might well write Rudy a letter of commendation when a critical order was shipped on time, or to tell him how proud he was that the plant looked so trim when a group of foreign engineers (or the governor) visited the plant last week.   Letters from the president should not be reserved for charity appeals or golden-anniversary congratulations.   They should be used whenever occasion warrants, bringing the employees closer to the company.   Some companies send these letters to employees at their homes, where the wife and children can also read them and take an increasing interest and pride in their association with the company.

In some companies a loudspeaker system enables the president to talk to Rudy in person.   This has been used very successfully by many industries to transmit the dynamic personality, enthusiasm, and optimism of the chief executive to the men and women at their desks and machines.   But the microphone seldom flatters, and not all executives are born broadcasters.   The medium of communication should be attuned to the personality of the executive.

Neither the loudspeaker system nor any other system of communication should be limited to messages of exhortation or rosy reports of achievements. Channels of communication should be used primarily to enable the company's top management and its rank-and-file employees to *understand each other better*—not merely to overwhelm with propaganda.   Channels of communication are most effective when used to discuss common problems, forecast future progress, answer inquiries, and disclose information about the company.   No channel of communication is effective unless it has prestige in the mind of the employee.

One frequently overlooked channel of communication is the local newspaper. Some managements discover the local newspaper only when a strike is imminent or has been begun, and then fill its pages with anguished screams of wounded righteousness.   By then it is too late to do a constructive job.   The local paper is a daily or weekly message.   It can be used to tell the president's story not once but repeatedly.   It can tell a message in different ways again and again and again.

It can tell its story in words.   It can tell it better in pictures.   It can tell the story by way of an educational advertisement or a lively, human-interest news story.   Sometimes a published letter to the editor is a good medium.   Contact with the local newspapers must be carried on by someone in management who knows his jobs, who lays out a long-range program, and follows it through with imagination and tact.   And it must be done *continuously.*

In addition to advertisements and news stories in the local press, alert managements seek to establish good relations with the local newspapers and, most important, let the local press know that someone from management is available at all times to give the company's reaction to any development involving the company.   Such relations cannot be developed instantaneously when needed. They must be cultivated continuously.   Fortunately, many managements are becoming increasingly aware of the importance of the printed word, and do not shy away from the press or meet every press inquiry with "No comment." Community public relations are becoming increasingly recognized as an important factor in employee relations.

Some companies have even recognized the value of incorporating employee-relations material in their national newspaper and radio advertising, having discovered that good employee relations are an excellent source of public goodwill.

While the channels of communication from the president to Rudy are varied and more than one is available, it cannot be emphasized too strongly that the president's message must be sincere and must be consistent with Rudy's experience in the shop.   If the president tells Rudy how much he is interested in his welfare, but his foreman fails to deliver to Rudy a message from his wife that the sick baby has suddenly taken a turn for the worse, Rudy will take every message from the president with a grain of salt.   And the president's message about the company's fair-wage policy will be worse than wasted if Rudy finds he is getting less money than some other employee for the same work.

Channels of communication between the president and Rudy must be established, kept open, and used consistently and wisely.   But if the president should come to the conclusion that these channels of communication can be a synthetic substitute for a genuine interest in employee relations, he will one day suddenly and painfully realize his error.

Rudy to president.   The channels of communication from the president to Rudy are much easier to maintain than those in the reverse direction.   But the mere fact that communications in the reverse direction are difficult does not minimize the importance of maintaining these channels open and in operating condition.   The lack of knowledge of employee reactions in top-management circles is as vast as it is unfortunate.   It is rather surprising that the average industrial organization works as well as it does when it is considered that in so many cases the president has not the slightest idea how Rudy feels about the company, the company's policies, or the way the company treats him.

Of the various ways in which Rudy can communicate with management, the most dramatic is the strike.   A strike usually means that Rudy very definitely dislikes something and is taking extreme measures to show his dislike.   (Of course, it is possible that Rudy made no personal decision at all. For in some cases it is not Rudy but his union representatives who decide that a strike is necessary to show that Rudy disapproves of something.) But the strike is a wholly inadequate channel of communication, because (1) it does not tell the management exactly what is wrong (the reasons advanced by the strike leaders are seldom the real causes); and (2) by the time the dissatisfaction has attained the proportions of strike action, it is usually rather late to undertake constructive action. Unfortunately, some managements put off employee-relations functions as relatively less important than other management functions, until a strike suddenly makes employee relations their No. 1 problem.

An opinion survey is one means of communication some managements have provided in an effort to determine employee morale or employee reaction. This is usually a rather extensive program that may involve sending a lengthy questionnaire to each employee, with subsequent analysis of the returns, requiring very careful interpretation. This procedure may or may not get appreciable returns from the employees, and there is always a question whether the employees who do return a completed questionnaire are representative of the majority or whether it is only the cranks or those with an ax to grind who take the trouble to fill in and return the questionnaires.

Some employee-attitude surveys are made by personal interview of a selected portion of the employees. This is also an extremely elaborate procedure. Both these types of surveys may be objectionable in that they may arouse employee resentment if employees do not understand their purpose.

Some companies have, however, had good results from employee-attitude surveys.

Contacts. Because of these and other objections to formal employee-attitude surveys, some managements have been moved to consider more carefully the actual contacts they have with their employees in an effort to evaluate employee reaction through normal management channels. The number of contacts that management has with its employees, even aside from the direct contacts with line supervision, are seldom fully appreciated, even by management representatives themselves.

The line organization may be perfectly satisfactory for the transmission of instructions and information downward. It is an appropriate medium for the exercise of authority from the top down. It is not necessarily a good channel for transmitting employee reaction upward.

The reasons for this are fairly obvious. In the first place, the immediate supervisor is so close to the trees he may not be able to see the forest. He may be in such intimate contact with the employees whom he supervises every day that it may be difficult for him to select the significant employee reactions from the regular run-of-the-mine reactions which he gets from his employees almost every minute of the day. Obviously he cannot report every reaction that he obtains from his employees, or he would be doing nothing else.

In the second place, the immediate supervisor is rather hesitant about transmitting upward employee reactions that may be critical of the line organization. Some of these reactions may be critical of the immediate supervisor himself. Some of them may be critical of the upper levels of the line organization. Some of them may be critical of company policies. In any case, the immediate supervisor may fear that when he reports these reactions to his superior, the immediate supervisor himself may be criticized for his mishandling of the situation, or his clumsiness in transmitting instructions of upper supervision, or in application of company policy.

Just as his relationship with his immediate supervisor is the most important factor in the employee's work environment, so the relationship with *his* superior is the most important factor in the work environment of the immediate supervisor. The immediate supervisor's report to his superior is likely to be largely determined by (1) what he believes his superior would like to hear and (2) the possibility that his superior may criticize him.

The immediate supervisor may also fear that employee reactions which to him appear innocent may be considered by his superior to be a reflection on his own ability as a supervisor.

Furthermore, the immediate foreman has usually had a considerable amount of experience in being the bearer of bad news, and he does not like that role. Some elements of management may take out their dissatisfaction at the receipt of bad news by finding fault with the person who brings the bad news to them. It is obvious that this reaction is the surest way of plugging up that particular channel of communication.

Still another reason why the supervisor is not a good channel for the transmission of employee attitudes is that the supervisor himself is frequently subject to the same griefs as is the employee. If he cannot make his own griefs felt by his superiors, he feels that there is not much point in passing on the gripes and reactions of his subordinates. The ferment of foreman organization in recent years indicates that foremen themselves may not be too happy about their situation. In such cases, foremen may become insulators rather than conductors in the line of communication.

Grievance machinery. One important channel of communication is the formal grievance procedure.

While it is generally recognized that an adequate grievance procedure is the foundation of any sound collective-bargaining relationship, a formal grievance procedure is at best an imperfect instrument of communication between employees and management.

A careful analysis, however, of all grievances received is a necessary function for any management interested in the reactions of its employees. Where grievances are technically defined as being limited to questions of interpretation or violation of the collective-bargaining agreement, the technical definition of the grievance should not blind management to the human value inherent in all complaints, whether or not they fit the technical qualification of a grievance. Even where a grievance relates to something entirely beyond the control of management, it may still be significant and may shed light on matters within management's province.

Besides the grievance procedure, other sources of information concerning employee reactions are available to management and should be carefully considered. Union newspapers are a fruitful source of helpful information concerning employee reactions. If nothing else they may indicate areas in which employees may need constructive information to overcome misinformation received by employees from other sources. The columns of the local newspaper should be watched, particularly the letters to the editor, because they may disclose significant reactions.

Another source of information about employee reactions is found in letters from employees to various members of management. These should always be centralized in one place for handling and analysis, even though they are sent to particular individuals because the employee involved may personally know the individual addressed.

Staff channels. Whereas the line organization is immersed in the major problems of production, the staff organizations, such as the employee-relations department personnel, are free to observe, analyze, and determine the facts and factors that hinder or facilitate the functioning of the line organization. The line organization directs—the staff advises and assists the line.

The various staff elements of the organization must be impressed with the importance of providing unrestricted and directed flow of information from the employees to top management. All the management people involved in such matters as employment, employee counseling, employee training, safety work, welfare, transfers, disciplinary measures, labor relations, job analysis, time study, employee recreation, medical service, and all other staff functions should be trained to report accurately employee sentiment and significant employee remarks to a central place where these reactions may be analyzed and summarized. The significance of employee-attitude trends should then be determined, and periodic reports made to top management.

The contacts with employees made by the employee-relations staff, for example, are many and various, and range all the way from a preliminary employment interview, before the employee is hired, to an exit interview when the employee leaves, with many an important contact in between.

Making a record of exit interviews and filing them for future reference alone does very little good. The interviews must be analyzed and summarized so that a glance can show what departments may be trouble spots and what factors are most important in causing employees to leave. These cases should be analyzed not only from the viewpoint of correcting the condition of which the employee complains, but from the viewpoint of the influence of that condition and its correction upon the entire employee body. Intelligently utilized exit interviews can be a very important channel of communication between employees and management.

It should not be overlooked that the exit interview furnishes an excellent continuous survey of employee attitudes. Assuming that the turnover for the average plant in the United States is about 6 percent per month, it is obvious that in the course of a year as much as 72 percent of the total employee body will have passed through the plant and have left. Therefore, without running a special employee-questionnaire survey, the exit-interview technique alone would provide management with a continuous source of information from a significant proportion of employees.

Discipline records can be a very significant index of employee reaction. Discipline records can serve as a check on—

Employee policies
Employee screening
Employee placement
Supervision
The results of various employee policies in action

Collecting accurate and adequate records of all disciplinary matters in one central place for analysis and periodic reports to top management can be very helpful.

One point of employee contact which is not often appreciated is that made by safety inspectors, safety engineers, personal-protective-device distributors (such as safety-goggle stations), nurses, matrons, etc. These people have daily, repeated contacts with employees and necessarily discuss with them causes of accidents, means of accident prevention, health, safety, and sanitary conditions in the shop, and allied matters. These are quite personal matters, and frequently lead to extremely frank, unrehearsed, significant statements of opinion. If these management representatives are taught to make reports on employee reactions, and such reports are centralized in one place for analysis, management can have a very useful channel of communication from employees.

Another management source of information concerning employee reaction (but one which must be treated carefully in order to safeguard employee confidence) is the numerous employee-service contacts. Counselors, recreation leaders, and welfare people are frequently in a position to get important employee reactions to a very varied assortment of company policies. The same goes for grievance investigators, employee-training instructors, and other personnel people. But it is important to make the point that none of this information is of very much value and none of it reaches top management unless a deliberate procedure is established for communicating all these reactions to a central point for summary and analysis, with periodic reports to top management. The continuous function of coordinating these reports might be assigned to the research section of the employee-relations department.

Labor relations as a phase of employee relations. Labor relations, i.e., relationship with unions, are perhaps the most dramatic aspect of employee relations. They are also the area in which management is most apprehensive of the possibility of being divested of its authority and functions. They are the area most affected by legislation and government regulations. Accordingly, they are the area in which management is most sensitive and in which it is likely to take decisive action.

But the true relationship between management and employees depends only in part on management's relations with the union. Management's many contacts with the employees themselves are far more important in the determination of employee attitudes. If, in his everyday experience, the employee becomes convinced that management is sincerely interested in his welfare, that management is willing to listen to his suggestions and complaints, that management will give him a square deal, that management treats him like a human being—then it becomes a relatively difficult matter for the union to upset the basically sound relationship between employees and management. In fact, in such a situation, the union is not so likely to undertake an antimanagement attitude, for it will conclude that it can do more for the employees by working with management on a constructive plane.

On the other hand, if the employees have been treated arbitrarily, if they have been led to believe that management will not listen to their complaints or suggestions, if they are convinced that management regards every employee as a clock number rather than as an individual human being, then the employees are likely to express their frustration by extravagant demands through the union. The union is then more likely to adopt a quarrelsome, uncooperative attitude and to conduct antimanagement campaigns.

Important as they are, union relations are but one aspect of the employer-employee relation. And what is more significant for management, the kind of labor relations that any organization enjoys are likely to be in considerable measure the result of the kind of employer-employee relations that management has fostered.

The labor-relations section is that part of the employee-relations department through which all contacts with labor unions are channeled. It conducts all the correspondence with the unions, participates in grievance handling at approximately the third step, represents the company in arbitration cases, participates in negotiations, and conducts all necessary correspondence with government labor agencies.

It is highly desirable that all correspondence with the unions be centralized in one place in the company, and the labor-relations section is that place. Since the section studies and analyzes grievances at all levels, it can best determine the significance of various union demands and requests.

If, as is quite common, grievances are handled verbally by the foreman in the first step, the foreman should feel free to consult the labor-relations section if he is in doubt as to contract interpretation or company policy.   In the second step, the grievance is usually presented in writing to the superintendent. He, too, should be free to consult the labor-relations section if in doubt, and copies of all grievances and rulings on them should be sent to the labor-relations section for study and analysis.

If the superintendent's handling is not satisfactory to the aggrieved employee, the grievance may be appealed to the works manager or a board of top-ranking supervisors.   The head of the labor-relations section should sit with the works manager or be a member of the board, to present the human-relations aspect in any consideration of the grievance, and to interpret applicable company policies and observe them in operation.

It is obvious that, in handling grievances and arbitration cases, the labor-relations section must work in the closest possible harmony with the line organization.   That harmony will be subjected to much stress and strain, but it will prevail if the line organization wants to cooperate and the staff organization realizes the importance of maintaining the prestige of the line organization.

The labor-relations section's participation and analysis of grievances in the various steps, together with information from other sources, should enable it to transmit to top management periodic reports on the status of employee morale and on the operation of employee policies.   Such reports may constitute a human audit of the company, and top management will soon come to realize their importance.

One of the most important functions of the labor-relations section is the part it plays in contract negotiations.   Counsel should be available for consultation and drafting, but the lead in collective-bargaining negotiations should be taken by the labor-relations section, which should prepare the background material, recommend changes in the existing contract on the basis of past experience, study the union demands, prepare counterproposals, and participate in (or conduct) the actual contract negotiations.   Collective-bargaining negotiations are a warmly human selling job rather than an exercise in legal logic.

In conducting or participating in negotiations, the labor-relations section should be in complete harmony with the line organization every step of the way.   It is the line organization that will have to live with the agreement and administer it.   Line supervisors must completely understand what is involved, and should be given as much information as possible during the negotiations so that they may understand and accept the result.

Living under a collective-bargaining agreement.   Negotiating a collective-bargaining agreement is only the more dramatic phase of collective bargaining.   Far more important, from both management and employee standpoints, is the day-to-day operation under the agreement.

A collective-bargaining agreement is intended to stabilize the relations between the parties for the life of the agreement. Anything that interferes with peaceful operation under the agreement strikes at the foundation of collective bargaining.

Any dispute about the interpretation of a collective-bargaining agreement can and should be settled by arbitration if direct negotiations fail. Many collective-bargaining agreements provide that there shall be no strike, slow-down, boycott, or lockout during the life of the agreement, and that unsettled disputes about interpretation or violation of the agreement shall be taken to arbitration. Such provisions are the essence of collective-bargaining agreements.

But not all agreements provide for arbitration of disputes concerning interpretation or alleged violation of the agreement, although such provisions are becoming fairly customary. Where such provisions are not included in the agreement, the parties are not likely to agree to arbitration at the time that a dispute arises, because at that time tempers are likely to be ruffled, and the strained relationship is not conducive to an agreement concerning the matter to be arbitrated, the selection of the arbitrator, the rules for arbitration, etc. Consequently, there is no way to determine the correct interpretation of the contract, or whether either party has violated it, except a lengthy court proceeding, or a strike, or lockout.

Relations with unions are likely to be better if all contacts are made through the labor-relations section, whose primary concern is good *employee* relations. Such centralization also ensures that all written communications with the union are centralized through a single department, which should also be responsible for keeping the official record of union relations.

Employee-relations research. Just as product development depends on research, so is the application of good industrial-relations techniques helped by adequate research—research into the effectiveness of various employee-relations techniques and policies, and into the applicability of new techniques to the particular conditions of the plant.

Industrial-relations research is no ivory-tower project. It is a very practical, down-to-earth undertaking which may be of great assistance in the development of new employee policies. It can keep management abreast of developments in the rapidly changing field and determine whether techniques found to be successful elsewhere are applicable in a specific plant, or what modifications may be necessary to make such techniques successful.

The research section may conduct investigations into profit-sharing plans, various employee-security plans, retirement plans, employment-stabilization programs, etc., and be ready to make recommendations at the appropriate time. Or it may study the operation of an incentive plan in a given department, to determine whether it is applied fairly or whether there is evidence of limitation on production.

The research section should be able to advise management what the cost of a proposed personnel program (such as compulsory wearing of safety goggles, for example) may be, and what results may be anticipated from it.

The research section may make an exhaustive study of seniority systems—an extremely complicated and far-reaching matter—and reach conclusions that will guide the labor-relations section in the next collective-bargaining negotiations.

The research section may study the budget of the entire employee-relations department to determine whether the company is receiving dividends on its expenditures, and what sections are not making the most of their opportunity.

One of the most important functions of the research section is to forecast the possible adverse employee reactions that may be expected as a result of introducing new practices or policies, in order that advance steps may be taken to head off such adverse reactions or convert them into favorable channels.

Industrial-relations research may also be considered a means for keeping the entire employee-relations department alert and on its toes. It helps to prevent continuance of those things which are carried on simply as a result of inertia. Sometimes it is just as important to stop certain operations as it is to start others.

Another important field which may be assigned to the research section is that relating to company organization. There are relatively few companies with a separate staff department devoted to the never-ending task of studying the company's organization for the purpose of improving it.

The organization of a company cannot be divorced from its personnel. As personnel, conditions, products, and policies change, so must the organization of the company be modified in order that it may maintain and improve its efficiency and effectiveness. There is no one perfect type of company organization. The research section may have as one of its chief functions the study and observation of the company organization and the recommendation of changes in it.

One of management's chief obligations to its employees lies in the area of continuity of employment. The cost of turnover and unemployment compensation is a factor to be reckoned with. But far more significant are the intangible factors—employee morale, community prestige, public opinion—all of which are vitally affected by the insecurity and callousness of hire-and-fire employment practices on the one hand and by the stability and improved relations resulting from year-round employment on the other.

While few companies are so situated that they can guarantee year-round employment, a great many companies can do more than they have done to remove employment fluctuations. Employment stabilization affects all departments and many company policies. It requires careful preliminary research to determine how best to begin, and what are the various techniques and their relative merits. The research section of the employee-relations department is an appropriate department to do this preliminary research and to make recommendations for approval by top management.

Organization. Reference has been made to an employment section to recruit, interview, select, test, place, induct, and follow up new employees, transfer them from job to job, and terminate their employment when they leave; a job-analysis section to see that they are equitably paid; a training section to train them and open up new vistas of development; a health and safety section to assure their safety and good health on the job; an employee-service section to help them get properly adjusted and help their morale and sociability; a labor-relations section to deal with their representatives; and a research section to help keep the entire operation on its toes.

It is obvious that such departmentalization may not be necessary, and in small companies it may not be possible. However, in every case, the corresponding employee-relations function should be recognized, and the responsibility for it should be assigned to someone. In those cases in which the organization is too small to justify specialists in these various fields, full use should be made of labor-relations and industrial-relations consultants, local and national trade associations, and local industrial-relations associations.

Head man. All the activities of the employee-relations department are centralized in the head of the department, who should report directly to the chief operating head of the company. It is becoming more and more customary, especially in the larger companies, to find the head of the employee-relations department bearing the rank of vice-president, and reporting directly to the president.

If the head of the employee-relations department is made subsidiary to the head of the production, manufacturing, sales, or any other department, his effectiveness is greatly limited, and it becomes difficult if not impossible for him to render a company-wide service, or even to do an adequate job in any department.

The head of the employee-relations department must have certain essential characteristics. He should combine tact with conviction. He should be able to sell his program to the line organization and yet be prepared to resort to pressure when that is necessary. He should have a deep, abiding faith in the importance of the human factor. He should be able to accomplish his purpose through other people. He should be endowed with a passion for anonymity. He should be prepared not only to give credit where credit is due, but frequently to give credit to others when it is in fact due to himself.

While maintaining a due regard for the authority and prestige of the line organization, he should make himself respected by the line organization for his ability and knowledge of the field, his ability to predict the results of a given course of action, and his interest in the welfare of all employees of the company while bearing in mind the long-range interest of the company. He must know and understand the nature of company organization.

He must be able to sell himself and his program not only to the line organization but also to the operating head of the company.   He should continually impress the operating head, and the board of directors if necessary, with the importance of the human factor.   He should be able to report at all times on the status of employee relations and to prove the dollars-and-cents value to the company of improving its employee relations.

He should know how to fill the role of employee-relations spokesman in the community.

The head of the employee-relations department should be prepared for a never-ending task of correcting errors.   He should expect to help many without receiving a word of thanks.   He should be grateful if he is given the means and organization with which to continue doing his job.

6. A world to gain

The achievement of good employee relations means the attainment of that intangible known as employee "morale," but it means more.   *Good employee relations are the best guarantee any company can have of continued success in any field of endeavor.*

Employees who are proud of their company constitute the best possible advertisement any company can have, not only in the plant community, but wherever its employees go, and wherever they may have friends.   The salesman who is "sold" on his company is a far more enthusiastic salesman than one who merely sells a good product.   A customer or prospective customer who visits a supplier's plant can tell almost at once whether a good relationship exists between employees and management.   If high morale exists, the company can be assured of having available to it the pick of prospective employees, assuring it of an ever better organization.

Good employee morale *pays off* in dollars and cents.   Where good morale exists, employees put their hearts into their work, as well as their hands and brains.   They enjoy their work, and they do it better and more efficiently.   Higher efficiency means greater output and lower costs.   In fact, it is probable that in no other single field can management show so great a return for so little investment.   Appropriate encouragement can release untapped latent reservoirs of employee contributions to the success of the business.   Satisfied employees are eager to suggest improvements.   Satisfied employees take a personal interest in the welfare of the company.   Satisfied employees require far less supervision.   Satisfied employees cause less wear and tear on the machinery and equipment.   Satisfied employees cause less avoidable waste.   Satisfied employees are probably the most valuable single asset that any company can have.

Employees who appreciate their company do not leave it for other opportunities.   Nor are they as likely to demand transfers to other jobs or departments, except for the purpose of utilizing their highest skills.   The resulting stability in the working force is an important factor in achieving ever higher efficiency. Employee turnover is costly in many ways that are difficult to evaluate.

Aside from its dollars-and-cents value, aside from its humanitarian value in bringing satisfaction in place of spiritual repression to millions of people, the achievement of good employee relations has an intensely personal value to the men and women who make up management. For the only possible comple-ment of good employee relations is good management relations. Where good employee relations exist, management has the opportunity to lead rather than drive. Management is looked up to, rather than vilified. Management's role is voluntarily accepted by the employees, rather than being forced on them by concepts of authority and legal rights. Only where good employee relations exist can management fully devote its time and effort to managing the business, rather than be perpetually engaged in overcoming human friction. Good em-ployee relations are indeed the lubricant that makes an organization function smoothly.

In no other field can management reap so rich a harvest as in the field of improved employee relations. In no other field can so much be accomplished, both for the individual company and for our society. New, rich areas have been explored but remain to be fully developed and utilized.

The tremendous improvements which have been made in processes and equip-ment have their future counterpart in improvement in relationship that can and will be made between management and employees. Management's success in the future will be gauged largely by the progress it makes in improving that relationship.

Section 18

BUILDING BETTER RELATIONS
WITH STOCKHOLDERS

BY

J. C. DINE

BUILDING BETTER RELATIONS
WITH STOCKHOLDERS

Introduction

Among the many publics, surely stockholders relate closer and closer with management.

This section will review ways and means of keeping stockholders informed on your company. This should be an important part of your information program because while a flow of information alone may not guarantee stockholder loyalty and affection, a lack of communication will certainly cause misunderstanding and friction.

Conversely, in this age of communications, management may find it too easy to mistake a fat, colorful annual report, plus a plush annual meeting with the latest closed-circuit radio and television and promotional gadgets, for a winning information program.

Stockholder relations are, unfortunately, not that simple. A rounded program of information is the only consistent, professional, satisfactory approach. Stockholders want to be informed, not romanced; educated, not dazzled. Their requirements, actually, are simple—

Management (who)
Money (finances)
Materials (products, marketing, etc.)

The question: How to provide this information?

1. Facts for stockholders

If any member of management seriously questions the need for keeping his company's stockholders informed in the interests of good stockholder relations, he should call for help from his company attorneys to learn more about SEC regulations, stock-exchange rules, and other legal information requirements, and from his public-relations director to get better acquainted with the need and the benefits of honest, informative, consistent, and interesting communications.

Here are some of the facts he would be presented with:

His directors are elected by the stockholders. He is responsible to the board

of directors. *Ergo:* He should communicate with the stockholders, if only
for defensive reasons

On a more positive basis, his company will need stockholder approval for
certain action, such as stock options, disposal of assets as a whole, mortgaging of all property, increase or decrease in authorized stock

If new shares are to be issued, your No. 1 prospect should be your stockholder
—and he will be, if he feels confidence in and/or loyalty to the company

Your shareholder can be a help or a hindrance in your company's public-
relations efforts to communicate with the general public. It is just as easy
to make him a help

Your shareholders can also be a customer of your products or services

All this communicating provides a mirror in which he can see management
as it really presents itself to the stockholder

As Alexander Pope wrote in his translation of Homer's *Odyssey,* "An honest
business never blush to tell," and here is some of the information management
should cover:

Company policy.   Company research, public service programs, employee relations, keeping quality up and price competitive, advertising, benefits to
investors, its public relations attitudes, and its general accomplishments

Disposition of the sales dollars.   Payrolls, cost of materials, taxes, selling and
administrative expense, depreciation, dividends, reserves, research, business
development, etc.

The price story.   Reasons for higher prices or costs; explanations how lower
prices are giving customers more for less; how taxes, wages, material costs,
construction and replacement costs, etc., affect rising costs

Investment and ownership.   How investments make jobs and keep the wheels
of industry turning, how the enterprise system benefits both shareholders
and employees, the management's responsibility to the shareholders

"Image information."   How the company contributes to the economy
through jobs and job security, higher wages, lower costs, wider markets,
indirect employment of others, how its incentive program increases production through better employee relations, opportunities for all, direct
and indirect benefits to the plant communities, and evidence that the company is owned by a broad cross section of the American people

Company news.   New personnel, promotions, new assignments, research developments, new plans and equipment, new advertising plans, expansion,
new sales outlets, new resources, relevant legislation and court decisions,
industry-wide programs (especially when the company is involved), anni-
versaries (such as the birth of the founder, important expansion dates,
major discoveries or inventions, union contracts, etc.), honors achieved by
the company and its executives, recognition of older employees, special
awards to employees, unusual employee activities, statistical and financial
news, notice of annual and regional meetings, postmeeting news, and, of
course, spot news made by the company

2. Blocks to communications

In this age of communications, when most people are nearly drowned by messages on the radio and television, on billboards, in the mail and in magazines and newspapers, the threshold of credibility keeps slowly rising, probably in more or less direct relationship to the amount of information.

Therefore, it is a distinct danger for a company's communicators to assume their message will be read with the same enthusiasm (if not awe) with which it was prepared and disseminated.

These are some of the blocks to acceptance:

The shareholder has most likely been exposed to such news as recent stockholder suits seeking damages from accountants and company officials. (This may well make him more skeptical of company information.)

He may not understand business language, particularly that having to do with money. Can he be blamed for this when various official or industry agencies sometimes disagree on basics?

He may have unwarranted expectations of profit the company "should be" making and therefore will discredit the true facts

He may also have no basis for sound business judgment because he does not keep consistently informed on the company's business, or on business in general. (Has the company, therefore, created its own problem by not keeping him interested through easily understood communications?) He may never have been trained sufficiently in understanding business reports to keep him from misunderstanding expensive advertising, plant expansion, executives' salaries, etc.

He may, in general, be one of those reported in recent surveys who do not read financial news regularly or thoroughly, who criticize the very reports issued for their benefit on the grounds that they have *too many* figures, who may be so unschooled in business that they confuse profits with gross sales

3. Media for management

The list of media available to tell the company's story is long and growing and the company and its communicators would do well to remember the placard posted on the door of the Aldine Press, Venice, about the time Columbus discovered America: "Talk of nothing but business and dispatch that business quickly."

The communicator, indeed, must be aware of the constant competition for the shareholders' attention, and, again, he must make certain his material is informing his audience, not merely reinforcing his company's views. As Dr. Bernard Berelson, the sociologist, mournfully observed, "Some kinds of information on some kinds of issues brought to the attention of some kinds of poeple under some kinds of conditions will have some kinds of effects."

Rather than overconfidence in one medium, the company should consider the various media as parts of the bridge that should be built between the company and its shareholders: radio, television, newspapers, news magazines, financial and business publications, trade periodicals; advertising (which might be offered as reprints to shareholders) ; annual meetings; regional meeting reports; interim communications, such as general reports, "personal" letters from the chairman or president; welcome letters to new stockholders; company publications, such as newsletters and bulletins; dividend enclosures; participation in industry communications; shareowner surveys to determine who shareholders are, what their investment objectives are, etc.; reports to employees by including them in shareholders' distribution and through special employees' publications; reproduction and distribution of appropriate articles in the general press that may range from basic definitions of financial terms to a discussion of why stock prices fluctuate and to "how-to-invest" articles on how to teach simple economics to schoolchildren; general articles on the techniques of investing, written under company auspices for the general benefit of stockholders; reports on general economic conditions such as inflations, methods of raising capital, and how they affect the company and its employees and stockholders; booklets dealing with investing; information courses for investors and students; displays in prominent windows and other public areas; preparation of speech material and discussion outlines; detailed statistical reports for securities analysts and similar groups, as well as appearances before such groups; the sometimes overlooked, but very important, annual and quarterly reports; and personal, informative, and courteous responses by top management to stockholder letters.

4. "Dear public(s)"

There are, as any public-relations practitioner will gladly tell you, a number of "publics," and only the uninitiated communicator would believe he has reached them all through, say, distribution of the annual report. While many may be linked, each group should be considered an entity when communications are being prepared.

The 20,000,000 plus shareholders might be divided as follows:

Sophisticated shareholders, who understand business and accounting details and who look for figures

The more typical shareholders, who lack such knowledge and who want only essential facts, presented simply

The professional group, bankers, institutions, pension trust funds, mutual funds, the business and financial press, trust officers, specialists, insurance companies, investment counselors, corporate investors, security analysts, etc.

Women stockholders, who may look for a particular type of information, and who might, for example, attend the annual women investors' clinics of the Federation of Women Shareholders in American Business

Employees
Unions
Students
Potential stockholders, to reach in answer to queries about the company

Of these groups, the most demanding, obviously, will be the professional or near professional investors.   Each will have his own private routine for checking figures.   One looks at the income statement, comparing gross to net; another checks the balance sheet for current financial strength.   Others weigh total assets and total current liabilities, the nature and amount of each item, the type and size of investments, the amount of cash, current assets, and the vulnerability of inventory—all this to synthesize the financial stability of the company and to determine how sensitive it might be to a business recession—a task obviously far over the heads of most investors.   These financial sophisticates might even need an *expanded* annual report, or a technical addendum.

Since 1899, companies applying to the New York Stock Exchange for the listing of their securities have entered into a listing agreement with the Exchange covering a code of performance.   Initially, there were three items of agreement, two of which dealt with mechanical necessities of the Exchange.

The third will be of interest here.   It represented the Exchange's interest in the need of investors for regular financial reports by Exchange companies.   This need had been long recognized but previously unfilled.   With the support of popular demand for such information, and interest on the part of corporate management, the Exchange sought to make the publication of annual financial statements a standard practice among listed companies.

(This was far from accepted practice once; in 1866, for example, one well-known company told the Exchange it had not made any reports or published statements for 5 years.)

The New York Stock Exchange's public-relations program is not only of major importance to American business, but is also a source of information to those who own shares.   The basis for the public-relations program is education about investing, about the economy, about the contributions of the financial community to that economy—and all carried out in such a manner that the *Saturday Review* called the program "solid . . . well thought out and intelligently executed."

The New York Stock Exchange, of course, may be called on for information by companies and by shareholders.

As the Exchange's vice-president has said, "We don't want a nation of unhappy shareowners.   We do want a nation of informed investors."

Inevitably, the question arises, "How far can a corporation go in reporting to the public without damaging itself competitively?"

The answer, of course, is that so much information is now available legally and ethically to competitors that most reporting falls far short of any real com-

petitive value.   Because so much information may be had from government
and industry reports, most companies operate in fishbowls, at least as far as
competitive snooping is concerned.

5. The annual meeting

It is easy for the newcomer to wonder about the intense concentration of so
much talent on a meeting that takes 3 or 4 hours out of one day out of 365.

The answer, of course, is that the annual meeting, if properly planned, promoted, and presided over, can be a jewel in the corporate diadem.

Planning.   Some well-organized companies start planning for the next annual
meeting almost as soon as the last one is finished.   Such plans might include
logistics (such as transportation) ; lighting, proper staging; press facilities and
information; amplification equipment—which should be carefully tested; the
agenda (including any tours and demonstrations) ; reprints and publications,
films and other visual presentations; premeeting conferences with the company
lawyers and public-relations experts, anticipating questions and preparing answers in advance; preparation for questions by studying recent mail and reading
recent news reports; distribution of the annual report; box lunches (in the case
of companies which still consider them stylish) ; distribution of postmeeting
reports; preparation of press kits and other news information, arrangements for
photographers, and news distribution of photos; arrangements for such mechanics as counting of proxies and voting; distribution of any souvenirs (samples of company products, gifts, calendars, etc.).

Promotion.   Communications with shareholders (and the news media) should
be far more than perfunctory notification of the meeting.   The shareholders
should be told why they should come, benefits they will derive from attending,
and, if necessary, how to get there.   Shareholders should be made to feel like
participants, not spectators.

Presiding.   Some experts recently agreed that the single most important in-
gredient of an annual shareholders meeting is the chairman.   He must control
with a firm hand, yet with patience, humor, and dignity.   He must get the
business of the meeting finished, he must get good questions, and he must
answer them informatively or turn them over to someone who can; he must not
appear arbitrary, impatient, or uninformed; he must not tolerate rudeness or
undue theatricals or abusive questions.   (The chairman of a well-known company a year or so ago answered an insulting question by barking, "You may sit
down."   And the surprised shareholder did!)

Perhaps one reason for rigid control of the annual meeting was the cynical
remark of one professional observer that he had never heard from the floor one
single suggestion that found its way to effective action by the company.   On
the other hand, other constructive "professional shareholders" feel that the
independent stockholder's role at annual meetings depends largely on the atti-

tude of management, and that the stockholder is practicing "corporate democracy," subject to the acceptance or nonacceptance of management.

Some professional stockholders do not have such a solid view, but take a savage delight in attempting to create all sorts of excitement through various ruses—some humorous, others bizarre and destructive. These people are obviously interested only in drawing press coverage. They ask emotional or insulting questions. They use bullhorn blasts. They may arrogantly call attention to the large number of shares they own.

Most chairmen will fall back on *Robert's Rules of Order* or *Cushing's Manual* [1] with the wistful but helpless knowledge that neither is ideal because both men were really only adapting the rules of parliamentary procedure to deliberative meetings of religious, educational, and fraternal organizations. Annual stockholders' meetings demand a very different approach.

The *New Yorker* magazine, in a review of various annual meetings, reported how one chairman reacted to an impasse: "This meeting is not being run by Robert's. It's being run by me." Although probably justified, the remark triggered an anxious explanation by an official of the American Society of Corporate Secretaries.

But just how *is* a chairman supposed to react when he is blithely asked (as one was) by a shareholder, "Sir, just what do you do that's worth $150,000 a year to us?"

This may not necessarily be considered a constructive question, but it is what chairmen more and more are being forced to face up to, and it is one of the reasons why the man running the meeting should be well briefed, well organized, and well prepared to control the meeting and not default to General Robert.

6. What shareowners want to know: a checklist

Kind of company
Products or services
Location and location of its installations
Number of employees
Number of customers (clients)
Relative position in industry (by volume, by capacity, by capitalization, by number of employees, by number of shareowners, by years in business)
Top company executives (their accomplishments, where they came from, how long with company, shareholdings)
The board of directors (background of each, any important board changes and why)
Earnings and dividends (growth, dividend history, stock dividends, rights, relevant company policies, comparison with competition)
Financial administration (sources of fixed capital; key ratios, including current assets to current liabilities, capitalization—common to preferred,

[1] Robert was a United States Army engineer whose "rules" were published in 1876. Cushing, a lawyer, published his manual in 1846.

funded debt to surplus, sales to inventory, net income to total assets, net income to net worth; financial statements, inventory condition and policies)

General financial figures (reconciliation of the surplus and reserve accounts, consolidated income statements and balance sheets going back a certain number of years, nature and size of any reserves, history of the company's earnings and dividends, how much of profits is due to increased inventory evaluation, expense items, details on contingent liabilities)

Production (comparison of production rates over past 25 years, or life of company; recent equipment installation; changes in production methods; trends in operating costs; program to improve efficiency; plans for new products)

Employee relations (union status and new contract developments, union leaders if prominent, employee benefits, pension program, promotion policy, health and safety, incentive awards, comparison of these with other companies in the industry)

Advertising (philosophy and goals, campaign reviews and forecasts, advertising and promotion budgets, media schedule, market data, ratio of advertising to sales, major broadcast and print media plans, description of major promotion campaigns)

Sales (how salesmen are selected and trained, relations with customers, sales plans and policies)

Research (achievements of the research department, major personnel, appropriations, ratio of research to sales, joint industry research activity, ratio of basic to applied research, objectives)

Company activities (trade-association activities, convention displays, cooperative advertising, participation in plant city activities, charitable donations, chambers of commerce or boards of trade activity, any problems vis-à-vis local, state, or national regulations and restrictions, general civic responsibility)

Business outlook (sales and earnings forecast, relevant findings by government economists or banks; probable effect of predicted developments on company's sales, prices, earnings, production; general business outlook, competition from other industries and from other companies in its industry)

Means of communicating with stockholders (letters from the president, folders and dividend enclosures, stockholder magazines, newsletters, announcements and minutes of stockholder meetings, institutional advertising and news, annual meetings, regional meetings and conferences, visits to shareholders' homes and offices, and visits by shareholders to the company)

Section 19

HOW TO BUY BUSINESS INSURANCE

BY

Curtis B. Lilly

HOW TO BUY BUSINESS INSURANCE

Introduction

"Insurance is an extremely complicated thing" is the plaintive cry of most insurance buyers who are not fully versed in the field, and it is also the proud boast of the insurance industry. As a result, many purchasers of insurance simply abdicate their responsibilities and turn them over to the insurance industry, either to their brokers or agents or to their direct-writing companies. This is a unique situation. It is highly doubtful that there is any other product or service that is purchased by a customer where the customer turns over the full responsibility for the development and implementation of the purchasing program to the person supplying the product.

It is our purpose in this section to attempt to lift the shroud of complexity from the problem of developing and implementing a business-insurance program. We hope to show how to evaluate the business's exposures to financial loss and the ways in which insurance can be used to protect the corporate assets and financial standing of the business.

The comments in this section are limited to the development and implementation of insurance programs for manufacturing, retail, contracting, and service businesses. They are not intended to cover personal insurance. These two businesses, that is, personal insurance and business insurance, are vastly different. One of the first things that a person charged with the responsibility for the business-insurance program has to understand and recognize is that his own experience with personal insurance has very little, if any, bearing or relationship to the provision of insurance for business operations.

It is not our intent to review every individual type of policy available. Our basic purpose is to review the need for insurance, if indeed there be any, and to discuss the development of the necessary coverages to fulfill those needs rather than to discuss the individual types of policies offered by the insurance industry. Similarly, our comments will be principally geared to the general insurance lines and will not include any particular reference to pension or profit-sharing plans which sometimes use insurance in part. We will touch only briefly upon the employee-benefit coverages, which, since they are basically considered as a fringe benefit for employees, are not really a part of the program of protection and indemnification that is reflected by the general insurance program.

1. Insurance—its purpose and use

As soon as a person goes into business, he is automatically faced with certain risks, which if handled improperly could put him out of business. Economical purchasing of materials and supplies, proper pricing of products, proper extension of credit, use of money, development of new products, sound employee-employer relations, protection of property—all these are risks that face every business. In addition, there are other factors which will control the success or failure of a business, such as the national and international economic and political picture, the development of competitive and replacement markets, and many others which also have an effect on the operations of any individual business.

It is quite apparent that the individual businessman has no control over a number of these basic factors. There are other factors which he definitely can control by virtue of his own efforts and abilities. Then there are other risks which are common, not only to the new business operations, but also to others with similar problems.

It is this latter category of risks that insurance was originally designed to handle. *Insurance,* whether it be a group of people or corporations banding together to share their own exposures to loss, whether it be a policy purchased from a mutual company, or whether it be a policy purchased from a stock insurance company, *is intended to provide indemnification for losses that the insured could not otherwise stand individually.* It is a sharing of the risk between many so that in the event of an unforeseen circumstance, the insured individual will be able to avoid complete financial ruin by having others share the burden of loss with him. For the protection granted by this sharing of risk he pays a premium, as do all other participants, and these premiums pay for the losses.

In the operation of any large company, certain types of losses are inevitable. You cannot run a large store and have thousands of people coming in every day without having somebody get hurt on your premises. You cannot employ hundreds of people without some workmen being injured on the job. You cannot operate a production line with many different motors without having an occasional motor burn out. You cannot operate a fleet of vehicles without having accidents and resultant damage to your vehicles. You cannot ship all your production in small packages by any means at all without having an occasional lost package. You cannot operate a utility with above-ground transmission and distribution lines without having an occasional storm or other climatic disturbance tear down some of those lines. Occurrences of this type are essentially normal operating expectations for the particular operations involved.

Within reasonable limits, you could not consider the occurrence of these losses as *unforeseen* circumstances, and therefore they really should not be a proper subject for insurance. Insurance's primary purpose is to protect the insured against the unexpected loss that could have a deleterious effect on the financial stability of the company. The insurance program should not be used as a tool to shift the responsibility for normal operating losses from the business to the insurance company. If insurance is purchased for the purpose of transferring responsibility, it must be recognized that insofar as that particular loss area is concerned, the insurance company will have to charge more for premiums than the losses total in order to stay in business. The only real justification for such purchases would be where the insurance company's services, such as loss prevention, claim handling, etc., are desired or where, as in the case of workmen's compensation, coverage is generally required by statute.

It should also be noted that it is generally poor practice to provide coverage for exposures wherein the ultimate possible loss is negligible in relation to the financial stability and structure of the business.

All of these principles must be measured in relation to your own business. A $2,000 or $3,000 unexpected loss, for example, could be the breaking factor for one small business, whereas it may represent no more than petty cash to a larger firm. Similarly, the larger firm has a greater spread of risk within its own operations than does a smaller company, and therefore the relationship of the premium to the size of the potential loss is quite different for the two firms. Take the example of a manufacturer who has one motor which costs $5,000 to replace. Assume that he can insure it for mechanical and electrical breakdown for $250. A much larger company may have 30 of the same type motors. At the same rate of premium, the cost of one year's premium to insure all 30 motors would be more than the cost of any one motor itself. In such a case it might be more reasonable to buy a spare motor with the year's premium than to insure all the motors.

A business's insurance program should be designed to fit its own particular requirements. It should not be simply an accumulation of policies that were purchased for various exposures that came up from time to time. Rather, it should be designed to fulfill a definitely established insurance-buying philosophy. The program should also contemplate a consistency of protection and action. By that we mean if you insure property against damage by fire on the basis of the current replacement value, then it would not be reasonable to insure damage by a boiler explosion on a depreciated value basis. If a loss occurs, the recovery should be the same, regardless of what the cause of the loss may have been.

The evaluation of whether or not to provide coverage should be based on the possibility of loss. The premium for the coverage will reflect the probability of loss. In this vein, it should also be kept in mind that if the premium for a broad-based exposure, such as fire, windstorm, or other such things that are common to most businesses, is high, it is only a reflection of the high risk involved and is generally all the more reason to buy the insurance. On the other hand, if the premium on a narrow-based exposure such as motion-picture-cast insurance, officers-and-directors-liability coverage, professional-liability coverage, etc., is high, it is basically a reflection of a relatively small spread of risk among a limited number of insureds. We will discuss briefly how to bring the costs within reason on such exposures in the section dealing with insurance markets and purchasing concepts.

No matter how well the insurance program may be put together, there are almost invariably indirect costs that result from an unexpected loss which no amount of insurance can pay for. To illustrate, let us take the case of a workmen's-compensation accident where an employee was injured on the job and was unable to work for 3 weeks. At the time of the accident there is invariably a substantial amount of time lost not only by employees who may be directly helping the injured man, but also by other employees who are merely spectators or who simply spend time discussing the accident. Next comes the problem of the time lag before the man can be replaced. Then comes the loss of efficiency and production because the new man is not so experienced as the injured worker. And all this does not take into consideration the time spent by various people in the company in filling out and processing forms, etc.

It has been estimated that the hidden cost of a workmen's-compensation claim is four times as great as the direct cost that is reflected by the medical and indemnity claim. Similarly, the direct-damage claim can be paid in full and the loss of profit from lost production can be recovered, but no amount of insurance can bring back the loss of customers that had to go to somebody else to fulfill their needs. No insurance can keep the momentum of a growing company moving. And no insurance, nor any amount of advertising, can completely sustain public acceptance until you can put your products back on the market.

Insurance cannot be a substitute for the continuous operation of the smooth-running, efficient company. It is therefore far more beneficial to try to prevent the loss in the first place rather than to try to salvage the most you can following a loss by collecting the insurance proceeds.

One of the primary functions of the good insurance company is to work with management to establish effective loss-prevention procedures. The details of the services that you should expect in this regard are more fully outlined in the part of this section entitled "Services that you should receive."

It must always be recognized that the size of your operations will determine how much personal attention and service and underwriting flexibility you will be able to obtain from the insurance underwriters. Regardless of size, however, it is essential to make a proper evaluation of your risks and to develop your objectives, even if they cannot be readily achieved at the present, simply to be sure that when coverages are available to you, they fit into your desired total program and do not provide you with a lot of unnecessary things.

2. The evaluation of operations and needs for insurance

The proper use of insurance depends upon complete understanding of the direct and indirect loss potentials of your own operations as well as recognition of statutory requirements. Too many insurance programs are constructed simply by accumulating policies without any real direction or basic philosophy behind their purchase. In order to produce an effective program that does the desired job at the most economical price, it is essential to evaluate your own operations carefully and then to determine the insurance-buying philosophy to follow in connection with the ability to absorb loss and to pay the premiums required.

This type of evaluation should be made by every insured, so that it has definite goals in mind of what is desired in a total insurance program. There may very well be times when, because of its size, an insured may not have the buying power to get exactly what it wants and it has to settle for what the insurance industry has to offer. However, this does not minimize the importance of having a complete understanding of overall objectives so that it can be determined how any offering made by the insurance company fits into the total program. If such a philosophy is adopted and periodically reviewed to reflect changing conditions, an insured will have taken the first step to avoid overinsurance and underinsurance.

The balance of this part has been developed to reflect the type of questions that should be asked in order to completely evaluate exposures to loss. A complete evaluation is the cornerstone of the establishment of a corporate insurance-buying philosophy. This philosophy can only be established by management. It cannot be made by insurance brokers or agents, as it is unrealistic to expect a completely objective evaluation of operations and corporate objectives from anyone whose income is derived from what he can sell. Management cannot abdicate this responsibility.

Space naturally precludes the inclusion of all questions that should be reviewed in the development of this insurance-buying philosophy. However, we have tried to incorporate many of the principal questions that will be germane to such a review and will at least indicate the type of questions that should be asked. There are many others that will be peculiar to any specific industry or operation which must also be incorporated in the review before the desired insurance-buying philosophy can be properly developed.

Property damage questionnaire. The following questions will, for the most part, apply to all types of operations, and whether the indicated exposure exists or not, the questions should still be reviewed to make sure that the loss potential has been explored.

Principal locations
a-1   Address (complete and accurate) _____

a-2 Purpose of use _____

a-3 Owned or leased _____

a-4 Total area _____

a-5 Number of floors _____

a-6 Construction: Walls _____

                  Roof _____

                  Floors _____

a-7 Nearest public hydrants _____

a-8 Sprinklered _____

a-9 Watchmen _____

a-10 Other sprinkler or burglary alarms or supervisory services _____

a-11 Geographical exposures: Flood _____

                           Earthquake _____

                           Tornado _____

                           Hurricane _____

                           Landslide _____

                           Subsidence _____

                           Other _____

a-12 Replacement values of owned properties:

                           Building _____

                           Machinery _____

                           Furniture and fixtures _____

                           Materials and supplies _____

                           Finished stock

                               average _____

                               maximum _____

a-13 Leased machinery or other leased property for which you are responsible:

                           Type: _____

                           Replacement value: _____

a-14 Property of others on premises for which you are responsible:

                           Dies and molds _____

                           Property being processed _____

                           Sold but not delivered _____

                           Other _____

a-15 Maximum cash or negotiable securities on hand:

                           Payroll _____

                           Other cash _____

                           Securities _____

a-16 Are physical inventories taken by each department or by someone not connected with the department? _____

a-17 Are two signatures required on checks over $250? _____

a-18 How frequently are outside audits made and how extensive are they? _____

a-19 How frequently are bank balances reconciled by someone other than the person making the regular daily entries? _____

a-20 Number, size, and type of boilers _____

    a-21 Number of other types of machinery:
        Compressors _____ Generators _____
        Motors (over 10 HP) _____ Transformers _____
        Refrigerating systems _____ Pressure vessels _____
        Major production machines _____
    a-22 Value of engineering drawings _____
    a-23 Any overhead cranes _____
    a-24 Any waterfront facilities _____
    a-25 Number and type of vehicles owned:
               Private passenger _____
               Commercial _____

The above questions should be completed for *each principal location*. The first group of questions relate primarily to the fire-insurance rating formulas and the underwriting markets that could be utilized.

The review of geographical exposures should be looked at not only in terms of the individual exposure for the particular location being covered by this questionnaire, but also for the general area of the country in which the property is located.

Developing the correct, accurate values for the various categories of property is important not only in establishing the amount of insurance, but in also making sure that you comply with coinsurance requirements which will thereby enable you to avoid being penalized at the time of a loss.

Questions *a*-13 and *a*-14 are intended to bring up these particular points for review. All too often there is no concrete understanding between lessor and lessee, or the owner and the processor, with respect to the responsibility for property on the lessee's or processor's premises. This situation often results in duplicate insurance being carried by both owner and processor or lessor and lessee, or in no insurance being carried and both parties relying on "general practices of the trade" to establish responsibility. We suggest that if the answers to these questions indicate that there are substantial values involved, definite concrete action should be taken to assign responsibility and provide for it accordingly.

Questions *a*-15, *a*-9, and *a*-10 relate to the need for coverage protecting money and securities, merchandise, office equipment, etc. While burglary, robbery, and theft account for substantial losses each year, the biggest crime losses arise out of the dishonest acts of employees. Questions *a*-16 through *a*-19 are intended to reflect certain obvious potential loss practices and a few of the checks and balances that can be used to reduce the exposure.

As is the case with most questions, *a*-20 and *a*-21 are brought up just to review the potential. If the indications are that serious exposures do exist, then much more detailed answers will have to be developed to fully evaluate the problem.

The importance of *a*-22 is related primarily to engineering papers or any other similar important papers which could not easily be duplicated or reproduced. In establishing the value of such property, it is important to make sure to include all development time in such value.

The question concerning the existence of waterfront facilities is important to make sure that such facilities would be included in the description of the plant premises. It is also important in determining the inherent liabilities that are created by the existence of such facilities.

Secondary locations (warehouses, processing, sales offices, etc.)
b-1 Address (complete and accurate) _____

_____

b-2 Purpose of use _____
b-3 Owned or leased _____
b-4 Sprinklered _____
b-5 Type of property and average and maximum values—

	Average	Maximum
Raw materials	_____	_____
Finished inventory	_____	_____
Furniture and fixtures	_____	_____
Property being processed	_____	_____

b-6 Geographical exposures: Flood _____
                                 Earthquake _____
                                 Tornado _____
                                 Hurricane _____
                                 Landslide _____
                                 Other _____

In developing the pertinent information for the secondary locations, such as warehouses, processing locations, sales offices, property at exhibits, etc., it is most important to be accurate in the determination of the address of the location. The prime reason here is that there may be several rates applying to different sections of the building, or to different buildings within the same complex. In order to get the most favorable rate treatment, it is necessary to be able to accurately determine the location in which the property is being stored or processed.

In establishing values it is important to note not only the maximum and average values, but the basis of valuation. For example, are the finished-inventory figures shown on a selling-price basis or on a manufacturing-cost basis? Are the furniture and fixture figures reflected on a full-replacement-value basis or on a depreciated-value basis? Is the property being processed valued at the value which existed before any processing was done, or is it increased to reflect the increased value that has been added in the course of processing? Insurance can be purchased on any of these bases, and it is important to be able to correlate the values that determine the limits of insurance with the basis of valuation that will be used in the settlement of a loss.

Transit

c-1   Annual sales in United States _____

c-2   Normal terms of sale in United States _____

c-c   Normal terms of purchase of raw materials _____

c-4   Value of shipments made to customers at your risk by—
        Rail _____
        Air _____
        Public truckmen _____
        Own trucks _____

c-5   What type of bill of lading is generally used? _____

c-6   Amount of shipments of own property between your own or subcontractors' locations _____

c-7   Usual method of shipment between own locations _____

c-8   Maximum value any one conveyance _____

c-9   Value of salesmen's samples: Total _____
                        Maximum individual _____
                        Number of salesmen _____

c-10 Maximum amount of cash in transit
        (payroll or otherwise) _____

c-11 Amount of regular shipments of machinery for servicing or repair _____
_____

c-12 Annual export shipments _____

c-13 Countries where principal volume of shipments go _____
_____

c-14 Usual term of export sale _____

c-15 Are export shipments handled by freight forwarder? _____

The main purpose in the questions relating to the transit exposures is to definitely establish responsibility for any damage that might occur to property in transit.   It is also intended to emphasize that the transportation exposure is not limited to the delivery of manufactured goods, but is also involved in the shipment of incoming materials and supplies.   It also covers the sending out of machinery and equipment for servicing and repair as well as internal shipments between plants and/or warehouses.

The question of responsibility is not simply one of ownership as it relates to the buyer and seller, which in many cases can be indecisive in itself, but it is also a question of the degree of responsibility, either assumed or denied by the shipping company.   Question c-5 is intended to bring out this particular problem, so as to make sure that the warranties and conditions that are normal to most transportation policies relating to bills of lading coincide with your actual operations.

Questions c-12, c-13, c-14, and c-15 relate to export shipments which bring about similar vague questions of responsibility, but which have to be handled in a different manner.

Special situations

d-1 Do you own or lease electronic data processing equipment? _____

d-2 Are media and source data kept apart? _____

d-3 Are there any valuable paintings or other objects of art on any of your premises? _____

d-4 Do you own or lease any watercraft or aircraft? _____

d-5 Do you own or lease any railroad rolling stock? _____

d-6 Do you own or are you responsible for roads, bridges, water supply, or waste disposal systems? _____

d-7 Do you own or are you responsible for any unusually priced animals? _____

d-8 Do you use any precious metals in your operation? _____

d-9 Do you have any off-shore facilities? _____

The basic purpose in the above questions is to investigate the potential exposures that often exist in a corporation which can often be overlooked, and which, if not properly taken care of, can represent a substantial financial exposure. It is not intended that they will fully cover *all* special situations, but they reflect the type of question that should be asked. If the answer to any of these questions is "yes," considerable further exploration needs to be done with regard to that particular problem.

Indirect or consequential damage questionnaire. The principal indirect loss that results from damage to your property is the loss of future earnings. Business-interruption, or use-and-occupancy insurance as it is sometimes called, provides the protection that a corporation needs for this loss of future earnings. The details of the business-interruption coverage and the variety of forms that are available are discussed in the third part of this section. The following questions are designed simply to ascertain whether or not there is a problem.

a-1   What are your annual net sales? _____

a-2   What is the cost of materials and supplies? _____

a-3   What is your ordinary payroll (hourly)? _____

a-4   Do you have an unemployment compensation credit? _____

a-5   Are sales seasonal? _____

a-6   Do you have extensive contractual sales? _____

a-7   Is production battery type or in-line type? _____

a-8   Estimated time to restore total facility _____

a-9   Estimated time to replace major equipment _____

a-10 In the event of a shutdown are there other facilities (owned, leased, or outside contractors) available to replace your productive capacity? _____

a-11 Is there any interdependency between plants? _____

a-12 Are any materials or supplies obtained from a sole source? _____

a-13 Is there any one customer that takes a major portion of your production?
_____

a-14 What is your source of power? _____

a-15 Do you have properties that you lease to others? _____

a-16 What effect will a loss of research and development equipment or data have on future corporate growth? _____
_____

a-17 Is refrigeration or any other form of temperature or humidity control essential to the continuance of your operations? _____

Questions *a*-1, *a*-2, and *a*-3 should be answered for each principal location and are intended to reflect the general range of the annual exposure to loss. While there will be many individual refinements in developing the proper values depending upon the type of form selected, generally the net sales less the cost of materials and supplies will give the value which would be used if the business-interruption insurance were written on a gross earnings basis. If written on a two-item basis, this gross earnings figure would have to be modified by the exclusion of the ordinary payroll (generally considered to be most of the hourly payroll). This ordinary payroll can then be separately insured, either in full or in part, or it can be excluded as desired.

One of the reasons for buying ordinary-payroll coverage is to protect an unemployment tax credit that may have been established over the years. If a fire or other casualty should shut down your plant for any extended period of time, the unemployment-compensation account would be severely drained by the unemployment checks collected by idle workers during the period of restoration. Under such circumstances, it is quite probable that you will lose the existing tax credit for many years to come and, depending upon the size of the payroll, this increased expense could be a sizable factor in the profitability of future operations. Ordinary-payroll insurance can be purchased to enable you to continue paying your idle workers for stipulated periods of time, or it can be used to reimburse your unemployment-compensation insurance account to maintain your tax credit.

The type of business-interruption policy required will be governed largely by the answers to questions *a*-5 and *a*-6. If sales are seasonal, it is generally desirable to try to arrange a reporting form of business-interruption insurance. You can then maintain adequate protection by having high limits of insurance, but still maintain reasonable premium levels by adjusting to the actual exposure incurred during the course of the policy period. Such forms are available under the filings of certain major underwriting organizations and some of the companies that specialize in industrial insurance. But the reporting form policy is not generally available under the standard form.

Most business-interruption policies are limited to providing recovery for the loss of profits and continuing expenses and payroll expenses that would have been earned during the period of shutdown. It is quite possible, in certain

industries, that the loss of a contract because of an inability to fulfill a requirement could create a loss that would go far beyond the actual time that it takes
to restore the damaged property. The additional loss, because of the loss of
contracts, would not be recoverable under the normal business-interruption
form. If there is such a problem reflected by the answers to question *a*-6,
special steps have to be taken to provide the necessary coverage.

The severity of a potential loss is the purpose behind the questions *a*-7, *a*-8,
a-9, *a*-10, and *a*-11.

The question relating to the battery type or in-line type of production facilities is asked to determine whether a loss anywhere in the course of manufacture
will shut down the entire plant. This is what could be called an in-line type
of production.

If the loss would only reflect a loss of production of the particular unit or
battery of equipment that was damaged, this would be a battery type of production loss. The balance of the production units would not be affected by the
loss of any other production unit.

One of the factors most often overlooked in evaluating the need for business-
interruption insurance is the length of time that it takes to obtain major pieces
of production machinery. It is not always the biggest machine that takes the
longest to replace, so that a careful evaluation is necessary to determine where
any trouble spots are.

The question of any interdependency between plants is chiefly designed to
pinpoint any situation that might develop whereby a loss at one plant would
affect not only that plant but others as well. This could be particularly true
in any operation that might be a combination of manufacturing and retailing
where, in addition to actually producing the product, the corporation also re-
tails the production. In such cases, the loss of productive capacity at the plant
would not only shut down the plant and lose the direct manufacturing profit;
it would also have a serious effect on any retailing operations. It might shut
them all down, thus losing the profit at that location in spite of the fact that
there was no damage there. This is a contingent business-interruption loss
within a company's own structure.

There are other major contingent exposures which are reflected by questions
a-12 and *a*-13. Question *a*-12 is designed to determine whether or not the
plant could be shut down because of an inability to obtain a vital material or
processing operation because of damage occurring at a supplier's or processor's
plant. Similarly, question *a*-13 is designed to determine whether or not the
plant could be shut down because a major customer simply could not take the
production.

The question of power interruption is a vital one in the evaluation of potential loss arising out of an interruption of production. This needs a complete
exploration with respect to whether you generate your own power or whether
it is supplied by a public utility; whether the public utility has sufficient backup

facilities to keep your power coming in under all circumstances; what standby power equipment and what alternate methods of generation are available; and how long will they take to put into operation. All these are questions that should be thoroughly explored.

The basic business-interruption forms are geared to the loss of profit and continuing expenses that result from an inability to manufacture. There are other income-producing exposures which are not geared to production, but are geared to the use of a facility. Accordingly, question a-15 is designed to determine whether or not there are any properties that you lease to others from which you derive an income which would be lost if the property were damaged or destroyed.

Question a-16 is intended to bring to the insured's attention the potential losses that could develop from damage or destruction of any part of his research or development program. The loss of the equipment or building facilities can easily be taken care of in a normal manner by direct-damage insurance. The problem comes about where you may have experiments in process which are undergoing time tests, etc., where the actual value of the particular object might be one-thousandth of its true value in terms of the time, effort, and importance to the research project that it is a part of. Accordingly, whenever there is an exposure of this nature, careful study must be made *before* the loss in order to establish a proper basis for valuation in the event a loss does occur.

A second major indirect loss potential that exists in a research and development operation is the loss of potential market because of the delay in completing experiments, testing, etc. This is an extremely difficult subject to put to any kind of evaluation. Any protection for this kind of exposure will not fall within the purview of the normal policy forms and coverage must be tailor-made.

Question a-17 is designed to bring up the question of a potential contamination loss that might result from the breakdown of refrigerating equipment. Like many of these questions, one leads to another, and the question of contamination then should be followed through and reviewed to check other sources of possible contamination, such as breakage of ammonia lines, inadvertent mixing of foreign bodies into foodstuffs, etc.

The second part of question a-17 is geared primarily to the potential shutdown and resultant loss of profit and continuing expenses (business interruption) that might result from a mechanical breakdown or other perils occurring to vital machinery.

In addition to the principal indirect or consequential loss exposures just described, there are also other miscellaneous types of indirect loss potentials. Some of these exposures are reflected by the following questions.

b-1 What are your maximum and average values of Accounts Receivable?

b-2 Are Accounts Receivable handled at one centralized accounting office?
_____

b-3 Can Accounts Receivable records be easily duplicated from manufacturing orders, shipping orders, sales slips, etc.? _____

b-4 Are Accounts Receivable records microfilmed? _____

b-5 What is bad-debt and uncollected account average for past 3 years?

Domestic _____

Export _____

b-6 Could export sales be increased with more liberal terms of sale? _____

b-7 Are top-management personnel and research and development personnel under contract of employment? _____

b-8 Are any pension or welfare funds handled as separate trusts? _____

b-9 Do your plant buildings conform to the present building codes? _____

The first four questions above are designed primarily to establish whether or not there is a loss potential that would result from damage to or the destruction of the Accounts Receivable records. The cost of the record books themselves is a direct-damage cost, but the cost to reestablish the records is an indirect cost not provided by the direct-damage policies. Furthermore, the direct-damage policies do not provide recovery for any inability to collect the accounts receivable because of the destruction of the records. It is essential to know what the maximum potential loss might be because of an inability to collect accounts receivable and, second, what it would cost to restore the records. This is an exposure that could well break a business if not properly protected, and only a complete evaluation can tell whether or not it is more feasible to insure the exposure or to take steps to duplicate the records or to combine the two approaches.

Questions *b*-5 and *b*-6 are primarily geared to develop the potential need for domestic or foreign credit insurance. The use of foreign-credit insurance can be a vital tool in enabling you to substantially expand export sales. It is not necessary to be a giant of industry to have a profitable export operation with substantially reduced risks by the use of foreign-credit insurance which will protect not only the credit exposure but, to a large degree, the political risks that are always present in the exporting field.

Question *b*-7 is intended to simply bring to management's attention the loss potential that could exist from "industrial espionage," particularly in the area of research and development. Insuring this potential loss hazard is an extremely difficult job. The primary purpose in bringing up the question is to make sure that the potential hazard is recognized, so that if the insurance markets do begin to offer this coverage on a definite basis, you will be in a position to evaluate the desirability of obtaining this protection.

The purpose behind question *b*-8 is to determine whether or not the insured is required, under the Federal Disclosure Act, to provide fidelity insurance for the trustees handling the pension or welfare funds.

Question b-9 is designed to bring out the possibility that in the event of a major building loss, particularly in an urban area, you may not be allowed to rebuild any damaged property with materials of like kind and quality as existed at the time of the loss but rather with materials that would comply with the existing building codes. In addition, you may be required not only to replace the damaged property with materials that satisfy the current codes, but also to demolish the undamaged portion of the building and restore that with materials that would comply with the current codes as well.

Liability questionnaire. The previous sections deal with the evaluation of the potential losses arising out of damage to your own property. The second basic area of loss potential arises out of the possible claims that could result from damage to or the destruction of property owned by others, or because of bodily injury, sickness, disease, or death resulting therefrom, that might be sustained by members of the public because of some action on the insured's part.

The following questions are designed to determine whether there are potential liability exposures in various areas.

c-1 What are annual net sales? _____

c-2 What is the amount of annual sales made to the United States government? _____

c-3 What is the amount of annual export sales? _____

c-4 To what areas are exports shipped? _____

c-5 What use is made of your product by your customer? _____

c-6 Are there any doctors or nurses retained as employees? _____

c-7 Are there any elevators or escalators on any of your owned or leased premises? _____

c-8 Are there any railroad sidetracks at the principal premises? _____

c-9 Are there any pier or wharf facilities at the principal locations? _____

c-11 Do you own or lease any watercraft? _____

c-12 Have you assumed any liability of others under any lease agreements, contracts, purchase orders, etc.? _____

c-13 Have you agreed to provide any liability insurance for any other person or entity under any contract or agreement? _____

c-14 Do you do any advertising? _____
If so, what is annual budget for—
                              Radio and TV _____
                              Newspapers _____
                              Magazines _____
                              Trade publications _____
                              Other _____

c-15 How many vehicles do you own? _____

c-16 How many vehicles do you lease under long-term contract? _____

c-17 What is the radius of operation of these vehicles? _____

c-18 Do your employees use their own cars on company business? _____

c-19 Do you design any products? _____

      Establish specifications? _____

      Act as consulting engineer? _____

The questions relating to sales are designed to review the questions of product liability. Sales to the government, for example, can in many cases be reasonably excluded from product-liability coverage depending upon the wording of the contract with the government. The questions relating to the amount and area of export sales are intended to determine whether or not any adjustments need to be made in the basic policies to provide worldwide protection.

Question c-5 relating to the use to which your product is put by your customers is intended to reflect the question of the adequacy of the limit of liability. It is quite apparent that the manufacturer of a vital component part of a commercial airliner can have far greater potential liability as a result of one occurrence than could the manufacturer of a small toy.

Question c-6 is intended to determine whether there is any malpractice-liability exposure on the part of the insured. At the same time, it brings up for consideration any arrangements that may be made between the insured and the doctor or nurse which relate to the doctor's or nurse's individual liability and whether or not the insured has assumed any responsibility for providing protection therefor.

The intent behind questions c-10 and c-11 is to simply bring up the questions whether or not aircraft or watercraft are ever used on your behalf, either under lease or under charter. Generally speaking, everybody is fully aware of the liability hazards inherent in the ownership of a car, airplane, or watercraft. Not everybody, however, is aware of the liabilities implicit in the operation of leased, chartered, or nonowned vehicles.

Similarly, everybody is fairly cognizant of his responsibilities for his own operations, but may not be so careful to properly evaluate the assumptions of liability that he may enter into under contract or agreements. He may enter into such contracts or agreements without even realizing that there are assumptions of liability or "hold-harmless" agreements contained therein. Questions c-12 and c-13 are designed to reflect the two major areas where you may have such problems in contracts or agreements; one being the assumption of somebody else's liability, and the second being the agreement under contract to provide insurance for another party.

The questions c-15, c-16, c-17, and c-18 relating to automobile exposures are self-explanatory, but are necessary to the proper evaluation of the risk. The type of trucking operation and the territory through which it is conducted are quite important in the evaluation of the necessary limits of liability.

The balance of the questions is designed to pinpoint specific exposures such as advertising liability, professional liability, marine liability, etc.

The foregoing questions and comments have been developed on a very general basis. Each major type of business operation, such as manufacturing, commercial, contracting, or service operations, will have problems that are peculiar to its industry. For example, the contracting business has a complete area of insurance that is used very little by other segments of industry, that is, the purchasing of surety bonds. Similarly, the commercial risks have a much greater emphasis on proper valuation and protection of leasehold improvements, whereas the service type of operation, such as country clubs, marinas, and others of similar nature, might be interested in rain insurance for particular exposures.

It is not possible to cover in this book all questions that would have a bearing on the development of a proper insurance program for any particular type of business enterprise. It is the intent to try and emphasize that the insurance program of any business should be built on the basis of the evaluation of the insured's own requirements and should not be built on the evaluation of individual policies as offered by the insurance industry.

3. Principal coverages and how they satisfy the needs

Now that we have reviewed the exposures to financial loss that face the company, the next problem is what course of action to follow. The exposures that are uncontrollable may not be insurable at the present time, but should not be completely discarded from mind as a potential financial risk, since the insurance industry and/or the government are continually exploring additional areas of protection which may be in the public interest. Two illustrations of the creation of new insurance facilities for areas that were completely uninsured in the past are the nuclear energy insurance pools for both direct-damage and liability exposures and the foreign-credit insurance facilities. Similar protections may be developed for flood exposure and other similar types of disaster losses that are now difficult to insure.

The balance of exposures to financial loss generally fall into two categories—

1. Those exposures where the risk can be eliminated
2. Those exposures where the risks are such that they cannot be eliminated without a detrimental effect on a business and which are of sufficient size to suggest the sharing of the risk through commercial insurance

It is not our purpose to review the infinite number of policy forms that could be utilized for the protection of any company's business. We intend to treat only the general areas of protection that would be required and to try to point out some of the principal features of the major insurance policies that the insured should be cognizant of, and some of the normal warranties and conditions and exclusions that he should be aware of.

It is essential to recognize that we are not in any way attempting to discuss the detail, terms, conditions, insuring agreements, or exclusions of any particular forms of policy. The insured must read and understand his own policy, keeping in mind that it is a contract between the insurance company and himself. In consideration of the premium that he is paying to the insurance company, they will undertake to reimburse him for certain damages arising out of certain given circumstances. There is no policy in the general insurance field that is an "all-loss" policy, and it is, therefore, necessary for the insured, in order to avoid any possible misunderstandings, to be aware of the limitations of the coverage that he has purchased.

Property damage
Principal locations

FIRE AND SUPPLEMENTAL PERILS. The extent of the coverage afforded under standard fire and supplemental perils policies varies in slight degree from state to state and it also varies between rating organizations and major underwriting organizations. In any case, most people consider and acknowledge that the term "fire and supplemental perils" would cover basically fire, lightning, wind, hail, explosion (other than the explosion of steam equipment), aircraft and vehicle damage, smoke damage, riot, civil commotion, vandalism, malicious mischief, and sprinkler leakage. If coverage is written with one of the major underwriting groups, the forms that they have developed include all of the perils under one form. Under the standard form of writing fire insurance, however, it is generally necessary to add various endorsements for the extended-coverage perils, vandalism and malicious mischief, and sprinkler leakage.

In the event that coverage is placed on a standard basis where coverage has to be added by endorsement, it is essential that all policy forms be made concurrent and provide the same perils. If there are several contributing policies and coverage is not concurrent, then the insured will not be fully protected and will suffer a portion of the loss himself in the areas of the nonconcurrency. For example, let us assume that four policies are written for $25,000, each covering a property worth $100,000. Let us assume that they are all written to apply to the same property and are subject to the same terms and conditions except that one policy does not have the extended-coverage endorsement on it, whereas the other three do. Let us then assume a $30,000 windstorm loss. Since only three-quarters of the amount of insurance was properly extended to include the windstorm peril, then the insured would only collect three-quarters of the loss and he would have to absorb the other 25 percent himself. The allocations of the coverage are based on the amounts of fire insurance even though the loss may be caused by a peril other than fire.

Fire insurance is written not only to apply at a specific location, but also to apply to property of a specific named insured. It is therefore essential that in issuing a policy the complete and proper named insured be utilized, so that coverage will be afforded to all of the entities having an insurable interest in the property.

Fire insurance can be written to cover a specific type of property, such as buildings, machinery and equipment, stock, or furniture and fixtures, or it can be written to cover all contents or on a blanket basis to cover all real and personal property. In addition to applying to the property of the named insured, the fire-insurance policy generally extends coverage to apply to similar personal property of others held in trust or on consignment and personal property of others that the insured may be liable for while such property is in his custody on the described premises. Coverage is sometimes also extended to apply to employees' personal property.

The major underwriting fire-insurance policies also extend coverage to apply to any new buildings or structures that may be built on the insured premises. This extension of coverage also applies to the contractor's interest to the extent that the insured has assumed liability therefor, and it also applies to materials and supplies, equipment, and machinery that are necessary to this new construction. If the construction takes place at a different location than that which is already insured, then builders-risk coverage will be required.

It is generally better to try to blanket as many items together under one amount of insurance as possible. It would be better, for example, to write a $1,000,000 policy to cover all real and personal property at a specific location rather than to cover $500,000 on the building and another $500,000 on the contents, or on an even more specified basis, $500,000 on the building, $250,000 on the machinery and equipment, and $250,000 on the stock.

If the insurance is written on a specified basis, such as illustrated above, it is apparent that the insured has considerably less flexibility in protection against any fluctuation of values or erroneous estimate of values that might develop in any particular category. It is thus preferable to blanket these various types of property under one amount of insurance to give the insured that additional flexibility.

One exception to this suggestion, however, would be where there might be a problem of severe fluctuation in inventory values, in which case it might be better to insure the inventory on a reporting basis, so that the insured could have adequate limits of liability, yet still pay premium only on the basis of the actual values at risk. Under this illustration, it would be desirable then to insure the building and all contents, other than inventory, on a blanket basis and to insure the inventory on a separate reporting form basis.

The advantages of blanketing coverage are even more apparent when blanketing coverage over two or more locations. Under this combination, the total amount of insurance applying to all locations that are blanketed together would be available for a loss at any one of the locations. Thus, if the insured moves property back and forth between plants, the total limit for all locations will not change. Under a blanket basis he would be fully protected and he would continue to satisfy the total coinsurance requirements. If he insured each location separately, adjustments in values would have to be made every time there was a major movement of property between locations.

Most fire insurance is written on a coinsurance basis. The basic purpose of the coinsurance clause is to make sure that the insured uses a proper value, so that the underwriter can get a fair premium for his assumption of risk. By accepting the coinsurance clause, the insured obtains the benefit of a substantially reduced rate in comparison with what he would pay on a flat-rate basis if he did not accept a coinsurance clause. In actual practice the flat rates are rarely used nowadays and almost everything is based on a coinsurance rate.

Under the terms of the coinsurance clause, the insured must maintain an amount of insurance that is at least equal to a stipulated percentage (generally either 80 or 90 percent for fire insurance) of the value of the property at risk at the time of the loss. If he fails to maintain the proper amount of insurance, he will become a coinsurer and will participate in the loss to the extent that he did not live up to his original obligation.

To illustrate, let us assume that an insured has property valued at $100,000 as of the time of the loss and the insurance is written on an 80 percent coinsurance basis. Therefore, under the terms of the coinsurance clause, he is required to carry at least $80,000 insurance. Let us now assume that the insured either was not aware that the value of the property had gone up to $100,000 or he had simply not increased his amounts of insurance, but in any event was only carrying $60,000 insurance at the time of the loss. If the insured suffered a $20,000 loss, he would only collect $15,000, since he was only carrying 75 percent of the amount of insurance that he had agreed to carry by the terms of the coinsurance clause ($60,000 divided by $80,000 equals 75 percent).

It is thus apparent that where there are major fluctuations in values, it is virtually impossible for an insured to be certain that he has satisfied the terms of the coinsurance clause at any given time.

The penalty provisions of the coinsurance clause can be waived by the insurance company for a given period of time by use of an agreed-amount clause which stipulates that the insurance company agrees that the amount of insurance carried is sufficient to satisfy the terms of the coinsurance clause. This clause is generally available to an insured only if he submits values on a regular annual basis and the values are supported by appraisals.

One of the most important aspects of the coinsurance clause is to make sure that the basis for establishing the amounts of insurance are in conformity with the valuation clause in the policy. It is the values determined by the valuation clause in the policy that govern the question of compliance with the coinsurance clause. Therefore, it is absolutely essential that an insured establish the amount of insurance on the same basis that will be used at the time of the loss.

All fire-insurance policies are written so as to provide recovery on the basis of the actual cash value of the damaged property at the time of the loss. Unless other provisions are made, the actual cash value will be the basis for loss adjustment. The term "actual cash value" means the present-day replacement cost of the damaged property, determined as of the date and at the place of the loss, less physical depreciation. *The depreciation factor applied is the physical depreciation and not the book depreciation.*

It is often possible and generally desirable to adjust the basic policy terms so that the recovery, at least for the building, machinery and equipment, and furniture and fixtures, will be on the basis of the present replacement cost without any deduction for physical depreciation. The addition of the repair-and-replace endorsement requires the adjustment of the values to 90 percent of the *replacement* value of the building, machinery, and equipment, and at the same time generally requires a 90 percent coinsurance clause. This coinsurance clause, however, can be nullified by the use of an agreed-amount endorsement.

Under the forms used by the major fire-insurance underwriting groups or associations, such as the Factory Insurance Association, Factory Mutuals, Improved Risk Mutuals, and others using the preferred risk rating tables, the value of stock also is subject to a separate valuation clause. Under their standard "value-of-stock" clause, finished inventory is insured on a selling-price basis; stock in process is insured on the basis of the replacement cost of the raw materials and supplies plus a proper proportion of overhead as well as any labor or other charges incurred up to the time of the loss; and raw materials and supplies are insured on a replacement basis.

The same extensions of coverage can be added by specific endorsement to the balance of the fire-insurance company offerings, but in those cases, unlike the forms of the F.I.A. and Factory Mutuals, this property will then be subject to coinsurance based on the values developed by the particular valuation clause attached to the policy. There is no coinsurance in the F.I.A. or Factory Mutuals form for coverage applying to stock.

It is important for an insured to clearly understand, if he uses a repair-and-replace endorsement, just what is covered by the endorsement and what is not. There are certain types of property, in addition to stock, that are normally excluded from the repair-and-replace endorsement. These properties would be such items as patterns, dies, molds, jigs, templates, and drawings. These can be insured on a replacement basis if proper provision is made. It is invariably wise for the insured to arrive at a definite understanding with the insurance company about the value of such property. Since the policy is subject to a coinsurance clause, it is best to eliminate any problems about compliance with the provisions of this clause before the loss occurs if at all possible.

In addition, there are certain other types of property, such as electronic data processing media, manuscripts, blueprints, microfilm, and similar types of property that might have a special valuation above and beyond the actual cost to replace. In such cases, special provisions must be made with the insurance company in the same manner that you would for dies and molds, etc., to predetermine the basis on which the insured wishes to be paid in the event of a loss. This basis can then also serve as a basis for establishing the amount of insurance.

The perils insured under a fire and supplemental peril policy are fortuitous in nature, and while proper operating procedures, maintenance, and protection can minimize some of the major perils, there is no way to eliminate them altogether. The values of the property involved and the potential losses are also extremely high in relation to the premiums paid. Accordingly, it is almost invariably found that this is a proper subject for the sharing of risk by means of the purchase of commercial insurance.

BOILER AND MACHINERY. The exposures to loss arising out of the ownership, maintenance, operation, or use of boilers, pressure vessels, machinery, and electrical apparatus can be basically broken down into two categories:

1. A potential happening that will occur within the object which may damage not only the object itself, but other property as well
2. A potential loss occurring only within the object itself

In the first category would be such things as a boiler explosion or the explosion of a pressure vessel, or the release of any flywheel or any other object turning at high speeds where centrifugal force could throw the object away from its primary station causing damage to other property. In the second category would be losses such as the burning, bulging, or cracking of boiler tubes, the breaking of a part or the whole of a mechanical machine into two or more parts, or the burning out of electrical apparatus.

Under the first category, the premiums for boiler-and-machinery insurance for those objects are generally higher in relation to the total potential damage than would be the case under a fire-insurance policy. However, the differential between the premium and loss potential is still very substantial. This differential coupled with the fact that losses still can occur regardless of how well engineered the risk may be, indicates that these objects are generally a proper subject for sharing the risk through commercial insurance.

In the second instance where a loss occurring in the object can do no damage to anything other than the object itself, it becomes a measurement of the premium as compared to the total cost to repair or replace the object. Objects that fall into this category may well be in the area where self-assumption of risk is quite feasible. This, of course, depends upon the individual circumstances reflecting the number of objects, the value of the objects, the age of the objects, and the premiums that would be paid for protection through commercial insurance.

If insurance is bought, particularly in regard to the first set of circumstances, it is important to recognize that when establishing the limit of insurance, consideration must be given not only to the value of the object itself, but also to the total potential damage that might be caused by an insured accident.

The boiler-and-machinery coverages are written in the same basic manner as the fire insurance in the sense that the basic policies provide for recovery based on the actual cash value of the damaged property. This may be amended by endorsement to adjust the basis of loss recovery to a full-replacement-value basis.

There is a growing trend toward combining the boiler and fire coverages under one policy. The primary purpose behind this move is to eliminate the areas of controversy that exist where a loss may be the combined result of a boiler explosion and a resultant fire. Under the boiler-and-machinery policy, the boiler underwriter would be liable only for the damage caused by the explosion. Under the fire policy the fire underwriter would be liable only for the damage resulting from the ensuing fire. It is perfectly obvious that it would be an extremely difficult task to determine accurately what damage was caused by which peril. Similarly, there are other areas of potential controversy concerning electrical fires and the explosion of pressure vessels. All of these areas of potential controversy would be eliminated if both the fire and boiler-and-machinery perils are written under one policy with the same underwriter and with the same loss adjuster.

There is also a growing tendency in the boiler-insurance industry to get away from the old basis of limited definitions of objects and limited definitions of accidents. The blanket group plan basis of insuring did provide automatic coverage for newly acquired objects so long as they fell within a classification of object that was already insured.

The current trend, however, is to insure all objects on a comprehensive basis and to specifically exclude those objects which you do not wish to insure. Under this "comprehensive" approach any new objects that are installed and are not a part of a previously insured class would automatically be covered. This comprehensive approach also enables you to eliminate objects on a specific basis, or by class, or by general purpose. In this manner you can either insure or eliminate, for example, production machinery, motors under 100 horsepower, transformers under 1,000 kva, or any other general type of object or size of object. The comprehensive coverage is written subject to a deductible, the size of which is a key factor in underwriting the premium for the risk. When using the comprehensive approach, it is generally desirable to use a deductible that would eliminate most of the maintenance losses and also the smaller equipment that you would not insure normally on a specific-item basis anyway.

CRIME. Crime-insurance policies cover several different areas, some of which lend themselves to fairly accurate assessment of the loss potential, while others have a very indefinite loss potential that could range from a nominal loss to a catastrophic loss that could put a business out of operation.

The loss potential of money and securities is an example of a coverage that can be fairly accurately evaluated to determine whether or not the risk warrants the provision of commercial insurance, or whether it is of such nominal nature as to justify the self-assumption of the risk. The exposure can vary from a nominal amount of cash, used solely for petty-cash purposes, up to rather substantial amounts as reflected by a major retail exposure or by a company that pays on a cash payroll basis.

The provision of proper safeguards when the money or securities are on the premises can minimize the risk and thus reduce the premiums required. If the exposure is at all substantial, it will not be possible to completely eliminate the risk, and therefore the sharing of the risk through commercial insurance is generally warranted.

Similarly, the exposure for the loss of money while being conveyed outside of the premises can also be protected or minimized by the use of armored-car services, or the use of the insured's own armed guard, or the adoption of a corporate policy that requires that money being transported away from the premises be kept to nominal amounts in any one transit. The use of the armored-vehicle service for all practical purposes transfers the responsibility to the armored-vehicle company, and it is doubtful that any further coverage on the part of the insured is required, provided that he makes certain of the adequacy of the protection and guarantees given by the armored-car service.

When an armored-car service is not used and the insured uses his own employees for the transportation of money, he must be aware of the conditions in the policy relating to the number of messengers that might be out at any one time; the definition of who is actually covered while transporting the money or securities; and whether or not there is any requirement in the policy relating to guards accompanying the messengers.

Burglary insurance is another area where it is possible to make a realistic evaluation of the loss potential. This evaluation would be largely dependent upon the type of commodity that would be involved, both as to its value and as to its ease of handling. Here again, proper protection of the premises can substantially reduce the probability of loss, but it will not eliminate it completely. Thus, there should be a measurement of the premiums versus the potential losses to determine whether a sharing of the risk through commercial insurance would be in order.

Burglary, as used in the insurance contract, is a very specific and limited phrase. In order to qualify as a burglary, there must be visible evidence of a forceable entry. Without such evidence there can be no burglary under the terms of the policy and therefore no coverage. It is therefore generally advisable to amend the standard burglary coverage to include theft, which will broaden the coverage substantially and eliminate the restrictive conditions that exist under the limited burglary coverage.

While many millions of dollars are paid out by insurance underwriters each year for burglary, theft, and robbery or holdup losses, by far the largest amount of crime losses arise out of the infidelity of employees. Unfortunately, the great majority of fidelity losses are uninsured and similarly the great majority of those that are insured are grossly underinsured.

Fidelity coverage should be written for all employers to cover all employees. All too often a mistake is made by limiting coverage to certain positions or to those people that handle money, and no thought is given to the possibility that major losses can be incurred without the embezzler ever touching any cash. One further common fallacy is the thought that not too much can be taken at one time without it becoming apparent, and thus there is no need for anything more than modest amounts of insurance. This is a completely erroneous line of thought, as a study of the major fidelity losses confirms that these major losses invariably extend over a lengthy period of time. It is also important to recognize that no matter how trustworthy a person is, a change in personal fortunes or misfortunes can be responsible for a complete change in an individual's personality, and the most trusted employee can become the most unsuspected embezzler.

Determining the proper amount of fidelity coverage to carry is much like trying to establish the proper limits of liability for automobile and general liability exposures. The insured can never be certain that he has adequate coverage until the loss actually occurs. However, in an effort to at least establish some guidelines, the American Institute of Accountants and the Surety Association of America formed a joint committee several years ago to establish a formula that could be used to at least provide guidelines to an insured regarding a *minimum* amount of fidelity insurance to carry. This formula is basically geared to the net assets of the company and the sales volume, and should be reviewed by any insured before establishing the amount of fidelity insurance to carry.

One other important area to consider in the crime-insurance field is the potential loss that might arise through forgery. The standard method of providing forgery insurance limits coverage to the forgery of checks, drafts, money orders, and other similar instruments that promise to pay a sum certain in money. The standard depositor's forgery coverage does not cover any loss that might arise out of the forgery of stock certificates, bills of lading, warehouse receipts, or other negotiable instruments. If such instruments present a hazard to the insured, it is possible to extend the forgery coverage by endorsement to include all issued instruments.

Another feature of the standard approach to the provision of forgery coverage is that normally coverage is excluded for losses caused by employees. This is done on the theory that the coverage for dishonest employees is provided under the fidelity section. However, the employee exclusion can be deleted from the forgery coverage which thus, in effect, gives an additional, although limited, amount of protection for losses caused by employees. Since most major losses do involve some amount of forgery, this is an effective and economical way of providing additional protection against a major loss.

The forgery of credit cards is not covered by the basic forgery policy, even if amended as suggested, since the credit card is issued by the credit-card company, not by the insured. This coverage can be added by special endorsement to protect the corporate obligations and also the individual obligations of the officers and their spouses. Similarly, the forgery coverage can be, and often is, extended to apply to the personal accounts of officers and their wives.

MISCELLANEOUS PERILS. The aforementioned types of insurance, that is fire and supplemental perils, boiler and machinery and crime, can be applied to almost any operation. In addition to the perils already covered, there are other perils that are either peculiar to a particular industry, peculiar to an individual location, or peculiar to the geographical location of the premises. Such miscellaneous additional perils would include earthquake, flood, water damage, collapse, subsidence, and others of similar nature.

Some of these particular perils, such as water damage and earthquake, can be individually insured on standard forms, and others, such as collapse, can be individually insured by the use of excess markets. Generally speaking, however, the most economical way to provide coverage for these miscellaneous perils is not to isolate them, but to write coverage on what is known as a difference-of-conditions basis. "Difference-of-conditions" simply means the provision of coverage on an all-risk basis, but excluding the perils that are normally covered by the fire and supplemental peril policies, boiler-and-machinery policies, the crime policies, and certain uninsurable perils such as war risk, etc. Any other particular peril that the insured does not wish to insure can also be excluded, and it is often beneficial in the premium negotiations to make such deletions. For example, just the mention of earthquake coverage generally scares most underwriters. Therefore, if the insured has no property which would be subject to a possible earthquake loss, it would be prudent to agree to delete earthquake from a difference-of-conditions policy. This would allow the underwriter to breathe more deeply, and possibly he will be more realistic in establishing the necessary premiums for the balance of the exposures.

This difference-of-conditions coverage can be written to apply to any portion of the property at risk—that is, it can be applied to stock only, contents only, building only, or any combination. It is generally offered by the excess or surplus lines markets, although some of the standard markets are now beginning to use their own forms under special filings.

It is important for an insured to read the insuring clauses and the exclusions even more carefully, perhaps, than in other forms of property-damage insurance inasmuch as there is no basic standard for these coverages. The phrase "water damage," for example, may be defined to mean one thing under one policy and quite another thing under a different policy. Similarly, flood can mean the rising of navigable waters under one policy and can mean any rising water under another policy.

Secondary locations. When considering the problems of insuring secondary locations such as warehouses, sales offices, outside processing locations, etc., the insured must recognize that he does not have the control over such locations that he would have over his own location.   Thus, the protection, maintenance, and general operations may be handled in such a manner as to be more conducive to loss than would his own operations.

Because of these factors, it is generally desirable to provide insurance protection on as broad an all-risk basis as can be reasonably developed.   On this basis all perils would be covered except those which are specifically excluded.   Therefore, anything that was not thought of specifically would be covered automatically under an all-risk approach as long as it was not specifically excluded.   On the other hand, if the insured should follow a basic concept of insuring on a named-peril basis, anything that was not thought of would be uninsured.

If it is decided to follow the approach of providing only named perils, this type of coverage can be written on a multiple-location fire reporting policy which is acceptable in most states.   The fire reporting policy can be endorsed to include the extended coverage perils, vandalism, malicious mischief, and sprinkler leakage.

If the all-risk approach is desired, the same fire multiple-location reporting policy can be used with difference-of-conditions coverage added to provide the combined all-risk protection.   Or, inland-marine markets can be used to combine the secondary location coverages with the transit coverages on an all-risk basis.   In the inland-marine field, there is a number of different available policy forms such as the manufacturers-output policy, commercial-property floater, transit and location forms, and others which are available through standard markets and tailor-made forms which are available through the excess and surplus lines markets.

The use of outside locations, particularly warehouses and processors' locations, generally indicates a continuous flow of property and, therefore, fluctuating values.   It is desirable to carry these suggested types of insurance on a reporting basis, so that adequate limits of liability may be established for these locations, yet have the premium predicated on the actual values at risk rather than on the limits of protection.

It is not at all uncommon to find that the person charged with the responsibility, for instance, is often the last one to be notified of the movement of property.   It is, therefore, also advantageous to include in any such reporting form policy, an automatic provision extending coverage to any unnamed location.

The questions of proper valuation of the property and the description of the property covered or excluded are basically the same as were discussed in the previous portion of this section relating to property damage at principal locations.

Transit.   Inland transit insurance is written to protect property during the course of transit from the time it leaves the point of shipment till the time that it arrives at its final destination.   Coverage can be written on a very limited form or it can be written on a very broad form.

Under the limited forms, the description of property covered will be limited to certain classes of material, and the risks against which the policy will provide protection will be named perils rather than an all-risk concept. In addition the means by which the transit is to be accomplished will also be restricted.

The broader form on the other hand can be written to provide protection for all personal property against all risks of loss during the course of transit by any conveyance.

It is essential to review the policies carefully because there is a tendency to buy coverage for a particular exposure and then to assume that this same policy will grant coverage for any transit risks.

Another feature of the transit policies that has to be watched carefully is the clause relating to the types of bills of lading under which it is permissible to ship the property and still retain coverage under the transit policy. The broader form will generally give you the automatic right to accept and ship under released-value bills of lading.

When covering all shipments of property, including incoming, outgoing, and interplant shipments, it is generally easier to tie the premium adjustment to the total sales of the corporation rather than to try to keep track of all of the shipments. The rates can be established on a composite basis to be applied to any base, but the sales figure is most commonly used because it is most readily available.

The need for transit insurance is largely dependent upon the volume of shipments, the maximum value contained in any one vehicle, the commodity being shipped, and the past experience. This is a type of coverage where the maximum loss in any one incident does not have the financial catastrophe potential that a major fire would have, yet the value can be rather substantial in certain circumstances. One of the basic uses of transportation insurance, in addition to the protection of the property, is the use of the insurance company's claims services as a substitute for the insured's own traffic department in following up claims with common carriers.

Ocean marine insurance covering the movement of merchandise or equipment is generally written on an all-risk basis and extends from the time the property leaves the inland point of shipment until it arrives at final destination. There are some limiting factors depending upon the area to which the property is being shipped, but basically the coverage applies on a warehouse-to-warehouse basis.

While most coverage is now written on an all-risk basis, it is possible to write it on several more limited forms which could produce a premium saving. If the insured is shipping by the container type of shipment, where the merchandise is packed in the container at his own premises, sealed by his own employees, and shipped without ever being opened until it arrives at the final destination, where it is then opened either by the customer or the insured's own employee, it might be well to consider the provision of insurance on a basis of covering marine perils only, rather than on an all-risk basis. The propriety of such a reduction in protection would of course depend upon the volume of shipments and the experience that had been accumulated by the insured.

War-risk coverages are generally added by the issuance of a companion policy which covers the same shipments as the all-risk coverage. Under the war-risk policy, coverage is more limited, unless it has an extension to apply to the property while on land.

One of the major features of providing ocean marine coverage is that it will give the shipper general-average protection. Under maritime law, damages occurring to a ship during the course of a voyage can, under certain circumstances, be allocated on a pro rata basis against all parties that have any interest in the voyage. This is known as a general-average claim. Protection for general-average claims is a part of the open-cargo policy. If the shipper has an open-cargo policy, then the insurance company will assume the duties of providing the necessary bonds and handling all the paper work involved in the development of the general-average allocation, and will pay the portion of the claim that would be assessed against the shipper.

Special situations. The previous discussions concerning the types of insurance and how they should be applied to the exposures that have been developed were primarily geared to the insuring of normal everyday property that would be found in almost any type of operation. Oftentimes unusual exposures exist which are not readily recognized and which are, therefore, handled in a standard, but inadequate, way. When the loss occurs, it is a little too late to recognize the differences and make adaptations in the policies to suit these differences.

Some of the types of special situations to look for are—

FINE ARTS. In a number of instances paintings, sculptures, or other particular works of art may be displayed in an executive's office. The particular problems in this case would be (1) establishing value, and (2) the desire to provide complete all-risk coverage with as few exclusions as possible. None of the standard forms of insurance providing protection against loss from various perils would provide a proper valuation clause for such an object of art unless it was specifically endorsed thereon. The exclusions that would be pertinent to the general line of insurance for a manufacturing or retailing operation, even if difference-in-conditions coverage is carried, would not be acceptable when it comes to insuring fine arts. Both of these problems are overcome by insuring under a specially drawn fine-arts floater.

CAMERAS OR SIMILAR EQUIPMENT. Here again it is a question of proper valuation and complete all-risk coverage required for any instrument, such as a camera, projector, microscope, or a similar instrument, that might utilize expensive lenses. This exposure could arise in a research lab, wherever photography might be a part of the operation, or where a company does its own microfilming of valuable papers and Accounts Receivable records.

ROADS, RAILROADS, AND BRIDGES. This is a unique type of special situation that would be particularly pertinent to the pulp and paper industry. The problem with these exposures is the provision of protection for perils that might otherwise be normally excluded such as flood, landslide, earthquakes, and subsidence. In addition, there is the question of establishing a reasonable value which might not fit the normal concept of replacement value or depreciated value.

WATERFRONT FACILITIES. Here the property would be subjected to a different type of damage occasioned by vessels docking at the facilities, which would not be contemplated in the normal vehicle coverage under the standard coverage endorsements.

AUTOMOBILE PHYSICAL DAMAGE. This is not so much an unusual type of exposure as one that is normally handled as a separate item due to the transient nature of the risk. Automobile comprehensive-and-collision coverages can be written on either a stated-amount basis or an actual cash-value basis. Under the stated-amount approach the insured and the insurance company agree on establishing a specific value for the particular vehicle as of the inception of the policy. Any total loss will be paid on the basis of the agreed value. The "actual cash value" is basically the same as it is in any other form of insurance in that it means the depreciated amount, but it is important to recognize that it is *physical depreciation* and not book value that establishes the amount that should be insured and the amount that should be collected in the event of a loss.

LIVESTOCK OR OTHER ANIMALS. This is an exposure that is almost invariably excluded from any normal property insurance program, and thus special coverage has to be taken out to protect the financial value of livestock or special animals. The problems of insuring such animals are much more closely related to the provision of accident and health insurance or life insurance for individuals than they are to providing property insurance.

There are many other special situations, such as the ownership of vessels or aircraft, the existence of offshore drilling facilities, and many others of similar nature which may be peculiar to any given industry. Specific coverage is generally available for all such exposures. These individual coverages are specifically designed for the particular problem and should be considered as specific insurance. Any master contracts that might normally cover the property on the premises should be considered as excess coverage and endorsed accordingly.

It is important to recognize that even though the exposure may be unusual and have to be handled in a specific manner, it should still be evaluated in the light of the overall philosophy of insurance buying before coverage is purchased to insure the unusual situation. For example, if a corporation has decided to assume the first thousand dollars of any property-damage loss, it would not be realistic to insure a $750 camera on an all-risk basis simply because it is different from the normal.

Indirect or consequential damage. The objective of any business is to make a profit, and you can only make a profit if you can continue to operate. The use of plant facilities, machinery, equipment, and almost all other types of tangible property are simply tools used to achieve the basic objective. The loss potential that might arise from direct damage to the physical facilities is generally readily recognized. Many businesses still have not recognized that they have a major indirect loss potential if their direct-damage loss is sufficient to interfere with their production or to cause additional expenses in order to continue to make the profit that is the objective of business.

The standard business-interruption forms for either manufacturing or non-manufacturing operations all have basically the same elements of protection. The primary function of a business-interruption policy is to provide recovery for the loss of profits suffered by the insured during the period of time it takes to restore the damaged property to its normal operating efficiency. In addition to paying for the loss of net profit, business-interruption insurance also pays for the recovery of normal continuing expenses such as salaries of key people, taxes, advertising costs, insurance expenses, etc., that would have been earned had no loss occurred.

The coverage also provides protection for any expediting expenses that are incurred to shorten the period of time that it takes to restore the damaged property to its normal efficiency. These expediting expenses are recoverable under the business-interruption policy only to the extent that they reduce the loss that the insurance company would otherwise have to pay if the expediting expenses were not incurred. For example, if a plant were shut down for 10 days because of damage to the facilities, and the normal loss of net profits and continuing expenses was $10,000 a day, the underwriters would be faced with a potential loss of $100,000. If by working repair crews overtime the period of time necessary to restore the damaged property is reduced from 10 to 6 days, thus reducing the insurance company's potential loss by $40,000, the insured would be able to recover any *extra* amount that he would have to pay because of the overtime, provided that the overtime premium did not exceed the $40,000 by which the loss would be reduced. It must be noted, however, that if the insured elects to incur expediting expenses in order to get back into production faster and the expenses are greater than the amount by which the loss would be reduced, then there will be no recovery for that extra amount under the business-interruption policy.

The establishment of the proper amount of insurance should be geared to the evaluation of the maximum time that it might take to restore the property. It is important to consider not only the time to reconstruct the building, but also the time required to replace the machinery. The most commonly selected figure for establishing a limit of insurance is the annual value of the net profit and continuing expenses. If the estimated period of restoration is less than a year, it is generally found that while it is possible to reduce the amount of insurance required, the rates go up with the reduction in the amount of insurance, and the net premium differential between the shorter term policy and the annual policy is generally not a significant amount.

Even though annual figures are generally used to establish the limit of insurance, it is important to note that the limit of *recovery* is the dollar amount of insurance and is not limited to 12 months following the date of the loss, nor is it limited to the policy period. Thus, in the event of a partial loss the insured could collect until the amount of insurance is exhausted, regardless of how long it takes to restore the property. If it took 2 years to replace a particular machine that affected a part of the operation, the insured could have full coverage for the loss in spite of the fact that he had bought insurance only on an annual basis.

Most business-interruption policies are subject to coinsurance requirements. The primary difficulty with complying with coinsurance requirements in a business-interruption policy is the fact that the test of compliance is based on the values at risk for the 12-month period *immediately following the loss*. It is, therefore, apparent that in order to be sure that he has complied with the coinsurance requirements, an insured must continually reevaluate his anticipated future operations or, alternatively, must deliberately purchase an amount of insurance in excess of his needs simply to be sure that the coinsurance requirements are met. An agreed-amount clause can be issued in most cases to nullify the penalty provisions of the coinsurance clause. This is an agreement between the insurance company and the insured that the amount of insurance in force is considered to be insufficient to satisfy the requirements of the coinsurance clause for a stipulated period of time. It is generally necessary to submit a report of values to the insurance company before they will issue such an agreed-amount clause.

Another alternative is the use of a premium adjustment form whereby the limits of insurance are established as estimates and the final earned premium is determined on the basis of the values that were actually at risk.

Business-interruption policies can be written in several different ways, but the two most common fire forms are the two-item form and the gross-earnings form. Basically, the two forms are quite similar. Under the two-item form one amount of insurance is established for the loss of net profits and continuing expenses, and a second amount of insurance is established for coverage of the so-called ordinary-payroll exposure.

The ordinary-payroll coverage is most often written for shorter periods of time than the protection granted for the loss of net profits and continuing expenses. The basic theory behind this reduced limit of protection for ordinary-payroll coverage is that in the event of a total loss it is generally not feasible to try to maintain the entire labor force of the company during the period of time that it takes to restore the property. The shorter period of protection does, however, allow the insured to continue to pay the entire labor force during short-term shutdowns or partial shutdowns arising out of insured damage, so that he may commence operations after the property has been restored with the same labor force that he has trained. Therefore, he can minimize the loss of efficiency that might otherwise result by having to obtain and train a new labor force.

The usual period of time selected for the ordinary-payroll coverage is 90 days, although it can be written for shorter periods of time or longer periods, or it may be excluded in its entirety.

The gross-earnings form originally provided one limit for the loss of net profits and continuing expenses including ordinary-payroll coverage. Other differences between the two forms were technical and relatively minor. The single limit of the gross-earnings form covering the same exposures that are insured under the two-item form by two separate limits gives greater flexibility to the insured. Thus, under the gross-earnings form the insured was purchasing a total amount of insurance that included the full amount of ordinary-payroll exposure, whether such coverage was desired or not. The gross-earnings form can now be amended by endorsement either to exclude ordinary-payroll coverage or to provide it for limited periods of time. This form also had the provision that the amount of loss would be reduced by any expense that could be eliminated if it was not necessary to enable the insured to start up production with the same quality of service or performance that existed at the time of the loss.

The amount of gross earnings is determined by taking the net sales and deducting the cost of materials and supplies. The coinsurance percentages are based on these figures. The amount of recovery, however, is based on the gross earnings, as previously defined, less any expenses that are not necessary to start up production with the same quality and performance. Thus, the insured has to purchase insurance on one basis in order to satisfy the coinsurance clause, but can collect only on a reduced basis.

In establishing the amount of insurance for the net profits and continuing expenses under the two-item form, it is possible to deduct not only the cost of materials and supplies, but also any expenses that would be discontinued during the course of restoration. Thus, an insured can recover on the same basis that he uses to establish the amount of insurance. The difficulty with this form, however, is that when the insured reduces the amount of insurance by the expenses that he expects to discontinue at the time of a loss, he is predetermining the course of action that he expects to take at the time of loss, and he loses the flexibility that he would have under the gross-earnings form.

Both the two-item form and the gross-earnings form are geared to the loss of profits and to the continuing expenses suffered by the insured during the period of time it takes to restore the damaged property. As indicated in Part 2 of this section, in some industries there can be a loss of contract sales that extends beyond the period of time that it takes to restore the damaged property.

In order to provide protection for this contingency, it is generally desirable to write the insurance on a gross-profits form where the measure of recovery is the loss of sales during the policy period, rather than the loss of profit during the period of restoration. This form is not readily available in the standard domestic markets, and if this type of protection is needed, coverage must generally be obtained through the use of the surplus or excess lines markets, or from one of the major industrial fire-insurance underwriting organizations.

The actual-loss-sustained form that is most often used in the boiler-and-machinery insurance field is very similar to the normal fire-insurance gross-earnings form except that it generally automatically excludes the ordinary-pay-roll coverage, which then has to be put back in by endorsement if it is so desired.

The boiler-and-machinery business-interruption coverage can be written with variable limits of liability for different types of objects insured. It is not necessary to buy the same amount of insurance for transformers or miscellaneous electrical apparatus that would be desired for the boiler-explosion exposure. The limits can be selected in keeping with the estimated time that it would take to restore the particular type of object insured. Each limit is generally subject to its own coinsurance percentages, but as with the fire-insurance policies, the coinsurance provisions can be voided for stipulated periods of time by the submission of reports of values.

In considering the objects to be insured under a boiler-and-machinery business-interruption policy, special consideration must be given to the loss potential that might result from an interruption in the power supply. If the insured owns its own generating facilities, the coverage would be treated in the same manner as any other piece of equipment. However, if the power is provided by public utilities or any other outside source, special off-premises power-interruption coverage would be required.

The boiler-and-machinery insurance companies also have available a "valued" form which provides protection on the basis of a stipulated daily amount which will be paid for each day that the total production of the plant is lost because of an insured accident to the insured equipment. This type of form is most beneficial where the production is constant and not subject to seasonal fluctuations. In using this valued form, it must be recognized that the limit of daily indemnity is payable in full only if the plant is totally shut down. Partial shutdowns will be recoverable on a correspondingly reduced basis. For example, if the plant suffers a 50 percent shutdown, then only 50 percent of the daily amount of insurance will be payable under the valued form business-interruption policy.

The loss that can cause the interruption in production can come from a number of different causes. Fire and windstorm are the two most prominent conditions that normally come to mind when it comes to this evaluation, and these perils are covered under the fire and extended-coverage approach. Normally, coverage should also be provided for vandalism, malicious mischief, and sprinkler leakage (if applicable). Consideration must also be given to the potential business-interruption losses that might occur from a boiler explosion or breakdown, or from damage to machinery or electrical apparatus.

Business-interruption insurance for losses caused by perils other than those normally covered by the fire and supplemental peril policies and the boiler-and-machinery policies, which would include such exposures as flood, earthquake, collapse, water damage, etc., is not standard in form and generally has to be tailor-made and written through the surplus lines or excess insurance markets.

The above discussion of the various business-interruption forms relates primarily to the exposure that would result from damage to the insured's own property. It is quite possible that an insured plant can be shut down just as quickly and just as effectively by a loss occurring at either a prime supplier's plant or at a principal customer's plant. If the insured's process is dependent upon a single processor or supplier for any part of the processing or the supplying of any particular material, it is necessary to investigate all possible secondary sources of supply and to review the amount of inventory that is maintained on hand or at the supplier's premises that could be used by the insured. If this evaluation shows that a major loss occurring at his supplier's premises could interrupt the flow of material into his plant and thus shut him down, then it would be desirable to purchase a contingent business-interruption policy insuring the loss of profit at his plant that results because of damage occurring at the supplier's plant. The dollar exposure would be the same as the insured's own business-interruption exposure. It will simply be a different cause of loss that will be insured.

A similar exposure exists if the major portion of the insured's production is made for a particular customer. If the customer's plant cannot accept the insured's production because of damage occurring to it, then his plant will be effectively shut down until he can establish additional markets for his production.

In addition to the aforementioned forms which are basically designed for use by manufacturing or mercantile operations, there are other types of policies designed for the protection of the loss of income that results from special types of situations.

A typical example of this type of form would be the rent-insurance form which provides for the protection of the loss of rental income to a landlord if the leased premises are damaged by an insurable peril. Such rent insurance can be written for the usual fire and supplemental perils, extended coverage, vandalism, malicious mischief, and sprinkler leakage, and it can also be written under the boiler-and-machinery insurance coverages. The amounts of insurance under this type of policy would be geared to the rental income that would be lost during the time it would take to restore the damaged premises.

Each lease should be reviewed to determine whether or not there is an abatement clause in it which would eliminate the lessee's responsibility to pay rent if the premises were damaged by fire, or any similar type of casualty, so that they could not be used. If there is no abatement clause in the lease, then the lessee is the one that generally needs to provide this protection, because he will still have the obligation to pay the rent regardless of whether he has the use of the premises or not.

Similar types of specialty coverages are available for the protection of commissions of selling agents where the selling agent's income is dependent upon the manufacturer's ability to supply merchandise to the agent to sell. Another similar exposure is the loss of tuition and fees at schools.

In some situations, the indirect loss does not necessarily mean a curtailment in production and loss of profits, but it does mean that alternate methods have to be used to continue the production, which thus generates extra expense. Part of such extra expense would be recoverable under a basic business-interruption policy providing that the amount of loss otherwise payable by the insurance company would be reduced by at least as much as the extra expense. There are, however, occasions when in order to maintain customers and for other reasons, an insured may decide to incur additional expenses above and beyond what would be recoverable under the basic policies. For example, a machine shop that suffered damage by an insured peril might well decide to subcontract the work out to other shops, even at a premium, in order to maintain customer relations by completion of the contract. Another example would be where a facility actually produced no income or profit, such as an insured's own warehousing operation, where a loss at the warehouse would simply mean that additional space would have to be obtained to continue operations, but a premium might have to be paid for such space. This would also be an area where an extra-expense policy would be applicable.

Another form of indirect loss potential that needs special treatment arises where an insured may make improvements to a leased property and then lose the value of the improvement because damage occurring to the balance of the property is sufficient to cause cancellation of the lease. As an illustration, let us assume that a tenant of a store building put a new storefront on the building, including show windows, etc., and a major fire burns out 50 percent of the building, but does not damage the improvements. If the building is restored, there is no problem. If the lease permits or provides for termination if the damage is 50 percent or more, then the insured may lose the value of his improvements even though they were not damaged. In order to protect this possible exposure, it is necessary to write leasehold-interest insurance which will provide protection for this type of loss.

Another indirect exposure arises from the possibility of the demolition of an undamaged portion of a building by order of civil authority and the additional expenditures that might be required in order to rebuild the building in conformity with the present-day building codes. Demolition and increased costs of construction coverage can be added by endorsement to building insurance policies that will provide protection for these exposures.

The protection of the Accounts Receivables can be taken care of either by insuring the records or by duplicating through microfilm or some other process, or by the use of duplicate records. Insurance can be written for this exposure which will not only pay for the cost to reconstruct the records, but will also pay for the receivables that are lost because of the inability to collect following the destruction of the records.

The insurance written for this type of exposure is geared basically to the fire-insurance rate, but is adjusted with credits or debits depending upon the type of receptacle in which the accounts-receivable records are kept when they are not being worked upon. Coverage is usually written on a reporting basis, so that the insured would be able to maintain a satisfactory limit of protection, yet pay premium on the actual exposure at risk.

Another type of consequential insurance that can be used beneficially in the sales campaigns of companies is credit insurance. Under this type of coverage the insured is not concerned particularly with the question of physical damage occurring at a customer's premises, but he is interested in insuring the solvency of his customer. Credit insurance would provide reimbursement for unpaid accounts in the event that the customer goes bankrupt and cannot pay his bills.

There are a very limited number of insurance companies in this field and the forms are fairly standardized. However, they are quite complicated in the application of formulas and other conditions that relate to the amount of protection that would be available for an insured at any given time for any particular customer. This coverage is almost always written with a very substantial deductible which is geared to the insured's normal bad-debt figures. The amounts of protection for an individual customer depend upon the customer's credit rating *at the time of shipment* rather than at the time the order was taken. If the customer's credit rating has decreased between the time the order was taken and the time the property is shipped, the limit of recovery could be substantially reduced from what was anticipated at the time the order was accepted.

Similar credit-insurance facilities are available for export shipments through the Foreign Credit Insurance Association and through the Export-Import Bank. These policies are written, basically, to cover against the insolvency of the customer, and, in addition, provide protection for any loss that the shipper might suffer through political risks in having his property quarantined, seized, or nationalized.

Liability. There are two basic liability exposures to which almost all business enterprises are subjected. These are—

1. The liability arising out of the insured's general operations, meaning the maintenance, operation, and use of his premises, the activities of his employees, and the liability that arises out of the use of his products

2. The liability that might arise out of the ownership, maintenance, operation, or use of automobiles

When talking about liability, we are talking about the responsibility for damage
to property of others, or for injury to members of the public.

Unlike insurance for damage to an insured's own property, where he knows
the value of the property and therefore the possible loss, the liability exposure
cannot be measured accurately, because it cannot be determined what amount
of damage will be sustained until the loss occurs. It is, therefore, vital to provide adequate limits of liability insurance that will take care of the extreme
losses as well as the smaller claims which are more likely to occur.

There is sometimes a tendency to restrict the limits of liability that are purchased, particularly by smaller concerns, to something in the neighborhood of
the net assets of the company. The theory generally advanced supporting this
approach is that if the assets of the company are only $300,000, it is unneces-
sary to provide liability insurance for a greater limit than $300,000. This is
completely erroneous reasoning, because the assets of the company will always
be subject to attachment *after* the liability limits of the insurance program are
exhausted. Therefore, the lower the limits of insurance, the more susceptible
the assets come to being used to satisfy an uninsured claim.

Limits of liability can generally be purchased in one of two basic ways. The
first is the method that has been in use for many, many years—the selection of
a limit of liability for each person that might be injured in an accident, a secondary limit for all persons that might be injured in one accident, and a third
limit for the amount of property damage that would be involved in one accident.
An alternate to this approach is the increasingly popular combined single
limit that establishes one limit overall for all claims that may be brought against
the insured as the result of any one accident or occurrence.

The liabilities arising out of the general operations of an insured can be
covered in several different ways. There are the schedule policy forms, such
as the manufacturer's and contractor's form, the owner's, landlord's, and tenant's
form, and other similar forms that have been designed to insure a specific
exposure. And then there is the more commonly used form, the comprehensive general-liability policy. The primary difference is that under the schedule
form of policy, the insured selects specific exposures that he wants to insure and
purchases insurance to protect him against such claims. Under the comprehensive form, the insured is theoretically providing coverage not only for the
known hazards that exist at the beginning of the policy period, but also for
any new hazards that might develop during the policy year. It should be
noted, however, that even though the comprehensive general-liability form is
probably the broadest of the basic policy forms available, it still has its own
limitations, conditions, and exclusions, and therefore should not be construed

to apply to all liability exposures that might arise during the course of the policy period.

The rating structure should develop the same cost for any specific exposure regardless of whether that exposure is insured under a schedule policy form or under a comprehensive form. Accordingly, the comprehensive general-liability form is invariably used unless the insured is purchasing insurance for an additional interest or some specific exposure that has nothing to do with his operations, but for which he has assumed an obligation to provide insurance. Therefore, our comments will be geared primarily to the protection afforded under the standard comprehensive general-liability policy.

Under the provisions of the comprehensive general-liability form, the insurance company agrees to pay on behalf of the insured any claims that may be brought against him, if he is legally liable therefor, which arise out of his operations. In addition to paying any claims, the insurance company will also provide legal defense against any alleged claims, whether valid or not, as long as the cause of the action falls within the terms of the general-liability policy.

The bodily-injury insuring agreement will pay for claims that arise from bodily injury, sickness, disease, or death resulting therefrom, arising out of an occurrence insured under the policy. It will not pay for the so-called personal-injury type of claims such as libel, slander, defamation of character, invasion of privacy, etc. These additional coverages can be added to the comprehensive general-liability policy by endorsement. The normal personal-injury endorsement will pick up the libel, slander, defamation of character, etc., type of claim, except for claims arising out of broadcasting and advertising activities.

The newer form of the comprehensive general-liability policy provides protection for claims arising out of an "occurrence." The older forms, unless amended by endorsement, provided coverage only if the claim arose out of an "accident." The term "occurrence" includes not only anything that would be covered by the term "accident," but in addition covers claims that might result from repeated exposure to a given condition that results in either bodily injury, sickness, disease, or property damage.

Under the basic insuring agreements protection is granted for liability arising out of the insured's operations and also for any liability that he may assume under contract. The contractual-liability coverage, however, is restricted later on in the policy, by the exclusions and definitions, to limit the contractual protection to apply only to "incidental" contracts which are lease of premises, easement agreements, railroad-sidetrack agreements, elevator or escalator maintenance agreements, and agreements required by municipal ordinance. Thus, if an insured assumes any liabilities under any other agreements or contracts, he does not have automatic protection under the comprehensive general-liability policy. This can be amended either by endorsing the policy to pick up specific assumptions of liability or by endorsing it on a blanket basis to pick up all assumptions of liability.

It should be noted that when a blanket contractual-liability endorsement is added to the policy, it is, in effect, a separate grant of coverage and is subject to its own basic terms and conditions, insuring agreements, and exclusions. Therefore, changes that may be made in the basic comprehensive general-liability policy will not automatically be made in the blanket contractual-liability coverage. For example, the extension of the basic policy to include personal-injury coverage would not extend the personal-injury coverage to the blanket contractual-liability endorsement unless it is so stated. Similarly, the deletion of any particular exclusion that is in both the basic policy form and in the blanket contractual endorsement form would not apply to both unless it is specifically so stated.

The basic policy form generally covers liability exposures existing in or occurring in the United States or Canada. With respect to the products-liability exposure, however, coverage is extended to apply on a worldwide basis provided that the product that causes the claim was originally designed for sale or use in the United States or Canada. Therefore, any product that is manufactured for export outside of the United States or Canada would not be covered by the products-liability provision of the general-liability policy unless the territorial definition is amended. Similarly, an employee traveling abroad on a business trip would not be protected by the general-liability policy unless the territorial definition has been extended.

The exclusions in the comprehensive general-liability policy fall into three basic categories—

1. Exclusion of exposures that are generally otherwise insured. In this category would be the exclusion of the automobile exposure, employer's-liability coverage, workmen's compensation, etc.
2. Exclusion of exposures that the underwriters do not generally want to insure under any circumstance. The principal exclusions in this category would be the liability for the cost of recalling defective, or allegedly defective products, claims resulting from such recall, professional liability, liability for damage to property owned by the insured, or any other amendment in the property-damage liability coverage that would have the effect of changing the third-party liability policy into a first-party property damage policy.
3. Exclusion of exposures which the underwriters do not generally want to assume without having an opportunity to evaluate and underwrite them individually. These are exclusions that can be deleted and have coverage afforded for an additional premium charge. Some of the major exposures along this line would be liability for damage to property of others in your care, custody, or control; the liquor-law liability exclusion; and the blasting, explosion, and underground property exclusions (known as the x, c, u exclusion).

Automobile-liability insurance can be written on either a scheduled basis or on a comprehensive basis.

On a scheduled automobile policy, the insurance is granted only for a particular vehicle, but under certain conditions it does apply to any newly acquired or additional vehicles. The policy applies to the ownership, maintenance, operation, or use of the particular automobile and would not provide coverage for any liability arising out of the operation, maintenance, or use of any hired or leased car. Nor would it apply to any liability for the operation of any nonowned car, such as an employee's use of his own car on company business.

On a comprehensive basis, the policy applies to any liability arising out of the ownership, maintenance, or use of *any* vehicles, and in addition, provides coverage automatically for hired vehicles or nonowned vehicles, unless they are excluded by notation in the declarations of the policy.

With respect to providing coverage for hired vehicles, it should be noted that the coverage is generally a contingent coverage and applies only if the primary coverage provided by the owner was inadequate, or for some other reason did not apply to the particular accident.

In view of the fact that the general-liability policy specifically excludes automobile exposures, it is generally advisable to provide the automobile insurance and the general-liability insurance in the same insurance company, so that there is less possibility of dispute between insurance companies regarding claims arising out of the controversial loading and unloading hazard.

Special types of liability situations, such as advertisers' liability, architects' and engineers' professional liability, other types of professional liability, marine liabilities, officers' and directors' liability, liquor-law liability, and aviation liability, are generally handled as separate situations and most often are written by only a few underwriters who specialize in the particular problem.

The umbrella liability form has come into increasing use as a means of providing catastrophe limits over and above the coverages provided by the basic policies. The basic policies generally considered under an umbrella policy are the comprehensive general liability, automobile liability, employer's-liability section of the workmen's-compensation coverage, and advertisers' liability. From a premium point of view, the use of the umbrella liability policy is often more economical than simply providing increased limits under the basic coverages. There are no rating schedules for umbrella liability, and consequently the insurance-company underwriters have more flexibility to use their own judgment in establishing the premium that they require for the particular risk.

In addition to providing catastrophe limits, the umbrella liability form generally provides broader coverage than is normally written under the basic policies. Any coverage that is afforded under the umbrella liability form which is not covered by a basic policy is subject to a fairly substantial deductible, generally $10,000 or $25,000. Thus the insured is protected on a catastrophe basis against the remote exposures not covered by the basic policies, but he would not be covered for small claims.

In reviewing any umbrella liability proposal, it is important to ascertain whether or not the coverage being offered will provide legal defense against any claims brought against you. The evaluation of the defense provisions should encompass not only the question of whether the umbrella liability underwriter will participate in the defense of a claim that is covered by a basic policy, but also whether the umbrella liability underwriter will provide defense for claims that come under the areas that are insured under the umbrella policy which are not insured under the basic policies.

The foregoing comments can be applied basically to almost all business operations. Each type of business endeavor, however, has somewhat different exposures, and therefore may require different adjustments in the provision of their basic liability coverages. For example, the provision of personal-injury coverage (covering claims for false arrest, libel, slander, defamation of character, etc.) would be far more important to a retailer than it would be to a manufacturer. Similarly, a contractor would be much more concerned about the provision of blanket contractual-liability coverage and the elimination of the general exclusions relating to blasting, excavating, and other underground work, than would a manufacturer. The special types of liability, such as professional liability or malpractice, or errors and omissions coverage, would apply primarily to professional services rendered by the insured. The main point is to make sure to evaluate the operations to determine whether or not some of these exposures exist in the insured's operations.

4. General comments on employee-benefits insurance

The cost of employee-benefit insurance is, generally speaking, the largest portion of the total insurance expenditures of almost any business.

The employee-benefit coverages that we speak of provide for—

An income if employees are sick or disabled and cannot earn their usual income
Reimbursement for hospital, surgical, and medical expenses
Death benefits

In the provision of insurance for the continuing income of a disabled worker there are two breakdowns, namely, those benefits that are payable because of occupational injuries or illness (workmen's compensation), and benefits that are payable for nonoccupational accidents and illnesses.

Workmen's-compensation benefits are established by state legislation in all of our states and territories. These benefits are changed periodically by the various legislatures to keep up with the economy, the general wage levels, and the cost of medical services. The provision of the necessary guarantees for the payment of benefits to the employees varies from state to state. There are at the present time six states that prohibit the use of commercial insurance to satisfy the obligations of the employer to his employees. In these six states the coverage is provided by state funds.

In the other states insurance is either required or permitted. In some of the states where insurance is permitted, the employer is also allowed to self-insure the risk if he so desires and can satisfy the state authorities that he has sufficient financial resources to absorb the cost of such a self-insured program. In order to satisfy the authorities it is generally necessary to put up financial security in the form of bonds, or excess or catastrophe insurance policies, or both. It is also generally advisable to retain an outside service which has the personnel and facilities to provide loss prevention and inspection work that is so necessary in keeping accident frequency down. This service will also provide the necessary claim-handling service in the cases where the compensation board of the particular state is involved.

The rates for compensation insurance are established by the state rating authorities, and all carriers writing business in a particular state are obliged to use the same rate schedule. Each classification of business has a basic manual rate in each state. The manual rate is adjusted periodically to reflect the loss experience that has been developed within that particular classification of employment.

Although the requirements differ from state to state, most employers will be subject to experience rating also. Under the experience-rating concept, the individual employer is measured against the average for his industry in the state. If his experience is better than average, then he enjoys a credit as compared to the manual rate. If his experience is worse than the average, he will be penalized with a debit rate as compared to the manual rate. The experience-rating application is compulsory for all those employers who develop enough premium to be qualified for experience rating. The qualifications vary somewhat from state to state. Here again all insurance companies providing workmen's-compensation coverage are obliged to use the same experience-rating modification factor.

Inasmuch as the manual rates and the experience modification factors are all determined by state rating authorities for use by all insurance companies, the only area where the employer has an option about the ultimate cost of his program lies in the manner in which he is going to develop the premium.

The starting point for all premium adjustment plans is the "standard premium," which is developed by multiplying the manual rate by the experience modification factor and then by the developed payroll. This standard premium will be the same regardless of whether the insurance is written by a stock company or a mutual company. Under the premium-discount method of premium determination, the standard premium as developed by the audit of the payroll is the final premium. This is then modified by a discount factor that is geared simply to the volume of the standard premium. The size of the discount varies by state, and it also varies depending upon whether or not the insurance carrier is a stock or a mutual company. The discounted premium, where a stock company is writing the insurance, is then the final premium. Where a mutual company is writing the insurance, the discounted premium is then subject to the dividend of that particular mutual company.

The principal alternate to the premium-discount, or guaranteed-cost program of premium development is a retrospective plan. This plan is more fully discussed in the part of this section dealing with insurance markets and purchasing concepts.

There are also loss ratio dividend plans that are a combination of the premium discount and retrospective plans.

There are several things to watch out for when writing workmen's-compensation insurance. It should be remembered that the workmen's-compensation policy insures the employer for the statutory obligations that he has under the workmen's compensation law of the states which are specifically named in the policy. If he becomes subject to the workmen's compensation laws of a state not listed in the policy, he will *not* have the benefit of protection under the standard workmen's-compensation policy. This can be amended by the addition of an all-state, or universal, endorsement to the policy which in effect provides reimbursement protection for the employer for any obligations that he may have in any states not listed in the policy.

In addition, it should be noted that in some states the requirements for an employer to become eligible under the workmen's compensation laws may not be met, and therefore employees that he may have in that particular state would not be covered by any protection whatsoever. This situation can be remedied by putting a voluntary-compensation endorsement on this policy which extends benefits to any employee in any state who does not come under the workmen's compensation law of any state.

It is also important to recognize the limitations in benefits in certain of the states. This is particularly true in regard to the coverage for medical expenses. Certain states have limited protection insofar as the reimbursement for medical expenses is concerned, and in these states it is common practice to endorse the workmen's-compensation policy to voluntarily provide higher limits of medical-expense coverage for employees who may be injured in those states.

In certain states coverage does not apply to executive officers unless the policy is properly endorsed to reflect the intent to grant such coverage.

The second feature of the standard workmen's-compensation policy is that it provides liability protection to the employer for any suits or claims that may be brought against him arising out of an injury or illness to an employee. This protection would be necessary where the suits may be brought by a third party, such as an employee's wife, or claims made for medical expenses or doctor's fees that the workmen's-compensation board does not believe are reasonable, and thus are not covered in full under the workmen's-compensation benefits. The normal limit of protection in this employers'-liability section is $25,000. In view of current-day attitudes towards suits and the size of awards being granted by judges and juries, it is found that most employers increase this limit of employers'-liability protection to at least $100,000. The increased premium charge for this addititonal protection is usually quite nominal.

The occupational disease laws of most states are not quite so all-inclusive as the protection for occupational accidents. This is another reason to maintain adequate limits of employers'-liability coverage.

It should also be noted that in some states the acceptance of the workmen's compensation law as provided by the legislature is purely voluntary, and an employer can elect to reject the Workmen's Compensation Act and all of its ramifications. If an employer does elect to reject the Workmen's Compensation Act under such conditions, an employee who would be injured in the course of his occupation would have to sue his employer. The employer, however, by the rejection of the Workmen's Compensation Act also loses the protection of his common-law defenses, making it very difficult to defend against most claims made by employees. As a result, there are very few companies that elect to decline the workmen's compensation law.

The workmen's compensation laws of the various states also vary in the extent to which they will provide benefits to employees working out of the state and out of the country. It is therefore desirable, when employees may be working abroad for any extended period of time, to make sure that the policy is endorsed with a foreign-coverage endorsement which extends the basic workmen's-compensation benefits of the state of hire of the employee to any United States citizen abroad. This foreign-coverage endorsement does not extend the workmen's-compensation benefits to foreign nationals, nor is it in any way intended to comply with any laws or regulations that might exist in the foreign country relating to the provision of workmen's compensation or similar coverage.

Nonoccupational accidents and illnesses also require insurance by the employer in certain states. However, coverage is often provided by employers in other states, regardless of whether or not they are required by law to furnish such protection. Even in the statutory states benefits are quite often provided by employers in excess of the statutory requirements.

The usual form of accident-and-sickness insurance or disability insurance is for a relatively short term, with 26 weeks being the most common period of coverage. The accident-and-sickness coverage provides solely for a reimbursement of income during the period that the employee is unable to earn his normal living because of a nonoccupational accident or disease. The benefits are usually determined as a percentage of the employee's normal earnings in the same manner as compensation benefits. Or, they may be derived from an incremental schedule which is also geared to earnings. This coverage is generally written with a waiting period so as to exclude the payment of income benefits for any nominal situation that keeps the employee out of work for only a day or two.

While workmen's compensation and disability insurance together provide some protection for the employee's loss of income during periods of short-term disability, there has been nothing that would pay for the really catastrophic situation where an employee was totally and permanently disabled. In recent years, long-term-disability insurance has been developed to take care of this major exposure.

The general philosophy of the long-term-disability insurance is protection against a total disability which would prevent the employee from ever working again. Accordingly, the main objective is to provide an income from the commencement of the disability, either for life or at least until the normal retirement age. In order to make the premium for this coverage realistic, the coverage is generally written with a substantial waiting period before the payments commence. The waiting periods may vary anywhere from 30 days to 6 months or to a year, but it seems that the most common waiting period being utilized by industry today is a 6-month waiting period.

The long-term-disability coverage is generally written to apply to both occupational and nonoccupational disabilities. Benefits are generally established as a percentage of the basic income, but without the relatively low limits that normally are provided by workmen's compensation or short-term-disability benefits. The programs can be tailor-made to suit any particular requirements. The normal percentage of basic earnings that is used to establish the benefits generally runs between 50 and 70 percent, up to a maximum benefit of $1,000 per month. Benefits payable under the long-term-disability program are generally offset by other benefits that might be collectible under workmen's compensation, other disability insurance programs, or from the disability provisions of the Social Security program.

When developing a long-term-disability program, it is important to make sure that it dovetails with the disability provisions in any pension or profit-sharing plan, as well as with any short-term-disability program that may be in existence, workmen's compensation, and Social Security benefits.

Hospitalization insurance is well known in its general purpose. There are two basic approaches to the problem of providing hospitalization coverage. One basis is known as a service-type program and is generally used by most of the Blue Cross organizations. Under the service-type program, coverage is generally available for the cost of semiprivate hospital room and board accommodations and all of the miscellaneous hospital expenses. The hospitalization policy covers only charges made by the hospital and will, therefore, not pay for charges made by doctors, surgeons, anesthetists, or other technicians who may be called upon for special tests. Under the service-type plan the benefits are generally limited by a period of time rather than by a dollar limit.

The alternate approach is the provision of stipulated limits of recovery for the two major categories of expense. That is, a separate limitation, both as to daily amount and the total amount, would apply for room and board charges, and a separate limit would apply to the charges for miscellaneous hospital expenses.

Under most hospitalization plans there is some degree of coverage for outpatient charges which are made by the hospital for the use of their facilities when a confinement is not involved. The extent of the benefits in this particular area varies considerably and therefore should be checked carefully. Hospitalization insurance is generally written to apply to the employee and to his dependents.

Most group-insurance companies have recently incorporated in their hospitalization policies a "coordination-of-benefits" clause. This is designed to eliminate the situation where a person could be insured as an employee under one group-insurance plan, and as a dependent under the group-insurance plan of his spouse, and consequently make a profit by being sick. The application of the coordination-of-benefits clause varies somewhat among companies, and not all companies recognize it. The basic purpose is to have the benefits charged to the program that insures the person as an employee. Any differential between the actual expense and the benefits received under the employee program would be covered under the group program where the person was insured as a dependent.

The advent of the Federal Medicare program and the various state Medicaid programs has created many conflicting, contradictory, and confusing situations. At this writing, so many of them are still in such a state of flux that we can give no concrete advice on the relation of a standard hospitalization program with these two governmental programs. It is extremely important, however, to recognize the existence of this problem, so that you can work out a satisfactory combination of benefits with your insurance carrier.

Surgical-medical insurance is designed to pay the doctor's fees, or a portion thereof for the services he renders. Anesthetist's charges are often included as part of the surgical schedule. The standard surgical schedule pays a stipulated amount for any surgical procedure. At the present time, the majority of surgical schedules are geared to a fixed dollar limit. It is anticipated, however, that surgical insurance will be purchased more and more on what is known as a "relative-value schedule," wherein the payment for each surgical procedure is measured against every other surgical procedure in terms of its complexity, and the protection is bought in units. This gives a greater spread between the complex and simple operations than is the case with a schedule with a fixed dollar limit.

Medical insurance is designed to pay the doctor for treating illnesses that do not require surgery. This coverage can be bought to apply to hospital visits only, or in its broadened form, can apply to home and office visits as well.   The normal procedure in this case is to provide a limit of a fixed number of dollars per visit for a stipulated period of time up to a maximum dollar amount.

Blue Shield surgical-medical programs often contain service provisions whereby the doctors and surgeons who participate in the Blue Shield program agree that they will not charge a person more than the benefit indicated in the regular Blue Shield schedule if the employee has annual earnings less than certain stipulated levels.   The existence of the service-type contracts and the income levels at which they are effective vary between the many different Blue Shield programs.

While the basic hospitalization and surgical-medical programs take care of the normal illnesses often encountered in the raising of a family, there are still tremendous expenses that are incurred for major illnesses not covered by the basic hospitalization and surgical-medical programs.   Major-medical coverage has been designed to cover this gap in protection.   This major-medical insurance is primarily catastrophe insurance to apply to virtually all expenses incurred as a result of accidents or illnesses.   It is not necessary that the person be hospitalized in order to come under the major-medical coverage.   This coverage will protect you against major expenses incurred while confined at home, and will pay for the doctor's and surgeon's charges that may exceed the amounts collectible under the surgical-medical program.   It will also pay for any hospital expenses incurred after the exhaustion of the basic hospitalization program as well as nursing costs.   The major-medical insurance is written as catastrophe insurance and is, therefore, generally written subject to deductibles and on a participating basis.

Group life insurance was originally designed to provide a burial-expense benefit for employees.   In the last few decades this coverage has been expanded substantially in many areas, so that it not only continues to perform its original purpose, but also now provides sufficient amounts to serve as a basic cornerstone of an employee's overall life-insurance program.   At times it is also used as an inducement by employers to attract key personnel.

The principle of group life insurance is simply the averaging of the life-insurance rate for all employees covered under the plan and charging only for the pure mortality charges plus administrative charges.   This is the lowest-cost form of life insurance an employee can obtain, particularly where the administrative requirements of many states limit the amount of premium that can be charged to the employee for contributory insurance.   Thus the employer is invariably paying a part, if not all, of the cost of this insurance.

In most states there is no limit on the amount of group life insurance that can be established for any one class of insured employees, although there are still some states that have a $40,000 limit.   It should, however, be noted that the premiums for anything over $50,000 of group life insurance have to be declared in accordance with the schedule established by the Federal government as additional remuneration to the employee and taxes paid on that premium.

One of the features of group insurance is that all people in a given class are eligible for this insurance without having to be individually underwritten from a medical, moral, or financial point of view. Thus, the advantage to some employees is twofold in that it provides protection at the lowest possible cost for the employee, and second, it guarantees that he can get the insurance which he might not be able to get as an individual.

In life insurance, and some of the hospitalization and surgical plans, the employee is also guaranteed the right to convert his group insurance from a group program to an individual policy upon the termination of his employment under the group plan. While he has to pay the premium that would be payable for the age at which he is making this conversion, he nevertheless is at least assured of having an insurance market to provide him with the coverage that he requires.

The requirements to establish a "group" for the provision of various types of group insurance varies among companies. In some cases it is possible to get group insurance for groups of four employees or more. On smaller groups of this type, the coverage that is available is generally a predetermined package policy offering by the insurance company, and they may require some amount of individual underwriting, particularly as regards medical history.

As groups grow larger, the inflexible package policies offered by the insurance company begin to change and the insured is given the flexibility to develop the program that he requires. Thus, it is apparent that as the account grows in size, the importance of the insurance aspect of it becomes less and less because it becomes a self-rated risk over a period of time, and the insurance company's function then becomes one primarily of service rather than of providing insurance protection.

When the group becomes almost completely experienced rated on their own account (and it does not take more than 150 employees with most group programs to achieve this level), the true cost of the program is not so much the premiums that are charged, but—

The net costs that are retained by the insurance company as its cost of doing business

The reserves that are retained by the insurance company as its protection against termination of coverage

The losses that are developed by the benefits being granted

In most cases, the losses will be the same, if the benefits are the same, regardless of who the insurance carrier is, and thus the only true measure among competitive carriers is the service that they provide, the amount of retention, and the reserves.

In order to get a true evaluation of the cost of the program, it is necessary to make sure that when you are comparing retentions of various companies, you include all items that make up the retention. Many companies will leave the taxes out of the figures that they consider to be a retention, while other companies will include it. Second, some companies will not include any of the reserves that they call "statutory reserves," nor do they include assessments made by the states for disability insurance. Others will include these items. It is apparent that you must obtain a breakdown of these items when comparing insurance companies, and that you do not simply compare what one insurance company calls "retention" with what another insurance company will call its "retention."

Similarly, with regard to reserves, it is necessary to find out whether or not any unused reserves are returnable to the insured at the time of termination, or whether the reserves belong to the insurance company. It should be determined from the insurance company whether its agreements regarding the handling of reserves apply at any time, or only if the policy is terminated on an anniversary date. It is common practice among many group-insurance companies to stipulate that they are accountable only for any earned dividend or accounting of reserves if the termination is made on an anniversary date. If termination is effected at any time other than an anniversary date, the insurance company may not be accountable to the insured for the money that it has been holding for years to pay the contingent expenses that would be developed at termination.

Travel-accident insurance is written to provide accidental death and dismemberment benefits for employees who are accidentally killed or injured during the course of travel on company business. Coverage can be extended so as to apply to all travel, including both business and pleasure, or, as is more commonly done, it can be written to apply only while the employee is traveling on a business trip. If the coverage is written only for business travel, it is generally advisable to make sure that the policy is extended to grant coverage for so-called "personal deviations" during the course of the business trip. Thus, if an employee was away on a business trip for two weeks or more and during the weekends he did a little traveling for his own personal pleasure, such travel would be covered inasmuch as the basic purpose of the trip was a business trip.

In addition to providing accidental death and dismemberment coverage, the travel-accident policies can also be extended to provide medical-expense benefits and weekly-indemnity coverage. If the policy is limited solely to business travel, then the coverages provided under both the medical-expense and weekly-indemnity provisions are generally a duplication of the benefits that would be available to the employee under the workmen's compensation laws. The need for additional weekly-indemnity coverage may still be pertinent because of the relatively low benefits that are available to the higher-paid employees under the workmen's compensation laws, but in most cases, the medical-expense coverage would be fully taken care of by the compensation laws, except in those states that have restricted or limited medical provisions.

If the travel-accident policy is written to provide coverage for personal travel as well, then the medical-expense coverage would be a duplication of the available group-hospital, surgical-medical, and major-medical coverage and would be really necessary only as an additional limit of coverage, or where there may be no basic group-hospital, surgical-medical, or major-medical coverage. Similarly, the weekly-indemnity coverage for a policy that provides for personal travel would act as additional coverage and may not be necessary if the employee has accident-and-sickness coverage on both the short-term and long-term basis.

This travel-accident coverage can be bought in a variety of ways. The most limited form is one which provides protection only while traveling on specified types of conveyances, such as aircraft. The next step up the line in broadening coverage would be a policy that would provide coverage while traveling in any public conveyance, and the next step would be one that would provide coverage while traveling in any conveyance, including private passenger automobiles. The form that we find most commonly used, however, is one that provides coverage for any accident occurring while on a business trip. This coverage is written like any other group-insurance coverage, so as to provide protection on an automatic basis to various classes of employees. It can be written to provide protection for specified individuals, but this is generally the most cumbersome and the most expensive way of providing coverage.

Generally speaking, the insured employee has the right to designate his beneficiary under the accidental death and dismemberment provisions, and as with the group-life insurance, the manner in which the beneficiary is designated should be carefully worked out with the employee's own attorney to make sure that he gets the full benefits from any applicable tax laws relating to the payment of the proceeds of such group travel-accident or life-insurance policies. At the present time, the tax applications are not exactly the same for travel-accident benefits as they are for group-life benefits, and consequently both areas should be thoroughly explored when making the appropriate beneficiary designation.

5. Insurance markets and purchasing concepts

Having thoroughly evaluated the operations of the company to determine what the risks are and what type of protection you wish to obtain, you now must find the best way to implement the desired program. There are many people that still consider insurance to be pretty much of a standardized commodity and believe that the same product can be produced by any insurance company, and therefore, it does not matter much what approach is taken, since all companies will provide the same protection at the same cost. This is not correct, especially for the larger buyers. There *can* be competition—not only among similar types of insurance companies, but also among different insurance markets.

There are three basic types of insurance companies—stock, mutual, and reciprocal.

The basic difference between stock and mutual companies is simply that the stock insurance company is owned by the investors who have put up their money for the capitalization of the company and therefore are entitled to the profits that the company may make. The mutual insurance company is owned by the policyholders, and any profits that they make are distributed to the policyholders in the form of dividends. A reciprocal insurance company is, for all practical purposes, almost the same as a mutual company.

It used to be that agents and brokers represented stock companies only, whereas mutual insurance companies were represented by their own salesmen. It can no longer be assumed, however, that the stock insurance companies are represented only by agencies and brokers. There are several large stock insurance companies that while espousing the agency philosophy, nevertheless operate completely as direct writers. By the same token, there are mutual companies that pay commissions and are now being represented by brokers rather than by their own direct salesmen. And there are other companies that operate in both manners.

Similarly, the dividend is no longer the sole property of the mutual company. There are again several major participating stock companies, and there are also stock insurance companies which operate on the usual fixed or guaranteed cost concept, and at the same time offer various participating plans for certain classes of business. It is, therefore, apparent that in the selection of an insurance company, the differential between stock and mutual is no longer of any significant difference. The more progressive brokers have recognized the need to make available to their insureds the total insurance market rather than one limited segment of it. Therefore they represent both stock and mutual companies on either a commission basis or a fee basis.

The principal differences among companies is not so much the type of company, but the rating bureau the company belongs to and the rate filings it has made with the various state governmental authorities. Basically, all members of a particular rating bureau are committed to follow the filings of that bureau and must use the same rates as their fellow members. Therefore, the competition among these types of companies is minimized. There are, however, some areas where some degree of flexibility is allowed the individual underwriter, and in these areas you would be able to anticipate some element of competition.

The differences between the major mutual and stock company rating bureaus are relatively slight. In many cases they use exactly the same basic rate filings. Another area that the insured can look to for competition is the large major companies that have made independent rate filings, so that their rate structure is different from that to which the bureau members subscribe.

Separate rate filings are also made by some of the companies that specialize in a particular line of insurance. The different rate filings may mean nothing more than a deviation from the standard, or it may mean a completely separate approach to the development of the rating structures. For example, the fire rates which are used by almost all stock and mutual companies are developed on the fundamental premise that the *construction of the building* is the paramount factor in the establishment of the proper rate for any particular insured. This basic rate is then adjusted by credits or debits, depending upon the type of protection afforded and the risk of the occupancy exposures and other factors, to come up with a final rate. The Factory Mutual companies take a diametrically opposed approach based on the premise that the *occupancy* is the paramount factor. The basic occupancy charge is then adjusted by credits and debits for building construction and protection to arrive at a final rate.

The point is not which approach is correct, but recognition of the fact that two contrary rate structures, or rating philosophies, have been used by major insurance companies for over 100 years. Both have survived, so that neither one can be considered right and the other wrong. Thus, an insured must recognize that there is no absolute rating structure or formula. If a company submits a proposal that differs substantially from other quotations, it does not necessarily mean that the company submitting this quotation is a cut-rate company.

In addition to the standard insurance markets as represented by the stock and mutual companies, there is also a substantial market known as the excess or surplus lines market. These companies are not licensed to do business in most states. This might present some problems at the time of a loss, but if the insured stays with the surplus lines carriers that are on the "approved" list of most states, he is not likely to have too much of a problem. The primary function of these excess or surplus lines companies is to provide an insurance market for those risks that the standard markets will not provide. Originally, this was construed to apply only to situations where the normal markets have the coverage available, but have declined to provide the coverage for a particular insured for various reasons. As corporate insurance buyers became more sophisticated and recognized that the standard insurance markets do not always provide the coverage that the insured wants, the surplus and excess lines markets became more prominent in providing coverage for individual situations where the standard marketing procedures and forms were not flexible enough to do the job required.

Many of the approved excess or surplus lines companies are domestic companies, while a substantial number are European companies, the majority being British. In addition to the companies there are the underwriters at Lloyd's, who account for the largest portion of the excess business by far. It is important to recognize that when dealing with Lloyd's, the policy issuance is delayed even longer than it is in the domestic market. Accordingly, coverage is continued on binder for much more extended periods of time than would be reasonable to expect if the insurance had been placed with a domestic company. Unlike the domestic operations (where most binders are issued by the insurance company), when insurance has been purchased in Lloyd's, the insured generally gets what is called a "cover note" (in lieu of a binder) issued by the broker—not by Lloyd's. It simply indicates that the broker, whether it be a London broker or a United States broker, has placed insurance on behalf of the insured in Lloyd's, subject to the indicated terms and conditions. In many cases Lloyd's will not take 100 percent of the line and the balance of the exposure is placed with other British or European companies. Separate cover notes are supposed to be issued with one showing the percentage of coverage provided by Lloyd's and the second showing the percentage of coverage provided by the other companies. The insured should insist upon a listing of the companies that are providing this coverage and the percentage of their participation.

One further marketing approach for any insured to keep in mind is the use of underwriting groups or associations. These organizations have been established for the most part to create the capacity required for a particular situation. These groups, such as the Factory Insurance Association, Improved Risk Mutuals, United States Aircraft Insurance Group, Associated Aviation Underwriters, American and Foreign Insurance Association, American Hull Insurance Syndicate, and others are made up of various insurance companies participating on a predetermined basis in the coverage that is underwritten by a central underwriting managing office. The Factory Mutuals are a similar type organization, although they do retain a greater degree of underwriting responsibility by the individual companies than do most of the other similar associations. The Factory Mutuals, however, do rely upon an association-owned engineering and loss-prevention department for their inspection and safety-engineering work and for the development of their rates and the handling of their claims.

In the associations, there are varying types of commitments among the member companies. In some cases the member companies participate jointly and severally, so that in the event one of the participating companies should be unable to fulfill its commitment, the remaining companies subscribing to the association will be liable for the unfulfilled commitment. On the other hand there are some association agreements whereby each participating company is responsible for its own share only, and if any one participating member cannot fulfill its obligations, the insured would be unprotected for that percentage of the coverage that was being afforded by the company that did not meet its obligation.

In addition to the aforementioned type of association and underwriting group, there are other associations that have been put together to provide protection for a given class of industry, such as the Oil Insurance Association, Food

Industries Federation, and Building Owners Federation. These associations often offer substantial benefits in comparison with the normal way of handling insurance. Such improvements are possible because concentrated underwriting in a particular area enables an underwriter, or a group of companies, to evaluate a particular type of exposure more intensively than they could by treating it as normal business and class underwriting.

The main thing for an insured to keep in mind is that there are different types of companies; different underwriting philosophies; and specialty situations that should be evaluated before accepting or rejecting any particular type of insurance market. The services that the insured should receive from whatever market is finally selected are discussed in the next part of this section.

Choosing the right carrier on the basis of its ability to provide the necessary service, coverage, and at the proper price is the cornerstone of the development of a sound insurance program. The proper price, however, is dependent to a large degree upon how the insurance requirements are marketed. In this area the insured must recognize that the tendency within the insurance industry is to provide coverage on a standard basis. It is then up to the insured in many cases to suggest alternative marketing concepts that might be beneficial to his overall program, but which may or may not be suggested to him by his insurance brokers or insurance companies.

Insurance rates are basically established on a class basis whereby the total losses in a given class of business for a given type of exposure are divided by the total amount of dollars of exposure to develop a base rate for the future. This is admittedly a gross oversimplification of the development of insurance rates, but it is necessary to understand what the basic premise is before you can evaluate the propriety of deviation.

As we have briefly discussed in the part of this section dealing with workmen's-compensation insurance, "experience rating" is a system followed in all states, whereby an individual insured's rates are deviated from the established standard either by a credit or a debit, depending upon that insured's individual experience over a stipulated period of time. Similar experience-rating credits and debits are used in the general-liability and automobile insurance fields, although not so all-inclusive or compulsory as the workmen's-compensation application of the experience-rating modifications.

The formulas used to develop the experience modification factors differ in some states. Thus, the modifications in some states may be more responsive to large single losses, whereas in other states a frequency of smaller claims might have a more marked effect on the modification than would a large single claim. In all cases, however, it is apparent that as the insurance premium increases, the insured comes closer and closer to being a self-insured risk that is simply retaining the insurance company for an element of catastrophe protection and for its inspection and claims service.

At this point consideration can well be given to the desirability of self-insuring the risk.

Self-insurance of workmen's-compensation exposures, where permitted by law, is usually feasible only where there are substantial operations under relatively close control. A single plant that employs 5,000 employees would be far more likely to be a reasonable subject for self-insurance than would an operation that had 25 plants employing 200 employees at each, even though the total number of employees is the same. One of the areas that can be beneficially handled in a self-insured workmen's-compensation program is the cost of the claim-handling service and the inspection service. Where it is under tight control, such services can often be obtained for less money than would be the percentage charges which are included in the net cost of an insured program and with equally satisfactory results. In addition, a self-insured program avoids the necessity of paying state taxes, which have to be paid by a commercial insurance company on the premiums.

Even when a workmen's-compensation program is self-insured, there is still a practical necessity of providing catastrophe protection against a major industrial fire, explosion, or other casualty that could kill or injure many employees, creating a completely unexpected and unforeseen liability that could have serious adverse effects on the financial structure of the insured. This type of catastrophe coverage would come into play whenever the losses were substantially greater than the anticipated losses.

Self-insurance of other areas of exposure to financial loss is not quite so practical because, with the exception of group insurance, the premiums are in most cases substantially lower than the exposures. For example, a fire-insurance exposure, even at a rate of $0.50 per $100 of value, would only develop a $500 annual premium for $100,000 worth of protection, and if the $100,000 worth of property is subject to a possibility of one loss, it would be unrealistic to self-insure or to self-assume this risk in order to save $500.

There are, however, some areas where the value of the property at risk is not sufficient to justify the premium expenditures required. For example, a store might elect to carry plate-glass insurance because of its particular location and because the premium, in relation to the replacement cost of a large pane of glass, is realistic. On the other hand, a chain of department stores, having 25, 30, or more stores would probably not find it feasible to provide plate-glass insurance, inasmuch as the total premiums for all stores would be more than the cost of the replacement of several panes of glass during the course of each policy year.

Similarly, minor values being transported are often not insured because of the relationship of the premium to the values at risk. General-liability and automobile-liability insurance because of their large loss potential are subjects that are rarely considered for self-insurance. Only the largest companies could feasibly consider these subjects as proper ones for self-insurance, and even then prudent management would probably decide upon providing catastrophe protection.

Because of its extremely large premium, group insurance is one of the subjects most often looked at in terms of a possible self-insured program. In spite of the large number of dollars being paid for employee benefits coverages in the areas of hospitalization, surgical-medical, major-medical, life, and accident-and-sickness insurance, the benefits take up the major share of the premium dollar, and the insurance company's portion is relatively small. Regardless of whether the program is insured or self-insured, the benefits will be the same and the net benefit cost will be approximately the same, so that the only area that can be improved upon by a self-insured program is the area of cost that would be retained by the insurance company. The principal areas of saving would be the reduction in the general administrative expense (although this would not be completely eliminated by a self-insured program) and the elimination of the need to pay state premium taxes.

There are a number of aspects of a group-insurance program that have decided drawbacks to them if a self-insurance program is adopted. For example, group life insurance cannot be feasibly self-insured because of the requirement that a terminated employee must have the right to convert his group-insurance policy to an individual policy. If the exposure is self-insured, there is no policy to convert, and unless special arrangements can be made with an insurance company to provide coverage for all terminated employees (which is highly doubtful), the insured has no means of satisfying his legal obligation to provide the conversion right.

With respect to the hospital, surgical-medical, and major-medical coverages, a self-insured plan again runs into conversion problems in certain states where it is mandatory, and in addition it puts the burden on the insured for policing the benefits to avoid duplication and overpayment. The group-insurance industry has effected a coordination-of-benefits program which is subscribed to by most companies and most insureds. This program is designed to prevent an employee from collecting more than the total amount of the expense actually incurred for an illness or accident. The insurance companies are equipped to police this type of program, whereas an individual insured is not.

The accident-and-sickness area of group insurance is one area that might be effectively self-insured inasmuch as accident-and-sickness coverage is no more than an insured salary-continuation plan and there can be some small savings in self-insuring this risk area. There are usually no major exposures in the short-term accident-and-sickness program, because the benefits payable to any individual employee are not excessive. Nor is the period of time for which coverage is granted of too long duration. Therefore, no one claim will have a serious effect on the total experience. Second, since most accident-and-sickness programs exclude occupational accidents or illnesses, there would be little likelihood of having any great number of employees subjected to the same exposure.

672 J. K. LASSER'S BUSINESS MANAGEMENT HANDBOOK

Having seen that pure self-insurance is not often practical to any large degree for any but the largest insurers, we are still faced with the possibility that a certain degree of self-insurance might be feasible. As a result, "retrospective rating" has been developed, and is used particularly in workmen's compensation and to a lesser degree in the general-liability and automobile insurance fields, which provide a certain element of limited self-insurance.

The retrospective-rating formula basically consists of the following items:

A basic premium for the insurance company's general administrative expenses. This is a percentage of the standard premium that would otherwise be charged. The standard premium is the same premium that would be the basis for the premium-discount type of final premium adjustment

An excess-loss premium, which is the pure insurance charge made for the cost of claims that exceed a given figure. If the insured selects a $10,000 loss limit in a retrospective-rating plan, this simply means that no loss will go into the plan for more than $10,000. When any loss exceeds $10,000, the excess of $10,000 will be charged directly to the insurance company and will not become a factor in the plan. This excess-loss premium is a pure insurance charge

Actual incurred losses. This is the predominant factor in the development of the retrospective-rating plan and interim adjustments are made while the claims are still open. The final retrospective premium is not determined, generally, until all of the claims have been closed or until the maximum has been reached

A loss-conversion factor. This is applied to the actual losses and constitutes the charge by the insurance company for handling the claims

A preliminary retrospective premium. This is developed by the sum of the basic premium, the excess-loss premium, and the converted losses

A tax factor. This reflects the premium tax for the states involved

The final retrospective premium. This is developed by the multiplication of the tax factor by the preliminary retrospective premium

A nonstock factor. If the retrospective plan is written by a mutual company or a participating stock company, an additional factor known as the nonstock factor is then applied to the final retrospective premium and the dividend applied after that

Under this formula the insurance company is guaranteed a certain minimum premium, and the insured is guaranteed that he will have a specific maximum premium regardless of what his loss experience is for the period in question. Within the minimum and maximum the insured makes his own premium by his own loss experience.

The retrospective-rating approach makes the net premium for a given year much more sensitive to the experience in that year than would be the case if the coverage were written on a premium-discount basis, in which the experience of the particular year has no immediate effect on the net premium of that year.

It is thus apparent that if an insured has a high experience debit in workmen's compensation that has been developed because of unusual circumstances, and he has every expectation that his loss picture will improve substantially in the coming year, he has a very good possibility of effecting an immediate benefit by using a retrospective-rating plan. On the other hand, an insured who has a substantial experience modification credit has already evidenced the fact that his operation is better than the average, and he will have to maintain a very fine loss-prevention program and loss record in order to match the premium that is developed by a premium-discount plan.

Retrospective plans for workmen's-compensation insurance can be evaluated with some degree of confidence, particularly if a true and honest evaluation of the company's loss-prevention activities is taken into consideration and if a stop-loss factor is inserted in the plan to minimize the shock effect of any particular claim.

Retrospective plans are also available for general-liability and automobile insurance exposure. However, claims in these areas are generally not so predictable as they are in workmen's compensation, and accordingly retrospective-rating plans on liability exposures are much more of a pure gamble than is the case with workmen's compensation.

The insurance companies generally have a tendency to try to put as much coverage together under one retrospective plan as possible, so that if they get hurt in one area, they will have the benefits of the other premiums to level off the total costs. They also have a tendency to emphasize the desirability of a 3-year retrospective plan. Before making any decision on this particular point, it is important to recognize that there is often very little difference between the basic premium percentage that is charged for a 1-year plan and that which is charged for a 3-year plan. Since all other factors are geared to losses, the only advantages in the 3-year plan as opposed to the 1-year plan are the slight reduction in the basic premium and a possible reduction in the maximum or the minimum premiums, although in many cases the reduction in the minimum premium would only be effective at unrealistic loss levels.

When general liability, automobile liability, and workmen's compensation are all put together, it is possible for the insured to select his own maximums and minimums, which in turn would then directly control the percentage that would be charged for basic premiums. In some cases it might be better to select high maximum premiums and low minimum premiums, which would have the effect of reducing the basic premium charge. If you desire to protect yourself against assuming a high maximum, it is possible to buy what is known as retrospective-penalty insurance, which is a policy that would pay the additional charges above and beyond the normal up to the maximum retrospective, thus enabling the insured to have the benefits of the low basic without a severe penalty in the event of adverse loss experience. The cost of the retrospective-penalty insurance would have to be added as a fixed cost in determining the overall benefits of the program.

There are modifications of a retrospective plan used by many companies in which the standard premium is adjusted on the basis of the payment of a divident predicated on the pure loss experience during the particular year. This is a simplified form of retrospective and generally provides little penalty in the event of adverse loss experience. However, the benefits are not so great as they might be under a pure retrospective plan. Various companies have different names for this type of plan, but they can generally be identified as loss-ratio dividend plans. The mechanics of these plans simply mean that you establish your standard premium in the same manner as you would for any other workmen's-compensation policy, whether it be written on a guaranteed cost basis or retrospective plan, and then the dividend or participating return is predicated on the pure loss experience. For example, if the loss experience is 40 percent, the dividend might be 13.5 percent. If the loss experience is 45 percent, the dividend might be 11.7 percent. If the loss experience is 30 percent, the dividend might be 17 percent.

Another form of semi-self-insurance is the use of deductibles. This type of approach to a partial self-insured plan is not appropriate to workmen's-compensation insurance. In most cases it is also not particularly adaptable to the normal general-liability or automobile-liability exposures unless there is a tremendous frequency of loss and arrangements are made with the insurance company to investigate all claims, regardless of whether they come in under the assumed deductible or not. This can be a dangerous situation because of the possibility of late reporting of accidents which might tend to inflate the ultimate claim settlements or be prejudicial to the effectiveness of the insurance protection.

Deductibles in liability are most commonly used where catastrophe insurance is being sought and where there is no frequency of loss. This would best be illustrated by an umbrella liability policy where anything that was not insured by the primary coverages would be subject to an uninsured deductible of $10,000 or $25,000. It would also be pertinent to such special types of exposures as errors and omissions, professional liability, etc. In most of these cases the deductibles under this catastrophe type of exposure would be at least $10,000.

The primary use of deductibles arises in the area of property insurance. Most fire-insurance companies, for example, now have approved filings for the writing of deductible insurance, although some of the schedules may not be particularly attractive in the credits that they grant for the absorption of risk. The purpose of the smaller deductibles is to eliminate from the experience picture the small, relatively nominal losses that might be an inherent part of the business operations. If these are insured in full, the insurance company must eventually charge more than an equal amount of premium just to pay these nominal losses, which can be eliminated from the experience by the use of a deductible. When following this approach, the deductible level can be anywhere up to $5,000 or $10,000, depending upon the frequency and severity of past experience.

An alternate use of the deductible is for those situations where there is little frequency in loss, and the premium returns in the form of rate reductions are sufficiently attractive to gamble on the premise that over a long period of time the premium savings will more than offset the amount of loss that would be absorbed under one or two claims. This latter approach is used particularly where there is a limited base of insurance to start with and where there are substantial values involved. In such situations, each insured has to pay a heavy premium to create enough of an insurance pool to pay for the losses that may occur to the few insureds that are participating. If one of the insureds in this particular pool writes his coverage at a low deductible and starts collecting small losses, he is, in effect, passing on his own normal loss experience to the other members of the pool and increasing the cost of everybody else's catastrophe protection. At the same time he is getting back his own premium by the collection of small losses at the expense of the other members of the pool. It is therefore generally desirable to write insurance on a high deductible basis when you are participating in a limited exposure field.

Deductibles can be written on either a dollar basis, a time basis, or a percentage basis. Each has some merit, but the dollar basis is the only one where the insured has an absolute knowledge of the amount that any one loss can affect his financial position. On a time basis, that is, if it is written on a 1- or 2-day deductible basis, as is often the case with boiler-and-machinery insurance, the amount of the loss can vary depending upon the time of the year and the particular location at which the loss occurred. Similarly, a percentage basis will likewise vary depending upon the size of the loss or the value of the property.

In addition to the straight deductible, which simply means that the insured pays any loss up to the deductible amount and the insurance company pays everything over that amount, there is also a type of deductible known as either a disappearing deductible or a franchise deductible. Under the franchise deductible a percentage in excess of 100 percent of the amount of the loss over the deductible is actually paid by the insurance company, so that if the loss is big enough, the full amount of the deductible is paid. For example, let us assume that we have a policy with a $5,000 franchise deductible, and under the terms of the franchise clause the insurance company will pay 125 percent of the amount of any loss over $5,000, but in no event more than the full amount of the loss. If we have a loss of $4,000, the insurance company pays nothing because the loss is under the $5,000 deductible limit. If the loss is $10,000, the insurance company pays 125 percent of the $5,000 which is in excess of the $5,000 deductible, or $6,250. If the loss is $25,000, then the amount that the insurance company would pay would be 125 percent of $20,000 or $25,000, and thus any loss over $25,000 would be paid in full under the terms of this franchise deductible clause.

One other feature to consider in the use of deductibles is the fact that in major lines it is often desirable to establish a limit on how much will be absorbed in deductibles during the course of the policy period. The insured may select a $10,000 deductible per loss and be perfectly happy with that insofar as any one loss is concerned, but he would not particularly like to have an unlimited number of $10,000 losses occur during the course of the policy. In order to limit the ultimate liability that might be absorbed in any given period of time, an aggregate stop-loss cover can generally be arranged, so that the total amount of losses absorbed under a deductible plan will not exceed a stipulated amount in a given period of time.

No discussion of insurance markets or marketing concepts would be complete without an evaluation of the benefits and drawbacks arising out of the use of package policies. There are a myriad of package-policy forms approved by the various rating bureaus, and in addition, there are a number of different package policies that have been created by individual companies. Generally speaking, package policies can be divided into two basic groups—those that combine similar coverages, and those that combine dissimilar coverages.

From a coverage point of view the combination of similar types of coverage is generally beneficial to an insured, because it enables him to adopt consistent assumption of risk and standardization of protection. This combination also has a further benefit in that it eliminates the potential controversy that might develop between two different insurance companies if a loss involved more than one peril or exposure. The combination of dissimilar types of insurance under one policy jacket, such as liability and property coverages, achieves no benefit whatsoever in terms of improving the coverage in either area.

From a cost point of view the smaller buyer of insurance may benefit to the extent that the underwriter will be able to reduce the costs that he needs for administrative expenses, and from the fact that most package policies, at least in the property-damage area, are written on a deductible basis which should minimize the cost of paying and handling small claims. The larger buyer does not generally realize any benefits in either coverage or cost that he could not otherwise get by the use of all available insurance markets.

While there may be some benefits to the smaller buyer in the area of cost, there are also serious disadvantages that arise primarily from the mechanical aspects of writing and using package policies. For example, in an effort to simplify the policy preparation standardized endorsements have been developed. In many instances these endorsements do not give as broad coverage as would otherwise be available in the normal manner.

Another disadvantage to the package policy is that the premiums are often lumped together without any indication of how the premium was computed.

Thus, when additional exposures are added during the course of the policy period, there is no way for the insured to determine how the additional premiums being charged for the increased exposures compare with the charges made at inception. Still another disadvantage is the fact that the combination of dissimilar coverages in one policy jacket creates a considerable amount of confusion for the inexperienced insurance buyer in trying to determine what he actually has.

These last two conditions make it extremely difficult to evaluate any competitive quotations, and the insurance buyer has a tendency then to abdicate his responsibilities and to rely completely on the man that is selling him the package policy. This in turn tends to lead towards a "captive-account" situation, which is hardly ever beneficial to an insured.

6. Services that you should receive

The insurance program that is ultimately developed really has two functions, one being the provision of protection against liability claims, the reimbursement for damages, loss of profits, or the payment of expenses, and the other being the performance of certain services, such as claim handling and loss-prevention work.

The importance of these services varies from coverage to coverage and to some degree with the size of the insured. Each basic type of coverage has differences in the service requirements, and within each coverage, of course, the requirements will further differ depending upon the type of operation. As a general guide, however, we will simply set forth some of the more general comments relative to the services that the insurance company should offer to you.

Fire insurance. The basic purpose of the fire-insurance inspections that should be received from the insurance carrier is to assist in maintaining properties and conducting operations in such a manner as to minimize the loss potential. The nature of the operation and the size of the potential loss will determine the frequency and the scope of the inspection service granted. It is quite apparent that a large industrial chemical complex will have a far greater number of fire-protection engineering problems than would a service station.

Since the fire-insurance premium is not generally based on the loss experience of an individual account, except in the case of major concerns, it can be assumed that since the insurance company cannot recover the losses from an insured through the operation of any direct loss-rating plan or similar device, they have as much interest in preventing the loss in the first place as the insured, and therefore real consideration should be given to any recommendation submitted by the insurance companies. There will be differences of opinion about the importance or the economic feasibility of complying with all recommendations that may be submitted, but all recommendations should at least be thoroughly reviewed and evaluated.

In many cases the fire-insurance company's engineering staff, if given proper information before changes are made or new construction begun, can point out improvements in the facility that, if made at inception, will be beneficial and not expensive. If they are delayed until after completion of the facility, they will still be beneficial, but then they can become quite expensive and therefore are often not completed. In addition, the fire-insurance company's engineering department can on occasion make suggestions when reviewing contemplated construction that can improve not only the fire protection, but also in some cases can improve the efficiency of the operation as a whole. This is particularly true where the fire insurance is handled by one of the major underwriting organizations.

A further service that the fire-insurance company will often make available is an estimating or appraisal service. In some cases, such as in the case of the major fire-insurance underwriting groups, this service actually is as extensive as a full-scale commercial appraisal. Some of the individual insurance companies, on the other hand, may only provide rough estimates of the general cost of the facility.

Boiler and machinery. The principal services furnished by the boiler-and-machinery insurance companies are twofold: first, to inspect the insured equipment to try to anticipate and prevent losses arising in the first place, and second, to meet the statutory requirements for inspection of various pieces of equipment.

Workmen's compensation. This coverage is generally one of the most expensive parts of the corporation's insurance program; and since it is directly loss rated for all operations except the smallest, it is extremely important to understand the importance of the services that are available. By the nature of the coverage, this is not a catastrophic type of insurance in the same sense as a fire-insurance policy, and consequently the selection of an insurance company should be based to a large degree on the service that they can offer rather than on the evaluation of the pure insurance aspects.

The insurance company should be expected to cooperate fully in the periodic review of claims to make sure that each individual claim is promptly handled. In all accounts that are subject to experience modification factors (which would be the great majority of industrial and commercial accounts), every claim has a very decided effect on the future cost of workmen's-compensation insurance. It is therefore imperative that prompt action be taken in handling a claim and that continuous review be applied by the insurance company to make sure that reserves for pending claims do not remain in the experience records after the claim has been settled. Unnecessary reserves established by the insurance company in the experience modification computations increase the premiums substantially.

Regular procedures should be established to review the details of these claims with the insurance company on either a quarterly, semiannual, or annual basis.

The frequency of such a review will depend upon the size of the account and the frequency of claims.

The second major function that should be provided by the insurance company in the workmen's-compensation field is loss-prevention work. It is fundamental that an experience-rated line of insurance such as workmen's compensation can be most improved by a reduction in the number of accidents. No insurance company can make a plant accident-free. All they can do is to assist management in developing safety consciousness among employees. In this regard some companies provide more effective service facilities than do others, but the main impetus for a successful safety program still must come from within the management of the insured corporation. The insurance companies can only show how. It is up to the individual company to do the required work. This means establishing internal inspections, safety committees, etc., as well as having insurance company inspections. But most importantly, it means the creation and perpetuation of an attitude of safety.

Liability. The services that should be expected from the insurance company with regard to liability coverages, both automobile and general-liability exposures, vary depending upon the size of the premiums involved. In smaller premium cases the claim burden is going to fall on the insurance company, and it is therefore pretty much their concern how much loss-prevention service they apply to an account. It is sound business to follow through with any reasonable recommendation that may be made by the insurance company to prevent accidents.

As the size of the account increases, the premium becomes much more of a loss-rated situation, somewhat like workmen's compensation, although the claims are not predetermined by statute. Therefore, it becomes increasingly important to work closely with the insurance company to develop the proper loss-prevention activity and in addition to make sure that the insurance company is following the insured's philosophy of claim payments.

In this regard it should be noted that many insureds, particularly those that deal with the public, often take a very liberal attitude and advocate quick settlement of all liability claims, even to the extent of paying a lot of small claims where no liability actually exists. This is in effect a goodwill type of philosophy. On the other hand, some insureds take a more conservative attitude. They realize that it is their direct cost that is being affected by the claim payment. They often follow the philosophy that claims should be paid only where there is genuine liability and all attempts to collect nuisance claims should be opposed.

It is imperative that after you have established the claim-handling concept that *you* want, which may not necessarily coincide with what the insurance company wants, you must insist on adherence to this philosophy by the claim department of your insurance carrier.

One other factor involved in the services required of your liability carrier is the provision of inspections to satisfy statutory requirements, particularly with regard to escalators and elevators.

Crime. The principal services that you should look for from the insurance company with regard to the crime exposures are the loss-prevention services that are offered by many crime underwriters for their larger accounts. These entail evaluation of the potential direct loss from burglary, theft, robbery, etc., and also involve the complete evaluation of accounting procedures to try to anticipate any weak spots that might exist which could create an opportunity for fidelity claims.

The services that the insurance companies offer are related only to the coverages that they provide. In contrast to this, insurance brokers are basically representatives of the insured and should provide services not only for coverages that they have sold, but other services as well. We believe that the good broker will provide you with the following services.

Evaluation of the corporate operations. The competent professional insurance man should be regularly in touch with his insured and be fully knowledgeable about his operations and his future plans, so as to be able to take care of the existing insurance needs and to anticipate future requirements.

Establishment of a corporate insurance-buying philosophy. Knowing the operations and its inherent problems, including where the production bottlenecks are, what the supply problems are, the marketing problems, etc., and knowing what the future plans are, the competent professional insurance man can be of immeasurable help in assisting management to determine a reasonable corporate insurance-buying philosophy. Too many corporate programs are developed as an accumulation of policies without any basic philosophy behind them.

Evaluation of alternative insurance markets. Having assisted in the development of the corporate insurance-buying philosophy, the truly competent broker is then in a position to be able to make the proper evaluation of all the available insurance markets that will best fulfill the objectives of the corporation.

He should not limit his exploration to his own normal commission-paying markets, because no matter how big the broker may be, his markets still represent only a segment of the total insurance-marketing facilities, particularly for large insureds, and there is no one market that can always produce the best program for every insured. The truly competent broker will, if necessary, negotiate a service fee with the insured if the best market does not pay a commission. With such professional help, the insured can then rest assured that his broker has evaluated the stock-company markets, the direct-writing markets, the foreign markets, the domestic excess markets, and the various underwriting associations as well as the reciprocal groups.

Negotiation of coverage. Here again it is a question of the competent broker being able to make the differentiation between an unrealistically low initial cost, which may be based on factors other than exposures and loss experience, and which may be increased substantially shortly after the coverage is placed, as compared with a sound, economical cost.

The truly competent broker will evaluate all available markets, but will offer coverage only where there is the proper financial stability, protection, loss-prevention and claim-handling services, and the proper price.

Loss prevention. The selection of the proper insurance market is a vital factor in the control of losses, but the broker is generally the one that has to do the selling job on management to originate and perpetuate proper loss-prevention programs. No insurance company, or for that matter no insured alone, can develop a truly worthwhile loss-prevention program without the full cooperation of the other. It is always a dual project, and it is the broker's job to get such a program off the ground and keep it in motion, and to augment the insurance company's services wherever possible with his own knowledge and experience.

Assistance in claim handling. The test of the efficacy of any insurance program is when claims occur. It is too late at that time to correct the errors made in the development of the program and the provision of coverage. The competent broker will be able to assist you in the mechanical aspects of getting full payment for losses occurring within the contract provisions. He will not, nor should he, be able to get payment for items not covered under the terms and conditions of the policies.

Administration. The simplification of administrative procedures and responsibilities within the insured's own organization is another major function of the competent insurance broker and his staff. He can be of considerable assistance in helping the insured establish proper claim-reporting procedures, following through on safety recommendations, distributing premium charges between subsidiary companies or divisions, establishing an insurance register, and other similar functions.

All the above functions are what the broker's commission dollar is paying for. But always remember, no matter how good your broker is, it must be kept in mind that his remuneration comes from what he sells. Therefore, there has to be a natural tendency, either conscious or unconscious, for him to push his product—insurance policies.

For this reason it is imperative to retain control of the insurance program and not abdicate responsibilities by letting the broker make basic decisions that should be made by the insured company.

There is a third area that the insured can look to for assistance on all facets of his insurance program and that is the growing area of the independent insurance consultant. When we use the term "insurance consultant," we do not mean those insurance brokers who hold themselves out to be consultants as well as brokers, but we refer solely to those who are completely independent and who do not sell insurance at all. Such individuals can give an insured an unbiased evaluation of his problems and the potential solutions, since his remuneration does not come from the selling of any insurance policies.

The services rendered by a true consultant follow fairly closely those that are offered by the broker except for the basic difference in viewpoint from which recommendations are generated. This would be especially true in such areas as the development of the insurance-buying philosophy that should be followed by the insured, and also in the area of the consideration of alternative markets or insurance-buying techniques that may or may not be advanced by the broker, but which are known to the consultant because of his specialized interest and experience in a particular field.

Most consultants limit themselves to work in the commercial and industrial fields and do not become involved with the general insurance of personal lines. Accordingly, they often have a greater depth of experience than most brokers, whose time, of necessity, must be spread over commercial and personal lines insurance, as well as the administrative handling of their own brokerage office, the handling of the details of their clients' accounts, and many other time-consuming functions that tend to limit the time that they have to devote to pure insurance matters.

It should never be considered that a consultant is in competition with a broker, nor can he possibly replace the broker or the direct-writing insurance salesman. The broker performs many services that would be impossible for the consultant to offer.

The consultant's primary function is to make sure that management is aware of what can be done with respect to the development and implementation of a sound insurance program. Whether any action is taken to follow his recommendations is not the concern of the consultant.

BY

JAMES GREENE

HOW TO DO BUSINESS ABROAD

Introduction

One of the more remarkable developments in American industrial history in recent years has been the growing involvement by American companies in the international marketplace. This development is not confined to any one industry, nor is it confined to large companies. The growth of many foreign national economies in the 1950s brought them to levels that at least approximated conditions in the United States economy. Consequently, many American manufacturers found their products, frequently with only minor adjustments, readily acceptable in a number of foreign countries. Other factors have been at work, too. Reconstruction in Europe in the late 1940s and early 1950s required massive infusions of American technical know-how and equipment. Foreign aid to developing countries has been utilized to purchase and install American equipment. Improved communications and transport have also helped to make foreign business practices less unfamiliar and foreign markets less remote. A gradual easing of trade barriers has opened many national frontiers to foreign goods.

While interest in Europe has been especially keen, United States investments overseas are relatively evenly placed around the world. These investments are linked closely to our exports. A recent study by the Department of Commerce indicates that approximately one-third of all commercial exports are shipped to foreign affiliates of the United States exporter. This trend is blurring the traditional distinctions that have been made between exporting and other types of foreign activity. To do business abroad today, the manufacturer must be willing to follow up a successful export effort with more permanent commitments to foreign markets, or risk losing what business has been established.

In addition to this requirement, however, American exporters have undoubtedly been lured to invest in many foreign markets because of their dynamic growth rates. Expansion in some foreign markets is permitting United States firms to build sales well beyond what would be possible were they to remain solely domestic companies.

1. Determining the approach

The method by which any individual company attempts to do business abroad is the result of many factors. The nature of its product, the financial and managerial resources of the company, the strength of the competition, the short- and long-term goals of top management are all matters that bear heavily on how the company will move into foreign markets.

If the company wishes to sell abroad merely to dispose of excess production or to provide some hedge against the cyclical nature of its industry, it may satisfy its requirements with very little change in its organization and at relatively little expense, choosing to export indirectly, or appointing a single man in its sales organization to establish foreign representation.

At the other extreme, the company's top management may well decide that a major move should be taken to do business overseas, and to build this to the point where foreign profits are equal to, or greater than, profits from operations in this country.

The discussion which follows attempts to outline approaches for companies at either extreme or at some middle point between them. Major emphasis is placed on exporting, since traditionally companies which have developed a successful export program have also developed sources of information and guidance that make the move to other, more involved methods of doing business abroad relatively easy.

2. Does a market exist?

Unquestionably, a company interested in overseas business must make an early determination whether the potential market for its product overseas is sufficiently large to justify efforts to capture it. In many firms this question has already been answered by the number of unsolicited orders that have come in from abroad or from agencies in the United States that are purchasing on behalf of customers overseas. For other companies, the question may be answered because major competitors have already developed the foreign market, or markets, and demonstrated that a demand exists. Nonetheless, for many smaller companies the answer is not so obvious and must be researched.

In these cases, consultation with the nearest United States Department of Commerce field office will often permit the manufacturer to determine whether the product, or products virtually identical to it, are currently being exported from the United States. If the product is not one that normally enters international trade, the Department of Commerce field office can usually indicate in which foreign countries the product is manufactured and sold locally. If the company finds that the product is not traded at all in a foreign country, it must determine whether a demand can be created for a new product there.

This process may be relatively inexpensive or a costly project. Consultation with customers in the United States who are active overseas may provide a ready answer in instances where the product is sold to industry. Initial field trips by technical representatives to one or more key foreign markets may provide enough information to convince the company it has a market overseas.

Consumer products may be tested through the use of export intermediaries in the United States (see below), which are often willing to test-market new products with the understanding that if the demand is there, they will be granted the representation.   Many companies test-market through arrangements with foreign importer-wholesalers.   A more expensive, though usually more valid answer, can be obtained by commissioning an initial market-research study by a reputable agency.   Such a study may be commissioned through the company's existing advertising agency or domestic market-research adviser, or directly through a foreign agency.[1]

3. Indirect exporting

Indirect exporting is a term used for the sale of goods for foreign consumption to an intermediary agency in the United States.   This contrasts with "direct" exporting in which the United States exporter sells directly to an agency located abroad, which may be the end consumer of the item, or may resell it.

A thoughtful economy usually dictates that a company seeking to do business abroad should initially examine the idea of indirect exporting thoroughly, and only discard it if necessary.   There are essentially three basic methods of indirect exporting—

1. Through sales of products to purchasers here who intend to use the product abroad
2. Through the assignment of some or all export markets to an intermediary United States company
3. Through formation with other companies making the same or similar products of a Webb-Pomerene association (see page 691)

Sales to United States purchasers.   Thousands of United States companies do a lucrative "export" business without ever shipping a product overseas. There are numerous agencies here interested in purchasing products for use abroad.   Although selling to such agencies may not, in a narrow sense, constitute "doing business abroad," United States suppliers to these agencies are frequently called upon to install or repair machinery overseas.   Moreover, such sales have often led the American manufacturer to become involved in more direct forms of exporting, and beyond this, to licensing or investment to keep business originally built up by a United States intermediary.

Among United States purchasers of goods for use or resale overseas are export merchants, purchasing offices of foreign governments or large foreign enterprises, prime contracting companies for overseas projects, and United

[1] A useful volume in choosing such an agency is *Bradford's Directory of Marketing Research Agencies and Management Consultants in the United States and the World,* published by Bradford's Directory of Market Research Agencies, Middleburg, Va.

States government agencies, particularly the Department of Defense and the Agency for International Development.

The American manufacturer interested in selling to this group of buyers has the choice of establishing a special sales force to solicit sales from such agencies, or of assigning these sales calls to domestic salesmen. Generally, companies use existing domestic salesmen whenever possible, at least initially. Since most export merchants are located in port cities, the manufacturer often assigns responsibility for sales to these customers to the branch office nearest the port involved. Again, since most purchasing offices of foreign governments are located either in Washington, D.C., or in one of the three or four largest cities, the manufacturer may designate the nearest branch to seek the foreign sales.

A sufficiently large number of major corporations here centralize their foreign and domestic purchasing in one United States office to encourage their supplier companies to assign sales responsibility for both domestic and foreign sales to the salesmen who are already calling upon these companies.

Sales to intermediary companies. Another form of indirect exporting, and one that has been a permanent fixture in our export trade since the nation's beginnings, is the sale of goods for export through intermediary trading companies. Under arrangements worked out and usually embodied in a written contract, the manufacturer assigns to an independent trading company responsibility for sale of the manufacturer's product overseas. The arrangement may cover all the manufacturer's products or only a single product. The assignment may be for all markets except the United States (and frequently Canada) or for only a limited area of the world.

Depending upon the specific arrangement, the intermediary company may buy from the manufacturer and resell overseas, carrying all credit risks involved in selling to an overseas customer, or the intermediary may operate as an agent, receiving a commission on sales, but leaving the manufacturer to carry the financial risks.

Margins and commissions, of course, depend upon those common in the industry involved. Frequently, however, the intermediary is granted a slightly larger margin or commission because of the higher costs usually involved in developing foreign sales.

Combination export managers. Many of these intermediary trading companies act simultaneously as the export department of allied, but noncompetitive, United States manufacturers, a fact that gives rise to the term "combination export manager." In many cases, these combination export managers operate under the letterhead of the United States manufacturer. To all intents and purposes foreign customers or distributors are dealing with the manufacturer's "export department," or, more loftily, its "international division."

In addition to promoting sales overseas, the combination export managers handle all details incident to exporting from the port of exit to the overseas customers, all billing, and collection. All queries received from abroad are forwarded to the management office for action.

Qualifications. Combination export managers usually specialize in one or a few product lines, e.g., aircraft parts, automotive equipment, housewares, sporting goods. All offer a United States manufacturer an established distribution system overseas, and many have their own sales branches or subsidiaries in foreign markets. Some may provide their manufacturing clients with assistance in establishing licensing agreements or joint ventures abroad when it is clear that a major market is being closed to import of the product.

As trading companies with established foreign ties, these intermediaries can frequently offer a manufacturer a far less expensive export outlet than the manufacturer could establish on his own. Since they also handle all details connected with exporting, the manufacturer is spared the expense of setting up its own department or the necessity of diluting the efforts of salesmen or sales managers by assigning them responsibility for export as well as domestic sales.

Some disadvantages. Although the use of intermediaries can be an extremely useful and relatively inexpensive method of entering the export trade, the method does have its drawbacks, most of which are unavoidable in commercial arrangements of this kind. While the manufacturer is enjoying the economies that come from sharing an export department with other manufacturers, he must accept, too, the fact that the department and its overseas network can devote only a fraction of their time and effort to any single manufacturer's product. If the product requires any special technical skills to be sold or used properly, it may be extremely difficult to find an intermediary trading company with the necessary skills. Moreover, when the manufacturer decides to end its arrangement with the trading company, the latter may, and frequently does, seek overseas representation for a competitor of its former client in order to fully utilize the special skills developed in handling the previous account. And finally, when sales go far over $1 million a year, management generally decides that the company should have a full-time export department of its own rather than continue to share the profits on overseas sales with an independent company. At this point it may have to suffer a sharp drop in such overseas sales as it is developing its own distribution network. Many companies, of course, would put the ceiling much lower, believing that a company doing $300,000 to $400,000 a year in export should have its own export department and be exporting directly.

Advantages of the combination export manager. As with so many generalizations on business practices and policies, however, these objections to indirect exporting through a combination export manager are open to some large exceptions. Certain types of manufactured products, among them housewares, automotive-repair equipment, hand tools, toys, and sporting goods have traditionally been traded internationally through intermediary companies. Orders for these goods are generally made in small volumes that must be consolidated at some point for economies of distribution, a function that the combination export manager can often perform better than any individual manufacturer. Similarly, sales of highly technical electronic equipment or laboratory instruments are often made internationally through trading companies which can combine complementary equipment from several manufacturers and thereby offer complete installations when no single manufacturer could do so. For this reason, one may find large, well-established international companies exporting products of this kind through an intermediary company.

Then, too, some overseas markets are simply too small to make it worthwhile for an individual manufacturer to establish direct export channels. Some intermediary companies have close and long-standing relationships with these small foreign markets, know the requirements and possibilities in the markets well, and can consolidate shipments of highly diverse products into one large shipment to obtain lower freight rates.

Some large companies that could well afford their own foreign marketing network have decided to concentrate their direct export sales efforts on their best-selling, highest-profit items, and assign the foreign sales of other products to an intermediary company. Or these manufacturers may conserve their marketing efforts, concentrating them on the foreign area of greatest potential—frequently Europe—while assigning markets of lower potential to an intermediary company. Combination export managers, however, are wary of receiving too small a share of the foreign markets to make their efforts worthwhile. Generally, a manufacturer can work out a method that satisfies the needs of both parties.

Not an either/or situation. It would be foolish, however, to assume that the choice between indirect and direct exporting is an either/or situation. The manufacturer may decide to export directly to certain markets and indirectly to others, or may export certain products directly and others indirectly. The manufacturer may decide it is most efficient or most profitable to export directly to certain major foreign customers, while all other exports are channeled through a combination export manager.

Choosing a combination export manager. If, after an examination of its position, a company decides to utilize the services of an export intermediary for some products, markets, or customers, it is a relatively easy task to locate such an agency. In addition to assistance available from Department of Commerce field offices, which maintain lists of reputable intermediaries, there are export promotion offices in many states which can recommend intermediary companies located within the manufacturer's own state. In addition, the Agency for International Development in Washington published in 1962 a five-volume *Directory of Combination Export Managers.* The volumes are divided by the broad category of products handled, e.g., fuels, chemicals, raw materials. The volumes contain names, addresses, product specialties, and other pertinent data.

While the directory was drawn up primarily as a guide to purchasing by foreign governments using AID funds, the list includes combination export managers selling all types of products all over the world.

After drawing up its own short list of possible representatives, the manufacturer can apply the same evaluation techniques it would use for domestic distributors—size of company, staff, current lines handled, number of salesmen, number of overseas outlets, etc.

Intermediary companies generally have a preferred method of operation. Either they purchase in a domestic transaction from the manufacturer for resale overseas, or they operate as agents, forwarding orders to the manufacturer directly and receiving a commission as compensation.

Cooperative exporting. Special mention should be made of United States manufacturing companies that are already active in international markets and are willing to cooperate with other allied but noncompetitive manufacturers in helping them to build an export business. A number of large American companies are willing in this way to permit independent manufacturers to utilize their foreign distribution channels. Generally, their margins or commissions match those of the intermediate trading company, and they usually offer the same range of services as the combination export management company.

The Department of Commerce calls this its "piggyback" program. The Department maintains lists of companies in various fields that have indicated a willingness to cooperate with other United States manufacturers in this way. The advantages or disadvantages of using this method of exporting are roughly the same as those for using a combination export manager. Some observers, however, note a special problem in piggyback arrangements. Since these companies are interested only in handling the exports of allied manufacturers, they may create potential conflicts of interest as a result of handling the exports of a company that is a competitor of one of their own domestic customers or suppliers.

Webb-Pomerene associations. Although the United States antitrust laws provide harsh penalties for competing American companies that collude to set prices or divide markets, some careful exceptions are made for the export field. These exceptions are embodied in the Webb-Pomerene law, or the Export Act of 1918. The intent of this law is to allow United States companies ordinarily competing in the market here to join in a common marketing organization for export. This was to permit our manufacturers to compete in export markets with highly cartelized foreign industry.

The price paid for this exception to United States antitrust law, however, is close scrutiny by the Federal Trade Commission, which has jurisdiction over Webb-Pomerene associations. Bylaws and full descriptions of the functions proposed for such an association must be filed with the Commission, which may require changes to bring the association's activities within the exceptions granted.

Generally, a Webb-Pomerene association is—

A central selling agency for each of its members, taking foreign orders, negotiating sales, and handling all details of shipment, or

A central coordinating agency directing the export efforts of members and
retaining certain export functions, but leaving actual overseas sales to be
developed by the agents of individual members, or

A central organization buying outright the products of members and reselling
them abroad, or

A central agency calling and running meetings at which members may periodically meet to discuss prices in export markets, the activities of foreign
competition, and to exchange statistical information on export shipments
in the industry

In their heyday between the two World Wars there were several hundred
Webb-Pomerene associations in American industry handling nearly 20 percent
of all United States exports. In recent years, however, their number has gradually declined, and it is rare for a new association to appear in the Federal
Trade Commission's roster, despite the fact that the Commerce Department has
been promoting Webb-Pomerene groups as a useful exporting mechanism for
smaller companies.

Reasons for current unpopularity. The reasons industry has shunned the
Webb-Pomerene mechanism in recent years are not entirely clear. Undoubtedly, vigorous antitrust enforcement in the postwar period has made many a
company shy away from operating under narrow "exceptions" to the antitrust
laws. More to the point, perhaps, is the fact that the Department of Justice
has instituted several proceedings against Webb-Pomerene groups for allegedly
operating in ways not covered by the exceptions under the original act. Undoubtedly, many companies do not treat as real the distinction the law makes
between "domestic" and "export" markets, and many more companies resist the
notion that it would be useful for them to be in association with their competitors, even though only for the export market.

Companies wishing to explore the possibilities, however, can consult the
Federal Trade Commission in Washington. This agency is prepared to outline
for interested companies the various operations that may be legally established
under the law and may assist companies in drawing up draft proposals for a
Webb-Pomerene association to be sent to competitor companies.

Given the attitude of the Justice Department, however, the American company contemplating joining or helping to establish a Webb-Pomerene group
needs expert legal advice from the outset, in addition to the guidance of the
Federal Trade Commission.

4. Direct exporting

Those companies that reject the notion of assigning an independent agency
in the United States to launch them in foreign markets usually turn to direct

exporting. This is the method that places the least demands upon the company's financial or managerial resources. Despite the small demand on the company created at the outset, however, the company that enters direct exporting haphazardly may well wind up losing money rather than making it.

Properly planned and executed, a company export program can not only increase profits directly through increased sales, but can open wide opportunities for the company in more complex and more rewarding forms of foreign activity. It can, as well, attract the interest of foreign companies searching for special arrangements in the market here. A well-run export-marketing organization can be a sensitive antenna for technical and other developments in foreign markets that may either threaten the company and its product line, or open new avenues for application of the product.

Organizing for overseas business. Where overseas prospects justify it, or plans require it, the company may go immediately to direct exporting to overseas distributors or end users, bypassing any intermediary agency. The company must determine where responsibility for the export program or other overseas business will be placed within the company. Companies currently active overseas usually organize in one of the following ways:

The general sales manager or chief sales executive is asked to preside over the export effort in addition to his normal domestic duties

An export unit is established within the existing corporate marketing organization; an export manager who reports to the general sales manager is appointed

An export unit distinct from the corporate marketing organization is established. The manager reports to the same level of management as does the general (domestic) sales manager

An export unit is established with a manager reporting to the executive in charge of corporate development

An international division is established with export as its only initial activity, but with a mandate to develop other forms of foreign business

A separate subsidiary company in the United States is established to purchase from producing elements of the parent company for resale overseas

A separate subsidiary company is established in a foreign country to similarly purchase from United States producing elements of its parent company for resale in all foreign markets

Special patterns have been developed by multidivisional companies composed of many divisions making dissimilar products. While many of these have established a single international division which is a microcosm of the domestic company, a number have found the duplication of skills involved in this method too great, or the lines of authority between product divisions and overseas production units too weak. A number of these firms have found at least a temporary solution in establishing a corporate staff group which lends marketing, financial, and legal guidance to product divisions that operate as largely autonomous units, both domestically and overseas. Others have made individual divisions fully autonomous subsidiaries with their own corporate staff, while the "parent" acts primarily as a holding company.

The first four patterns enumerated above, obviously, are utilized by companies whose major overseas business is composed of exporting from the United States. Generally, foreign licensing in such companies is supervised not by the export unit but by production units.

Seven prototypes. The prototype charts reproduced here show several patterns that have been adopted by many American companies to handle their exports and other overseas business. In some of these, the export unit is primarily a sales and marketing organization; in others, the export organization undertakes all shipping, billing, and collections for foreign markets as well.

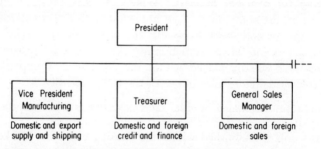

Fig. I. Part-time export activity of domestic personnel.

American companies are sharply divided on whether the export organization of the company should include only sales, or whether other functions connected with export are sufficiently different from the respective domestic function to be duplicated in the export unit. Much depends upon the size and quality of

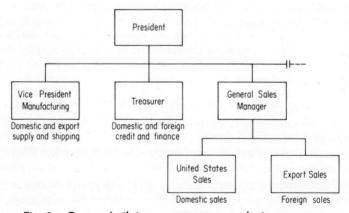

Fig. 2. Exports built into a corporate marketing structure.

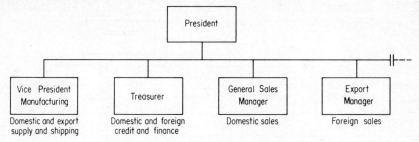

Fig. 3.   The separate Export Department.

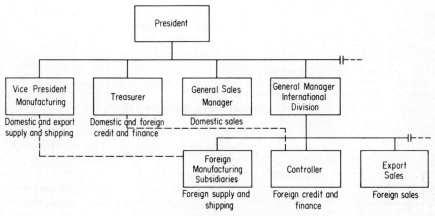

Fig. 4.   International Division A.

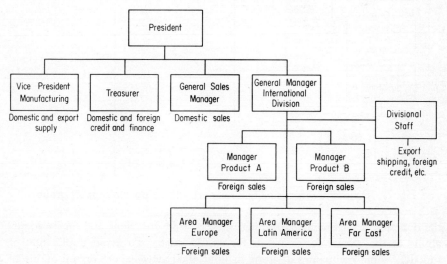

Fig. 5.   International Division B.

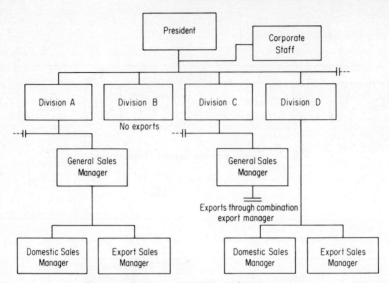

Fig. 6.   Divisional responsibility for export.

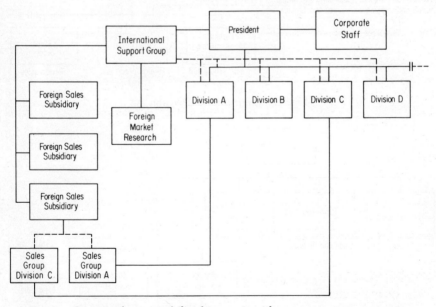

Fig. 7.   Divisional responsibility for export with corporate support group.

the domestic department performing these postsale functions and on its adaptability to the special requirements for export sales.   To avoid duplication of function, some companies attempt to limit their new export organizations to sales.   These companies argue that the necessity of duplicating billing and shipping functions for the export field, if it develops into a necessity, will become obvious in due course.

Assigning export functions. Exporting will involve the company in the same range of functions as those connected with domestic selling. While this statement seems obvious, it is not uncommon for companies to overlook it. They assign a man the title of export manager, charge him with building export sales, and let him flounder in uncertainty about who will handle all the details involved after he has closed a sale.

Consequently, a company will enhance its chances of success in exporting if it has placed definite responsibility for all functions directly connected with exporting. Below is a list of these main functions, and an indication of where they are frequently assigned within companies. Titles refer to managers in the domestic company, although in the international divisions of many companies similar titles are held by personnel within these divisions:

Function	*Assignment*
Supervision of an intermediary trading company	General sales manager
Supervision of foreign agents and distributors	General sales manager Export manager
Market planning for export	Marketing manager Export manager
Advertising and promotion	Advertising manager General sales manager Export manager
Financial and credit policy	Export manager Treasurer Controller
Export shipping	Traffic manager Export manager Independent freight forwarder
Billing and collections	Billing department Export manager
Legal and tax problems	Legal department Corporate secretary

Western Hemisphere trade corporations. To promote trade within the Western Hemisphere, United States law provides American manufacturers with an important tax concession embodied in the Internal Revenue Code of 1954. In effect, a manufacturer here may establish a separate United States company to handle its trade in the Western Hemisphere; so long as this separate company derives 95 percent of its income from sources outside this country, and 90 percent from the active conduct of the business, and apart from "incidental purchases" does all its business in the Hemisphere, it qualifies for a 14-point reduction in the normal United States tax.   As of this writing, this would mean a tax burden of about 34 percent rather than 48 percent.

Several hundred such WHTCs have been set up, purchasing from their parent companies here and selling the product overseas.   To qualify the income as "foreign," these companies are careful to arrange for title to the goods to be passed outside this country.   Purchases from the United States parent must be at "arm's length," that is, at prices the parent would charge an independent purchaser in a similar transaction.   Failure to meet the arm's-length test may often result in the Internal Revenue Service's reallocating income from the WHTC back to the parent, and the imposition of full taxes on the reallocated sum.   Passive types of income such as royalties or dividends from subsidiary sales companies may accrue to a WHTC, but only within the 10 percent limit. Consequently, most American firms limit their WHTCs to trading and manufacturing abroad through branch operations.

For several years, the Treasury attempted in a series of court challenges to require the WHTC to have "substance" abroad, e.g., active sales branches and other assets established to "penetrate" foreign markets in the Hemisphere. After consistently losing these cases, the Treasury has apparently abandoned this attempt.   Today, many WHTCs simply operate as shadow corporations without offices or staff.   Sales to Western Hemisphere markets are passed through the WHTC and title is passed to the foreign customer outside the United States.

Many others, however, have a great deal of substance, with multiple branches abroad, and many have their chief or central branch in San Juan, Puerto Rico. A recent examination by the Department of Commerce indicates that a growing number of WHTCs are engaging in manufacturing via foreign branch offices to reap the full advantages of the tax reduction.

Direct foreign representation.   Most United States manufacturers actively engaged in export have arranged for their own direct representation in foreign markets.   They may choose either an agent, a distributor, or a company-owned sales outlet such as a branch or subsidiary company.

To some extent, the normal sales pattern of an industry will determine whether a company will choose an agent or a distributor.   If inventory must be maintained abroad, a distributor is usually chosen.   For large or custommade machinery, agents are normally used; at the other extreme, consumer soft goods are usually sold through distributors operating as wholesaler-importers reselling to retail outlets in the country.   In many markets, customers may prefer to deal with agents, since this permits the customer direct contact with the manufacturer of the products they wish to buy.   In other markets, distributors may be preferred.   Companies generally investigate the normal method in use in a particular market before making any choice or entering into any contractual obligations.

Selection of a representative.   Finding an agent or distributor in a foreign country may be a simple matter; finding a good agent or distributor is usually even more difficult in a foreign market than it is in this country. In some cases, American firms have helped to finance a new distributor in opening a business because all candidates were rejected as unsuitable.

When the company cannot dispatch someone to the country on a personal trip, or when it doubts that potential sales would justify such a trip, the company may seek help from the Department of Commerce field office nearest to corporate headquarters, or consult with the Department's Bureau of International Commerce in Washington. Over the past few years the information on potential distributors and agents in foreign markets collected by the Bureau has increased greatly. In many cases, the Bureau is willing to undertake to gather further information on potential representatives for an American exporter. Another source of information may be other manufacturers here who make allied but noncompetitive equipment. The overseas distributor for, say, an office-machinery maker may be willing and able to take on a line of office furniture or accessories. A third possible source is the foreign country's embassy. Most embassies here have commercial sections familiar with the industrial and commercial networks existing in their countries.

Use of contracts. Manufacturers ordinarily use a slightly amended version of their domestic distributorship or agency agreements for overseas. When the parties to the contract come from different countries, it is, of course, necessary to stipulate which of the two countries' laws will apply. It is necessary, too, to designate an agency to arbitrate disputes; the International Chamber of Commerce is commonly named as the agency. Because of their remoteness from the United States headquarters, foreign distributors are frequently requested to file monthly reports on sales, inventories, collections, and other matters, as well as copies of their regular profit-and-loss statements and balance sheets. These materials help the manufacturer to properly evaluate the distributor's performance.

Motivating the representative. Techniques for evaluating and motivating foreign distributors and agents have advanced rapidly in recent years. A major motivation has been and continues to be money. Consequently, most schemes to motivate the representative focus on helping him to sell more of the company's product. Techniques successfully used by one distributor are passed quickly to all distributors, describing their impact on sales in the recent past. Visits by sales management and technical personnel are scheduled regularly for important distributors. Regional sales-management centers have been established by many companies to bring home-office policies and techniques closer to the representatives, to plan and run periodic regional sales meetings, and to learn more about the special problems and challenges being met daily by the representative.

Less expensive than these overseas sales supervisory offices is the annual or biannual sales meeting held in the United States or abroad, at which all distributors and agents are brought together for a meeting lasting from 1 day to a week. The manufacturer usually bears all costs of the meeting, while the representatives pay for their own travel and lodging. One small New Jersey company spent $5,000 to sponsor a special sales meeting in a resort in West Germany, a sum that included all expenses of representatives and their wives at the resort. The meeting included sessions on marketing, technical aspects of the product, future outlook for the industry served by the product, and methods of training salesmen. The expense paid off in an immediate increase in foreign sales to a higher plateau and far more cordial relations between the manufacturer and the foreign representatives.

Company-owned sales organization. While direct foreign investment is generally thought of as principally investment in production facilities, in fact large sums have been invested by American companies in overseas sales and management subsidiaries and branches. Such sales organizations often precede any investment in production facilities. In addition to sales responsibilities, the branches or subsidiaries are often charged with collecting and analyzing the data necessary for a decision to make an investment in production facilities.

In countries where the company's export volume appears to justify it, the company may establish the foreign installation to serve only that single national market, yet charge it with overseeing distributors and agents in the general geographic area and with planning for other company activity in the area.

The decision whether a branch or a subsidiary is to be established is dependent on many factors. Tax factors are usually very important; the branch as a part of the United States company has no "profits" of its own. Its earnings are part of the company's profit and subject to immediate tax in the United States, less any local taxes paid. If the branch is expected to lose money for a number of years before becoming profitable, then the American company might welcome this opportunity to charge off losses against United States profit while it builds up sales in a foreign market. However, once the branch begins making money, many companies convert it to a subsidiary, which has its own profit-and-loss statement and balance sheet. In most cases, the subsidiary is then subject only to local taxes and may plan and execute its operations as a distinct company. The parent company here is subject to United States taxes on the subsidiary's earnings only when the profit is remitted to this country in the form of dividends.

Many companies, however, eschew the establishment of foreign branches. They sometimes fear that the branch exposes the total assets of the corporation to negligence suits that may occur against the company in a foreign country. They may fear that in establishing a local tax base for the branch operations, local tax authorities may demand to see the complete company records in order to allocate a percentage of profits to the branch. Again, this is a subject on which competent legal counsel in the United States, and frequently in the foreign country concerned, is especially valuable. Discussion with other companies with either branch or subsidiary operations in the country is also valuable, since national regulations in many countries affecting importing, distribution, sales, and contract negotiation differ in application between branch and subsidiary operations.

5. Manufacturing investment

Companies eager to serve a foreign market, but unable to export competitively to it, frequently decide on direct investment in the market. Most companies approach such a commitment with caution, and weigh at length the various methods open to them on the basis of their past history in the market. Is a joint venture feasible or desirable? Is an acquisition feasible or desirable? How soon, on the basis of the figures assembled, will the company realize the payback of its investment? Is local political and economic stability sufficient to ensure reasonable conditions over the payout period? Are concessions or other forms of assistance available to incoming capital? Are obstacles placed before such capital? Are the management resources of the company up to the demands of an additional production facility in a foreign market?

In assessing the value of a direct investment, most companies utilize a checklist adapted from similar lists used for investment in new domestic production facilities. Obvious additions to a domestic checklist concern the freedom of capital to enter the country, limits on the percentage of ownership by foreigners, restrictions on the repatriation of capital or remittance of earnings in the form of interest, royalties, and dividends, requirements of the use of foreign managers or other foreign personnel, limits on the import of raw material and components, and a host of other restrictions that may apply to foreign-owned industry in the country involved.

Sources of information. Sources of the type of information needed are many. The problem is more often applying the information collected to the particular requirements of the proposed investment. Administrative and legal codes in many countries are vague, and it is frequently impossible to determine in advance whether a given operation or a particular approach will be permitted by foreign authorities who have very wide areas of discretion.

Sources used by companies, in addition to information they may collect on field trips to the country, include—

Representatives or licensees already located in the country
U.S. Department of Commerce's Bureau of International Commerce
United Nations and its specialized agencies, such as the International Labor
    Organization, Food and Agricultural Organization, United Nations International Development Organization, etc.
Private services, including the National Industrial Conference Board, the

Economist Intelligence Unit of London, Business International, or the
Gallatin Service in the United States

Other private agencies, including banks, market-research agencies, management consultants, and advertising agencies.

A number of foreign governments maintain, within their United States embassies or in separate offices, investment-promotion and information services
that are capable of providing a wide assortment of information on their own
country, and are, of course, authoritative sources for information on government
regulations and policies.

6. Licensing

Foreign licensing is viewed by many companies as a middle ground between
simple exporting and full-scale foreign investment. It provides a means of
producing within foreign markets and escaping high import tariffs without the
commitment of large amounts of capital or management attention. In many
cases, licensing is useful in serving smaller markets that would not in any case
support a complete production facility devoted to one product. In other cases,
high political and economic risks in a foreign country will induce the United
States manufacturer to license his products in the country to avoid exposing
capital and other corporate assets.

The manufacturer may agree to license the production and sale of the product in the local market, or he may simply "contract" out the "manufacture" of
the product, buying from the producer at an agreed-upon price and handling
all the marketing in the local or adjacent markets. This method is most common in industries where local production is necessary to serve the market, but
where the distribution and selling costs represent a large proportion of the final
sale price and hence a proportionately larger percentage of the total profit.
Generally, however, United States manufacturers license the foreign manufacturer to produce and sell the product in a specified territory.

Exclusivity in the territory is usually granted, but various developments in
foreign regulations, particularly in Western Europe, have called into question
whether a patent holder may legally restrict a licensee to sales in a single national market. Today, exclusivity in a market is usually implied in contracts—
the licensee is explicitly licensed to manufacture and sell the product in, say,
"all of France." Should a licensee in fact sell outside his national market, he
is presumably selling in a market in which rights have been retained by the
licensor or assigned by the patent holder to another third party. In such instances, the third party has recourse to the courts.

License agreements, of course, cover much more than patented property.
They often include unpatented manufacturing know-how, trademarks or brand

names, material or equipment necessary for a manufacturing process, technical or engineering advice and assistance, improvements developed by the licensor, marketing assistance and advice, and often managerial assistance. It is not uncommon for a licensor to invest some capital as a minority equity partner in a licensee's company. Companies that license abroad frequently obtain and exercise options to convert royalty or other payments from a licensee to equity.

In instances where unpublished know-how or other industrial property is to be paid for in equity in a foreign company, a special ruling from the Internal Revenue Service is necessary to permit the equity to be acquired without the imposition of current United States tax.

Compensation paid under licensing agreements may come in varying forms. Where basic knowledge of the process is to be transmitted, and this knowledge is easily duplicated once it is disclosed, the licensor may ask for a substantial "disclosure" fee, payable at the outset, or in installments that are distinct from any other payments. In addition, management or technical fees may be charged, based upon the expense incurred by the licensor to transmit the information properly.

Depending on the agreement and the industry involved, royalty payments may range from a fraction of 1 percent to 20 percent and over in, say, agreements covering trade names for cosmetic or fashion designs.

As in many matters concerning overseas business, expert legal counsel is needed to protect the company in negotiating licensing contracts. Tax treaties between the United States and foreign countries, or even between two foreign countries, may help the United States firm to plan the tax treatment of income from licensing agreements. In addition, different forms of income are subject to different rates of tax in many countries, e.g., royalties may be subject to withholding tax in some countries, while "fees" are not.

Disadvantages in licensing. While licensing offers the company numerous advantages over either exporting or direct investment, it has its disadvantages. License agreements may be terminated by either party, and the United States manufacturer may have created a competitor as a result of the transfer of manufacturing or other know-how that is not, or could not be, the substance of a patent. Moreover, the American company may be called upon to expend considerable attention by its management and technical personnel to launch a new licensee, or to solve the frequent problems that occur in this form of foreign production. The licensee has his own line of business in addition to that for which he is licensee; in the former he reaps the total profit, while in the latter he shares it with the foreign licensor. Moreover, the licensor, to protect his own interest, must be involved in policing the licensing process to be certain that the licensee is conforming to standards of quality and marketing, and is reporting accurately on production and sales.

7. Importance of tax planning

The company operating internationally has a special advantage over purely domestic companies—the possibility of exercising options that can reduce the tax level on earnings and release additional sums for dividends, reinvestment, or reserves. While legal experts deplore attempts by a company to evade taxes, or to distort normal commercial operations to reap the benefits of "tax gimmicks," they nonetheless stress the value of tax planning for the internationally active company.

This is because such a company is operating in multiple jurisdictions, often linked together by tax and other treaties which present the company with a wide range of choices. To become involved in this maze without attention to the tax consequences may often result in the company's bearing a far higher tax burden on its total business than the current burden on domestic business in the United States.

For the smaller firm, as for the larger company, tax planning is part of the company's total development plan. Properly structured, with the aid of legal counsel, tax planning can enhance the chances of success in the company's growth plan.

No review of this kind can present an exhaustive list of the factors to be considered in setting up a proper tax review in the international field. Yet here are a few of the necessary questions to be answered.

Should we establish a base company in a country which has a low tax rate on foreign income? This base company could purchase our United States exports for resale in third markets and generate income subject to a low tax that could be used for reinvestment abroad. (The Revenue Act of 1962 provides for current United States tax on the income of such subsidiaries in certain cases, but substantial benefits from tax planning are still possible.)

If we intend to license in or invest in Country X, with what foreign countries in addition to the United States does Country X have tax or other treaties, or special trading relationships?

Does Country X offer any special incentive for new investment, or for investment in a particular region? What is its tax treatment of various types of commercial organization, and what is the net effect in remitting dividends or profits to the United States?

Does Country X offer any special incentives for new companies that export and would there be a benefit to our company's overall profit were we to export from Country X to certain markets?

What are the tax differences, if any, among various types of financing of a venture in Country X? What is the most desirable debt-equity ratio from a tax standpoint, and do we have options that might be exercised in this field?

8. Impact of regionalism

The trend towards regionalism among the nations of the world has caused companies to align their plans for overseas investment and marketing with the plans of these various blocs. It has become possible, and it is becoming increasingly easy, for a company to service many foreign nations from a single foreign manufacturing facility without encountering tariffs or other traditional barriers to transactions across borders.

The most prominent of these blocs is the European Economic Community, which includes France, Germany, Belgium, Italy, the Netherlands, and Luxembourg. Associated with, but not full members of this group are Greece, Turkey, and Israel. Associated also, but less than full members, are a number of countries including Surinam and others, primarily in Africa, that were once part of the French empire.

Other groups include the European Free Trade Association, embracing Britain, Switzerland, Sweden, Norway, Denmark, Austria, and Portugal. Finland is associated with this group, which is designed as an area of completely free trade in industrial products.

Most of the nations of South America and Mexico are involved in a Latin American Free Trade Association for removal of tariffs and other barriers between its members. Concessions being made between members on tariff levels have already resulted in many companies serving several Latin markets from a single source of supply within the area.

Another group is represented by the Central American Common Market, including the five Central American states. Exchanges between the members of this group are already free, and the enlarged market they offer collectively has attracted a large number of companies to establish production within this area.

9. Mandatory controls

In early 1968, the U.S. imposed controls on the outflow of dollars from the country, on the repatriation of earnings from overseas operations, and on short-term financial assets held overseas by U.S. firms. At the outset, the controls prohibit new outflows to Continental Europe, restrict investments in a special category of nations, including the United Kingdom, Canada, and Japan, and hold investments in approved "less-developed" countries to slightly more than was invested in the 1965–1966 period. Local borrowing is not included in the controls. Reinvestments of foreign earnings are held to 35 percent of the annual average for 1965–1966. Percentages are likely to change from year to year. Those firms investing less than $100,000 a year are exempt, and special treatment will be accorded to companies making initial foreign ventures. The Office of Direct Foreign Investment in the Department of Commerce will administer the controls.

Section 21

HOW THE LAW CONTROLS THE COMPETITIVE RELATIONSHIPS OF A BUSINESS

BY

JERROLD G. VAN CISE

HOW THE LAW CONTROLS THE
COMPETITIVE RELATIONSHIPS
OF A BUSINESS

Introduction

An antitrust attorney dropped in at the Department of Justice in Washington shortly after the imposition of jail sentences in the electrical conspiracy case. He sought out the chief of the trial section responsible for instituting this litigation, shook his hand warmly, and said: "Thank you." When the surprised section chief asked why he was being thanked, the attorney responded: "Because now, for the first time, my clients are calling me 'Sir.'"

There is some truth in this story. The incentive of a businessman to seek the advice of antitrust counsel has been on the increase in recent years, due to the steadily expanding role that is being played by the laws on trade regulation in today's economy. But the respect accorded by the businessman to this advice has been noticeably stimulated in some industries by the current series of jail sentences imposed in antitrust proceedings brought against local plumbers in Las Vegas, small businessmen in Columbus, and big businessmen in Philadelphia. The failure today of an executive to know the application of these laws to his business may cause him to forfeit tomorrow his freedom to engage in this business.

There is, however, another—far more substantial—reason for a deferential approach by the businessman to our antitrust statutes. He should honor these laws because his right to profit from trade and commerce depends in large part upon the successful operation of their provisions. As the laws on trade regulation go, so—in a very real sense—goes free enterprise in our nation.

It seems appropriate, therefore, to include in this handbook a brief nontechnical discussion of what a businessman should know about the antitrust laws. Four questions commonly asked with respect to this legislation will be taken up in these pages and briefly answered in lay language, unmarred by citation of or quotation from legal authority. Any reader then desiring a more extended treatment by the author of the subject matter, with the details which delight the lawyer, may consult one of the publications listed in the footnote.[1] The four questions that are to be considered here are as follows:

---

[1] *Understanding the Antitrust Laws*, Practising Law Institute, New York, 1966, 382 pp. (prepared for the lawyer), and *The Federal Antitrust Laws*, American Enterprise Institute, Washington, D.C., 1965, 80 pp. (written for the layman).

1. Why were the antitrust laws enacted?
2. What do they say?
3. When do they apply?
4. How are they enforced?

1. Why the antitrust laws were enacted

A businessman normally engages in trade or commerce for profit. Without the incentive of some material reward, he would seldom devote his time or risk his money in private enterprise. If nothing could be gained, nothing would be ventured.

This right of a businessman to profit from trade and commerce, however, is man-made; and what man has given can, of course, be—and in some countries has been—taken away. It is the objective of our antitrust laws to make unnecessary in this country any such attack upon private profits. That objective is sought through the employment of statutory guidelines requiring the private interest of industry in money to serve the public interest of society in mankind. A passing glance at the history of trade regulation will make clear that underlying motivation of this legislation.

Private profits. In many areas of the world the profit motive of private businessmen has been under almost continuous attack as sinful. Thus, during medieval times, church saints viewed all profit as unjust, and preached that profit-taking businessmen would be punished in the hereafter. In more recent times, in Iron Curtain countries, antichurch sinners have similarly condemned private profit, and have proceeded to make sure that such businessmen are penalized in the here and now.

In contrast, in this country, the profit incentive of private industry has rarely been under serious attack. Rather, in colonial days, the early settlers discovered through trial and error that their survival was possible only if the production of the necessities of life was stimulated through the award of the fruits of industry to the industrious; and in more modern times, their descendants subsequently found that they benefited most when the wheels of their economy were turned by businessmen reaching for the carrot of cash. As a result, both of our major political parties and most of our American people have become firm believers in individual initiative.

In short, while private profit is banned as a vice in the Union of Soviet Socialist Republics, it is blessed as a virtue in the United States of America.

Private restraints. This opposition to private profit in other areas of the world has been premised, of course, upon the conviction that businessmen engaging in trade or commerce tend inevitably to seek their returns—not by competing on the merits in offering merchandise of the highest quality at the lowest price—but from restraints of trade. Socialists and communists believe that selfish motivation will first drive private profiteers either to conspire with or to destroy their competitors. Thereupon, it has been thought, the victorious businessmen will next proceed to use their control of industry to extort high prices from the consumer, to impose low wages upon the laborer, and eventually to control the body politic.

This conviction that businessmen will seek to profit from engrossing, rather than from engaging in, trade is not entirely lacking in support from the pages of history. For example, in the Industrial Revolution, manufacturers and middlemen notoriously sought to profit from restraints of trade at the expense of other members of society. Indeed, the indifference in those days of private interests to the public interest was even summarized by an American capitalist in the revealing declaration: "The public be damned."

The reasoning of this hostile approach to private profits—compounded in part from fantasy but in part also from fact—has led revolutionaries to the view that such profit is not only a moral, but also an economic and political sin. The solution of the confiscation of private business has therefore been proposed and has, unfortunately, been all too often adopted abroad.

Regulation of trade. Any such opposition to the profit system in this country has largely been forestalled, however, by the adoption of our antitrust laws. Our forefathers similarly feared, and to a degree suffered from, trade restraints. Nevertheless, they felt that private initiative had proven to be too valuable a source of creative energy during the history of our nation to be lightly discarded.

Our practical ancestors accordingly decided that the interest of a businessman in money—much like his attraction to women—needed only to be channelized by legislation into productive and away from destructive uses. Our antitrust —and marriage—laws resulted. A series of antitrust statutes was drafted to prohibit businessmen from engaging in antisocial restraints of trade. In this manner the profit motive was not only retained, but was simultaneously tamed to serve as a safe source of industrial power on our continent.

It seems ironic that abroad, purported virtue has begotten sin; whereas here, so-called sin has given birth to virtue. On the one hand, the communist has sought, for purportedly virtuous reasons, to repress private profits and has thereby produced a far greater evil, namely, the police state. On the other hand, the capitalist has, for allegedly selfish reasons, merely regulated private initiative and from this has come our free world. The roads to heaven and hell are not always clearly marked.

2. What the antitrust laws say

These reasons for the enactment of the antitrust laws understandably have dictated their content. Collectively, the resulting statutes direct the businessman to earn his profits in a competitive economy, through vying with other businessmen in offers of newer, better, and more varied goods and services on more attractive terms. In such a free economy, reliance is placed upon informed consumers to choose between these competitive offers and to award the prize of profits to the businessman who best merits their patronage.

The antitrust laws assume, in other words, that a businessman who profits in a competitive society is making a contribution for which he is equitably entitled to compensation. The legislation therefore intervenes only when he attempts instead to profit from private restraints which disserve rather than serve this economy. Three sets of these laws have been enacted.

Sherman Antitrust Act. The Sherman Antitrust Act, enacted in 1890, is the first of these congressional commandments whose objective is to require the businessman to earn his profits in a competitive economy. It is a broadly phrased statute which, in the manner of an emancipation proclamation, declares that our society must be free from unreasonable restraints of trade.

Section 1 of this statute is directed at joint restraints. Its language proscribes any contract, combination, or conspiracy of a businessman with any customer, any competitor, or any other person whose purpose or effect is to restrain competition so substantially as to constitute an unreasonable restraint of the interstate or foreign trade of the United States. The Section, in this manner, condemns obvious competitive abuses by agreement between businessmen, such as price-fixing, boycotts, division of markets, and tying arrangements. But it also reaches other concerts of action when a factual analysis of their objectives and operations reveals that they unreasonably restrict competition to a substantial degree in a substantial market.

Section 2 of the statute is aimed at both individual and joint restraints. It provides that no businessman, whether alone or in concert with any others, should maliciously attempt to obtain, or purposely exercise, the power to fix prices in or to exclude others from the interstate or foreign trade of the United States. It thereby seeks to forestall the end result of unreasonable restraints, namely, monopoly. The reasoning of this provision is that if it is unreasonable under Section 1 to restrict, it is even more unreasonable under Section 2 to eliminate competition to a substantial degree in a substantial market.

The conduct forbidden by these two Sections of the Sherman Act represent present, direct, and substantial restraints of competition, which threaten the very existence of competition in our free economy. Accordingly, the Act further provides that persons who engage in such unreasonable restraints of trade may be severely punished in actions brought by the Department of Justice and by private parties. Thus, Sherman Act violators may be sentenced to jail, fined up to $50,000 for each offense, divested of their property, and subjected to court injunctions, in government proceedings; and may be enjoined and required to pay threefold the damages suffered by victims of the unlawful conduct, in private suits.

Clayton and Robinson-Patman Acts. The Clayton Act, which was initially enacted in 1914 and was thereafter amended in 1936 by the Robinson-Patman Act and in 1950 by the Celler-Kefauver Act, is another of the congressional enactments intended to require the businessman to earn his profits in a competitive economy. It supplements the emancipation proclamation of the Sherman Act with a form of civil-rights legislation whose purpose is to guarantee equal rights to the small businessman to compete in the marketplace free of certain defined restraints from larger business organizations.

Section 2 of the Act, as amended by the Robinson-Patman Act, in essence declares that the small businessman should be entitled to purchase commodities at the same prices with the same services as those which his suppliers make available to his more powerful competitors, in the absence of just cause for a difference in treatment. Initially, the Section bans discrimination in price in the sale of commodities of like grade and quality in interstate commerce when the effect may be substantially to lessen competition. Next, it outlaws discriminatory brokerage arrangements between sellers and buyers of goods. Finally, it prohibits discrimination in paying for and/or providing services or facilities when they are not made available on proportionately equal terms to all competing customers. The Act then provides for certain exemptions from its prohibitions, e.g., where savings in costs justify discrimination in price and where competitive offers justify discrimination with respect to prices, services, and facilities. Finally, the Robinson-Patman Act concludes with provisions which make buyers liable for the knowing receipt of unlawful price discrimination, and which outlaw malicious price cuttting, whether in the form of discriminatory or of unreasonably low prices.

Section 3 of the Clayton Act is designed to permit the small businessman to negotiate with suppliers and distributors with the same freedom as is enjoyed by those of his competitors having greater bargaining power. The Section condemns the lease or sale of commodities on the condition that the lessee or purchaser refrain from doing business with competitors of the lessor or seller, where the effect may be substantially to lessen competition. It thereby outlaws total-requirement contracts, tying arrangements (which make available desirable commodities only on condition that less desirable products are taken), and undertakings that a lessee or vendee deal exclusively with the lessor or vendor, whenever the competitive freedom of the contracting outlet in selecting its suppliers is thereby unduly limited.

Section 7, on its part, is intended to guarantee that both small and big business will compete on the basis of the merits of their goods and services, without the assistance of unearned competitive strength obtained through a corporate acquisition. The Section proscribes (with minor exceptions) the purchase by a corporation of the stock or assets of another corporation engaged in commerce where the effect may be substantially to lessen competition. In this manner a more affluent corporation is prevented from gaining a substantial competitive advantage over smaller companies where this strength is obtained from acquiring its competitors, or buying up its suppliers and customers, or merging its purchasing power and resources with those of other corporations.

The practices forbidden by these and other Sections of this Act (e.g., Section 8, which bans interlocking directors between competitors) differ from those which are dealt with in the Sherman Act. They do not necessarily represent presently existing restraints of trade which directly threaten the existence of competition in our economy, as does the conduct proscribed by the earlier statute; but are rather potential or indirect threats to competition in the sense that, if they succeed in destroying small business, they will eliminate a major source of competition. For this reason, only one form of these potential restraints of trade, namely malicious price cutting in violation of the Robinson-Patman Act, is punishable by fines and jail. The other violations of the Clayton and amendatory acts, however, are sufficiently discouraged by the retention of the remedies of injunctions, divestiture, and treble damages in Department and/or in private actions, comparable to those specified in the Sherman Act, and by the addition of a provision for cease-and-desist orders to be entered in administrative proceedings brought by the Federal Trade Commission.

Federal Trade Commission Act. The Federal Trade Commission Act, passed originally in 1914 and amended subsequently in 1938, is still another statute designed to ensure that the businessman earn his profits in a competitive economy. As we have seen, the Sherman Act proclaims that our economy must be free of unreasonable restraints; and the Clayton and related acts protect the right of small, as well as large, companies to do business in this free economy. The Federal Trade Commission Act now completes this trilogy of trade regulations with what might be termed an "honest-ballot statute." It provides that all businessmen must abstain from unfair and deceptive conduct, so that the choice by consumers in electing between such competing small and large suppliers will be based on the value to the buyers of the proffered goods and services.

Initially, Section 5 of this Act condemns unfair methods of competition in interstate or foreign commerce. This reaches what are thought of as incipient violations of the other antitrust statutes and any other conduct which might impair free and fair competition in the marketplace.

Thereafter, the Section continues with a sweeping ban on all unfair or deceptive acts or practices in such commerce. This further prohibition embraces such widely varying antisocial conduct as false advertising, fictitious list pricing, fraudulent guarantees, gambling sales devices, misleading representations, and outright fraud.

The Federal Trade Commission Act, by this Section 5, deals with even less tangible threats to a competitive economy than the conduct prohibited by the Sherman, Clayton, and amendatory acts. Accordingly, it provides that violations of its provisions may only be proceeded against in administrative proceedings brought by the Federal Trade Commission. But once a Commission cease-and-desist order has been entered warning a respondent not to engage in a particular unfair act or practice, any further violation of this nature is punishable by penalties of up to $5,000 per day for each day of a continuing offense.

With this addition of the Federal Trade Commission Act to the other trade-regulation statutes, there emerges a reasonably clear and remarkably consistent picture of the economy envisioned by these laws. In that economy, profits must be earned in competitive markets, in which large and small sellers vie for the patronage of free and informed buyers. The Sherman Act safeguards the "competitive" markets; the Clayton Act insures the presence of both "large and small" sellers; and the Federal Trade Commission Act endeavors to make possible "free and informed" buyers. There are miscellaneous other federal and state statutes, such as those dealing with fair trade, foreign trade, and specially regulated industries, but this supplemental legislation represents special details of little interest in a general antitrust survey.

Critics admittedly delight in describing the antitrust laws as confused and inconsistent. In support of their unfavorable reviews, moreover, they point to individual strokes of the legislative brush which have, on occasion, produced crude statutory language, as in the case of the Robinson-Patman Act. A disinterested observer who will step back sufficiently to merge the three major antitrust laws into the composite antitrust legislation, however, will find from this perspective that there will emerge a remarkably comprehensive and comprehensible congressional painting. The subject matter thus revealed may be the "Three Graces" or the "Three Furies," depending upon one's school of antitrust thought, but the identity of this trinity will certainly be more apparent than in most modern art. Once trade regulation is approached as an integrated totality, the whole is far clearer than its several statutory parts.

3. When the antitrust laws apply to relations with customers

These antitrust laws apply essentially to three relationships of a business, namely, to those with suppliers and customers, to those with competitors, and to those with internal divisions and subsidiaries. These relationships will now be dealt with in the order in which they have been listed.

The preceding discussion of the purposes and provisions of the antitrust laws reasonably indicates when the prohibitions of these laws will apply to the relationships of a business with its suppliers and customers. The teaching of this legislation is that a businessman is free to invite others to sell to and buy from him, in order to enable him to compete more effectively with their assistance; but he may not unduly interfere with, or unfairly influence, their competition. His profits must be derived from the voluntary support of merchants, not from the involuntary submission of mercenaries.

This application of antitrust principles to these so-called "vertical" relationships of a businessman may roughly be grouped into three categories: (1) his preliminary contacts in deciding whether or not to deal with suppliers and distributors, (2) his subsequent contracts with these parties, and (3) his prices and terms in doing business with such parties.

Customer contacts. A businessman in a free society is entitled to choose his friends, his political party, and his religion. This freedom also extends to the selection of his suppliers and his customers. A competitor operating in a free market may in good faith deal or not deal with whom he pleases.

This liberty of choice, however, must be extended reciprocally to his suppliers and to his customers. The businessman may advise his customers with respect to any competitive activity, but he may not automatically accept or reject them for their failure to conform to that advice. Specifically, he may not require a potential seller or buyer, as a condition of being permitted to do business with him, to surrender his independence in a manner which would be unlawful if it were formalized in a written contract. For example, the threat of refusal to deal may not be used to dictate the purchases of, or to limit the territories of, or to control the resale prices charged by one's customers, in a manner which would restrain trade in violation of the Sherman and Robinson-Patman Acts.

This mutual freedom of selection by sellers and buyers, moreover, may not be distorted by deception, bad faith, fraud, or oppression. The Federal Trade Commission Act, as previously noted, seeks to free the channels of trade from unethical acts and practices which contaminate and eventually clog the flow of commerce. Thus, franchisors must make full disclosures of all material facts before inducing uninformed applicants to invest their savings in a franchised operation.

Customer contracts. A businessman is likewise free to enter into such forms of agreements as may be reasonably necessary to do business with the sellers and the buyers that he selects. Thus, he may assure an outlet that it has been selected as his exclusive distributor. In addition, if he franchises the latter to do business by use of the former's trade name, he may obligate the outlet to purchase such distinctive supplies as may be required to provide the public with the products associated with the franchised name. Finally, he may establish objective, nondiscriminatory standards for the resale of his products—such as those which require a customer to use its best efforts to promote the products in (but not solely in) defined areas of primary responsibility, maintain reasonable servicing facilities, and refrain from unfair practices—and may further provide that breach of such standards will constitute just cause for terminating their relationship.

These agreements may not, however, go beyond what is necessary to enable a business organization to profit from competing in its market with the assistance of its suppliers and customers, and seek further to gain from restraining the competition of those vendors and vendees in their respective markets. For example, a businessman should hesitate to prohibit his dealers from obtaining any and all goods and services from other suppliers, in violation of the Clayton Act, or to regiment the resale prices, customers, and markets of those dealers in a manner outlawed by the Sherman Act (unless saved by fair-trade legislation).

A small businessman, who is otherwise unable to enter into or remain in a market, may possibly negotiate at arms length with equally small and vulnerable outlets to form a more restrictive relationship for their mutual survival than is described above.   Thus, a newcomer probably may require reciprocal exclusive dealing from its customers in order to launch a new product or service in competition with entrenched establishments.   But a substantial seller with strong commercial claws cannot successfully hide under any such sheep's clothing of small business and claim a privilege to dominate its dealers.   What would be a defensive act for a young lamb would be offensive action by the lion of an industry.

Discrimination in price.   A businessman, finally, has substantial freedom in pricing his products, so long as he does not thereby threaten the competitive freedom of others.   For example, he may sell the same grade and quality of a product under differing brands at differing prices, provided that each brand of the product is offered to—and thus cannot injure competition with—each of his customers.   In addition, his prices for the same grade and quality of the identical commodity may vary between classes of buyers, permitting wholesalers to purchase at lower rates than retailers, and retailers to buy at lower levels than consumers, as competition between these classes is not affected. Also, he may sell a particular grade and quality of a product at one price to one customer, and sell an unlike grade and quality of the same product at a lower price to another customer, if the latter grade and quality is inferior in physical content and in customer appeal.

A seller may not, however—without affirmative justification—safely sell to competing buyers the same grade of a commodity at substantially different prices, or on terms significantly affecting those prices, over a substantial period of time. Nor may he make payments for or offer to provide, to some purchasers of a commodity, certain services and facilities (e.g., in the form of advertising assistance, warehousing, free goods, and special packaging), without making a comparable offer to other customers competing in the resale of this commodity. This is because his inducement of purchases from favored outlets—through providing them with significant benefits in the form of lower prices and better promotions—will handicap other buyers who compete with the favored purchasers, and may even foreclose other sellers from doing business with the preferred outlets.   Sellers may not thus profit from sales obtained by discriminatory prices or through discriminatory promotions, which injure the competition of others in violation of the Robinson-Patman Act, unless their conduct is justified under its statutory provisions by cost savings attributable to differences in methods of sale and delivery (in the case of differing prices) or by the necessity to meet in good faith competitive offers (in the event of differing prices or promotions).

It is worth adding that buyers as well as sellers are forbidden to profit from these restrictive acts and discriminatory practices.   For example, a buyer may not use his selection of essential suppliers as a means of coercing the latter to refuse to sell to other buyers; nor require these sources of supply to regiment the price and territories of such other buyers; nor knowingly induce the receipt of preferential discounts, allowances, services, and facilities to the injury of competition from such other buyers. It will be recalled that Eve was equally guilty when she persuaded Adam to profit from a forbidden acquisition and was therefore required to share in the first known punishment of divestiture in the history of trade regulation.

4. When the antitrust laws apply to relations with competitors

The antitrust principles applicable to the relationships between competitors, in similar fashion, distinguish between conduct which is consistent and that which is inconsistent with a free economy. A businessman may enjoy profits earned in fair and informed competition with other members of his industry.

He may not, however, enhance such profits with monetary returns obtained through conspiracy with or control over these competitors.

This application of antitrust principles to what are sometimes called the "horizontal" relationships between a businessman and his competitors may also be divided, for convenience, into three categories: (1) his informal contacts with his competitors, (2) his more formal contracts with these competitors, and (3) his problems in the event that he should seek to control the latter.

Competitor contacts. Whether he is engaged in playing golf or in practicing his trade, a businessman is permitted to compete vigorously. On the one hand, he may enjoy personal friendships with his opponents. On the other, however, he may utilize his ingenuity to beat them. The mere fact that he may succeed, and in the process may make life difficult for others, will not expose him to successful attack.

His competition with others, however, should be bona fide. He may not derive his profits from an outward show of rugged rivalry, while secretly softening the impact of his struggles—much like the purported practices of professional wrestlers. Thus he would do well to avoid commercial courtesies inconsistent with competition, such as the confidential disclosure to his competitors of the intimate details of his business, a friendly discussion with them of his contemplated price moves, or an assurance of loyal adherence to their policies and programs. Undue familiarity with competitors often breeds a course of action in contempt of the Sherman Act—conduct which is particularly suspect because cloaked in the secrecy of silence.

His competition with other members of his industry should also be fair. Unconscionable conduct in the form of the bribery of competitors' employees, predatory below-cost pricing, disparagement of competitive products, and foreclosure of substantial markets by a network of total-requirement contracts, would conflict with the Federal Trade Commission Act. Succinctly stated, he should seek neither to fix the competitive race nor to foul the individual participants in that race.

Competitor contracts.   A businessman is likewise permitted to enter into contractual relationships with his competitors, if his purpose is to improve the opportunities of all to compete.   Thus, he may join in forming trade associations for the collection, averaging, and distribution of industry statistics with respect to past transactions, in order to facilitate informed competition.   Again, he may participate in industry service organizations which are established to conduct national advertising promotions, to provide more efficient equipment, and to develop new-product markets, in a manner which would be beyond the resources of the smaller individual members.   Such industry-wide cooperation to enhance competition is becoming increasingly essential if small business is to contend on equal terms with big business.

Competitors, however, should not go beyond the promotion of, and instead attempt to regulate, their competition.   Regardless of good motives, profits are suspect when earned by companies which collectively determine the products, limit the production, fix the prices, regulate the practices, or select the persons to be recognized as authorized outlets in their industry.   The attendant curtailment of competition in the form of boycotts, blacklists, white lists, divisions of markets, and price-fixing represents per se violations of the Sherman Act.   The antitrust laws assume that self-regulation will inevitably become selfish regulation, and they will have none of it.

There are, of course, lines of commerce which of necessity require some limitation upon competition if they are effectively to serve the public.   The communications, power, railroad, and securities industries are illustrative.   But to what extent competition should be encouraged or discouraged in these lines of commerce had best be left to the government agencies authorized by law to regulate them.   Any restraints approved by disinterested public officials should safeguard the consumer from the excessive profits which might otherwise result from restrictions imposed by interested private parties.

Monopolization of trade.   It follows from this discussion that—if a group of competitors may not lawfully control the prices of, or determine the persons who may participate in, an industry—necessarily a single person or a single group of persons should not be permitted to do so.   For profits are suspect whether they are derived from the cooperation of conspirators or the coercion of a monopolist.

It is true, as above explained, that a private businessman may safely strive to surpass his competitors.   He is entitled to the fruits of any special skills, superior products, natural advantages, or patents covering inventions conceived by him.   He may not, however, maliciously seek to profit by predatory tactics intended to suppress the competition of others, such as by cutting off rivals from essential sources of supply, coercing customers into refusing to deal with those competitors, and malicious price cutting. Rule-or-ruin tactics designed to force competitors either to surrender their independence or to leave the industry are obviously prohibited both by the letter and the spirit of the antitrust laws.

The businessman, indeed, may not safely enjoy monopoly profits even when they are derived from normal business practices, if this action is consciously taken in order to obtain or to retain the power to regulate by private edict the price levels of and the participants in the industry. For example, long-term leasing may not be used to control a line of commerce. Once more, it should be stressed that the antitrust laws permit private enterprise to engage in business for profit only so long as its earnings are derived from the competition of alternative suppliers who vie for the favor of free and informed buyers. Unless monopoly power is thrust unwillingly upon him, a businessman is forbidden to decide what is best for an industry on any theory that what is best for his company is necessarily best for the country. Benevolent as well as malevolent dictatorship is proscribed by the laws on trade regulation.

5. When the antitrust laws apply to relations within the corporation

There remains the issue of the manner in which the antitrust laws relate to the internal organization of a business. Here, the application of the guiding legal principles, in distinguishing between the licit and the illicit, is difficult. Nevertheless, the regulatory approach is the same, namely, that a businessman should derive his profits from creative competition rather than from restrictive restraints.

Three phases of these internal relationships of a corporation merit special attention, namely, (1) its size, (2) its structure, and (3) its growth through mergers and joint ventures.

Corporate size. The industrialist of today is permitted to marshal a vast aggregation of capital funds, physical properties, and mobilized manpower under a single corporate banner. The resulting size of the assembled host at times dwarfs even the resources of local and state governments. This concentration of competitive power is viewed by our antitrust laws as an inevitable phenomenon of a world of big problems, like big trade unions and big federal government.

The greater the size of the corporation in a particular line of commerce, however, the greater is its potential strength. This size, if short of monopoly power, does not violate the antitrust laws; but it affords the opportunity for profit—making from abuses in the uses of this strength. Thus, a refusal by a major manufacturer to deal with alleged price-cutters and transhippers may unduly regiment the prices and territory of its dealers in violation of the Sherman Act, even though this supplier has no overall monopoly of its line of commerce. Similarly, the discriminatory reduction by this large company of the prices of an advertised brand of product in order purportedly to meet the prices of unadvertised brands of weaker manufacturers may unreasonably beat, rather than merely meet, the latter prices, and therefore cannot always be justified under the Robinson-Patman Act.

The larger the size of a corporation, moreover, the more careful it must be to avoid any use of the small irregularities of trade which may be overlooked if engaged in by the minor members of an industry, but can scarcely go unnoticed when promoted nationally by the major members. Confusing labels, deceptive claims, incomplete offers, fictitious pricing, and unlawful lotteries—which divert the trade of the unsuspecting consumer from the moral to the amoral supplier— not only are illegal, but also are lethal when utilized by big business.   The intercontinental range of the Big Lie launched by a corporate Goliath is far more destructive today than any localized falsehoods flung from the slingshot of a defiant David.

Corporate structure.   The modern industrialist is likewise free to engage in multiple businesses.   Whether he operates a local confectionery store or a national dairy chain, he may vertically integrate his manufacturing, warehousing, and retailing functions under one management, may horizontally distribute his products in differing local markets, and may add from time to time supplemental lines of commerce.   The objective of the antitrust laws would be frustrated if American industry was "Hinduized" into strict caste or craft guilds, each limited to a single economic function, and was further "Balkanized" into Lilliputian locals confined to single geographical areas.

Liberty to innovate and to integrate, however, may give competitive advantages to a multibusiness corporation in its competition with a single-business company.   Accordingly, it must be cautious in using the commercial strength of one of its businesses or divisions in a manner to secure profits for another of its integrated businesses or divisions which were not fairly earned by the latter in the marketplace.   Thus the employment of reciprocity, by which the purchasing power of one corporate unit is deployed to force sellers to purchase in return from another unit of the corporation, gives to the integrated enterprise added returns attributable to coercion rather than to competition, in violation of the Sherman and Federal Trade Commission Acts. Similarly, the use of the profits derived in one market to subsidize predatory pricing in another may financially underwrite malicious competition, in defiance of the Robinson-Patman Act.

The separate incorporation of each business and each division of an integrated organization into subsidiaries of a common parent will particularly invite attack upon any such diversion of the corporate troops of a big corporate brother to surround and win an otherwise even fight engaged in by a smaller member of the corporate family.   It will permit an allegation to the effect that two distinct persons are combining to restrain unduly the trade of another.   Failure to seek separate charters for the differing businesses of an integrated organization will not, of course, safeguard the multiline company from the laws on trade regulation, since some of the laws do not require the joint action of two distinct persons; it merely makes the application of these statutes more difficult. Needless to say, a corporate omission cannot justify sins of antitrust commission.

Mergers and joint ventures. An industrialist, finally, may also utilize his capital resources to acquire the stock or assets of other corporations. True, his subsequent profits from the acquisition will be reaped in a field in which he had not initially sown; but the resulting harvest may nevertheless be gleaned by him, so long as he is satisfied with the fruits of honest husbandry. For unless buyers may buy, then sellers may not sell; and if a seller may not sell his business when this is to his advantage, he will have far less of an incentive to devote his funds and his future in building up this business.

The purchaser of the stock or assets of another company, nevertheless, will violate Section 7 of the Clayton Act and one or more of the Sections of the Sherman Act, if he acquires a significant and successful competitor, or buys a series of suppliers or customers representing a substantial share of a substantial market. In the first case, the subsequent profits of the combination of two viable competitors will in part arise from limiting, if not eliminating, competition between the previously contending companies. In the second case, the resulting returns of the purchaser taking over major sources of supply or distribution will to a degree be attributable to controlling, if not foreclosing, access to the acquired assets by his competitors. Special circumstances, such as an economic necessity for combined operations in order to meet competition or to forestall insolvency, may justify such horizontal or vertical mergers; but the burden of establishing this defense, where the restraint is not *de minimis,* must be assumed by the purchaser.

The industrialist who avoids any such horizontal or vertical transactions may still seek to acquire the stock or assets of an unrelated business, or to share in a joint venture creating an unrelated business. These forms of growth by acquisition are less likely to face antitrust attack. The Department of Justice and the Federal Trade Commission, however, are currently urging before the courts that even these transactions may on occasion be vulnerable, e.g., when they restrain potential competition between the contracting parties, or give undue strength to those parties in their competition with others, or accelerate a trend toward increased concentration in industry. Under these circumstances, any such conglomerate acquisition or joint venture preferably should be considered only where the facts demonstrate that it will tend to erode, rather than to erect, barriers to competition, by expanding the industrial markets involved.

6. How the antitrust laws are enforced

Having covered the purposes, provisions, and applications of the antitrust laws, we now turn to the final problem of enforcement. We have seen that the laws on trade regulation require a businessman to earn his profits through his participation in a competitive economy.   But what is to prevent him from pocketing his profits and withholding his competitive contribution?   On occasion, the propensity to sin of fathers who engaged in trade restraints during the Industrial Revolution may have descended to the children of this generation.

The answer to this final question of antitrust enforcement is to be found in (1) the compliance procedures established by individual companies, (2) the coercive proceedings instituted by public and private plaintiffs, and (3) certain cooperative programs which may be joined in by government and industry.

Compliance procedures.   The voluntary procedures for antitrust compliance of American industry are limited only by the resourcefulness of counsel and the resources of his company.   Crime in antitrust, when discovered, does not pay today; and the bigger the company, the more painful may be its fall from grace.   By and large, therefore, responsible executives are accustomed to take steps along the lines of the following: to authorize trade regulation surveys, to issue directives correcting any trade restraints thereby discovered, and to establish policing programs to insure and record the future competitive virtues of the company.

These compliance procedures, when properly administered, have been found to be effective in safeguarding both management and corporation from the civil and criminal penalties for antitrust violation.   Individual companies have had on occasion to limit their scope, however, in order to meet the competition of unlawful practices pursued in disregard of the antitrust laws by others.   Compliance by a company with the nondiscriminatory policies of the Robinson-Patman Act and the fair-competition requirements of the Federal Trade Commission Act, for example, is not always possible in the face of the loss of business resulting from the defiance of these laws by competitors.

The reputable businessman is aware of these occasional trade irregularities in his industry because of his occasional forced participation in their violations, as above described; but he is powerless to free his company and his industry from the unlawful practices without assistance from the government.   This is because the antitrust statutes forbid him either to conspire with, or to coerce, other members of his industry to join him in complying with any private regulation of trade, however laudable may be his motives.   Indeed, any industry policeman who seeks to impersonate a government prosecutor in seeking antitrust compliance merely exposes himself in turn to prosecution.

Coercive proceedings.   The involuntary proceedings which may be brought by the government to compel antitrust compliance on the part of those who will not voluntarily conform to these laws range from the criminal and civil actions of the Department of Justice, through the injunctive and treble-damage suits of private persons, to the sweeping administrative procedures of the Federal Trade Commission.   The potential punishment for antitrust violation, as previously explained, correspondingly embraces fines, jail, injunctions, divestiture, and treble damages—plus thereafter living much of one's life with lawyers to insure against contempt of court or Commission orders. At the day of recent antitrust judgments, there has been much weeping and wailing and gnashing of teeth.

The funds of public and private plaintiffs are nevertheless limited, and their knowledge of trade practices is often more so. It follows that a Federal patrolman or a private detective is not always available to drive to the scene of every antitrust crime, because of shortages of manpower and equipment, and even if he were, he would not always know whom to apprehend. There are therefore still some persons in some industries who will gamble the future of their persons and property in return for the present temporary enjoyment of the gains from as yet undiscovered trade restraints.

The occasional businessman who thus professes and simultaneously profanes his faith in a free competitive economy raises a serious problem for government, for industry, and for society. His competitors know who he is, but may not act; whereas government may act, but is unable to do so. With a little bit of luck, the beatnik businessman sometimes avoids being caught.

Partnership in regulation. In recent years, however, a practical procedure has been evolving which on the one hand permits the responsible majority in an industry to advise how the stream of commerce can be cleansed of any such contaminating trade abuse, and on the other enables the government—on the basis of this advice—to take corrective action against any irresponsible minority which thereafter continues its polluting practices. This procedure requires the cooperation of the Department of Justice or of the Federal Trade Commission. The latter, however, has taken the lead in enlisting the assistance of businessmen in such cooperative trade regulation.

Initially, under such a partnership arrangement, an industry group may draft a guide, rule, or rules which condemn an unreasonable or unfair trade restraint, and may submit its proposal to the Department or to the Commission. The government agency then may approve or disapprove the suggestion, and may advise whether and to what extent the industry may police the prohibited conduct. Thus, disinterested laboratories may be authorized to test products to determine whether they measure up to their advertised claims. Again, professional staffs may investigate practices to see whether or not they conform to approved standards. An appeal from any adverse findings may then be taken to an impartial body and the results may be publicized.

Subsequently, under some of these cooperative enforcement programs, the industry group may request one of the government agencies to take action against any recalcitrant violator of an approved guide or rule. For as previously explained, a trade organization may only propose how to deal with, but may not itself coercively dispose of, recalcitrant restraints. Their enforcement functions should be limited much in the manner of the church in earlier days in dealing with unlawful conduct by the clergy, where a priest might be unfrocked by the church for a crime, but had to be turned over to the secular arm of the state for any corporal punishment.

Conclusion

A few years ago the writer had the privilege of addressing a trade group on the "do's" and "don't's" of the antitrust laws. When he finished, a member of the audience asked permission to come forward and make a few remarks. Upon reaching the microphone, the latter explained that he had recently been in jail for an alleged unlawful trade restraint. He thereupon described his experiences in being handcuffed, confined in the penitentiary, and required to associate with criminal companions; and he concluded with the statement that he wished that he had acquired his knowledge of the antitrust laws "before rather than afterwards."

This anecdote—like that in the introduction to this section—underscores our need to acquire a working understanding of the laws on trade regulation. As previously stated, the safety of one's individual person and property may otherwise be in danger.

We need more, however, than a knowledge of the antitrust laws. We must also desire compliance with their provisions. Otherwise the role of management itself in our economy may be jeopardized. It will be recalled that when the feudal aristocracy of France no longer earned its prerogatives in competitive warfare, it was guillotined. It is essential, therefore, that the industrial aristocracy of this country continue to justify its profits by competitive marketing, or, in less drastic form, it "could happen here." It has been said that one either learns from history, or repeats it.

In conclusion—a word to the businessman who on occasion states that he would be "happy" to comply with the antitrust laws if only they were "clarified." Such a businessman might ask himself whether the famous observation of a great humorist with respect to the Bible is not equally applicable to his alleged antitrust confusion. Is it not possible that:

"It is not what I don't understand that troubles me; it is what I understand all too well"?

Section 22

ADVERTISING AND THE LAW

BY

JOSHUA LEVINE

ADVERTISING AND THE LAW

Introduction

Today, it is practically impossible to conduct a business enterprise, large or small, without being affected by laws relating to advertising. Whether it be a classified ad for a salesman or a TV commercial on a network telecast, the "rules of the game" must be observed. Unfortunately, many of these rules are not so clearly defined as they might be, and their interpretation will require the professional skills of your counsel. Furthermore, our legislative, judicial, and administrative bodies are constantly at work in this rapidly developing field. Accordingly, all this section can hope to accomplish is to indicate to you some problem areas and to give you a bird's-eye view of the law. The emphasis will be on the Federal statutes, although some general references will be made to state laws and to nongovernmental regulatory bodies.

1. Federal Trade Commission Act

Powers and procedures. The Federal Trade Commission Act empowers the Federal Trade Commission to prevent unfair methods of competition or unfair or deceptive acts or practices in commerce. Under this broad power the Commission has jurisdiction over advertising which is "misleading in a material respect." Pursuant to its authority under the act, the Federal Trade Commission staff monitors broadcasts and telecasts of commercial announcements and reviews advertising in newspapers and other publications. It also invites complaints from consumers and businessmen who believe that they are injured or threatened with injury by reason of certain advertising.

The Federal Trade Commission is authorized to issue complaints, hold hearings thereon, and issue a cease-and-desist order if such an order is warranted by the evidence. If not appealed from within the prescribed time, the order becomes final and binding. The violation of any final cease-and-desist order may bring on serious penalties—up to $5,000 for each violation (and in the case of a continuing violation, each day of such continuance is a separate offense). The Commission also has the power to request a court to enjoin the dissemination of any false advertisement of a food, drug, device,[1] or cosmetic. In addi-

---

[1] "Device" is defined in the Federal Food, Drug, and Cosmetic Act as "instruments, apparatus, and contrivances, including their component parts, and accessories, intended

tion, where the use of a food, drug, device, or cosmetic which is falsely advertised may be injurious to health, or where advertisements of any such products are disseminated with intent to defraud or mislead, whether or not the item advertised is injurious to health, the Commission may refer the matter to the Department of Justice for the institution of criminal proceedings which could lead to fine and imprisonment.

Very frequently an offending advertiser is afforded an opportunity by the Federal Trade Commission to either informally or formally agree to alter his advertising in certain respects so as to bring it into conformity with what the Commission believes is proper under the law. The formal agreement is in the form of a consent order which has the same force and effect as a cease-and-desist order issued after a hearing and, like the latter, is circulated to the public. However, the Federal Trade Commission allows the advertiser to enter into such a consent order without an admission on his part that he has violated the law, and the order will so state. The informal agreement to modify advertising is ordinarily not published (although the Commission reserves the right to do so) and, where it can be worked out, is to be preferred over the consent order, particularly because a violation of the agreement does not incur any of the penalties which flow from the violation of an order. The Commission is not obliged to enter into consent orders or informal agreements and may always insist upon a cease-and-desist order which makes a public finding of wrongdoing on the part of the advertiser. While FTC complaints may be successfully defended, it frequently entails a great deal of expense and unfavorable publicity.

Under its rules and regulations the Federal Trade Commission will afford businessmen assistance in determining, in advance, whether a proposed course of action, if pursued, may violate any of the laws administered by the Commission and, where practicable, will give them the benefit of the Commission's views in the form of a written advisory opinion. Any request for such an opinion should be addressed to the Secretary of the Commission in Washington, D.C., and include full and complete information regarding the proposed course of action. Conferences with members of the Commission's staff may be held before or after submittal of the request. Advisory opinions are usually published, but without any references to the particular company or brand involved. The Commission reserves the right to reconsider and modify or rescind any advisory opinion which it issues, but its rules and regulations declare that in such event the information submitted to it will not be used as the basis for a proceeding.

From time to time the Federal Trade Commission issues valuable rules and guides which indicate the Commission's view with respect to various practices.

---

(1) for use on the diagnosis, cure, mitigation, treatment, or prevention of disease in man or other animals; or (2) to affect the structure of any function of the body of man or other animals.''

These rules and guides fall into three general groups: Trade Practice Conference Rules, FTC Trade Regulation Rules, and FTC Guides. Copies of all of these are available at the office of the Bureau of Information, Federal Trade Commission, Washington, D.C.

Trade Practice Conference Rules. These rules represent a declaration by the Federal Trade Commission and by those industry members which formally accept them that certain practices are unfair methods of competition. Some of these rules relate to advertising and sales promotion. Over 150 industries have been made the subject of Trade Practice Conference Rules and you will find them listed as an appendix to this section on page 742.

FTC Trade Regulation Rules. These rules cover certain very specific problems in particular industries and state the FTC position with respect to them. Since this is a relatively new procedure, only eight sets of rules of this type are now in effect. They relate to—

1. Deceptive Use of "Leakproof," "Guaranteed Leakproof," etc., as Descriptive of Dry Cell Batteries
2. Advertising and Labeling of Sleeping Bags as to Size
3. Misuse of "Automatic" or Terms of Similar Import as Descriptive of Household Electric Sewing Machines
4. Deception as to Nonprismatic and Partially Prismatic Instruments Being Prismatic Binoculars
5. Misbranding and Deception as to Leather Content of Waist Belts
6. Deceptive Advertising and Labeling of Previously Used Lubricating Oil
7. Deceptive Advertising and Labeling as to Size of Tablecloths and Related Products
8. Deceptive Advertising as to Sizes of Viewable Pictures shown by Television Receiving Sets
9. Failure to Disclose That Skin Irritation May Result from Washing or Handling Glass Fiber Curtains and Draperies and Glass Fiber Curtain and Drapery Fabrics

At this time there are pending proceedings to establish Trade Regulation Rules concerning—

The prevention of the unlawful granting or furnishing of discriminatory advertising payments or promotional allowances, services, or facilities to customers competing in the resale of men's and boys' tailored clothing
Incandescent Electric Light Bulbs
Advertising of non-prescription Analgesic Drugs
Deception as to Transistor Count of Radio Sets and Walkie-Talkies

FTC Guides. The Commission has adopted certain guides which are administrative interpretations of laws administered by the Commission and are issued for the guidance of the public. These guides may relate to a practice common to many industries or to specific practices of a particular industry. Such guides have been issued on the following subjects:

Deceptive Labeling and Advertising of Adhesive Composition
Advertising Allowances and Other Merchandising Payments and Services
Avoiding Deceptive use of the Word "Mill" in the Textile Industry
Bait Advertising
Cigarette Advertising
Debt Collection Deception
Advertising Fallout Shelters
Advertising of Guarantees
Mail Order Insurance Industry
Deceptive Pricing
Advertising Radiation Monitoring Instruments
Advertising Shell Homes
Shoe Content Labeling in Advertising
Tire Advertising

At this writing the Federal Trade Commission is considering issuing a guide to retail credit transactions as well as one for the dog and cat food industry.

False or misleading advertising of a product or service. An advertisement may be false or misleading either because of what is expressed or implied by the use of words, sound, or pictorial representation or by any combination of these. Also, the failure to state a material fact may cause a similar result. Major areas of false and misleading advertising are as follows:

Misrepresenting the effectiveness or the nature, quality, or characteristics of any product. However, harmless "puffing" is permitted through the use of terms such as "best looking," "best tasting," "most beautiful," "finest," and similar expressions of opinion not made as a representation of fact

Misrepresenting the composition of any product, e.g., advertising that the product contains grape flavor when in fact the flavor does not come from grapes but from some artificial source

Defaming a competitor, falsely disparaging his products or services, or making false or deceptive comparisons with his products

Misrepresenting the character or state of a business, e.g., calling oneself a manufacturer when not engaged in such an activity or not absolutely controlling the manufacture of his product

Misrepresenting the affiliation of the advertiser with persons, firms, or organizations

Misrepresenting the financial standing of the advertiser, or the length of time in which he has engaged in business

Misrepresenting the status of facilities or personnel, e.g., falsely stating that one has plants all over the country or that certain employees are engineers or have other professional qualifications

Misrepresenting the origin of a product, e.g., stating or implying that a product is made in the United States if, in fact, the whole or a substantial part of the product is made outside the United States, or falsely stating or implying a product is made in another country

Misrepresenting as new, products which are used, secondhand, or rebuilt, or made from previously used materials

Characterizing a product as being new (in the sense of being different) for a period of longer than six months. Test marketing covering not more than 15% of the population and a period of not more than six months may be conducted in good faith before the time limit on the use of the term "new" begins to run. This time limit may be curtailed or extended on a showing of exceptional circumstances warranting such action

Misrepresenting or passing off, directly or by inference, one's products as the product of another manufacturer. Such misrepresentation may occur in a variety of ways, including the simulation of competitors' advertising, his business names, his trademarks, and packaging

Misrepresenting tests, surveys, awards, or certifications

Representing that a testimonial was unsolicited when such was not the fact. Furthermore, testimonials may not be used to make false statements about a product even though such statement may be the honest opinion of the person making it. The classic example of such a false statement is a testimonial from a user who says, "Your pills cured me of cancer." In any event, testimonials should not cover areas beyond the individual's competence to diagnose and prescribe for himself and should always be based on the actual experience of the individual

Misrepresenting a job or business opportunity

Misrepresenting the method or process by which a product is made, e.g., custom-made, handmade, union-made, homemade, vat-dyed, damask, engraved, etc., when such is not the case

Misrepresenting that a product or service is the only one with certain characteristics or features

Misrepresenting that a product conforms to a certain legal or official standard

Misrepresenting the quality, weight, number, or size of a product

Failing to conspicuously disclose any conditions attached to a "free" offer. If one has to buy something in order to get the free goods, such condition must be clearly set forth in the offer at the outset. Even if the condition is shown, the free offer may be deceptive if the price of the product which must be purchased has been increased or if the quantity of the product has been reduced to cover in whole or in part the cost of the free goods

Failing to disclose all of the material terms and conditions of a guarantee, i.e., what is guaranteed, who guarantees it, for how long, the manner in which the guarantor will perform, and what the purchaser must do to get the benefits of the guarantee

Advertising a list or suggested retail price when such price is significantly higher than the actual price at which the product is sold generally; or misrepresenting a price as a bargain or special price, or making misleading price comparisons

Engaging in bait advertising, i.e., offering to sell a product which the advertiser does not truly want to sell, but rather offers to create a lead to a prospective customer whom he hopes to switch to a higher-priced or more profitable item

2. Special statutes enforced by the Federal Trade Commission which affect the advertising of furs, textiles, and wool products

A detailed set of rules for the labeling, invoicing, and advertising of furs, textiles, and wool products will be found in the Fur Products Labeling Act, the Wool Products Labeling Act, and in the Textile Fiber Products Identification Act and in the regulations promulgated pursuant to each of these statutes. These laws are designed to protect the purchaser against the misrepresentation of fur, wool, and textile products and are intended to supplement the provisions of the Federal Trade Commission Act. They are enforced by the Commission, which in proper cases may issue a cease-and-desist order, may seek a court injunction, and, in the case of wool products, may resort to condemnation.

3. Federal Food, Drug, and Cosmetic Act

This act is designed primarily to regulate the composition and the labeling of foods, drugs, cosmetics, and devices and the advertising of prescription drugs. However, the Food and Drug Administration, which administers the act, also asserts jurisdiction over certain other advertising.

"Labeling" is defined in the regulations to include all written, printed, or graphic matter accompanying an article at any time while such article is in interstate commerce or is being held for sale after shipment or delivery in interstate commerce. From this it is evident that if a circular is inserted in a carton of a food, drug, cosmetic, or device, such circular comes within the definition of "labeling." In addition, point-of-sale material set up on the counter of a drugstore or a grocery store and displayed in conjunction with the product itself, and promotional material generally used by the dealer in promoting the sale of the product, have been held to be "labeling" within the scope of the definition.

Also of interest is the special power which the Food and Drug Administration may exercise in connection with the advertising of drugs and devices—and this is aside from the clearly granted statutory authority which it has to regulate the advertising of prescription drugs. Under the Federal Food, Drug, and Cosmetic Act the Food and Drug Administration may declare that a drug or device is misbranded (and therefore violates the law) if its label fails to bear adequate directions for use. The regulations under the act provide that "adequate directions for use" means directions under which the layman can use a drug or device safely and for the purposes for which it is intended. However, directions for use may be inadequate, among other reasons, because of the failure to mention on the label all of the purposes or uses for which the product is recommended or suggested in advertising. Of course, if all such uses and purposes are mentioned on the label, but the product is ineffective for any of them, then the product is deemed to be misbranded for that reason. This is popularly called the "squeeze play," and here is an example of how it can operate. Let us consider an over-the-counter drug that bears a label showing its ingredients, that it is recommended for the relief of upset stomach, and that the dose is one to two tablets. No mention is made on the label that the product may be used for the treatment of an ulcer. However, the manufacturer of the drug advertises that his product is a remedy for an ulcer. In this situation the Food and Drug Administration can declare that the product does not bear adequate directions for its use because the label does not state that the drug is recommended for ulcers. Accordingly, the product is misbranded. As indicated above, if the label did state that the drug could be used for the treatment of an ulcer, but in truth and in fact the product is ineffective for such purpose, here again the product would be deemed to be misbranded.

Violation of the antimisbranding provisions of the Food, Drug, and Cosmetic Act is a crime punishable by fine and imprisonment. The Administration is also authorized to seize an offending product and to move in court to have it condemned, and to have an injunction issued against such violations.

4. Postal laws

The Federal postal laws prohibit the use of the mail for fraud, for obscene or lascivious matter, and for advertisements relating to abortions or representing anything as applicable for the prevention of conception (although there has been some liberality in the enforcement of the law with respect to the last), or for any matter which tends to incite arson, murder, or assassination, or which advocates the overthrow of the United States government or of any local level of government. In addition, no matter relating to a lottery may be placed in the United States mails (see part entitled "Contests and lotteries"). In connection with all of the foregoing, it should be kept in mind that just about every newspaper and magazine in the United States is entered as second-class mailing matter, and every advertisement in those publications thus becomes subject to the postal laws.

5. Other regulation of advertising

State and local. There are many state statutes directed against false and misleading advertising and against special advertising practices, such as bait advertising, obscene or salacious advertising, contraceptive advertising and advertising of lotteries. Other state laws regulate the advertising of securities, specific commodities, occupations and professions, banks, insurance, sales below cost, outdoor and billboard advertising, use of flags, names and likenesses of people, and names of nonprofit organizations in advertising, and the representation in advertising that the sales tax is being absorbed by the seller. It should also be mentioned that there are local ordinances which regulate certain advertising practices. Some of them are in the same categories as above outlined and others cover special situations such as going-out-of-business sales and other similar special sales.

Special Federal statutes. The Federal government also regulates advertising in certain particular areas pursuant to its powers under special statutes. Under its taxing power over alcoholic beverages, the Internal Revenue Service regulates the advertising of alcoholic beverages; the Federal Communications Commission, which has the obligation to ensure that radio and television stations are operating in the public interest, exercises certain control of advertising practices in broadcasting and telecasting media; the Securities and Exchange Commission, which is charged with the regulation of securities and securities markets, has jurisdiction over the advertising of securities; and advertising by banks and savings-and-loan associations is regulated by other Federal agencies under existing securities legislation.

Private groups. Those who administer special industry-adopted codes, better business bureaus, and advertising media exercise certain policing activities over advertising. In the case of the better business bureaus, their sole power is to persuade and to develop community pressure in favor of appropriate advertising practices. Advertising media have the power to reject any advertising which they consider to be improper, and one media trade association, the National Association of Broadcasters, has established standards of advertising practices which it interprets and enforces by requesting members to refuse to carry advertising which violates its standards. As examples, the NAB TV Code prohibits the use in television commercials of physicians, dentists, or nurses, or actors depicting them, where such commercials are for services or over-the-counter products involving health considerations; and the NAB TV and Radio Codes have rules against the disparagement of competitive products. The various radio and television stations which are members of the National Association of Broadcasters generally observe the interpretations and rulings of the NAB.

6. The use of names and likenesses of individuals—the right of privacy

Generally speaking, either by statute or court decisions, the various states prohibit the use of a living person's name, photograph, or other likeness in advertising unless he has given his written consent thereto. In Utah, Oklahoma, and Virginia these laws are also applicable, under certain circumstances, to deceased persons.

7. Defamation

Since the law regarding libel and slander is broad in its application, it is obvious that it applies to advertising matter and that anyone who makes a defamatory statement may be held liable therefor.

8. Illustrations of money, stamps, savings bonds, and other securities

Coins may be depicted in advertising, but the use of advertising matter on coins (e.g., stickers on pennies) is not permitted. Neither United States nor foreign paper money may be shown in print advertising (except numismatic advertising in black and white and in reduced or exaggerated size) or filmed commercials. It is not clear whether such money may be depicted in taped commercials. Illustrations of United States Savings Bonds or other United States securities or obligations may not be employed in advertising, nor may illustrations of United States postage stamps (except in black and white for philatelic advertising). Canceled foreign postage stamps may be shown in all advertising.

9. Illustrations of flags, coats of arms, and other similar symbols

Neither the flag of the United States, the United Nations flag, nor the flag of any of the states may be used in advertising. Under various state statutes this rule also applies to the shield, seal, and coat of arms of the United States and to other symbols of the national government and of the respective state governments. With some exceptions, the various foreign countries object to the depiction of their flags in advertising. The policy of a particular country should be ascertained from its embassy or consulate.

10. References to armed forces, government, White House, President, and certain national and local nonprofit organizations

Most government agencies and departments request that references to them in advertising first be submitted for their approval. It is particularly recommended that no reference be made in advertising to the Department of Defense or to any of its components, materials, equipment, military insignia, or personnel without first clearing such reference with the office of the Secretary of Defense.

The fact that a product is in compliance with a particular Federal standard or is government-inspected or is of a specific government grade may, under certain circumstances, be advertised.

The use of the name or likeness of the President or that of his wife in advertising is forbidden, and it has been the long-standing policy of the White House to object to any reference to it in advertising.

The American National Red Cross is opposed to any reference to it or to representations of its personnel in uniform or identified by its Red Cross insignia in connection with the sale or advertising of any product or service. References to the Boy Scouts of America in connection with merchandise which is not made or distributed under specific authorization of that organization is prohibited.

A New York State statute specifically forbids the use for advertising purposes, without prior written consent, of the name, symbol, or other identification of a nonprofit organization organized exclusively for religious, benevolent, humane, charitable, educational, hospital, patriotic, fraternal, or veterans' purposes, or to promote the study or the advancement of the arts or sciences, or to sustain or promote the musical or performing arts.

11. Contests and lotteries

There are several Federal antilottery statutes in addition to various state laws on the subject.   The most effective and best known of the Federal laws is the postal lottery law.   There is also the criminal broadcasting lottery statute and the Federal Trade Commission Act, which has been interpreted to declare lottery schemes to be unfair methods of competition.   Under the law three elements must be present before a lottery exists.   They are: prize, consideration, and chance.   If any one of these is missing, there is no lottery.   Obviously, prize can never be eliminated from this type of scheme.   Accordingly, the efforts of advertisers and promoters have been directed at avoiding either consideration or chance.

Consideration usually involves the payment of money or the expenditure of substantial time or effort.   For example, if a manufacturer places a $10 bill in every thousandth package of his product, consideration will be furnished by those who purchase the product, even though the price of such product is not increased.   Similarly, if a box top or label must accompany a contest entry, consideration will be deemed to be present.   If a detailed facsimile may be furnished instead of the actual box top, the effort involved in making it will usually be construed as consideration.   On the other hand, the mere requirement that the contestant mail a coupon on which he writes his name and address and even the name of the advertised product will not result in a finding of consideration.   Under the Federal rules, the need for the contestant to go to a store to register, or to pick up an entry blank, and even to return to learn whether he is a winner, will not be deemed as consideration.   A number of the states, however, take a stricter view of what is consideration and prohibit the promotion in their jurisdictions of certain contests and drawings which are legal under existing Federal laws.

In connection with chance, it is important to note that a scheme or contest may be illegal if the awards will be based even only in part on chance.   That is why in all contests, where prize and consideration are present, the rules are required to provide that duplicate prizes will be awarded in the event of a tie. Otherwise, it would be strictly a matter of chance whether a contestant's entry is the best and gets the whole prize or his and another's entry are equally the best and therefore divide the prize.   This problem cannot be avoided by giving the prize to the one whose entry bears the earliest postmark, because here again, the element of chance will determine how the tie should be broken.

In any contest where the element of consideration cannot or should not be eliminated, the sponsor may avoid the element of chance by making the contest one of skill. The most common way of doing this is to give a prize for the best statement on a given subject, or the best slogan, etc. In such situations the contestant must be told what standards of merit, skill, or ability will be used in determining the best entry and impartial judges must follow these standards in determining the winner. It is important to remember that "best" contests must be susceptible to the application of skill and intelligence. The awarding of a prize for "the most interesting signature" would not be construed as a contest of skill.

Because the United States postal laws prohibit the mailing of any matter relating to a lottery (e.g., publications containing ads, letters containing entries, letters to the winners, etc.), all contest schemes which are the least bit questionable as to legality and which may involve the use of the United States mails for any aspect thereof should be submitted to the United States Post Office Department for a ruling before the contest is offered. In addition, because of the variety of state laws dealing with lotteries, the contest should also be reviewed from the point of view of the applicable state statutes.

12. Price-saving coupons and premium offers

Coupons which offer a price reduction for a particular product or which offer a premium, and which are issued and ultimately redeemed by the manufacturer are legal in all the states except when employed in connection with the promotion of certain products. There is some local legislation which restricts or prohibits the use of coupon and premium offers in connection with alcoholic beverages or with bakery, confectionery, petroleum, tobacco, and other products. Furthermore, some states require that coupons must be redeemable for cash, and accordingly they usually bear a statement that they are redeemable for a small fraction of a cent. In addition, provision should be made in price-reduction coupons that the entire sales tax on the purchased item is to be paid by the consumer. It is also advisable to set forth the expiration date of the offer and the geographical area within which the coupon or premium offer will be recognized. It should be noted that the use of price-reduction coupons might violate certain state fair-trade statutes by thus effecting a reduction in the fair-traded price of the product.

13. Cooperative advertising and merchandising

The Robinson-Patman Act, which is generally enforced by the Federal Trade Commission,[2] provides, among other things, that a seller of a product may not

[2] Parties injured by violation of the act may sue in the Federal courts for triple damages and such parties or the United States Attorney General may seek court injunctions against violations.

make payment to the buyer for a service or facility furnished by the buyer unless he also makes that payment available on proportionately equal terms to competitors of the buyer.   It also provides that a seller may not discriminate in favor of one buyer by furnishing a service or facility to him without making such service or facility available to all competing buyers on proportionately equal terms.   Cooperative advertising or merchandising programs fall within the scope of the act.   Under the law, it is incumbent on the seller who offers a cooperative advertising or merchandising program to make certain that the offer is actually made known to all competing customers.   Furthermore, the plan must be so geared that all of them may take advantage of it in the normal course of their business.   One way of providing for this is to offer alternative services of comparable value, so that all competing buyers may participate on a proportionately equal basis.   Such a program may entail television advertising, radio advertising, ads in publications, handbills, displays, and other forms of advertising.   No payment should be made or service furnished unless and until the buyer has completed his part of the bargain, and no payment should be made in excess of the amount actually disbursed by the buyer.

14. Copyright and unfair competition

Advertisements may be afforded the protection of statutory copyright by having each and every publication of the ad accompanied by a copyright notice, i.e., © followed by the name of the advertiser or by the initials of the advertiser if its full name is set forth elsewhere in the advertisement.   Advertisements in publications do not require a statement of the year of first publication, but many other types of ads do.   Within a reasonable time after first publication, two copies of the advertisement with the notice should be filed with the Register of Copyrights, Washington, D.C., together with an application for copyright and the filing fee of $6.   A copyright is valid for 28 years and may be renewed for another 28 years.   However, as of this writing there is under consideration in the United States Congress a bill to make major revisions in the present copyright law.   If the bill now in Congress is passed, and the indications are that it will be, the term of copyright will be generally for the life of the author plus 50 years after his death.   However, in the case of a "work made for hire" (and much advertising may fall into this category), the copyright will last for 75 years from first publication or 100 years from the creation of the work, whichever is shorter.

Meanwhile, pending action on the new copyright legislation, a special congressional resolution provides that at the present time no copyrighted works shall fall into public domain at the conclusion of their renewal term of copyright, and copyright protection for such works is being extended on a year-to-year basis.

Normally, broadcast material does not need the protection of statutory copyright because it is not regarded as having been published and under general principles of law will be fully protected against copying without the formality of notice or registration.   Such protection will continue as long as the material remains unpublished.

No copyrighted or unpublished matter should be used in an advertisement without the permission of the owner.   In this connection, it should be remembered that just about every newspaper and magazine published in the United States is copyrighted.   The use of quotation marks around the copied material, with credit to the owner, does not permit the use of such material.   Actual consent is required.   The ideas expressed in copyrighted matters are not protected, but the manner of expressing them is.

Contrary to popular belief, material contained in letters belongs to the writer and not to the recipient.   Accordingly, no letter should be used in advertising without the consent of the writer.

While titles of songs, books, movies, and stage plays are not protected by copyright, they may be protected under the general law of unfair competition if they have attained popularity.   Similarly, advertising matter which has not been copyrighted, but which has become associated in the public's mind with a particular product, also may under certain circumstances be protected from use by others under the law of unfair competition.

Care must be exercised when purchasing photographs and art for use in advertising.   The agreement of purchase should clearly spell out the purchaser's rights therein.   The mere purchase of a print of a photograph does not give the purchaser the right to reproduce it in advertising.   Also, the right to reproduce in advertising, when granted, is not an exclusive right unless it is so provided in the instrument of purchase either by the grant of all property rights or by an express grant of exclusivity.   The purchaser should also be certain that the person who is selling the print with the right to reproduce it in advertising has the authority to grant such right.   Finally, while it is generally true that reproduction rights accompany the ownership of a work of fine art unless the artist specifically reserves them, the law of the State of New York is that the right to reproduce a work of fine art remains with the artist unless he specifically transfers it.   Where a work of art or a photograph includes the likeness of an individual, the laws relating to right of privacy should be kept in mind (see part entitled "The use of names and likenesses of individuals—the right of privacy").

15. Trademarks

The law of trademarks deserves consideration because of the effect that advertising may have on continued trademark protection.   Just to provide a few examples, aspirin, linoleum, escalator, and cellophane were all once registered trademarks which are now available for generic use by anyone.   Marks such as these became generic terms in the United States when the public ceased to regard them as identifying a particular source for a product. In other words, aspirin is no longer a brand of acetylsalicylic acid. It is the product itself. Good trademark usage in advertising can help to prevent, but not ensure against such loss of trademark rights.

A trademark should be used as an adjective and not as a noun or verb. It also should not be used as a possessive or in the plural form. It is important that the trademark be associated with the generic name of the product—not always, but at least once in each ad, and preferably in connection with the first or most prominent mention. The trademark should always be shown with an initial capital letter, and it is desirable to otherwise set it apart with italics, quotes, underlining, bold-faced type, or other means. If the trademark has been registered in the U.S. Patent Office, such fact should be shown. The most widely employed method is to place an "R" in a circle next to the first or most featured use of the mark. Otherwise it may be referred to as "Registered in U.S. Patent Office" or "Reg. U.S. Pat. Off." If a trademark has been registered in a state, it may be referred to as "registered trademark" or "Reg. TM." A trademark should never be represented as having been registered before registration is actually effected. Prior to registration it may be referred to as "TM," but from a legal point of view this designation is of no advantage.

16. Closing note

This section has covered a wide variety of the major legal problems relating to advertising, but only in a most cursory manner. The aim is to serve to alert you, the businessman, to some situations which entail concerns of a legal nature. Your counsel should take it from there.

Appendix

Artificial Limb Industry
Barre Granite Industry
Beauty and Barber Equipment and Supplies Industry
Bedding Manufacturing and Wholesale Distributing Industry
Blueprint and Diazotype Coaters Industry
Braided Rug Industry
Brick and Structural Clay Tile and Allied Products Industry
Buff and Polishing Wheel Manufacturing Industry
Building Wire and Cable Manufacturing Industry
Button Jobbing Industry
Candy Manufacturing Industry
Canvas Cover Industry
Carbon Dioxide Manufacturing Industry
Catalog Jewelry and Giftware Industry

Cedar Chest Manufacturing Industry
Chemical Soil Conditioner Industry
China Recess Accessories Industry
Cocoa and Chocolate Industry
Combination Storm Window and Door Industry
Commercial and Industrial Floor and Vacuum Machinery Industry
Commercial Dental Laboratory Industry
Common or Toilet Pin Industry
Concrete Burial Vault Manufacturing Industry
Construction Equipment Distributing Industry
Corset, Brassiere, and Allied Products Industry
Cosmetic and Toilet Preparations Industry
Cotton Converting Industry
Covered Button and Buckle Manufacturing Industry
Crushed Stone Industry
Curled Hair Industry
Cut and Wire Tack Industry
Cut Stone Industry (Building Stone)
Doll and Stuffed Toy Industry
Electrical Contracting Industry
Electrical Wholesalers Industry
Embroidery Industry
Engraved Stationery and Allied Products Industry of the New York City Trade
    Area
Environmental Testing Equipment Manufacturing Industry
Fabricators of Ornamental Iron, Bronze and Wire Industry
Feather and Down Products Industry
Fine and Wrapping Paper Distributing Industry
Fire Extinguishing Appliance Industry
Fluocarbons Industry
Folding Paper Box Industry
Fountain Pen and Mechanical Pencil Industry
Fresh Fruit and Vegetable Industry
Frozen Food Industry
Gladiolus Bulb Industry
Golf, Baseball and Athletic Goods Industry
Grocery Industry
Gummed Paper and Sealing Tape Industry
Hand Knitting Yarn Industry
Handkerchief Industry
Hearing Aid Industry
Hosiery Industry
House Dress and Wash Frock Manufacturing Industry
Household Fabric Dye Industry
Household Furniture Industry
Ice Cream Industry (District of Columbia and Vicinity)
Industrial Bag and Cover Industry

Infants' and Children's Knitted Outerwear Industry
Interior Marble Industry
Jewelry Industry
Knitted Outerwear Industry
Kosher Food Products Industry
Ladies' Handbag Manufacturing Industry
Library Binding Industry
Low Pressure Refrigerants Industry
Luggage and Related Products Industry
Macaroni and Noodle Products Industry
Manifold Business Forms Industry
Marking Devices Industry
Masonry Waterproofing Industry
Melamine Dinnerware Industry
Metal Awning Industry
Metal Clad Door and Accessories Manufacturing Industry
Metallic Watch Band Industry
Milk Bottle Cap and Closure Industry
Millinery Industry
Millwork Industry
Mirror Manufacturing Industry
Mopstick Industry
Motor Vehicles-Retail Installment Sale and Financing
Musical Instrument and Accessories Industry
Narrow Fabrics Industry
Nursery Industry
Office Machine Marketing Industry
Oil Heating Industry of the New England States
Oleomargarine Manufacturing Industry
Optical Products Industry
Orthopedic Appliance Industry
Outlet and Switch Box Manufacturing Industry
Paint and Varnish Brush Industry
Paper Bag Industry
Paper Drinking Straw Manufacturing Industry
Parking Meter Industry
Peat Industry
Phonograph Record Industry
Photoengraving Industry of the Southeastern States
Piston Ring Industry
Plastics Housewares Industry
Pleasure Boat Industry
Popular Priced Dress Manufacturing Industry
Portrait Photographic Industry
Poultry Hatching and Breeding Industry
Preserve Manufacturing Industry
Private Home Study Schools Industry

Public Refrigerated Storage Industry
Public Seating Industry
Putty Manufacturing Industry
Rabbit Industry
Radio and Television Industry
Rayon and Silk Dyeing, Printing and Finishing Industry
Rayon, Nylon and Silk Converting Industry
Razor and Razor Blade Industry
Rebuilt, Reconditioned and Other Used Automotive Parts Industry
Refrigeration and/or Air-Conditioning Contracting Industries
Residential Aluminum Siding Industry
Resistance Welder Manufacturing Industry
Ribbon Industry
Ripe Olive Industry
Sardine Industry
Saw and Blade Service Industry
School Supply and Equipment Industry
Scrap Iron and Steel Industry
Seam Binding Industry
Set-Up Paper Box Industry
Shoe Finders Industry
Shrinkage of Woven Cotton Yard Goods Industry
Slide Fastener Industry
Stationers Industry
Steel Bobby Pin and Steel Hair Pin Manufacturing Industry
Subscription and Mail Order Book Publishing Industry
Sun Glass Industry
Tie Fabrics Industry
Tire and Tube Repair Material Industry
Tobacco Distributing Industry
Tobacco Smoking Pipe, and Cigar and Cigar Holder Industry
Toilet Brush Manufacturing Industry
Tomato Paste Manufacturing Industry
Trade Pamphlet Binding Industry of the New York City Trade Area
Tubular Pipings and Trimmings Manufacturing Industry
Tuna Industry
Umbrella Industry
Uniform Industry
Upholstery and Drapery Fabrics Industry
Venetian Blind Industry
Vertical Turbine Pump Industry
Wall Coverings Industry
Walnut Wool Industry
Warm Air Furnace Industry
Waste Paper Dealers and Packers Industry
Watch Case Industry
Watch Industry (Respecting the terms "Waterproof," "Shockproof," "Non-

Magnetic," and related Designations, as applied to Watches, Watchcases and
Watch Movements)
Water Heater Industry
Waterproof Paper Industry (Asphaltic Type)
Wet Ground Mica Industry
Wholesale Confectionery Industry (Philadelphia Trade Area)
Wholesale Confectionery Industry
Wholesale Plumbing and Heating Industry
Wine Industry
Wire Rope Industry
Wood Cased Lead Pencil Industry
Woodworking Machinery Industry
Work Glove Industry
Yeast Industry

INDEX

Mortgage loans, long-term, 33–34
  selecting type of, 33
  short-term, 33
Mutual insurance companies, 666
Myers, D'Alton B., 78

NASA (National Aeronautics and Space Administration), 349
National Association of Broadcasters, 736
National Consumer Panel of the Market Research Corporation of America, New York, 502
National Housing Act, 58
National Planning Association, 103
  Center of Economic Projections of, 101
Natural disaster, 152
Navy, U.S., 344
  Special Projects Office, 344
Neuner, John J. W., 435
New York Stock Exchange, public-relations program of, 609
New York Terminal Warehouse Company, 46
New Yorker magazine, 611
Newspapers, local, in establishing good employee relations, 590–591
Nielson, A. C., Company, Chicago, 501–502, 540
Nonpersonal selling, 517
Nontaxable transactions in buying and selling businesses, 172–176
  statutory merger or consolidation, 172–173
  stock-for-assets acquisition, 174–175
  stock-for-stock transaction, 173–174
Notes, of customers, internal control for, 459
Numerical file, 401

Objectives, determining, 124–125
Occupational distribution of embezzlers, 479–480
Ocean-marine insurance, 642–643
Office expenses, internal control of, 465
Oil Insurance Association, 668
Olin Mathieson, 344
On-account payments, internal control of cash receipts from, 456–457
1001 Embezzlers (United States Fidelity and Guaranty Company), 477, 479
Operating routines, standardized, as phase of internal control, 441–443
Opinion surveys, employee relations and, 592

Orders, size of, and marketing productivity, 286–287
Organization, basic helps in, 142
  checking efficiency of, 143–144
  control and, 140–142, 144
  developing pattern of, 135–138
    defining responsibility by job description, 136
    delegating authority to handle responsibility, 136
    fair compensation, 136–138
      retirement pay, 137–138
    formulating and communicating goals, 135–136
    progress evaluation, 138
    selection and training of personnel, 138–139
  distribution and, 144
  for efficient management, 120–144
  errors to avoid in building, 143
  financing and, 144
  function of, 130–135
    control, 134–135
    operational, 132–134
    planning, 130–132
  good, delegation of authority in, 128–129
    need for control in, 129–130
    ten commandments of, 138
  for good employee relations, 600
  growth pattern of delegation of authority and, 140
  levels of, 139–140
  for overseas business, 693–694
  personnel and, 144
  as phase of internal control, 438–439
  planning and, 144
  principles of, 123–128
    centralizing control, 126–127
    classifying or functionalizing operations, 126
    departmentalizing, 126
    determining objectives, 124–125
    ensuring coordination, 127–128
    formulating policies, 125–126
    freedom of top management, 128
    recruiting and training personnel, 127
  product and, 144
  production and, 144
Organization manual, 143–144
Ortho Pharmaceutical Corporation, 349
Overhead, defined, 311
  excessive inventories and, 311–312
  fringe benefits and, 312
  insurance and, 312
  maintenance and, 312
  utilities and, 313
Overhead budget, manufacturing, 377–378